SWEDISH:
A COMPREHENSIVE GRAMMAR

SECOND EDITION

Routledge Comprehensive Grammars

Comprehensive Grammars are available for the following languages:

Cantonese
Catalan
Danish
Dutch
Greek
Indonesian
Japanese
Modern Welsh
Modern Written Arabic
Slovene
Swedish
Ukrainian

Tiles of related interest

Colloquial Swedish
by Philip Holmes and Gunilla Serin

SWEDISH: A COMPREHENSIVE GRAMMAR

SECOND EDITION

Philip Holmes and Ian Hinchliffe

Routledge
Taylor & Francis Group

LONDON AND NEW YORK

First edition published 1994
by Routledge

Reprinted with corrections 1998

Second edition published 2003
by Routledge
11 New Fetter Lane, London EC4P 4E1E

Simultaneously published in the USA and Canada
by Routledge
29 West 35th Street, New York, NY 10001

Routledge is an imprint of the Taylor & Francis Group

Typeset in Times New Roman by Phil Holmes
Printed and bound in Great Britain by
TJ International Ltd, Padstow, Cornwall

British Library Cataloguing in Publication Data
A catalogue record for this book is available from the British Library

Library of Congress Cataloging in Publication Data
Holmes, Philip, 1944
      Swedish: a comprehensive grammar / Philip Holmes and Ian Hinchliffe –
2nd ed.
            p. cm. – (Routledge comprehensive grammars)
      1.   Swedish – Grammar. I. Hinchliffe, Ian. II. Title. III. Series.
      PD5112.H66 2003
      439.782,421– dc21
2003010196

ISBN 0–415–27883–X (hbk)
ISBN0–415–27884–8 (pbk)

CONTENTS

Preface   ix
Symbols and Abbreviations Used in the Text   xi

Chapter 1 Nouns   1

Introduction 101
A   Gender rules 102–105
B   Miscellaneous points of gender 106–110
C   Plural noun forms – the declensions 111–119
D   Miscellaneous points on indefinite plural forms 120–123
E   Special uses of the singular and plural 124–127
F   Noun homonyms 128
G   The genitive 129–30
H   The form of the indefinite article 131
J   The form of the definite (end) article 132–135
K   The use of the indefinite and definite (end) article 136–143

Chapter 2 Adjectives   58

A   Form and order 201–207
B   The indefinite declension 208–216
C   The definite declension 217–226
D   Adjectival nouns 227–231
E   Comparison of adjectives 232–245

Chapter 3 Pronouns   112

A   Personal pronouns – forms 301
B   Subject and object pronouns 302–309
C   Reflexive pronouns 310–313
D   Emphatic pronouns 314–315
E   Possessive adjectives and pronouns 316–324
F   Demonstrative pronouns 325–328
G   Determinative pronouns 329
H   Indefinite pronouns 330–360
J   Interrogative pronouns 361–368
K   Relative pronouns 369–373

Chapter 4 Numerals   196

A   Forms of numerals 401–405
B   The use of cardinal numbers 406–410
C   The use of ordinal numbers 411
D   Fractions 412–413
E   Dates 414–415
F   The time 416

Chapter 5 Verbs   213

A   Forms 501–517
B   The use of the tenses 518–533
C   Ways of expressing mood 534–538
D   Transitive, intransitive and reflexive verbs 539–541
E   S–forms of the verb and the passive 542–553
F   Compound verbs 554–559
G   Some problem verbs 560–561

Chapter 6 Adverbs   292

A   Form 601–605
B   Function 606–612
C   Location and movement 613–614
D   Some difficult adverbs 615–616

Chapter 7 Prepositions   322

A   Introduction 701–704
B   Simple and compound prepositions 705–719
C   Prepositional use 720–731

Chapter 8 Conjunctions   404

A   Coordination and subordination 801–803
B   Coordinating conjunctions 804–809
C   Subordinating conjunctions 810–819
D   Other subordinators 820–822
E   Some problem conjunctions 823

Chapter 9 Interjections 901–908   428

Chapter 10 Sentence Structure and Word Order 434

A Sentence elements 1001–1008
B Phrases 1009–1014
C Main clause word order – basic positions 1015–1018
D Subordinate clause word order – basic positions 1019–1020
E Order within positions 1021–1025
F Main clause transformations 1026–1036
G Subordinate clauses 1037–1043
H Emphasis 1044–1048
J Ellipsis 1049–1053

Chapter 11 Word Formation 516

Introduction 1101
A Affixation 1102–1109
B Compounding 1110–1119
C Expressive formation 1120–1122
D Abbreviation 1123–1124
E Foreign influences on Swedish 1125–1131
F Conversion 1132–1135

Chapter 12 Orthography 559

A Symbols and sounds 1201–1203
B Spelling 1204–1205
C Small and capital letters 1206–1210
D Miscellaneous 1211–1213

Chapter 13 Punctuation 1301–1312 573

Linguistic Terms 583

Short Bibliography 590

Index 593

PREFACE

We have two aims in writing this book:

- To describe various style registers in contemporary written and spoken Swedish.

- To provide a source of reference for the student and teacher, in order to help non-native learners develop fluency when speaking and writing Swedish.

We have attempted to write an English-language grammar for Swedish with as comprehensive an approach as that found in grammars already available for the major world languages.

A substantial Index is provided to both Swedish and English key words as well as to grammatical concepts.

Where possible we have retained traditional linguistic terminology and a traditional structure. In Chapter 10 (Sentence Structure and Word Order), however, users are advised to study Section A before turning to the chapter as a source of reference. This is because, for the first time, the positional scheme for sentence structure developed by the Danish linguist Paul Diderichsen has been adapted for the English learner of Swedish.

Any grammar is a snapshot of something both multi-faceted and swiftly changing. Some of our observations will probably be invalid in twenty years' time; others (such as the acceptance of the written forms **ska** and **sa** or the increasingly widespread use of comparative constructions with **mer** and **mest**) would have raised eyebrows only a few years ago.

However, we trust we have not been deluded into accepting uncritically some assumptions made about the language which we regard as unfounded. To take one example: the forms **mig**, **dig**, **sig** still hold the high ground in cultivated written Swedish. The trend towards **mej**, **dej**, **sej** is not as strong as some observers have imagined.

The starting point in our account has been what Swedes write or say in the early 21st century. We have used the findings of modern research to test traditional rules against actual practice. A living language is too complex to be embodied in a simple system of rules, and there are invariably a number of grey areas in syntax and grammar. Here we have attempted to guide learners towards what is generally considered to be good usage. To do this we have chosen to relegate outmoded expressions, slang and peripheral phenomena to notes within the text.

A book of this kind requires hundreds of examples. In some cases these have been specifically constructed to help in the learning/teaching process. In other cases examples from books, newspapers, radio and television have been adapted to simplify this process. Our own translations have been provided for the vast majority of examples and may be regarded as an additional aid in the task of learning how to render Swedish accurately into English.

Swedish: A Comprehensive Grammar is unashamedly comparative in nature. By concentrating on some of the questions most frequently raised by English learners of Swedish we hope that this book may provide some practical answers.

We wish to thank Jyrki Pietarinen for many valuable suggestions for improvements.

We wish also to thank Peter Graves of Edinburgh University, Kersti Börjars of Manchester University and Els-Marie Widén-Karlsson of Växjö and, last but by no means least, Katie Lewis, for their invaluable assistance and advice in the final stages of this project. All remaining errors and omissions are ours alone. We would also like to thank the many undergraduate learners of Swedish in The University of Hull's Department of Scandinavian Studies who, albeit unwittingly, have served as guinea-pigs.

Finally, we would like to thank our wives and families for tolerating our long-term extra-marital relationships with various word processors.

SECOND EDITION

The first edition of this book came out in 1993, and the 1998 reprint included a number of corrections and updates and some additional examples. These versions of the book preceded the publication of *Svenska Akademiens Grammatik* in 1999.

This second edition involves a number of major changes to the structure and content of the book, among which are:

- The addition of a new chapter, Chapter 11 Word Formation.
- The provision of a single Chapter 1 on Nouns rather than the original two – Nouns and Nouns – Forms with Articles.
- Substantial changes to Chapter 1, including a categorisation of noun declensions that accords with the new scheme proposed in *Svenska Akademiens Grammatik*.
- The addition to Chapter 10 on word order of a section on phrases.
- Numerous changes of detail and examples throughout, with the overriding aim of simplifying the arguments and eliminating duplication.

Consequently, it should be noted that section numbering in this version differs from that in the first edition.

Phil Holmes and Ian Hinchliffe
Hull and Killeberg, June 2003

SYMBOLS AND ABBREVIATIONS USED IN THE TEXT

(att), nå(go)n	word or part of a word omitted or added
växt/vuxit	alternatives
***ordföranden**	incorrect usage
-C	ends in a consonant
-V	ends in a long vowel
-ska, inna, etc.	word ending in **-ska, -inna,** etc.
/or, -t, -na	inflexional endings
-0	no plural ending
skriv/er	verb stem + inflexional ending
x → y, x > y	x changes into y
x ↔ y	y refers to or agrees with x
0	no preposition (Chapter 8)
I, II, IIa, IIb, III, IV	verb conjugations
hetat*	irregular verb form
/sa/	approximate pronunciation using normal Swedish spelling
dok'torer	stress on syllable following mark
för|be|red|else|r	division into word formation elements or morphemes

adj.	adjective	fem.	feminine
adv.	adverb	FS	formal subject
art.	article	FV	finite verb
aux.	auxiliary	gen.	genitive
C	complement	IO	indirect object
CA	clausal adverbial	indef.	indefinite
coll.	colloquial	inf.	infinitive
Conj.	conjugation	intr.	intransitive
conj.	conjunction	irr.	irregular (verb)
conjunct.	conjunctional	*lit.*	literally
coord. conj.	coordinating conjunction	masc.	masculine
def.	definite	MC	main clause
DO	direct object	n.-n.	non-neuter
end art.	end (definite) article	n.	neuter
		NFV	non-finite verb
Eng.	English	NP	noun phrase
FE	first element	O	object

FS	formal subject
FV	finite verb
gen.	genitive
IO	indirect object
indef.	indefinite
inf.	infinitive
intr.	intransitive
irr.	irregular (verb)
lit.	literally
masc.	masculine
MC	main clause
n.-n.	non-neuter
n.	neuter
NFV	non-finite verb
NP	noun phrase
O	object
OA	other adverbial
O/C	object/complement
obj.	object(ive)
para.	paragraph
part.	participle
pl.	plural
prep.	preposition
–prep.	no preposition
+prep.	with preposition
pron.	pronounced
RS	real subject
S	subject
SC	1. subordinate clause,
	2. subject complement
sing.	singular
sub. conj.	subordinating conjunction
subj.	subject
T	topic
tr.	transitive

1   NOUNS

101   Introduction

A   GENDER RULES
102   Non-neuter by meaning
103   Non-neuter by form
104   Neuter by meaning
105   Neuter by form

B   MISCELLANEOUS POINTS OF GENDER
106   Masculine and feminine
107   Particularly difficult suffixes
108   Nouns with uncertain gender
109   Gender of proper nouns
110   Gender of abbreviations and foreign loans

C   PLURAL NOUN FORMS – THE DECLENSIONS
111   Introduction
112   The first declension: plurals in **-or**
113   The second declension: plurals in **-ar**
114   The third declension: plurals in **-er**
115   The fourth declension: plurals in **-r**
116   The fifth declension: plurals in **-n**
117   The sixth declension: zero plurals
118   The seventh declension: plurals in **-s**
119   Nouns – plural indefinite forms: predictability

D   MISCELLANEOUS POINTS ON INDEFINITE PLURAL FORMS
120   Types of noun with no plural form
121   Nouns with special collective forms
122   Nouns with no singular form
123   Nouns – plural indefinite forms: summary

E   SPECIAL USES OF THE SINGULAR AND PLURAL
124   Nouns which are singular in English but plural in Swedish
125   Nouns which are singular in Swedish but plural in English
126   Singular for the quantity expressed
127   Plural for the measure of quantity

F   NOUN HOMONYMS
128   List of Swedish noun homonyms

G   THE GENITIVE
129   The form of the genitive
130   The use of the genitive

H   THE FORM OF THE INDEFINITE ARTICLE
131   The indefinite article

J   THE FORM OF THE DEFINITE (END) ARTICLE
132   The definite (end) article
133   The form of the definite singular
134   Choice of the definite plural ending
135   Nouns – forms with end article: summary

K   THE USE OF THE INDEFINITE AND DEFINITE (END) ARTICLE
136   Introduction
137   Swedish has a definite (end) article – English has no article
138   Swedish has a definite (end) article – English has an indefinite article
139   Swedish has no article – English has a definite article
140   Swedish has no article – English has an indefinite article
141   Swedish has an indefinite article – English has no article
142   The use of the definite article to indicate possession
143   Differences in the position of the articles in Swedish and English

---

101   Introduction

(a) Different types of noun are:

(i) Proper nouns:

Gustav; **Malmö**; **Sverige** Sweden; **IKEA**

(ii) Common nouns:

Concrete: **katt** cat; **stol** chair; **hus** house; **flicka** girl
Abstract: **glädje** joy; **sjukdom** illness; **begåvning** intelligence; **mjukhet** softness

(b) Nouns may also be classified as:

(i) Count nouns, i.e. concrete things and creatures: **bulle** bun; **träd** tree; **student**
student. Some abstracts are count nouns: **skratt** laugh; **färg** colour.

(ii) Non-count nouns, i.e. substances: **vatten** water; **bensin** petrol; **luft** air. Some abstracts are non-count nouns: **vithet** whiteness; **lycka** happiness. Also: **pengar** money.

(c) Swedish has two noun genders, non-neuter and neuter (but see also 305), shown by the form of the indefinite and definite article (see 131ff. below). (Some grammars use the term 'common' for 'non-neuter'. Others use 'n-word' or 'en-word' for non-neuter noun and 't-word' or 'ett-word' for neuter noun.) About 75% of all nouns in newspaper text are non-neuter. In many cases either the form of the noun (usually its final syllable) or the meaning of the noun may provide a clue to its gender.

(d) Plurals are indicated by a number of different endings according to declension (see 112–118).

A   GENDER RULES

102   Non-neuter by meaning

The following types of noun are non-neuter by meaning:

(a) Human beings:

> **en fader** a father; **en lärare** a teacher; **en svensk** a Swede; **en kvinna** a woman

Note 1: *Exceptions*: **ett barn** a child; **ett biträde** an assistant (and others in -biträde); **ett geni** a genius; **ett helgon** a saint; **ett original** an eccentric; **ett proffs** a professional; **ett snille** a genius; **ett syskon** a sibling; **ett spöke** a ghost; **ett vittne** a witness; nouns ending in -ombud and -råd when referring to people: **ett statsråd** a cabinet minister; **ett skyddsombud** a safety representative; **ett fnask** a prostitute; **ett fyllo** a drunk.

For how to use adjectives and pronouns with these nouns see 211(d), 306.

Note 2: Nouns of neuter gender do not alter their gender when used to depict a human being:

Han är stark som ett lejon.	He's as strong as a lion.
Han är som ett monster mot sin fru.	He is a monster to his wife.

(b) Animals:

> **en fisk** a fish; **en duva** a dove; **en hund** a dog; **en spindel** a spider

Note 1: *Exceptions*: **ett bi** a bee; **ett djur** an animal (and others in -**djur**); **ett får** a sheep; **ett föl** a foal; **ett höns** a hen; **ett kreatur** a beast; **ett lamm** a lamb; **ett lejon** a lion; **ett sto** a mare; **ett svin** (and compounds in -**svin**).

Note 2: Higher animals are often treated as masculine irrespective of their true gender: **elefanten** – **han** the elephant – he; **örnen** – **han** the eagle – he.

Note 3: Nouns ending in -a which denote animals are often treated as feminine irrespective of their true gender: **råtta** – **hon** rat – she; **åsna** – **hon** ass – she.

See also 106.

(c) Days and parts of the day, months, seasons, festivals (see 415):

> **en fredag**, a Friday; **en vardag**, a weekday; **en morgon**, a morning; **en timme**, an hour; **en minut**, a minute; **en sekund**, a second; **en mild januari**, a mild January; **våren**, (the) spring; **hösten**, (the) autumn; **sommaren**, (the) summer; **vintern**, (the) winter; **julen**, Christmas; **påsken**, Easter; **midsommaren**, Midsummer

Exceptions: **ett dygn**, a day (and a night: i.e. a 24-hour period); **ett kvartal**, a quarter; and all expressions for periods of a year and longer: **ett år**, a year; **ett årtionde**, a decade; **ett sekel**, a century.

(d) Trees, flowers, shrubs and bushes:

> **granen** the fir tree; **apeln** the apple tree; **rosen** the rose

Exception: **ett träd** a tree (and compounds in **-träd**)

(e) Lakes and rivers:

> **Vänern; Bodensjön** Lake Constance; **Klarälven; Rhenen** the Rhine

(f) Cardinal numbers, fractions (see 406, 412f.):

> **en etta** a (number) one; **en fjärdedel** a quarter; **en åttondel** an eighth

Exceptions: **ett hundra** a hundred; **ett tusen** a thousand

(g) Many tools:

> **en hammare** a hammer; **en såg** a saw; **en spik** a nail

Exceptions: **ett lod** a plumb; **ett städ** an anvil; **ett verktyg** a tool, and other compounds in **-järn**: **ett strykjärn** an iron

103   Non-neuter by form

Nouns with the following endings are non-neuter by form:

> -a   **en saga** a fairy tale; **en lampa** a lamp; **en fluga** a fly

Exceptions: **ett drama** a drama; **ett delta** a delta; **ett dilemma** a dilemma; **ett hjärta** a heart; **ett schema** a timetable; **ett öga** an eye; **ett öra** an ear (see 116)

-ans	**en ambulans** an ambulance; **en leverans** a delivery
-ant	**en fabrikant** a manufacturer; **en praktikant** a trainee
-are	**en mätare** a meter, a gauge; **en behållare** a container

Exceptions: **ett altare** an altar; **ett ankare** an anchor

-dom	**en sjukdom** an illness; **kristendomen** Christianity
-else	**en rörelse** a movement; **en styrelse** a board of directors

Exception: **ett fängelse** a prison

-ens	**en konferens** a conference; **en frekvens** a frequency
-het	**en svaghet** a weakness; **en personlighet** a personality
-ik	**trafiken** the traffic; **en publik** an audience

Exceptions: **ett lik** a corpse; **ett fik** a café

-(n)ing   **en parkering** a car park

Exceptions: **ett ting** an object; **ett sting** a sting

-ion   **en station** a station; **en religion** a religion

Exception: **ett stadion** a stadium

-ism	**realismen** realism; **socialismen** socialism
-nad	**en byggnad** a building; **en tystnad** a silence

104   Neuter by meaning

The following types of nouns are neuter by meaning:

(a) Many geographical locations that are proper nouns (except lakes and rivers, see 102(e)). Their neuter gender is revealed below in the ending of the adjective:

Asien är överbefolka*t*.	Asia is overpopulated.
Sverige är avlång*t*.	Sweden is oblong.
Småland är bergig*t*.	Småland is rocky.
Stockholm är stor*t*.	Stockholm is big.
Sahara är torr*t*.	The Sahara is dry.

(b) Trees ending in -träd and berries:

ett äppelträd an apple tree; **ett plommonträd** a plum tree; **ett hallon** a raspberry; **ett körsbär** a cherry

(c) Letters of the alphabet:

> **ett a** an a; **ett z** a z

(d) Some nouns formed from pronouns, adverbs, interjections, conjunctions and prepositions:

> **nuet** the present; **jaget** the ego; **ett nej** a no

Note: When the infinitive (usually with **att**) is used as a noun, a predicative adjective is inflected as if the infinitive has neuter gender (see 518(b)).

105 Neuter by form

The following types of noun are neuter by form:

(a) Nouns ending in:

> *-ande* (present participles used as abstract nouns):

> **ett antagande** an assumption; **ett ingripande** an intervention

Exceptions: In some cases nouns in -ande denote a person and are then non-neuter (117(a)(iii)):

> **en sökande** an applicant; **en ordförande** a chairperson; **en studerande** a student

> *-ende* (present participles used as abstract nouns):

> **ett leende** a smile; **ett utseende** an appearance

Exceptions: In some cases nouns in -ende denote a person and are then non-neuter (cf. 117(a)(iii)): **en gående** a pedestrian

> *-eri*   **ett batteri** a battery; **ett bryggeri** a brewery

Exception: **en periferi** a periphery

> *-um/-eum/-ium* (bi- and polysyllabic nouns from Latin):

> **ett faktum** a fact; **ett museum** a museum; **ett gymnasium** an upper secondary school

(b) Foreign loans ending in the following syllables:

> *-em*   **ett problem** a problem; **ett system** a system
> *-iv*   **ett adjektiv** an adjective; **ett stativ** a tripod
> *-tek*   **ett apotek** a pharmacy; **ett bibliotek** a library

B MISCELLANEOUS POINTS OF GENDER

106 Masculine and feminine

(a) The sex of humans and animals is often shown lexically:

Male	*Female*
man man	**kvinna** woman
pojke boy	**flicka** girl
gubbe old man	**gumma** old woman
far father	**mor** mother
bror brother	**syster** sister
kung king	**drottning** queen
prins prince	**prinsessa** princess
hingst stallion	**märr** mare
tupp cockerel	**höna** hen

(b) The endings **-e** and **-a** on nouns denoting humans and animals often indicate masculine and feminine respectively (cf. also 218ff):

Males: **pojke** boy; **gubbe** old man; **kille** chap, guy; **tomte** gnome; **hane** male; **oxe** ox; **make** spouse (i.e. husband)

Females: **flicka** girl; **gumma** old woman; **kvinna** woman; **häxa** witch; **hona** female; **katta** (female) cat; **maka** spouse (i.e. wife)

This also applies to personal names:

Men's names: **Ebbe, Ove, Åke, Tore, Olle, Folke, Yngve, Tage, Inge.**

Women's names: **Ebba, Eva, Åsa, Tora, Ulla, Lena, Maria, Gunilla, Inga.**

Exceptions: **Anne, Marianne, Marie, Susanne, Yvonne, Signe.**

(c) The endings **-inna, -ska** normally indicate female:

en väninna a (girl/woman) friend; **en kassörska** a (female) cashier; **en skådespelerska** an actress

Note 1: Functional feminines (job titles indicating gender) are becoming less frequent:

en lärarinna 'a woman teacher' is now **en lärare**.

Note 2: Matrimonial feminines (honorary titles accorded to the wives of professional people) have almost died out, but were common until the 20th century:

en professorska a professor's wife; **en biskopinna** a bishop's wife

(d) Many nouns that were formerly specifically male are now gender neutral:

läkare doctor; **tekniker** technician; **professor** professor

In order to distinguish gender the words **manlig** ('male') or **kvinnlig** ('female') are used: **en kvinnlig läkare** 'a female doctor'

Note 1: Compare: **kvinnoläkare** gynaecologist (of either gender)
  kvinnlig läkare woman doctor
But note: **kvinnopräst** woman priest

Note 2: Most nationality nouns indicate gender, e.g. **en tysk** (m.)/**en tyska** (f.) a German person (see 229)).

Note 3: Other nouns in **-man** are increasingly gender neutral: **en talesman** a spokesperson.

Note 4: In hospital terminology **en sjuksköterska** 'a nurse'; **en syster** 'a sister' are of either gender, as is **en barnmorska** 'a midwife'.

(e) Människan ('human being') is always referred to as **hon** ('she').

(f) Klockan (indicating time, see 416 (c)) is referred to as **hon** ('she'), whereas **klockan** (= 'the clock', 'watch') is referred to as **den** ('it'):

Hur mycket är klockan? Hon är fem.
What time is it? 5 o'clock.

Hur mycket kostar klockan? Den är gratis!
What does the watch cost? It's free!

107 Particularly difficult suffixes

(a) About fifty commonly used nouns end in **-skap**:

Non-neuter are:

bekantskap acquaintanceship; **egenskap** property; **fångenskap** captivity; **gemenskap** community; **kunskap** knowledge; **vetenskap** science; **vänskap** friendship

Neuter are:

budskap message; **främlingskap** estrangement; **författarskap** authorship; **landskap** province; **medlemskap** membership; **mästerskap** championship; **redskap** tool; **sällskap** society

(b) About fifty nouns end in **-ent**:

Non-neuter (mostly people) are:

> **accent** accent; **agent** agent; **cement** cement; **disponent** manager; **docent** university lecturer; **klient** client; **konsument** consumer; **patient** patient; **president** president; **procent** per cent; **student** student

Neuter (mostly abstract concepts) are:

> **argument** argument; **departement** department; **dokument** document; **element** element; **experiment** experiment; **moment** moment

(c) About twenty-five nouns end in **-at**:

Non-neuter (mostly people, animals, plants and instruments) are:

> **kandidat** candidate; **soldat** soldier; **delegat** delegate; **advokat** advocate; **senat** senate; **apparat** piece of equipment; **pirat** pirate; **demokrat** democrat; **kamrat** friend; **traktat** treaty; **tomat** tomato

Neuter (mostly substances and abstract concepts) are:

> **mandat** parliamentary seat; **proletariat** proletariat; **plakat** placard; **klimat** climate; **format** format; **pensionat** cheap hotel; **preparat** preparation; **referat** report; **resultat** result; **attentat** attempted assassination; **sulfat** sulphate; **pastorat** parish; **korrelat** correlative; **citat** quotation

(d) Nouns in **-al**:

Non-neuter are:

> **signal** signal; **liberal** liberal; **lokal** premises; **areal** area

Neuter are:

> **ideal** ideal; **material** material; **original** original; **kapital** capital

108 Nouns with uncertain gender

(a) A number of nouns take either gender. These include the following (the more usual gender is given first):

baconen/baconet (pl. -0)	the bacon
bolstern/bolstret (pl. **bolstrar/bolster**)	the bolster
borren/borret (pl. **-ar** or -0)	the drill
hemvistet/hemvisten (pl. **-er**)	the abode

jacket/jacken (pl. -0 or –ar)	the socket
kumminen/kumminet (pl.-0)	the cumin
mjället/mjällen (pl.-0)	the dandruff
näbben/näbbet (pl. -ar or -0)	the beak
paraplyet/paraplyn (pl. -er, -n)	the umbrella
tacket/tack-en (pl. -0)	(the) thanks
testet/testen (pl. -er)	the test
tjärnen/tjärnet (pl. -ar or -0)	the tarn

See 112–117 for plural endings.

(b) Particularly uncertain are concrete non-count nouns indicating substances:

fotogen paraffin; **koffein** kaffein; **morfin** morphine; **latex** latex; **nylon** nylon; **muslin** muslin

Note: In regional colloquial language the gender of some nouns differs from that found in standard written Swedish.

Written Swedish has non-neuter gender for: **apelsin** orange; **bakelse** cream cake; **brunn** well; **spik** nail; **sylt** jam; **såg** saw; **tvål** soap.

Written Swedish has neuter gender for: **grus** gravel; **hekto** hectogramme; **kilo** kilogramme; **lasarett** hospital; **lås** lock; **rede** nest; **snus** snuff; **tjog** score.

109 Gender of proper nouns

Like common nouns, proper nouns have grammatical gender. This is determined by (a) their meaning, (b) the gender of their hyperonym, (c) the gender of their final element.

(a) Meaning:

(i) People have non-neuter gender: **den duktiga Ylva** (the) diligent Ylva.

(ii) Continents, countries, cities, etc. have neuter gender (see 104(a)): **det vackra Paris** beautiful Paris.

(b) Hyperonym-based gender implies that the gender is determined by the logical class or type word: **en ny Peugeot** 'a new Peugeot' (**en bil**, 'a car' is understood), **ett gott Chianti,** 'a good Chianti' (**ett vin**, 'a wine' is understood).

(c) Final element determines gender: **den hotade Nordsjön** the endangered North Sea (**en sjö** a sea); **den smala Doverkanalen** the narrow Straits of Dover; **Gibraltarsundet är också smalt** The Straits of Gibraltar are also narrow.

(d) The gender of some common groups of names is as follows:

Non-neuter:

People and animals: **Helena blev glad** Helena was happy.
Planets: **Pluto är mycket liten** Pluto is very small.
Streets: **Kungsportsavenyn är lång** Kungsportsavenyn is long.

Neuter:

Continents, land areas, mountains, countries, provinces and towns. Asien är stort.
Some organisations and companies: **Jaguar är framgångsrikt** Jaguar is successful.

110   Gender of abbreviations and foreign loans

(a) Abbreviations

(i) In most cases when the etymology of an abbreviation is no longer obvious there is a tendency to treat the abbreviation as a neuter singular concept:

LO (Landsorganisationen) är oenigt i frågan
LO (The Swedish Trade Union Confederation) is divided on the matter.

FN är starkt.   The United Nations is strong.
(plural: **Forenta Nationerna**)

Note: For some indigenous words the gender is the same as for the unabbreviated noun.

en mc = en motorcykel	a motorcycle
JO-n = Justitieombudsmannen	the Ombudsman
en bh = en bysthållare	a bra
KB (= Kungliga Biblioteket) är stängt.	The Royal Library is closed.

(ii) Foreign abbreviations, especially English ones, are generally treated as neuter:

Jag fick ett långt SMS.	I received a long text message.
det mäktiga USA, FBI, CIA	the mighty USA, FBI, CIA
ett wc	a WC
det välorganiserade SAS	the well-organised SAS company

(b) Foreign loans

Most loans, like 75% of all Swedish nouns, are non-neuter:

Ryder-cupen the Ryder Cup	cf. **en pokal** a cup
en kindergarten	cf. **en barnträdgård**

In cases where the loan takes neuter gender, this is usually the result of influence from a cognate Swedish word:

ett fait accompli	cf. **ett faktum** fact
ett team	cf. **ett lag**
ett jobb	cf. **ett arbete**
ett city a city centre	cf. **ett affärscentrum**
ett game	cf. **ett spel**

C PLURAL NOUN FORMS – THE DECLENSIONS

111 Introduction

Swedish has seven ways of forming the plural of nouns. These declensions are outlined in paragraphs 112–118 below. There are also some irregular plural forms detailed in these paragraphs. For a key to predicting the plural forms of nouns quickly and accurately, see 119.

112 The first declension: plurals in **-or**

(a) The first declension includes:

(i) Only non-neuter nouns.

(ii) Many bisyllabic and polysyllabic nouns in **-a**:

   flicka girl; **gata** street; **lampa** lamp

(iii) A very few nouns ending in a consonant:

   ros rose; **toffel** slipper; **våg** wave

(b) Basic rule:

The final **-a** of first declension nouns is replaced by the plural ending **-or**.

en flicka	a girl	**två flickor**	two girls
en blomma	a flower	**två blommor**	two flowers
en gata	a street	**två gator**	two streets

(c) Nouns in **-el**, **-er** drop the vowel of their final syllable before adding **-or**:

en toffel	a slipper	**två tofflor**	two slippers
en åder	a vein	**två ådror**	two veins

(d) Nouns ending in a consonant simply add **-or** to the stem:

en ros	a rose	**två rosor**	two roses
en våg	a wave	**två vågor**	two waves

Note 1: The following nouns have a common plural form for both of their singular forms:

en flagg *or* **en flagga**	**två flaggor**	two flags
en spån *or* **en spåna**	**två spånor**	two chips (of wood)

Note 2: The following nouns properly belong to other declensions, but possess an alternative plural ending in **-or**:

en katt, katter/kattor	
(by analogy with **en katta** a she-cat)	cat, cats
en kollega, kolleger/kollegor	colleague, colleagues
en svan, svanar/svanor (poetic)	swan, swans
en vad, vader/vador	calf, calves (of the leg)

(e) Even though the plural ending is always spelled **-or** in written Swedish, in spoken Swedish it is frequently pronounced as if it were spelled **-er**.

(f) The definite plural form of first declension nouns is formed by adding **-na** to the plural form (see 134(a)):

flickor	girls	**flickorna**	the girls
tofflor	slippers	**tofflorna**	the slippers
rosor	roses	**rosorna**	the roses

113　The second declension: plurals in -ar

(a) The second declension includes:

(i) Only non-neuter nouns (with one exception, see (f) below), many of them of indigenous origin.

(ii) Many monosyllabic nouns ending in a consonant:

hund dog; **mun** mouth; **arm** arm

(iii) Some monosyllabic nouns ending in a vowel:

sjö lake; **å** river; **ö** island

(iv) Nouns with unstressed endings in **-e, -el, -en, -er, -dom, -(n)ing, -lek, -is**:

pojke boy; **fågel** bird; **fröken** unmarried woman; **syster** sister; **sjukdom** illness; **tidning** newspaper; **storlek** size; **potatis** potato

(b) Basic rule:

Second declension nouns add the ending **-ar** to the stem to form the plural.

en hund	a dog	**två hundar**	two dogs
en bro	a bridge	**två broar**	two bridges
en ö	an island	**två öar**	two islands

(c) Nouns ending in **-e** drop this letter before adding the plural ending **-ar**:

en pojke	a boy	**två pojkar**	two boys
en kudde	a pillow	**två kuddar**	two pillows

(d) Polysyllabic nouns ending in **-el, -en, -er** drop the vowel in the final syllable before adding **-ar** (see also (e) and (f) below and 114(e)):

en fågel	a bird	**två fåglar**	two birds
en öken	a desert	**två öknar**	two deserts
en vinter	a winter	**två vintrar**	two winters

Note 1: This group also includes a number of loans previously possessing an s-plural (see also 118):

en blazer – blazrar; en jumper – jumprar; en reporter – reportrar; en container – containrar.

Note 2: Some other nouns in unstressed syllables in **-l, -n, -r** also drop the final vowel:

en djävul	a devil	**två djävlar**	two devils
en afton	an evening	**två aftnar**	two evenings
en sommar	a summer	**två somrar**	two summers

Note 3: **En fjäril – två fjärilar** a butterfly – two butterflies.

(e) Two nouns ending in **-er** modify the root vowel and drop the **-e** of their final syllable before adding **-ar**:

en dotter	a daughter	**två döttrar**	two daughters
en moder	a mother	**två mödrar**	two mothers

(f) There is one neuter noun in the second declension, which forms its plural like **vinter** (d) above:

ett finger	a finger	**två fingrar**	two fingers

(g) Monosyllabic nouns with a short vowel and ending in **-m** or **-n** double the final consonant before adding **-ar**:

en lem	a limb	**två lemmar**	two limbs
en gom	a palate	**två gommar**	two palates
en mun	a mouth	**två munnar**	two mouths

(h) The definite plural of second declension nouns is formed by adding **-na** to the indefinite plural form (see 134(a)):

hundar	dogs	**hundarna**	the dogs
fingrar	fingers	**fingrarna**	the fingers
mödrar	mothers	**mödrarna**	the mothers
munnar	mouths	**munnarna**	the mouths

114   The third declension: plurals in **-er**

(a) The third declension includes:

(i) Both non-neuter and neuter nouns.

(ii) Many monosyllabic nouns ending in a consonant:

en park a park; **en dam** a lady

(iii) Many nouns of foreign origin, including most foreign nouns with final stress:

en möbel a piece of furniture; **en regel** a rule; **en armé** an army; **en restaurang** a restaurant; **en trottoar** a pavement; **ett bryggeri** a brewery; **ett paraply** an umbrella

(iv) A number of nouns which modify the root vowel in the plural (see (h) and (j) below):

en hand	a hand	**två händer**	two hands
en bok	a book	**två böcker**	two books

Non-neuter nouns ending in **-het**, **-nad**:

en dumhet	a blunder	**två dumheter**	two blunders
en byggnad	a building	**två byggnader**	two buildings

(b) Basic rule:

Third declension nouns add the plural ending **-er** to the stem:

en park	a park	**två parker**	two parks
en månad	a month	**två månader**	two months

(c) Polysyllabic nouns ending in a stressed syllable add the plural ending **-er** in accordance with the basic rule. These nouns are invariably of foreign origin:

en armé	an army	**två arméer**	two armies
ett geni	a genius	**två genier**	two geniuses
en ragu	a ragout	**två raguer**	two ragouts
en meny	a menu	**två menyer**	two menus
en essä	an essay	**två essäer**	two essays
en miljö	an environment	**två miljöer**	two environments
en station	a station	**två stationer**	two stations
en direktör	a director	**två direktörer**	two directors
en geolog	a geologist	**två geologer**	two geologists
en emigrant	an emigrant	**två emigranter**	two emigrants
en autograf	an autograph	**två autografer**	two autographs

(d) Non-neuter polysyllabic nouns ending in unstressed **-or** add the plural ending **-er** in accordance with the basic rule, but in the plural the stress shifts to the **-or** syllable:

en pro'fessor	a professor	**två profe'ssorer**	two professors
en 'doktor	a doctor	**två dok'torer**	two doctors
en 'motor	an engine	**två mo'torer**	two engines

Note 1: Some words ending in **-or** already have the stress on the final syllable even in the singular form:

en ma'jor	a major	**två ma'jorer**	two majors
en korri'dor	a corridor	**två korri'dorer**	two corridors

Note 2: This shift in stress is also found in the following nouns with other final syllables:

en 'konsul	a consul	**två kon'suler**	two consuls
en 'kansler	a chancellor	**två kans'lerer**	two chancellors

(e) Polysyllabic nouns ending in unstressed **-el, -en, -er** drop the **-e** of the final syllable before adding the plural ending **-er** (cf. 113(d)):

en muskel	a muscle	**två muskler**	two muscles
en sägen	a legend	**två sägner**	two legends
en fiber	a fibre	**två fibrer**	two fibres

(f) Nouns of foreign origin ending in **-eum**, **-ium** drop the the final syllable **-um** before adding the plural ending **-er**:

ett laboratorium	a laboratory	**två laboratorier**	two laboratories
ett museum	a museum	**två museer**	two museums

Nouns ending in unstressed **-a** drop this **-a** before adding the plural ending **-er**:

ett drama	a drama	**två dramer**	two dramas
en historia	a history	**två historier**	two histories

(g) The following nouns double their final consonant before adding the plural ending **-er**:

en vän	a friend	**två vänner**	two friends
en gnet	a nit	**två gnetter**	two nits
en get	a goat	**två getter**	two goats
en nöt	a nut	**två nötter**	two nuts

This involves the shortening of the vowel except in the case of **vän** where the vowel is already short.

(h) The following nouns modify their root vowel as well as adding the plural ending **-er** or **-r**:

Vowel change:

a → ä

en and	a duck	**två änder**	two ducks
en brand	a fire	**två bränder**	two fires
en hand	a hand	**två händer**	two hands
ett land	a country	**två länder**	two countries
en natt	a night	**två nätter**	two nights
en rand	a stripe	**två ränder**	two stripes
en strand	a beach	**två stränder**	two beaches
en tand	a tooth	**två tänder**	two teeth

a → ä

en bokstav	a letter of the alphabet	**två bokstäver**	two letters of the alphabet
en stad	a town	**två städer**	two towns

å → ä

en spång	a plank	två spänger	two planks
en stång	a pole	två stänger	two poles
en tång	a pair of tongs	två tänger	two pairs of tongs

o → ö

en bot	a penance	två böter	two penances, fines
en ledamot	a member	två ledamöter	two members
en son	a son	två söner	two sons

(j) The following nouns both modify and shorten their root vowel and double the final consonant before adding the plural ending -er:

en fot	a foot	två fötter	two feet
en rot	a root	två rötter	two roots
en bok	a book	två böcker	two books
		(NB Spelling)	

(k) Bi- and polysyllabic non-neuter nouns in -al normally take the plural ending -er (see also 107(d)):

| en pedal | a pedal | två pedaler | two cups |
| en areal | an area | två arealer | two areas |

Note: The following nouns in -al are only found in the plural (cf. 124):

arkivalier archives; kemikalier chemicals; viktualier victuals

(l) The definite plural of third declension nouns is formed by adding -na to the plural form (cf. 134(b)):

parker	parks	parkerna	the parks
arméer	armies	arméerna	the armies
muskler	muscles	musklerna	the muscles
museer	museums	museerna	the museums
händer	hands	händerna	the hands

115 The fourth declension: plurals in -r

(a) The fourth declension includes only non-neuter nouns ending in a vowel (not -a):

en ko a cow; en linje a line; en aktie a share; en hustru a wife

(b) Basic rule: fourth declension nouns add **-r** to the stem to form the plural.

(c) Fourth declension nouns are of the following kinds:

(i) A few monosyllabic non-neuter nouns:

en sko	a shoe	**två skor**	two shoes
en tå	a toe	**två tår**	two toes
en mö	a maiden	**två mör**	two maidens

Also: **klo** claw; **vrå** corner; and nouns in **-bo**: **Uppsalabo** inhabitant of Uppsala; **sambo** life partner.

(ii) Some non-neuter nouns ending in **-e**, particularly in **-ie**, **-je**:

en kastanje	a chestnut	**två kastanjer**	two chestnuts
en aktie	a share	**två aktier**	two shares
en fiende	an enemy	**två fiender**	two enemies

Others: **same** Sami; **pinje** pine.

Note: **en bonde – två bönder**, a farmer – two farmers, (Vowel change!)

(iii) Some non-neuter nouns ending in **-else**, **-arie**:

en rörelse	a movement	**två rörelser**	two movements
en bibliotekarie	a librarian	**två bibliotekarier**	two librarians

Note: **ett fängelse – två fängelser**, a prison – two prisons, (Neuter gender!)

(iv) Some non-neuter nouns ending in other unstressed vowels, especially **-o**, **-u**:

en bastu	a sauna	**två bastur**	two saunas
en studio	a studio	**två studior**	two studios

Also, **farstu** porch; **jungfru** virgin; **duo** duo; **radio** radio.

Note: Some neuter nouns in **-o** take the **n**-plural however:

ett kvitto – två kvitton areceipt – two receipts

Also with n-plural: **fiasko** fiasco; **intermezzo; motto; tempo; veto** (See 116).

(d) The definite plural for fourth declension nouns is formed by adding **-na** to the indefinite plural form.

bastur	saunas	**basturna**	the saunas
fiender	enemies	**fienderna**	the enemies

116   The fifth declension: plurals in **-n**

(a) The fifth declension includes:

(i) Only neuter nouns.

(ii) Almost exclusively nouns ending in a vowel.

(b) Basic rule:

Fifth declension nouns add the ending **-n** to the stem to form the plural.

ett hjärta	a heart	**två hjärtan**	two hearts
ett ansikte	a face	**två ansikten**	two faces
ett märke	a mark	**två märken**	two marks
ett bi	a bee	**två bin**	two bees
ett piano	a piano	**två pianon**	two pianos
ett rally	a rally	**två rallyn**	two rallies
ett strå	a straw	**två strån**	two straws
ett knä	a knee	**två knän**	two knees
ett frö	a seed	**två frön**	two seeds

(c) Notice the following irregular plural forms of three frequent nouns regarded as belonging to the fifth declension:

ett öga	an eye	**två ögon**	two eyes
ögat	the eye	**ögonen**	the eyes
		colloquial	
		pronunciation /ögona/	
ett öra	an ear	**två öron**	two ears
örat	the ear	**öronen**	the ears
ett huvud	a head	**två huvuden**	two heads
colloquial			
pronunciation /huve/		/huven/	
huvudet	the head	**huvudena**	the heads
colloquial			
pronunciation /huvet/		/huvena/	

(d) Nouns in **-ande**, the majority of which were originally present participles, are inflected according to the fifth declension (see also 105(a)):

ett anförande	a statement	**två anföranden**	two statements
ett meddelande	a message	**två meddelanden**	two messages

Note 1: A small number of nouns in **-ande** denote persons and occupations, and they are then inflected according to the sixth declension with **-0** plural (cf. 117(a)(iii)):

en ordförande	a chairperson	**två ordförande**	two chairpersons
en studerande	a student	**två studerande**	two students

Note 2: Because of the large number and high frequency of the neuter nouns, it is common to find such contaminations as **två *studeranden, två *ordföranden** (cf. 105(a)).

(e) The names of the letters of the alphabet belong to this declension:

ett a	an a	**två a-n**	two a's
ett b	a b	**två b-n**	two b's

(f) The definite plural for fifth declension nouns is formed by adding **-a** to the indefinite plural form (see 134(c)):

ansikten	faces	**ansiktena**	the faces
teman	themes	**temana**	the themes

Note: For three important exceptions: **öga** eye; **öra** ear, **huvud** see 116(c).

117   The sixth declension: zero plurals

(a) The sixth declension includes:

(i) Both neuter and some non-neuter nouns.

(ii) Many neuter nouns ending in a consonant:

> **ett barn** a child; **ett hus** a house; **ett golv** a floor

(iii) All non-neuter nouns ending in **-are, -ande, -ende, -iker** and some in **-er** which denote people and professions (cf. 105(a)):

> **en lärare** a teacher; **en studerande** a student; **en gående** a pedestrian; **en elektriker** an electrician; **en partner** a partner

(iv) Neuter nouns ending in **-ment, -gram, -tek, -at**:

> **ett departement** a department; **ett program** a programme; **ett bibliotek** a library; **ett lektorat** a lectureship

(v) Names for berries and fruits ending in **-on**:

> **ett hallon** a raspberry; **ett smultron** a wild strawberry; **ett lingon** a cowberry

(b) Basic rule:

Sixth declension nouns add the ending -0 (zero) to the stem to form the plural, i.e. the indefinite plural is identical to the indefinite singular form (cf. English 'sheep'):

ett får	a sheep	**två får**	two sheep
ett hus	a house	**två hus**	two houses
en lärare	a teacher	**två lärare**	two teachers

(c) Most neuter nouns of this declension ending in a consonant + **um** have two or more possible indefinite plural forms. They may remain unchanged (-0 plural) or may replace the **-um** by either **-a**:

ett faktum	a fact	**två faktum/fakta**	two facts
ett datum	a date	**två datum/data**	two dates
ett centrum	a centre	**två centrum/centra/**	

See 133(g).

(d) En officer (alternative form: **officerare**) 'an officer', has the indefinite plural form **(två) officerare**.

(e) Definite plural forms follow two basic rules (see 134(d)f.):

1   Neuter nouns of the sixth declension add **-en** to the indefinite plural.

hus	houses	**husen**	the houses
problem	problems	**problemen**	the problems

Note 1: Neuter nouns of the sixth declension ending in unstressed **-el**, **-en**, **-er** drop the **-e** of the final syllable before adding the definite plural ending **-en** (see 134(e)):

två segel – seglen	two sails – the sails
två tecken – tecknen	two signs – the signs
två piller – pillren	two pills – the pills

Note 2: By analogy with other declensions some frequent neuter nouns of the sixth declension ending in a consonant possess an alternative form in colloquial Swedish (see 134(d)).

2   Non-neuter nouns of the sixth declension add **-na** to the indefinite plural.

musiker	musicians	**musikerna**	the musicians
studerande	students	**studerandena**	the students

Note: Non-neuter nouns of the sixth declension ending in **-are** drop the final **-e** before adding the definite article **-na** in the plural (see 134(g)):

två lärare – lärarna	two teachers – the teachers
två fiskare – fiskarna	two fishermen – the fishermen

(f) The following sixth declension nouns have irregular plural forms or plural definite forms:

broder	brodern	två bröder	bröderna	brother
fader	fadern	två fäder	fäderna	father
man	mannen	två män	männen (cf. 1205(c))	man
gås	gåsen	två gäss	gässen	goose
lus	lusen	två löss	lössen	louse
mus	musen	två möss	mössen	mouse
mil	milen	två mil	milen	Swedish mile
tum	tummen	två tum	tummen (cf. 1205(c))	inch

118   The seventh declension: plurals in -s

(a) The seventh declension includes:

Non-neuter loans retaining their foreign character but with stress not on the final syllable:

en happening, en musical, en farm, jeans

Note that, when the loan becomes familiar in Swedish, an indigenous plural may be employed instead:

reporters	→ **reportrar**	**royalties**	→ **royaltyer**
jumpers	→ **jumprar**	**babies**	→ **babyar/babyer**
		designers	→ **designer**

(b) Factors tending to favour the use of the s-plural with loans include:

(i) A structure that does not easily allow the use of other plural endings: **trailers, receivers** (though *Svenska Akademiens ordlista* only lists **trailrar, receivrar**).

For the sake of pronunciation it is more convenient to retain the s-plural here.

Notice the problems inherent in, for example: ***sprinklrar, *partnrar**

Note: The 0-plural is used as an alternative in some cases: **två bestseller, två partner**.

(ii) The loan has a meaning which rarely requires its use in the singular:

odds, gags, pickels, cornflakes, pumps, shorts, blinkers

(c) A major problem in employing many loans is the formation of a definite plural form, as the usual choices **-na**, **-a**, **-en**, may all provide difficulties:

*designersen, *designersarna

Yet the alternative 0-plural, e.g. **två designer**, is here still felt to be unnatural to many Swedes who use **designer** in the plural.

Where there is a collective sense in the plural, the s-plural is considered to belong to the stem. These nouns are then regarded as having a 0-plural, and **-en** is added to form a plural definite:

jeansen	the jeans	**gagsen**	the gags

Note: In certain words ending in **-s** the borrowed s-plural has at some time in the past been regarded (falsely) as part of the singular stem and a Swedish plural ending added:

en keps	a cap	**två kepsar**	two caps
en räls	a rail	**två rälsar**	two rails

119 Nouns – plural indefinite forms: predictability

(a) Plurals of Swedish nouns are very largely predictable. The decisive factors in the choice of a plural ending are:

1 Gender – whether the noun is non-neuter or neuter gender.
2 Whether the non-neuter noun has stress on the last syllable.
3 Which of certain distinctive suffixes is found in the non-neuter noun without stress on the last syllable.
4 Whether the neuter noun ends in a vowel or a consonant.
5 Whether the neuter noun ending in a vowel has stress on the last syllable.

(b) There are six main rules for predicting plural forms of nouns:

1 Non-neuter nouns ending in unstressed **-a** have a plural in **-or**:

en flicka **två flick*or*** girl(s)

2 Non-neuter nouns ending in unstressed **-e** have a plural in **-ar**:

en pojke **två pojk*ar*** boy(s)

3   Non-neuter nouns with stress on the last syllable have a plural in **-er**:

en armé   två arméer   army (armies)

4   Neuter nouns ending in a stressed vowel have a plural in **-er**:

ett geni   två genier   genius(es)

5   Neuter nouns ending in an unstressed vowel have a plural in **-n**:

ett yrke   två yrken   profession(s)

6   Neuter nouns ending in a consonant have a plural in -0 (i.e. no plural ending):

ett barn   två barn   child(ren)

(c) It is possible to formulate a number of additional rules for accurate prediction:

7   Non-neuter nouns ending in suffix **-are** have a plural in -0:

en lärare   två lärare   teacher(s)

8   Non-neuter nouns ending in suffix **-er** have a plural in -0:

en tekniker   två tekniker   technician(s)

9   Nouns (always non-neuter) ending in suffix **-(n)ing** have a plural in **-ar**:

en tidning   två tidningar   newspaper(s)

10 Nouns (always non-neuter) ending in the suffixes **-het, -nad, -tion** have a plural in **-er**:

en nyhet   två nyheter   (piece(s) of) news
en byggnad   två byggnader   building(s)
en station   två stationer   station(s)

Note 1: It is often difficult to predict the plurals of monosyllabic non-neuter nouns ending in a consonant. Such nouns add **-ar** or **-er**:

en bil	**två bilar**	car(s)
en färg	**två färger**	colour(s)
en hund	**två hundar**	dog(s)
en park	**två parker**	park(s)

Note 2: Nouns ending in unstressed -el, -en, -er tend to drop the -e in the final syllable and add -ar:

en fågel	**två fåglar**	bird(s)
en vinter	**två vintrar**	winter(s)
en fröken	**två fröknar**	unmarried woman (women)

Notice, however, that some loanwords ending in unstressed -el, -en, -er take -er:

en muskel	**två muskler**	muscle(s)
en neger	**två negrer**	negro(es)

(d) Plural predictability chart

		Plural	Example	Rule	Section
NON-NEUTER					
No stress on last syllable	ends in -a	+or	flickor	1	112
	ends in -e	+ar	pojkar	2	113
Stress on last syllable		+er	arméer	3	114
NEUTER					
Ends in vowel - with stress		+er	genier	4	114
Ends in vowel - without stress		+n	äpplen	5	116
Ends in consonant		+0	barn	6	117

D MISCELLANEOUS POINTS ON INDEFINITE PLURAL FORMS

120 Types of noun with no plural form

The following types of noun generally have no plural form:

(a) Verbal nouns describing an action:

ett bugande	a bow	(cf. **en bugning – två bugningar**)
ett mördande	a murder	(cf. **ett mord – två mord**)

Note: In cases where such verbal nouns have lost their original verbal significance they are inflected according to the fourth declension:

ett leende	a smile	**två leenden**	two smiles
leendena	the smiles		

Verbal nouns describing people belong to the sixth declension (cf. 117(a)):

en studerande	a student	**två studerande**	two students

(b) Abstract nouns:

godhet goodness; **köld** cold; **sötma** sweetness; **längtan** longing; **fattigdom** poverty; **adel** nobility; **glädje** joy

Note: Plurals of abstract nouns express a countable quantity, and occur only infrequently:

Hans döttrar var skönheter.	His daughters were beauties.
Du pratar dumheter!	You're talking nonsense!

(c) Substances and materials:

guld gold; **kött** meat; **kol** coal; **snö** snow; **dagg** dew; **nylon** nylon; **rost** rust; **luft** air; **mjölk** milk

Plurals of such words, usually formed with -er, are used to indicate types or makes of a substance:

teer teas; **viner** wines; **tyger** types of cloth

(d) Collective nouns:

boskap cattle; **folk** people; **avkomma** progeny

(e) Weights and measures are not usually used in the plural after cardinal numbers (cf. English '6 foot tall', '2 pound of potatoes', see also 126f.):

två kilo smör	two kilos of butter
nittonmeterlånga lastbilar	nineteen-metre-long trucks

(f) Bi- and polysyllabic non-neuter nouns ending in -an (cf. also 133(c)). These nouns often 'borrow' a plural form from other synonymous words:

en önskan	a wish	**två önskningar**	two wishes
en tävlan	a competition	**två tävlingar**	two competitions
en anmälan	a report	**två anmälningar**	two reports
en predikan	a sermon	**två predikningar**	two sermons
en begäran	a demand	**två krav**	two demands
en början	a beginning	**två inledningar**	two beginnings

Note: **Ett gisslan** 'hostage', has only one form for both singular and plural and in the definite singular and plural.

121 Nouns with special collective forms

A few nouns possess a special collective (non-count) form:

en ärta 'a pea'; count plural: **två ärtor** 'two peas'; collective: **ärter** 'peas' (in general)

Hur många ärtor har du på tallriken?
How many peas do you have on your plate?

Vi åt ärter och fläsk idag.
We ate pea soup and pork today.

en mygga 'a mosquito'; count plural: **två myggor** 'two mosquitoes'; collective: **mygg** 'mosquitoes' (in general)

Det var två myggor i tältet.	There were two mosquitoes in the tent.
Här finns mycket mygg.	There are a lot of mosquitoes here.

en bräda 'a plank'; count plural: **två brädor** 'two planks'; collective: **bräder** 'planks' (in general)

Vi behöver tre brädor till.	We need three more planks.
Vi säljer bräder.	We sell planks.

en polis 'a policeman'; count plural: **två poliser** 'two policemen'; collective: **polis** 'the police (force)'

Poliserna kom i två bilar.	The policemen came in two cars.
Polisen kom i två bilar.	The police came in two cars.
Polisen kom i en bil.	The policeman came in a car.

en man 'a man'; count plural: **män** 'men'; collective: **man** (organised group of men or women); **mannar** (colloquial and for a group)

Ett dussin män satt där.	A dozen men were sitting there.
en officer och tio man	one officer and ten men
en besättning på 500 man	a crew of 500
Mannarna klarade strapatserna.	The men coped with the hardships.

122   Nouns with no singular form

The following nouns are usually encountered only in the plural:

Declension:

1	**anor** lineage; **bannor** scolding; **brillor** glasses; ***byxor** trousers; **inälvor** bowels; ***matvaror** foodstuffs; **skulor** swill; **sopor** rubbish; **åthävor** gestures; **kläder** clothes
2	***föräldrar** parents; ***pengar** money; **småpojkar** small boys; **bränningar** surf
3	**annaler** annals; **arkivalier** archives; **ferier** holidays; ***finanser** finances; **förfäder** forefathers; **gotter** sweets; ***grönsaker** vegetables; **kalsonger** underpants; **kemikalier** chemicals; **later** manners; **räkenskaper** accounts; **ränker** machinations; **specerier** groceries; **viktualier** victuals; **repressalier** reprisals; **griller** whims; ***böter** fine
4	**choser** affectations; **dubier** doubts
5	***glasögon** spectacles; ***hängslen** braces
6	**livsmedel** groceries
7	**shorts** shorts; **jeans** jeans

Singular forms of the nouns marked * do exist in certain set phrases, and singulars are conceivable for some other nouns listed:

Det köpte jag för en billig peng.	I bought it for a small sum.
	(cf. 124(k))

finansens värld	the world of finance
Han ställdes till räkenskap.	He was brought to book.
räkenskapens dag	the day of reckoning
en slitstark byxa	a hard-wearing trouser

123 Nouns – plural endings: summary

Alternative forms are shown in brackets. Numbers refer to sections.

Section	Singular	Plural	Section	Plural ending	Meaning
112 First declension					
Non-neuter	en flicka	flickor		-or	girls
	en toffel	tofflor			slippers
	en ros	rosor			roses
	–	sopor	122		rubbish
113 Second declension					
Non-neuter	en hund	hundar		-ar	dogs
	en ö	öar			islands
	en pojke	pojkar			boys
	en tiger	tigrar			tigers
	en gangster	gangstrar			gangsters
	en dotter	döttrar			daughters
	–	småpojkar	122		small boys
114 Third declension					
Non-neuter	en park	parker		-er	parks
	en meny	menyer			menus
	en motor	motorer			engines
	en muskel	muskler			muscles
	en hand	händer			hands
	en fot	fötter			feet
	en hobby	hobbyer			hobbies
	en rabbi	rabbier			rabbis
	–	kläder	122		clothes
Neuter	ett geni	genier			geniuses
	ett museum	museer			museums
115 Fourth declension					
Non-neuter	en ko	kor		-r	cows
	en linje	linjer			lines
	en trio	trior			trios

Section	Singular	Plural	Section	Plural ending	Meaning
116 Fifth declension					
Neuter	ett ansikte	ansikten		-n	face
	ett foto	foton			photo
	ett öga	ögon			eye
	–	glasögon	122		spectacles
	ett antagande	antaganden			assumptions
	ett schema	scheman			timetables
117 Sixth declension					
Neuter	ett får	får		-0	sheep
	ett segel	segel			sails
	ett centrum	centrum (centrer/			
		centra)	117(c)		centres
	–	livsmedel	122		groceries
Non-neuter	en lärare	lärare			teachers
	en studerande	studerande			students
	en hammare	hammare/hamrar			hammers
	en musiker	musiker			musicians
	en designer	designer	118		designers
	en man	män			men
118 Seventh declension					
Non-neuter	en musical	musicals		-s	musicals
	en trailer	trailers (trailrar)			trailers
	–	jeans			jeans

E   SPECIAL USES OF THE SINGULAR AND PLURAL

124   Nouns which are singular in English but plural in Swedish

In addition to those nouns listed in 122 which have no singular form in Swedish, the following differences in usage may be noted:

(a) There was no furniture in the room.   **Det fanns inga möbler i rummet.**
     I bought a new piece of furniture.   **Jag köpte en ny möbel.**

(b) Have you any information about it?   **Har du några upplysningar om det?**
     I have been informed that . . .   **Jag har fått upplysning om att . . .**

(c) My income and expenditure . . .   Mina inkomster och utgifter . . .
     They live on a good income.   De lever på en bra inkomst.
     Buying a car is a big expense.   Att köpa bil är en stor utgift.

(d) A good knowledge of Swedish . . .   Goda kunskaper i svenska . . .
     The tree of knowledge . . .   Kunskapens träd . . .

(e) He is making good progress.   Han gör stora framsteg.
     The victory was a step forward.   Segern var ett framsteg.

(f) The news is on TV every night.   Nyheterna är på TV varje kväll.
     I have got some news (a piece of
     news) for you.   Jag kan tala om en nyhet för dig.

(g) Business is good.   Affärerna går bra.
     A good piece of business . . .   En god affär . . .

(h) I need some good advice.   Jag behöver några goda råd.
     A good piece of advice . . .   Ett gott råd . . .

(j) A fine of 500 crowns . . .   Femhundra kronors böter . . .

Note that **bot** means 'penance'.

(k) I have no money.   Jag har inga pengar.

Peng in the singular is only encountered in idioms: **en vacker peng, en billig peng** [See 122].

(l) I had finished my homework at   Jag var färdig med läxorna kl. 6.
     6 o'clock.

     I have finished my history homework but I have my Swedish left.
     Jag är färdig med historieläxan, men jag har svenskan kvar.

(m) Other words which regularly occur in the plural in Swedish where English has a singular:

     skällsord (pl.) abuse; **applåder** applause; **kontanter** cash; **bevis** (pl.)
     evidence

Note: Swedish has a plural where English often uses a singular noun with certain expressions with fractions (413(c)):

dela något i två halvor   divide something in half

125 Nouns which are singular in Swedish but plural in English

(a) Swedish has a number of singular nouns which correspond to plural ideas in English:

aska-n	ashes
folk-et	(the) people
havre-n	oats
innehåll-et	contents, ingredients
lokal	premises
lön-en	wages
massan	the masses
moral-en	morals
narkotika-n	drugs, narcotics
protokoll-et	minutes
rekvisita-n	(stage) props
sprit-en	spirits
statistik-en	statistics
tack-et	thanks
trappa-n	stairs, steps

This applies especially to cases where English has 'a pair of':

en bälg	(a pair of) bellows
en passare	(a pair of) compasses
en pincett	(a pair of) tweezers
en sax	(a pair of) scissors
en trappstege	(a pair of) steps, stepladder
en tång	(a pair of) tongs
en våg	(a pair of) scales

Notice that 'several pairs of scissors' = **flera saxar**, and so on.

(b) Notice the use of Swedish singular where English uses a plural form of the noun in reciprocating constructions:

Ska vi byta plats?	Shall we change places?
Ska vi skaka hand?	Shall we shake hands?
Hon blev god vän med honom.	She made friends with him.

(c) Others:

medeltiden	the Middle Ages
medelklassen	the middle class(es)
tull(en)	(the) Customs

126 Singular for the quantity expressed

In expressions such as those given below the noun indicating the measure of quantity is usually in the singular form regardless of the quantity involved. Notice that the English 'of' has no equivalent in these expressions.

en kilometer	one kilometre
femtio kilometer	fifty kilometres
en mil	one Swedish mile (= 10 km)
två mil	two Swedish miles
en meter (tyg)	one metre (of cloth)
tre meter (tyg)	three metres (of cloth)
ett kilo (smör)	one kilo (of butter)
fyra kilo (smör)	four kilos (of butter)
ett hekto (mjöl)	one hecto (of flour) (= 100 gram)
sex hekto (mjöl)	six hectos (of flour)
en fot	one foot
två fot	two feet (or: foot)
en liter (mjölk)	one litre (of milk)
tre liter (mjölk)	three litres (of milk)
(det kostar inte) ett öre	(it doesn't cost) an öre
(det kostar) femtio öre	(it costs) fifty öre

Exception: **krona**

en krona	one crown (unit of currency)
två kronor	two crowns
det kostar tio kronor	it costs ten crowns

Note: Less common are:

en famn ved	one cord of wood
två famnar ved	two cords of wood
en skäppa havre	one bushel of oats
två skäppor havre	two bushels of oats

127 Plural for the measure of quantity

Plural forms of the nouns in 126 are encountered when the measure of quantity rather than the quantity expressed is of prime importance:

Nu har vi bara de sista kilometrarna kvar.
Now we only have the last kilometres left.

De extra fem kilona smör gjorde att han inte kunde lyfta lådan.
The extra five kilos of butter meant that he could not lift the box.

Han hade flera litrar med sig när han reste ur landet.
He had several litre bottles (of spirits) with him when he left the country.

Han stod och hotade henne med sina åttio vältränade kilon.
He stood threatening her with his 80 well-trained kilos.

F NOUN HOMONYMS

128 List of Swedish noun homonyms

Some Swedish nouns have either two different genders or two different plural forms or both, indicating differences of meaning. Sometimes the words have different accent (word stress) in the singular definite and indefinite forms. The following is a list of the most frequent homonyms.

Singular indefinite	Plural indefinite	Meaning
en bak	bak	behind, seat
ett bak	bak	bake
en bal	balar	bale
en bal	baler	ball, dance
en bank	bankar	sandbank
en bank	banker	bank, financial institution
en bas	basar	foreman, supervisor
en bas	baser	(1) base, (2) basic substance
en bok	bokar	beech tree
en bok	böcker	book
en byrå	byråar	bureau, chest of drawers
en byrå	byråer	bureau, office of government, department
en bål	bålar	(1) trunk, body, (2) bowl
ett bål	bål	bonfire
en damm	dammar	(1) dam, (2) reservoir, pond
damm (-et-)	–	dust
ett element	element	radiator, heater
ett element	elementer	element, fundamental
en fax	faxar	fax machine
ett fax	fax	fax message
fil (-en/-et)	–	soured milk, yoghourt
en fil	filar	file, rasp
en fil	filer	row, lane (of road)
en form	formar	mould
en form	former	form, shape

en grund	grunder	reason, ground(s)
ett grund	grund	shallow, sandbank
en gång	gångar	path
en gång	gånger	time, occasion
en gång	–	gait
en knäck	knäckar	toffee
ett knäck	knäck	income from extra work
en kur	kurar	shed
en kur	kurer	cure
en lag	lagar	law
ett lag	lag	team, group
en lager	lagrar	laurel
ett lager	lager	(1) store, (2) layer
ett land	länder	country
ett land	land	(1) plot of land, (2) province
en led	leder	(1) joint, (2) way, route
ett led	led	(1) link, (2) row, (3) generation
en lock	lockar	lock of hair, curl
ett lock	lock	lid
en lår	lårar	packing case
ett lår	lår	thigh
en mask	maskar	worm
en mask	masker	mask
en not	notar	seine net
en not	noter	(1) musical note, (2) written note
en nöt	nötter	nut (edible)
ett nöt	nöt	creature, beast
en plan	planer	(1) plan, (2) sports pitch
ett plan	plan	(1) plane, (2) aeroplane
en pris	prisar	pinch (e.g. of salt, snuff)
ett pris	priser	price
ett pris	pris	prize, reward
en ras	raser	race of people or animals
ett ras	ras	landslide
en regel	regler	rule, law
en regel	reglar	(1) door bolt, (2) beam
en rev	revar	fishing line
ett rev	rev	reef, sandbank
en slav	slavar	slave
en slav	slaver	Slav
en stav	stavar	staff, pole
en stav	stäver	(wooden) stave (in a barrel etc.)
ett stånd	stånd	status, class, level
ett stånd	ständer	estate e.g. **de fyra ständerna**

en val	valar	whale
ett val	val	(1) choice, (2) election
en vad	vader	calf (of leg)
en vad	vadar	seine net
ett vad	vad	(1) bet, (2) appeal, (3) ford
en vals	valsar	roller
en vals	valser	waltz
en våg	vågar	balance, scales
en våg	vågor	wave

G   THE GENITIVE

129   The form of the genitive

(a) Basic rule:

Add **-s** to the indefinite or definite singular, indefinite or definite plural form.

Indefinite singular genitive
en flickas a girl's
ett barns a child's

Definite singular genitive
flickans the girl's
barnets the child's

Indefinite plural genitive
flickors girls'
barns children's

Definite plural genitive
flickornas the girls'
barnens the children's

There are, however, other genitive endings listed below and also many periphrastic forms of the genitive (See 729).

(b) Unlike English, no apostrophe is used with the genitive **-s**:

ett barns ansikte   a child's face

(c) Scandinavian place names ending in a consonant usually take an **-s** (but cf. (e) below):

Gripsholms slott Gripsholm Castle; **Dalslands kanal** the Dalsland Canal

(d) Names ending in **-s**, **-x** and **-z** usually have no s-genitive and no apostrophe (but cf. (g) below):

Lukas evangelium Luke's gospel; **Topelius dikter** Topelius' poems; **SAS terminal** SAS's terminal; **Marx "Das Kapital"**; **Schweiz järnvägar** Switzerland's railways

An apostrophe is used if a misunderstanding might otherwise arise:

Engels' skrifter Engels' writings

Note 1: Names ending in an s-sound and silent **e** as well as those in **-sj**, **-tj** sounds usually take an **-s**:

Alices äventyr i underlandet Alice's Adventures in Wonderland; **Sjostakovitjs fjärde symfoni** Shostakovich's Fourth Symphony

Note 2: Genitives of acronyms are written with a colon +s:

LO:s regler   LO's rules

(e) Some Scandinavian place names, especially those ending in a vowel, may have a genitive without **-s** in set phrases:

Uppsala domkyrka Uppsala Cathedral; **Solna Centrum** Solna Centre; **Huddinge sjukhus** Huddinge hospital; **Visby ringmur** Visby's Walls; **Malmö hamn** Malmö harbour

Note: **Falu gruva** (from **Falun**)   Falun's mine

(f) Adjectival nouns may also take an s-genitive (see also 227(c)):

de gamlas besparingar the old people's savings; **den döendes sista ord** the dying man's last words; **det godas seger** the triumph of good

(g) Latin genitives are used in some loanwords and names:

Kristi himmelsfärd the ascension of Christ; **Jesu liv** the life of Jesus; **Berzelii park** Berzelius Park; **Bacchi son** son of Bacchus

There is a double Latin genitive in: **i Jesu Kristi namn** in the name of Jesus Christ

Note:

Olaus Petris kyrka (← **Petri**)   Olaus Petri's Church
Pompejis sista dagar (← **Pompeji**)   the last days of Pompeii

(h) There are many remnants of the Old Swedish genitive case after the preposition **till**:

(i) With an **s**-genitive:

> **till fots** on foot; **till skogs** to/in the forest; **till havs** to/at sea; **till sjöss** to/at sea; **till torgs** to market; **till fjälls** to the mountains; **gå till bords** go to (the) table; **gå till sängs** go to bed

Note: In some cases the stem vowel is shortened and the final consonant devoiced when the -s is added: **hav** (pronounced /haːv/), 'sea' → **(till) havs**, (pronounced /hafs/), '(to) sea'; **skog** (pronounced /skɯːg/, 'forest' → **(till) skogs** /skɯks/, 'to the forest'.

(ii) With an **a**-genitive or **o**- or **u**-genitive (old genitive plural) after **till**:

> **gå till väga** set about; **gå någon till handa** be of help to someone; **vara till salu** be for sale; **ta till orda** start to speak

130   The use of the genitive

(a) Swedish uses the genitive in -s much more often than English uses s-genitives. The s-genitive is very frequent in Swedish, especially in the written language, and corresponds both to English genitive constructions with 's or s' and to expressions with 'of' (but cf. 729):

pojkens far	the boy's father
pojkarnas far	the boys' father
Amerikas upptäckt	the discovery of America
en hjältes död	the death of a hero
Englands drottning	the Queen of England
Sveriges huvudstad	the capital of Sweden
Stockholms stad (but cf. 729(f))	the town of Stockholm

(b) After a noun in the genitive form the noun following does not take an end article:

bergets topp	the top of the hill
skolans rektor	the headmaster of the school
flickornas föräldrar	the girls' parents

This often involves a conscious transformation from the English:

The end of summer		**Sommarens slut**
Def. art. *No art.*	→	*Def. art.* *No art.*

Note: A rare exception is where the noun is a title or proper name:

Jag tycker om Mobergs Utvandrarna. I like Moberg's *The Emigrants.*
En resa till sjöfåglarnas Färöarna. A journey to the Faeroes of the sea birds

(c) If a name comprises a group of words, the genitive is usually placed on the last word of the group, the group genitive:

Bo Janssons far	Bo Jansson's father
mannen på gatans åsikter	the views of the man in the street
Kungen av Danmarks bröstkarameller	King of Denmark's Cough Drops [a proprietary brand in Sweden]
Karl den Stores rike	Charlemagne's kingdom
Forskning och Framstegs redaktör	the editor of *Forskning och Framsteg*

Note 1: In lists, however, each element should in correct written Swedish have an -s:

*Åke och Lisas lillayster → **Åkes och Lisas lillasyster** Åke's and Lisa's little sister

Note 2: A noun or pronoun in apposition, when it is pre-positioned, takes the same case as the noun to which it refers, in these examples the genitive:

Under ordförandens, doktor Svenssons, frånvaro ...
During the Chairman, Dr Svensson's, absence ...

(d) Notice the following special uses of the **s**-genitive in Swedish:

(i) In certain set expressions to indicate a quality:

medelålders herrar	middle-aged men
de stackars barnen	the poor (unfortunate) children
den satans lymmeln	the damned wretch
ett jädrans väder	damned awful weather

(ii) The genitive of measurement:

ett par timmars sömn	a couple of hours' sleep
en tvåliters vinflaska	a two-litre wine bottle
ett fyrtiominuters TV-program	a forty-minute TV programme

(iii) 'Kind(s) (sort(s), type(s)) of':

En sorts, sorters (from **en sort**), **ett slags, slags** (pronounced /slaks/, from **ett slag**):

en sorts radiomottagare	a sort of radio receiver
sju sorters kakor	seven kinds of cake
ett slags frukt	a type of fruit
Det finns två slags statsmän.	There are two kinds of statesman.

Note how adjectives are used before and after **sorts** and **slags**. (See also 223(a)(ii))

> **en ny sorts vin/ett nytt slags vin**   a new type of wine
> **en sorts egendomlig insekt**   a kind of strange insect

Note: **Ett slags** has now lost its status as a noun and functions like an indeclinable adjective cf. **allsköns** 206(c). A frequent mistake is to write e.g. *****en slags ny blomma**, 'a kind of new flower', where the indefinite article agrees with **blomma**. This kind of attraction is grammatically incorrect (see also 214, 223(a)(ii)).

(iv) The explicative genitive:

> **Lövens långa sjö**   the long lake Löven
> **avhållsamhetens dygd**   the virtue of abstinence

(v) Genitives in names:

> **Jag handlar hos Olssons.**   I always shop at Olsson's.
> **mitt emot Pettersons**   opposite Petterson's
> (i.e. **Pettersons hus**)

> **Överstens (familj) kommer på besök.**
> The colonel's family are coming on a visit.

(vi) **S**-genitive corresponding to English superlative + 'in' + place name:

> **Sveriges rikaste man**   the richest man in Sweden

(vii) The objective genitive is best avoided. **Olof Palmes mord** would suggest that Palme committed murder: use **mordet på Olof Palme.**

(e) In spoken Swedish there are many different prepositional expressions corresponding to the English genitive construction with 'of'. There are also some cases when the Swedish equivalent to English constructions with 'of' involves no genitive marker at all. For a detailed account of these, see 729.

H   THE FORM OF THE INDEFINITE ARTICLE

131   The indefinite article

The indefinite article in Swedish is **en** for non-neuter nouns and **ett** for neuter nouns:

> *en* **flicka** a girl   *ett* **äpple** an apple
> *en* **arm** an arm   *ett* **barn** a child

J THE FORM OF THE DEFINITE (END) ARTICLE

132 The definite (end) article

In Swedish the definite article (or end article) singular is added to the end of the noun as a suffix: **-en/-n** for non-neuter nouns and **-et/-t** for neuter nouns.

The definite (or end) article plural is **-na** for nouns ending in the plural indefinite in **-or, -ar, -er** (mostly non-neuter), **-en** for nouns ending in the plural indefinite in **-0** and **-a** for nouns ending in **-n** (mostly neuter). (see 134)

Singular: *Plural:*

flickan the girl   **äpplet** the apple   **flickorna** the girls   **äpplena** the apples
armen the arm   **barnet** the child   **armarna** the arms   **barnen** the children

133 The form of the definite singular

(a) Basic rule:

Most Swedish nouns ending in a consonant add **-en** or **-et** according to gender, whilst those ending in a vowel add **-n** or **-t** according to gender.

en lön	**lönen**	the salary
en firma	**firman**	the firm
ett företag	**företaget**	the company
ett yrke	**yrket**	the profession

(b) Nouns ending in **-er, -el, -en, -or**:

(i) Non-neuter nouns ending in stressed **-el, -er, -or** (mostly loanwords) add **-en** according to the main rule:

> **materielen** the material; **klientelen** the clientele; **officer(e)n** the officer; **spanjoren** the Spaniard; **korridoren** the corridor; **metaforen** the metaphor

(ii) Non-neuter nouns ending in unstressed **-er, -el, -or** (see 113(d), 114(d), (e)) add **-n**:

> **brodern** the brother; **dottern** the daughter; **fadern** the father; **modern** the mother (***fadren** 'the father', ***modren** 'the mother' are archaic); **åkern** the field

> **fågeln** the bird; **cykeln** the cycle; **handeln** the trade; **möbeln** the piece of furniture; **regeln** the rule; **doktorn** the doctor; **motorn** the engine; **rektorn** the head teacher; **reaktorn** the reactor; **professorn** the professor

Note 1: In South and West Sweden the forms **cyklen, nycklen** are often found.

Note 2: **En himmel** ('heaven' or 'sky') has several alternative forms with end article singular: **himlen/ himmelen/himmeln.**

(iii) Neuter nouns ending in unstressed **-el, -er** (see 117(e) Note) add **-et** according to the main rule, but drop the final **-e** of the stem:

ett exempel	an example	**exemplet**	the example
ett finger	a finger	**fingret**	the finger

Similarly: **alstret** the product; **bullret** the noise; **lagret** the store; **lägret** the camp; **mönstret** the pattern; **silvret** the silver; **vädret** the weather

Note :The small number of neuter nouns which end in stressed **-er** (loanwords) take **-et**:

maneret the fashion; **kvarteret** the area, block

(iv) Nouns of both genders ending in unstressed **-en** drop the **-e** of the stem before adding the end article singular:

en socken	a parish	**socknen**	the parish
en öken	a desert	**öknen**	the desert
ett vapen	a weapon	**vapnet**	the weapon
ett tecken	a sign	**tecknet**	the sign

Note 1: *Exceptions*: **siden – sidenet** silk; **bäcken – bäckenet** pelvis

Note 2: A few nouns in unstressed **-en** possess no special definite form:

en fröken	an unmarried woman	**fröken**	the unmarried woman
examen	a degree	**examen**	the degree

Similarly: **kulmen** culmination; **orden** order; **borgen** surety; **lekamen** body; **lösen** stamp duty; **myrten** myrtle; **tentamen** examination.

Note 3: A few nouns in stressed **-en** take the endings **-en** or **-et** according to gender:

kaptenen the captain; **fenomenet** the phenomenon

(c) Nouns in **-an**:

Many non-neuter nouns ending in **-an** (see 120(f)), have no special definite form. These are often abstracts derived from verbs:

anmälan notification; **ansökan** application; **antydan** hint; **begäran** request; **början** beginning; **fruktan** fear; **förtvivlan** desperation; **gisslan** hostage; **inbjudan** invitation; **längtan** longing; **predikan** sermon; **strävan** striving; **tvekan** doubt; **tävlan** contest; **undran** wonderment; **vägran** refusal; **väntan** expectation; **ängslan** anguish; **önskan** wish

None of these nouns has a plural form but see 120(f).

Note: Neuter nouns ending in **-an** do, however, possess a definite form:

ett lakan	a bedsheet	**lakanet**	the bedsheet

(d) Contractions of the definite form in colloquial language:

(i) In colloquial Swedish non-neuter nouns ending in **-are** drop the final **-e** before adding the end article:

läraren	→	**lärarn**	the teacher
källaren	→	**källarn**	the basement

Note 1: A similar alternative short definite form is found in colloquial Swedish in the following nouns:

aborren	→	**aborrn**	the perch
ekorren	→	**ekorrn**	the squirrel
sommaren	→	**sommarn**	the summer

Note 2: There is a clear semantic distinction between **herrn** ('the gentleman') and **Herren** ('the Lord', i.e. 'God').

(ii) Alternative forms similar to those found in (b) above are the following colloquial forms for non-neuter nouns ending in **-l, -r**:

direktören	→	**direktörn**	the director
dörren	→	**dörrn**	the door
karlen	→	**karln**	the chap

Note: The final **-l** is not pronounced in any of the forms of **karl**.

(iii) Notice the common contractions:

staden	→	**stan**	the town
dagen	→	**dan**	the day

The short forms of these words are always found in spoken and often in colloquial written Swedish. They are also found in many compounds: **verkstan** 'the workshop'; **riksdan** 'Parliament'

(e) Nouns ending in stressed **-i, -é, -ä** and **-ö** (loanwords) also vary in their definite singular form according to gender (see 114(c)).

(i) Non-neuter nouns usually have the short form nowadays:

industrin industry; **energin** energy; (*but*: **Svenska akademien** the Swedish Academy); **armén** the army; **idén** the idea; **europén** the European; **essän** the essay

(ii) Neuter nouns usually retain the long form in written Swedish:

konditoriet (*or* **konditorit**) the café; **fotografiet** (*or* **fotografit**) the photograph; **knäet** (*or* **knät**) the knee; **träet** (*or* **trät**) the wood; **fröet** (*or* **fröt**) the seed; **kaféet** (*or* **kafét**) the café

(f) Bisyllabic or polysyllabic nouns ending in **-eum**, **-ium** (loanwords, see 114(f)) usually drop the **-um** before adding any endings:

museum	**museet**	**två museer**	**museerna**	museum
decennium	**decenniet**	**två decennier**	**decennierna**	decade

But cf.

aluminium	**aluminiumet**	(no plural)	aluminium
	(aluminiet)		

(g) Nouns ending in **-um** usually add **-et** to the stem and often possess several alternative definite forms (cf. 117(c)):

Indef. sing.	*Def. sing.*	*Indef. plural*	*Def. plural*
album	**albumet**	**två album**	**albumen**
('album')			
datum	**datumet**	**två datum**	**datumen**
('date')	**datum**		
faktum	**faktumet**	**två faktum**	**faktumen**
('fact')	**faktum**	**fakta**	**fakta**
centrum	**centrumet**	**två centrum**	**centrumen**
(Eng. 'centre')		**centra**	**centra**

(h) Notice the change of stem vowel in:

en historia	**historien**	**historier**	**historierna**
('story')			

(j) In some non-neuter nouns ending in **-n** the **-e** of the article drops and the **-n** of the article is assimilated in colloquial Central Swedish, especially in fixed expressions:

Låt maten tysta mun (munnen)!
Don't talk with your mouth full! (*lit.* Let your food silence your mouth!)
Kapten (kaptenen) stod på däck.   The captain stood on deck.

(k) Nouns ending in **-m**, **-n** after a short vowel double the **m** or **n** before adding the end article or plural ending (see also 1205):

hem	**hemmet**	**två hem**	**hemmen**	home
medlem	**medlemmen**	**två medlemmar**	**medlemmarna**	member
man	**mannen**	**två män**	**männen**	man
vän	**vännen**	**två vänner**	**vännerna**	friend

134   Choice of the definite plural ending

For plural indefinite forms see Chapter 1, C, D. For plural definite forms by declension, see 112(f), 113(h), 114(l), 115(d), 116(f), 117(e), 118(c). Gender and declension are, however, of little significance in determining the choice of the plural article form. The determining factor is the form of the plural indefinite.

(a) Plurals in **-or**, **-ar** (always non-neuter) add **-na**:

en gata	**två gator**	**gatorna**	the streets
väg	**två vägar**	**vägarna**	the roads

Note: The plural definite ending **-ne**, which was used especially for masculine nouns with plurals in **-ar**, **-are** (**pojkarne** 'the boys'; **hundarne** 'the dogs'; **lärarne** 'the teachers'), is now archaic.

(b) Plurals in **-er** (neuter and non-neuter) add **-na**:

ett vin	**två viner**	**vinerna**	the wines
en film	**två filmer**	**filmerna**	the films

(c) Plurals in **-n** (always neuter) add **-a**:

ett rike	**två riken**	**rikena**	the kingdoms
ett antagande	**två antaganden**	**antagandena**	the assumptions

(d) Most nouns of both genders with no plural form (0-plural), except those in (f), (g) below, add **-en**:

ett bord	**två bord**	**borden**	the tables
en mil	**två mil**	**milen**	the (Swedish) miles

Note: By analogy with other declensions some sixth declension neuter nouns ending in a consonant possess an alternative plural definite form in colloquial Swedish (though not in S. Swedish):

ett hus	**två hus**	**husen (husena)**	the houses
ett träd	**två träd**	**träden (träna)**	the trees
ett barn	**två barn**	**barnen (barna)**	the children
ett huvud	**två huvud**	**huvuden (huvudena)**	the heads

Forms in **-a** are still regarded as colloquial and should not be used in writing.

Nouns which modify their root vowel but take a 0-plural take **-en** in the plural definite, even though they do have a distinct plural form:

en man	**två män**	**männen**	the men
en gås	**två gäss**	**gässen**	the geese
en mus	**två möss**	**mössen**	the mice
en lus	**två löss**	**lössen**	the lice

See also 117(f).

(e) Neuter nouns ending in **-el**, **-en**, **-er** drop the **-e** of the stem before adding the plural end article **-en**:

ett exempel	**två exempel**	**exemplen**	the examples
ett tecken	**två tecken**	**tecknen**	the signs

(f) Neuter nouns ending in **-er** usually behave as those in (e) above:

ett blomster	**två blomster**	**blomstren**	the blooms
ett hinder	**två hinder**	**hindren**	the obstacles

Note: However, there is a tendency for some of these nouns to develop alternative plural definite forms in speech:

ett fönster	**fönstret**	**fönster**	**fönstren/**	the windows
			fönsterna	
ett nummer	**numret**	**nummer**	**numren/**	the numbers
			nummerna	

Also: **fruntimmer** 'woman' (derogatory); **bekymmer** 'worry'; **papper** 'paper'.

(g) Nouns (neuter and non-neuter) with 0-plurals and which end in **-are** drop the final **-e** before adding the plural end article **-na**:

en läkare	**två läkare**	**läkarna**	the doctors
bagare	**två bagare**	**bagarna**	the bakers

Note: Only two nouns in **-are** are neuter:

ett altare	**två altare (altaren)**	**altarna**	the altars
et ankare	**två ankare (ankaren)**	**ankarna**	the anchors

(h) Non-neuter nouns ending in **-er** with 0-plurals add **-na**:

indier	**två indier**	**indierna**	the Indians

(j) Nouns with a 0-plural (neuter and non-neuter) ending in **-s** add **-en**:

ett tricks	**två tricks**	**tricksen**	the tricks
ett par jeans	–	**jeansen**	the jeans

(k) Some nouns have no special plural definite form (although some of these may possess alternative distinct plural definite forms, shown in brackets below). They comprise largely:

(i) Nouns with a plural indefinite ending in **-a** (see also 117(c)):

> **aktiva** the assets; **data** the data; **examina** the degrees; **fakta** the facts; **lexika** (**lexikonen**) the dictionaries; **tentamina** the examinations; **passiva** the debts; **pronomina** (**pronomenen**) the pronouns

(ii) Nouns with a plural indefinite ending in **-i**:

cembali (cembalorna) the harpsichords; foci (fokusarna) the foci or focuses; tempi (tempona) tempos or tempi

135 Nouns – forms with end article: summary

Alternative forms and selected stems are shown in brackets. Figures refer to sections in the text.

Non-neuter Singular		Neuter Singular	
133(a)	arm-en	133(a)	barn-et
133(a)	flicka-n	133(a)	äpple-t
133(b)	fågel-n	133(b)	exempl-et (from exempel)
133(b)	moder-n	133(b)	fingr-et (from finger)
133(b)	rektor-n	–	
133(b)	ökn-en (from öken)	133(b)	vapn-et (from vapen)
133(b)	materiel-en	133(b)	kvarter-et
133(b)	kapten-en	133(b)	fenomen-et
133(c)	början		
133(d)	lärare-n (or lärar-n)		
133(d)	direktör-en (or direktör-n)		
133(d)	stad-en (or stan)		
133(e)	industri-n (or industri-en)	133(e)	fotografi-et (or fotografit)
		133(g)	centrum-et (or centret or centrum)
		133(g)	faktum-et (or faktum)
		133(f)	muse-et (from museum)
133(e)	armé-n	133(e)	knä-t (or knä-et)
Plural		*Plural*	
134(a)	armar-na	134(d)	barn-en
134(a)	flickor-na	134(c)	äpplen-a
134(b)	filmer-na	134(b)	viner-na
134(d)	män-nen (from man)	133(d)	program-men (1205)
134(g)	bagar-na (from bagare)		
134(h)	indier-na (from indier) tricks-en	134(e)	fönstr-en (coll. fönster-na) 134(j)
		134(e)	exempl-en (from exempel)
		134(d)	hus-en (coll. hus-ena)

K THE USE OF THE INDEFINITE AND DEFINITE (END) ARTICLE

136 Introduction

In most cases the same principle applies in Swedish as in English, namely that concepts *familiar* from the context take a definite article whilst *unfamiliar* concepts take an indefinite article:

Flickan hade inte sett *en ekorre* tidigare. *Ekorren* kom fram till henne.
The girl hadn't seen *a squirrel* before. *The squirrel* came up to her.

Swedish article use may be seen as a series of contrasts or choices between three forms of the noun:

(a) Noun without article:

For count nouns the form without article (**bil**, **hus**) is contrasted both with the form with indefinite article (**en bil**, **ett hus**) and with the form with definite article (**bilen**, **huset**). Use of count nouns without an article tends to imply an abstract sense, concentrating on the content or idea behind the noun rather than indicating one specific case of the noun:

Generality	*Specific example*
Har du bil?	**Har du en bil?**
Have you got a car?	Have you got a car?
Vi åt kyckling till middag.	**Vi åt en kyckling till middag.**
We had chicken for lunch.	We had a chicken for lunch.
Fru Lund var på resa.	**Fru Lund var på en resa.**
Mrs Lund was travelling.	Mrs Lund was on a journey.
Du måste läsa läxa till i morgon.	**Du måste läsa läxan till i morgon.**
You must do your homework for tomorrow.	You must do the homework for tomorrow.

(b) Noun with indefinite article:

This is usually found in the case of count nouns for concepts unfamiliar from the context (see examples above):

Generality	*Type or sort*
Bonden hittade bara sten på markerna.	**Peter hittade en sten på stranden.**
The farmer found only stone in his fields.	Peter found a stone on the beach.

With count nouns indicating substances etc., the use of the indefinite form indicates a limitation of the generality and stresses a type or sort:

Granit är en hård sten.
Granite is a resistant rock.

In contrast with the noun without article, it may also have a figurative sense:

Literal	*Figurative*
Chaplin var clown.	**Skolans rektor var en clown.**
Chaplin was a clown.	The headteacher was (i.e. behaved like) a clown.

(c) Nouns with definite article:

When there is assumed common knowledge of a context, Swedish often has the definite form even in many cases where English does not:

Han er i staden.   He is in town.

A whole species or family may be denoted by either definite singular or indefinite plural:

Älgen/Älgar finns över hela Sverige.
The elk is/Elk are to be found throughout Sweden.

137   Swedish has a definite (end) article – English has no article

(a) Abstract nouns in a general sense:

Svenskarna älskar naturen.   Swedes love nature.
Han fruktade döden och helvetet.   He feared death and hell.

(i) This applies especially to nouns depicting aspects of human life and thought such as:
arbetet work; **eländet** misery; **industrin** industry; **kommunismen** Communism; **litteraturen** literature; **lyckan** happiness; **mänskligheten** humankind; **sömnen** sleep; **ungdomen** youth; **vetenskapen** science; **äktenskapet** marriage; **ödet** fate

(ii) This applies also to words denoting human qualities and emotions:

kärleken love; **hälsan** health; **förnuftet** reason; **skönheten** beauty; **hatet** hate; **stoltheten** pride

(iii) The general sense may be linked to specific circumstances:

Hur går affärerna?   How is business?
Erfarenheten visar det.   Experience shows this.

(iv) Set phrases include:

enligt traditionen	according to tradition
i verkligheten	in reality
på modet	in fashion
i praktiken	in practice
till utseendet	by appearance

(b) Proverbs are a special case of (a):

Konsten är lång men livet är kort.	Art is long but life is short.
Kärleken är blind.	Love is blind.
Historien upprepar sig.	History repeats itself.
Sånt är livet.	Such is life.
Människan spår men Gud rår.	Man proposes but God disposes.

(c) Types and groups in a collective sense:

Människan är bara en naken apa.	Man is only a naked ape.
Priserna har stigit jämt.	Prices have risen constantly.

(d) Institutions and locations:

Han har gått till arbetet.	He has gone to work.
Olle går i skolan/kyrkan.	Olle goes to school/church.
Lars åker till sta(de)n/är i sta(de)n.	Lars is going to town/is in town.
Erik ligger på sjukhuset	Erik is in hospital.

(e) Days of the week, seasons, festivals and mealtimes (but see also 723ff.):

På fredagarna åker vi hem.	On Fridays we go home.
På vintern spelar vi ishockey.	In winter we play ice-hockey.
Hösten är vacker.	Autumn is beautiful.
Vi ses på nyårsdagen!	See you on New Year's Day!
förra veckan	last week
juldagen	Christmas Day
i gryningen	at dawn
i skymningen	at dusk
Middagen serveras klockan åtta.	Dinner is served at 8 o'clock.

Exceptions: Festivals ending in **-afton**:

julafton Christmas Eve; **midsommarafton** Midsummer's Eve; **påskafton** Easter Saturday; **nyårsafton** New Year's Eve

Note: With the verb **äta** and the preposition **till** expressions for mealtimes are used without the article:

Vi äter middag klockan åtta.	We eat dinner at 8 o'clock.
Vad äter du till frukost?	What do you eat for breakfast?

(f) Names of streets, lakes, squares, parks and public places:

Kungsgatan, Västerbron, Humlegården, Vänern, Storsjön, Siljan, Skansen

Exceptions:

(i) Street names ending in **-gränd, -plan: Odenplan, Berzeliigränd.**

(ii) Street names including a proper name in the genitive and written as two words: **Gustav Adolfs torg, Frölunda torg** (see 129(f)).

(g) Materials and substances:

vattnets fryspunkt	the freezing point of water
Brödet är dyrare än förr.	Bread is more expensive than before.

(h) Titles and vocative expressions when not followed by a name:

Tack, doktorn!	Thank you, doctor!
Hej, lilla gumman!	Hallo, little lady!

(j) Titles comprising a noun in the neuter or referring to a woman:

prinsessan Diana	Princess Diana

But note the following titles without end article:

ingenjör Ågren	Mr Ågren, the engineer
direktör Olsson	Mr Olsson, the director

(k) Nouns after the following words:

båda or **bägge**:	**båda pojkarna**	both boys	347
den här etc.:	**den där hunden**	that dog	222(b), 326(b)
den, det, de etc.:	**den mannen**	that man	326
förra:	**förra veckan**	last week	224(b)(v)
hela:	**hela vintern**	all winter	224(a)
halva:	**halva priset**	half price	224(a)
vardera, etc.:	**på vardera sidan**	on each side	336

138 Swedish has a definite (end) article – English has an indefinite article

(a) Prices:

Osten kostar hundra kronor kilot.
Cheese costs a hundred crowns a kilo.

(b) Wages and frequency of occurrence:

Han tjänar femhundra kronor i timmen/veckan/månaden.
He earns five hundred crowns an hour/a week/a month.

tio gånger om dagen/året
ten times a day/a year

139 Swedish has no article – English has a definite article

(a) Some idiomatic phrases involving instruments and pastimes after verbs like **lyssna på, titta på, spela, dansa**:

Han spelar piano.	He plays the piano.
De lyssnar på radio.	They listen to the radio.
Flickan dansade tango.	The girl danced the tango.
Han talar i telefon.	He's on the phone.
Ska vi gå på bio?	Shall we go to the cinema?

(b) Grammatical terms:

Ordet får bestämd artikel.	The word takes the end article.
Det finns i preteritum.	It is found in the past (tense).

(c) With certain expressions involving proper names:

Vi är bjudna till Janssons.	We're invited to the Janssons'.
Vi brukar bo på Hilton.	We usually stay at the Hilton.

This is also the case when using English proper names in Swedish:

Jag läste detta i Times.	I read this in *The Times*.
John satt på British Library.	John was sitting in the British Library.

(d) Others (set phrases):

tala sanning	speak the truth

i norr	in the North
till vänster	to the left
på höger sida	on the right-hand side
Han är son till Ingmar Bergman.	He is Ingmar Bergman's son.
Delblanc är författare till boken.	Delblanc is the author of the book.
Han har inte fått tillfälle att göra det.	He has not had the chance to do it.
Att han hade mage att göra det!	That he had the gall to do it!

Note: Expressions involving **ett flertal**:

ett flertal studenter	a majority of the students.

(e) After the following words:

nästa:	**nästa tåg**	the next train
samma:	**samma dag**	the same day
fel:	**fel hus**	the wrong house
rätt:	**på rätt sätt**	in the right way
följande:	**följande år**	the following year
föregående:	**föregående dag**	the previous day
motsvarande:	**motsvarande uttryck**	the corresponding expression
vederbörande:	**vederbörande tjänsteman**	the appropriate official

See also 223(e).

(f) With some superlatives (but cf. 241(g)):

billigast möjliga bil	the cheapest possible car
till högsta pris	at the highest price
av bästa kvalitet	of the best quality

140 Swedish has no article – English has an indefinite article

(a) Nouns denoting nationality, profession, trade, religion or political belief used as a subject complement:

Sven-Göran är svensk.	Sven-Göran is a Swede.
Han blev lärare.	He became a teacher.
Herr Weber är katolik.	Mr Weber is a Catholic.
Moberg var socialist.	Moberg was a Socialist.

The noun does, however, take an indefinite article in three important instances:

(i) When preceded by a qualifier:

Han är en god katolik.	He is a good Catholic.

Hon är en gammal socialist.	She is an old Socialist.

(ii) After certain prepositional expressions:

Hon är gift med en lärare.	She is married to a teacher.
Hon är dotter till en präst.	She is the daughter of a priest.

But:

Han blev utbildad till arkitekt.	He was trained as an architect.

(iii) When followed by a restrictive relative clause:

Han var *författare*, men han blev så småningom kritiker.
He was an author, but he eventually became a critic.

Han var *en författare som* debuterade på 80-talet.
He was a writer who made his debut in the eighties.

(b) When the noun follows **som** (= 'in the capacity of') no article is used in Swedish:

Som professor fick han tala vid mötet.
As (a) professor he was allowed to speak at the meeting.

Som barn var han alltid glad.
He was always happy as a child.

Som kristen måste du uppföra dig ordentligt.
You must behave properly as a Christian.

Note: However, when the noun follows **som** (= 'like a') an indefinite article is used, as in English:

Du talar som en professor.	You speak like a professor.
Han var glad som ett barn.	He was as happy as a child.
Han uppförde sig som en kristen.	He behaved like a Christian (even though he was an atheist).

(c) In many idiomatic expressions with a singular count-noun when only one is obvious and inferred:

De väntar barn.	They are expecting a child.
Han kan inte skaffa arbete/bostad.	He cannot find a job/a home.
Han måste skaffa bil.	He must get a car.
Vi bygger villa.	We are building a house.
Eva måste skriva brev till dem.	Eva must write a letter to them.

Hon väntar på svar.	She is waiting for an answer.
Har du telefon?	Do you have a phone?
Vi tog taxi.	We took a taxi.

In this sense nouns denoting equipment and clothes are often found in the form without article in Swedish:

Bilen har turbomotor.	The car has a turbo engine.
Huset har källare.	The house has a basement.
Eva har kjol och blus på sig idag.	Eva has a skirt and blouse on today.

(d) In other idiomatic expressions:

med hög röst in a loud voice; **med stor majoritet** with a large majority; **vid gott humör** in a good mood; **i stor skala** on a large scale; **få plats** get a seat; **ta plats** take a seat; **ha bråttom** be in a hurry; **ha rätt att** have a right to; **ha feber** have a temperature; **röka pipa** smoke a pipe; **det är fråga om** it is a question of; **som följd av** as a result of; **med vinst/förlust** at a profit/loss; **på avstånd** at a distance; **i nödfall** in an emergency

(e) In expressions after the following words:

vilken etc.	**Vilken vacker dag!**	(See 368)
	What a beautiful day!	

mången etc.	**Mången diktare har skrivit om döden.**	(See 349 Note)
	Many a poet has written of death.	

hur . . . än	**Hur stor ledare han än är, måste han lyda lagen.**	
	However great a leader he is, he must obey the law.	

(f) In some expressions of quantity with **mycket, lite, hundra**, etc. (see also 404):

hundra män	a hundred men
lite öl	a little beer
mycket vin	a lot of wine
tusen demonstranter	a thousand demonstrators
bara få människor	only a few people

(g) The indefinite article in Swedish corresponds in some instances to English 'a piece of':

ett snöre	a piece of string
en tvål	a piece of soap

en möbel	a piece of furniture
en nyhet	a piece of news
en läxa	a piece of homework

141 Swedish has an indefinite article – English has no article

Notice the following expressions in which **en** means 'about', 'approximately'.

Hon har en fyra, fem barn.
She has four or five children.

Jag har bara en femtio, sextio kronor.
I only have fifty or sixty crowns or so.

142 The use of the definite article to indicate possession

(a) The definite article is often employed in Swedish with parts of the body and articles of clothing if it is clear who these belong to (see also 323); English uses a possessive adjective in these cases:

Hon ska tvätta håret/händerna.	She is going to wash her hair/hands.
Han skakade på huvudet.	He shook his head.
Jag fryser om fötterna/händerna.	My feet/hands are frozen.
Nils bröt benet.	Nils broke his leg.
Barnen tog av sig skorna.	The children took off their shoes.

The possessive need not refer to the subject:

Ha sa åt flickorna att tvätta händerna.
He told the girls had to wash their hands.

However, where the precise ownership of an article of clothing or part of the body needs to be indicated to avoid ambiguity, Swedish like English has a possessive:

Hon lade sin hand i min.
She placed her hand in mine.

Tjuven stoppade sin hand i min ficka.
The thief put his hand in my pocket.

Jag satte på hans hatt.	I put his hat on.
(Cf. **Jag satte på hatten.**	I put my hat on.)

(b) Notice the following construction locating various aches and pains, which requires different renderings in English (cf. 721(d)(i) Note 2):

Han har ont i ryggen/magen/huvudet/benet.
He has a pain in his back/stomach ache/headache/a pain in his leg.

143   Differences in the position of the articles in Swedish and English

Note:

en halv liter	half a litre, a half-litre [See 413]
en halvtimme (en halv timme)	half an hour, a half-hour
ett sådant svårt problem	such a difficult problem [See 328]
ett alltför fåfängt hopp	too vain a hope
en ganska lång väg	rather a long way
en lika fin föreställning	just as fine a performance
hela vintern	the whole winter [See 339(c)]

2 ADJECTIVES

A   **FORM AND ORDER**
201   Introduction to forms and use
202   The basic rule
203   Variations – neuter form
204   Variations – plural and definite form
205   Variations – **liten** and **gammal**
206   Indeclinable adjectives
207   The order of adjective attributes

B   **THE INDEFINITE DECLENSION**
208   The use of the indefinite form
209   The double subject
210   The complement precedes the subject
211   Constructions according to meaning
212   Words indicating measurement or degree
213   **Ärter är gott; engelska är tråkigt**
214   Cases of attraction
215   The independent adjective
216   Indefinite use of adjectives: summary

C   **THE DEFINITE DECLENSION**
217   Introduction
218   Compulsory ending in **-a**
219   Compulsory ending in **-e**
220   Variations between **-e** and **-a** with masculines
221   The use of the definite declension – introduction
222   Front article and end article (double definition)
223   No end article after certain words
224   No front article but an end article
225   Neither a front article nor an end article
226   The definite use of adjectives: summary

D   **ADJECTIVAL NOUNS**
227   Introduction
228   The forms and use of the adjectival noun
229   Nationality words
230   Complete nominalisation

231   Intermediate forms

E   COMPARISON OF ADJECTIVES
232   Introduction
233   Comparison with the endings **-are, -ast**
234   Comparison with the endings **-re, -st** plus modification of the root vowel
235   Irregular comparison
236   Comparison with **mer(a), mest**
237   Comparison of compound adjectives
238   Adjectives deficient in the positive, positive and comparative, or superlative
239   Adjectives which do not compare
240   The comparative is indeclinable
241   Inflexion of the superlative
242   Similarity, dissimilarity and reinforcement
243   The absolute comparative
244   The absolute superlative
245   Adjectives – use of the positive, comparative and superlative: summary

A   FORM AND ORDER

201   Introduction to forms and use

Adjectives are inflected in Swedish. Adjectives, both attributive and predicative, change form according to the gender and number (and in a few cases the form) of the noun or pronoun with which they agree. The indefinite forms of the adjective are used both attributively and predicatively, while the definite forms are only used attributively:

	Indefinite	*Definite*
Attributive	**en ung flicka** a young girl	**den ung***a* **flickan** the young girl
	unga flickor young girls	**de unga flickorna** the young girls
	ett stor*t* **hus** a big house	**det stor***a* **huset** the big house
	stora hus big houses	**de stora husen** the big houses
	en industrialiserad värld an industrialised world	**den industrialiserad***e* **världen** the industrialised world
	ett industrialisera*t* **land** an industrialised country	**det industrialiserad***e* **landet** the industrialised country

industrialiserade länder	**de industrialiserade länderna**
industrialised countries	the industrialised countries

Predicative *Singular* *Plural*

flickan är ung	**flickorna är unga**
the girl is young	the girls are young
huset är stor*t*	**husen är stora**
the house is big	the houses are big
världen är industrialiserad	
the world is industrialised	
landet är industrialisera*t*	**länderna är industrialiserade**
the country is industrialised	the countries are industrialised

(a) Notice that the definite declension of the adjective usually employs the front (or adjectival) article **den**, **det**, **de**. (See 222ff.)

(b) In the definite declension the adjective has two forms, one ending in **-a**, one ending in **-e**. (See 217ff.)

(c) After *copular verbs* like **vara**, **bli**, **heta**, **verka**, the adjective comprises a *predicative complement* (see 1006) and is inflected according to the subject or object to which it refers (see 208).

202   The basic rule

(a) There is no distinctive marker for the non-neuter singular indefinite (basic or dictionary) form of the adjective, but the neuter singular form adds **-t**, and both the plural indefinite and the definite (singular and plural) add **-a**. The basic rule is shown for the adjective **fin** 'fine' in the diagram:

Non-neuter singular indefinite
(Basic form)
fin

Neuter singular indefinite

Plural indefinite (and definite of both genders, singular and plural)

fin*t*   **fin*a***

Notice that there is no distinction made between non-neuter and neuter plural form. Examples:

en fin bok	**ett fint vin**	**fina böcker, fina viner**
a fine book	a fine wine	fine books, fine wines

(b) The basic rule (shown in this form for comparison with 203ff.):

	Basic form	Neuter	Plural/Definite	
Ending:	-0	-t	-a	
	blek	blek*t*	blek*a*	pale
	rolig	rolig*t*	rolig*a*	funny

The large group of adjectives which inflect according to this rule includes:

(i) Many monosyllabic adjectives ending in a consonant or consonant group:

arg angry; **bar** bare; **dyr** expensive; **ful** ugly; **gul** yellow; **hemsk** horrible; **jämn** even; **klok** wise; **lugn** calm; **mjuk** soft; **norsk** Norwegian; **rak** straight; **sen** late; **torr** dry; **van** common.

(ii) Polysyllabic adjectives ending in -al, -bar, -ell, -ig, -isk/-esk, -iv, -är, -(i)ös:

lokal local; **katastrofal** catastrophic; **dyrbar** valuable; **underbar** wonderful; **aktuell**, topical; **traditionell** traditional; **fattig** poor; **dålig** bad; **självisk** selfish; **grotesk** grotesque; **attraktiv** attractive; **expressiv** expressive; **reaktionär** reactionary; **preliminär** preliminary; **ambitiös** ambitious; **generös** generous.

203 Variations – neuter form

The basic pattern shown in 202 is found with a number of minor variations for a minority of adjectives, which are, however, relatively frequent. These are detailed in 203-205. (In the summary of form given below -V = vowel, -$\underline{V}$ = long vowel, -C = consonant.)

Variations predominantly in the neuter form are found in:

(a) Adjective ending in a long vowel:

	Basic form	Neuter	Plural/Definite	
Ending:	-$\underline{V}$	-V+tt	-$\underline{V}$+a	
	fri	fri*tt*	fri*a*	free

This group includes: **blå** blue; **grå** grey; **ny** new; **rå** raw; **slö** dull.
The vowel is shortened in the neuter form. In the plural two words possess alternative forms: **blå/blåa, grå/gråa.**

Exception: **bra** see 206(b).

(b) Monosyllabic adjectives ending in a long vowel +t:

	Basic form	*Neuter*	*Plural/Definite*	
Ending:	-<u>V</u>+t	-V+tt	-<u>V</u>+t+a	
	vit	**vit*t***	**vit*a***	white

This group includes: **våt** wet; **het** hot; **fet** fat; **slät** smooth; **söt** sweet.

The vowel is shortened in the neuter form.

Exception: **lat** (see (l) below).

(c) Polysyllabic adjectives ending in a long vowel +t:

	Basic form	*Neuter*	*Plural/Definite*	
Ending:	-<u>V</u>+t	-<u>V</u>+t	-<u>V</u>+ta	
	konkret	**konkret**	**konkreta**	concrete

This group includes many loanwords: **adekvat** adequate; **akut** acute; **delikat** delicate; **desperat** desperate; **diskret** discreet; **moderat** moderate; **privat** private; **separat** separate.

(d) Adjectives ending in a short vowel +tt:

	Basic form	*Neuter*	*Plural/Definite*	
Ending:	-V+tt	-V+tt	-V+tt+a	
	lätt	**lätt**	**lätt*a***	easy

This group includes: **blott** mere; **flott** smart; **mätt** full; **nätt** neat; **rätt** correct; **platt** flat; **tafatt** clumsy; **trött** tired; **violett** violet.

(e) Adjectives ending in a consonant +t:

	Basic form	*Neuter*	*Plural/Definite*	
Ending:	-C+t	-C+t	-C+t+a	
	intressant	**intressant**	**intressant*a***	interesting

This group includes:

(i) A number of loanwords: **abstrakt** abstract; **exakt** exact; **briljant** brilliant; **distinkt** distinct; **elegant** elegant; **intelligent** intelligent; **kompetent** competent; **latent** latent; **perfekt** perfect; **robust** robust.

(ii) Some indigenous monosyllabic adjectives: **brant** steep; **fast** firm; **kort** short; **stolt** proud; **trist** sad; **tyst** silent.

(iii) The past participles of some second conjugation verbs (group II(b), see 531): **köpt** bought; **låst** locked; **läst** read; **sällsynt** rare; **upplyst** enlightened; **vidsträckt** widespread.

(f) Adjectives ending in a long vowel **+d**:

	Basic form	*Neuter*	*Plural/Definite*	
Ending:	<u>V</u>+d	-V+tt	-<u>V</u>+d+a	
	glad	**gla**tt	**glad**a	happy

This group includes: **bred** broad; **död** dead; **god** good; **röd** red; **sned** slanting; **spröd** crisp; **vid** wide; **blid** mild; **solid** solid.

Note: Polysyllabic adjectives ending in -id do not, however, usually possess a neuter singular form (see (l) below):

> **gravid** pregnant; **stupid** stupid; **mongoloid** mongoloid

(g) Adjectives ending in a short vowel **+dd**:

	Basic form	*Neuter*	*Plural/Definite*	
Ending:	-V+dd	-V+tt	-V+dd+a	
	högljudd	**höglju**tt	**högljudd**a	loud
	obebodd	**obebo**tt	**obebodd**a	uninhabited

This group includes:

(i) Past participles of third conjugation verbs (see 531): **anförtrodd** confided; **omsydd** re-sewn; **försmådd** disdained; **nådd** reached; **avskydd** despised; **strödd** strewn; **varskodd** warned; **åtrådd** desired.

(ii) Some others: **infödd** indigenous; **omstridd** disputed; **oavsedd** unintended.

Exception: **rädd** afraid (cf. (l) below).

(h) Adjectives ending in a consonant **+d**:

	Basic form	*Neuter*	*Plural/Definite*	
Ending:	-C+d	-C+t	-C+d+a	
	hård	**hår**t	**hård**a	hard

This group includes:

(i) Past participles of second conjugation verbs (Group II(a) (see 531)): **använd** used; **avspänd** relaxed; **berömd** famous; **bestämd** determined; **byggd** built; **frikänd** liberated; **fylld** filled; **glömd** forgotten; **lärd** learned; **skrämd** frightened; **spänd** tense; **stängd** closed; **tänd** lit; **utnämnd** nominated.

(ii) Some others: **absurd** absurd; **avsevärd** considerable; **blind** blind; **blond** fair; **enskild** private; **grund** shallow; **mild** mild; **nöjd** pleased; **oerhörd** unprecedented; **ond** evil; **rund** round; **sund** sound; **vild** wild; **värd** worth(y).

(j) Adjectives ending in a short vowel +**nn**:

	Basic form	*Neuter*	*Plural/Definite*	
Ending:	-V+nn	-V+n+t	-V+nn+a	
	sann	**san***t*	**sann***a*	true

This group includes: **grann** attractive; **nogrann** careful; **tunn** thin.

(k) Adjectives ending in a short vowel +**m**:

	Basic form	*Neuter*	*Plural/Definite*	
Ending:	-V+m	-V+m+t	-V+mm+a	
	ensam	**ensam***t*	**ensam***ma*	alone

This group includes:

(i) Many monosyllabic adjectives: **dum** stupid; **from** pious; **grym** cruel; **ljum** lukewarm; **stum** dumb; **tom** empty; **öm** tender.

(ii) Adjectives ending in -**sam**: **bekymmersam** troubling; **beslutsam** decisive; **blygsam** shy; **hjälpsam** helpful; **långsam** slow; **pinsam** painful; **tveksam** doubtful; **verksam** active; **våldsam** violent.

(l) Some adjectives are not used attributively in the neuter singular form. Most of these qualify nouns denoting human beings:

lat lazy; **rädd** afraid; **kry** healthy; **pigg** fit; **pryd** prudish; **vred** angry; **ledsen** sad; **höger** right; **vänster** left; **rigid** rigid (see also Note to (f) above); **disträ** absent-minded.

When used predicatively they do not possess a neuter form:

Barnet var rädd.   The child was afraid.

204 Variations – plural and definite form

(a) Adjectives ending in -**ad**:

	Basic form	*Neuter*	*Plural/Definite*	
Ending:	-a+d	-a+t	-a+d+e	
	sofistikerad	**sofistikera***t*	**sofistikerad***e*	sophisticated

Note the ending **-e** in the plural/definite form. This group includes:

(i) Past participles of first conjugation verbs (see 531): **aktad** respected; **befriad** liberated; **delad** divided; **filmad** filmed; **granskad** checked; **krossad** crushed; **laddad** loaded; **missad** missed; **nekad** denied; **orsakad** caused; **plockad** picked; **rensad** cleaned; **skadad** injured; **testad** tested; **övertygad** convinced; **dramatiserad** dramatised; **frapperad** struck; **koncentrerad** concentrated; **nationaliserad** nationalised.

(ii) Adjectives which are inflected like past participles in (i), some of which originally were past participles: **befogad** warranted; **beskaffad** constituted; **besläktad** related; **kortfattad** concise; **mångfacetterad** multi-faceted; **passionerad** impassioned; **rutinerad** experienced; **sinnad** minded.

(b) Adjectives ending in unstressed **-el/-er**:

	Basic form	*Neuter*	*Plural/Definite*	
Ending:	-el/-er	-el/-er+t	(drop e) -l/-r+a	
	ädel	**ädel***t*	**ädl***a*	noble
	vacker	**vacker***t*	**vackr***a*	beautiful

This group includes:

(i) Many bisyllabic adjectives: **bister** forbidding; **bitter** bitter; **diger** thick; **mager** thin; **munter** merry; **nykter** sober; **sober** sober; **säker** sure; **tapper** brave.

(ii) Adjectives ending in **-abel, -ibel**: **acceptabel** acceptable; **diskutabel** debatable; **veritabel** veritable; **riskabel** risky; **sensibel** sensible; **flexibel** flexible.

(c) Adjectives ending in unstressed **-en**:

	Basic form	*Neuter*	*Plural/Definite*	
Ending:	-en	-e+t	(drop e) -n+a	
	mogen	**moge***t*	**mogn***a*	ripe
	sliten	**slite***t*	**slitn***a*	worn

This group includes:

(i) Past participles of verbs of the fourth conjugation (strong verbs) (cf. 531): **begraven** buried; **bjuden** invited; **drucken** drunk; **frusen** frozen; **gripen** seized; **kommen** arrived; **riden** ridden; **skriven** written; **slagen** struck; **struken** ironed; **stulen** stolen; **tagen** taken; **tvungen** forced; **vriden** twisted; **vuxen** adult.

(ii) Many other adjectives: **angelägen** urgent; **avlägsen** distant; **belåten** satisfied; **benägen** disposed; **besviken** disappointed; **egen** own (see 223 (iii)); **erfaren** experienced; **förmögen** wealthy; **galen** mad; **gedigen** solid; **häpen** astonished; **kristen** Christian; **ledsen** sad; **medveten** conscious; **naken** naked; **nyfiken** curious; **sorgsen** sad; **storslagen** grandiose; **vaken** awake; **öppen** open.

205   Variations – **liten** and **gammal**

(a) Liten ('little') is unique in two respects:

(i) It changes stem in the plural:

	Basic form	*Neuter*	*Plural only*	
Indefinite	**liten**	**litet**	**små**	little

(ii) Uniquely, it possesses a singular definite form **lilla** which differs from the plural indefinite and definite (cf. 217ff.):

	Basic form	*Neuter*	*Plural only*
Definite	**lilla**	**lilla**	**små**

Examples: **en liten flicka**   **ett litet barn**   **små flickor/barn**
a little girl   a little child   little girls/children

den lilla flickan   **det lilla barnet**   **de små flickorna/barnen**
the little girl   the little child   the little girls/children

Note 1: It is possible to form a neuter indefinite from **små**, namely **smått**, but this is usually found in set phrases or used nominally or adverbially:

Allting är smått härhemma.   Everything is so small here at home.
smått och gott   all kinds of nice little things
Han är smått förälskad i henne.   He's a little in love with her.

Note 2: The noun **lillan**, found only with the end article, means 'the little girl', while **lillen** means 'the little boy'. Notice also: **en liten** 'a little baby'; **lite(t) av varje** 'a little of everything'

(b) Gammal ('old') is unusual as regards its plural (and definite) form:

gammal   **gammalt**   **gamla** (one **m**, 1205(d))

206   Indeclinable adjectives

The following types of adjective are indeclinable, i.e. do not add an inflexional ending in either the indefinite or the definite declension, but see also 236:

(a) Adjectives ending in -e: **ett främmande språk**, a foreign language.

This group includes:

(i) All present participles (see 532): **en oroväckande utveckling** a disturbing development; **ett påfallande intresse** a marked interest; **de hotande översvämningarna** the threatened floods.

(ii) **ense** agreed; **gängse** current; **ordinarie** usual, permanent; **vilse** lost; **öde** deserted; **ömse** mutual; **(bli) varse** to notice.

(iii) Many participial adjectives, i.e. adjectives that were originally participles, but have become isolated from the verb as the verbs have changed: **beklämmande** depressing; **betryggande** adequate; **enastående** unique; **ovidkommande** irrelevant; **tidsödande** time-consuming; **rasande** angry.

(iv) **beige** beige; **gyllene** gold(en); **orange** orange (cf., however, (d) Note below).

(v) Comparative forms in **-are/-re** (see 232ff., 240).

(b) Adjectives ending in **-a**: **fem bra filmer** five good films.

This group includes:

(i) Adjectives which are also adverbs (see 602): **annorlunda** different(ly); **sakta** slow(ly); **noga** careful(ly); **stilla** calm(ly); **långväga** long-distance.

(ii) Adjectives ending in **-tida**: **forntida** prehistoric; **framtida** future; **medeltida** medieval; **nutida** present; **samtida** latter-day, contemporary; **sentida** of our time.

(iii) Other adjectives in **-a**: **allehanda** all kinds of; **allena** alone; **barfota** barefoot; **bra** good; **enahanda** monotonous; **enda** only; **enstaka** individual; **extra** extra; **laga** lawful; **lila** mauve; **olaga** illegal; **omaka** ill-matched; **prima** first class; **ringa** insignificant; **rosa** pink; **samma** same; **sekunda** second class; **udda** odd; **äkta** genuine.

(c) Many adjectives ending in **-s**:

This group includes:

(i) Adjectives ending in a consonant **+s**:

   ett medelålders biträde a middle-aged assistant

Other: **gammaldags** old-fashioned; **sams** agreed; **stackars** poor, pitiable; **allsköns** diverse, all kinds of.

(ii) Adjectives ending in **-es**:

   många invärtes åkommor many internal complaints

Others: **avsides** secluded; **inbördes** reciprocal; **inrikes** domestic; **utrikes** foreign; **urminnes** ancient.

(iii) **gratis** free: **flera gratis böcker** several free books.

Note: Exceptions: adjectives ending in long -is, -os, -us, -ös inflect according to the basic rule (202):

en grandios sal	ett grandiost slott	grandiosa salar/slott
a grandiose hall	a grandiose castle	grandiose halls/castles

en nervös student	ett nervöst barn	nervösa studenter/barn
a nervous student	a nervous child	nervous students/children

Other examples: **vis** wise; **seriös** serious; **diffus** diffuse; **precis** precise.

(d) Others, including adjectives formed from nouns and adverbs:

slut finished; **fel** wrong; **släkt** related; **kvitt** quits; **lagom** just enough; **redo** prepared; **sönder** broken; **kul** fun; **bakom** stupid; **fjärran** distant; **framåt** go-ahead; **idel** sheer; **lutter** sheer; **lönt** worth; **pyton** horrible; **solo** solo; **toppen** great.

Note 1: Some recent loans belong to this group:

allround, gay, selfmade, up-to-date

Note 2: In colloquial Swedish one or two of the adjectives listed in (a)–(d) above are sometimes inflected:

ett par lagoma vantar	a perfect pair of gloves
ett beigt tyg, orangea byxor	a beige material, orange trousers

(e) Some indeclinable adjectives may be used both attributively and predicatively:

Jag slog fel nummer.	I dialled the wrong number.
Det är fel att slå sina barn.	It is wrong to hit your children.
en öde ö	a desert island
Landet var öde och obebott.	The country was desolate and uninhabited.

Also: **bra** good; **gratis** free; **kul** fun.

(f) Some indeclinable adjectives are only used attributively:

de stackars flickorna	the poor girls
det dåtida Stockholm	the Stockholm of that time
i fjärran länder	in foreign parts

Also: **inbördes, avsides, allsköns, allehanda, framtida, ömse, enstaka, gyllene, laga, olaga, långväga, idel** (for meanings see (a)–(d) above).

(g) Some indeclinable adjectives are only used predicatively:

Fönstret är sönder.	The window is broken.
Jag är ense med dig om detta.	I am in agreement with you on this.
Arbetet var slut för dagen.	Work was over for the day.
De är släkt med varandra.	They are related to each other.

Also: **varse, kvitt, samma, (o)sams, redo** (for meanings see (a)–(d) above).

207 The order of adjective attributes

(a) The order of adjective attributes in Swedish is not always as in English. It is only possible to provide some general guidelines for this:

(i) The more permanent the quality indicated, the nearer it is placed to the noun it qualifies:

uppstruket svart hår = svart hår som är uppstruket
black hair combed up

den pittoreska svensk staden = den svenska staden som är pittoresk
the picturesque Swedish town

en arg rödhårig grabb = en rödhårig grabb som är arg
an angry, red-haired lad

Sometimes adjective and noun form a fixed expression and cannot be separated:

det världsberömda Röda korset   the world-famous Red Cross

(ii) Generally speaking, the longer or more complex adjective is placed nearest to the noun, so that participles are often found in this position:

det mörka omoderna rummet   the dark, old-fashioned room
en rik prisbelönt författare   a rich, prize-winning author

(iii) Adjectives indicating size or quantity *are not* placed nearest, while those indicating nationality and colour *are* placed nearest:

det stora vita huset   the big, white house
en liten svensk bil   a small, Swedish car

(iv) **Liten, ung, gammal** are *not* generally placed nearest the noun, although they may occupy this position when the noun indicates a person. Compare:

en liten röd stuga   a small, red cottage
en söt liten flicka   a pretty little girl
en intelligent ung man   an intelligent young man
en trevlig gammal gubbe   a nice old man

Translation of English expressions such as 'a little old house' thus presents some difficulty. One solution is to expand the Swedish to **ett litet och gammalt hus** or to use a relative clause. Swedish speakers tend to avoid this kind of juxtaposition.

(b) Notice the difference between English and Swedish word order in:

en så(dan) lång tid	such a long time	cf. 328
en sådan vacker hatt	such a beautiful hat	cf. 328
ett halvt kilo	half a kilo	cf. 413

Note: In remnants of archaic expressions or in colloquial or dialectal use the attribute is sometimes placed after the noun:

fågel blå	blue bird
Han vattnar sina fålar fem.	He waters his five foals.
i dagarna tre	for three days
sak samma	never mind
Eva lilla	little Eva

Cf. the inversion of the possessive in: **Fader vår** ('Our Father' in the introduction to the Lord's prayer,) and in colloquial use in: **far min** 'my father'; **bror din** 'your brother'; **gården deras** 'their farm'; **frugan min** 'my wife' (the last two with the noun in the definite).

B   THE INDEFINITE DECLENSION

208   The use of the indefinite form

(a) The indefinite form of the adjective may be used attributively with no word preceding the adjective + noun if the noun is non-count (101(b)) or plural:

god mat	**vacker***t* **väder**	**lång***a***, rak***a* **vägar**
good food	beautiful weather	long, straight roads

(b) The indefinite form of the adjective may be used attributively after:

- the indefinite articles **en, ett**

- indefinite pronouns or adjectives: **många, någon, ingen, varje, var, varannan, varenda, en annan, en sådan** (and their inflected forms, Chapter 3H)

- **vilken, sådan** (and their inflected forms) in exclamations (368, 328)

- **flera, alla, många, få** (Chapter 3H)

- cardinal numbers in the plural (Chapter 4)

Non-neuter	Neuter	Plural
en ny bil a new car	–	två ny*a* bilar two new cars
	ett ny*tt* hus a new house	två ny*a* hus two new houses
–	–	många ond*a* gärningar many bad deeds
någon älskvärd manniska some kind person	något älskvär*t* barn some kind child	några älskvärd*a* människor/barn some kind people/children
ingen lämplig plats no suitable place	inget lämplig*t* ställe no suitable place	inga lämplig*a* platser/ställen no suitable places
en annan vacker sång another beautiful song	ett annat vacker*t* drama another beautiful drama	andra vackr*a* sånger/dramer other beautiful songs/dramas
en sådan rolig bok such an amusing book varje nybyggd båt every newly built boat	ett sådant rolig*t* sällskap such an amusing group varje nybygg*t* höghus every newly built block of flats	sådana rolig*a* böcker/sällskap such amusing books/groups
–	–	flera vackr*a* flickor several pretty girls
	–	få dumm*a* studenter few stupid students
vilken fin utsikt! what a fine view!	vilket fin*t* slott! what a fine castle!	vilka fin*a* utsikter/slott! what fine views/castles!
sådan tråkig läsning! what boring reading!	sådant tråkig*t* väder! what boring weather!	sådana tråkig*a* dikter/hus! what boring poems/houses!

(c) The indefinite form of the adjective may be used predicatively:

(i) As a subject complement:

Dikten är svår.	The poem is difficult.
Dramat är också svår*t*.	The drama is also difficult.
Dikterna/dramerna är svår*a*.	The poems/dramas are difficult.

(ii) As an object complement:

Han målade stolen grön, bordet grön*t* och väggarna grön*a*.
He painted the chair green, the table green and the walls green.

(iii) As a predicative attribute:

Han gick bedrövad bort.
He left dejected.

Den gamle mannen dog lugn och lycklig.
The old man died calm and happy.

(d) When used predicatively the adjective (complement, see 1006) normally agrees with the noun (subject or object):

Flickan är vacker.	The girl is pretty.
subj ← *subj comp*	
Barnet är vacker*t*.	The child is pretty.
subject ← *subj comp*	
Flickorna/Barnen är vackr*a*.	The girls/children are pretty.
subject ← *subj comp*	
Studenterna gjorde läraren ledsen.	The students made the teacher sad.
subject *object* ← *obj comp*	

However, in 209–215 below various cases are detailed in which agreement deviates from this norm. An important case is that in which the adjective as subject complement agrees with a subordinate clause or an infinitive phrase as subject (in other words agreement is not with a noun phrase). In this case the adjective takes a neuter ending:

Att han aldrig kommer att vinna Nobelpriset är otänkbar*t*.
It is unthinkable that he will never win the Nobel Prize.

Att få vandra i skogen vid skymningen är magisk*t*.
To wander in the forest at dusk is magical.

209   The double subject

(a) When there are two or more subjects the complement is usually in the plural form:

Erik och Anders och Nils var hemskt smutsig*a*.
Erik and Anders and Nils were awfully dirty.
Konungen och drottningen är älskad*e* *av många*.

The King and Queen are loved by many people.

(b) There are, however, a number of important cases where the form of the adjective is determined by the meaning of the subject:

(i) When the double subject is regarded as one indivisible idea, the adjective is found in the singular:

Allt buller och jäkt är här bannlyst.
All bustle and stress is banned here.

Lag och rätt är hotad.
Law and order is threatened.

(ii) Både ... och. Here two alternatives out of two are implied, and a plural complement is therefore required:

Både han och hon var bjudn*a*.
Both he and she were invited.

(iii) Såväl ... som. Again, two alternatives out of two requires a plural complement:

Såväl hans mor som hans syster är rödhåriga.
Both his mother and his sister are red-haired.

(iv) Antingen ... eller, varken ... eller. Here practice varies:

1   If each subject is in the singular, then the complement will be in the singular:

Varken han eller hon var bjuden.
Neither he nor she was invited.

2   If the subject comprises both singular and plural, then the complement assumes the number of the subject placed nearest to it:

Varken läraren eller barnen var intresserad*e*.
Neither the teacher nor the children were interested.

Varken barnen eller läraren var intresserad.
Neither the children nor the teacher were interested.

3   If the two singular subjects have different genders, then the construction with a complement is best avoided altogether. If used, the complement assumes the gender of the subject placed nearest to it.

210   The complement precedes the subject

It is now common to find the complement – when placed at the beginning of the sentence – in the neuter form irrespective of the gender or number of the noun it qualifies. This is especially true of adjectives like **karakteristiskt, typiskt, gemensamt, viktigt, väsentligt**:

> **Karakteristisk*t* för isländskan är de många böjningsändelserna.**
> Characteristic of Icelandic is the many inflexional endings.

> **Gemensam*t* för de tre nordiska folken är deras tro på demokrati.**
> Common to the three Nordic peoples is their belief in democracy.

> **Inte minst viktig*t* är allmänhetens inställning till de mentalsjuka.**
> Not least important is the public's attitude to the mentally ill.

This type of construction may be elliptical:

> **(*Det* som är) karakteristisk*t* för isländskan är de många böjningsändelserna.**

In these cases the complement is a subject complement, but is regarded as an object complement. It is used to provide emphasis. Such complements should only be used in the neuter when:

1   the subject is vague, and
2   the complement precedes the subject:

cf.   **Foga*t* till denna skrivelse är en lista.**
       Complement   Subject
       A list is attached to this communication.

211   Constructions according to meaning

In these cases the inherent meaning of the subject overrides the grammatical number; in other words, sense overrides form. Therefore, with subjects denoting a collective, the complement is often found in the plural.

(a) The pronoun **man** (330) is singular, but is often found with a plural complement, especially in spoken Swedish:

> **Man var enig/enig*a* om beslutet.**
> They were united on the decision.

Man var tvungen/tvungna att göra något.
They were forced to do something.

(b) Folk possesses a plural complement when it denotes people, individuals:

Folk är mer intresserade av idrott än politik.
People are more interested in sport than in politics.

Svenska folket är uttråkade.
The Swedish people are bored.

Notice, however, when the adjective is used attributively:

lite(t) folk	few people	(not **få**)
ungt folk	young people	(not **unga**)

(c) Par, barn. Complements to these nouns are found in the neuter, but when referring to them the pronouns **de**, **han** or **hon** are used:

Ett ungt par kom in. *De* var lyckliga.
The young couple came in. They were happy.

Det lilla barnet var vackert. *Hon/han* hade blont hår.
The child was pretty. She/he had blond hair.

(d) With neuter nouns denoting people a neuter form is used attributively, but a non-neuter predicative complement is often used. There are a number of nouns ending in **-råd** ('secretary in the civil service'), **-biträde** ('assistant') which often cause confusion. Here natural gender tends to override grammatical gender as regards complement and pronominal reference. When referring to these nouns the pronouns **han** and **hon** respectively are used:

Det unga statsrådet var säker på sin sak. *Hon* hade läst på.
The young cabinet minister was sure of her case. She had read up on it.

Affärsbiträdet blev orolig. *Han* hade stulit pengar.
The shop assistant grew uneasy. He had stolen some money.

Incongruence of this kind is most noticeable and thus best avoided when the predicative complement immediately follows the verb:

Statsrådet blev nervös.   The government minister grew nervous.

This can easily be avoided:

Statsrådet Karl Karlsson blev nervös.
Minister Karl Karlsson grew nervous.

(e) Titles of published books and newspapers which are plural are regarded as non-neuter singular for purposes of agreement:

Dagens Nyheter är pålitlig.
Dagens Nyheter is reliable.

Heidenstams Karolinerna är något långrandig.
Heidenstam's *The Charles Men* is somwehat long-winded.

212 Words indicating measurement or degree

These cases are rather similar to those in 209. If the whole (group or collective) is intended rather than the part, the singular form of the complement should be used:

Antalet stipendier är otillräcklig*t*.
The number of grants is insufficient.

If the individual parts are intended, then the plural is used:

Över hälften av pojkarna var sjuk*a*.
Over half of the boys were sick.

Ett flertal poliser blev skadad*e*.
A majority of the policemen were injured.

213 Ärter är gott; engelska är tråkigt

In cases where the subject has a general, abstract or collective sense the neuter indefinite form of the adjective is often used:

Ärter är go*tt*.	Peas are nice.
Sill är go*tt*. (NB **sill-en**)	Herring is nice.

Here it is not the peas/herring itself which is good, but the idea of (eating) peas/herring. Such expressions may be regarded as ellipted forms, for example:

Cf. **Färsk sill är go*tt*.**	Fresh herring is good.
Att äta färsk sill är go*tt*.	Eating fresh herring is good.
Det är go*tt* med färsk sill.	Fresh herring is good.

The use of the neuter complement is also found with school subjects etc.:

Engelska är tråkig*t*.	English is boring.
Ishockey är populär*t* i Sverige.	Ice hockey is popular in Sweden.

This lack of agreement occurs only when the noun is in the form without article (singular or plural) or in the indefinite singular with article. It is especially frequent with subjects not normally found in the plural:

Politik är rolig*t*.	Politics is fun.
Röda hund är smittsam*t*.	German measles is contagious.
Motionsgymnastik har blivit populär*t*.	Keep-fit has become popular.
Stövlar är omodern*t*.	Boots are old-fashioned.
(= Det är omodern*t* att gå i stövlar.)	

But when the meaning is more closely defined, by the end article or an additional complement, then the complement must agree:

Svensk ishockey är populär.	Swedish ice hockey is popular.
Hans engelsk är tråkig.	His English (written style) is boring.
De gula ärterna var goda.	The yellow peas were good.
Den färska sillen var god.	The fresh herring was good.
De svarta stövlarna är omoderna.	The black boots are old-fashioned.

Compare:

Rosor är vacker*t*. (= Att hålla sig med rosor är vacker*t*)
Roses are nice.

Rosor är vackra. (= Blommorna är vackra)
Roses are lovely.

214 Cases of attraction

Involuntary lack of agreement is often caused by the writer or speaker losing sight of the subject:

*En stor del av brevet var oläslig*t*.
A large part of the letter was illegible.

Should read: **oläslig** to agree with **en del**.

*Är något av rummen lediga?
Is one of the rooms free?

Should read: **ledigt** to agree with **något**.

*På kyrkogården ligger en av lärarna begravna.
One of the teachers is buried in the churchyard.

Should read: **begraven** to agree with **en**.

In the cases above, the writer has inflected the complement according to a word other than the subject. This is frequent in structurally complex sentences or when the order is varied for emphasis:

*Kritisk var professorns anförande.
The professor's address was critical.

Should read: **kritiskt** to agree with **(ett) anförande**.

*Riktigheten av dessa uppgifter kan läsaren få bekräftade.
The reader can obtain confirmation of the veracity of these facts.

Should read: **bekräftad** to agree with **riktigheten**.

215   The independent adjective

The adjective is normally used either attributively or predicatively, and subordinated to the noun. Sometimes, however, the adjective functions independently. There are various intermediate stages between adjective and noun (see Adjectival nouns, D below), but one or two types of independent adjective occur always in the neuter form:

(a) Colours:

Jag tycker om blått och grönt.	I like blue and green.
Vitt vann spelet.	White won the game.

(b) Nominalised adjective retaining its adjectival ending (always in the neuter form):

Man skall löna ont med gott.	You should reward evil with good.
Något nytt hade inte kommit fram.	Nothing new had come out.

216   Indefinite use of adjectives: summary

(Not including the comparative and superlative)

1 Attributive

	Non-neuter sing.	Neuter sing.		Plural	
208(a)	god mat	vackert väder		långa raka vägar	
208(b)	en - någon ingen en annan en sådan varje vilken } ny säng	ett - något inget ett annat ett sådant varje vilket } nytt bord		två många några inga andra sådana alla vilka } nya sängar/bord	

2 Predicative

208(c)	Bilen är stor men huset är litet.
	Han målade bordet brunt och stolarna gröna.
	Han levde sitt liv lugn och lycklig.
209	Både han och hon var bjudna.
210	Karakteristiskt för isländskan är de många böjningsändelserna.
211	Folk var tokiga.
213	Färsk sill är gott.
215	Rött och vitt vore vackert.
206	Det var ett äkta gammaldags julfirande.

C   THE DEFINITE DECLENSION

217   Introduction

The ending denoting the definite declension of the adjective has two possible forms:

1   An a-form: **den roliga historien**   the funny story
2   An e-form: **den roligaste filmen**   the funniest film

In most cases -a is used but in some well-defined cases -e is compulsory. There remains one area in which -e and -a are alternatives, namely in adjective + noun constructions denoting male persons. The rules indicating the choice of ending are set out in 218–220.

Note 1: **Små** does not take the definite ending **-a**:

    de små flickorna   the small girls

Note 2: The ending in **-a** is optional for **blå, grå**:

    den blå(a) himlen   the blue sky

See 203(a).

218   Compulsory ending in -a

The ending in **-a** is compulsory in the following cases:

(a) In all adjectives qualifying plural nouns except those in 219(a)–(d):

de fina blommorna	the fine flowers
de långa breven	the long letters

(b) In all adjectives qualifying neuter nouns except those in 219(a)–(d):

det vackra trädet	the beautiful tree
det maskinskrivna brevet	the typed letter
landets nya statsråd	the country's new cabinet minister

(c) In all adjectives qualifying non-neuter nouns referring to female persons:

den gamla (kvinnan)	the old woman
den sjuka (kvinnan)	the sick woman
den äldsta (kvinnan)	the oldest woman
Kära Ulla!	Dear Ulla
den engelska drottningen Viktoria	the English Queen Victoria

(d) With **människa**

den goda människan	the good person

219   Compulsory ending in -e

The ending in **-e** is compulsory in the following cases:

(a) After **-ad**, i.e. in past participles of first conjugation verbs:

den nymålade stugan	the newly painted cottage
det nymålade huset	the newly painted house
de nymålade båtarna	the newly painted boats

(b) In present participles (in **-ande, -ende**), which are indeclinable (see 206(a)):

den nuvarande kungen	the present king
det leende ansiktet	the smiling face
de badande flickorna	the bathing girls

(c) In comparative forms ending in **-are, -re**, which are indeclinable (233ff., 240):

den varmare rocken	the warmer coat
det grövre brödet	the coarser bread
de större äpplena	the larger apples

(d) After **-ast**, i.e. in some superlatives (233, 241):

den vackraste flickan	the prettiest girl
det mjukaste täcket	the softest quilt
de senaste nyheterna	the latest news

(e) In adjectival nouns referring to male persons:

den gamle (mannen)	the old man
den sjuke (mannen)	the sick man
den äldste (mannen)	the oldest man
den svenske krigarkungen Karl XII	the Swedish warrior king Charles XII

(f) With proper names (fixed expressions) denoting male persons:

Erik den helige Saint Erik; **Karl den store** Charlemagne; **Röde Orm** Red Orm; **Käre Erik!** Dear Erik

(g) In some fixed titles **-e** is used for either sex:

förste bibliotekarie	Chief Librarian
andre styrman	Second Mate

220 Variations between **-e** and **-a** with masculines

See also 218f.

(a) In formal written language (and in the spoken language of South and West Sweden) **-e** is usual when describing a male person:

den unge pojken	the young boy
Evas trevlige kusin	Eva's nice cousin

(b) In informal written language either **-e** or **-a** is used:

den unge/unga pojken

(c) In everyday spoken language (except in South and West Sweden) **-a** is used:

den unga pojken

(d) In written language and formal spoken language (except in South and West Sweden) **-e** has a higher stylistic value than **-a**:

	hennes gamle make	her elderly spouse
cf.	**hennes gamla gubbdjävel**	her old devil of a husband

(e) With nouns in **-are** and those denoting occupations **-e** is frequent if the reference is gender neutral:

den svenske medborgaren	the Swedish citizen
den utomodentlige läraren	the excellent teacher

221   The use of the definite declension – introduction

There are four types of definite construction in which adjective and noun may be combined:

Type	*Front article etc.*	*Definite adjective*	*Noun*	*End article*	*Section*
1	**den** the	**långa** long	**resa** journey	**-n**	222
	det där that	**fina** fine	**hus** house	**-et**	
2	**Peters** Peter's	**långa** long	**resa** journey	**-0**	223
	hennes her	**fina** fine	**hus** house	**-0**	
	denna this	**kalla** cold	**vinter** winter	**-0**	
3	**0** the	**Röda** Red	**kors** Cross	**-et**	224
	0 the	**hela** whole	**år** year	**-et**	

Type	Front article etc.	Definite adjective	Noun	End article	Section
4	0	**kära** dear	**barn** child	-0	225
	0	**(med) största** (with) greatest	**nöje** pleasure	-0	

Type 1: Front article and end article (double definition)
Type 2: No end article after certain words
Type 3: No front article but an end article
Type 4: Neither a front article nor an end article

222 Front article and end article (double definition)

(a) When the adjective precedes the noun in the definite form an additional definite article is usually added in front of the adjective:

resa*n*	the journey
den* långa resa*n	the long journey

This front (or adjectival) article has the following forms:

den for non-neuter singular nouns:

den långa resan	the long journey

det for neuter singular nouns:

det stora huset	the big house

de for plural nouns of both genders:

de långa resorna	the long journeys
de stora husen	the big houses

This is the most frequent use of the definite declension.

Note: It is only in spoken Swedish that one can distinguish between the unstressed front article in **den begåvade studenten** ('the gifted student') and the stressed demonstrative in **den begåvade studenten** ('that gifted student'). See also 325ff. No such ambiguity is present in the form **den studenten** which can only be demonstrative ('that student').

(b) The noun also takes an end article after demonstratives **den här, det här, den där, det där, de här, de där** (326(b)(i)):

den här långa resan	this long journey
det här stora huset	this big house
de här långa resorna	these long journeys
de här stora husen	these big houses

(c) The presence of both a front article and an end article is termed double definition because both the noun and the adjective possess their own article. These two correspond to a single article in English:

the new car	***den* nya bil*en***
the old ladies	***de* gamla damer*na***

Double definition may be considered a misnomer since the noun is actually defined three times; once by adding the definite ending to the adjective:

den* nya bil*en	cf. *en* **ny bil**

223   No end article after certain words

After the following types of word the adjective takes the definite ending but the noun does not take an end article:

(a) The genitive (129ff.):

Svenssons nya bil	Svensson's new car
bilens nya däck	the car's new tyres
pojkarnas gamla mormor	the boys' old grandmother

Exceptions: in the following cases the adjective is inflected according to the indefinite declension (0, -t, -a) (202ff.):

(i) The genitive of measurement (130(e)(ii)):

ett trettiminuters långt program	a 30-minute-long programme
tre timmars mödosam vandring	three hours' strenuous walk
ett fem våningars nybyggt hus	a newly built five-storey building

(ii) With **en sorts, ett slags** (130(e)(iii)):

en sorts mörk choklad	a kind of dark chocolate
ett slags grönt tyg	a sort of green material
flera slags persiska mattor	several kinds of Persian rug
	(*NB plural noun in Swedish*)

(iii) After a genitive or possessive **egen** is inflected according to the indefinite declension (-0, **-t**, **-a**) (204(c)):

mammas egen lilla hemlighet	Mummy's own little secret
deras eget fina hus	their own fine house

Note 1: After the indefinite article **egen** ('own') behaves as a normal adjective in the indefinite:

Han har ett eget hus.	He has a house of his own.
Egna barn är en fröjd att ha.	It is a joy to have children of one's own.

Note 2: After a front article **egen** does take a definite ending:

den egna torvan	one's own plot

Note 3: When **egen** = **säregen** ('peculiar') it does take a definite ending even after a genitive or possessive:

Hans egna uppträdande förvånade alla.	His peculiar behaviour astonished everyone.

(iv) After a genitive or possessive, **salig** is indeclinable when it is used to mean 'late', 'dead':

fru Holmstrands salig man	Mrs Holmstrand's late husband
hennes salig man	her late husband

When **salig** = 'delighted' it is inflected according to the basic rule (202).

(b) The possessive (316ff.):

min vackra flickvän	my beautiful girlfriend
hans tunga väska	his heavy suitcase
dess höga tak	its high ceiling
deras okunniga lärare	their ignorant teacher

Note: In colloquial Swedish it is becoming common to omit the definite adjective ending after **var sin**, **var sitt**, etc. (320(j)):

Pojkarna fick var sin ny cykel.	The boys received a new bicycle each.

The analogy is with **varje** ('every') (see 208(b)):

varje ny cykel	every new bicycle

In written Swedish the definite form is still found, however:

Pojkarna fick var sin nya cykel.	The boys received a new bicycle each.

(c) The demonstrative **denna, detta, dessa** (326(b)(ii)):

denna mörka skog	this dark wood
detta vackra träd	this beautiful tree
dessa mörka skogar	these dark woods

dessa vackra träd   these beautiful trees

Note: In Southern and Western Swedish dialects **denna, detta, dessa** are followed by the end article:

> **denna nya skolan**   this new school
> **detta nya huset**   this new house

(d) The relative pronoun **vars** (372):

> **Mannen, vars lilla son är sjuk, är mycket orolig.**
> The man, whose little son is ill, is very concerned.

(e) The words **samma** 'the same'; **nästa** 'the next'; **följande** 'the following'; **föregående** 'the previous'; **vederbörande** 'the (person) concerned' (cf. 139(e)):

> **samma dumma fråga**   the same silly question
> **nästa fina helg**   the next fine weekend

(f) The personal pronoun (this is rare):

> **'Du gamla, du fria, du fjällhöga Nord'**
> 'You ancient, you free, you mountainous North'

224   No front article but an end article

This is an abbreviated form of double definition in which the front article is omitted when the expression becomes familiar, assuming the nature of a set phrase, or before certain words. See 222. Compare:

> **Vita huset (i Washington)**   the White House (in Washington)
> **det vita huset (i skogen)**   the white house (in the forest)

Notice also that the construction without front article forms one concept and therefore has one stress:

> **Vita 'huset**   the 'White House
> **det 'vita huset**   the white 'house
> **svenska 'folket**   the Swedish people (a familiar concept)
> **det 'peruanska ' folket**   the Peruvian people (a less familiar concept)

This construction is becoming widespread and is very common in newspaper style, especially headlines. It is often found with certain frequent adjectives in their basic forms as well as in the comparative and superlative form:

gammal old; **ung** young; **sen** late; **ny** new; **hög** high; **låg** low; **stor** big; **liten** small; **god** good; adjectives in **-(i)sk**; adjectives in **-(l)ig**.

Examples:

stora flickan	the big girl
gamla gardet	the old guard
katolska kyrkan	the Catholic Church
kungliga livgardet	the Royal Life Guards

See 1208 for use of capital letters in proper names.

(a) No front article is possible with the words **hela** 'the whole'; **halva** 'half the'; **själva** 'the very'; **rena rama/blotta** 'sheer':

hela året om	all year round, the whole year through
till halva priset	at half price
i själva verket	in reality
Själva drottningen kom.	The queen herself came.
Det är rena rama sanningen.	It is the plain and simple truth.
med blotta ögat	with the naked eye

Note: Similar in type are the following:

sena natten	late at night
ljusa dagen	broad daylight
bleka döden	pallid Death

Note the following points about constructions with **hela, halva**:

(i) If **hela** (= 'the whole') has a front article this comes immediately after it (339(c)):

hela den anslagna tiden	the whole of the time allocated

(ii) The possessive also comes immediately after it, and is indefinite (see 317(d), 339(c)):

hela mitt liv	throughout my life

(iii) Compare the following constructions:

Kan du ge mig hela kakan?	Can you give me the whole (entire) cake?
Kan du ge mig den hela kakan?	Can you give me the whole (uncut) cake?
Kan du ge mig halva äpplet?	Can you give me half the apple? (The apple is whole.)

Kan du ge mig det halva äpplet?   Can you give me the half apple?
(The apple has already been cut.)

(b) The front article is often omitted in the following types of fixed expression:

(i) In names of geographical locations:

Kungliga slottet	the Royal Palace
Gamla stan	the Old Town
Stilla havet	the Pacific Ocean
Förenta staterna	the United States

(ii) With nationality adjectives:

Svenska Akademien	the Swedish Academy
franska revolutionen	the French Revolution
brittiska flottan	the British fleet

(iii) With words denoting location:

på högra sidan	on the right-hand side
på övre våningen	on the upper floor
i yttre skärgården	in the outer skerries
i mellersta lådan	in the middle drawer

(iv) With compass points:

Norra Ishavet	the North Polar Sea
södra stambanan	the southern main line
östra delen av staden	the eastern part of town
västra halvklotet	the western hemisphere

(v) With ordinal numbers and other words denoting series (see also 225(b)):

på tredje våningen	on the third floor
första världskriget	the First World War
för andra gången	for the second time
förra tisdagen	last Tuesday
senaste numret av tidningen	the latest issue of the newspaper

(vi) With some superlatives (cf. 225(c)):

mesta tiden	most of the time
största delen	the largest part
högsta beloppet	the greatest sum

(vii) With colours:

gula febern	yellow fever
Röda korset	the Red Cross
svarta tavlan	the blackboard
gröna vågen	the green movement

(viii) In some forms of address (cf. 225(a)):

Bäste rektorn!	Dear headmaster, (in a letter)
Lilla gumman!	Little woman!

(ix) Others:

Gamla testamentet	the Old Testament
Sahlgrenska sjukhuset	the Sahlgren Hospital

225 Neither a front article nor an end article

This is a relatively infrequent construction. There are three main types:

(a) In some forms of address, with proper nouns and other expressions denoting relationships:

Käre far!	Dear Dad!
Snälla farmor	Dear Gran
Lilla vän!	My dear!
Gamle herr Nilsson	Old Mr Nilsson
Lille Albert	Little Albert

Cf. 224(b)(viii).

(b) With some ordinal numbers (cf. 224(b)(v)):

Ta första bästa buss!	Take the first available bus.
i andra hand	second hand
åka första klass	go first class

(c) With some superlatives:

i sista stund	at the last moment
med största nöje	with great pleasure

See also 244.

226   The definite use of adjectives: summary
(Not including the comparative and superlative)

Non-neuter singular	Neuter singular	Plural

1 Double definition

220(a)	den gamle (gamla) gubben –	–	–

222(a)	den	det	de
222(b)	den här } nya bilen	det här } nya huset	de här } nya bilarna/
	den där	det där	de där } husen

2 No end article

223(a)	Svens	Svens	Svens
	firmans	firmans	firmans
223(b)	min	mitt	mina
223(c)	denna	detta	dessa
223(d)	vars } nya bil	vars } nya hus	vars } nya bilar/hus
223(e)	samma	samma	samma
	nästa	nästa	nästa
	följande	följande	följande
	föregående	föregående	föregående

3 No front article

224(b)(i)	Gamla stan
224(b)(ii)	svenska språket
224(b)(vii)	Röda korset
224(b)(iii)	högra sidan
224(b)(iv)	östra stadsdelen
224(b)(v)	andra gången
224(b)(vi)	största delen
224(b)(vii)	svarta tavlan
224(a)	hela dagen
224(a)	själva tanken
224(b)(viii)	lilla gumman

4 Neither front article nor end article

225(a)	Käre far!
225(b)	första klass
225(c)	i sista stund

D   ADJECTIVAL NOUNS

227   Introduction

The adjective is normally subordinated to the noun, but in certain cases it may attain a degree of independence. In the following cases an adjective is used independently of the noun.

(a) The noun may readily be supplied:

Gamla bilar är billigare än nya (bilar).
Old cars are cheaper than new ones.

Jag har en gammal bil och skulle gärna köpa en ny (bil).
I have an old car and would like to buy a new one.

Vill du köpa den stora tårtan? Nej, jag tar den lilla (tårtan).
Do you want to buy the big cake? No, I will have the small one.

en bekant (person)
an acquaintance

både unga tennisspelare och gamla (tennisspelare)
both young tennis players and old ones

den långhårige (mannen)
the long-haired man

Alla de äldre (människorna) var trötta.
All the older people were tired.

In these cases the adjectival noun retains its adjectival inflexion in singular and plural:

en bekant – två bekanta
an acquaintance – two acquaintances

(b) The noun is not usually supplied. This type is the one usually regarded as the 'adjectival noun':

en anhörig a relative; **an arbetslös** an unemployed person; **en blind** a blind person; **en döv** a deaf person; **en handikappad** a disabled person; **en mentalsjuk** a mentally ill person; **en sakkunnig** an expert; **en värnpliktig** a national serviceman

de blinda the blind; **de döva** the deaf; **de handikappade** the disabled

Note that in the singular definite of such expressions the form in **-e** is always used to indicate masculines (see also 218–219):

den blinde = den blinde (pojken, mannen) the blind boy/man
den blinda = den blinda (flickan, kvinnan) the blind girl/woman

A non-neuter form is generally used to refer to a person or to a non-neuter noun omitted but understood:

en blind   a blind person
den okände   the stranger
Du är den ende.   You are the only one.

Schuberts bästa symfoni är Den ofullbordade.
Schubert's best symphony is the *Unfinished*.

A neuter form generally refers to an unlimited, unspecified amount or quantity or to a neuter noun omitted but understood:

det enda vi kan göra   the only thing we can do
det sista han gjorde   the last thing he did
det nya i boken   the new element in the book
det svåraste att förstå   the most difficult thing to understand
det bästa jag vet   the best thing I know

(c) Notice that the adjectival noun takes a genitive in **-s**:

den okändes ansikte   the face of the stranger
det möjligas konst   the art of the possible

Jag tycker mer om den nya modellens form än den gamlas.
I like the shape of the new model better than the old one's.

Den stora flickans hår var mörkare än den lillas.
The big girl's hair was darker than the little girl's.

228 The forms and use of the adjectival noun

(a) Both English and Swedish often use adjectival nouns in the plural definite to indicate persons:

de unga the young; **de sjuka** the sick; **de gamla** the old; **de döda** the dead; **de fattiga** the poor; **de arbetslösa** the unemployed.

(b) However, as may be seen from the examples in 227, Swedish has gone much further than English, as the article form and adjectival ending alone indicate number *and* gender. In Swedish adjectival nouns are formed from:

(i) The indefinite form of the adjective:

en blind a blind person; **en svart** a black person; **en bekant** an acquaintance; **en död** a dead person; **ett ont** an evil (a pain).

(ii) The non-neuter singular form of the adjective:

den gamle the old man; **den gamla** the old woman.

(iii) The neuter singular form of the adjective:

det nya the new thing; **det goda** the good thing; **det löjliga** the stupid thing; **det fatala** the fatal thing.

(iv) The superlative form of the adjective:

Det var det minsta vi kunde göra.
It was the least we could do.

(v) Present participles:

de närvarande those present; **en gående** a pedestrian; **en studerande** a student; **de sörjande** the mourners.

(vi) Past participles:

den okände the unknown man, the stranger; **undertecknad** the undersigned.

(c) Adjectival nouns in Swedish may also correspond to the following in English:

(i) A common noun:

de röstande the voters

(ii) An abstract noun:

det fördelaktiga i detta the advantage of this

(iii) A clause:

Detta är det betydelsefulla. This is what is important.

(iv) Adjectives which are now treated as nouns, with a plural in **-s**:

de vuxna the adults; **de gröna** the greens; **de konservativa** the Conservatives; **de nygifta** the newly-weds; **de misstänkta** the suspects; **de intellektuella** the intellectuals.

(d) Unlike English, Swedish does not require the additional word 'one' in cases where the count noun (101(b)) is omitted (cf. 227(a)):

Olle köpte en ny bil men jag hade bara råd med en gammal.
Olle bought a new car, but I could only afford an old one.

Olle har två bilar. Hans favorit är den röda men jag gillar den blå bäst.
Olle has two cars. His favourite is the red one, but I like the blue one best.

De nygifta var de enda utan bil.
The newly married couple were the only ones without a car.

See also 360.

229   Nationality words

(a) Nationality words:

In most cases the noun for the language is identical with that for the female inhabitant, both of them first declension.

Country	Adjective	Male inhabitant	Female inhabitant	Language
(i) Male inhabitant = nationality adjective:				
Sverige	svensk -t –a	svensk-en	svenska-n	svenska-n
Danmark	dansk -t -a	dansk-en	danska-n	danska-n
Tyskland ('Germany')	tysk -t -a	tysk-en	tyska-n	tyska-n
(ii) Male inhabitant different from adjective (notice the wide variety of forms for male inhabitants):				
Storbrittanien	engelsk -t –a	engelsman-nen	engelska-n	engelska-n
Frankrike	fransk -t-a	fransman-nen, män-nen	fransyska-n	franska-n
Norge	norsk -t -a	norrman-nen, män-nen	norska-n	norska-n
Ryssland	rysk -t -a	ryss-en, -ar-na	ryska-n	ryska-n
Spanien	spansk -t -a	spanjor-en, -er-na	spanjorska-n	spanska-n
Finland	finsk -t -a	finländare-n, -0-na (finne-n, -ar-na)	finska-n	finska-n
Island	isländsk -t -a	islänning-en, -ar-na	isländska-n	isländska-n
Belgien	belgisk -t -a	belgare-n, belgier-n	belgiska-n	
USA/Förenta staterna	amerikansk -t -a	amerikan-en, -er-na	amerikanska-n,	engelska-n
Kina	kinesisk -t -a	kines-en, -er-na	kinesiska-n	kinesiska-n

Note: Adjectives and nouns of nationality are not written with capital letters unless they start a sentence. See 1207(e)(iii).

(b) English nationality expressions of the type 'the English, the Greeks, the French, the Norwegians' are never translated using the adjectival noun in Swedish. There are separate common nouns for these in Swedish:

engelsmännen the English; **fransmännen** the French; **holländarna** the Dutch; **irländarna** the Irish

230 Complete nominalisation

(a) In cases such as the nationality noun the adjective takes on nominal inflexion:

> **svensk -t, -a**, Swedish → **en svensk, svensken, svenskar, svenskarna,**
> a Swede

Other examples of complete nominalisation of the adjective are:

De har en unge/två ungar.	They have one kid/two kids.
De har just fått en liten.	They have just had a baby.
lillan	small female child
lillen	small male child
högern	the Right (in a political sense)
vänstern	the Left (in a political sense)
gulan, vitan	the yolk, white (of an egg)
fett-et	fat
vilt-et	game (wild animals)
djup-et	the deep
grund-et	the shallows

Note: To express the plural of **en liten, lillen** and **lillan** one would use **små** or **de små**:

> **En mamma kom in med sina små.**   A mother came in with her little ones.

Notice the following:

> **en död** a dead person (but **en död** a death, **döden** = (the) death)
> **den döde** the dead man
> **den döda** the dead woman
> **de döda** the dead (people)

231 Intermediate forms

Some adjectival nouns represent forms intermediate between adjective and noun:

En fullmäktig ('a delegate') has a definite form in **-en** but an adjectival plural in **-e. En anhörig** ('a next of kin') has no end article form, but an adjectival plural in **-a**.

Nästa ('a neighbour') is only singular:

> **Man skall älska sin nästa.**   One shall love one's neighbour.

Närmaste ('nearest and dearest') is only plural:

mina närmaste   my nearest and dearest

Note the alternative forms: **käraste -n, -0 (käresta -n, -or,** fem. only), dearest

E   COMPARISON OF ADJECTIVES

232   Introduction

Swedish adjectives possess a basic (positive) form which is inflected according to number, gender and species (definite/indefinite, see B, C above), a comparative form which is uninflected and a superlative form which is inflected according to species alone (definite declension). There are four main types of adjective comparison:

1   The endings **-are, -ast** are added to the positive (see 233):

    glad, gladare, gladast   happy, happier, happiest

2   The endings **-re, -st** are added to the positive and its root vowel is modified (see 234):

    stor, större, störst   big, bigger, biggest

3   A different stem from that of the positive is used (irregular comparison) (see 235):

    liten, mindre, minst   small, smaller, smallest

4   The words **mer, mest** are used with the positive (see 236):

    typisk, mer typisk, mest typisk   typical, more typical, most typical

Note: See also 236(b) below for inflection of the adjective with **mer, mest.**

233   Comparison with the endings **-are, -ast**

Most Swedish adjectives add **-are** to the positive in order to form the comparative, and **-ast** to the positive to form the superlative. These include those adjectives whose indefinite declension is noted in 202, 203 (a)–(f), (h)–(l) (Past participles ending in **-dd** (203(g)) compare using **mer, mest** (236(a)), but see also 236 Note 3.) For the comparison of adverbs see 605.

(a) The vast majority of these adjectives simply add **-are** and **-ast**:

Positive	Comparative	Superlative	Meaning
glad	gladare	gladast	happy
rolig	roligare	roligast	amusing
trött	tröttare	tröttast	tired
sen	senare	senast	late
grann	grannare	grannast	pretty

(b) Some ending in **-el**, **-en**, **-er** drop the final **-e** of the stem (see 204(b),(c)):

riskabel	riskablare	riskablast	risky
mogen	mognare	mognast	mature, ripe
mager	magrare	magrast	thin

(c) Some adjectives ending in **-m** double the **-m** before adding **-are**, **-ast** (see 203(k)):

dum	dummare	dummast	stupid
långsam	långsammare	långsammast	slow

(d) Adjectives ending in unstressed **-a** drop the **-a** before adding **-are**, **-ast**:

sakta	saktare	saktast	slow
udda	uddare	uddast	odd

234 Comparison with the endings **-re, -st** plus modification of the root vowel

The following adjectives form a small but frequently encountered group:

Positive	Comparative	Superlative	Vowel change	Meaning
stor	större	störst	o → ö	big
grov	grövre	grövst	o → ö	coarse
låg	lägre	lägst	å → ä	low
lång	längre	längst	å → ä	long, tall
trång	trängre	trängst	å → ä	narrow
få	färre	-	å → ä	few
små	smärre	-	å → ä	small
ung	yngre	yngst	u → y	young
tung	tyngre	tyngst	u → y	heavy
hög	högre	högst	No change	high

235 Irregular comparison

(a) Form:

The following adjectives form their comparative and superlative by employing a different stem. They form a small but frequently encountered group.

Positive	Comparative	Superlative	Meaning	
god, bra	bättre	bäst	good	see also (b) below
(godare)	(godast)			
dålig	sämre	sämst	bad	see also (c) below
	värre	värst		see also (d) below
	(dåligare)	(dåligast)		
ond	värre	värst	bad	
	(ondare)	(ondast)		
gammal	äldre	äldst	old	
liten	mindre	minst	little	
många	fler	flest	many	see also (e) below
mycket	mer(a)	mest	a lot	see also (e) below

(b) 'Good – better':

The usual equivalents are: **god – bättre – bäst**. The alternative **godare – godast** is used to indicate 'pleasant tasting'.

(c) 'Bad – worse':

The usual equivalents are: **dålig – sämre – sämst**. The alternative **dåligare – dåligast** is found in colloquial Swedish to indicate poor health.

(d) 'Worse – worst':

The choice is: **värre – värst** or **sämre – sämst**.

Värre – värst indicates that something is endowed with more of a bad property:

ett annat, värre lidande	another, worse suffering
Det var den värsta lögn jag hört.	That was the worst lie I've heard.

Sämre – sämst indicates that something is endowed with less of a good property:

de sämre lottade i livet   those worse-off in life
byxor av sämre kvalitet   trousers of worse quality

Han blir sämre (= sjukare) för var dag som går.
He gets worse every day.

Compare:

Vädret är värre idag.   The weather is worse today.
(i.e. The weather was already bad yesterday.)

Vädret är sämre idag.   The weather is worse today.
(i.e. The weather was good yesterday.)

(e) 'More' – 'most'

The choice is: **mer(a)** – **mest** or **fler** – **flest**. Mer(a) – mest are used with non-count nouns (see 101(b)):

Vill du ha mer kaffe?   Would you like more coffee?
Han fick mest pengar.   He got most money.
Det mesta arbetet gör han själv.   Most of the work he does himself.

Fler – **flest** are used with count nouns (see 101(b)):

De var många fler människor än vi.   They were many more than us.
Jag måste köpa fler böcker.   I must buy more books.
De flesta svenskar tycker om sill.   Most Swedes like herring.

Note 1: **flera** = several, a number of, various different (see 351(c)):

flera unga studenter   several young students

In a sense it is an absolute comparative (see 243).

Note 2: If a comparison is implied when using **de flesta**, the noun following takes an end article (see 353(c)(d)):

Vem fick de flesta rösterna?   Who got most votes?

If no comparison is implied (i.e. if **de flesta** is an absolute superlative, see 244) the noun has no article:

De flesta (människor) visste inget.   Most people did not know anything.
De flesta bilar har blinkers nuförtiden.   Most cars have indicators nowadays.

236 Comparison with mer(a), mest

(a) Adjectives compared with **mer(a)** and **mest** form a large and varied group including:

(i) Most past participles, and all past participles and other adjectives ending in **-ad** (204(a), 531):

komplicerad	**mer(a) komplicerad**	**mest komplicerad**
complicated	more complicated	most complicated
snabbfotad	**mer(a) snabbfotad**	**mest snabbfotad**
fleet-footed	more fleet-footed	most fleet-footed

Note 1: Exception: adjectives ending in a long **-a + d**:

glad	**gladare**	**gladast**
happy	happier	happiest

Note 2: Past participles ending in **-d**, **-t** may compare either with **mer(a)**, **mest** or with inflexional endings:

en mer(a) bortskämd (bortskämdare) flicka	a more spoiled girl
en mer(a) förskräckt (förskräcktare) man	a more terrified man

Note 3: Those adjectives ending in **-d**, **-dd**, **-t**, **-en** formed with non-verbal suffixes but appearing to have the form of past participles, tend to have inflexional comparatives:

en högljuddare församling	a noisier gathering
en vidsyntare person	a more broad-minded person
ett angelägnare ärende	a more urgent errand

Note 4: Past participles ending in **-en** compare using inflexional endings rather more commonly by analogy with those adjectives ending in **-en** that are not formed from verbs:

en frusnare (mer(a) frusen) brevbärare	a colder postman

Many participles of strong verbs used as adjectives have become remote from the original verb. In cases where their meaning becomes specialised, there is a tendency to adopt an inflexional comparative:

en drucknare sjöman	a more drunken sailor

Similarly: **galen** crazy; **storslagen** grandiose; **svullen** swollen; **öppen** open; **avlägsen** remote.

(ii) All present participles (in **-ande**, **-ende**) (206(a), 532):

motbjudande	**mer(a) motbjudande**	**mest motbjudande**
repulsive	more repulsive	most repulsive
ingående	**mer(a) ingående**	**mest ingående**
detailed	more detailed	most detailed

(iii) Most adjectives ending in **-isk** (202(b)(ii)):

fantastisk	**mer(a) fantastisk**	**mest fantastisk**
fantastic	more fantastic	most fantastic
typisk	**mer(a) typisk**	**mest typisk**
typical	more typical	most typical

Note 1: An exception is **frisk**:

frisk	**friskare**	**friskast**
healthy	healthier	healthiest

Note 2: The very few adjectives ending in **-esk** are sometimes compared with **mer(a)**, **mest** by analogy with those ending in **-isk**:

grotesk	**groteskare**	**groteskast**
(mer(a) grotesk)	**(mest grotesk)**	
grotesque	more grotesque	most grotesque
pittoresk	**pittoreskare**	**pittoreskast**
(mer(a) pittoresk)	**(mest pittoresk)**	
picturesque	more picturesque	most picturesque

(iv) Many (otherwise indeclinable) adjectives ending in **-a**, **-e**, **-s** (see also 206):

annorlunda	**mer annorlunda**	**mest annorlunda**
different	more different	most different
gängse	**mer gängse**	**mest gängse**
customary	more customary	most customary
gammaldags	**mer gammaldags**	**mest gammaldags**
old-fashioned	more old-fashioned	most old-fashioned

But notice: some adjectives ending in **-a** (see 206(b)) which are normally indeclinable in the positive (indefinite declension) add **-re**, **-st** but do *not* modify the root vowel:

noga careful	**nogare**	**nogast**
sakta slow	**saktare**	**saktast**
stilla peaceful	**stillare**	**stillast**
ringa lowly	**ringare**	**ringast**

(v) The longer and more complex an adjective is, the more likely it is to compare using **mer** and **mest**. Compound adjectives and adjectives derived from other word classes (especially those with stressed suffixes) may use either **-are**, **-ast** or **mer**, **mest**:

framgångsrik -are, -ast successful
or **mer framgångsrik, mest framgångsrik**

formell -are, -ast formal
or **mer formell, mest formell**

(vii) There is an increasing tendency to use **mer**, **mest** as an alternative to inflexional comparisons:

Det är mest troligt att premiärministern avgår.
It is most likely that the Prime Minister will resign.

(vii) Notice also:

van accustomed	**mer(a) van**	**mest van**

(b) Note particularly that adjectives comparing with **mer(a)**, **mest** are inflected according to the indefinite or definite declension:

ett mer(a)/mest komplicerat fall	a more/most complicated case
mer(a) komplicerade fall	more complicated cases
det mer(a)/mest komplicerade fallet	the more/most complicated case
de mer(a)/mest komplicerade fallen	the more/most complicated cases
en mer(a)/mest ingående skildring	a more/most detailed description
mer(a) ingående skildringar	more detailed descriptions
den mer(a)/mest ingående skildringen	the more/most detailed descriptions
mer(a)/mest ingående skildringarna	the more/most detailed descriptions

237   Comparison of compound adjectives

Compound adjectives comprising two adjectival elements (see 1115f.) form their comparisons in one of three ways:

(a) The final element compares by adding **-are/-ast** or **-re/-st** (for those adjectives that compare in this way see 233, 234):

högtidlig	**högtidligare**	**högtidligast**	formal
kortvarig	**kortvarigare**	**kortvarigast**	brief
godmodig	**godmodigare**	**godmodigast**	good-humoured

(b) The whole compound is compared with **mer(a)**, **mest** if the final element would normally be compared with **mer(a)**, **mest** (see 236):

långsökt	**mer(a) långsökt**	**mest långsökt**	far fetched
kortfattad	**mer(a) kortfattad**	**mest kortfattad**	concise

(c) In a few well-defined instances only the first element compares. Note that the first element in these expressions then becomes an independent adverb and is thus inflexible:

lättillgänglig	**ett lättare tillgängligt material** a more easily available material
mörkblå	**en mörkare blå kostym** a darker blue suit
glesbefolkad	**glesare befolkade öar** more sparsely populated islands
	det glesast befolkade området the most sparsely populated area

238   Adjectives deficient in the positive, positive and comparative, or superlative

(a) Some adjectives with a comparative in **-re**, superlative in **-erst/-st** and which denote place have no positive form, but derive from an adverb or preposition (see also 607):

Positive	Comparative	Superlative	Meaning
borta	**bortre**	**borterst**	away, furthest away
(hit)	**hitre**	**hiterst**	here, nearest
(Place in relation to other elements and to the speaker)			
(inne)	**inre**	**innerst**	in, innermost
(ute)	**yttre**	**ytterst**	out, outermost
(i mitten)	–	**mitterst**	in the centre
(mellan)	–	**mellerst** '	between, in the middle
(Place in relation to other elements and the centre)			
(under)	**undre**	**underst**	below, at the bottom
(över)	**övre**	**överst**	above, at the top
(ner)	**nedre**	**nederst**	down, at the foot of
(Place in vertical order in relation to something)			
(bakom)	**bakre**	**bakerst**	behind, at the very back
(fram)	**främre**	**främst**	forward, at the very front
(Place in horizontal order in relation to something)			

Examples:

Han sitter i inre rummet.	He is sitting in the inner room.
på övre våningen	in the upper storey
på en av de främre bänkarna	on one of the front benches
i mellersta Sverige	in central Sweden

Note 1: The comparative form may not be used predicatively.

Note 2: Several of these adverbs may be compared with **längre** and **längst**:

(**borta**), away – **längre bort**, further away – **längst bort** furthest away

Others are: **in, ut, ner, upp, fram**

(b) Some adjectives exist only in the superlative form:

näst next; **sist** last

Note that **sist** means 'last' in the sense of 'final'. 'Last' in the sense of 'latest' is properly rendered in Swedish by **senast** (see 233(a)):

Spielbergs senaste film	Spielberg's latest film
Chaplins sista film	Chaplin's last film

But this distinction often breaks down:

Spielbergs sista film Spielberg's latest film; **Tack för sist** (lit.) Thank you for the last time (a Swedish politeness used when meeting someone again after having been entertained by them)

Some adjectives possess no superlative form:

få, färre	few, fewer
små, smärre	small, smaller (minor)

239 Adjectives which do not compare

Because of their absolute meaning, some adjectives possess no comparative or superlative form:

allsmäktig almighty; **död** dead; **barhuvad** bare-headed; **barnlös** childless; **enögd** one-eyed; **fyrkantig** square; **gratis** free; **gravid** pregnant; **medeltida** medieval; **äkta** genuine, etc.

This group includes adjectives combined with the (colloquial) prefixes **jätte-, toppen-, ur-, skit-, as-** or prefixed by a noun:

jättestor gigantic; **toppenbra** fantastic; **urdålig** terrible; **skitbillig** very cheap; **aspackad** dead drunk; **dödstrött** dead tired; **stenrik** filthy rich.

240 The comparative is indeclinable

The comparative formed with **-are/-re** retains the same form for both indefinite and definite irrespective of gender or number:

> **Han har en äldre bror. Den äldre brodern heter Lars.**
> He has an older brother. The older brother is called Lars.

> **Han har ett äldre hus. Det äldre huset ligger vid sjön.**
> He has an older house. The older house is by the lake.

> **de äldre bröderna/husen**
> the older brothers/houses

Compare indeclinable adjectives in **-e**, 206(a).

241 Inflexion of the superlative

(a) When used predicatively the superlative in **-ast/-st** is either left uninflected (indefinite declension) or inflected (definite declension). Cf.:

> **Dina rosor är vackrast.**
> Your roses are most beautiful.

> **Dina rosor är de vackraste i rummet.**
> Your roses are the most beautiful in the room.

(b) When used attributively the superlative is always inflected (definite declension):

den vackrast*e* rosen	the most beautiful rose
det vackrast*e* huset	the most beautiful house
de vackrast*e* husen	the most beautiful houses

Notice that one may say either of the following:

den yngsta av de två barnen	(*lit.*) the youngest of the two children
den yngre av de två barnen	the younger of the two children

(c) Superlatives whose uninflected form ends in **-ast** (233 above) add **-e**:

Den där flickan var vackrast.	That girl was most beautiful.
den vackraste flickan	the most beautiful girl

(d) Superlatives whose uninflected form ends in **-st** with modification of the root vowel (234 above) add **-a** (masculines either **-e** or **-a**, 220):

Den där tårtan är störst.	That cake is biggest.
den största tårtan	the biggest cake
Den där pojken är störst.	That boy is biggest.
den störste/största pojken	the biggest boy

Notice that superlatives whose stem differs from that of the positive (235) also take **-a** (masculines in **-e** or **–a** (220):

Deras bil var äldst.	Their car was oldest.
den äldsta bilen	the oldest car
Deras son var äldst.	Their son was oldest.
den äldste/äldsta sonen	the eldest son

(e) Superlatives formed using **mest** + present participle (236(a)(ii)) are uninflected because the present participle is never inflected:

den mest ingående skildringen	the most detailed depiction

(f) Superlatives formed from **mest** + past participles (236) vary as to their inflected form according to the conjugation of the verb from which the participle derives (see also 531). Notice that the adjective in this construction is always inflected in the definite:

den mest älskade prinsessan	the most beloved princess
det mest berömda dansstället	the most famous dance hall
den mest sjungna visan	the most sung folk song

Masculine:

den mest berömde/berömda detektiven	the most famous detective
den mest avskydde/avskydda tyrannen	the most detested tyrant

The superlative with **mest** + past participle etc. used predicatively inflects according to number, unlike superlatives in **-ast/-st**:

Det fallet var mest komplicerat.	The case was most complicated.
De fallen var mest komplicerade.	The cases were most complicated.

(g) The superlative is often used in the definite form without the front article (221, 224(b)(vi)):

minsta barnet	the smallest child
högsta kortet	the highest card
äldste sonen	the eldest son
yngsta dottern	the youngest daughter
bästa sättet	the best method
senaste modet	the latest fashion
närmaste/närmsta vägen	the shortest route

This is especially frequent with adjectives depicting place (see 238):

översta hyllan	the top shelf
nedersta trappsteget	the lowest step
yttersta vänstern	the extreme left

In some set phrases the superlative may be used without either front article or end article (221, 225):

Stig av vid närmaste station!	Get off at the nearest station.
i största hast	in great haste
i bästa fall	at best

Note: The superlative after **som** is generally used when a person or thing is compared with itself under different circumstances. This often corresponds to 'at its' in English:

Trafiken är som värst vid midsommarhelgen.
The traffic is at its worst over the Midsummer weekend.

Då vattnet stod som högst blev vi rädda.
When the water had reached its deepest we were afraid.

242 Similarity, dissimilarity and reinforcement

(a) Phrases with **som** are used to link two elements that are similar:

Han är lika intelligent som jag.	He's as intelligent as me/I (am).
Han talar samma dialekt som jag.	He speaks the same dialect as me/ I (do).
Din mössa är likadan som min.	Your cap is like mine.

Note: Subordinate clauses expressing similarity often begin with **som om** with the past tense or **skulle** or the subjunctive:

Sven låter som om han var/vore full.	Sven sounds as if he was/were drunk.
Det ser ut som om det skulle bli snö.	It looks as if there's going to be snow.
Det verkar som om det blir bra.	It seems as if it's going to be OK.

(b) The adjective **lik, -t, -a** and the verb **likna** are also used to express similarity:

Jag är lik min bror.	I am like my brother.
Jag liknar min bror.	I resemble my brother.

(c) In order to express dissimilarity the particle **än** is used:

Whisky är starkare än öl.	Whisky is stronger than beer.
Hans dialekt är annorlunda än din.	His dialect is different from yours.

(d) The adjective **olik, -t, -a** is also used to express dissimilarity:

Hans dialekt är olik din.	His dialect is unlike yours.
Det är olikt honom.	It is unlike him.
Bröderna är mycket olika varandra.	The brothers are very unlike each other.

(e) The words **ännu, mycket, ändå, allt** may sometimes be used to reinforce the comparative:

De har en ännu bättre bil än vi (har). They have an even better car than us.

(f) The word **allra** may be used to reinforce the superlative (see 612(b)):

den allra vackraste kvinnan	the most beautiful woman
den allra första blomman	the very first flower

(g) 'The more . . . the more' is expressed in Swedish by the bracketing expression **ju . . . desto . . .** , or **ju . . . ju . . .**, **ju . . . dess . . .** . Notice the inversion in the second clause:

Ju mer(a) hon äter, desto mer(a) vill hon ha.
The more she eats, the more she wants.

Ju fullare han blir, desto pratsammare blir han.
The more drunk he gets, the more talkative he becomes.

243 The absolute comparative

When the second part of the comparison is not stated in Swedish, the element of comparison may disappear in part or in whole. This is known as the absolute comparative, as opposed to a relative comparative. English has no absolute comparative, and the Swedish construction is often translated as 'rather X', 'quite Y'.

Relative comparative
Penningsumman han vann var större än han väntat.
The sum of money he won was larger than he expected.

Absolute comparative
Han har vunnit en större penningsumma.
He has won a fairly large sum of money.

Other examples of the absolute comparative:

Det har inte blivit någon större temperaturförändring.
There has been no great change in temperature.

De åkte in i ett mindre samhälle.
They came into a fairly small community.

Det kom en grupp högre tjänstemän.
A group of senior officials arrived.

Han har ådragit sig en lättare hjärnskakning.
He has suffered a mild concussion.

De tog sig en längre promenad.
They took quite a long walk.

Note also:

mindre vatten (= små sjöar)	smallish lakes
en kortare tid	rather a short time
en äldre herre	an elderly gentleman

244 The absolute superlative

The absolute superlative is used when the speaker/writer wishes to show that something possesses a quality to a very high degree, without directly comparing it to anything else. The use of the superlative in this way is an exaggeration. Notice that the absolute superlative rarely occurs with end article.

Relative superlative
De bästa vännerna i vår klass var Ulf och Per.
The best friends in our class were Ulf and Per.

Absolute superlative
De var de bästa vänner (i världen).
They were the best of friends.

Note: Other examples of the absolute superlative:

den (allra) största försiktighet	the greatest care
den djupaste tystnad	the deepest silence
i högsta grad	to a very high degree
i värsta fall	in the worst case
inte den minsta aning	not the slightest inkling
med varmaste hälsningar	kindest regards
med största nöje	with great pleasure
med minsta möjliga tidsspillan	with the least possible delay
tyg av den (allra) sämsta kvalitet	material of the very worst quality

245 Adjectives – use of the positive, comparative and superlative: summary

Attributive	*Predicative*

A POSITIVE
Indefinite (202–205, 207–216)

en rolig man	Mannen är rolig.
en rolig film	Filmen är rolig.
en skadad arm	Armen är skadad.
ett roligt program	Programmet är roligt.
roliga filmer	Filmerna är roliga.
roliga program	Programmen är roliga.

Definite (217–226)

den rolige mannen
den roliga filmen
den skadade armen
det roliga programmet
de roliga filmerna
de roliga programmen
de skadade armarna

B COMPARATIVE
Indefinite (232–236, 240)

en roligare man	Mannen är roligare.
en roligare film	Filmen är roligare.
ett roligare program	Programmet är roligare.
ett större fel	Felet är större.
en mer(a) ingående skildring	Skildringen är mer(a) ingående.
ett mer(a) komplicerat fall	Fallet är mer(a) komplicerat.
roligare filmer	Filmerna är roligare.
roligare program	Programmen är roligare.

Attributive	*Predicative*

Attributive	*Predicative*
större fel	Felen är större.
mer(a) ingående skildringar	Skildringarna är mer(a) ingående.
mer(a) komplicerade fall	Fallen är mer(a) komplicerade.

Definite (240)
den roligare mannen
den roligare filmen
det roligare programmet
det större felet
den mer(a) ingående skildringen
det mer(a) komplicerade fallet
de roligare filmerna
de roligare programmen
de mer(a) ingående skildringarna
de mer(a) komplicerade fallen

C SUPERLATIVE
Indefinite (241)

Mannen är roligast.
Filmen är roligast.
Armen är mest skadad.
Skildringen är mest ingående.
Programmet är roligast.
Filmerna är roligast.
Programmen är roligast.

Definite (241)
den roligaste mannen
den roligaste filmen
den mest skadade armen
den mest ingående skildringen
det roligaste programmet
de roligaste filmerna
de roligaste programmen

3   PRONOUNS

A   PERSONAL PRONOUNS
301   Personal pronouns – form, table

B   SUBJECT AND OBJECT PRONOUNS
302   The first person – **jag, vi**
303   The second person – **du, ni**
304   Forms of address in Swedish
305   The third person
306   **Han, hon** and nouns indicating a person but not a gender
307   **Ett ungt par** – **det** or **de**?
308   Table showing the major uses of **det**
309   The use of **det**

C   REFLEXIVE PRONOUNS
310   The use of reflexive pronouns
311   Some exceptions to the main rule
312   The ethical dative
313   'Each other', 'one another' – reciprocal pronouns

D   EMPHATIC PRONOUNS
314   Emphatic pronouns in English – personal pronoun in Swedish
315   **Själv**

E   POSSESSIVE ADJECTIVES AND PRONOUNS
316   Possessive adjectives and pronouns
317   The use of possessive pronouns
318   **Dess**
319   **Hans** or **sin**? – basic use
320   **Hans** or **sin**? Further implications of the basic rule
321   Possessive pronouns in pejorative expressions
322   'A friend of mine'
323   Possessive pronoun in English – definite article in Swedish
324   Personal and possessive pronouns in comparisons with **än** and **som**

F   DEMONSTRATIVE PRONOUNS
325   The form of demonstrative pronouns
326   The use of demonstrative pronouns
327   **Samma, densamma**
328   **Sådan, dylik, slik**

G	DETERMINATIVE PRONOUNS
329	Determinative pronouns

H	INDEFINITE PRONOUNS
330	**Man**
331	**Varje, var, varenda**, etc., table of forms and use
332	**Varje, var**
333	**Var och en, varenda**, etc.
334	**Varannan**
335	**Varandra**
336	**Vardera, någondera, ingendera,** etc.
337	Prices: '50 euros each'
338	Distribution: '1 teaspoonful to every 5 litres'
339	**All (allt, alla)** etc.
340	**Annan, den andra**
341	**Någon (något, några)**
342	**Somlig**
343	**Ingen (inget, inga)**
344	**Ingen** or **inte någon?**
345	**Ingen, inte någon** – a schematic summary
346	Translation of 'some' and 'any' into Swedish
347	**Båda**
348	**Mycket**
349	**Många**
350	**Inte för mycket ärter, tack!**
351	**Mer, fler**
352	'Most', **mest**, etc. – a schematic overview of Swedish use
353	'Most', 'most of', etc.
354	**Lite, litet**
355	**Få**
356	**Mindre, färre, minst**
357	**Lagom**
358	Swedish pronominal compounds with **som helst**, and English 'whoever', 'whatever', etc.
359	Concessive 'whoever', 'whatever', etc.
360	'One' used to replace a noun

J	INTERROGATIVE PRONOUNS
361	Interrogative pronouns, introduction and form
362	**Vem? Vilka?** in direct questions
363	**Vad?** in direct questions
364	**Vad för?** etc. in direct questions
365	**Vilken?** etc. in direct questions
366	Interrogative pronouns in indirect questions
367	Interrogative pronouns in direct and indirect questions
368	**Vilken (vilket, vilka)** = 'What (a)' + noun in exclamations

K   RELATIVE PRONOUNS
369   Relative pronouns, introduction and form
370   **Som**
371   **Vilken, vilket, vilka**
372   **Vars** and the genitive forms of the relative pronoun
373   **Vad** and **vad som**

A   PERSONAL PRONOUNS

301 Personal pronouns – form, table

Singular		*Subject*	*Object*	*Possessive*	*Reflexive*
1	person	**jag** I	**mig (mej)** me	**min** my, mine	**mig (mej)** me
2	person familiar	**du** you	**dig (dej)** you	**din** your, yours	**dig (dej)** you
2	person formal	**ni** you	**er** you	**er** your, yours	**er** you
3	person masculine	**han** he	**honom** him	**hans/sin** his	**sig (sej)** himself
3	person feminine	**hon** she	**henne** her	**hennes/sin** her, hers	**sig (sej)** herself
3	person non-neuter	**den** it	**den** it	**dess/sin** its	**sig (sej)** itself
3	person neuter	**det** it	**det** it	**dess/sin** its	**sig (sej)** itself

Plural		*Subject*	*Object*	*Possessive*	*Reflexive*
1	person	**vi** we	**oss** us	**vår** our, ours	**oss** us
2	person familiar	**ni** you	**er** you	**er** your, yours	**er** you
2	person formal	**ni** you	**er** you	**er** your, yours	**er** you
3	person masculine, feminine, non-neuter, neuter	**de** they	**dem** them	**deras/sin** their, theirs	**sig (sej)** themselves

The table above does not include neuter and plural forms of the possessive pronouns (see 316–324). Subject and object pronouns are dealt with in 302–309, reflexive pronouns in 310–312.

Comments on the form, spelling and pronunciation of personal pronouns:

(a) Jag is almost invariably pronounced /ja/, i.e. without the final **-g.**

(b) Although **mig, dig, sig** are the most commonly encountered forms in written Swedish, there is a tendency to spell **mig, dig, sig** phonetically **(mej, dej, sej)** in personal correspondence and in dialogue in contemporary fiction.

(c) In spoken Swedish the possessive pronouns for 1st and 2nd persons plural **(vår/vårt, er/ert)** have colloquial singular forms **(våran/vårat, eran/erat)** which exist alongside the standard written forms (see 316 (d)).

(d) In most spoken Swedish the 3rd person plural pronouns **de** and **dem** are both pronounced /dom/ (short vowel), except in liturgical and formal language. For a number of years the writing of **dom** has been generally accepted as an alternative to **dem** (object) in personal correspondence and in dialogue in contemporary fiction, though standard Swedish retains **dem.** This practice has not extended to the use of **dom** as a front article before the adjective: **de rika** /dom rika/ 'the rich'.

Note: In South Sweden and Finland the pronunciation of **de** is often /di/.

(e) The following points, while less important, are worth noting:

Note 1: Formerly the 2nd person pronouns were written with capital initial letters in correspondence. This practice is now less common in personal correspondence, but capital letters are still sometimes used in business correspondence. (See 1206(c)(ii).)

Note 2: In very colloquial Swedish the **d-** of **du/dig/dej** is frequently omitted following a verbal ending in **-r:**

Ser'u nåt? (= **Ser du något?**)	Can you see anything?

Note 3: The antiquated 2nd person plural pronoun **I** (corresponding roughly to the English 'ye') is no longer used, except in some dialects and occasionally in liturgical language. **I** is always written capitalised and must be combined with a special form of the verb ending in **-n.** (See 517.) The object, reflexive and possessive pronoun corresponding to **I** is **eder.** The possessive forms **(eder, edert, edra)** may still be encountered in very formal language (see 304(a), Note 2).

Note 4: Shortened spoken forms of the 3rd person singular pronouns are sometimes used in dialect. **Han, hon, den** are pronounced /en/, or /n/ after a vowel. **Det** is pronounced /et/, or /t/ after a vowel. **Honom** is pronounced /en/, as /n/ after a vowel, or sometimes /han/ (like the subject form). **Henne** is pronounced /na/.

Jag har aldrig sett 'en/han.	I've never seen 'im.
Jag gav 'na pengarna	I gave 'er the money.
Här har du geväret. Ta't!	Here's your rifle. Take it!

B　SUBJECT AND OBJECT PRONOUNS

302　The first person – jag, vi

(a) **Jag** (subject) and **mig** (object) refer to the speaker in the singular:

Jag heter Jan.	My name is Jan.
Kalla mig inte för Janne!	Don't call me Janne.
De skrev ett brev till mig.	They wrote a letter to me.

(b) **Vi** (subject) and **oss** (object) refer to the speaker in the plural:

Vi är tvillingar.	We are twins.
Kan du skilja mellan oss?	Can you tell us apart?
Du gav oss en blomma.	You gave us a flower.

Note 1: **Vi** may also be used by royalty to signify a speaker in the singular ('*pluralis majestatis*', cf. English 'the royal we'):

Vi, Carl XVI Gustav, med Guds nåde ...　　We, Carl XVI Gustav, by the grace of God

Note 2: **Vi** is also occasionally used as a form of address. See 304(c)(ii).

God morgon. Hur mår vi idag?　　Good morning. How are we feeling today?

Note 3: Note the idiomatic expressions:

mig veterligen	as far as I know/to my knowledge
oss emellan	between ourselves/between you and me

303　The second person – du, ni

There are two pairs of 2nd person singular pronouns in Swedish: **du** (subject form with **dig** as the corresponding object form) and **ni** (subject form with **er** as the corresponding object form). Both of these pronouns render English 'you'. For differences in usage see (a) and (b) below.

The 2nd person plural pronoun is **ni** (subject), **er** (object). See (c) below.

(a) **Du (dig)** is the familiar form of address, used with people or animals.

Är det du, mamma?	Is that you, Mum?
Jag vill gärna träffa dig igen.	I would like to meet you again.

From the 1960s onwards, as old class barriers have become less marked, **du** has become almost universally accepted in Sweden. Nowadays most people working in the same firm or building will use **du** to one another. **Du** is generally used between younger people, and people of roughly the same age and social standing meeting socially. Generally only older people, those who grew up with clear 'rules' about the use of the familiar **du** and the formal **ni**, remain more conservative, although there has recently been a revival of **ni** (see (b) below).

The use of **du** instead of **man** (see 330) is becoming increasingly frequent, a phenomenon that reveals the influence of English.

> **När du dyker blir världen som förvandlad.**
> When you go diving the world seems transformed.
> (Preferable is: **När man dyker . . .**)

Note 1: Capital initial letters are sometimes used for **du, dig** in personal and business correspondence (cf. 301(e) Note 1).

Note 2: When used in a pejorative expression, the English 'you' is sometimes rendered by the possessive adjective in Swedish (cf. 321).

> **Din jäkla idiot!**   You damned idiot!

Note 3: The verbs **dua/nia** mean 'to call someone **du/ni**' (perhaps best approximated in English by the concept of 'being/not being on first-name terms with someone'):

> **Som goda vänner har vi alltid duat varandra.**
> As good friends, we've always been on first name terms.

Note 4: Some Swedish idiomatic expressions with **du/ni**:

> **Kära du, har du inte hört?**   My dear fellow/girl, haven't you heard?
> **Du milde, vad här ser ut!**   My word, what a mess!
> **Snälla du/ni, hjälp mig!**   Please, help me!
> **Hör du, du ...**   Look here = I say ...

(b) When used in the singular **ni** and **er** provide a formal mode of address. They are used:

(i) When speaking to a stranger (especially an older person) whose name is not known (cf. 304(a)):

> **Ni har slagit fel nummer.**   You've dialled the wrong number.

(ii) In business letters addressed to a firm or an individual with whom the writer is not on first-name terms. In this context **Ni/Er** is sometimes spelt with an initial capital letter (see 1206(c)(ii)):

> **Vi tackar för den order Ni har sänt.**   We thank you for the order you sent.

(c) Ni and er may be used in the plural in all cases where the English 'you' refers to two or more people.

304   Forms of address in Swedish

Du and **ni** are not the only modes of address in Swedish.

(a) Titles

A conspicuously polite mode of address may be achieved in spoken Swedish by using a person's name and/or title and a third person construction (as if one were speaking of the person rather than to the person). The person may be addressed either by:

(i) Title and name:

> **Har fröken Ek bokat rum?**
> Have you booked a room, Miss Ek?

(ii) Name alone:

> **Vill Jan Eriksson komma fram, tack!**
> Jan Eriksson, would you please step forward.

(iii) Title alone (in the definite form):

> **Skulle herrn/damen vilja prova byxorna?**
> Would sir/madam like to try the trousers?

> **Kan inte doktorn komma snarast?**
> Can't you come at once, doctor?

> **Vill herrarna vara vänliga och gå den här vägen?**
> Kindly step this way, gentlemen.

Note 1: Most Swedish titles (**herr, fru, doktor, professor, intendent, direktör**, etc.) do not begin with a capital initial letter unless they start a sentence (see 1206 (c), 1207 (e)).

Note 2: Note the idiomatic 3rd person constructions used to address certain high ranks:
> **Har Ers/Eders Majestät/Ers Höghet/Ers Nåd varit här förr?**
> Has Your Majesty/Your Highness/Your Grace been here previously?

Note 3: Note the following colloquial uses of 'titles' in the definite form (cf. also 224(b)(viii)):
> **Har du en rök, grabben?**   Have you got a fag, mate? [*lit.* the boy]
> **Ska du åka med, tjejen?**   Want a lift, love? [*lit.* the girl]

(b) Impersonal and passive constructions

Uncertainty about appropriate modes of address has led Swedes to use a number of impersonal and passive constructions to avoid the issue.

Vad får det lov att vara?	What would you like? / Can I help you? (in a shop, for example)
Hur var namnet?	What is [*lit.* 'was'] your name?
Önskas socker?	Would you like some sugar?
Ska det vara ett kex till?	Would you like another biscuit?

(c) Other pronouns used as terms of address

Man and **vi** (and less frequently **han/hon**) are also used as terms of address.

(i) **Man** (see 330)

1   As a familiar term of address (in place of **du**) with a touch of ironical politeness and formality:

Varför är man alltid så sur?	Why are you always so grumpy?

2   As the equivalent of the English 'you' meaning 'one':

Man kan komma dit med tåg.	You can get there by train.
Man kan aldrig veta.	You/one never can tell.

(ii) **Vi** (see 302)

Like 'we' in English, **vi** is a familiar form of address, almost avuncular and a little patronising in tone. It may be used to address one or several persons.

Ska vi ta på oss skorna?	Shall we put our shoes on?

(Addressing, for example, a single child.)

Note: **Han/hon** (see 305) have an old-fashioned, rustic flavour when used as terms of address. In some dialects they remain a polite form of address, whereas in standard Swedish they tend to be a little derogatory:

Vill han veta hur man gör, så ska han få se.
If you want to know what to do, you can have a look.

Han kan göra som han vill, jag har haft nog!
You can do as you please, I've had enough!

305 The third person

(a) Han, hon

(i) **Han** (subject) and **honom** (object) refer primarily to:

1 Male persons:

Han var en stor man.	He was a great man.
Jag vet inget om honom.	I don't know anything about him.

2 Male animals:

Vilken tjur! Han är enorm!	What a bull! He's enormous!

Note: **Han** may also refer to so-called 'higher animals' (cf. 102 (b) Note 2) irrespective of their true gender.

(ii) **Hon** (subject) and **henne** (object) refer primarily to:

1 Female persons:

Min mor är gammal. Hon fyller 95 nästa år.
My mother is old. She will be 95 next year.

2 Female animals:

Kon äter inte. Hon är sjuk.
The cow won't eat. She's ill.

3 The nouns **människa** ('human being', 'humankind') and **klocka** (used when asking or telling the time, cf. 416(a)). See also 106(e)(f).

Människan föddes fri, och överallt är hon i bojor.
Man was born free, and everywhere he is in chains.

Hur mycket är klockan? Hon är halv fem.
What time is it? It's half past four.

4 Boats

Note 1: **Hon** and **henne** may also refer to nouns ending in -a describing animals (cf. 102(b) Note 3) irrespective of their true gender.

Note 2: In some dialects and poetic language **han/hon** may refer to other nouns with no natural gender (e.g. **solen**, 'the sun'; **liljan**, 'the lily'). This usage sounds provincial, quaint, or romantically poetic.

(b) Den, det

(i) **Den** serves as both subject and object form, and refers to a previously mentioned singular noun of non-neuter gender which does not describe a person:

Jag har en bok. Jag har läst den. Den står i bokhyllan.
I have a book. I have read it. It is in the bookcase.

(ii) **Det** serves as both subject and object form, and refers to a previously mentioned singular noun of neuter gender which does not describe a person (see 308ff.):

Jag har ett hus. Jag köpte det i fjol. Det är stort.
I have a house. I bought it last year. It is big.

(c) De, dem

De (subject) and **dem** (object) refer to one or more previously mentioned plural nouns, or two or more previously mentioned singular nouns, irrespective of gender:

Jag har flera hus. De är gamla. Jag vill sälja dem.
I have several houses. They are old. I want to sell them.

Jag har ett hus och en bil. De är gamla båda två. Jag vill sälja dem.
I have a house and a car. They are both old. I want to sell them.

306   Han, hon and nouns indicating a person but not a gender

Many Swedish non-neuter nouns indicate a person but not a gender (**gästen** 'the guest'; **konsumenten** 'the consumer'; **kusinen,** 'the cousin'; **läsaren** 'the reader'; **släktingen** 'the relative'; **ägaren** 'the owner'; etc.) while a smaller number of neuter nouns refer to people (**barnet** 'the child'; **statsrådet** 'the cabinet minister'; **hembiträdet** 'the home help'; etc.) See also 102(a) Note 1. Nouns from these two categories are usually referred to by **han** or **hon** depending on context and meaning. See also 211(d).

Patienten har lidit av blodbrist sedan hon fick sitt första barn.
The patient has suffered from anaemia since she had her first child.

Mitt barn började spela golf när han var bara fem år.
My child started to play golf when he was only five years old.

Skyddsombudet är inte här. Hon har ledigt idag.
The safety representative is not here. It is her day off today.

In cases where there is any doubt, or where the noun refers collectively to people of either sex, Swedish uses either **han** or **hon** individually, or **han eller hon, han/hon** or **han resp(ektive) hon**:

> **Vet konsumenten vilka rättigheter han har?**
> Does the consumer know what rights he has?

> **Studenten ska skriva om ett ämne som han eller hon väljer.**
> The student is to write on a subject of his or her choice.

Note: **Den, det** are not normally used in any of the above circumstances. **Den**, when used to refer to a person, tends to be derogatory:

> **Britta? Äsch, den!**   Britta? Huh, her!

307   Ett ungt par – det or de?

Sometimes formal numerical congruence of noun and pronoun sounds affected. A suitable plural form of the pronoun is readily used in spoken Swedish and all but the most formal written language when a singular noun refers to a collective idea, especially when people or animals are involved (for example, **allmänheten** 'the public', **befolkningen** 'the population', **herrskapet** 'the couple', **laget** 'the team', **familjen** 'the family'). See also 211(a)–(c).

> **Ett ungt par skadades vid en bilolycka.** *De* **kom från Malmö.**
> A young couple were injured in a car accident. *They* came from Malmö.

> **Det svenska folket har** *sig själva* **att skylla för sina problem.**
> The Swedish people have *themselves* to blame for their problems.

308   Table showing the major uses of det

Function of *det*	Used with	English equivalent	Refer to
refers to neuter noun	any verb	it	309(a)
complement of **vara, bli**	**vara, bli**	it, that	309(b)
complement of **vara, bli**	**vara, bli** + noun	it, this, that or any 3rd pers. pronoun	309(b)
demonstrative pronoun	used as a demonstrative	that, it, that one	309(c) 325–326
formal subject, place-holder	**vara, bli** + adj.	it	309(d)(i), 1003, 1033
formal subject	**vara, finnas**	there is/are	309(d)(ii)
formal subject/place-holder	any intransitive verb	0, there is/are + -ing	309(d)(iii),

Function of *det*	Used with:	English equivalent	Refer to:
when the real subject of the sentence is 'postponed'			1003, 1033
formal subject in passive constructions lacking a real subject	passive verb	there, 0	309(d)(iv), 551
refers to infinitive, adverbial clause or sentence and avoids need to repeat the same	any verb	it, that, 0	309(e)
object function	verbs expressing 'think', 'hope', 'say'	so	309(e)
object function	. . . **också** to render 'so' = 'also'	so	309 (e) Note
refers to a previous question			309(f)
predicate of **vara, bli**	**vara, bli**	0	
object of auxiliary verbs	auxiliary verbs	0	
object of **göra, veta**	**göra, veta**	0, so	
refers to noun, adj. or clause			309(g)
predicate of **vara, bli**	**vara, bli**	0, that	
predicate of **heta, kallas**	**heta, kallas**	that	
impersonal subject	impersonal verbs	it, there	309(h), 1003
indeterminate object	set phrases	0	309(j)

309 The use of **det**

(a) In many instances **det** refers back to a previously mentioned neuter noun (305(b)(ii)):

Jag har ett hus. Det är stort.   I have a house. It is large.

However, **det** is also used on many other occasions in Swedish. In these instances **det** does not always to correspond to English 'it'.

(b) **Det** is used as a complement with the verbs **vara, bli**:

Vad är det?   What is it/What is that?
Vem är det?   Who is it/Who is that?
Är det du, mamma?   Is it you, mum?

When **vara, bli** are followed by a noun or pronoun, **det** is used regardless of the gender or number of that noun or pronoun:

Vad är det? Det är en hund.	What is it? It's a dog.
Vem slog dig? Var det han?	Who hit you? Was it him?
Jag har en bil. Det är en Volvo.	I have a car. It's a Volvo.
Det var härliga tider!	Those were the days.

Note: **Hon**, not **det** is used with **vara** in expressions of time by the clock (see also 305(a)(ii) 3):

| **Hur mycket är klockan? Hon är tre.** | What time is it? It's 3 o'clock. |

(c) Det is used as a demonstrative pronoun (cf. 325–326).

(d) Det is used as a formal subject, or as a place-holder in existential sentences (cf. 1003, 1033).

(i) With the verbs **vara**, **bli** + adjective. The adjective appears in the neuter indefinite form (cf. 202) to agree with the impersonal **det**.

| **Det är enkelt att sy egna kläder.** | It's simple to sew your own clothes. |
| **Det blir svårt att sluta röka.** | It will be difficult to stop smoking. |

(ii) With the verbs **vara**, **finnas**, **fattas**, **saknas** used to render English 'there is', 'there is not', etc.

| **Det fanns en kvinna i bilen.** | There was a woman in the car. |
| **Det fattas en bit.** | There's a piece missing. |

(iii) As a formal subject (cf. 1003) when the real subject is postponed in the sentence (cf. 1033). There is not always an English equivalent for **det** used in this way, although it may sometimes be rendered by 'there is/are' + -*ing* form of the verb.

| **Det har hänt en hemsk olycka.** | A terrible accident has happened. |
| **Det bor många danskar här.** | There are a lot of Danes living here. |

(iv) In impersonal passive constructions (cf. 553):

| **Det skrivs mycket om henne.** | There is a lot written about her. |
| **Det hörs att du inte är svensk.** | I can hear you're not Swedish. |

(e) Det is used to refer back to an infinitive, infinitive phrase, adverbial phrase, clause or sentence, to avoid having to repeat it. There is not always an English equivalent for **det** used in this way:

Att springa är nyttig motion, men det tar tid.
Running is good exercise, but it is time-consuming.

Du sa, att han bor i USA, men det gör han inte.
You said he lives in USA, but he doesn't.

Jag behöver två exemplar redan idag. – Varför det?
'I need two copies today.' 'Why?'

Kaffe med grädde. Det smakar härligt.
Coffee and cream. That tastes delicious.

Used as the object of verbs like 'think', 'believe', 'hope', 'say', etc. **det** may usually be rendered in English by 'so':

Har han åkt hem? – Det tror jag./Jag hoppas det./Det sa han.
'Has he gone home?' 'I think so./I hope so./He said so.'

Note: **Det . . . också** or **det . . . med** may usually be rendered by 'so' in English:

Han var hungrig. Och det var vi också/med.   He was hungry. And so were we.

(f) Det is used as the complement of **vara, bli** or the object of one of the auxiliary verbs or **göra, veta**, when answering a question (or command) formulated with one of these verbs. English usually has no equivalent to **det** in these 'short answers'. **Det** usually starts the clause when used in this way.

Är du rik? – Ja, det är jag.
'Are you rich?' 'Yes I am.'

Kan hon svenska? – Nej, det kan hon inte.
'Does she know Swedish?' 'No, she doesn't.'

Vet du hans namn? – Ja, det vet jag.
'Do you know his name?' 'Yes, I do.'

Note: When the questions are formulated with other verbs, a suitable form of **göra** is used in the answer.

Vill du diska? – Det har jag redan gjort.   'Will you wash up?' 'I've already done so.'

(g) Det is used as a complement of **vara, bli, heta, kallas** to refer back to a noun, adjective or clause (cf. also (e) above). There is usually no equivalent in English when **det** is used in this way with **vara, bli**.

Hon ser snäll ut och det är hon.
She looks kind and she is.
Han heter Karl men han kallas sällan det.
His name is Karl, but he is rarely called that.

(h) Det is used, as 'it' in English, with a number of impersonal constructions (cf. 1003):

> **det händer att** 'it happens that', **det syns att** 'it is obvious that', **det tycks som om** 'it seems as if'.

Many impersonal verbs refer to weather conditions:

> **det blixtrar** 'there's lightning', **det blåser** 'it's windy', **det fryser** 'it's freezing', **det haglar** 'it's hailing', **det klarnar** 'it's clearing up', **det mulnar** 'it's clouding over', **det regnar** 'it's raining', **det snöar** 'it's snowing', **det töar** 'it's thawing', **det åskar** 'it's thundering'.

Note: Impersonal constructions are more common in Swedish than in English, and are often used where English would have a personal subject:

Det var roligt att . . .	I'm/We're glad that . . .
Det var tråkigt att	I'm/We're sorry that
Det är bäst att du går.	You'd better go.

(j) Det is used as an indeterminate object in certain set expressions in Swedish:

ha det bra/dåligt (ställt)	to be fortunate/badly off
ha det bättre än . . .	to be better off than . . .
ha det roligt/tråkigt	to have fun/to be bored

C REFLEXIVE PRONOUNS

310 The use of reflexive pronouns

See table in 301 for forms.

There are no special reflexive pronouns for the 1st and 2nd persons in Swedish. The ordinary object forms of the personal pronoun are used in a reflexive sense for these persons. Only 3rd person pronouns have a separate reflexive form, namely **sig** (singular and plural). Note that **själv** (**självt, själva**) is not a reflexive pronoun, but is used purely for emphasis (cf. 315).

The reflexive pronouns are never used as the subject of a clause (for expressions such as 'I myself am grateful' see 315), but they always refer to the subject. Reflexive pronouns are used only as the object of a verb or after a preposition.

> **Du har skurit dig.**   You have cut yourself.
> subject ←→ object

Jag stängde dörren efter mig.   I closed the door behind me.
subject ←→   prepositional object

Han hade hunden med sig.   He had the dog with him.
subject ←→   prepositional object

Compare:

Hon sköt sig.   She shot herself.
(**Sig** refers to the subject of the clause.)

Hon sköt henne.   She shot her.
(**Henne** refers to someone other than the subject of the clause.)

Note: A number of verbs used without reflexive pronouns in English are rendered by reflexive verbs in Swedish (cf. 541): **lägga sig** to lie down/go to bed; **sätta sig** to sit down; **gifta sig** to get married; **känna sig**, to feel; **skynda sig** to hurry; etc.

311   Some exceptions to the main rule

(a) After verbs followed by an object and infinitive construction (cf. 518 (a)(iii)) the reflexive pronoun normally refers to the object, and the personal pronoun refers to the subject of the main clause. This is because these constructions are generally regarded as ellipted forms (see 1050(b)).

Patienten bad sjuksköterskan förbereda *henne* **för operationen.**
(subj)   ←→   (obj)   ←→   (personal pronoun)
The patient asked the nurse to prepare her for the operation.
(cf. **Hon bad att sjuksköterskan skulle förbereda henne**.)

Läkaren bad sjuksköterskan förbereda *sig* **för operationen.**
(subj)   ←→   (obj)   ←→   (reflexive pronoun)
The doctor asked the nurse to prepare herself for the operation.
(cf. **Han bad att sjuksköterskan skulle förbereda sig**.)

Han hörde dem förbanna honom.   He heard them curse him.
Jag såg honom resa sig.   I saw him stand up.
Jag bad barnen tvätta sig.   I asked the children to get washed.

(b) The reflexive pronoun is sometimes used to refer not to the grammatical subject of a finite verb in a clause, but to the implied subject of an infinitive or noun phrase (cf. also 320(c)):

Det är viktigt att kunna försvara sig.
It is important to be able to defend oneself.

Hans försök att köpa sig samvetsfrid misslyckades.
His attempt to buy himself peace of mind failed.

Deras höga tankar om sig själva är frånstötande.
Their high opinions of themselves are repugnant.

(c) In some set phrases **sig** is used idiomatically:

i och för sig	in/by itself
en typ för sig	a peculiar type, one on his/her own
De/Vi bor var för sig.	They/We each live on our own.

312 The ethical dative

The reflexive pronouns are sometimes used in an obliquely reflexive manner to provide what is known as the ethical dative. This usage is not without parallel in English, but is more common in Swedish.

Gör dig inga bekymmer!	Don't make problems for yourself!
De har skaffat sig en båt.	They have got themselves a boat.
Han fick sig en omgång.	He got a good hiding.
Det var mig en baddare till gädda!	What a whopper of a pike!
Jag vet mig ingen råd.	I'm at a loss/at my wits' end.

313 'Each other', 'one another' – reciprocal pronouns

Varandra (or its colloquial form **varann**) serves a reciprocal function and may usually be rendered in English by 'each other', 'one another'. **Varandra** may be used with any plural personal pronoun or plural noun. **Varandras** is the genitive form for both **varandra** and **varann**.

Vi hade aldrig sett varandra förr.	We'd never seen one another before.
Tvillingarna avskyr varandra.	The twins detest each other.
Vi tryckte varandras händer.	We squeezed one another's hands.

Note: Some Swedish verbs may themselves take on a special reciprocal function by adding an -s (cf. 544). In such instances **varandra** becomes redundant in the Swedish and is omitted:

De slåss.	They are fighting one another.
Vi träffades i Lund.	We met each other in Lund.

D EMPHATIC PRONOUNS

314 Emphatic pronoun in English – personal pronoun in Swedish

(a) Swedish has no special emphatic (disjunctive) form of the pronoun, unlike, for example, French (*moi, toi,* etc.), but uses the personal pronouns for this function.

However, while English tends to use the object forms of the pronouns in emphatic positions, Swedish prefers the subject.

'Who said that? 'Him!'	**Vem pratade? – Han!**
'Hey, you!' 'Who, me?'	**Hallå där! – Vem, jag?**
She saw it was only us.	**Hon såg (att) det bara var vi.**

(b) Nevertheless Swedish uses an object form of the pronoun rather than a subject form in the following cases:

(i) With a preposition:

Jag vill åka. – Inte utan mig!   'I want to go.' 'Not without me!'

(ii) In constructions where a following verb or preposition linked with the pronoun makes the pronoun an object in the mind of the speaker:

Är det mig du vill träffa?
Is it me you want to see?

Var det henne vi fick brev från häromdagen?
Was it her we got a letter from the other day?

(iii) With expressions using **stackars**:

stackars mig/dig/honom   poor me/you/him

315   Själv

(a) Swedish **själv** (plural **själva**) corresponds to the emphatic 'myself', 'yourself', etc. There is a neuter form **självt**, but the basic form **själv** is often used even when referring to a neuter noun or pronoun.

Jag kan göra det själv.	I can do it myself.
Barnen själva bestämde.	The children themselves decided.
Hon är godheten själv.	She is kindness itself.
Säg själv vad du tror!	Tell us yourself what you think.
Barnet själv(t) sa ingenting.	The child itself said nothing.

Själv is always stressed in spoken Swedish. This is because **själv** is not used in a reflexive sense but merely emphasises the pronoun or noun to which it refers. Swedish uses **själv** rather than **mig**, **sig** etc. where 'myself' etc. can be left out of the English without altering the meaning of the sentence in which it occurs. (Note: This does not apply in the case of reflexive verbs! cf. 541). Compare:

Jag skar brödet själv.   I cut the bread myself.

Jag skar mig.	I cut myself.

For extra emphasis **själv** sometimes precedes a pronoun or noun to which it refers.

(i) Used before a pronoun **själv** (**själva** in plural) begins the sentence or clause and is followed by the inverted verb and subject:

Själv vågar jag inte säga något.	Myself, I daren't say anything.

(ii) Used before a noun **själva** (invariable, but see also 224(a)) immediately precedes the noun, which appears in its definite form, if it has one:

Själva kungen har sovit här.	The king himself has slept here.
Vi bor i själva London.	We live in London itself.

For further emphasis colloquial Swedish sometimes uses **självaste** (invariable) and the noun in the definite form:

Självaste kungen kunde inte ha det bättre.
The (very) king himself could not be happier.

(b) 'Myself' etc. may be reflexive and emphatic at the same time. In Swedish this is rendered by using the *reflexive pronoun* + **själv, -t, -a**:

Han hjälper bara sig själv.	He helps only himself.
Det säger sig själv(t).	It speaks for itself.
Det går av sig själv(t).	It works by itself.
Han går och pratar för sig själv.	He is talking to himself.

Note: **Själv** is used in a number of idiomatic expressions:

i själva verket	in actual fact
det är självaste den att	what an awful nuisance that
Han är inte sig själv idag.	He is not himself today.
Tack själv.	Thank you, too. (Stressed 'you', when someone has already thanked you for something.)

E POSSESSIVE ADJECTIVES AND PRONOUNS

316 Possessive adjectives and pronouns

In Swedish possessive adjectives and possessive pronouns have the same form. 'My' and 'mine' are both translated by **min** (**mitt, mina**), 'you' and 'yours' by **din** (**ditt, dina**), etc. In the following section the expression 'possessive pronoun' is used as a common term to include both types of word.

Form:	Non-neuter	Neuter	Plural
Singular			
1 person	**min** my, mine	**mitt**	**mina**
2 person familiar	**din** your, yours	**ditt**	**dina**
2 person formal	**er** your, yours	**ert**	**era**
3 person masculine	**hans/sin** his	**hans/sitt**	**hans/sina**
3 person feminine	**hennes/sin** her, hers	**hennes/sitt**	**hennes/sina**
3 person neuter	**dess/sin** its	**dess/sitt**	**dess/sina**
Plural			
1 person	**vår** our, ours	**vårt**	**våra**
2 person familiar	**er** your, yours	**ert**	**era**
2 person formal	**er** your, yours	**ert**	**era**
3 person masculine, feminine, neuter	**deras/sin** their, theirs	**deras/sitt**	**deras/sina**

Most possessive pronouns agree in number (and, in the singular, in gender) with the noun or nouns to which they refer, but the 3rd person forms **hans, hennes, dess** and **deras** are indeclinable. Possessive pronouns have no definite form.

(a) Din (ditt, dina) is the possessive pronoun corresponding to the familiar 2nd person singular pronoun **du. Er (ert, era)** is the possessive pronoun corresponding to the formal 2nd person singular pronoun **ni** (cf. 303).

(b) The formal 2nd person possessive pronoun **er** (**ert, era**) has an alternative form **Eder** (**Edert, Edra**), almost invariably written with a capital initial letter. This form is now antiquated and encountered only in liturgical and very formal language. It is also the possessive pronoun used in conjunction with the antiquated 2nd person pronoun **I** (cf. 301(e) Note 3).

(c) The possessive pronoun **sin** (**sitt, sina**) is reflexive and used only to refer to a 3rd person subject of the clause in which it occurs (cf. 319).

(d) In spoken Swedish the possessive pronouns **vår/vårt** and **er/ert** have colloquial singular forms which exist alongside the standard written forms.

Det är våran/eran skola.	It's our/your school.
Det är erat/vårat hus.	It's your/our house.

317   The use of possessive pronouns

(a) The choice of the possessive pronoun is determined by the pronoun or noun signifying the possessor. The form is determined by the gender and/or number of the noun signifying the possession:

Jag har en bil.	**Min bil är röd.**	**Bilen är min.**
I have a car.	My car is red.	The car is mine.
Vi bor i ett hus.	**Vårt hus är stort.**	**Huset är vårt.**
We live in a house.	Our house is big.	The house is ours.
Du har två katter.	**Dina katter är gamla.**	**Katterna är dina.**
You have three cats.	Your cats are old.	The cats are yours.

(b) On many occasions Swedish has the definite article where English uses a possessive pronoun. See 323.

(c) Adjectives preceded by a possessive pronoun take the definite form (223(b)):

min röda bil	my red car
ditt gamla hus	your old house

(d) The possessive pronouns are used only in the indefinite declension (208), even with words which normally require a definite form of the adjective and/or noun (223, 224):

av hela mitt hjärta	with all my heart
detta ditt förbiseende	this oversight of yours

Note 1: The possessive pronouns have no genitive form:

Det är min mors pengar, inte din mors.   It's my mother's money, not your mother's.

English expressions such as 'a friend of mine' have thus to be expressed in Swedish by other means (cf. 322):

I've met a relative of yours.   **Jag har träffat en släkting till dig.**

Note 2: Used in the neuter singular form Swedish possessive pronouns are encountered in a range of idiomatic usages:

Allt ditt är mitt.	All that I have is yours.
Han har gjort sitt.	He has done his bit.
Jag sköter mitt, du sköter ditt.	I'll mind my business, you mind yours.

Note 3: The forms 'Yours sincerely', 'Yours faithfully', etc. are usually rendered in Swedish by **Med vänlig hälsning** or **Med vänliga hälsningar**.

318 Dess

(a) The possessive pronoun **dess** ('its') is not very common outside written and formal spoken Swedish:

teatern och dess roll idag	the theatre and its role today
kärlek och dess följder	love and its consequences
Umeå och dess omgivningar	Umeå and (its) environs

(b) In colloquial and informal written Swedish **dess** is usually avoided, being replaced by:

(i) Omitting the possessive and using the definite form of the noun (cf. 323):

Hunden har stått här hela långa dagen, och ingen vet var ägaren finns (cf. **dess ägare**).
The dog has been here all day, but no-one knows where its owner is.

(ii) A prepositional construction and a pronoun:

Det var ett bra hotell men jag kommer inte ihåg namnet på det (cf. **dess namn**).
It was a good hotel, but I don't remember its name.
[*lit.* 'the name of it']

(iii) Repeating the noun in its genitive form:

Vi såg hunden men hundens husse såg inte oss.
We saw the dog, but its owner didn't see us.

(iv) An idiomatic usage of **sin** (**sitt, sina**) (cf. also 320(d)):

Läraren ställde tillbaka boken på sin plats.
The teacher put the book back in its place.

Note: **Dess** is also encountered in a number of adverbial expressions in both written and spoken Swedish:

innan dess	before then/that time
(in)till dess	up to that time
sedan dess	since then/that time
till dess (att)	until [as a conjunction]
dess bättre, dess värre	all/so much the better, all/so much the worse

319 Hans or sin? – basic use

(a) Introduction

In contrast to English, Swedish has two distinct ways of rendering the third person possessive pronouns: a reflexive form with **sin** (**sitt, sina**) and a non-reflexive form with **hans, hennes, dess, deras**.

(i) The reflexive possessives **sin** (**sitt, sina**) refer to possession by the subject of the clause:

Han älskar *sin* fru, *sitt* barn och *sina* föräldrar.
S ◄———— O — O ————►O
He loves his wife, his child and his parents.

Sin (**sitt, sina**) *cannot* be used to qualify the subject of the clause:

***Hans* fru älskar honom.**
S
His wife loves him.

(ii) The non-reflexive forms **hans, hennes, dess, deras** (indeclinable) do *not* refer to the subject of the clause:

Olle är sur. – Varför det?	**Åke gick ut med *hans* fru.**
S	S O
Olle is miserable. – Why?	Åke went out with his wife.

Hans, hennes, dess, deras may, however, qualify the subject or object of a clause:

***Hans* fru är lärare.**	**Jag har sett *hans* fru på skolan.**
S	O
His wife is a teacher.	I've seen his wife at the school.

(b) The basic use of **hans, hennes, dess, deras**

Hans etc. is used when:

(i) Qualifying the subject of a sentence or clause:

> *Deras* **barn är mycket duktiga.**   Their children are very clever.

(ii) Referring to an object which is not owned by the subject of the sentence or clause:

> **Lasse är Ivars chaufför. Han kör *hans* bil.**
> Lasse is Ivar's chauffeur. He drives his [i.e. Ivars's] car.

(c) The basic use of **sin (sitt, sina)**

Sin (sitt, sina) agrees in gender and/or number with the noun which it qualifies or replaces. Although used idiomatically in a number of ways (see 320), basically **sin (sitt, sina)** should be used only when *both* of the following conditions are fulfilled:

(i) **Sin (sitt, sina)** must relate to the subject of the clause, which may be a noun or a 3rd person pronoun. (In other words, the possessor must be the subject of the clause).

(ii) **Sin (sitt, sina)** must qualify the object of the clause (the object may be a direct object, indirect object or prepositional object).

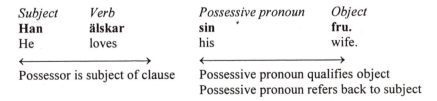

Subject	*Verb*	*Possessive pronoun*	*Object*
Han	**älskar**	**sin**	**fru.**
He	loves	his	wife.

Possessor is subject of clause   Possessive pronoun qualifies object
                                        Possessive pronoun refers back to subject

As a rule of thumb, it may be said that a form of **sin, sitt, sina** can be used if the word 'own' can be inserted before the object in English.

> **Han skrev ett brev till sin dotter.**   He wrote a letter to his (own) daughter.

Note: **Sin (sitt, sina)** may precede the subject to which it refers:

| **I sina tal nämner han ofta krigstiden.** | In his speeches he often mentions the war years. |
| **Sina betyg är hon inte så stolt över.** | She is not very proud of her grades. |

(d) The use of **sin (sitt, sina)** or **hans, hennes, dess, deras** changes the meaning of a sentence completely:

Eva älskar sin man.	**Ulla älskar hennes man med.**
Eva loves her [own] husband.	Ulla loves her [i.e. Eva's] husband too.

Sara och Sten bor hos hans mor.	Sara and Sten live with his mother.
Sara och Sten bor hos sin mor.	Sara and Sten live with their mother.

320 **Hans** or **sin**? Further implications of the basic rule

(a) Hans etc. is always used when the possessive is part of the subject even with 'double subjects':

Han och *hans* fru går ofta på bio.
He and his wife often go to the cinema.

Eleverna och *deras* lärare försvann.
The pupils and their teacher vanished.

(b) Hans etc. is always used with the subject of a subordinate clause:

De tycker att *deras* lärare är tråkig.
They think that their teacher is boring.

Compare the following example where the possessive qualifies the object of the subordinate clause:

Jag tror inte att han gillar sitt jobb.
I don't think he likes his job.

(c) Sin (sitt, sina) is used in object and infinitive constructions (with no finite verb in the clause) to refer to the *implied subject* of the clause rather than its grammatical subject:

Jag hörde *henne* ropa på *sin* man.   I heard her call her husband.
S   IS ←————— O

Strictly speaking the use of **sin** (**sitt, sina**) in such instances contravenes the basic rule. The subject (**jag** in the above example) is not the possessor; the possessive pronoun does not relate to the grammatical subject of the clause (cf. 319(c)). The apparent anomaly is, however, explained if we consider that the constructions above are ellipted forms: in the expanded versions the relationship of **sin** to the subject of the clause becomes clear (cf. 1049ff.).

Jag hörde att *hon* ropade på *sin* man.
S   S ←————— O
I heard that she called her husband.

Confusion may arise when the subject of the sentence or clause and the object in an object and infinitive expression (518(a)(iii)) are both 3rd person:

Han bad städerskan städa sitt rum.
[Whose room is being cleaned?]

Ulf såg Lars sparka sin hund.
[Whose dog is being kicked?]

Sometimes the use of the non-reflexive 3rd person possessive pronouns will clarify the issue:

Han bad städerskan städa hennes rum.
He asked the cleaner to clean her room.

Han bad städerskan städa hans rum.
He asked the cleaner to clean his room.

On other occasions only a full clause will do:

Ulf såg att Lars sparkade sin hund.
Ulf saw Lars kick his [i.e. Lars'] dog.

Ulf såg att Lars sparkade hans hund.
Ulf saw Lars kick his [i.e. Ulf's] dog.

Note: **Sin (sitt, sina)** sometimes replaces **ens** (330) in infinitive constructions with an implied subject:

Det är inte lätt att hålla sina löften.   It is not easy to keep one's promises.

(d) Sin (sitt, sina) and attraction

In spoken Swedish especially, the construction of certain sentences may lead to an idiomatic use of **sin (sitt, sina)** rather than **hans, hennes, dess, deras**, even though the possessor is not the grammatical subject of the clause. This phenomenon is known as *attraction*. Attraction occurs primarily because the distance between the true subject and the possessive pronoun is greater than the distance between the possessive pronoun and another expression which readily 'attracts' the pronoun in the mind of the speaker/writer.

Hans avgång berövar regeringen av en av _sina_ ärligaste män.
Subject   *Possessive pronoun*
His departure deprives the government of one of its most honest men.

(e) Sin (sitt, sina) and comparison

Sin (sitt, sina) is used in abbreviated comparisons with **än**, and sometimes with som. (See also 324.)

Han är längre än sin fru.	He is taller than his wife.
Hon vet mer än sin bror.	She knows more than her brother.
De är lika fattiga som sin far.	They are as poor as their father.

Hans, hennes, etc. are, however, invariably used if the comparison is expanded by the addition of a finite verb:

Han är längre än hans fru är.	He is taller than his wife is.
Hon vet mer än hennes bror gör.	She knows more than her brother does.

Note: In most cases the context will make the meaning clear, but the use of **sin (sitt, sina)** in unexpanded comparisons can create confusion. Compare:

Han älskar golf mer än sin fru.	= mer än han älskar sin fru.
Han älskar golf mer än hans fru.	= mer än hans fru gör.

(f) Sin (sitt, sina) and cleft sentences

Sin (sitt, sina) is used idiomatically as a predicate of the verbs **vara** and **bli** in certain cleft sentences (cf. 1048). The condition for this is that sin (sitt, sina) would be used in the unexpanded version of the sentence.

Det är sin man (som) hon älskar.	It is her husband (whom) she loves.
(Compare: **Hon älskar sin man.**)	

(g) Sin in passive constructions

In passive constructions (542ff.) **sin (sitt, sina)** is used to qualify the agent when the possessive pronoun refers to the 3rd person subject of the clause:

Han räddades av sina barn.	He was saved by his children.

(h) Sin in appositional phrases

In short appositional phrases, and in relative clauses with no relative pronoun or finite verb, **sin (sitt, sina)** is used even though it does not necessarily qualify the object or refer to the subject of the sentence or clause:

Han bor i Lund, sin födelsestad.	He lives in Lund, the town of his birth.

(j) Var sin (var sitt, var sina)

Swedish expresses regular distribution of an item or items by using the idiomatic **var sin** (var sitt, var sina) (sometimes written as one word: **varsin** etc.). **Var** is indeclinable in this usage, while the choice of **sin, sitt** or **sina** is determined by the gender and number of the following noun. **Sin, sitt** or **sina** are used even with 1st and 2nd person subjects in this instance. (See also 223(b) Note.)

Barnen fick var sitt äpple.	The children got an apple each.
Vi satt och läste i var sin bok.	We sat reading a book each.
De fick var sina tre kakor.	They got three buns each.

(k) Sin (sitt, sina) in some common expressions

In a number of common idioms and expressions the normal rules for the use of **sin** (sitt, sina) do not apply:

Det tar oss på sin höjd 5 år.	It will take us 5 years at the most.
Har ni ställt bilen på sin plats?	Have you put the car back in its place?
Det var mycket snö på sina håll.	There was a lot of snow in places.
Publicera artikeln i sin helhet!	Publish the article in its entirety.
Vad i all sin dar gör du?	What on earth are you doing?

(l) Other 3rd person pronouns and **sin (sitt, sina)**

The 3rd person pronouns listed below, which have their own genitive forms, also 'borrow' the forms **sin, sitt** and **sina** for reflexive use. The distinction is exactly the same as that between **hans** and **sin** explained in 319 above: **sin (sitt, sina)** can only qualify the object of the clause, and then only if that object is owned by the subject of the same clause. Thus:

Pronoun	*Section*	*Genitive*	*Reflexive genitive*
man	(330)	**ens**	**sin, sitt, sina**
var och en	(333)	**vars och ens**	**sin, sitt, sina**
alla	(339)	**allas**	**sin, sitt, sina**
andra	(340)	**andras**	**sin, sitt, sina**
någon etc.	(341)	**någons**	**sin, sitt, sina**
ingen etc.	(343)	**ingens**	**sin, sitt, sina**
båda	(347)	**bådas**	**sin, sitt, sina**
många	(349)	**mångas**	**sin, sitt, sina**
vem	(362)	**vems**	**sin, sitt, sina**
vilka	(362, 365)	**vilkas**	**sin, sitt, sina**

321 Possessive pronouns in pejorative expressions

Idiomatically Swedish uses the possessive (not the personal) pronoun in pejorative expressions addressed directly to a person (see also 303(a) Note 2). This gives rise to a wide range of expressions such as:

> **Din dumbom!** You knucklehead!; **Din dumma åsna!** You stupid ass!; **Era lathundar!** You lazy devils! [*lit.* 'dogs']; **Ditt nöt!** You ass!; **Din sentimentala tok!** You old softie!; **Era stackare!** You poor things!

The possessive pronoun is also used in similar expressions when the speaker addresses him/herself:

> **Jag, min dumsnut**   I, fool that I am

Note: There is, however, no equivalent 3rd person usage of the possessive pronoun in this sense.

> **Han, dumma åsna, sa nej.**   He, fool that he was/the fool, said no.
> **De, lata som de är, gör inget.**   They – lazy devils! – don't do a thing.

322 'A friend of mine'

Swedish has no direct equivalent to possessive pronoun constructions like 'a friend of mine', 'a brother of hers', etc. These are usually expressed by a construction with **till** and the relevant personal pronoun, although, as indicated by the examples below, other constructions are also used.

He's a friend of mine.	**Han är vän till mig.**
Aren't you a neighbour of ours?	**Är inte du granne till oss?**
She's a sister of theirs.	**Hon är syster till dem.**
He has no children of his own.	**Han har inga egna barn.**
He's a friend of us all.	**Han är allas vår vän.**
There are only three of us.	**Vi är bara tre stycken.**
That's no business of yours.	**Det angår dig/er inte.**

323 Possessive pronoun in English – Definite article in Swedish

English possessive pronouns qualifying parts of the body or articles of clothing are rendered by the definite article in Swedish in cases where there is no doubt about the ownership. In practice this means that the definite article is used in most instances when the subject(s) of the verb and the possessor(s) of the direct or prepositional object are identical (cf. 142).

> I've not broken my leg, have I?   **Jag har väl inte brutit benet?**

Take your shoes off!	**Ta av dig skorna!**
He has lost his memory.	**Han har tappat minnet.**

The definite article is far more commonly used than the possessive pronoun in Swedish when referring to parts of or qualities of inanimate objects (cf. 318).

Bilen tappade ett av hjulen.	The car lost one of its wheels.
Träden fäller löven på hösten.	Trees shed their leaves in autumn.
Diamanter förlorar aldrig glansen.	Diamonds never lose their sparkle.

324 Personal and possessive pronouns in comparisons with **än** and **som**

In Swedish as in English it is common to omit the predicate verb when a comparison is made (cf. 1051(b)). Although the norm is to use the subject form of the pronoun, the object form of the pronoun may be used in comparisons with **än** and **som** when the verb is omitted, particularly in colloquial Swedish. This is especially true with 1st and 2nd persons singular and plural. (Colloquial English accepts the object form for all persons.)

Du är yngre än jag/än mig.	You're younger than me.
Jag är lika glad som du/som dig.	I'm as happy as you.

However, if the predicate verb is retained then the subject form of the pronoun must be used:

Du är yngre än jag är.	You are younger than I am.
Jag är lika glad som du är.	I am as happy as you are.

Note also the use of **sin (sitt, sina)** rather than **hans, hennes, dess, deras** to qualify something compared with a third person subject. (See also 320(e).)

F   DEMONSTRATIVE PRONOUNS

325 The form of demonstrative pronouns

Non-neuter singular	*Neuter singular*	*Plural (non-neuter and neuter)*	*Meaning*
den här	**det här**	**de här**	this (one), these
den där	**det där**	**de där**	that (one), those
denna/denne	**detta**	**dessa**	this (one), these
den	**det**	**de/dem** (see 326(c)(ii) below)	that (one), those

Note 1: The form **denne** is frequently used when referring to a person of male gender. (cf. 220, 326 Notes 2 and 3).

Note 2: The demonstrative pronouns **den, det**, **de** are identical in form with the front article (cf. 222(a)), but are pronounced with stronger stress.

326 The use of demonstrative pronouns

(a) There are two Swedish alternatives corresponding to the English 'this', etc.

- **Den här** etc. is common in spoken and informal written Swedish.
- **Denna/denne** (**detta, dessa**) occur mostly in written Swedish.

There are two Swedish alternatives corresponding to the English 'that', etc.:

- **Den där** etc. is common in spoken and informal written Swedish, and. usually refers to something tangible or present, i.e. something to which the speaker can point.

- **Den** (**det, de**) is equally common in both spoken and written Swedish. Although **den** (**det, de**) is often used to refer to something concrete, it is the alternative generally preferred when referring to something of a more abstract nature, something to which one cannot point:

Jag är född i det där huset år 1939. Senare det året började andra världskriget.
I was born in that house in 1939. Later that year the Second World War broke out.

(b) Used attributively

(i) **Den här, den där**, etc. + noun + end article
   Den (**det, de**) + noun + end article

A noun qualified by one of these demonstrative pronouns takes an end article where possible:

Den dagen kommer aldrig.	That day will never come.
Vill du köpa det där huset?	Do you want to buy that house?
Jag gillar de förslagen.	I like those suggestions.
Den där Erik sjunger bra.	That Erik guy sings well.

(ii) **Denna/denne** (**detta, dessa**) + noun

A noun qualified by one of these demonstratives generally takes no end article.

Denna värld är inte rättvis.	This world is not just.
Dessa barn vet inte bättre.	These children know no better.
Har du sett denne man?	Have you seen this man?

Note: In colloquial Swedish, however, the end article may sometimes be added. (See 223(c) Note)

(c) Used pronominally

(i) Demonstrative pronouns may also be used independently of a noun.

They then assume the gender and number of the noun which they imply. Note that the English word 'one' in 'this one', 'that one' has no equivalent in Swedish.

Ta det här äpplet, inte det där.
Have this apple, not that one.

Bland alla hans tavlor är de här nog finast.
Of all his paintings these are probably the best.

Detta, det här, etc. may also refer to a previous clause (cf. **vilket** 371(b)).

Han sa att han hade gift sig. Detta visste jag förut.
He said he had got married. I already knew that.

(ii) Note that **de** (those) has the distinct object form **dem** when used pronominally:

Jag tar de här skorna, inte dem.	I'll have these shoes, not those.

Note 1: Where English uses 'this' ('that', 'these', 'those') as subject of the verb 'to be' with a following noun as predicate, Swedish uses the neuter singular **det här** (**det där, detta, det**) regardless of the gender or number of the following noun (cf. 309(b)):

Detta var hans sista ord.	These were his last words.
Det här är min fru.	This is my wife.
Vad är det för en bil?	What kind of car is that?

Note 2: **Denna, denne, detta, dessa** have genitive forms in **-s**, although these are rarely used in modern Swedish. The genitive **dennes** abbreviated to **ds** is used in formal business correspondence in the same way as 'instant' (abbreviated to 'inst.' = of this month) in English:

I Ert brev av den 9 ds	In your letter of the 9th inst

Note 3: In written Swedish the demonstrative **denna** etc. (but not **den här** etc.) is used in much the same way as the English expression 'the latter'. This can sometimes help avoid ambiguities. In such instances **denne** is used to refer to a single male.

Han pratade med mannen men denne kunde inte hjälpa honom.
He spoke to the man but the latter could not help him.

The English 'the former ... the latter' is rendered in Swedish by **den förra** (masculine form: **den förre**) ... **den senare**.

Note 4: Demonstrative pronouns have a range of idiomatic uses in both languages:

så här, så där	like this, like that
sålunda	in this/that way
herr den och den	Mr so and so
på den och den platsen	at such and such a place
vid den och den tiden	at such and such a time

327 Samma, densamma

Non-neuter	Neuter	Plural	Meaning
samma/samme	samma	samma	(the) same
densamma/densamme	detsamma	desamma	the same

(a) **Samma** is only used attributively. There is no article in Swedish before **samma** and no end article on the following noun. A masculine singular form **samme** exists but is rarely encountered.

>**Vi ses imorgon. Samma tid, samma plats.**
>See you tomorrow. Same time, same place.

>**Det är samma gamla hus och samma gamla människor som bor i dem.**
>They are the same old houses and the same old people who live in them.

(b) **Densamma** etc. (written as one word) is only used pronominally. Apart from a few common exceptions of the type noted below **densamma** etc. is generally reserved for more formal written Swedish; in spoken Swedish it is more common to use **samma** + suitable noun. **Densamme** is used when referring to a male in the singular (see 220).

>**Hon är alltid densamma.**   She's always the same.
>**Alla frågar detsamma.**   Everyone is asking the same thing.

Note: **Detsamma** occurs in a number of idiomatic expressions:

>**God jul! Tack, detsamma!**   Happy Christmas! Thanks, the same to you.
>**Det gör mig detsamma.**   It's all the same to me.
>**med detsamma**   immediately, at once
>**i detsamma**   at that very moment

328   Sådan, dylik, slik

Non-neuter	Neuter	Plural	Meaning
sådan	sådant	sådana	such
dylik	dylikt	dylika	similar, such
slik	slikt	slika	such

Sådan (like the much less frequently encountered **dylik** and **slik**, see Note 2 below) is used both attributively and pronominally. **Sådan, sådant** and **sådana** are often pronounced (and occasionally spelled) **sån, sånt** and **såna** (short vowel sound).

When **sådan (sådant)** is used with a singular noun it is usually preceded by the singular indefinite article. (Contrast English, which has 'such a/an' only before a count noun.)

Jag har aldrig sett en sådan lycka.	I've never seen such happiness.
Du är ett sådant dåligt exempel!	You're such a bad example!
Sådana ovanor tolereras inte.	Such bad habits will not be tolerated.

Sådan etc. may also serve the function of English expressions such as 'like this/that', and when followed immediately by **här** or **där** often renders 'this/that kind of':

Jag vill gärna ha en sådan dator.	I'd love a computer like that.
Köp en slips eller något sådant!	Buy a tie or something similar.
Sådana här böcker är oumbärliga.	Books like this are indispensable.
Ett sådant där fel är vanligt.	That kind of error is common.

Note 1: **Sådan** etc. may be translated into English in various other ways:

Jag tar fem sådana.	I'll have five of those/these.
Sådant händer.	Things like that/this do happen.
Sånt är livet!	That's life!
Ett sånt liv!	What a commotion! [cf. 368]
Sådan är hon!	That's the kind of person she is.

Note 2: **Slik** and **dylik** are archaic, but **dylik** is still used in some formal expressions or when the speaker wishes to be slightly ironic.

Student söker möblerat rum eller dylikt.	Student seeks furnished room or similar.
Dylika metoder godkänns inte idag.	Methods like those are unacceptable today.

G DETERMINATIVE PRONOUNS

329 Determinative pronouns

Sometimes the demonstrative **den** (**det, de**) not only points out (i.e. 'demonstrates')
but also defines or restricts (i.e. 'determines') by directing attention to what
follows. In such instances it is known as a determinative pronoun. In spoken
Swedish determinatives are nearly always stressed.

(a) Used attributively:

Non-neuter	*Neuter*	*Plural*
den + noun without end article + **som** . . .	**det** + noun without end article + **som** . . .	**de** + noun without end article + **som** . . .

When the determinative qualifies a noun, the noun has no end article. By contrast,
the demonstrative **den** (**det, de**) (325ff.) requires an end article. Compare:

Demonstrative
De turister*na* fick mycket sol.
Those tourists got a lot of sun.

Determinative
**De turister *som* åkte till Island fick mycket sol, medan *den* grupp *som*
åkte till Italien fick regn varje dag.**
Those tourists who went to Iceland got a lot of sun, while the group that went
to Italy had rain every day.

A determinative is used when the information that follows (typically a clause
introduced by **som** or **där**) is essential to the sentence. Frequently some kind of
contrast is stated or implied. If, on the other hand, the information that follows is
proffered merely as an afterthought – often signalled in English by the fact that it is
presented within commas – a demonstrative is used. Compare:

Determinative
De bilar *som* jag gillar bäst tillverkas i Japan.
Those/The cars I like best are made in Japan.

Demonstrative
De bilar*na* – som jag förresten aldrig riktigt gillat – säljs inte längre.
Those cars, which incidentally I never really liked, are no longer on sale.

A Swedish determinative is often rendered in English by the definite article 'the' (rather than the demonstrative 'this/that') especially with a singular noun.

Island har mycket att bjuda den turist som gillar äventyr.
Iceland has a lot to offer the tourist who likes adventure.

Note 1: **Som** as an object or prepositional object is frequently omitted after determinatives (cf. 370(c)).

Har du sett den film jag pratade om?   Have you seen the film I spoke about?

Note 2: When the determinative qualifies the subject, some native speakers tend to use the definite form of the noun rather than the determinative in spoken and informal Swedish.

Turisterna som åkte till Island fick mycket sol, medan gruppen som åkte till Italien fick regn varje dag. (cf. above)

Note 3: In spoken Swedish the determinative is always stressed, unless followed by an adjective:

ˈ **Den bok hon läser heter Utvandrarna.**   The book she's reading is *The Emigrants*.

Den ˈ **enda bok hon har läst är Utvandrarna.**   The only book she's read is *The Emigrants*.

(b) Used pronominally

Non-neuter			*Neuter*			*Plural*		
subj	obj	gen	subj	obj	gen	subj	obj	gen
den	**den**	**dens**	**det**	**det**	**(dess)**	**de**	**dem**	**deras**

The determinative pronoun used independently corresponds in all but its genitive forms (which are now rarely used in Swedish and missing in English) with the 3rd person pronouns.

In cases where Swedish uses a determinative pronoun in this way, English may have 'that', 'those', 'the one(s)', 'he/him', 'she/her', 'anyone' or a noun (e.g. 'the man (who)', 'the person (who)', etc.).

De här husen är mycket bättre än de som har rivits.
These houses are much better than the ones which have been pulled down.

Det är dens uppgift som går sist att släcka ljuset.
It's the job of the person who goes last to switch off the light.

Island har mycket att bjuda dem som gillar äventyr.
Iceland has a lot to offer those who like adventure.

Note 1: When the determinative is used without a noun **de som** is now accepted as an object form in place of **dem som.**

Staten straffar de som bryter mot lagen.   The state punishes those who break the law.

Note 2: After a preposition both the subject and object form of the plural determinative are found. This depends upon the role that the speaker allocates to the determinative. Does the preposition govern the determinative (object form only: 1) or is the determinative regarded as an integral part of the following relative clause (either subject: 2; or object form: 3)?

1   **Av dem som sökte läkarhjälp blev bara fem allvarigt sjuka.**
    Of those who sought medical help only five became seriously ill.

2   **Av de som sökte läkarhjälp blev bara fem allvarigt sjuka.**

3   **Av dem som läkaren hjälpte blev bara fem allvarligt sjuka.**
    Of those whom the doctor helped only five became seriously ill.

Note 3: Where English uses a determinative pronoun before a noun in the possessive case ('that of . . .' etc.) Swedish prefers the genitive form of the noun (see also 729 (o)):

Today's cars are much safer than those of yesterday.
Dagens bilar är mycket säkrare än gårdagens. [= yesterday's]

H   INDEFINITE PRONOUNS

330   Man

Subject	Object	Possessive	Reflexive
man	en	ens sin (see (b) below))	sig (see 310)

Man (object form **en**; reflexive form **sig**) renders English 'one'. However, **man** is far more common in Swedish than the rather stilted 'one' in English. It is encountered in both written and spoken Swedish in many instances where colloquial English would use 'you', 'we', 'they', 'people', etc. (In Swedish **du, dig, ditt** are generally used only when addressing a person directly, or in conjunction with general imperatives, but see also 551.)

Man kan aldrig vara för säker.	One/You can never be too sure.
Vem hjälper en om man blir sjuk?	Who helps you if you become ill?
Man dricker mycket te i Kina.	They drink a lot of tea in China.
Man säger att han är stenrik.	People say he is filthy rich.
Man ska alltid städa efter sig.	You should always tidy up after you.
Man erkänner allmänt att	It is widely acknowledged that

(b) Man has two possessive forms, **ens** and **sin** (**sitt, sina**), both of which are rendered in English by 'one's'. These forms are not interchangeable.

Ens is used to qualify the subject of a clause, or an object which is not owned by the subject of the clause.

Ens ord misstolkas lätt!
One's words are easily misinterpreted!

När man röstar på en politiker tror man aldrig att han ska komma att ta bort ens rättigheter.
When you vote for a politician you never think he is going to take away your rights.

Sin (**sitt, sina**) is used to qualify the object of the clause when the subject of the clause is the possessor. (See also 319(c).)

Man måste göra sin plikt.   One must do one's duty.

(c) Man is sometimes used in colloquial Swedish as a polite or mildly ironical substitute for **jag**:

Får man vara med?
May I join you?

Hur länge får man stå här och vänta?
How long do I have to stand here waiting?

(d) Man is also used as a term of address in Swedish (cf. 304(c)(i)).

Note 1: Although **man** may refer to one or several people, strictly speaking it is a singular non-neuter pronoun, as indicated by the singular form of the adjective in the following example:

Man är glad när solen skiner.   People are happy when the sun shines.

However, colloquial and informal written Swedish has many examples of plural predicates/correlates with **man**. See 211(a).

Man var tvungna att fly från stormen.   People were forced to escape the storm.
Man ser inte lika mycket av varandra idag. People don't see as much of one another today.

Note 2: As the examples in this paragraph show, **man** frequently corresponds to English 'people'/'they' etc. referring to some unspecified group. Colloquially **folk** or **de** is also used in Swedish, although certain linguists maintain a distinction between **man** (which may be considered to include the speaker) and **de/folk** (which does not). Thus:

Man säger han är rik.   They say he's rich (and I agree).
De säger han är rik.   They say he's rich (but I'm not so sure).

Note 3: **En** used as a subject is an antiquated alternative form to **man**:

En skulle kunna tro att   One would think that

331   **Varje**, **var**, **varenda**, etc., table of forms and use

Form			Use	
Non-neuter	*Neuter*	*Plural*	*Attributive*	*Pronominal*
varje	varje	–	yes	after preposition
var	vart	–.	yes	yes
var och en	vart och ett		–	+ **av** + noun yes
				or pronoun
varenda	vartenda	–	yes	rare
varenda en	vartenda ett		–	+ **av** + noun yes
				or pronoun
varannan	vartannat –		yes	yes
–	–	**varandra**	– ·	yes

332   **Varje**, **var**

Varje (indeclinable) and **var** (non-neuter), **vart** (neuter) correspond to English 'every', 'each'. These two forms are synonymous but differ in usage.

(a) Used attributively

Varje is more common before a noun, especially in spoken Swedish:

Jag brukar gå dit varje dag.	I usually walk there every day.
Varje språk har sina svårigheter.	Every language has its difficulties.

However, **var/vart** is preferred before an ordinal number:

Val äger rum vart fjärde år.	Elections take place every four years. [*lit.* 'every fourth year']

Note: A special form (**varannan**, **vartannat**) is used to render English 'every other/every second/every two' etc. (See 334.)

Han brukar hälsa på varannan vecka.	He usually calls in every other week.

(b) Used pronominally

Used without a following noun **var** usually signifies 'each' in the sense of 'per person' etc. (cf. also **var sin** 320(j)). For Swedish renderings of 'each' in prices, see 337.

Pojkarna fick ett äpple var.	The boys got an apple each.
Vi betalade femtio kronor var.	We paid fifty crowns each.

Varje is only used pronominally after a preposition:

Fem påsar med 2 ägg i varje.	Five bags with two eggs in each.
lite(t) av varje	a bit of everything

Note: The expressions **var för sig**, **vart för sig**, etc. correspond to the English 'separately', 'individually', etc.:

De bor var för sig.	They each live on their own.

333   Var och en, varenda, etc.

Var och en and **varenda** (and their neuter forms: **vart och ett** and **vartenda**) are more emphatic than **var**. They correspond to English 'each one/every one' and 'each and every/every single', etc.

Var och en is only used pronominally, but may frequently be followed by **av** + a pronoun or a plural noun with the end article.

Var och en betalade för sig.	Each person paid for himself.
Hon gav var och en av oss ett kex.	She gave each of us a biscuit.
Vart och ett av barnen mår bra.	Each of the children is well.

Varenda is followed by a noun without an end article:

Det finns fel på varenda sida.	There are errors on every single page.
Vartenda hus ska målas.	Each and every house is to be painted.

Note 1: 'Every single one' is rendered colloquially by **varenda en**, **vartenda ett**.

Varenda en av tavlorna blev stulen.	Every single one of the pictures was stolen.

For further emphasis the forms **varendaste en**, **vartendaste ett** are used (cf. 315(a)(ii) **självaste**.)

Note 2: **Var och en** (but not **vart och ett**) has a genitive form **vars och ens**. However, this sounds clumsy in modern Swedish and **varje människas** or some construction with **alla** is usually preferred. (See also 320(l).)

Det är vars och ens plikt att	It is everyone's duty to
(*better:* **Det är varje människas plikt att**)	
Det är vars och ens ensak.	That's every one's own private affair.

Note 3: **Envar** (**ettvart**) is now archaic, apart from the expression **alla och envar** ('every man jack'). Formerly these words had the same range of usage as **var och en** (**vart och ett**) but now, if used, generally refer only to people.

Envar svarade för sig.	Everyone answered for himself.

334 Varannan

Varannan (vartannat) is used with the singular indefinite form of the noun and corresponds to English 'every other', 'every second', 'every two'. (For forms such as 'every third' etc. cf. 332 (a).)

Varannan and **vartannat** are used both attributively and pronominally:

Hon kom varannan dag.	She came every other day.
Vartannat hus var rött.	Every other house was red.

Note: Used idiomatically, **vartannat** indicates a haphazard order. Grammatical gender has no significance in this idiomatic usage:

Allting låg om vartannat.	Everything was higgledy-piggledy.
Inbillning och verklighet om vartannat.	Fantasy and reality all mixed up.

335 Varandra

Varandra is actually the plural form of **varannan (vartannat)**. However, **varandra** is limited in meaning to 'one another', 'each other' and is only used pronominally.

De älskar varandra.	They love each other.
Alla blev trötta på varandra.	Everyone grew tired of one another

Varandra has a genitive form **varandras**:

Vi lånade varandras bilar.	We **borrowed** each other's cars.

See also reciprocal verbs, 544.

336 Vardera, någondera, ingendera, etc.

Non-neuter	Neuter	Plural	Meaning
vardera	vartdera	–	each, either
någondera	någotdera	–	some, any, either
ingendera	ingetdera,		
	intetdera	–	none, neither
endera	ettdera	–	one, one of these
–	–	bådadera	both

Although the words above conveniently fulfil a specific semantic function (especially when used pronominally, suggesting 'each of them', 'neither of them', 'both of them', etc.), they are rarely used in Swedish today. Modern Swedish prefers a suitable form of **var/varje, någon, ingen** or **båda**. Note that, when used attributively, **vardera, någondera**, etc. are followed by the singular definite form of the noun or by **av** + the plural definite form of the noun.

De gick inte med på någotdera av kraven/på någotdera kravet.
They would not accept either of the demands/either demand.

Är det Volvo eller Saab som är Sveriges största företag? Ingetdera!
Is it Volvo or Saab that is Sweden's biggest company? Neither!

Hotellet och vädret – bådadera var en besvikelse.
The hotel and the weather – both were a disappointment.

Also:

i ingetdera fallet	in neither case
endera dagen	one of these days

Note 1: **Inte . . . någondera/någotdera** must sometimes be used instead of **ingendera/ingetdera**. (See 344, 345.)

Note 2: In modern Swedish **båda delarna** is more commonly used than **bådadera**. **Båda två** is preferred when referring to people.

Vill du äta nu eller senare? Båda delarna.	Do you want to eat now or later? Both!
Träffade du Olle eller Hans? Båda två.	Did you meet Olle or Hans? Both of them.

337 Prices: '50 euros each'

Swedish **styck** or **stycket** is often used where English has 'each' in the sense 'apiece'. (Cf. 332(b).)

slipsar för trettio kronor styck(et)	ties for thirty crowns each
Priset per styck är	The price per unit (each) is
biljetter à 50 euro styck	tickets at 50 euros each

338 Distribution: '1 teaspoonful to every 5 litres'

Swedish has no distributive particle (cf. for example German *je*) and thus no convenient way of expressing numerically equal distribution. However, Swedish sometimes uses **varje** in such instances (cf. English 'every'), even though **varje** is otherwise found only before singular nouns (cf. 332).

Ta en tesked på (varje) fem liter vatten.
Take 1 teaspoonful to (every) 5 litres of water.

en riksdagsman för (varje) 20 000 väljare
one MP for every 20,000 voters

Bilen förbrukar endast en liter bensin på (varje) 5 mil.
The car uses only 1 litre of petrol every 50 km.

339 All (allt, alla) etc.

All (allt, alla) may be followed by a noun without the end article or by a noun with the end article. These alternative forms correspond closely to English 'all' and 'all the' respectively.

Non-neuter	Neuter	Plural	Meaning
–	**allt**	**alla**	all, everything, everyone
all + noun	**allt** + noun	**alla** + noun	all *(universal)*
all + noun + end art.	**allt** + noun + end art.	**alla** + noun+end art.	all (of the) *(specific)*
hela + noun + end art.	**hela** + noun + end art.	**hela** + noun+end art.	the whole/all (of the)

(a) All (allt, alla) + noun without end article (universal application)

All (allt, alla) combined with a noun without the end article corresponds to English 'all' + noun and has a universal implication. **All (allt, alla)** agrees in gender and number with the following noun.

All mat är dyr nuförtiden.	All food is expensive these days.
Allt hopp är ute.	All hope is gone.
Han tycker om alla djur.	He likes all animals.

All or **allt** with a singular count noun without the end article often corresponds to English 'every':

Han har all utsikt att lyckas.	He has every prospect of success.
Du har all anledning att vara arg.	You have every reason to be angry.

Note also:

Tåget går alla dagar utom söndag. The train runs every day except Sunday.

(b) All (allt, alla) + noun + end article (specific application)

When **all (allt, alla)** is used with the definite form of the noun it indicates a specific application.

Alla eleverna gjorde samma fel.	All (of) the pupils made the same error.
Du får all den hjälp du behöver.	You'll get all the help you need.

All (**allt, alla**) is also used in this sense with a determinative pronoun (329), a demonstrative pronoun (325) or a possessive pronouns (316ff.) and a following noun or pronoun.

Hon förlorade alla sina vänner.	She lost all (of) her friends.
Åt du upp allt det där själv?	Did you eat all (of) that yourself?

(c) Hela followed by the noun in the definite singular form renders English 'all', 'all of the' when this may be replaced by with 'the whole' (cf. 224(a)):

Han jobbar hela dagen.	He works all day.
Jag sprang genom hela staden.	I ran all through the town.
Har du läst hela boken?	Have you read all of the book?

Note that the noun has no end article when **hela** is used with a possessive pronoun.

Vi älskar dig med hela vårt hjärta.	We love you with all of our heart.

Note 1: **Hela** is used with a front article only when an adjective precedes the noun. The front article follows **hela**:

Hela den gamla delen av huset förstördes i branden.
The whole of the old part of the house was destroyed in the fire.

Note 2: Used in the indefinite form with count nouns **en hel** (neuter, **ett helt**; plural, **hela**) corresponds to English '(a) whole':

Grisen åt en hel banan, ett helt äpple och tre hela grapefrukter.
The pig ate a whole banana, a whole apple and three whole grapefruits.

Note 3: Notice forms like **hela 2 liter** ('a full 2 litres'), where **hela** followed by an expression of measurement takes the indefinite form of the noun.

(d) Allt and **allting** used by themselves correspond to English 'all' = 'everything':

Allt/Allting jag har är ditt.	All/Everything I have is yours.
Han vet allt/allting om sport.	He knows all about sport.
inte för allt/allting i världen	not for everything in the world
Du är mitt allt.	You're everything to me.

Notice that these neuter forms are used even when referring to a non-neuter noun:

Det fanns ingen mat kvar. Han hade ätit upp precis allt.
There was no food left. He had eaten absolutely everything/all of it.

In most instances **allt** and **allting** are interchangeable. **Allt** is, however, preferred when combined with a neuter adjective in expressions such as:

Allt roligt är förbjudet.	Everything that's fun is forbidden.
Han tycker om allt svenskt.	He likes everything Swedish.
Jag är allt annat än glad.	I'm anything but happy.

(e) Alla (plural) used by itself corresponds to English 'all' = 'all people', 'everyone', 'everybody':

Alla kan inte ha rätt.	Everybody can't be right.
Hon överraskade oss alla.	She surprised us all.

Note: **Alla** is an indefinite 3rd person *plural* pronoun, while English 'everyone, everybody' is 3rd person *singular*. This difference between the two languages becomes apparent in the congruences with adjectives and verbs respectively.

Alla var trötta och smutsiga.	Everybody was tired and dirty.

Alla has a genitive form **allas** (see also 320(I)):

Hon var föremål för allas blickar.	She was the object of everyone's gaze.
för allas vår skull	for all our sakes
allas vår vän	a friend of us all

(f) For the use of **alls**, **allt**, **alltmera** and **allra** as amplifiers with adjectives, see 612(b).

(g) Alltsamman, allesamman; alltihop, allihop(a), etc.

These are 3rd person pronouns. In their singular forms (**alltsamman, alltsammans, alltihop**) they correspond to English 'everything', usually in the sense of 'the whole lot'.
In their plural forms (**allesamman, allesammans, allihop, allihopa**) they correspond to English 'everybody', 'all of us/you/them'.

These pronouns are encountered almost exclusively in colloquial and informal written Swedish, and are far more restricted in use than **allt**, **allting** (cf. (d) above) and **alla** (cf. (e) above).

Jag köpte alltihop.	I bought everything/the whole lot.
Jag är trött på alltsamman.	I'm tired of everything.
God natt allesamman!	Good night, everybody!
Allihop(a) gömde sig i skogen.	All of them hid in the forest.

Note: The following phrases and idioms with **allt** etc.

en gång för alla	once and for all
allt som allt	all in all

hans allt i allo	his right-hand man
allahanda, allsköns (*both indeclinable*)	all manner of (+ nn in indefinite form)
överallt	everywhere
på alla sätt	in every way
åt alla håll	in every direction
allt emellanåt	every now and then

340   Annan, den andra

	Non-neuter	Neuter	Plural	Meaning
Indefinite	(en) annan	(ett) annat	andra	another (one), others
Definite	den andra	det andra	de andra	the other(s)

Instead of **den andra** Swedish sometimes prefers **den andre** when referring to a masculine noun.

(a) Annan etc. agrees in gender and number with the noun to which it refers. It is used both attributively and pronominally:

Eva och en annan tjej vann.	Eva and another girl won.
Huset är för dyrt. – Köp ett annat!	'The house is too dear.' 'Buy another.'
Den andra kjolen är snyggare.	The other skirt is nicer.
Var är de andra?	Where are the others?

When used pronominally **annan** etc. may take a genitive **-s**. (See also 320(l))

Jag tog en annans hatt.	I took another person's hat.
Han stjäl ofta andras idéer.	He often steals other people's ideas.

(b) Annan (**annat, andra**) after an indefinite pronoun frequently corresponds to English 'else'.

Någon annan har varit här.	Someone else has been here.
Vilka andra var på festen?	Who else (plural) was at the party?

Compare also: **alla andra** 'everyone else'; **någonting annat** 'something else'; **ingenting annat** 'nothing else'; **allt annat** 'everything else'; **mycket annat** 'much else'; **lite(t) annat** 'little else'.

Annan and **andra** have genitive forms in **-s**:

Hans bil är större än alla andras.	His car is bigger than everyone else's.

Note 1: **Annars** (= 'otherwise') – not **annat** – is combined with the interrogative pronouns **vem**, **vad** (and also **var, vart, hur**) in expressions corresponding to English 'who else?', 'what else?', etc. (But

see also Note 2 below.) Note also the word order in such instances:

> **Vem kunde det annars vara?**   Who else could it be?
> **Var kan vi annars leta?**   Where else can we look?

Note 2: When English 'else' means 'in addition' rather than 'instead' Swedish sometimes uses **mer/mera** with **vem** and **vad**. **Mera** is never used in this way with **vilken, alla, allt, litet**.

> **Vad sa han mer(a)?**   What else did he say?

Note 3: Note the idiomatic renderings:

> **någon annanstans/ingen annanstans**   somewhere else/nowhere else

(c) '(The) One . . . the other'

The Swedish expression **den/det ena . . . den/det andra** corresponds to English '(the) one . . . the other' used pronominally. **Ena** and **andra** both have masculine forms in **-e**:

> **Den ena gick ut när den andra kom in.**
> One went out when the other came in.

> **Den enes död, den andres bröd.**
> One man's meat is another man's poison.
> [*lit.* 'One man's death, the other's bread.']

> **Å ena sidan . . . , å andra sidan . . .**
> On (the) one hand . . . , on the other (hand) . . .

(d) 'Another'

Swedish has three forms of expression that correspond to English 'another', depending on meaning.

(i) Another = 'a different' = **en annan, ett annat**. Gender is determined by the noun referred to or implied.

> **Jag vill ha en annan bil.**   I want another [i.e. a different] car.
> **Sälj ert hus och köp ett annat!**   Sell your house and buy another.

Note: **Andra** (sometimes **några andra**) provides a corresponding plural form:

> **Jag tycker inte om de här skorna. Jag köper snart andra.**
> I don't like these shoes. I'm going to buy some others [i.e. different ones] soon.

(ii) Another = 'an additional' = **en/ett . . . till** etc.
Gender is determined by the noun referred to or implied.

Vi behöver en bil till.	We need another [i.e. an additional] car.
Behåll ert hus och köp ett till!	Keep your house and buy another (one).

Note: **Några till** provides a corresponding plural form:

Jag tycker om de här äpplena. Jag tror jag köper några till.
I like these apples. I think I'll buy some more.

(iii) 'One another' = **varandra** (see 335).

Note 1: English 'one' is not translated after **en annan, den andra, en . . . till**, etc.

Jag vill ha en annan.	I want another one.
Ta ett päron och ge det andra till Eva!	Take a pear and give the other one to Eva.

Note 2: **Ytterligare** is sometimes used instead of **till** with a numeral and a plural noun. Note the difference in the relative positions of **till** and **ytterligare**.

Jag fick vänta 25 minuter till.	I had to wait another twenty-five minutes.
Jag fick vänta ytterligare 25 minuter.	

Note 3: **Annan, den andra**, etc. occur in a number of idiomatic expressions.

på ett eller annat sätt	somehow or other
ett eller annat	something or other
av en eller annan anledning	for some reason or other
Jag har annat att göra.	I've other things/better things to do.
Var är de båda andra?	Where are the other two?
bland andra (bl.a.)	among others [i.e. persons]
bland annat (bl.a.)	among other things
en och annan gång	now and again
gång efter annan	time after time
Jag var allt annat än nöjd med det.	I was anything but satisfied with it.
Ingen annan än statsministern vet om det.	Nobody but/No one other than the PM knows.

Note 4: In familiar speech **en annan** has two idiomatic functions. Used attributively it may sometimes be imbued with a meaning similar to English 'regular', 'proper':

som en annan idiot	like a proper fool
som en annan Tarzan	like a regular Tarzan

Used pronominally it provides a circumlocutive (usually ironic) form for **jag**:

Här går en annan och sliter.	Here I am, working my fingers to the bone.

Note 5: In vague expressions of time English '(the) other' etc. is rendered idiomatically in Swedish:

the other day	**häromdagen**
the other evening	**häromkvällen**
the other year	**häromåret**

341 Någon (något, några)

Non-neuter sing.	Neuter sing.	Plural	Meaning
någon	**något**	**några**	some, any

Note the following colloquial pronunciations: **någon** /nån/; **något** /nåt/; **några** /nåra/; **någonting** /nånting/; **någonstans** /nånstans/

(a) Used attributively

(i) **Någon** etc. is used attributively before a noun without the end article. The form is determined by the gender and number of the following noun. Used in this way **någon** etc. usually renders English 'some', or 'any' in questions and negative statements.

Några barn satt och lekte.	Some children sat playing.
Har du någon mat hemma?	Have you any food at home?

(ii) When asking questions Swedish tends to use **någon/något** before a count noun in the singular where English has either 'a/an' + singular, or 'any' + plural. (See also 346(c)(i) Note 2.)

Finns det någon skola i byn?	Is there a school in the village?
Har hon någon bror?	Has she a brother (any brothers)?

However, Swedish **en/ett** before a noun is retained in cases where English has 'one'. **En/ett** used in this way is stressed when spoken.

Har hon ˈen bror eller flera?	Does she have one brother or several?

Note 1: Used attributively **några** may also mean 'a few' (= **några få**)

för några dagar sedan	a few days ago
om några veckor	in a few weeks' time
Jag har några stycken.	I have a few.

Note 2: Note also

på något sätt	somehow
på ett eller annat sätt	somehow or other

(b) Used pronominally

(i) **Någon** etc. is also used pronominally. The gender and number depend on the noun to which **någon** refers.

Vi är utan mat. Har du någon?	We have no food. Do you have any?
Vi är utan vatten. Har du något?	We have no water. Do you have any?
Några av barnen blev sjuka.	Some of the children became ill.

(ii) **Någon** = 'someone'. Used pronominally **någon** may also translate 'someone', 'somebody', 'anyone', 'anybody' (see also 344ff. for forms in negative statements). **Någon** is a third person singular non-neuter pronoun. The plural form **några** renders 'some people'.

Någon har glömt sin hatt.	Someone has forgotten his hat.
Har någon ringt?	Has anyone phoned?
Jag måste prata med någon.	I have to talk to somebody.
Några tror att han är galen.	Some people think he's mad.

Note 1: **Någon** and **några** have the genitive forms **någons** and **någras**. (See also 320(1).)

Någons katt har tagit vår kanariefågel.	Someone's cat has taken our canary.
enligt någras mening	according to what some people think

Note 2: **Någon** meaning 'someone' etc. is not used pronominally with an adjective as in English. Swedish usually prefers a construction with a relative clause instead.

Hon gifte sig med någon som är lång och mager.
She got married to someone tall and thin.

But note **någon annan** = 'someone else', **någon annans** = 'someone else's'.

Note 3: 'Anyone' = 'anyone at all' is usually rendered in Swedish by **vem som helst** (see 358).

(iii) **Något** = 'something'. Used pronominally **något** and the longer form **någonting** are synonymous and render English 'something', 'anything' (see also 344ff. for forms in negative statements). **Något/någonting** are third person singular neuter pronouns.

Hör du något?	Can you hear anything?
Det är någonting jag inte förstår.	That's something I don't understand.

Note 1: As in English **något**, **någonting** may be combined with an adjective.

Någonting rött låg på marken.   Something red lay on the ground.

But note, **något annat** = 'something else'.

Note 2: **Något** (but not **någonting**!) is also used adverbially to translate the English 'somewhat' = 'slightly', 'a little' as an alternative to **lite(t)**.

Kjolen kunde vara något längre.	The skirt could be slightly longer.
Vi saktade farten något.	We reduced our speed somewhat.

342 Somlig

Non-neuter	Neuter	Plural	Meaning
somlig	**somligt**	**somliga**	some

Somlig is not commonly used in Swedish. Although it corresponds to English 'some', it should not be regarded as a synonym of **någon** (341). The idiomatic usages of these words differ considerably. There is often some idea of comparison when **somlig**, etc. is used (i.e. 'some, but not others'):

> **Somliga gör si, andra gör så.**   Some do this, others do that.

The singular forms, used only with non-count nouns, are rarely encountered.

> **Somligt vin är nästan vitt.**   Some wine is almost white.

Note: The plural form has a genitive in **-s** when used pronominally.

343 Ingen (inget, inga)

Non-neuter singular	Neuter singular	Plural	Meaning
ingen	**inget (intet)**	**inga**	no, none, not . . . any

The neuter singular form **inget** has an alternative form, **intet**, but this is rarely used in modern Swedish outside a limited range of set phrases such as **intet ont anande** ('unsuspectingly'), **intetsägande** ('non-committal'), etc.

(a) Used attributively

Used attributively before a noun **ingen** etc. correspond to English 'no', 'not a', 'not any'. The form is dependent on the gender and number of the following noun.

> **Ingen människa är fullkomlig.**   No man is perfect.
> **Det var ingen dum idé.**   That's not a bad idea.
> **De har inga barn.**   They haven't any children.

Note, however, that **inte . . . någon** etc. must sometimes be used instead of **ingen** etc. (344ff.).

(b) Used pronominally

(i) Ingen etc. are also used pronominally. They then correspond to English 'none', 'not any', 'not . . . one'. The form depends on the gender and number of the noun implied:

Ingen av oss förlorade jobbet.	None of us lost our job.
Har vi inget bröd?	Have we no bread?/
	Haven't we got any bread?
Vill du ha pengar så har jag inga.	If you want money I don't have any.

Note, however, that **inte . . . någon** etc. must sometimes be used instead of **ingen** (344ff.).

(ii) Ingen = 'no-one'. Used pronominally **ingen** may also translate 'no-one', 'nobody'. Note, however, that **inte . . . någon** etc. must sometimes be used instead of **ingen** (344ff.).

Ingen kan tjäna två herrar.	No one can serve two masters.
Jag känner ingen med det namnet.	I know no one by that name.

Ingen is a 3rd person singular non-neuter pronoun. With the plural form **inga** (= 'nobody', 'no people', 'none') Swedish maintains a distinction that English does not have:

Det var inga jag kände på festen.	There was no one I knew at the party.

Ingen has a genitive form **ingens**. (See also 320(l))

Det var ingens fel att han dog.	It was no-one's fault he died.

(iii) Inget = 'nothing'. Used pronominally **inget (intet)** or **ingenting** may also render 'nothing', 'not anything'.

Vi letade men fann ingenting.	We searched but found nothing.
Han äger inget av värde.	He owns nothing of value.

Note, however, that **inte . . . något** etc. must sometimes be used instead of **inget** (344ff.).

Note 1: While **inget** (= 'nothing') and **inga** (= 'no people') may be combined with an adjective, the non-neuter singular **ingen** (= 'no-one', 'nobody') is rarely used in this way. Swedish usage often prefers a relative clause instead.

Inget gott kan komma av det.	No good can come of it.
Det finns inga gamla i byn.	There are no old people in the village.

but:

Ingen som är berusad får komma in	No one drunk is to be let in.
Den som är berusad får inte komma in.	

Note 2: Added to **ingen, inte någon**, etc. the word **alls** has the force of English 'at all'.

Hon har inga pengar alls.	She has no money at all.
Ingenting alls kunde få mig att sjunga.	Nothing at all could get me to sing.

(cf. also 345 Note 4, 358f.)

Note 3: In phrases such as the following, where the idea is that of 'not (a single) one', **ingen/inget** in the subject position may be replaced by **inte en/ett** (with stress on **en/ett**). In the object position **ingen/inget** may be replaced by **inte en/ett enda** (with the stress on **enda**):

Inte ' en av eleverna klarade provet.	Not (a single) one of the pupils passed the test.
De klarade inte ' ett enda prov.	They didn't pass a single test.

Note 4: **Ingen** etc. is used in a range of idiomatic expressions.

ingen annan/ingen annans	no-one else/no-one else's
inget (ingenting, intet) annat	nothing else
Det är inget annat än skandalöst.	It's nothing short of scandalous.
Han levde på inget annat än vatten.	He lived on nothing but water.

Note also:

Han försvann i tomma intet.	He disappeared into thin air.
Han är en riktig nolla.	He's a real nobody.

344 Ingen or inte någon?

Swedish maintains a distinction similar to English in the usage of 'no'/'not . . . any':

Inga nyheter är goda nyheter.	No news is good news.
Jag har inte fått några nyheter.	I have not received any news.

As the table in 345 shows, **ingen** etc. is consistently preferred to **inte . . . någon** etc. in the subject position. In the object position, however, **ingen** etc. generally appears only in a main clause with simple verb forms. In other cases:

ingen	is replaced by	inte någon
inget/intet	is replaced by	inte något
inga	is replaced by	inte några
ingenting	is replaced by	inte någonting
ingendera	is replaced by	inte någondera
intetdera/ingetdera	is replaced by	inte någotdera
(ingenstans	is replaced by	inte någonstans – adverb)

345   Ingen, inte någon – a schematic summary

Main clause		Subordinate clause
Subject position		
Ingen såg mig.	Simple verb	**Jag sa, att ingen såg mig.**
(See also Note 1)		
Ingen har sett mig.	Complex tense	**Jag sa, att ingen hade sett mig.**
Ingen kan se mig.	Modal aux. + verb	**Jag sa, att ingen kunde se mig.**
Object position		
Jag såg ingen. (Note 2)	Simple verb	**Jag sa, att jag inte såg någon** (Note 5)
Jag har inte sett någon. (Note 3)	Complex tense	**Jag sa, att jag inte hade sett någon.**
Jag vill inte se någon.	Modal aux. + verb	**Jag sa, att jag inte ville se någon.**
Jag tyckte inte om någon.	Object after compound verb	**Jag sa, att jag inte tyckte om någon.**
Jag pratade inte med någon. (Note 4)	Object after verb + preposition	**Jag sa, att jag inte pratade med någon**

Note 1: Note the difference between:

Är det ingen mat till mig?	Is there no food for me?	(Anticipates answer 'No')
Är det inte någon mat till mig?	Isn't there any food for me?	(Anticipates answer 'Yes')

Note 2: When used in the object position with a simple verb **ingen** etc. are often replaced by **inte någon** etc. in the spoken language.

Jag såg inte någon bil/inte någon.   I didn't see a car/anyone.

Note 3: In more formal situations **ingen** etc. may occasionally be encountered before the main verb. In a main clause **ingen** etc. (and, if applicable, its correlative) then precedes the main verb (cf. 1031(e)):

Jag har ingenting sagt och vill ingenting säga.
I have said nothing and don't wish to say anything.

In a subordinate clause **ingen** etc. (and, if applicable, its correlative) then precedes the finite verb (cf. 1031(e)):

Han sade, att han inga pengar hade.   He said he had no money.
Jag visste att hon ingenting ville stjäla.   I knew she wouldn't steal anything.

Note 4: Note that there is a degree of flexibility in the word order when expressions with **inte . . . alls** (343 Note 2) are used in subordinate clauses:

Jag sa, att jag inte har någon lust alls att . . . I said I don't feel (in the slightest) like . . .
Jag sa, att jag inte alls har någon lust att . . .

Note 5: For the position of **inte** in the subordinate clause, see 1031.

346   Translation of 'some' and 'any' into Swedish

Swedish does not maintain the same idiomatic distinctions between 'some' and 'any' as English. The rules for the translation of English 'some' and 'any' and their compound forms into Swedish may be summarised thus:

(a) 'Some' = **någon (något, några)**

Most often English 'some' (and compound forms) is rendered by Swedish **någon** etc. (and compound forms). (See 341)

Can I be of some use?	**Kan jag vara till någon nytta?**
I have some flowers for you.	**Jag har några blommor till dig.**

There must be someone somewhere who knows something about this.
Det måste finnas någon någonstans som vet någonting om detta.

(b) 'Some' = 'a little' = **lite(t)**

When English 'some' is used partitively to signify 'an unspecified amount of' rather than 'any at all' (i.e. the opposite of 'none') it is usually rendered in Swedish by **lite(t)** (indeclinable, see 354). Sometimes **lite(t)** may be omitted, especially before items in a list.

I've brought some cheese with me.	**Jag har tagit lite(t) ost med mig.**
Buy some cheese, bread and butter.	**Köp ost, bröd och smör!**
Pour some for me, please.	**Slå upp lite åt mig, är du snäll!**
May I offer you some cakes?	**Kan jag få bjuda på lite kakor?**

Note: **Någon** etc. is retained in instances where 'some' suggests 'some . . . or other':

Jag har någon ost hemma, men jag vet inte vad det är för sort.
I've some cheese at home, but I don't know what kind it is.

(c) 'Some' = 'some (but not all) of'

(i) 'Some of' + a plural count noun is rendered by **några av** in Swedish.

Some of the pupils are ill.	**Några av eleverna är sjuka.**

Note 1: 'One of' + a plural count noun is translated by **någon av, något av** in Swedish when the actual quantity is of no concern. (Cf. 341 (a)(ii)) Compare:

Du borde läsa någon av hans böcker.	You ought to read one of his books [or more].
Jag har läst en av hans böcker.	I've read one of his books [i.e. a single one].

Note 2: 'Either of' + plural count noun is usually translated by **någon av, något av** in Swedish (but see also 336):

Have you met either of the twins?	**Har du träffat någon av tvillingarna?**

(ii) 'Some (of)' + a non-count noun or singular count noun is rendered by Swedish **en del (av)** (literally 'a part of'):

Some white wine is very sour. **En del vitt vin är mycket surt.**
I saw only some of the machinery. **Jag såg bara en del av maskineriet.**

(d) 'Some' + numeral = 'approximately'

'Some' before a cardinal number is translated by **ungefär** or **omkring** (literally 'approximately'). (Cf. also 407(a))

He died some fifty years ago. **Han dog för omkring 50 år sedan.**

(e) 'Some' = 'some . . . or other'

'Some' followed by a noun used in the sense 'some . . . or other' is translated by **någon (något, några)** in Swedish. (See 341)

Some boy (or other) phoned you. **Någon pojke ringde till dig.**

(f) 'Some' = 'an extraordinary'

In familiar style the stressed 'some' before a noun expressing the meaning 'an extraordinary', 'quite a' may be rendered in Swedish by **något till** (regardless of the gender of the following noun):

That's some car you had there! **Det var något till bil du hade där!**

(g) 'Some . . ., some' = 'some . . ., others'

The expressions 'some . . ., some . . .' and 'some . . ., other' are usually translated by **somliga . . ., andra . . .**:

Some days are good, others bad. **Somliga dagar är bra, andra dåliga.**
Some people sat, some stood. **Somliga satt, andra stod.**

(h) 'Any' in negative statements

In negative statements and statements expressing doubt or uncertainty 'any' (and its compound forms) is usually translated by **inte . . . någon**, etc. or **ingen**, etc. (and compound forms). **Ingen** is only used with a simple verb (cf. 345).

He has not spoken to anyone. **Han har inte talat med någon.**
I haven't any money. **Jag har inga pengar.**

Before a non-count noun, or the words **mer, fler,** Swedish seldom has a word corresponding to English 'any':

She has never eaten any pork.	**Hon har aldrig ätit fläsk.**
I don't want any more presents.	**Jag vill inte ha fler presenter.**

Note:

hardly/scarcely any	**nästan ingen (nästan inget, nästan inga)**
hardly/scarcely anyone	**nästan ingen**
hardly/scarcely anything, next to nothing	**nästan ingenting**

(j) 'Any' in interrogative statements

In positive interrogative statements 'any' (and its compound forms) is usually translated by **någon (något, några)** (cf. also (m) below). Note however, that when used in a partitive sense in interrogative statements 'any' is usually rendered by **lite(t)**. See (b) above.

Have you any letters for me?	**Har du några brev till mig?**
Did you find anything?	**Hittade du något?**
Have you any coffee?	**Har du lite kaffe?**

(k) 'Any' in conditional statements

In conditional statements 'any' (and its compound forms) is usually rendered by **någon (något, några)** etc.

If there had been any elk in your garden you would no doubt have seen them.
Om det hade funnits några älgar i trädgården hade du nog sett dem.

(l) 'Any of'

(i) 'any of' + a plural count noun is usually rendered by **inte några av** or **inga av** in negative sentences, or by **inte . . . någon/något av** or **ingen/inget av** if the sense is 'not a single one of' (= **inte en/ett enda av**). (See 345 for the difference in usage between **inte några** and **inga**.)

I haven't read any of your letters.	**Jag har inte läst några av dina brev.**
Didn't you read any of the books.	**Läste du ingen av böckerna?**

Note: 'None of', 'neither of' + a plural count noun as a subject of the clause is translated by **ingen av.**

None of the drivers came to work.	**Ingen av förarna kom till jobbet.**
Neither of her parents came.	**Ingen av hennes föräldrar kom.**

(ii) 'Any of' + a plural count noun is translated by **några av** in positive interrogative sentences, or by **någon/något av** if the sense is clearly 'a single one of'.

Have you any of the cakes left?	**Har du några av kakorna kvar?**
Did any of your friends visit you?	**Kom någon av era vänner på besök?**

(iii) 'Any of' + a non-count noun or singular count noun may be rendered in Swedish by **någon del av** (= 'any part of') when the noun refers to something which is made up of various components.

Do we need to replace any of the machinery?
Behöver vi byta ut någon del av maskineriet?

Otherwise a form of **någon** or **ingen** is used:

Has he lost any of his hair yet?	**Har han tappat något hår än?**
She didn't inherit any of her money.	**Hon ärvde inga av sina pengar.**

(m) 'Any' = 'no matter which', etc.

'Any' meaning 'no matter which' etc. is usually rendered in Swedish by a pronominal compound with **som helst** (cf. 358f.).

'Which train do I take?' 'Any.'	**Vilket tåg tar jag? – Vilket som helst.**
Anyone can see you're ill.	**Vem som helst kan se att du är sjuk.**

Note, however:

If anyone can do it, you can!   **Om någon (alls) kan göra det, så är det du.**

(n) 'Any' = 'all, every'

'Any' in the sense of 'all', 'every' is translated by **alla** + plural form of the noun (cf. 339) or **varje** + singular form of the noun (cf. 331f.).

a familiar voice to any listener	**en välkänd röst för alla lyssnare**
at any rate, anyway, in any case	**i varje fall**

(o) 'Any' + comparatives

(i) 'Any' before an adverbial comparative has no equivalent in Swedish:

He couldn't walk any further.   **Han kunde inte gå längre.**

(ii) 'Any' after a comparative + 'than' is rendered by **någon**, etc.:

He plays better than any pro.   **Han spelar bättre än något proffs.**

(p) 'Any' = 'any possible', 'any . . . . that you may have'

The adjective **eventuell** (**eventuellt, eventuella**) is used to translate 'any' in phrases such as the following:

I'll answer any questions later.
Jag svarar på eventuella frågor senare.

Any complaints should be made in writing.
Eventuella klagomål framförs skriftligt.

(q) 'Any' = 'any (single) one'

'Any one' (written as two separate words with strong emphasis on 'one') does not readily translate into Swedish.

You can have any one of these books.
Du kan få vilken som helst av de här böckerna, (men bara en).

347 Båda

Swedish **båda** and its variant **bägge** (both indeclinable plural pronouns) correspond to English 'both'.

(a) Used attributively

Båda and **bägge** may be used attributively before a noun, in which case they are usually followed by the definite form of the noun.
Båda bilarna är röda.	Both (of the) cars are red.
Han har kört bägge bilarna.	He has driven both of the cars.

Note, however, that **båda** and **bägge** are not followed by the definite form of the noun after a possessive pronoun or genitive expression.

Båda hans söner är gifta.	Both his sons are married.
diken på vägens båda sidor	ditches on both sides of the road

Note 1: If an adjective follows **båda, bägge** the front article (221f.) is usually inserted before the adjective:
Båda de nya bilarna är röda.	Both (of the) new cars are red.

Note 2: Idiomatic usage does not always require the definite (end) article on nouns following **båda**, **bägge**. The end article is not generally used where English has 'both' rather than 'both of the':

    En gång med dörrar i bägge/båda ändar. A corridor with doors at both ends.

If **båda** or **bägge** used attributively is preceded by the front article (221f.), a possessive pronoun or a demonstrative pronoun, it corresponds in meaning to the English 'the two', 'these two', etc. (Used in this way **båda/bägge** have less stress in speech.)

De båda bilarna krockade.	The two cars crashed.
De båda bröderna förolyckades.	The two brothers died in the accident.
Deras båda systrar överlevde.	Their two sisters survived.

Used attributively **båda**, **bägge** do not have a genitive form. This is indicated instead by the noun which **båda**, **bägge** precedes.

båda bilarnas motorer	both the cars' engines
mina båda systrars män	my two sisters' husbands

(b) Used pronominally

When **båda**, **bägge** are used pronominally they are often followed by **två**. See also 336 Note 2.

Båda (två) var uttröttade.	They were both worn out.
Hon gömde båda (två) i skåpet.	She hid them both in the cupboard.

Note 1: Swedish has no direct equivalent to 'both of us', 'both of them', etc. **Båda**, **bägge** are sometimes replaced by **två** in expressions with a personal pronoun.

Båda är professionella musiker.	Both of them are professional musicians.
Han var alltid en god vän till oss båda.	He was always a good friend to both of us.
Jag tänker ofta på er två.	I often think of you two/both of you.

Note 2: Used pronominally, **båda** (but not **bägge**!) has a genitive form in **-s**. (See also 320(l).)
    Det ligger i bådas intresse.   It is in the interest of both of them.

Note 3: Note the following (see also 823(e)):

Hon är både okunnig och dum.	She is both ignorant and stupid.
Både han och hans fru kom.	Both he and his wife came.

348 Mycket

For the most part the uses of Swedish **mycket** and English 'much' run parallel. **Mycket** can generally translate 'much' used pronominally or before a singular non-count noun. **Mycket** also renders English phrases such as 'a lot (of)', 'a good deal of', etc.

Hur mycket ost åt du? Mycket!	How much cheese did you eat? A lot.
Mycket återstår att göra.	There's a lot left to be done.

Note 1: **För mycket** is used idiomatically in expressions such as the following (cf. also 355(a) Note):

Du har tagit en banan för mycket.	You have taken one banana too many.
Studenten fick tre poäng för mycket.	The student got 3 marks too many.

Note 2: Swedish **mycket** also corresponds to the English adverb 'very'. (See 612.):

Schäfern är en mycket hängiven hund.	The Alsatian is a very devoted dog.

'Very much' is usually rendered in Swedish by **väldigt mycket**, but note the idiomatic expression **Tack så väldigt mycket** – 'Thank you very much'.

Note 3: The non-neuter and definite forms (**mycken**, **myckna**) are now all but obsolete. **Mycket** is used with substances, materials, etc. regardless of number and gender. See also 350.

mycket ost, mycket vatten, mycket ärter   a lot of cheese, a lot of water, a lot of peas

The definite form sounds contrived:

På grund av det myckna regnandet blir årets skörd dålig.
Because of the large amount of rain/As a result of all the rain, this year's harvest will be poor.

Note 4: Some other expressions with **mycket** or 'much':

Vi tjänar lika mycket.	We earn the same. [*lit.* 'equally much']
Han är inte så mycket att se på.	He's not much to look at.
Han är inte mycket till fotbollsspelare.	He's not much of a footballer.
Jag är inte så mycket för kaffe.	I'm not all that fond of coffee.
Det är inte särskilt bra.	That's not much good.
Det är inget vidare bra.	That's not very good.

349 Många

For the most part the uses of Swedish **många** and English 'many' run parallel. **Många** may also be rendered as 'a lot of', 'lots of' followed by a plural noun (but cf. 350 below). **Många** is used pronominally in the plural and attributively before a plural noun:

Hon har många CD-skivor.	She has a lot of CDs.
Jag har inte hittat många fel.	I've not found many errors.
Hur många av er kan simma?	How many of you can swim?
Många av bilarna var stulna.	Many of the cars were stolen.

Många has a genitive form in **-s** meaning 'many people's'. (See also 320(l).)

Mångas föräldrar var fattiga på den tiden.
Many people's parents were poor in those days.

Note: **Mången** (non-neuter) and **månget** (neuter) correspond to English 'many a' + noun. They are followed by the singular form of the noun without article. These forms sound archaic in modern Swedish, and can often be avoided.

| **Mången soldat har stupat förgäves.** | Many a soldier has fallen in vain. |
| Better is: **Många soldater** | |

The neuter form **mångt** now occurs only in the expression **i mångt och mycket** = 'in many respects'.

350 Inte för mycket ärter, tack!

Swedish often uses **mycket** before a collective or plural noun where the emphasis is on the quantity as a whole rather than the individual items which make up the quantity (see 121). English renders this in a number of ways. (Cf. also **litet** (354) and **få** (355).)

Det finns mycket fisk i havet.	There's a lot of fish in the sea.
Hur mycket pengar har du?	How much money do you have?
Inte för mycket ärter, tack!	Not too many peas for me, please!
Det är mycket bilar på vägarna.	There are a lot of cars on the roads.
Det var inte mycket folk där.	There weren't many people there.

Note: Conversely, **många** is rendered by 'much' in English when Swedish plurals correspond to English non-count nouns (cf. 124):

| Did he give you much information? | **Gav han dig många upplysningar?** |
| We haven't much evidence of this. | **Vi har inte många bevis på detta.** |

351 Mer, fler

(a) **Mer** or **mera** may be used pronominally to refer to a singular or non-count noun or attributively before the noun, and is usually rendered by 'more' in English. (See also 235(e).)

Jag har mycket tålamod, men du har mer.
I have a lot of patience, but you have more.

Jag har mer arbete än jag klarar av för tillfället.
I have more work than I can cope with at present.

Note: For **mer** in adjectival comparisons see 236. For **mer** in adverbial comparisons see 605(e).

(b) **Fler** or **flera** relates to a plural noun and is usually rendered by 'more' in English. (See also 235(e))

Han har fler(a) bröder än systrar.
He has more brothers than sisters.

Han har många syskon, men jag har fler.
He has a lot of brothers and sisters, but I have more.

Note, however:

Alla vill ha mer pengar.   Everyone wants more money.

(c) Fler(a) renders English 'several' and is used pronominally or attributively with a plural noun. Used pronominally (especially of people) **flera** is synonymous with **många** (see 349). The pronominal **flera** has a genitive form in **-s**.

Hon har flera vänner i England.   She has several friends in England.
Flera har skrivit och klagat.   Many people have written to complain.
på fleras begäran   in response to many people's requests

Note: Although synonymous with **flera**, **åtskilliga** is less common and almost solely reserved for more formal language.

Åtskilliga bland besättningen blev sjösjuka.
Several/A number of the crew were sea-sick.

Used attributively before a singular noun without an end article **åtskillig(t)** means 'considerable', 'a good deal of'.

åtskilligt obehag   a great deal of discomfort

(d) 'The more . . . , the more . . .' is generally rendered by Swedish **ju . . . desto . . .**, **ju . . . ju . . .** or **ju . . . dess . . .** (cf. also 242(g)). The choice of **mer** or **fler** is determined according to the criteria in (a) and (b) above. Notice the inverted word order in the second clause.

Böcker! Ju fler man läser, desto fler vill man ha!
Books! The more you read, the more you want.

Ju mer arbete jag gör, ju mer verkar jag få.
The more work I do, the more I seem to get.

Note the following expressions:

med mera (m.m.)	etc., and so on (singular/non-count nouns)
med flera (m.fl.)	etc., and so on (plural nouns)
alltmer	more and more (singular/non-count nouns)
alltfler	more and more (plural nouns)

352 'Most', **mest**, etc. – a schematic overview of Swedish use

(a) 'Most', **mest**, etc. as adjectives – summary

	Non-neuter	353	*Neuter*	353	*Plural*	353
most + noun	**den mesta glassen**	(a)(i)	**det mesta regnet**	(a)(i)	**de flesta flickor**	(c)
most of + noun	**största delen av min tid**	(b)	**största delen av vinet**	(b)	**de flesta rösterna**	(d)

(b) 'Most', **mest**, etc. as pronouns – summary

	Singular	353	Plural	353
most (subj.)	**det mesta**	(e)(iii)	**de flesta**	(e)(iv)
most (obj.)	**mest**	(e)(ii)	**flest**	(e)(v)
most of it, most of them	**största delen**	(e)(i)	**de flesta**	(e)(iv)

353 'Most', 'most of', etc.

English expressions with 'most', 'most of', etc. are rendered in a number of ways in Swedish. (Cf. 352.)

(a) 'Most' + singular noun

(i) English 'most' + singular noun or non-count noun may be translated into Swedish by **den mesta, det mesta** + singular noun with the end article:

| Most rain falls in the sea. | **Det mesta regnet faller i havet.** |
| He ate most ice-cream. | **Han åt den mesta glassen.** |

However, in many instances, this sounds contrived in Swedish. Often Swedish idiom prescribes a different mode of expression:

Regnet faller för det mesta/huvudsakligen i havet.
Most rain falls in the sea.

Han åt mer glass än någon annan.
He ate more ice cream than anyone else.

(ii) Sometimes the form **mest** + noun without end article is used, when **mest** qualifies the object of a clause and indicates some kind of comparison. Note, however, that this may lead to ambiguity with the use of **mest** as an adverb (cf. (e) below, and 607(d)):

| **Han åt mest glass.** | He ate most ice-cream. *Or* |
| | He ate mostly ice-cream. |

(b) 'Most of' + singular noun

English 'most of' + singular or non-count noun may be rendered by Swedish **största delen av** + singular noun in the definite form.

We spend most of our time here.	**Största delen av vår tid tillbringar vi här.**

(c) 'Most' + plural noun

English 'most' + plural noun signifying 'most X in general' or 'X as a whole' is generally rendered by Swedish **de flesta** + noun in the indefinite plural form (cf. the absolute superlative 244). Note, however, that this construction is usually seen only in subject positions (cf. (d) and note below).

Most children like animals.	**De flesta barn tycker om djur.**

(d) 'Most of' + plural noun, 'the most' + plural noun

English 'most of' + plural noun or 'the most' + plural noun is generally rendered by Swedish **de flesta** + noun in definite plural form.

Most (of the) children said they liked animals.
De flesta barnen sa att de tyckte om djur.

He got the most votes.	**Han fick de flesta rösterna.**

In these examples a specific comparison is implied. Cf. (c) above and 243, where this is not the case.

Note: Sometimes **de flesta** + noun in definite plural form is replaced by **flest** + noun in indefinite plural form when used with the object or prepositional object of a clause.

Han fick flest röster.	He got most votes.

(e) 'Most' used pronominally

(i) **Största delen** is used to refer to a singular or non-count noun, irrespective of gender. **Största delen** renders 'most (of it)':

Han har inte mycket pengar.	He hasn't much money.
Största delen ger han bort.	He gives most (of it) away.

(ii) **Mest** renders 'most' as an indefinite pronoun, usually in the object form.

Han åt mest – som vanligt.	He ate most – as usual.

However, if the speaker is thinking of a plural noun **de flesta** or **flest** is used (cf. (iv) and (v) below).

(iii) **Det mesta** renders 'most' as an indefinite pronoun, usually in the subject form. **Det mesta** is often followed by **av** + clause:

Det mesta av det du säger är inte sant.
Most of what you say isn't true.

(iv) **De flesta** renders 'most' in the sense 'most of them', 'most people', etc. and refers to a plural noun:

Jag samlar folkvisor på CD.	I collect folk songs on CD.
De flesta gick efter en timme.	Most (people) left after an hour.

(v) **Flest** renders 'most', 'the most' referring to a plural noun, but is characteristically used only as the object or prepositional object when some kind of comparison is intended. **Flest** is not used in the sense 'most people' (cf. (iv) above).

Alla mina vänner samlar CD-skivor. Jag har flest.
All my friends collect CDs. I have (the) most.

(f) For 'most' used with superlatives, see 236.

Note the following expressions with **mest**, 'most', etc.

För det mesta är han mycket pålitlig.	For the most part he's highly reliable.
Sin mesta tid tillbringar han borta.	He spends most of his time away from home.
Han sover mest hela dagen.	He sleeps practically all day.
De är som folk är mest/flest.	They are like most people.
Det var på sin höjd tio gäster där.	There were, at (the) most, ten guests there.
Han gjorde det bästa av situationen.	He made the most of the situation.
Vad vill du helst göra?	What would you most like to do?

354 Lite, litet

Lite and its more formal alternative **litet** (also usually pronounced /lite/) are used to render the meanings of both 'little' and 'a little' in conjunction with a non-count noun.

Sometimes **lite(t) grann** or **lite(t) grand** may be preferable when translating English 'a little', to avoid any possible confusion. Otherwise the difference between English 'little' and 'a little' is expressed by the degree of stress given to Swedish **lite(t)** in the spoken language. **Lite(t)** meaning 'a little' is unstressed. **Lite(t)** corresponding to 'little' is stressed, or prefaced by **bara** for emphasis.

All these forms are indeclinable and may be used attributively and pronominally:

Det är (bara) lite mjölk kvar.	There's little milk left.

Jag har lite grann hemma.	I have a little at home.
Gör litet och säg ännu mindre!	Do little and say even less.

Note 1: **Lite(t)** is nearly always used with substances, materials, etc. regardless of number and gender. (Cf. **mycket** 348.)

lite ost, lite vatten, lite grönsaker	a little cheese, a little water, a few vegetables
Jag har lite pengar.	I have (a) little money.

Note 2: **Lite(t)** corresponds to English 'few' in expressions such as the following (cf. also 348 Note 1 and 355(a)):

Du har tagit en banan för lite.	You have taken one banana too few.
Studenten fick tre poäng för lite.	The student got three marks too few.

Note 3: **Föga** corresponds to pronominal 'little' but it is old-fashioned and rarely encountered in modern Swedish.

Det är föga som jag kan göra.	There's little I can do.

Note 4: Note the following expressions and phrases:

Är det inte lite svårt?	Isn't it rather difficult?
Jag gjorde det lilla jag kunde.	I did what little I could.
Den lilla engelska jag kan hjälpte inte.	The little English I know was of no help.

Note 5: **Lite(t)** (like English 'little') may also be used adverbially in Swedish. See 612(a).

355 Få

(a) **Få** is used attributively and pronominally, and may usually be rendered by English 'few' or 'few people' (but not 'few things' = **få saker**). However, **få** is more literary in style than English 'few', and in the spoken language Swedes often prefer constructions with **inte många** (= 'not many').

Få saker irriterar mig mer.	Few things irritate me more.
Man ser få sådana bilar i dag.	You see few cars like that today.
Få (människor) har lidit som han.	Few people have suffered as he has.
Du är en av de få han litar på.	You're one of the few he trusts.

Note: **Lite(t)**, not **få**, corresponds to English 'few' in expressions such as the following (cf. also 348 Note 2):

Du har tagit en banan för lite	You have taken one banana too few.
Studenten fick tre poäng för lite.	The student got three marks too few.

(b) Swedish uses **några få** or **några stycken** where English has 'a few' and 'a few people'. **Några få** is most often used attributively before a plural noun, and sometimes **få** is omitted. **Några stycken** is most often used pronominally referring to a plural noun.

Jag har flugit några (få) gånger.	I have flown a few times.

Kan jag få ta några stycken?	May I have a few?
Några (få) människor klagade.	A few people complained.

Note 1: Sometimes **ett fåtal** (= 'a small number') is used in more formal Swedish, especially when the impression is that the exact quantity has been counted. **Ett fåtal** may be followed by the plural indefinite form of the noun:

Mötet samlade bara ett fåtal åhörare.	The meeting attracted only a few listeners.

Note 2: **Rätt många** corresponds to English 'a few' used colloquially to mean 'a good few'.

Han har varit där rätt många gånger!	He's been there a few times!

Note 3: **Så** is usually added before the word **få** to form the negative **inte så få** (= 'not a few'):

De har inte så få problem.	They have not a few [i.e. a lot of] problems.

356   Mindre, färre, minst

Swedish **mindre**, **minst** usually corresponds to English 'less', 'least' (referring to a non-count noun). **Färre** corresponds to English 'fewer' (referring to a count noun). However, a form of **färre** corresponding to English 'fewest' does not exist in standard Swedish. Swedish uses **minst** instead. These words may be used attributively or pronominally.

Du har bara lite mat, hon har mindre, men jag har minst.
You have only a little food, she has less, but I have least.

Här bor inte många, men snart blir de ännu färre.
There aren't many people living here, but soon there will be even fewer.

357   Lagom

Although the Swedish **lagom** ('just right', 'just enough') is, strictly speaking, an adverb (cf. 612) or adjective (206(d)), it may sometimes fulfil a function similar to that of a pronoun.

Jag har inte gott om pengar men jag har lagom.
I haven't a lot of money, but I've got just enough.

358   Swedish pronominal compounds with **som helst**, and English 'whoever', 'whatever', etc.

The commonest interrogative pronouns (see 361) serve as indefinite pronouns by adding the indeclinable **som helst**:

vem som helst	anyone, anybody (at all/you like, etc.)

vad som helst	anything (at all/you like, etc.)
vilken som helst (non-n)	
vilket som helst (neuter)	any, any one (at all, etc.)
vilka som helst (plural)	
när som helst	at any time (at all), whenever (you like)
var/vart som helst	anywhere (at all), wherever (you like)
hur . . . som helst	however + *adj., adv.* (you like, etc.)
hur som helst	any way at all, etc.

Note also:

ingen som helst (non-n)	none at all, not . . . any at all
inget som helst (neuter)	none at all, not . . . any at all
inga som helst (plural)	none what(so)ever
ingenting som helst	nothing what(so)ever

Generally **som helst** corresponds to English expressions with 'at all' as in 'anyone (at all)'. English often combines such indefinite pronouns idiomatically with tag phrases such as 'you like', 'you want', etc. Such additional phrases are not used in Swedish. Note, however, that phrases such as **vem du vill, vad du vill**, etc. are sometimes used as alternatives to **vem som helst, vad som helst**, etc. (**Du kan fråga vem du vill; Jag gör vad jag vill.**)

Vem som helst kan lära sig.	Anyone can learn.
Hon äter vad som helst.	She eats anything (at all).
Ta vilken bil som helst.	Take any car you want.
Tänk på ett tal, vilket som helst.	Think of a number, any number you like.
ingen som helst anledning	no reason at all

Note 1: **Vilken som helst** and **ingen som helst** are used both attributively and pronominally. **Vilken/ingen** agrees in gender and number with the noun to which it refers. Generally the noun appears between **vilken/ingen** and **som helst** although it may also occupy other positions (cf. 359(c)).

Note 2: For rules governing the choice of **var, vart** in the expressions **var (vart) som helst** see 613.

Note 3: **Inte någon . . . som helst** is sometimes preferred to **ingen som helst**. See 345.

Note 4: English 'anyone' used to translate **vem som helst** must not be confused with 'anyone' etc. used instead of 'someone' in interrogative and negative statements (cf. 341(b) ii).

359 Concessive 'whoever', 'whatever', etc.

(a) Swedish expresses ideas corresponding to English concessive clauses with 'whoever', 'whatever' etc. in a wide variety of ways. For Swedish equivalents to 'who ever', 'what ever', etc. properly written as two words and used interrogatively to mean 'who on earth?' etc., see (b) 7 below.

(b) 'Whoever'

	Remarks on usage	Singular	Plural	See examples
Whoever	= no matter who	vem (som) än	alla som ...	1, 2, 3
	= anyone who/ everyone who	den som ...	alla som ...	3, 4, 5
Whoever	= whoever you like/want etc.	vem som helst	vilka som helst	6
Who ever?	= who on earth?	vem i all världen	0	7

1   **Öppna inte dörren, vem som än kommer!**
     Don't open the door, whoever comes!

2   **Vem du än är, så kom fram med detsamma!**
     Come out at once, whoever you are!

3   **Säg till alla som kommer att jag är sjuk.**
     Tell whoever comes that I'm ill.

4   **Den som/Alla som stjäl åker fast förr eller senare.**
     Whoever steals is caught sooner or later.

5   **Jag vill tala med den som har hand om reklamationer.**
     I want to speak to whoever deals with complaints.

6   **Fråga vilka som helst som var med i kören!**
     Ask whoever you like who was in the choir!

7   **Vem i all världen gjorde det?**
     Who ever did that?

Note 1: **Vem som än** is used only as the subject of the clause. When this phrase is used as a predicate of the verb **vara** or **bli** (i.e. with a noun or personal pronoun), the **som** is generally omitted and **så** precedes the following clause. Cf. example (2) above.

Note 2: Note how Swedish renders the following type of phrase:

The President, or whoever it was...   **Presidenten, eller vem det nu var...**

(c) 'Whatever'

English	Remarks on usage	Swedish	See examples
Whatever	= no matter what	subj. **vad som än** ...	1
		obj. **vad ... än** ...	2
Whatever	= everything	subj. **allt som** ...	3
	= anything	obj. **allt**	4
Whatever	= the thing which	subj. **det som** ...	11
		obj. **vad/det som** ...	

English	Remarks on usage	Swedish	See examples
Whatever you like	= whatever you want	subj. **vad som helst** obj. **vad som helst**	4
What ever?	= what on earth	pronominal usage no noun **vad i all världen** **är/var det som . . .?** + noun **vad i all världen** **är/var det för . . .?**	9 10
Whatever + noun	= no matter what kind of + noun	subj. **vilken vilket,** **vilka** + noun **som än** . . . obj. **vilken vilket,** **vilka** + noun . . . **än** . . .	7
Whatever + noun	= all/any + noun = which that	subj. **all allt, alla** + noun **som** . . . obj. **all allt, alla** + noun	5
Whatever	= *negative* whatsoever	subj. **ingenting* alls** obj. **ingenting* alls**	6
No + noun whatever	= no + noun + at all	subj. & obj.: **ingen* som helst** + noun **ingen* alls** + noun **ingen*** + noun **alls** neuter: **inget* intet*,** plural: **inga***	8

* **Inte . . . någon** must sometimes be used in preference to **ingen** etc. See 345.

1   **Vad som än händer, tappa inte modet!**
     Whatever happens, don't be discouraged!

2   **Vad man än säger, tappa inte modet!**
     Whatever people say, don't be discouraged!

3   **Allt som smakar gott blir man tjock av.**
     Whatever tastes good makes you fat.

4   **Man får göra allt man vill/vad som helst.**
     You can do whatever you like.

5   **Hans sekreterare öppnar all post som kommer/all post han får.**
     His secretary opens whatever post comes/whatever post he gets.

6   **Han sa ingenting alls.**
     He said nothing what(so)ever.

7   **Vilka böcker du än har läst, så har du fått det om bakfoten.**
     Whatever books you've read, you've got it all wrong.

8   **Jag har ingen som helst lust att åka dit.**
I've no desire what(so)ever to travel there.

9   **Vad i all världen är det som har hänt?**
What ever has happened?

10   **Vad i all världen är det för böcker du har där?**
What ever books have you got there?

11   **Låt mig hämta det som/vad du behöver!**
Let me fetch whatever you need.

Note:

Jag försöker, kosta vad det vill.	I'll try, whatever the cost.
Jag försöker, hända vad som hända vill.	I'll try, whatever happens/come what may.
Jag gör det ändå.	I'll do it whatever/regardless.
Stenen, eller vad det nu var, träffade mig.	The stone, or whatever it was, hit me.
Ring eller skriv! Vilket som går lika bra.	Write or phone. It's the same to me, whatever.
Ska jag ringa eller skriva? – Vilket som!	'Shall I write or phone?' 'Whichever/Please yourself.'

(d) 'Whichever'

English	Remarks on usage	Swedish	See examples
Whichever + noun	= the noun who/which See determinatives 329	**den** + non-neuter nn **+ som** **det** + neuter noun **+ som** **de** + plural noun **+ som**	1
Whichever you like	= any one you wish	**vilken vilket, vilka** **som helst**	2, 3
Which ever + noun?		**vad är/var det för** **+ noun**	4

1   **Den lärare som sa det ljuger.**
Whichever teacher said that is lying.

2   **Rösta på vilken kandidat som helst.**
Vote for whichever candidate you like.

3   **Jag har tre pennor. Ta vilken som helst.**
I have three pens. Take whichever one you want.

4   **Vad var det för en lärare som sa det?**
Which ever teacher said that?

Note: For adverbial forms 'wherever', 'whenever', 'however', etc., see 616(e),(f).

360 'One' used to replace a noun

English 'one' ('ones') may be used idiomatically in place of a noun to avoid a repetition of that noun. Swedish usually has no equivalent to 'one' ('ones') used in place of a noun in this way, but uses a variety of techniques to express the idea.

(a) English indefinite article + adjective + 'one' (see 228(d))

> My mobile phone has broken, but I can't afford a new one.
> **Min mobil är sönder, men jag har inte råd med en ny.**

> There's only one hotel and it's an expensive one.
> **Det finns bara ett hotell och det är dyrt.**

> These shoes are too small, but I haven't any larger ones.
> **De här skorna är för små men jag har inte några större.**

(b) English definite article + adjective + 'one'

> Bergman's production of *The Magic Flute* is the best one I have ever seen.
> **Bergmans uppsättning av Trollflöjten är den bästa jag någonsin sett.**

(c) English 'one' standing alone

> He's a policeman, but he doesn't look like one.
> **Han är polis men ser inte ut som en sådan.**

(d) Other similar usages in English, where 'one' has a replacive function, are indicated below. The list is not exhaustive, but covers the most common examples.

English	Swedish	See section
another one = a different one	**en annan**, etc.	340(d)(i)
another one = an additional one	**en till**, etc.	340(d)(ii)
one another	**varandra**	335
any one	**vilken som helst**, etc.	358
each/every one	**varenda en**, etc.	333
every other one	**varannan**, etc.	334
which one?	**vilken . . . ?**, etc.	365
this/that one, etc.	**den här/den där**, etc.	325, 326(c)
the one that	**den som**, etc.	329(b)
the only one	**den enda**, etc.	228(d)

Note also:

one after the other	**den ena efter den andra**
I knew one Charlie Brown, who...	**Jag kände en (viss) Charlie Brown, som . . .**
No one man can hope to achieve so much.	**Ingen kan hoppas uppnå så mycket ensam.**

J   INTERROGATIVE PRONOUNS

361   Interrogative pronouns, introduction and form

(a) Interrogative pronouns introduce some form of a question. Interrogative pronouns in main clauses introduce a direct question (V-question, see 1036(b)); a question mark is placed at the end of the sentence. Interrogative pronouns in subordinate clauses introduce an indirect question.

(b) Form:

Usage.	Meaning	Non-neuter	Gen.	Neuter	Gen.	Plural	Gen.
362	who, whom, whose	**vem**	**vems**	–	–	**vilka**	**vilkas**
363	what	–	–	**vad**	–	**vad, vilka**	
365	which	**vilken**	+s	**vilket**	+s	**vilka**	+s
364	what kind of	**vad för en** **vad för någon** **vad för sorts** **vad för slags** **hur(u)dan**		**vad för ett** **vad för något** **vad för sorts** **vad för slags** **hur(u)dant**		**vad för (ena)** **vad för några** **vad för sorts** **vad för slags** **hur(u)dana**	
365	which (of two)	**vilkendera**	+s	**vilketdera**	+s	–	

362   Vem? vilka? in direct questions

Vem, vilka, etc. may be either the subject or object of a direct question. Swedish maintains a difference between singular and plural 'who' (**vem/vilka**), a distinction not present in English.

Vem vann guldet?	Who won the gold (medal)?
Vilka tog de andra medaljerna?	Who got the other medals?
Vem träffade du?	Who(m) did you meet?

Vem and **vilka** add **-s** to form a genitive. (See also 320(l).)

Vems är hatten?	Whose hat is it?
Vilkas bilar står därute?	Whose cars are outside?

Vem, vems and **vilka, vilkas** may be preceded by a preposition but, even in written Swedish, it is far more common for the preposition to stand at the end of the clause. This is almost invariably so in colloquial Swedish.

Vilka har du berättat detta för?   Who have you told this to?
Vems dotter blev han kär i?   Whose daughter did he fall in love with?

363   Vad? in direct questions

Vad ('what') is a neuter singular pronoun. **Vad** is used as either subject or object of a direct question. **Vad** is only rarely used with a noun (see Note 2 below): in such instances a form of **vilken** (365) is usually preferred.

Vad har hänt?   What has happened?
Vad gör ni?   What are you doing?

Although **vad** is also used to refer to things in the plural, **vilka** is used for 'what' in the plural, when some aspect of enumeration is present. Compare:

Vad har du i lådorna?   What have you got in all those boxes?
Vilka är de fyra årstiderna?   What are the four seasons?

Note 1: **Vad** is rarely preceded by a preposition when used pronominally. The preposition is placed instead at the end of the clause.

    Vad skär man ost med?   What does one cut cheese with?

In formal style a compound interrogative pronoun comprising **var** and preposition is sometimes used:

    Vari ligger problemet?   Wherein lies the problem?

Note also: **varav** ('of which'), **varmed** ('with which'), etc.

Note 2: **Vad** is used attributively only in certain idiomatic expressions, where it may be preceded by a preposition:

    I vad mån gäller föreskrifterna?   In what way do the regulations concern us?

Note 3: In colloquial Swedish **vad** is sometimes used in place of **eller hur?** to avoid repeating the verb and subject in a construction akin to English tag questions (615(b)). In such instances **vad** is invariably pronounced /va/.

    Det gjorde väl ont, vad?   I bet that hurt, didn't it?/I bet that hurt, eh?

Note 4: Swedes use **Vad?** freely to indicate that they have not heard what the speaker has said. A form more akin to English '(I beg your) pardon' but rarer in Swedish is **Hursa?** (= **Hur sa (du)?**). **Förlåt (mig)** and **Ursäkta (mig)** are usually reserved for genuine apologies.

Note 5: **Vilken (vilket, vilka)** is sometimes used as a predicate of the verb **vara** ('to be') in preference to **vad**. In such instances **vilken** agrees in number and gender with the noun to which it refers.

    Vilken är nästa hållplats?   What is the next stop?

364 Vad för? etc. in direct questions

(a) Swedish questions formulated with **vad för** + noun, **vad för en**, etc. correspond to English forms with 'what' + noun meaning 'what kind of?' These words, especially **vad för någon** etc., are colloquial in tone, but also occur in informal written Swedish.

> **vad för**
> **vad för någon (något, några . . .)**
> **vad för slags/sorts . . .**
> **vad för en (ett, ena . . .)**

(b) **Vad för, vad för sorts, vad för slags** (all indeclinable) are used with singular non-count nouns and plural nouns of all types. **Vad** may be separated from **för** (**för en, för slags**, etc.) by other words such as a finite verb, subject, etc.

Vad har du för planer i dag?	What are your plans today?
Vad för sorts mat tycker du om?	What (kind of) food do you like?
Vad för slags man skulle göra så?	What (sort of) man would do that?

Vad för sorts, vad för slags may be used without an accompanying noun.

> **Han säljer bilar. – Vad för slags?**   'He sells cars.' 'What kind?'

Note: The two indeclinable expressions **vilken sorts** and **vilket slags** have the same function and usage as **vad för sorts, vad för slags** but belong more to written Swedish than the spoken language. (See also 130(d)(iii).)

(c) **Vad för en/ett** are used before singular count nouns. **Vad för ena** is a colloquial form used only before nouns referring to people.

Vad för en bok läser du?	What kind of (a) book are you reading?
Vad för ett hus är det?	What kind of (a) house is it?
Vad för ena stackare är ni?	What kind of poor devils are you?

Except in certain idiomatic expressions (cf. Note 3 below) **vad för (en/ett)** and **vad för (någon/något)** are not used without an accompanying noun in Swedish:

> **De har en bil. – Vad för (en) bil?**   They have a car. What kind?

Note 1: **Vad för** (**vad för en, vad för slags**, etc.) are not normally preceded by a preposition. The preposition is placed instead at the end of the sentence:

> **Vad för ett hus bor ni i?**   What kind of a house do you live in?

Note 2: Colloquial Swedish frequently uses the expression **vad för något/någonting** (and analogous expressions) where **vad** alone (363) would suffice.

Vad sa du för någonting/något?	What did you say?
Var bor du någonstans?	Where do you live?
Vart gick de någonstans?	Where did they go to?

Note 3: Some idiomatic expressions:

Vad är du/han/hon för en?	What kind of person are you/is he/is she?
Vad är de för ena?	What kind of people are they?
Vad är det för dag i dag?	What day is it today?

Note 4: In recent years **hurdan** (non-neuter), **hurdant** (neuter) and **hurdana** (plural) have lost ground to expressions in (b) and (c) above and to the indeclinable adverbial form **hur**. Today they are rarely encountered apart from in one or two expressions.

Hurdant var vädret?	What was the weather like?

365 Vilken? etc. in direct questions

Vilken (vilket, vilka) is used both pronominally and attributively and corresponds to English 'which'. It is used of both persons and things, singular and plural. **Vilka** serves as the plural of **vem** (362) and under certain conditions as a plural for **vad** (363).

Vilken etc. may be preceded by a preposition, although it is more common for the preposition to stand at the end of the clause (especially in spoken Swedish).

Vilken etc. forms a genitive by adding **-s**.

Note that the English 'one' (after 'which' used pronominally or in the genitive) has no direct equivalent in Swedish.

Vilka skor är dina?	Which shoes are yours?
Vilken skola går du i?	Which school do you go to?
Vilkas bilar blev förstörda?	Whose cars were wrecked?
Vilket av husen är ert?	Which of the houses is yours?
En av dem ljuger – men vilken?	One of them is lying – but which (one)?

Note 1: **Vilkendera** (non-neuter) and **vilketdera** (neuter) may be used to indicate a choice between two or more alternatives, even though **vilken, vilket** normally suffices (cf. also 336). When used with a noun, the noun takes the definite form. **Vilkendera** and **vilketdera** have genitive forms in **-s**.

Vilkendera boken tycker du bäst om?	Which book/Which of the books do you like best?
Vilketdera förslaget är mest praktiskt?	Which suggestion is most practical?

Note 2: **Vilken, vilket, vilka** also serve other functions. See 368 for exclamations with **vilken**, and 371(b) for **vilken** as a relative pronoun.

366 Interrogative pronouns in indirect questions

All the interrogative pronouns may be used in indirect questions. In such instances interrogative pronouns are invariably used to introduce a subordinate clause (see 820 ff.). When interrogative pronouns are used as the subject of a subordinate clause they are followed by **som** (except **vad för (slags)** etc., **hurdan** etc. and **vilken sorts, vilket slags**). This **som** has no equivalent in English (see also 370 below).

Som is added as a subject marker when the subject is an interrogative pronoun or a phrase containing an interrogative as qualifier. **Som** is optional after elements other than the subject. Compare:

Jag undrar ...	I wonder ...
... vad (O) han gör.	... what he's doing.
... vad som (S) händer.	... what's happening.
... vilka skor som (S) är mina.	... which shoes are mine.
... vilka (O) (som) jag missade.	... who (plural) I missed.

367 Interrogative pronouns in direct and indirect questions

As subject in a main clause *i.e. in direct questions*	*As subject in a subordinate clause* *i.e. in indirect questions*
Vem har gjort det? Who has done it?	**Jag undrar, vem som har gjort det?** I wonder who has done it.
Vad har hänt? What has happened?	**Vet du, vad som har hänt?** Do you know what has happened?
Vilken väg är kortast? Which route is shortest?	**Vet du, vilken väg som är kortast?** Do you know which route is shortest?
Hurdant var vädret? What was the weather like?	**Jag undrar, hurdant vädret var.** I wonder what the weather was like.
Vad är det för något? What is it?	**Vet du, vad det är för något?** Do you know what it is?

As object in a main clause *i.e. in direct questions*	*As object in a subordinate clause* *i.e. in indirect questions*
Vem såg du? Who(m) did you see?	**Jag vet inte, vem du såg.** I don't know who(m) you saw.
Vad gör de? What are they doing?	**Jag undrar, vad de gör.** I wonder what they are doing.
Vilket äpple tog han? Which apple did he take?	**Vet du, vilket äpple han tog?** Do you know which apple he took?
Vad läser du för bok? What kind of book are you reading?	**Jag vet vad du läser för bok.** I know what kind of book you are reading.

368   Vilken (vilket, vilka) = 'What (a)' + noun in exclamations

Vilken, **vilket** or **vilka** agreeing in gender and number with the following noun is used in exclamations etc. in the same way as the English 'what' or 'what a'. (Cf. also **sådan**, 328 Note 1.) Note that there is no indefinite article in Swedish in such expressions.

Vilken härlig dag!	What a lovely day!
Vilket dåligt väder!	What awful weather!
Vilken tur vi hade!	What luck (we had)!
Vilka (dumma) idéer!	What (stupid) ideas!

K   RELATIVE PRONOUNS

369   Relative pronouns, introduction and form

(a) A relative pronoun refers back to one or more words (the 'correlative') in the same sentence.

(b) Form:

	Non-neuter	*Neuter*	*Plural*	*Usage cf.*
subject	**som**	**som**	**som**	370
object	**som**	**som**	**som**	370
(formal style) subject	**vilken**	**vilket**	**vilka**	371
(formal style) object	**vilken**	**vilket**	**vilka**	
subject	–	**vad som**	–	373
object	–	**vad**	–	373
(formal style) genitive	**vars**	**vars**	**vilkas**	372
(formal style) genitive	**vilkens**	**vilkets**	**vilkas**	372

370   Som

(a) Som is by far the most common relative pronoun, practically the only one used in conversation and common in all forms of written Swedish.

Som is indeclinable and may thus be used as a subject or object referring to a correlative of either gender or number.

Som corresponds to English 'who(m)', 'which' or 'that'. After 'such' and 'the same' **som** corresponds to 'as'.

Mannen, som bor i Malmö, har fyra barn som han aldrig sett.
The man, who lives in Malmö, has four children whom he has never seen.

Griskött som man äter kallas fläsk.
Meat from a pig that you eat is called 'pork'.

Är rummet sådant som ni önskade?
Is the room (such) as you wished (it to be)?

Jag har samma lärare som min syster.
I have the same teacher as my sister.

Note also the use of **som** in expressions such as:

Jag glömmer aldrig den dagen (som) jag vann Vasaloppet.
I'll never forget the day (when) I won the Vasa Ski race.

(b) Som + preposition

If **som** is combined with a preposition, the preposition must be placed at the end of the clause.

Jag vill ha en fåtölj som är bekväm att sitta i.
I want an armchair that is comfortable to sit in/in which it is comfortable to sit.

Städerna som de flyttar till är redan överbefolkade.
The towns they are moving to are already overpopulated.

If the length or complexity of a relative clause makes it impractical to place a preposition at the end of the clause, **som** is replaced by a suitable form of **vilken** etc., which, unlike **som**, may be preceded by a preposition. (Cf. 371(a)(i).)

(c) Omitting **som** (see 1040(b))

Som may be omitted when used as an object.

Pengar man har på banken ger ränta.
Money (that) you have in the bank yields interest.

Här är en rolig historia ni kommer att skratta åt.
Here's a funny story (that) you will laugh at.

In contrast to English usage **som** is never omitted when occupying the subject position.

Pojken som står därborta är min son.
The boy (who is) standing over there is my son.

Note: Position of **som** and correlative

When using the relative **som** it is important to remember that the correlative should stand directly before the relative pronoun in Swedish. If you say *Hunden fick ett ben av slaktaren som den åt upp, then the Swedish **som** refers to the butcher (= 'The dog got a bone from the butcher who(m) it ate up'). The sentence should read **Hunden fick av slaktaren ett ben som den åt upp** (= 'The dog got a bone from the butcher which it ate up').

A greater degree of latitude in the positioning of correlative and relative pronoun is permissible when **vilken** etc. is used, since it agrees in gender and/or number with the correlative (see 371).

371 Vilken, vilket, vilka

The gender and/or number of the correlative determines whether the form **vilken**, **vilket** or **vilka** is used as a relative pronoun. As a relative pronoun **vilken** etc. is rarely used other than in formal written Swedish and as in (b) below. **Vilken** etc. may not be used as a relative pronoun after **ingen**, **någon**, **sådan**, **samma** or a superlative. **Som** is used in such instances.

(a) As a rule **vilken** etc. should only be used instead of **som** in the following instances:

(i) When, for stylistic reasons, it is necessary for a preposition or prepositional phrase to precede the relative pronoun. The length and/or complexity of a relative clause may make it impractical, for example, to place a preposition at the end of the clause (cf. 370(b)).

Detta är brevet i vilket hon först skrev om sina upplevelser i skärgården.
This is the letter in which she first wrote about her experiences in the skerries.

en här, i spetsen för vilken stod en utmärkt general
an army, at the head of which was a distinguished general

(ii) To clarify the relationship between the relative pronoun and its correlative. In the following Swedish examples the respective use of the singular and plural forms makes clear whether the coin alone, or both key and coin, slipped into the crack.

I lådan finns en nyckel och ett mynt, vilket har glidit ner i en springa.
In the drawer are a key and a coin, which has slipped down into a crack.

I lådan finns en nyckel och ett mynt, vilka har glidit ner i en springa.
In the drawer are a key and a coin, which have slipped down into a crack.

(iii) When a noun or adjective is added after the relative pronoun. This attributive usage of the relative pronoun is rare outside formal written Swedish. **Som** is not be used in this way.

Man diskuterade arbetslösheten bland ungdomarna, vilket problem verkar bli allt större.
They discussed unemployment among young people, a problem that seems to be on the increase.

Bland rovdjuren finns kattfamiljen och hundfamiljen samt hyenorna, vilka sistnämnda utgör en övergångsform mellan de två andra.
Among the beasts of prey are the cat and dog families as well as the hyenas, the latter comprising an intermediate form between the other two.

(b) The neuter singular form of the pronoun, **vilket**, must be used when the relative pronoun refers to a complete clause. **Något som** is also used in this context, but not **som** alone (370).

Han är arbetslös, vilket förvånar mig.
He is unemployed, which surprises me.

Jag köpte en ny bil, vilket var dumt av mig.
I bought a new car, which was foolish of me.

Compare:

Hon sjöng en sång för mig som jag tyckte mycket om.
She sang me a song that I liked. [i.e. I liked the song that she sang]

Hon sjöng en sång för mig, något som/vilket jag tyckte mycket om.
She sang me a song – which I liked. [i.e. I liked the fact that she sang]

Note, however, the idiomatic usage of **som** in the following expressions:

Nu känner jag mig bra igen, som väl är.
Now I feel well again, which is a good thing.

Som naturligt är, försökte hon försvara sina barn.
She tried to protect her children, as is only natural.

372 Vars and the genitive forms of the relative pronoun

The genitive forms of the relative pronoun are followed by a noun in the indefinite form. (See 223(d))

(a) Vars

The indeclinable relative pronoun **vars** serves as the genitive form of **som** in the singular. **Vars** may be preceded by a preposition.

Damen, vars hund skäller hela dagen, är stendöv.
The lady whose dog barks all day is stone deaf.

Det är ett påstående vars giltighet jag ifrågasätter.
It is a statement the validity of which I question.

Familjen i vars hus vi bor kommer snart tillbaka.
The family in whose house we are living are soon coming back.

(b) Vilkens, vilkets

These are the genitive singular forms of the relative pronouns **vilken** and **vilket** (371). **Vilkens** and **vilkets** may be preceded by a preposition. They are rarely used today except in formal written Swedish.

(c) Vilkas is the genitive plural form of the relative pronoun. **Vilkas** may be preceded by a preposition.

Barn vilkas föräldrar arbetar kommer ofta hem till ett tomt hus.
Children whose parents work often come home to an empty house.

(d) In colloquial Swedish both **vars** and **vilkas** are often avoided by using a construction with the relative **som** (370) + preposition or a relative clause.

En man vars namn alla känner. → **En man som alla känner namnet på.**
A man whose name everyone knows.

Alla vilkas namn börjar på S. → **Alla som har namn som börjar på S.**
All those whose names begin with S.

373 Vad and vad som

Vad is indeclinable and can be considered to represent an indefinite neuter singular concept. **Vad** is not used attributively.

(a) Used as an object or after a preposition the relative pronoun **vad** = **det som** ('that which', 'what').

Jag gör vad jag kan.
I do what I can.

Uppskjut inte till morgondagen vad du kan göra idag!
Do not put off until tomorrow what you can do today.

Av vad du säger verkar problemet vara löst.
From what you say the problem seems to be solved.

(b) In a relative clause following **allt**, the word **vad** may be used as an object instead of **som**, although this usage is rather formal.

Hon ger allt vad hon äger till de fattiga.
She gives everything she owns to the poor.

Note: When combined with **allt**, the word **vad** may not be preceded by a preposition. The preposition must instead be placed at the end of the relative clause.
Allt vad jag har sett fram emot är borta.   Everything I've looked forward to is gone.

(c) When used as the subject of a relative clause **vad** is followed by **som**.

Vad som göms i snö kommer upp i tö.
What is hidden in the snow comes up in the thaw. [Swedish proverb]

Säg alltid vad som är sant.
Always say what is true.

Note: Observe the position of the verb in certain common idiomatic expressions where **vad** is used as the subject of a relative clause without **som**.
Vad mig angår är jag fortfarande intresserad.
As far as I am concerned, I am still interested.

Jag ramlade och, vad värre var, jag bröt benet.
I fell and, what is worse, I broke my leg.

Båten är gammal och, vad mera är, den läcker!
The boat is old and what is more it leaks!

4 NUMERALS

A   FORMS OF NUMERALS
401   Cardinal and ordinal numbers
402   **En, ett** or **ena**?
403   **Två-, tve-**, etc.
404   **Hundra, tusen, miljon**, etc.
405   Some other expressions indicating numerical quantities

B   THE USE OF CARDINAL NUMBERS
406   Notes on the use of cardinal numbers
407   Nouns formed with **-tal**
408   Age
409   Temperature
410   Mathematical expressions

C   THE USE OF ORDINAL NUMBERS
411   Notes on the use of ordinal numbers

D   FRACTIONS
412   Fractions formed from ordinal numbers
413   **Halv**, 'half', etc., 'quarter'

E   DATES
414   Years
415   Months, weeks, days

F   THE TIME
416   The time

A FORMS OF NUMERALS

401 Cardinal and ordinal numbers

List of cardinal and ordinal numbers. For the use of figures and words see 1212.

Cardinal			See section	Ordinal	
0	noll	zero	Note 5 below		
1	en, ett	one	402	första	first
2	två	two	403	andra	second
3	tre	three	403(b)	tredje	third
4	fyra			fjärde	
5	fem			femte	
6	sex			sjätte	
7	sju			sjunde	
8	åtta			åttonde	
9	nio			nionde	
10	tio			tionde	
11	elva			elfte	
12	tolv			tolfte	
13	tretton			trettonde	
14	fjorton			fjortonde	
15	femton			femtonde	
16	sexton			sextonde	
17	sjutton			sjuttonde	
18	arton		Note 6 below	artonde	
19	nitton			nittonde	
20	tjugo			tjugonde	
21	tjugoen (-ett)		402(c)	tjugoförsta	
22	tjugotvå			tjugoandra	
30	trettio			trettionde	
40	fyrtio			fyrtionde	
50	femtio			femtionde	
60	sextio			sextionde	
70	sjuttio			sjuttionde	
80	åttio			åttionde	
90	nittio			nittionde	
100	(ett) hundra		404	(ett) hundrade	
101	(ett) hundraen (-ett)			(ett) hundraförsta	
1000	(ett) tusen		404	(ett) tusende	
1001	(ett) tusenen (-ett)			(ett) tusenförsta	
3 254	tretusentvåhundrafemtiofyra		Note 3 below	tretusentvåhundrafemtiofjärde	
1 000 000	en miljon		404	en miljonte	
1 000 000 000	en miljard		404		

Note 1: There is no **och** between elements in compounded cardinal/ordinal numbers except in **Tusen och en natt**, *A Thousand and One Nights*. Compound numbers under a million are usually written as one word, unless this becomes inordinately long, in which case there is a gap after the thousands.

Note 2: Words for numbers 101–199, 201–299, etc. are written as one word in Swedish. Words for numbers over 1,000 tend to be compounded.

niohundranittioniotusen tvåhundrafjorton
nine hundred and ninety-nine thousand two hundred and fourteen

Note 3: The gap between the thousands in numbers written as figures corresponds to use of the English comma (see 1302(j)):

Swedish: **3 254**   English: 3,254

Note 4: Cardinal numbers may take a genitive in -s

de nios pris   The Nine's Prize

Note 5: **Noll** translates variously as 'nought', 'zero', 'oh', 'nil', 'love', 'duck'.

Note 6: **Arton** is a contraction of the older form **aderton**. This older form is still retained in more formal usage. The eighteen members of **Svenska Akademien** (the Swedish Academy of Letters) are referred to as **De aderton**.

Note 7: Pronunciation of some numerals:

Nio, tio and compounds in **-nio, -tio** are often pronounced /nie/, /tie/. The spelling **nie, tie** may also be encountered in colloquial Swedish. **Tjugo** is often pronounced /tjugi/, /tjugu/ or /tjuge/. **Tjugoett, tjugotvå**, etc. are often pronounced /tjuett/, /tjutvå/, etc.

Note 8: **Trettio, fyrtio**, etc. frequently appear in the shorter forms **tretti, fyrti**, etc., which correspond to the usual pronunciation of these numbers: **trettio** /tretti/, **fyrtio** /förti/.

Note 9: Ordinal numbers are derived from cardinal numbers by adding the suffixes **-dje, -de, -te, -nde**. Occasionally this requires some modification of the stems: cf. **åtta – åttonde, elva – elfte**.

Note 10: **Tjugonde, trettionde**, etc. are pronounced /tjugonde/, /trettionde/, etc., but notice: **tjugoförsta** /tjuförsta/ and **trettioförsta** /trettiförsta/, etc. (Cf. notes 7, 8 above.)

402   En, ett or ena?

(a) The choice of **en** or **ett** to translate the English word 'one' is determined by the gender of the following noun if there is one. See 101ff., 131.

en buss   one bus
ett tåg   one train

(b) Ett is used in general counting, calculating and time by the clock:

ett, två, tre	**tjugoett**	**hundraett**
one, two, three	twenty-one	a hundred and one

Klockan är ett.   It's one o'clock.

(c) If what is being counted is specified then a choice must be made between **en** and **ett** according to the gender of the noun being counted:

tjugoen hundar	twenty-one dogs	(cf. **en hund**)
trettioett barn	thirty-one children	(cf. **ett barn**)

Note also the use of the singular in expressions such as:

en och en halv dag	one and a half days	(cf. **en dag**)
ett och ett halvt år	one and a half years	(cf. **ett år**)

When the English '(the) one' is used as a pronoun or an attributive adjective the equivalent Swedish expression **den/det ena** is used (340(c)). **Ena** has a masculine form **ene**:

Den ene säger ett, den andre ett annat.
The one (*or:* One man) says one thing, the other (*or:* another) says another thing.

Jag har ont i (det) ena ögat.
One of my eyes hurts.

Den ena systern är död.
The one sister (*or:* One of the sisters) is dead.

en kyrka, vars ena torn är snett
a church, one tower of which is crooked

från det ena till det andra
from one thing to another

Note 1: The usual rules for the use of **en** and **ett** do not always apply in the case of compound words (cf. (a) above).

en enrumslägenhet	a one-roomed flat	(cf. **ett rum**)
enögd	one-eyed	(cf. **ett öga**)
en ettåring	a one-year-old	(cf. **ett år**)

Note 2: **en** sometimes means 'about', 'approximately'. See 141.

403 Två-, tve-, etc.

(a) 'Two' + noun in the definite declension (217) is often rendered by **båda** + noun:

de båda bröderna	the two brothers
mina båda systrar	my two sisters

See also 347.

(b) The form **tu** ('two') is used for **två** in certain fixed expressions.

på tu man hand	privately [i.e. 'between the two of us']
ett, tu, tre	all of a sudden [*lit.* 'one, two, three']

(c) Tvenne and **trenne** are archaic forms of **två, tre**.

(d) The prefix **tve-** (no longer used to form new words) is found in some words to indicate **två**:

> **tvedräkt** discord; **tvegifte** bigamy; **tvehågsen** in two minds; **tvetydig** ambiguous; **tvestjärt** earwig; **tveeggad** double-edged.

Otherwise **två-** is generally used as the first element in a compound:

> **tvåfärgad** two-tone; **tvåmanstält** two-man tent; **tvåstavig** bisyllabic; etc.

Note 1: **ett par = två**:
  ett par skor, a pair of shoes; **800 kronor paret** 800 kronor the pair; **ett äkta par** a married couple.

Note 2: **ett par = några få**:
  ett par hundra man a couple of hundred men; **ett par tre stycken** one or two.

404 Hundra, tusen, miljon, etc.

(a) Hundra, tusen are neuter nouns of the sixth declension with no separate plural form.

> **trehundra kronor**   three hundred crowns

Note that: 'a hundred' = **hundra** (cf. 140(f)), 'one hundred' = **ett hundra** or **etthundra**, 'a thousand' = **tusen**, 'one thousand' = **ett tusen**.

For numerals between 1100 and 1999 in dates and prices **hundra** is often used:

> **1500 kronor**   **femtonhundra kronor**
> **(År) 1968**   **nittonhundrasextioåtta**
> but: **2034**   **tvåtusenochtrettiofyra**

Note 1: Indeclinable **hundra, tusen** occasionally have the archaic forms **hundrade, tusende** (neuter 4th declension) (cf. ordinals).
  Må han/hon leva uti hundrade år!   May he/she live for a hundred years!
Note 2: A hundred thousand (100,000) = **hundratusen**.

(b) Miljon, biljon, miljard are non-neuter nouns of the third declension with a plural in **-er**.

> **tre miljoner människor**   three million people

Note that: 'a/one million' = **en miljon**.

Note the alternative spellings of these words: **million, billion, milliard**.

405   Some other expressions indicating numerical quantities

(a)   ett dussin = tolv
    ett dussin knivar   a dozen knives
    ett halvt dussin   half a dozen (NB word order, cf. 413(a))

(b)   ett tjog = tjugo
    Vi köpte ett tjog ägg.   We bought a score of eggs.

(c)   ett gross = 144
    ett gross häftstift   a gross of drawing pins

(d)   ett ris = 500 blad
    ett ris papper   a ream of paper

B   THE USE OF CARDINAL NUMBERS

406   Notes on the use of cardinal numbers

(a) The cardinals numbers themselves are regarded as neuter concepts in Swedish. However, Swedish has special forms of the cardinal numbers up to twelve that are used as non-neuter nouns, i.e. **en etta, en tvåa, en trea, en fyra, en femma, en sexa, en sjua, en åtta, en nia, en tia, en elva, en tolva** (plurals **ettor, tvåor, treor**, etc.) These are used to indicate:

(i) Numeral, i.e. 'a one', 'two threes', etc.

    Jag kan inte skilja på hans fyror och hans sjuor.
    I can't tell his fours from his sevens.

Notice that: **en nolla** means both 'a nought' and 'a nobody', 'an unimportant person'.

(ii) Number of house, bus, train, class, ward in a hospital:

    Han tar sjuan till arbetet.   He takes the number seven to work.

(iii) Size of flat:

    De hyr en trea i Tensta.   They have a five-room flat in Tensta.
                           [three rooms plus kitchen and bathroom]

(iv) Position in a race:

Vårt lag blev trea.　　　　　Our team came third.

(v) Road classification:

Vi tar E4-an till Stockholm.　　We will take the E4 to Stockholm.

(vi) Size of clothes, shoes, etc.:

Fyrtiettorna passar mig bäst.　　The (shoe) size forty-one fits me best.

(vii) Some coins, notes, etc.:

en femma a five-kronor coin; **en tia** a ten-kronor coin
cf. **en tjugolapp, femtilapp, hundralapp, tusenlapp.**

(viii) For clarification, over the telephone, for example (see 1202).

(b) The noun **stycken**, abbreviation **st.** (plural of **ett stycke**) is often inserted after numerals:

fem stycken apelsiner　　　　five oranges
Vi har beställt hundra stycken.　　We have ordered a hundred.
Kan jag få fem stycken?　　　Could I have five (of them)?

(c) Gång -en, -er is used to indicate frequency: **en gång** once; **två gånger** twice; **tre gånger** three times, etc.

(d) 'Twofold', etc.: Multiplication is indicated by employing derivatives of cardinal numbers formed with the suffixes **-faldig(t), -dubbel(t).** The suffix **-faldig(t)** corresponds to the English '-fold' in 'twofold', 'sixfold', etc. and is generally used in expressions where English has 'in duplicate', 'in triplicate', etc. The suffix **-dubbel(t)** corresponds to the English 'double', 'triple (treble)', 'quadruple', etc.

Det kostar dubbelt så mycket som förra året.
It costs twice as much as last year.

Syftet med resan var tvåfaldigt.
The purpose of the trip was twofold.

tredubbla fönster
triple glazing

Also: **flerfaldigt (-dubbelt)** several times; **mångfaldigt (-dubbelt)** many times.

Note: **Enfaldig** = stupid, simpleminded. **Enda** (= 'only one') or **enkel** is used instead to indicate 'single':

Han har inte en enda vän.	He hasn't a single friend.
En enkel till Luleå, tack.	A single (ticket) to Luleå, please.

(e) For the use of **var** (each, every) in regular distributions see 332(b).

407   Nouns formed with -tal

Neuter nouns may be formed by adding **-tal** to cardinal numbers. These nouns have the following meanings:

(a) An approximate number:

ett hundratal män	about a hundred men
ett tjugotal bilar	twenty or so cars, twenty-odd cars, some twenty cars

Words indicating an indefinite number may be derived from these nouns by adding **-s**:

hundratals män/bilar	hundreds of men/cars

See also 141.

(b) A decade or century:

Han dog på femtiotalet.	He died in the fifties. [i.e. 1950s, 1850s, etc.]
på 1900-talet (nittonhundratalet)	in the 20th century, in the 1900s
1200-talets korståg	the Crusades of the 13th century
2000-talet (tjugohundratalet)	the 21st century

Note 1: A related construction is also used to indicate the decade of a person's birth:

sjuttitalister	people born in the 1970s

Note 2: Swedish literary historians often divide periods according to decades:

Åttiotal och nittiotal	(writing from) the eighties and nineties (1880s, 1890s)
Tiotalister, fyrtiotalister	writers active in the 1910s/1940s

Note 3: Rare alternatives to using **-talet** are forms using **sekel (seklet)** and **århundrade (-t)**:

1800-talet = det nittonde seklet = det nittonde århundradet (1800–1899)	
Kärlek i tjugonde seklet	Love in the twentieth century

408 Age

There are a number of ways of expressing age. Compare:

Åke är tre år (gammal).	Åke is three (years old).
Åke är i treårsåldern.	Åke is three (years old).
Åke är en treåring.	Åke is a three-year-old.
Åke är en treårig pojke.	Åke is a three-year-old boy.

Note: He is in his fifties. **Han är i femtiårsåldern/Han har fyllt femtio.**
She is thirty something. **Hon är i trettiåren.**

409 Temperature

Swedes use the centigrade scale: **0°C (Celsius)** = 32° F

Termometern visar –5° C (fem minusgrader).
The thermometer reads minus five (degrees).

Idag är det fem grader kallt/minus fem.
Today it's minus five.

Termometern visar +15°C (femton plusgrader).
The thermometer reads (plus) fifteen (degrees).

Idag är det femton grader (varmt)/Idag är det plus femton.
Today it's fifteen degrees.

Idag är det 0°C (noll grader).
Today it is zero.

410 Mathematical expressions

(a) Note the following:

=	**(är) lika med**	equals
+	**plus**	plus
−	**minus**	minus
<	**större än**	greater than
>	**mindre än**	less than
˙ or . or ×	**gånger**	multiplied by
:	**delat med/dividerat med**	divided by
%	**procent**	per cent
‰	**promille**	per thousand, mille
√	**roten ur/av**	square root of

(b) Some mathematical expressions:

	att addera till to add to
	att subtrahera från to subtract from
$4 + 5 = 9$	**fyra plus fem är (lika med) nio**
$12 - 2 = 10$	**tolv minus två är (lika med) tio**
	att multiplicera med to multiply by
	att dela med to divide by
$6 \cdot 3 = 18$	**sex gånger tre är (lika med) arton**
$25:5 = 5$	**tjugofem delat med fem är (lika med) fem**
$2^2 = 4$	**kvadraten på två är fyra**
$10^3 = 1000$	**tio upphöjt till tre är (lika med) tusen**
$\sqrt{16} = 4$	**roten/kvadratroten ur sexton är (lika med) fyra**

Note 1: In modern Swedish maths books **200 × 45** is a measurement of area (200 by 45).

Note 2: The decimal point in English is a **decimalkomma** in Swedish

5,62   5.62

Note 3: The comma used to indicate thousands and millions in English usually has no equivalent in Swedish (cf. 401 Note 3):

3 000   3,000
4 567 000   4,567,000

C THE USE OF ORDINAL NUMBERS

411 Notes on the use of ordinal numbers

(a) Notice the following nouns derived from ordinal numbers (See also 407):

ett årtionde	a decade
ett århundrade	a century
ett årtusende	a millennium

(b) Ordinal numbers are found with the front article, or after a possessive or noun in the s-genitive form (but see also 224 (a)(v)ff.):

Det är den första idag.	It is the first (of the month) today.
Det är Olles tredje bil.	It is Olle's third car.
Det är hans andra fru.	It is his second wife.

(c) **Första, andra** (and compounds ending in **-första, -andra**) end in **-e** when referring to male persons (see 217, 219 (g)):

förste stadsläkare	principal medical officer

All other ordinals have one form only, ending in **-e**.

(d) Andra meaning 'second' should not be confused with **andra** (the definite form of **annan**) meaning 'other' (cf. 340). Notice the following:

Vi har sålt den andra bilen	We have sold the other car.
Många har en andra bil.	Many (people) have a second car.

(e) Notice that 'firstly', 'secondly', 'thirdly' = **för det första, för det andra, för det tredje**.

(f) Ordinal numbers are also frequently found in the names of kings and popes:

Erik den fjortonde	(King) Erik XIV
Pius den tolfte	(Pope) Pius XII

(g) Ordinal numbers are used to indicate frequency of occurrence:

en gång var fjortonde dag	once every fourteen days/a fortnight [cf. 332(a)]

Notice also:

varannan vecka	every two weeks/second week/other week [cf. 334]

(h) **1:a, 2:a, 3:e** are common abbreviations for **första, andra, tredje** and this series may be extended: **101:a, 103:e**. The colon and the final letter of the ordinal number may be omitted if the context makes it clear that an ordinal number is being used (cf. 415(b)).

3 pers. pres.	=	**tredje person presens** 3rd person present tense
21 lönegraden	=	**tjugoförsta lönegraden** the 21st point on the salary scale

Note: Some miscellaneous differences in the use of ordinals in English and Swedish:

ettans växel	first gear
första sidan	the front page
Vi tar sakerna i tur och ordning.	First things first.
Jag tänkte inte närmare på det.	I didn't give it a second thought.
min näst bästa kostym	my second best suit
staden nummer tre i storlek	the third largest town
vid första bästa tillfälle	at the first available opportunity

(j) Most fractions are formed from ordinal numbers. See 412 below.

D FRACTIONS

412 Fractions formed from ordinal numbers

(a) Fractions are largely formed from ordinal numbers by adding the noun suffix
-del (**en del** = 'a part', 'share') :

¼ = **en fjärdedel**
¾ = **tre fjärdedelar**
¼ l. = **en fjärdedels liter**

(b) Notice:

(i) In **en åttondel** (1/8), **en tiondel** (1/10) the **-de** ending of the ordinal number is
assimilated. This also applies to ordinals ending in **-onde**: **en artondel** (1/18).

(ii) In fractions constructed from ordinals such as **tjugoförsta**, **tjugoandra**, etc.
the suffixes **-första**, **-andra** are replaced by **-ente-** and **-tvåon-**:

en tjugoentedel (1/21)   **en tjugotvåondel** (1/22)

(c) Notice the use of fractions in Swedish where English has a cardinal number:

att dela något i fjärdedelar   to divide something into four

413 Halv,'half', etc.,'quarter'

(a) 'Half' = **halv, -t, -a** (adjective)

en halv sida	half a page [NB word order]
halva sidan	half the page
ett halvt äpple	half an apple
halva äpplet	half the apple
en och en halv månad	1½ months
ett och ett halvt år	1½ years
två och en halv månad(er)	2½ months

See also 416 (a)(c), 1105.9.

Note 1: **halv två, halv tio**, etc. = half past one, half past nine, etc. (Cf. 416.)

Note 2: Notice also the archaic forms:

halvannan månad 1½ months
halvtannat år 1½ years

(b) 'Half' = **hälft, -en, -er** (noun: 'a part/half share of something')

hälften av hans pengar	half (of) his money
första hälften av boken	the first half of the book
ta hälften var	take half each
bröd av hälften råg och	bread made from half rye and half
hälften vete	wheat
hälften så stor som	half as big as
hälften av pojkarna blev sjuka	half of the boys were ill
	[NB plural adjective, cf. 211]

(c) 'Half'= **halva,-n,-or** (noun: usually 'a small quantity of' [coffee, alcohol, etc.])

en halva brännvin	a half bottle of schnapps
halvan (*as in:* **helan och halvan**)	the second glass of schnapps

But note:

att dela något i två halvor	to divide something in half

(d) 'Half'= **halvt** (adverb)

halvt vansinnig	half insane
halvt på skämt	half jokingly, half in jest
halvt om halvt lova något	to half promise something

(e) 'Quarter' = (i) **en fjärdedel**, (ii) **en kvart(s)**. These are synonymous in:

en kvarts/fjärdedels mil a quarter of a (Swedish) mile (i.e. 1½ English miles); **ett kvarts kilo kaffe** ¼ kg of coffee; **ett kvarts sekel** a quarter of a century; **tre kvarts liter** ¾ litre.

But notice:

en kvart	a quarter of an hour [See also 416]
att dela något i fjärdedelar	to divide something into four

E   DATES

414   Years

(a) Years are most often written in figures in Swedish (cf. 1212), but when written in full they appear as one word. The word **hundra** is never omitted in Swedish.

1994 = nittonhundranittiofyra   nineteen ninety-four
1295 = tolvhundranittiofem   twelve ninety-five

Swedes use **tusen** in dates only for the years 1000–1099, 2000–2099, etc.

Island blev kristet år 1000 (tusen).
Iceland became Christian in the year 1000 (ten hundred or one thousand).

Note: Swedish does not use **och** in years, dates:

Huset blir betalt först år 2025 (tvåtusentjugofem).
The house will not be paid for until 2025 (two thousand and twenty-five).

For centuries see 407(b).

(b) The preposition 'in' before years in English has no equivalent in Swedish. (See 724(b).)

1990 avgick Carlsson.   In 1990 Carlsson resigned.

However, written Swedish frequently has **år** (= '(in the) year') before years expressed in numerals. This is almost invariably the case when such dates would otherwise begin a sentence.

Författaren är född (år) 1944.   The author was born in 1944.
År 1918 slutade första världskriget.   The First World War ended in 1918.

(c) Genitive of year dates:

2002-års val   the election of 2002
1954-års världsmästare   the world champion of 1954

415   Months, weeks, days

(a) Months of the year do not have a capital letter in Swedish unless they begin a sentence.

januari	**maj**	**september**
februari	**juni**	**oktober**
mars	**juli**	**november**
april	**augusti**	**december**

All months have non-neuter gender (see 102(c)). They do not have a plural form:

en kall januari   a cold January

November brukar vara grå.	November is usually grey.

(b) As in English the corresponding ordinal number is used to express the date in a particular month. Notice that Swedish does not generally have any equivalent for 'th', 'rd' or 'st' in English dates or for the word 'of' before the month in English idiom.

den 3 (tredje) januari 2005	3rd (the third of) January 2005

(i) Swedes often give dates beginning with the year on letterheads: **2003-10-04** = 4.10.2003 (British English) or: 10.04.2003 (US English). See 1312.

(ii) The preposition 'on' before dates in English has no equivalent in Swedish (see 724(b)).

(c) Days of the week do not have a capital letter in Swedish unless they begin a sentence: **måndag, tisdag, onsdag, torsdag, fredag, lördag, söndag.**

(d) Frequent use is made of the fact that Swedish diaries and calendars generally number the weeks of the year for ease of reference.

Jag är i London vecka 26.	I'll be in London in week 26 (i.e. end of June).

F THE TIME

416 The time

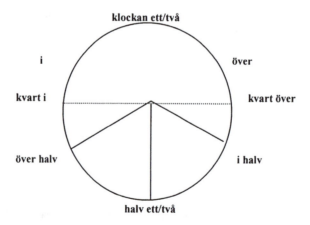

(a) 'What is the time?' etc.

(i) Examples:

Hur mycket är klockan?	What time is it?
Vad är klockan?	What is the time?
Klockan/Hon är ett.	It is one o'clock.
(See 106(f), 305(a)(ii) 3)	
Klockan är tolv.	It is twelve o'clock.
Klockan är en minut över ett.	It is one minute past one.
Klockan är fem (minuter) över tre.	It is five (minutes) past three.
Klockan är (en) kvart över fyra.	It is (a) quarter past four.
Klockan är 15 minuter över fyra.	It is fifteen minutes past four.
Klockan är 25 minuter över fem.	It is twenty-five (minutes) past five.
Klockan är fem (minuter) i halv sex.	It is twenty-five (minutes) past five.
Klockan är halv sex.	It is half past five.
Klockan är fem (minuter) över halv sex.	It is twenty-five (minutes) to six.
Klockan är 25 minuter i sex.	It is twenty-five (minutes) to six.
Klockan är 20 (minuter) i sex.	It is twenty (minutes) to six.
Klockan är kvart i sex.	It is a quarter to six.

In some cases the word **minuter** may be omitted, but as a general rule it is best retained.

(ii) 'Half past' an hour in English is always expressed as 'half (to)' the next hour in Swedish:

halv ett	half past twelve
halv midnatt	half past eleven in the evening

(iii) There are two ways of expressing time from twenty-one minutes past the hour to twenty-one minutes to the hour:

sex minuter i halv fyra = 24 minuter över tre = 3.24
tre minuter över halv två = 27 minuter i två = 1.33

(iv) The word **en** is usually omitted before **kvart** in expressions like **kvart i fem**, **kvart över fyra**, etc.

(v) The international 24-hour clock is used in Sweden:

kl.17.30 = 5.30 p.m.

Note that **fm = förmiddag** = a.m.; **em = eftermiddag** = p.m.

(b) 'What time . . . ?' etc.:

Hur dags går tåget?	What time does the train leave?
När går tåget?	When does the train leave?
Klockan tre.	At three o'clock.
Klockan fem och fyrtifem.	At five forty-five.
Klockan kvart i sex.	At a quarter to six.
kl. 05.45	(At) 05.45 [in timetables, etc.]

Note 1: **Hur dags/Hurdags** is pronounced /hurdax/.

Note 2: Swedish has no equivalent for the preposition 'at' before hours etc. Cf. above and also 724(b):

Möt mig klockan fem.	Meet me at five o'clock.

For this reason **klockan** is usually retained, unlike English 'o'clock':

Vi går klockan sju.	We leave at seven.

(c) Some other useful expressions of time:

vid ett-tiden	around one (o'clock)
vid halvtretiden	around half (past) two
Klockan/Hon är över tio.	It is after/past ten. [**klocka-n** is feminine]
på slaget sex	on the stroke of six
(på) prick(en) åtta	at eight o'clock sharp/on the dot
Klockan är mycket.	It's (getting) late.
ett dygn	a day = 24-hour period [from midnight]
en halvtimme	half an hour
Min klocka går rätt/före/efter.	My watch is right/fast/slow.
i dag om åtta dagar	one week today
fjorton dagar	a fortnight (two weeks)

5 VERBS

A   FORMS

501   Principal parts and generalised endings
502   First conjugation
503   Second conjugation
504   Irregular verbs of the second conjugation
505   Third conjugation
506   Irregular verbs of the third conjugation
507   Fourth conjugation: introduction
508   Fourth conjugation: gradation series **i – e – i – i**
509   Fourth conjugation: gradation series **y/(j)u – ö – u – u**
510   Fourth conjugation: gradation series **i – a – u – u**
511   Fourth conjugation: gradation series **a – o – a – a**
512   Fourth conjugation: gradation series **ä – a – u –u**
513   Fourth conjugation: minor gradation series
514   Verbs – forms: summary chart
515   Long and short forms
516   Verbs with alternative forms
517   Plural forms

B   THE USE OF THE TENSES

518   The infinitive – major uses
519   The infinitive in English and Swedish and the English gerund
520   The present tense
521   The present tense in English and Swedish and the English progressive (or continuous) tense
522   The past tense
523   The perfect tense
524   The pluperfect tense
525   The future tense
526   The future perfect tense
527   The future of the past
528   The future perfect of the past
529   Time planes
530   Compatibility of tenses
531   The supine and past participle
532   The present participle
533   Renderings of the English present participle into Swedish

C   WAYS OF EXPRESSING MOOD

534   Introduction
535   Modal auxiliary verbs

536   The subjunctive
537   The imperative
538   Conditional clauses

D   TRANSITIVE, INTRANSITIVE AND REFLEXIVE VERBS
539   Introduction
540   Transitive and intransitive verbs
541   Reflexive verbs

E   S-FORMS OF THE VERB AND THE PASSIVE
542   **S**-forms of the verb: form
543   **S**-forms of the verb: summary of use
544   The reciprocal
545   The deponent
546   Absolute use of the **s**-verb
547   The passive: introduction
548   The **s**-passive
549   Forms of **bli** + past participle
550   Forms of **vara** + past participle
551   **Man** etc. + active verb
552   Factors underlying the use of different passive forms
553   Differences in the use of the passive in English and Swedish

F   COMPOUND VERBS
554   Introduction
555   Inseparable verbs
556   Separable verbs
557   Separable or inseparable forms – stylistic differences
558   Separable or inseparable forms – semantic differences
559   Separable verbs – the position of the particle

G   SOME PROBLEM VERBS
560   Translation into Swedish of some problem verbs
561   Translation into Swedish of the verb 'to be'

A FORM

501 Principal parts and generalised endings

(a) The principal parts of the verb are the most useful forms to memorise, namely the three inflexional forms, infinitive, past and supine – since all the other forms may easily be derived from them (see 502–514):

Infinitive	Past	Supine	Meaning
arbeta	**arbeta***de*	**arbeta***t*	work

Imperative	Present	Present participle	Past participle
arbeta!	**arbeta***r*	**arbeta***nde*	**arbeta***d*, non-neuter
			arbeta*t*, neuter
			arbeta*de*, plural/def.

The stem is that part of the verb to which inflexional endings (marked in italic) are added. Swedish has both vowel stems:

arbeta/   conjugation I
sy/   conjugation III

and consonant stems:

kör/   conjugation II
skriv/   conjugation IV.

The supine is indeclinable and used together with forms of the auxiliary verb **ha**: **ha** to form the perfect infinitive, **har** to form the perfect tense and **hade** to form the pluperfect tense (see 523f.):

Jag har/hade *målat* huset.   I have/had painted the house.

The past participle functions largely as an adjective and helps to form one type of passive construction (see 531, 547, 549f):

Huset är *målat* vitt.   The house is/has been painted white.
Huset blev *målat* förra veckan.   The house was painted last week.

The present participle is most often used as an adjective or noun (see 532):

Boken är en *bitande* satir.   The book is a biting satire.
Ej *gående*.   No pedestrians.

The infinitive functions either as a verb together with a modal auxiliary or as a noun (see 518):

Vi ska *spela* fotboll.   We shall play football.
Att *spela* fotboll är roligt.   Playing football is fun.

The simple tenses, namely present and past, are those indicated by inflexion alone, e.g. **gå** go; **han går** he goes; **han gick** he went.

The complex tenses, namely the perfect and pluperfect, are those indicated by both inflexion and the use of an auxiliary verb, e.g. **att ha gått** to have gone; **han har gått** he has gone; **han hade gått** he had gone.

(b) The classification of Swedish verbs into four conjugations is an attempt to reduce and simplify a great number of different patterns of inflexion and variations of stem into a system it is possible to memorise. There are twenty-four such patterns in the summary in 514. The major division is into three conjugations of weak verbs (I, II, III) and one of strong verbs (IV). The division is made largely on the basis of the past tense form, as in English: 'work' is a weak verb ('work*s*, work*ed*', cf. **arbetar**, **arbeta*de***), 'drink' is a strong verb ('dr*i*nks, dr*a*nk', cf. **dr*i*cker, dr*a*ck**). Weak verbs in Swedish add an inflexional ending to the stem. Strong verbs in Swedish add no inflexional ending in the past, but change the stem vowel:

Weak past tenses:

Conjugation	Infinitive	Past	Meaning
I	**arbeta/**	**arbeta*de***	work/worked
II	**kör/a**	**kör*de***	drive/drove
	köp/a	**köp*te***	buy/bought
III	**sy/**	**sy*dde***	sew/sewed

Strong past tenses:

Conjugation	Infinitive	Past	Meaning
IV	**bit/a**	**b*e*t**	bite/bit
	bjud/a	**bj*ö*d**	invite/invited

Approximately 67% of Swedish verbs found in written texts belong to Conjugation I, and this is a growing group; 20% belong to Conjugation II, 1% to Conjugation III and 12% to Conjugation IV, but strong verbs are much more frequent in actual use (at 30%) than one might assume from this.

(c) It is possible to arrive at a generalised pattern of endings for Swedish verbs. The supine generally provides the most reliable indicator of conjugation.

Infinitive: vowel, usually -a	Present: -r	Past: -de/ -te, 0
-a I, II, IV other vowel III, IV	-ar I -er II, IV other vowel -r (IIa), III, IV (vowel -I II)	-ade I consonant -de IIa consonant -te IIb vowel -dde (IIa), III vowel change IV

Supine: -t	Past participle: -d/-t/en	Present Participle: -nde
-at I consonant -t II vowel -tt III, II (vowel change) -it IV (vowel change) -en IV	-ad I consonant -d IIa consonant -t IIb vowel -dd III, II, IV	-ande II, IV -ende III

(d) Some other forms dealt with in subsequent paragraphs are: subjunctives in 536, s-forms in 542f., the now virtually extinct plural forms in 517 and particle verbs in 556ff.

502 First conjugation

Main paradigm:

Infinitive	Present	Past	Supine	Past participle	Present participle	Meaning
arbeta/	arbeta/r	arbeta/de	arbeta/t	arbeta/d	arbeta/nde	work
studera/	studera/r	studera/de	studera/t	studera/d	studera/nde	study

(a) The infinitive = the stem. To the stem – which always ends in -a – are added the endings -r (present), -de (past), -t (supine), -d (past participle – this form also inflects for number and gender: see 531), -nde (present participle). The inflexion of the first conjugation is the most regular of all.

(b) In colloquial Swedish the -de/-t ending is often omitted in pronunciation of the past and supine in Central and Northern Sweden:

Just nu ropa' han på mig.	Just now he shouted for me.
Han har ropa' tidigare.	He has shouted earlier.

(c) Approximately half of frequent Swedish verbs belong to this conjugation.

(d) Nearly all newly formed verbs belong to this conjugation: e.g. **jobba** work; **mejla** (send an) e-mail; **missa** miss; **lifta** hitch a lift

(e) All verbs ending in **-era** belong to this conjugation e.g.: **parkera** park; **decentralisera** decentralise

(f) Some of the most frequent verbs of the first conjugation are in order of frequency:

visa show; **fråga** ask; **börja** begin; **tala** speak; **mena** mean; **berätta** tell; **verka** appear; **bruka** usually do; **spela** play; **bygga** build; **skapa** create; **rätta** correct; **kosta** cost; **kalla** call; **räkna** calculate; **arbeta** work; **sakna** miss; **lämna** leave; **vänta** wait; **handla** shop; **svara** answer; **öka** increase; **betrakta** look at; **förklara** explain; **öppna** open.

503 Second conjugation

Second conjugation verbs possess a stem ending in a consonant. There are two main types: verbs with stems ending in voiced consonants and those with stems ending in voiceless consonants. Those with stems in voiced consonants have past tenses in **-de** and past participles (non-neuter) in **-d**. Those with stems in voiceless consonants have past tenses in **-te** and past participles (non-neuter and neuter) in **-t**. The verbs ending in voiced consonants are called IIa verbs, those ending in voiceless consonants are called IIb verbs. As shown below, each of these main divisions is further subdivided. The second conjugation is a large and complex group of frequent verbs. The infinitive = consonant stem + **a**. To the stem are added the endings **-er** (present), **-de/-te** (past), **-t** (supine), **-d/-t** (past participle – NB This form also inflects for number and gender: see 531), **-ande** (present participle).

(a) IIa: Main paradigm:

Infinitive	Present	Past	Supine	Past participle	Present participle	Meaning
häll/*a*	häll/*er*	häll/*de*	häll/*t*	häll/*d*	häll/*ande*	pour

These verbs have stems in **-d, -g, -gg, -j, -l, -ll, -m, -mm, -n, -nn, -r, -v,** i.e. the voiced consonants. The past tense ends in **-de** and the past participle in **-d** (NB. This form also inflects for number and gender: see 531). There are some other important variations on the main paradigm; see (ii)–(ix) below.

Note: Two verbs with a stem in -l have no present tense ending; see (v) below.

(i) Stems ending in:

-g:	**inviga** inaugurate; **äga** own; **väga** weigh; **ringa** ring; **tynga** weigh down; **hänga** hang; **slänga** throw; **stänga** close
-gg:	**tigga** beg; **bygga** build
-j:	**böja** bend; **nöja (sig med)** be pleased with; **röja** clear; **dröja** delay; **avslöja** reveal (see also (viii) below)
-l:	**anmäla** report; **kyla** chill (but see (v) below)
-ll:	**anbefalla** order; **fylla** fill; **skylla** blame; **fälla** fell; **gälla** apply to; **ställa** place.
-m:	**döma** judge; **värma** heat
-n:	**nämna** mention
-v:	**väva** weave; **leva** live

(ii) Stems in **-r** (cf. also 511ff.):

Infinitive	Present	Past	Supine	Past participle	Present participle	Meaning
kör/*a*	kör/	kör/*de*	kör/*t*	kör/*d*	kör/*ande*	drive

These verbs assimilate the **-er** ending in the present tense, and thus present tense = stem.

Examples: **begära** desire; **föra** lead; **hyra** rent; **höra** hear; **lära** learn; **nära** nourish; **röra** move; **styra** govern; **störa** disturb; **tära** consume.

(iii) Stems in vowel + **d:**

Infinitive	Present	Past	Supine	Past participle	Present participle	Meaning
betyd/*a*	betyd/*er*	betyd/*de*	bety/*tt*	betyd/*d*	betyd/*ande*	mean

These double the -d and shorten the vowel in the past and past participle according to the main paradigm but also lose the -d and double the -t in the supine.

Examples: **föda** give birth; **glöda** glow; **antyda** hint; **pryda** adorn; **tyda** interpret.

Note: **breda** 'spread'; **träda** 'step'; **kläda** 'clothe'; **späda** 'dilute'; **råda** 'advise', also possess short infinitive, imperative and present tense forms e.g. **klä, klä!, klär**, etc. These verbs can therefore be classified as third conjugation (see 506, 515(b)).

(iv) Stems in consonant + **d**:

Infinitive	Present	Past	Supine	Past participle	Present participle	Meaning
använd/*a*	använd/*er*	använd/*e*	använn/*t*	använd	använd/*ande*	use

These verbs assimilate the -d of the past -de ending and drop the stem -d in the supine. In the past participle the -d is assimilated.

Examples: **anlända** arrive; **hända** happen; **sända** send; **tända** ignite; **vända** turn.

(v) Two verbs with stems in -**l** (cf. 511f.):

Infinitive	Present	Past	Supine	Past participle	Present participle	Meaning
tål/*a*	tål/	tål/*de*	tål/*t*	tål/*d*	tål/*ande*	put up with
mal/*a*	mal/	mal/*de*	mal/*t*	mal/t	mal/*ande*	grind

These verbs possess an unusual present form without an -**r** ending.

(vi) Stems in -**mm**:

Infinitive	Present	Past	Supine	Past participle	Present participle	Meaning
glömm/*a*	glömm/*er*	glöm/*de*	glöm/*t*	glöm/*d*	glömm/*ande*	forget

These verbs drop one -**m** in the past tense, supine and past participle (see 1205).

Examples: **skymma** obscure; **rymma** run away; **skämma** spoil; **klämma** squeeze; **skrämma** frighten; **gömma** conceal; **drömma** dream.

(vii) Stems in -**nn**:

Infinitive	Present	Past	Supine	Past participle	Present participle	Meaning
känn/a	**känn/er**	**kän/de**	**kän/t**	**kän/d**	**känn/ande**	know

These verbs drop one -**n** in the past, supine and past participle (see 1205).

Examples: **påminna** remind; **spänna** tension; **bränna** burn.

(viii) Stems in a short mutated vowel with intrusive -**j** in the infinitive and present tense, and a long vowel in other tenses:

Infinitive	Present	Past	Supine	Past participle	Present participle	Meaning
välj/a	**välj/er**	**val/de**	**val/t**	**val/d**	**välj/ande**	choose

Examples: **smörja** grease; **städja** hire; **vänja** accustom; **dölja** conceal; **kvälja** nauseate; **skilja** separate.

(ix) Stems in a mutated vowel in the infinitive and present only:

Infinitive	Present	Past	Supine	Past participle	Present participle	Meaning
bör/a	**bör/**	**bor/de**	**bor/t**	–	–	ought

Verbs like **böra** with stems in -**r** assimilate the -**er** in the present. Cf. (ii) above.

Examples: **göra** do, make (but see also 504); **töras** dare.

(b) IIb: Main paradigm:

Infinitive	Present	Past	Supine	Past participle	Present participle	Meaning
köp/*a*	köp/*er*	köp/*te*	köp/*t*	köp/*t*	köp/*ande*	buy

These verbs have stems ending in **-k, -ck, -n, -p, -pp, -s, -ss, -t, -x**, i.e. largely the voiceless consonants. The past tense ends in **-te** and the past participle in **-t**. (NB This form also inflects for number: see 531.)

Some verbs with stems in a consonant **+n** are IIa, see (a) above.

(i) Examples:

-**k -ck**: **rycka** snatch; **trycka** press; **tycka** think; **släcka** extinguish; **knäcka** crack; **räcka** reach; **förskräcka** scare; **sträcka** reach; **täcka** cover; **väcka** waken; **leka** play; **steka** fry; **ryka** fume; **åka** travel; **vräka** throw; **röka** smoke; **söka** seek; **skänka** donate; **tänka** think; **styrka** support; **märka** notice; **stärka** strengthen.

-**n**: **röna** experience; **kröna** crown; **synas** appear; **begynna** begin.

-**p**: **svepa** wrap; **döpa** baptise; **köpa** buy; **löpa** run; **hjälpa** help; **krympa** shrink; **skärpa** sharpen.

-**pp**: **klippa** cut; **släppa** release; **knäppa** button.

-**s**: **resa** travel; **hysa** house; **lysa** illuminate; **frysa** freeze; **låsa** lock; **läsa** read; **fräsa** hiss; **lösa** solve; **glänsa** gleam.

-**ss**: **kyssa** kiss.

-**x**: **växa** grow. (See also 504, 516.)

(ii) Verbs with stems ending in a vowel **+t**, whilst inflecting according to this paradigm, shorten the stem vowel in the past tense, supine and past participle forms (cf. also stems ending in consonant **+t** in (ii) below):

Infinitive	Present	Past	Supine	Past participle	Present participle	Meaning
möt/*a*	möt/*er*	möt/*te*	möt/*t*	möt/*t*	möt/*ande*	meet

Examples: **byta** exchange; **mäta** measure; **sköta** look after; **stöta** prod.

(iii) Special cases with deviant forms are stems in consonant **+t**:

Infinitive	Present	Past	Supine	Past participle	Present participle	Meaning
mist*a*	mist*er*	mist*e*	mist/	mist/	mist*ande*	lose

The -t is assimilated in the past tense, supine and past participle.

Examples: **gifta** marry; **lyfta** lift; **smälta** melt; **fästa** fix. Also: **vetta** face onto (see also 516).

504 Irregular verbs of the second conjugation

Some verbs conform broadly to the inflexion of the second conjugation (with largely regular present and past forms) but possess one or more irregular form. A hyphen before a past participle form in the table below indicates that it usually only occurs as a compound.

Infinitive	Present	Past	Supine	Past participle	Meaning
glädja	gläder	gladde	glatt	–	please
göra	gör	gjorde	gjort	gjord	do, make
gitta	gitter	gitte	gittat	–	be bothered
ha	har	hade	haft	-havd	have
heta	heter	hette	hetat	–	be called
kunna	kan	kunde	kunnat	–	can, be able
lägga	lägger	la(de) /la/	lagt /lakt/	lagd	lay, place
–	måste	måste	måst	–	must, have to
skilja	skiljer	skilde	skilt	skild	separate, part
skola	ska(ll)	skulle	skolat	–	shall, will
stöd(j)a	stöd(j)er	stödde	stött	stödd	support [see 516(d)]
säga	säger	sa(de) /sa/	sagt /sakt/	sagd	say
sälja	säljer	sålde	sålt	såld	sell
sätta	sätter	satte	satt	satt	place
(varda)	(varder)	vart	–	(vorden)	be, become
veta	vet	visste	vetat	–	know
vilja	vill	ville	velat	–	want
välja	väljer	valde	valt	vald	choose
vänja	vänjer	vande	vant	vand	grow accustomed
växa	växer	växte vuxit	växt vuxen		grow [see 516(e)]

Note 1: Some grammars either have a separate group for all irregular verbs or else group all strong and irregular verbs together.

Note 2: The verbs **kunnna, skola, vilja, veta** are modal auxiliary verbs (see also 535).

Note 3: The forms **skola** and **skolat** are rarely used nowadays.

505 Third conjugation

Main paradigm:

Infinitive	Present	Past	Supine	Past participle	Present participle	Meaning
sy	sy/*r*	sy/*dde*	sy/*tt*	sy/*dd*	sy/*ende*	sew

The stem ends in a stressed vowel other than -a. As in the first conjugation the infinitive = the stem. Endings are **-r** (present), **-dde** (past), **-tt** (supine), **-dd** (past participle) and **-ende** (present participle). The vowel is long in the infinitive but is shortened in the past, supine and past participle. (NB This last form also inflects for number and gender: see 531). The stem vowels involved are:

-e: **bete sig** behave; **förete** produce; **ske** occur; **te (sig)** appear.
-o: **anförtro** confide; **bo** live; **bero** depend; **glo** stare; **gno** rub; **gro** sprout; **ro** row; **sko** shoe (e.g. a horse); **sno** twist; **tro** believe; **varsko** warn.
-y: **avsky** detest; **bry sig** care; **fly** flee; **gry** dawn; **sky** avoid; **spy** vomit.
-å: **flå** flay; **förebrå** reproach; **förmå** be capable of; **klå** thrash; **må** feel; **nå** reach; **spå** predict; **så** sow; **åtrå** desire.
-ö: **strö** sprinkle; **förströ** divert.

This is a small and virtually non-productive group.

Note: The third conjugation also includes the deponent verb **brås** 'take after'.

506 Irregular verbs of the third conjugation

Some verbs conform broadly to the inflexion of the third conjugation (with largely regular present, supine and past participle forms) but possess one or more irregular forms. These irregular forms are marked * in the table. A hyphen before a past participle form in the table below indicates that it usually only occurs in a compound.

Infinitive	Present	Past	Supine	Past part.	Meaning
be	ber	bad*	bett	-bedd	ask
dö	dör	dog*	dött	–	die
få	får	fick*	fått	–	get, receive
ge	ger	gav*	gett/givit*	given*	give
gå	går	gick*	gått	–	walk, go
le	ler	log*	lett	–	smile
se	ser	såg*	sett	sedd	see
stå	står	stod*	stått	-stådd	stand
förstå	förstår	förstod*	förstått	förstådd	understand
påstå	påstår	påstod*	påstått	påstådd	assert
klä(da)*	klä(de)r*	klädde	klätt	klädd	dress
bre(da)*	bre(de)r*	bredde	brett	bredd	spread
rå(da)*	rå(de)r*	rådde	rått	rådd	advise
spä(da)*	spä(de)r*	spädde	spätt	spädd	dilute
trä(da)*	trä(de)r*	trädde	trätt	trädd	step

Note 1: In other grammars these irregular verbs are sometimes classified as Conjugation IV because they change their root vowel in the past tense form.

Note 2: In colloquial Swedish **stod** is sometimes pronounced /stog/.

Note 3: The last five of these irregular verbs may be variously classified, see 503(a)(iii) and Note.

507 Fourth conjugation: introduction

Nearly all strong verbs have stems ending in a consonant, and their infinitives are consonant stem +**a**. The present tense ends in -**er**, the supine in -**it** and the past participle in -**en**, present participle in -**ande**. (A very few verbs have supines in -**t**/-**tt** and one, **ligga**, has a supine in -**at**.) There is no inflexional ending for the past tense. What nearly all these verbs have in common is that they form the past tense form by changing the stem vowel, which may be changed again in the supine (but see 513). The same vowel is often found for the infinitive and present and for the supine and past participle.

Strong verbs are sub-divided into groups possessing the same vowel gradation series, i.e. the same vowels in the same principal parts. The fourth conjugation totals only a hundred or so verbs, but includes the most frequent verbs in Swedish. In the following lists arranged alphabetically within each gradation series the irregular forms are marked *. A hyphen before a past participle form in the table below indicates that it usually only occurs as a compound.

508 Fourth conjugation: gradation series **i – e – i – i**

Infinitive	Present	Past	Supine	Past part.	Meaning
bita	biter	bet	bitit	biten	bite
bli*	blir*	blev	blivit	bliven	be, become
driva	driver	drev	drivit	driven	drive, drift
glida	glider	gled	glidit	–	glide
gnida	gnider	gned	gnidit	gniden	rub
gripa	griper	grep	gripit	gripen	catch
kliva	kliver	klev	klivit	kliven	step, climb
knipa	kniper	knep	knipit	knipen	pinch
kvida	kvider	kved/kvidde	kvidit	–	whimper
lida	lider	led	lidit	liden	suffer
niga	niger	neg	nigit	–	curtsy
pipa	piper	pep	pipit	–	chirp
rida	rider	red	ridit	riden	ride
riva	river	rev	rivit	riven	tear, demolish
skina	skiner	sken	skinit	–	shine
skrida	skrider	skred	skridit	skriden	glide
skrika	skriker	skrek	skrikit	-skriken	shout
skriva	skriver	skrev	skrivit	skriven	write
slita	sliter	slet	slitit	sliten	wear out
smita	smiter	smet	smitit	–	run away
sprida	sprider	spred	spritt/spridit	spridd	spread [see also 516.]
stiga	stiger	steg	stigit	stigen	step, climb
strida	strider	stred/stridde	stridt/stritt	-striden	fight
svida	svider	sved	svidit	–	smart
svika	sviker	svek	svikit	sviken	fail, desert
tiga	tiger	teg	tigit	-tegen	be silent [see also 516.]
vika	viker	vek	vikit	viken	fold, yield
vina	viner	ven	vinit	–	whine
vrida	vrider	vred	vridit	vriden	twist

509 Fourth conjugation: gradation series **y/(j)u – ö – u – u**

Infinitive	Present	Past	Supine	Past part.	Meaning
bjuda	bjuder	bjöd	bjudit	bjuden	invite
bryta	bryter	bröt	brutit	bruten	break
drypa	dryper	dröp	drupit/drypt –		drip
duga	duger	dög	dugit	–	be suitable
flyga	flyger	flög	flugit	flugen	fly
flyta	flyter	flöt	flutit	-fluten	float
frysa	fryser	frös	frusit	frusen	freeze [intr.], be cold
gjuta	gjuter	göt*	gjutit	gjuten	cast [metal]
hugga	hugger	högg	huggit	huggen	chop
klyva	klyver	klöv	kluvit	kluven	split, cleave
knyta	knyter	knöt	knutit	knuten	tie, knot
krypa	kryper	kröp	krupit	krupen	creep
ljuda	ljuder	ljöd	ljudit	–	sound
ljuga	ljuger	ljög	ljugit	-ljugen	tell a lie
ljuta	ljuter	ljöt	ljutit	–	suffer [death]
njuta	njuter	njöt	njutit	-njuten	enjoy
nypa	nyper	nöp	nupit	nupen	pinch
ryta	ryter	röt	rutit	–	roar
sjuda	sjuder	sjöd	sjudit	sjuden	simmer, seethe
sjunga	sjunger	sjöng	sjungit	sjungen	sing
sjunka	sjunker	sjönk	sjunkit	sjunken	sink [intr.]
skjuta	skjuter	sköt*	skjutit	skjuten	shoot
skryta	skryter	skröt	skrutit	-skruten	boast
sluta	sluter	slöt	slutit	sluten	close, make peace
smyga	smyger	smög	smugit	-smugen	slink
snyta (sig)	snyter (sig)	snöt (sig)	snutit (sig)	snuten	blow one's nose
stryka	stryker	strök	strukit	struken	stroke, delete
suga	suger	sög	sugit	sugen	suck
supa	super	söp	supit	-supen	drink [alcohol]
tjuta	tjuter	tjöt	tjutit	–	howl
tryta	tryter	tröt	trutit	–	run short

510 Fourth conjugation: gradation series i – a – u – u

Infinitive	Present	Past	Supine	Past part.	Meaning
binda	binder	band	bundit	bunden	bind, tie
brinna	brinner	brann	brunnit	brunnen	burn [intr.]
brista	brister	brast	brustit	brusten	burst
dricka	dricker	drack	druckit	drucken	drink
finna	finner	fann	funnit	funnen	find
finnas	finns	fanns	funnits	–	be
förnimma	förnimmer	förnam	förnummit	förnummen	perceive
försvinna	försvinner	försvann	försvunnit	försvunnen	disappear
hinna	hinner	hann	hunnit	–	have time
rinna	rinner	rann	runnit	runnen	run, flow
sitta	sitter	satt	suttit	-sutten	sit
slinka	slinker	slank	slunkit	–	slink
slinta	slinter	slant	(sluntit)	–	slip
slippa	slipper	slapp	sluppit	-sluppen	avoid
spinna	spinner	spann	spunnit	spunnen	spin, purr
spricka	spricker	sprack	spruckit	sprucken	burst, crack
springa	springer	sprang	sprungit	sprungen	run
spritta	spritter	spratt	(spruttit)	–	give a start
sticka	sticker	stack	stuckit	stucken	prick, sting, run away
stinga	stinger	–	stungit	stungen	sting
stinka	stinker	stank	–	–	stink
tvinga	tvingar*	tvang*	(tvungit)	tvungen	force [See 516(f)]
vinna	vinner	vann	vunnit	vunnen	win

511 Fourth conjugation: gradation series a – o – a – a

Infinitive	Present	Past	Supine	Past part.	Meaning
dra	drar*	drog	dragit	dragen	pull
fara	far*	for	farit	faren	travel
gala	gal*	gol	galit/galt	–	crow
ta* (taga)	tar*	tog	tagit	tagen	take

512 Fourth conjugation: gradation series ä – a – u – u

Infinitive	Present	Past	Supine	Past part.	Meaning
bära	bär*	bar	burit	buren	carry
skära	skär*	skar	skurit	skuren	cut
stjäla	stjäl*	stal	stulit	stulen	steal
svälta	svälter	svalt	svultit	svulten	starve [intr.]

513 Fourth conjugation: minor gradation series

Infinitive	Present	Past	Supine	Past part.	Meaning
falla	faller	föll	fallit	fallen	fall
hålla	håller	höll	hållit	hållen	hold
gråta	gråter	grät	gråtit	-gråten	weep
låta	låter	lät	låtit	-låten	allow
komma	kommer	kom	kommit	kommen	come
sova	sover	sov	sovit	–	sleep
ligga	ligger	låg	legat*	-legad	lie
slå*	slår*	slog	slagit	slagen	hit
slåss*	slåss*	slogs	slagits	–	fight
svära	svär*	svor	svurit	svuren	swear
vara	är*	var	varit	–	be
äta	äter	åt	ätit	äten	eat

514 Verbs – forms: summary chart

Conj.	Para.	Stems	Infinitive	Present	Past	Supine	Past part.
Weak verbs (excluding irregular verbs)							
I	502	-a	arbeta/	arbeta/r	arbeta/de	arbeta/t	arbeta/d
IIa	503(a)	-g,-gg, -j,-l,-ll -m,-n	böj/a	böj/er	böj/de	böj/t	böj/d
	503(a)(ii)	-r	kör/a	kör/	kör/de	kör/t	kör/d
	503(a)(iii)	V+d	betyd/a	betyd/er	betyd/de	bety/tt	betyd/d
	503(a)(iv)	C+d	använd/a	använd/er	använd/e	använ/t	använd
	503(a)(v)	-l	tål/a	tål/	tål/de	tål/t	tål/d
	503(a)(vi)	-mm	glömm/a	glömm/er	glöm/de	glöm/t	glöm/d
	503(a)(vii)	-nn present	känn/a	känn/er	kän/de	kän/t	kän/d

Conj.	Para.	Stems	Infinitive	Present	Past	Supine	Past part.
	503(a)(viii)	-j+mut. in inf.,	välj/a	välj/er	val/de	val/t	val/d
	503(a)(ix)	mut. in inf. and present	bör/a	bör/	bor/de	bor/t	
IIb	503(b)(i)	-k, l, -n, -p,-pp, -s,-ss,-x	köp/a	köp/er	köp/te	köp/t	köp/t
	503(b)(ii)	V+t	möt/a	möt/er	möt/te	möt/t	möt/t
	503(iii)	C+t	mist/a	mist/er	mist/e	mist	mist
III	505	vowels other than -a	sy/	sy/r	sy/dde	sy/tt	sy/dd
IV	508	i e i i	bit/a/	bit/er	bet	bit/it	bit/en
	509	y/(j)u ö u u	bjud/a	bjud/er	bjöd	bjud/it	bjud/en
	510	i a u u	finn/a	finn/er	fann	funn/it	funn/en
	511	a o a a	dra(ga)	dra/r	drog	drag/it	drag/en
	512	ä a u u	bär/a	bär/	bar	bur/it	bur/en
	513	a ö a a	fall/a	fall/er	föll	fall/it	fall/en
	513	i å e e	ligg/a	ligg/er	låg	leg/at	leg/ad
	513	o o o o	komm/a	komm/er	kom	komm/it	komm/en
	513	å å ä å	gråt/a	gråt/er	grät	gråt/it	gråt/en
	513	ä ä å ä	ät/a	ät/er	åt	ät/it	ät/en

515 Long and short forms

(a) A number of frequent verbs possess shortened forms in the infinitive, present and imperative, while retaining the original longer form as an alternative that is now generally regarded as formal or archaic:

Infinitive	Present	Imperative	Past	Supine	Meaning
be (bedja)	ber (beder)	be (bed)	bad	bett	ask
dra (draga)	drar (drager)	dra (drag)	drog	dragit	pull
ta (taga)	tar (tager)	ta (tag)	tog	tagit	take
bli (bliva)	blir (bliver)	bli (bliv)	blev	blivit	be(come)
ge (giva)	ger (giver)	ge (giv)	gav	gett (givit)	give
ha (hava)	har (haver)	ha (hav)	hade	haft	have

Note 1: In colloquial Swedish there is often further syncopation in forms of the supine of the above verbs: **dragit → dratt, tagit → tatt, blivit → blitt**. These forms are avoided in writing.

Note 2: The longer forms are more frequently encountered in the integral forms of separable compound verbs (see F below): **utebliva, omgiva, avtag, bedraga**.

Note 3: The longer forms are still found in religious language:

Gud som haver barnen kär ...	God who loves children ....
Guds ord förbliver evinnerligen.	God's words remain eternally
de bedjande	those at prayer

(b) Second conjugation verbs with stems ending in -d after a vowel (503(a)(iii)) may in some cases drop this -d in the infinitive and present and are then classified as third conjugation (see also 506):

Infinitive	Present	Imperative	Past	Supine	Meaning
klä (kläda)	klär (kläder)	klä (kläd)	klädde	klätt	dress
bre (breda)	brer (breder)	bre (bred)	bredde	brett	spread
rå (råda)	rår (råder)	rå (råd)	rådde	rått	advise
trä (träda)	trär (träder)	trä (träd)	trädde	trätt	step
spä (späda)	spär (späder)	spä (späd)	spädde	spätt	dilute

(c) Notice the alternative forms of: **lägga** (past **lade**, less commonly **la**); **säga** (past **sa**, less commonly **sade**).

516   Verbs with alternative forms

(a) Some verbs may possess either (i) two distinct sets of principal parts, each belonging to a different conjugation, or (ii) differing forms within the same conjugation, or (iii) one part which varies. Examples (a hyphen before a past participle form in the table indicates that it usually only occurs in a compound):

Infinitive	Present	Past	Supine	Past part.	Meaning
(i) sprida	sprider	spridde (II)	spritt	spridd	spread
		spred (IV)	spridit (IV)		
(ii) svälja	sväljer	svalde (II)	svalt (II)	svald (II)	swallow
		sväljde (II)	sväljt (II)		
(iii) tiga	tiger	teg	tigit (IV)	-tegen (IV)	keep silent
			tegat (I)		

Variations are often dialectal, poetic or archaic in nature. In the following paradigms the most usual form is given first.

(b) Either first or second conjugation in the past tense and supine:

Infinitive	Present	Past	Supine	Meaning
frälsa	frälsar (I)	frälsade (I)	frälsat (I)	save (= redeem)
	frälser (II)	frälste (II)	frälst (II)	
fästa	fästar (I)	fästade (I)	fästat (II)	fasten, fix
	fäster (II)	fäste (II)	fäst (II)	
koka	kokar (I)	kokade (I)	kokat (I)	boil
	kokte (II)	kokt (II)	kokt (II)	

NB Present in **-ar**. Others: **betjäna** serve; **krysta** strain; **tjäna** serve (past part. **tjänad/tjänt**); **tala** speak (past part. usually **talad**); **mena** mean (past part. **menad/ment**); **skapa** create (past part. **skapad/skapt**); **spara** (pres. **sparar/spar**; past part. **sparad/spart**), save; **spela** play (past. part. **spelad/-spelt**); **svara** reply (past. **svarade/svarte**); **ana** suspect (past part. **anad**).

Notice:

Infinitive	Present	Past	Supine	Past part.	Meaning
betala	betalar	betalade (I)	betalat (I)	betalad (I)	pay
		betalte (II)	betalt (II)	betald (II)	
bringa	bringar	bringade (I)	bringat (I)		cause
		bragte (II)	bragt (II)		

(c) Either second or first conjugation in the past tense and supine:

Infinitive	Present	Past	Supine	Past part.	Meaning
mista	mister	miste (II)	mist (II)	mist (II)	lose
		mistade (I)	mistat (I)		

NB pres. in **-er**. Others: **koka** boil; **lyfta** lift; **leva** (past **levde**) live; **tala** (past **talade/talte**) speak.

(d) Variations within the second conjugation:

(i) Alternative past tense, supine:

Infinitive	Present	Past	Supine	Past part.	Meaning
förtälja	förtäljer	förtäljde förtalde	förtäljt förtalt	förtäljd förtald	tell

Others: **svälja**, swallow; **tämja (tämjde/tamde/tämde)** tame; **dväljas** dwell.

(ii) Alternative present:

Infinitive	Present	Past	Supine	Past part.	Meaning
stödja	stöder stödjer	stödde	stött	stödd	support

Others: **städja** hire.

(e) Either second conjugation or fourth conjugation in the supine or past tense or both:

Infinitive	Present	Past	Supine	Past part.	Meaning
växa	växer	växte (II) vuxit (IV)	växt (II) vuxen (IV)	-växt (II)	grow
begrava	begraver	begravde (II) (begrov) (IV)	begravt (II) begravit (IV)	begravd begraven	bury
rysa	ryser	ryste (II) rös (IV)	ryst (II)	–	shudder
(be)strida	(be)strider	(be)stridde (II) (be)stred (IV)	(be)stritt (II) (be)stridit (IV)	(be)stridd (II)	fight
duga	duger	dugde (II) dög (IV)	dugt (II)	–	suit, suffice
strypa	stryper	strypte (II) ströp (IV)	strypt (II)	strypt (II)	throttle

Others:
Like **rysa**: **fnysa** snort; **lyda** obey; **nysa** sneeze (supine **nyst/nusit**), **dyka** dive.
Like **(be)strida**: **sprida** spread.

(f) Either first or fourth conjugation in the past tense and supine:

Infinitive	Present	Past	Supine	Past part.	Meaning
simma	simmar (I)	simmade (I)	simmat (I)	–	swim
		sam (IV)	summit (IV)		

Others: **klinga (klang)** sound; **stupa (stöp)** fall; **tvinga (tvang)** compel.

(g) Notice the following difficult verbs:

(i) **Sluta – slutade** ('finish') is used intransitively.
Sluta – slöt ('close') is used transitively.
Frysa – frös ('freeze', 'feel cold') is used intransitively.
Frysa – fryste ('freeze') is used transitively.

(ii) **Besluta** ('decide') may be either Conj. I or Conj. IV:

  beslutade – beslutat (I)   **beslöt – beslutit (IV)**

(iii) **Tvinga** ('force') has an alternative past participle: **tvingad** or **tvungen**. Cf.:

Jag är tvingad att stanna (av någon).	I am forced to stop (by someone).
Jag är tvungen att gå nu. = **Jag måste gå nu.**	I am forced to/must go now.

The forms **tvang – tvungit** are archaic.

517 Plural forms

(a) Until the early 1900s written Swedish possessed a plural form for the tenses of the verb. Since that time these separate plural forms have gradually been abandoned, first in fiction in the early 1900s, then in 1945 in newspaper language, and post 1945 in legal and biblical language. With very few exceptions, what was previously the singular form is now used throughout the tense. However, some familiarity with plural forms facilitates the reading of older texts, and plurals are occasionally found in set expressions: **Obehöriga äga ej tillträde** ('No admittance without permission'), cf. **äger**. The table below gives the now archaic plurals in brackets after their present-day equivalents.

Conj. I	Conj. II	Conj. III	Conj. IV	Plural ending:

Present tense
1st person

vi kallar (kalla)	köper (köpa)	tror (tro)	skriver (skriva)	= infinitive

2nd person

| ni kallar | köper | tror | skriver | = stem +n/en |
| (I kallen) | (köpen) | (tron) | (skriven) | |

3rd person

de kallar (kalla)	köper (köpa)	tror (tro)	skriver (skriva)	= infinitve

Notice: **kan (kunna), är (äro)**

Past tense
1st person

–	–	–	vi skrev (skrevo)	past sing. +o
			vi drack (drucko)	vowel change+o
				See (b) below

2nd person

ni kallade	köpte	trodde	skrev	
(I kalladen)	(köpten)	(trodden)	(skreven)	past sing. +en/n
			drack (drucken)	

3rd person

–	–	–	de skrev (skrevo)	past sing. +o
			de drack (drucko)	vowel change +o
				See (b) below

Imperative
1st person

tacka (tackom)*	följ (följom)*	–	låt (låtom)*	stem +om

2nd person

kalla (kallen)	köp (köpen)	tro (tron)	skriv (skriven)	stem +en/n

* These forms corresponded roughly to 'Let us...' in English:

Tackom och lovom   Let us give thanks and praise (See also 537(a) Note.)

(b) In the past tense the plural forms of some strong and irregular verbs show a change of root vowel from the singular forms:

a → u	**brann (brunno), fann (funno)**
a → u	**skar (skuro), bar (buro)**
a → å	**bad (båado), gav (gåvo)**
a → o	**var (voro)**

(c) Notice also the following irregular plural forms in the past tense:

fick (fingo), gick (gingo)

B THE USE OF THE TENSES

518 The infinitive – major uses

For form see 501. The infinitive is the basic form of the verb and its dictionary form. It is inflexible, but is often preceded by the particle **att** (often pronounced /å/). The infinitive is not identical in form to the stem (501). Note that some verbs have no infinitive form, e.g. **lär, må, måste** (see 535) below. Sometimes the distinction is made between the present infinitive, e.g. **att köpa** 'to buy' and perfect infinitive, e.g. **att ha köpt** 'to have bought. The infinitive can take an s-passive ending (see 542). For use with the negative, see 1031(a).

(a) Verbal use

The following types of two-verb constructions involve the infinitive without **att**:

(i) Infinitive after modal auxiliaries: **kunna** be able; **skola** will, shall; **vilja** want to; **måste** have to; **böra** should; **tör** should; **må** may; **måtte** may; **månde** may; **lär** is said to; **låta** let; **få** be permitted to. See 535 below.

> **Han kan komma ikväll.**   He can come tonight.
> **Måste du göra det?**   Do you have to do that?

(ii) Infinitive after verbs which are modal equivalents: **behöva** need to; **besluta** decide to; **bruka** usually (do); **tänka** intend to; **börja** begin to; **fortsätta** continue; **ämna** intend to; **råka** happen to; **förmå** be able to; **försöka** attempt to; **nödgas** be forced to; **orka** be able to; **slippa** avoid; **törs våga** dare to; **sluta** stop; **hoppas** hope to; **lova** promise to; **lyckas** succeed in; **låtsas** pretend to; **verka** appear to; **vägra** refuse to; **önska** wish to.

> **De brukar resa utomlands på sommaren.**
> They usually travel abroad in the summer.

> **Du behöver väl inte gå.**
> Surely you don't need to go.

> **Han började förstå.**
> He began to understand.

Note 1: After the following verbs **att** is optional: **börjar (att)** begin; **försöker (att)** try; **slutar (att)** stop; **beslutar (att)** decide; **planerar (att)** plan.

Note 2: In spoken Swedish, newspaper style and informal written language there is a growing tendency to omit the **att** after **kommer**:

> **Det kommer inte hända mer.**   It will not happen any more.

(iii) Infinitive in object and infinitive constructions (see 1050(b)). Here the pronoun is the object of the finite verb, but the subject of the infinitive. This construction is often found after the verbs **se** see; **höra** hear; **låta** allow; **tillåta** allow; **anse** consider:

Vi såg honom göra det.	We saw him do that.
Vi har hört henne sjunga.	We have heard her sing.

(iv) Infinitive in passive object and infinitive constructions (or subject and infinitive: see 1050(c)):

Han sågs göra det.	He was seen to do that.
Hon hördes sjunga.	She was heard to sing.

(v) Infinitive in reflexive object and infinitive constructions (1050(b)). In these the verb is usually: **tro sig** think; **tycka sig** think; **anse sig** consider; **säga sig** claim; **påstå sig** claim:

Han trodde sig höra röster.   He thought he heard voices.
(= Han trodde att han hade hört röster)
Han anser sig vara förbigången.   He considers himself (to be) passed
over.

(b) Nominal use

The infinitive frequently functions as if it were a noun, and in these cases is usually found with **att**:

(i) Infinitive as subject:

Att fela är mänskligt, att förlåta är gudomligt.
To err is human, to forgive divine.

Notice that the predicative adjective is inflected as if the infinitive were a neuter noun. Notice also that **det** is often found as a formal and anticipatory subject in addition to the (grammatical) subject in the infinitive phrase:

Det	**är skönt**	**att bada i havet.**
It	is lovely	to bathe in the sea.
Formal subject		*Real subject*

See 309(d), 1003, 1033.

(ii) Infinitive as object (see 1005(e)):

Hon älskar att åka bil. (Cf. Hon älskar mat.)
She loves driving the car.

Jag föredrar att avgå. (Cf. **Jag föredrar öl.**)
I prefer to resign.

(iii) Infinitive preceded by a preposition (see 519(c)(iv), 1050(a)):

Han gick utan att säga något.   He left without saying anything.
Tack för att du kom!   Thank you for coming.

The infinitive is preceded by a preposition after many adjectives:

Han är galen i att simma.   He is mad about swimming.
Är du orolig för att uppträda?   Are you anxious about appearing?
Var säker på att släcka ljuset!   Make sure you switch off the light.

NB With expressions indicating intention **för att** (816) should be used rather than **att**:

Han kom hit för att vila sig.   He came here (in order) to rest.

(iv) Infinitive qualifying a noun, pronoun or adjective as attribute:

konsten att vinna inflytande   the art of gaining influence
Jag har ingenting att säga.   I've nothing to say.

519 The infinitive in English and Swedish and the English gerund

(a) English infinitive = Swedish infinitive. The use of the infinitive in the two languages is often identical:

(i) In two-verb constructions (see 518(a)(i)):

You really must come.   **Ni måste verkligen komma.**

(ii) In adjectival constructions:

It is not easy to do it.   **Det är inte lätt att göra det.**

(iii) In object and infinitive constructions (1050(b)):

He promised her to come the next day.
Han lovade henne att komma dagen därpå.

(b) English infinitive = Swedish full clause:

(i) With object and infinitive constructions verbs like 'want', 'wish', 'allow':

What do you want me to do?
Vad vill du att jag ska göra?

(ii) After 'wait for', 'long for', 'count on', 'rely on':

Were they waiting for the rain to stop?
Väntade de på att regnet skulle upphöra?

Can we count on you to give us a hand?
Kan vi räkna med att du ska hjälpa oss?

(iii) After an interrogative:

They don't know what to do.
De vet inte vad de ska göra.

(iv) After 'too' + adjective, or adjective + 'enough':

It was too dark for us to set out.
Det var för mörkt för att vi skulle kunna starta.

(v) After 'had better':

You had better hurry up!
Det är bäst (att) du skyndar dig!

(c) Swedish has no gerund (or verbal noun) like, for example:

The proof of the pudding is in *the eating*. Or: It's no use *crying* over spilt milk.

Instead, Swedish either has an infinitive or a full clause:

(i) English infinitive or gerund = Swedish infinitive:

He began to read/reading.	**Han började läsa.**
I can't bear to see/seeing you suffer.	**Jag står inte ut med att se dig lida.**
Do you intend to leave/leaving today?	**Tänker du resa idag?**
I prefer to travel/travelling by train.	**Jag föredrar att åka tåg.**
I like walking in the rain.	**Jag tycker om att gå i regnet.**

Also after verbs meaning 'continue', 'finish', 'give up', 'avoid', 'escape', 'want', 'need' (518(a)(ii)):

It has stopped raining.	**Det har slutat regna.**
We can't get out of going.	**Vi kan inte slippa gå.**

(ii) English gerund = Swedish full clause:

He went to bed, having first locked up.
Han gick och lade sig sedan han först låst dörrarna.

(iii) English possessive adjective + gerund = Swedish full clause:

My/Me being his brother has nothing to do with it.
Att jag är hans bror har ingenting med saken att göra.

He did it without my/me knowing it.
Han gjorde det utan att jag visste om det.

(iv) English preposition + gerund = Swedish preposition + infinitive:

After having eaten lunch, we went for a walk.
Efter att ha ätit lunch, gick vi på en promenad.

Note: A common mistake is to change the subject unwittingly after an expression of this kind:
*Efter att ha kört bilen i fem år, förstördes den i en krock.
After having driven the car for five years it was destroyed in a crash.
(Should read: **Efter att han/hon hade kört bilen . . .**)

(v) English preposition + gerund = Swedish preposition + **att**-clause

Here Swedish needs to insert the new subject, cf. 519(c)(iii) above.

We thanked him for coming.
Vi tackade honom för att han kom.

They were arrested for stealing a car.
De arresterades för att de stulit en bil.

520   The present tense

For form, see 501(c), 502–513. For use with the negative, see 1031(a). The present tense is used much as in English. For differences between Swedish use and English, see 521. The present tense has five main uses in Swedish:

(a) Instantaneous present, where the emphasis is on what is happening here and now:

Vad gör du Anders?	What are you doing, Anders?
Jag sitter och läser tidningen.	I'm sitting reading the newspaper.
Jag bifogar härmed min ansökan.	I enclose herewith my application.

(b) State present, where the emphasis is on the general and timeless:

Jorden går runt solen.	The earth goes round the sun.
Jönköping ligger vid Vättern.	Jönköping is on Lake Vättern.
Vattnet kokar vid 100° Celsius.	Water boils at 100° Celsius.

(c) Habitual present, where the emphasis is on regular repetition over a period:

Lektionerna börjar klockan 8.	Lessons begin at 8 o'clock.
Vi åker till Frankrike varje sommar.	We go to France every summer.

(d) Future action, especially with **bli**, **vara**, verbs of motion and phrases involving a distinct marker for future time (525):

Om en vecka reser jag bort.	I leave in a week.
Imorgon blir det regn.	There will be rain tomorrow.

(e) The historic (dramatic) present is used

(i) To create a dramatic illusion of 'now' in a narrative about the past. This is often the case in newspaper headlines or literary works:

Fem dör i gårdagens jordbävning.   Five die in yesterday's earthquake.

27 november 1896 bryter Strindberg upp från Klam och reser över Berlin och Danmark hem.
On 27 November 1896 Strindberg leaves Klam and travels home via Berlin and Denmark.

(ii) When the result of an action in the past is important, especially when relating to a book, play or work of art:

Strindberg skildrar det svenska samhället på 1870-talet.
Strindberg depicts Swedish society in the 1870s.

521 The present tense in English and Swedish and the English progressive (or continuous) tense

(a) Although the use of the present is often identical in the two languages (see 520) there are some minor differences of usage:

(i) Present in Swedish = past in English:

This is found with the past participle and is used when an action is completed in the past, but the (tangible) result of the action remains.

> **Operan är komponerad år 1860.** The opera was composed in 1860.
> **Slottet är byggt på 1300-talet.** The castle was built in the 14th century.

A very common example of this is the use of the present tense with **föda(s)** and **vara född**, '(be) born', when people are still alive:

> **När är ni född?** When were you born?
> **Jag är född den 10 december 1944.** I was born on 10 December 1944.

Notice, however, that with persons now dead the past tense of **föda(s)** is used:

> **Strindberg föddes 1849.** Strindberg was born in 1849.

(ii) Present in Swedish = perfect in English in the following cases when the action is continuing:

> **Det är första gången jag är här.** It is the first time I have been here.
> **Jag känner honom sedan 10 år.** I have known him for ten years.

(b) The English progressive tense (expressing a limited but not necessarily complete process that is in progress at a given time) is rendered in various ways in Swedish:

(i) Simple present tense (see 520(a)):

> **Vart går du?** Where are you going?
> **Jag sitter på arbetsrummet.** I am sitting in the study.

(ii) Two verbs in the present linked by **och**. These are typically a verb of location and a verb of action, the sense of location in the first verb having become weakened:

> **Han sitter och läser.** He is (sitting) reading.
> **Du står och ljuger!** You are (standing there) lying!

(iii) **Hålla på att** + infinitive equates to English 'be busy/involved with/in the process of' and stresses the fact that the action is still in progress.

> **Han håller på att skriva brev.** He is (busy) writing letters.

Huset håller på att byggas.   The house is (in the process of)
                                         being built.

Notice that **håller på att** sometimes means 'be on the point of/about to':

Jag håller på att dö av hunger.   I am dying of hunger.

522 The past tense

For form see 501, 502–513. For use with the negative, see 1031(a). The past tense
in Swedish (sometimes called the preterite (Sw. **preteritum**)) is a used to express
a completed action at a point of time in the past. Use of the past tense is largely as
in English.

(a) The past tense often involves an expression to mark this point in the past, i.e.
a time marker, often a temporal adverbial (607(a)):

I fjol/Då **reste vi till Grekland.**   Last year/Then we went to Greece.

This time marker may be understood in a longer narrative text:

**När vi kom till Aten *i somras* var det förskräckligt varmt. Det första vi
gjorde var att köpa solglasögon. Det var så bländande ljust. Sedan åkte
vi upp till bergen. Där var det lite svalka.**
When we arrived in Athens last summer it was awfully hot. The first thing
we did was to buy sunglasses. It was so bright it was dazzling. Then we went
up into the mountains. It was a bit cooler there.

(b) The past tense expresses a repeated action in the past; English uses 'used
to/would':

Som liten gallskrek han varje gång han inte fick sin vilja fram.
As a small child he used to yell/would yell every time he didn't get his own
way.

Note: Swedish often prefers **brukade** + infinitive to emphasise a sense of customary or repeated
action (see 518(a)(ii)).

(c) The past tense injects a note of politeness or caution into a demand or
intention with the modal auxiliary (cf. 535):

Kunde du tänka dig göra det?   Do you think you could do it?
(Instead of: **Kan du göra det?**)

(d) The past tense may have a modal sense, indicating an unreal situation (536(c)):

Om jag var president, skulle jag avskaffa all skatt.
If I were president I would abolish all taxes.

(e) Swedish past = English present:

This happens in some impersonal expressions describing first impressions or feelings:

Det var verkligen synd!	That is a real shame!
Det var dyrt!	That is expensive!
Det var varmt, det här!	This is hot!
Det var riktigt gott kaffe!	This is really good coffee!
Det var roligt att höra det!	I am glad to hear that!
Det var en annan sak	There is another thing
Hur var namnet?	What is your name, please?

(f) **Höll på att** + infinitive either means 'kept on (doing something)' or 'just avoided (doing something)' or 'nearly managed to (something)' (cf. 521(b)(iii)):

Hon höll på att gråta.	She kept crying.
Huset höll på att brinna upp.	The house very nearly burned down.
Engelsmannen höll på att vinna.	The Englishman almost won.

523   The perfect tense

For form see 501(a)(c), 502–13. For use with the negative, see 1031(a).

The perfect tense in Swedish is used to indicate a link between past and present, the relevance of a completed action in the past to a present situation. The tense indicates an indeterminate length of time and point in time, but the point of reference is usually the present. Cf. 522(a) above.

(a) The time adverbial (607(a)) is always vague or includes the present (cf. time adverbials with the past tense):

Vi har rest till Grekland förr, men nu föredrar vi Spanien.
We have been to Greece before, but now we prefer Spain.

Jag har bott här för länge sedan.	I (have) lived here a long time ago.
Nu har jag avslutat boken.	Now I have finished the book.

(b) Notice that the auxiliary verb **har** may be omitted in subordinate clauses (cf. 531(c)(ii)):

Då jag inte (har) fått svar på mitt förra brev, skriver jag en gång till.
As I haven't had a reply to my last letter I am writing again.

(c) With a suitable adverbial the perfect may indicate that an action has taken place and is still taking place (the 'inclusive perfect'):

De har varit gifta i många år.
They have been married for many years [and are still married].

cf. **De har varit gifta.**
They used to be married [but are no longer married].

(Cf. also (g) below.)

(d) The perfect may express a repeated or customary action:

Jag har plockat svamp här i många år.
I have been picking mushrooms here for many years.

Note: Swedish sometimes uses **har brukat** + infinitive to emphasise a sense of customary action (see 518(a)(ii)).

(e) The perfect may express the relationship between two events in the future when one completed action precedes another action (see 525(e)):

När jag har tvättat bilen kan vi dricka kaffe.
When I have washed the car we will have coffee.

(f) The Swedish perfect is often used to express English future perfect (cf. 525(e)):

När du kommer har jag nog avslutat boken.
When you come I will probably have finished the book.

(g) Swedish perfect = English past tense:

This is used when some action completed in the past has a connection with the present.

Vem har skrivit Röda rummet?
Who wrote *The Red Room*? [The novel still exists and is read.]

Var har ni lärt er svenska?
Where did you learn Swedish? [The knowledge of Swedish still exists.]

It is especially frequent in questions, particularly those including **aldrig** ('never')
and **någonsin** ('ever'):

Det har jag aldrig tänkt på.	I never thought of that.
Har ni sovit gott i natt?	Did you sleep well last night?

(h) Swedish perfect = English present when the English present is used idiomatically to express a past action:

Jag har glömt vad han heter.	I forget what he's called.
Jag har hört att de ska skiljas.	I hear that they are getting divorced.

524 The pluperfect tense

For form, see 501, 502–513. For use with the negative, see 1031(a).

(a) As in English, the Swedish pluperfect tense expresses an action in the past taking place before another action expressed by the past tense:

Innan han kom hit, hade han köpt blommor.
Before he came here he had bought flowers.

Sedan vi hade lagat bilen, åkte vi därifrån.
After we had repaired the car, we left.

(b) The pluperfect may express the result of a completed action:

Då hade vi redan gett upp allt hopp.
By that time we had already given up all hope.

(c) The pluperfect may indicate that an action had taken place and at some point in the past was still taking place (the inclusive pluperfect, cf. 523(c) above):

De hade varit gifta i många år, när de skildes.
They had been married for many years when they got divorced.

(d) The pluperfect (like the past: 522(d)) may have a conditional sense, sometimes indicating an unreal situation:

Om det bara inte hade varit så halt på vägen och om föraren hade varit nykter, hade de klarat sig.
If only it had not been so icy on the road and if the driver had been sober, they would have been all right.

(e) Notice that the auxiliary verb **hade** may be omitted in subordinate clauses (cf. 531(c)(ii)):

Jag vet inte vad jag hade gjort, om jag inte (hade) hittat dig.
I don't know what I would have done if I hadn't found you.

525 The future tense

As in English, there is no inflexional form of the verb in Swedish to indicate future. Future is more often expressed by the present tense than by the future tense proper, i.e. than **ska** + infinitive, **kommer att** + infinitive. For use with the negative, see 1031(a). The different ways of expressing future are thus:

(a) Present tense (501(c), 503–513, 520(d)):

(i) This often requires a time marker (607(a)) to avoid confusion:

Jag kommer snart.	I will come soon.
Tåget går om fem minuter.	The train leaves in five minutes.

(ii) A time marker is not always necessary with the verbs **blir** 'be'; **får** 'have'; **ser** 'see'; **kommer** 'come':

Blir det regn, tycker du?	Will there be rain do you think?
Får du tid att göra det?	Will you have time to do it?

Note: The verbs **tänker**, **ämnar** ('intend') indicate future intention:

Jag tänker/ämnar plantera potatisen nästa vecka.
I am thinking of planting/intending to plant the potatoes next week.

(iii) In subordinate clauses of both a temporal (812) and conditional (814) kind, the present tense is often used to indicate the future as in English.

När semestern börjar, åker vi ut på landet.   [Temporal]
When the holidays begin [= Once the holidays have begun], we (will) go to the countryside.

Om det snöar idag, går jag inte ut.   [Conditional]
If it snows today, I'm not going out.

(b) Kommer att + infinitive:

This construction is used to indicate simple future and is often used with a non-personal subject in objective expressions. The speaker intends nothing, nor does he take responsibility for the statement.

Det kommer att regna senare.	It will rain later.
Kommer det att funka?	Will it work?
Ni kommer att bli förvånade.	You will be surprised.

Note: In spoken Swedish there is a growing tendency to omit the **att** (cf. 518(a)):

Det kommer inte hända mer.	It won't happen any more.

(c) Ska + infinitive:

(i) This construction does not only indicate future but in addition has a modal sense (see 535(b) below). In contrast to **komma att** (see (b) above) this form, especially when used with a personal subject, indicates a firm intention of committing the action described at some point in the future.

Jag ska titta på TV ikväll.	I shall watch TV tonight.
[= intention, promise]	

Ska du resa imorgon?	Are you leaving tomorrow?
[= intention, promise]	

(ii) In the 3rd person **ska**, 'will', 'shall' often indicates simple future, i.e. it is merely temporal (see (b) above), especially when the subject is impersonal:

Ska tåget gå snart?	Will the train be leaving soon?
Det ska bli auktion på fredag.	There will be an auction on Friday.

Note 1: **Vill** = 'want to' and is stronger than **ska**. It never expresses simple future.

Note 2: Compare the different ways of expressing the future in Swedish and English in the following examples:

Det blir/kommer att bli mörkt snart.	It will be dark soon.
Du ska förstås inte följa med, Nils.	You will not be coming, of course, Nils.
Men jag vill ju följa med, pappa.	But I want to come, Dad.

See also 535(b)(iii) 2.

(d) Skulle + infinitive

(i) This construction is used to indicate the future in the past, i.e. something viewed as future from a point of reference in the past:

Igår sa jag att han skulle ringa mig idag.
Yesterday I said that he should ring me today.

Jag skulle just ringa honom, när han knackade på dörren.
I was just about to ring him when he knocked at the door.

(ii) It is also used in conditional clauses (see also 535(b)):

Om jag vore rik, skulle vi kunna köpa en ny bil.
If I were rich we would be able to buy a new car.

Om vi hade studerat mera, skulle vi ha klarat provet.
If we had studied harder we would have passed the exam.

(e) Perfect tense:

The perfect tense occasionally indicates an action taking place before another action in the future (cf. 523(e), 524).

När jag har ätit frukost, går jag till skolan.
[= ska jag gå ...]
When I have eaten breakfast I will go to school.

Nästa vecka vid den här tiden har vi nog kommit till Spanien.
[= ska vi ha kommit ...]
By this time next week we will probably have arrived in Spain.

Tror du att du har läst boken före skrivningen?
[= kommer att ha läst ...]
Do you think you will have read the book before the exam?

526 The future perfect tense

The future perfect tense is realised by the form **ska** or **kommer att** + **ha** + supine of the main verb. It expresses a state or action lasting up to a point in time in the future (cf. 523 perfect tense):

När det är dags för dig att gå till posten ska jag ha skrivit brevet färdigt.
When it's time for you to go to the post I will have finished the letter.

Innan nästa val kommer en förbättring av läget förmodligen att ha ägt rum.
Before the next election an improvement in this situation will presumably have taken place.

527 The future of the past

The future of the past is a tense realised by **skulle** + infinitive. It expresses a future state or action in relation to a point in time in the past. It is often used in indirect speech.

> **Då han äntligen kom skulle jag just gå och lägga mig.**
> When he finally arrived I was just about to go to bed.

528 The future perfect of the past

The future perfect of the past is a tense realised by **skulle** + **ha** + supine of the main verb. It expresses a state or action lasting between two points in time, both in the past. It is often found in indirect speech. This construction is also used in conditional expressions:

> **Han sa att han skulle ha målat om gästrummet innan mamma kom.**
> He said he would have repainted the guest room before Mum arrived.

> **Om jag hade vetat att du var sjuk, skulle jag ha besökt dig.**
> If I'd known you were ill, I would have visited you.

529 Time planes

There are two basic time planes in Swedish, a *now* plane and a *then* plane. The *now* plane includes the present, perfect and future tenses, the *then* plane includes the past, pluperfect and future in the past (**skulle** + infinitive):

NOW plane

Before now	*Now*	*After now*
Perfect:	Present:	Future:
Jag har skrivit	**Jag skriver**	**1 Jag skriver i morgon**
I have written	I write/am writing	I will write tomorrow
		2 Jag kommer att skriva i morgon
		I will write tomorrow
		3 Jag ska skriva i morgon
		I will write tomorrow
		Perfect:
		När jag har druckit kaffe, skriver jag brevet
		When I have had coffee, I will write the letter

THEN plane

Before then	*Then*	*After then*
Pluperfect:	Past:	Future of the past:
Jag hade skrivit	**Jag skrev**	**Jag skulle skriva**
I had written	I wrote	I was to write

530 Compatibility of tenses

It is not usual to change from one time plane to another (see 529 above) in mid-utterance. If a sentence begins in one plane it is usually completed in the same plane.

NOW:	**Jag säger,**	**att jag har tvättat bilen.**	*Before now*
	I am saying	that I have washed the car	
	Jag säger,	**att jag tvättar bilen.**	*Simultaneous with now*
	I am saying	that I am washing the car	
	Jag säger,	**att jag ska tvätta bilen.**	*After now*
	I am saying	that I will wash the car	

Jag har nog tvättat bilen, när du kommer. *After now*
I will probably have washed the car when you arrive.

THEN:	**Sven skrev,**	**att han hade målat huset.**	*Before then*
	Sven wrote	that he had painted the house	
	Sven skrev,	**att han målade huset.**	*Simultaneous with then*
	Sven wrote	that he had painted the house	
	Sven skrev,	**att han skulle måla huset.**	*After then*
	Sven wrote	that he would paint the house.	

The main function of the tense is to express not the time plane itself, but the relation of the speaker/writer to the plane by expressing 'before', 'simultaneous with' or 'after'.

On occasion a change of plane is possible when indicated by a adverbial expression of time:

Comparative
Vädret *var* [*then*] bättre förra veckan än det *har varit* [*now*] den här veckan.
The weather was better last week than it has been this week.

Indirect speech

Sven *skrev* [*then*] för en månad sedan att han *kommer* [*now*] om en vecka.
Sven wrote a month ago that he is/will be coming in a week's time.

Sometimes one may change plane in mid-sentence when a following clause has a new subject:

> **Turisterna *åkte* [*then*] till pyramiderna, som *ligger* [*now*] utanför Kairo.**
> The tourists *went* to the pyramids, which *are situated* outside Cairo.

531 The supine and past participle

(a) Summary table of forms (see also 501(a)(c), 502–513)

Conjugation	Supine	Past participle			Meaning
		n-n.	*n.*	*pl.*	
I	**arbetat**	**arbetad**	**arbetat**	**arbetade**	worked
IIa	**böjt**	**böjd**	**böjt**	**böjda**	bent
IIb	**köpt**	**köpt**	**köpt**	**köpta**	bought
III	**sytt**	**sydd**	**sytt**	**sydda**	sewn
IV	**bjudit**	**bjuden**	**bjudet**	**bjudna**	invited

(b) Notes on forms:

(i) In Conj. I, II, III the supine = the neuter past participle.

(ii) In Conj. IV the supine usually ends in **-it**, the neuter past participle in **-et**.

(iii) The past participle in Conj. IV drops the final **-e** in the plural (see 204(c)(i)):

Jag är bjuden.	I am invited.
Vi är bjudna.	We are invited.

(iv) The non-neuter singular of Conj. IIb past participles ends in **-t**.

Cf. **en nyköpt limpa – ett nyköpt hus**

(v) The past participle of strong verbs usually has the same stem vowel as the supine:

Infinitive	Present	Past	Supine	Past part.	Meaning
bjuda	**bjuder**	**bjöd**	**bjudit**	**bjuden**	invite
skriva	**skriver**	**skrev**	**skrivit**	**skriven**	write

(vi) The plural and definite form of the past participle of first conjugation verbs ends in **-e**, whereas those forms of the past participles of all other conjugations end in **-a** (see 219(a)).

(c) The distinction between supine and past participle is that the supine is used with the auxiliary verb **ha** to form the perfect and pluperfect tenses (523, 524), while the past participle is used with the auxiliary **vara** in a passive or adjectival manner (203(e)(g), 204(a)(c)). Swedish is the only Germanic language to make this precise distinction and it is one of recent date. Below are some notes on aspects of usage:

(i) The supine is indeclinable. With the auxiliary **har/hade** it forms the perfect and pluperfect tenses (523, 524):

Han har köpt en bil.	He has bought a car.
De hade köpt en bil.	They had bought a car.

(ii) The supine is frequently used without the auxiliary **har/hade** in all kinds of subordinate clauses, especially relative clauses (822):

Som du redan hört, ska vi resa i morgon.
As you have already heard, we will be leaving tomorrow.

Han sa, att han varit sjuk.
He said he had been ill.

(iii) The past participle inflects as an adjective, and is used both predicatively and attributively. When used attributively it may take both definite and indefinite forms (see also 201, 203(e)(g), 204(a)(c), 226):

	Indefinite	*Definite*
Conj. I	**en nytvätta*d* bil** a newly washed car	**den nytvätta*de* bilen** the newly washed car
	ett nymåla*t* hus a newly painted house	**det nymåla*de* huset** the newly painted house
Conj. IIa	**en stäng*d* dörr** a closed door	**den stäng*da* dörren** the closed door
	ett stäng*t* fönster a closed window	**det stäng*da* fönstret** the closed window

	Indefinite	*Definite*
Conj. IIb	**en nyköp*t* bil** a newly purchased car	**den nyköp*ta* bilen** the newly purchased car
	ett nyköp*t* hus a newly purchased house	**det nyköp*ta* huset** the newly purchased house
Conj. III	**en obebo*dd* stuga** a deserted cottage	**den obebo*dda* stugan** the deserted cottage
	ett obebo*tt* torp a deserted croft	**det obebo*dda* torpet** the deserted croft
Conj. IV	**en välskriv*en* uppsats** a well written essay	**den välskriv*na* uppsatsen** the well written essay
	ett välskriv*et* brev a twell written letter	**det välkriv*na* brevet** the well written letter

(iv) The past participle is also used as an adjectival noun (see 227ff.):

Den okände trädde in.	The stranger entered.
De inbjudna började anlända.	Those invited began to arrive.
en älskades namn	the name of a loved one

(v) The past participle is also used with forms of **vara** and **bli** to construct one type of passive (see 547(b), 549f.):

Bilen blev förstörd i kraschen.	The car was destroyed in the crash.
Huset är nymålat.	The house is newly painted.

532 The present participle

(a) The present participle is formed by adding:

(i) **-ande** to verbs with stems in unstressed **-a** (which lapses), or stems ending in a consonant:

arbeta/	**arbet/*ande***	I	work
böj/*a*	**böj/*ande***	IIa	bend
köp/*a*	**köp/*ande***	IIb	buy
skriv/*a*	**skriv/*ande***	IV	write

(ii) **-ende** to verbs with stems in a stressed final vowel:

bete/	**bete/*ende***	III	behave
gå/	**gå/*ende***	III irr.	walk
dö/	**dö/*ende***	III irr.	die

See also 501(a)(c), 502–514.

(b) Use

(i) As an adjective (note that Swedish usage sometimes prefers a present participle where English has a past participle):

- attributively (see 206(a)):

omfattande kunskaper	wide-ranging knowledge
en heltäckande matta	a wall-to-wall carpet
en ingående beskrivning	a detailed description

- predicatively:

Utvecklingen är oroväckande.	The development is disturbing.

(ii) As a noun:

Fifth decl. neuter: **ett inflytande** an influence; **ett erbjudande** an offer; **ett påstående** a statement. (See 116(d).) Sixth decl. non-neuter: **en ordförande** a chairperson; **en sökande** an applicant; **en studerande** a student. (See 117(e).) When used as non-neuter nouns the participles usually indicate people.

(iii) As an adverb (601(d)):

Han var påfallande lat.	He was strikingly lazy.
Vädret var övervägande mulet.	The weather was predominantly cloudy.

(iv) As a verb after **komma** 'come'; **gå** 'go'; **bli** 'remain', **ha** 'have':

Han gick visslande nerför vägen.	He walked down the street whistling.
Vi blev sittande.	We remained seated.

Note: In speech and informal writing a form with added -s is found, primarily as a free particle and after the verb **komma** (see also 542(c)):

Hon kom, medförandes en korg med ägg.	She arrived, bringing a basket of eggs.
Bilen kom farandes förbi i hög hastighet.	The car came past at high speed.

533 Renderings of the English present participle into Swedish

For translations of the other English '-ing' forms see 519 (gerund) and 521 (continuous tense).

(a) Swedish has two verbs in the same form (521(b)(ii)):

He lay sleeping.	**Han låg och sov.**
They stood watching the train.	**De stod och tittade på tåget.**

(b) Swedish has a finite verb and an infinitive (519(c)):

He continued writing.	**Han fortsatte att skriva.**
Do you like skiing?	**Tycker du om att åka skidor?**

(c) Swedish has an object and infinitive (519(a)(iii)):

I heard her shout(ing).	**Jag hörde henne ropa.**
They saw him run(ning) away.	**De såg honom springa bort.**

(d) Swedish has full clauses, whereas English has contracted sentences:

A woman wearing a green dress went up to a man sitting near the window.
En kvinna som hade en grön klänning på gick fram till en man som satt vid fönstret.

Alec left early, promising to be back later.
Alec gick tidigt, och lovade att komma tillbaka senare.

C WAYS OF EXPRESSING MOOD

534 Introduction

Mood is the attitude of the speaker to the activity expressed by the verb. Mood is expressed in a number of different ways, but primarily by using:

(a) Modal auxiliary verbs (535) together with the main verb:

Vi ska komma.	We shall come.
Jag måste gå.	I must go.

(b) Modal forms, i.e. the indicative, subjunctive (536) and imperative (537):

Det vore roligt om du kunde komma.
It would be nice if you could come. [subjunctive]

Var inte dum nu, Olle!
Don't be silly now, Olle!   [imperative]

(c) Conditional clauses (538):

Om jag hade sparat mer pengar, kunde jag ha rest utomlands.
If I had saved more money, I could have travelled abroad.

535   Modal auxiliary verbs

(a) Form: these verbs express mood when used together with the infinitive of the main verb.

Infinitive	Present	Past	Supine	Meaning
skola	ska (skall)	skulle	(skolat)	shall, will
kunna	kan	kunde	kunnat	be able
vilja	vill	ville	velat	will, want to
–	måste	måste	måst	must, have to
böra	bör	borde	bort	should, ought to
–	tör	torde	–	is probably
–	må	måtte	–	may, must
–	månde	–	–	may
–	lär	–	–	is said to
låta	låter	lät	låtit	let
få	får	fick	fått	may, be allowed to, must, have to

For use with negatives, see 1031(a).

(b) Notes on use:

(i) **Ska** (the spelling **skall** is falling out of use; past tense **skulle**): see 525(c) above on the future tense, and note also the following uses:

1   Polite use:
Jag skulle vilja be dig om en tjänst.   I would like to ask you a favour.

2   The conditional (see (v) **bör** 'ought to', below):
Om jag hade tid, skulle jag följa med.   If I had time I would come.

3   Necessity, duty:
Man ska tvätta håret ofta.   You must wash your hair often.

4   'Be about to':
Hon skulle just ringa.   She was on the point of phoning.

5   Opinion, assumption, possibility:
Ska det här vara roligt?   Is this supposed to be funny?

(ii) **Kan** (past tense **kunde**) has the following uses:

1   Possibility:
Kan du komma?   Can you/Is it possible for you to come?

2   Ability:
Jag kan köra bil.   I can drive.

3   Concession:
Det kan du ha rätt i.   You may be right.

Note: When not used as an auxiliary **kan** indicates ability in a language or field of knowledge:

Han kunde italienska.   He knew Italian.
Han kan allt om bilar.   He knows everything about cars.

(iii) **Vill** (past tense **ville**). Note also the following uses:

1   Polite use:
Jag vill/ville helst åka utomlands.   I want/would like to go abroad.

2   Subject's wishes:
Vill du ha ett glas öl?   Would you like/Will you have a glass of beer?

Notice the difference between **vill** (= 'wish') and **ska** (= simple futurity: 525(c)):

Vill du gå på bio?   Do you want/Would you like to go to the cinema?

Ska du gå på bio?   Are you going to the cinema?

(iv) **Måste** has the following uses:

1   Compulsion: in positive expressions **måste** = **får** = 'must', 'have to', 'be forced to':
Jag måste tyvärr gå nu. = Jag får tyvärr gå nu.
I must/have to/am forced to go now.

2   Concession: in negative expressions **måste inte** = **behöver inte** = 'do not have (need) to':
Du måste ju inte röka.
You don't have to smoke, you know.

NB   **får inte** = 'must not':
Du får inte röka härinne.
You must not/are not allowed to smoke in here!

(v) **Bör** (past tense **borde**) has the following uses:

1   Suitability or strong recommendation:
Du bör/borde absolut se hans senaste film.
You really should see his latest film.

Man bör göra sin plikt.
One should do one's duty.

NB English 'you should' indicating suitability is never translated as **skulle**, which is conditional (538).

Du bör/borde få lite frisk luft.
You should get some fresh air.

Cf. **Jag skulle få lite frisk luft, om jag kunde komma ut.**
I would get some fresh air if I could get out.

The past tense form **borde** is more polite and tentative than the present **bör**.

Du borde verkligen skriva en bok.
You really ought to write a book.

2   Assumption, possibility:
De bör vara mycket trötta efter den långa resan.
They must be/are probably very tired after the long journey.

(vi) **Torde** is used for assumption or possibility:

> **Borgen torde ha byggts på 1100-talet.**
> The stronghold was probably built in the 12th century.

Torde is usually found only in written Swedish.

(vii) **Må** is used for wishes, hopes, possibilities in many fixed expressions:

Vad som än må hända …	Whatever may happen …
Det må jag säga!	I must say!
Länge må hon leva!	Long may she live!

(viii) **Måtte** has the following uses:

1   Wish (cf. **må**: vii):
    Måtte du aldrig glömma det!   May you never forget it!

2   Certainty:
    Han måtte väl ha blivit lite försenad.
    He must have been slightly delayed.

(ix) **Månde**: similar to **må, måtte** (vii, viii), usually in set phrases:

> **Gör det, vad han än månde säga!**   Do it whatever he may (might) say.

(x) **Lär** is used for assumption or possibility:

> **Hon lär skriva dikter.**   She is said to write poetry.

Lär is usually found only in written Swedish.

(xi) **Låter** (past tense: **lät**) has the following uses:

1   Permit, give someone leave to:
    Låt mig fortsätta!   Let me (Allow me to) continue!

2   Refrain from changing ('leave'/'let be'):
    Låt cykeln stå kvar.   Leave the bike where it is.

3   Commission, undertaking:
    Hon lät sy om sin brudklänning.   She had her wedding dress altered.

See also 537(a) Note 1.

(xii) **Får** (past tense: **fick**):

1 Ask or receive permission:
   Får jag gå ut ikväll?   May I go out tonight?

2 Necessity:
   Jag fick ligga på sjukhuset.   I had to stay in hospital.

3 Be compelled:
   Vi fick stå ute i snön.   We had to stand out in the snow.

4 Have cause to:
   Jag får tacka er så mycket.   I must thank you so much.

5 Get to:
   Vi fick aldrig se pyramiderna.   We never got to see the pyramids.

NB The usual non-modal sense of **få** is 'receive':

   Jag fick en present i går.   I got a present yesterday.

It can also mean 'get someone to do something':

   Vi fick henne att spela piano.   We got her to play the piano.

536 The subjunctive

(a) Form:

	Infinitive	Present	Past	Supine	Meaning
I	välsigna	välsigne	–	–	bless
II	leva	leve	–	–	live
III	ske	ske	–	–	happen
IV	vara	vare	vore	–	be

The past subjunctive only has a special form for strong verbs, where it is formed from the past plural form (see 517). Whilst a century ago the subjunctive was frequently found in written Swedish it is now rare.

(b) The present subjunctive has a very restricted use in modern Swedish, largely to express a wish or prayer. It is found exclusively in fixed expressions:

   Leve konungen!   Long live the king!
   Gud välsigne dig, mitt barn!   God bless you, my child!
   Gud ske lov!   Thank heavens!

Tack vare din hjälp! Thanks to your help!
Bevare mig väl! Goodness gracious!
Det vete fan! The devil alone knows!

The role previously played by the subjunctive has been taken over by the modal auxiliary verbs (**skulle, bör**), adverbs (**nog, väl**) or certain phrases (e.g. **Det är troligt att** 'It is likely that')

(c) The past subjunctive is extremely rare in modern Swedish, and, outside dialect usage, as a distinct form is now found only in **vore** (from **vara**). It may be used to indicate a range of modal meanings, often the difficulty or impossibility of fulfilling something imagined:

Vore jag ung igen, skulle jag göra mycket annorlunda.
Were I young again, there are many things I would do differently.

The past subjunctive is often found together with **om** in conditional clauses (although the conjunction is, strictly speaking, unnecessary):

Om jag vore ung igen If I were young again

In constructions with **om** the past indicative is increasingly used (See 522(d), 524(d)):

Om jag var ung igen If I was young again

Swedish use conforms quite closely to English in this regard.

537 The imperative

(a) Form: the imperative = the stem, i.e. it ends in **-a** like the infinitive in conj. I, and in a stressed vowel in Conj. III and some irregular verbs, otherwise in a consonant.

Conj.	Infinitive	Imperative	Meaning
I	arbeta/	**Arbeta hårdare!**	Work harder!
IIa	släng/a	**Släng bort dem!**	Throw them away!
IIa	känn/a	**Känn på kvaliteten!**	Feel the quality.
IIb	hjälp/a	**Hjälp mig!**	Help me!
III	tro/	**Tro mig eller inte!**	Believe me or not!
IV	skriv/a	**Skriv en uppsats!**	Write an essay.
irregular	gå/	**Gå ut härifrån!**	Get out of here!
irregular	gör/a	**Gör något!**	Do something!
irregular	var/a	**Var inte dum!**	Don't be stupid!

For use with the negative, see 1031(a).

Note: In medieval Swedish the imperative had separate plural forms. These are now only found in fixed expressions (see also 517):

1st person plural: -om:

Sjungom studentens lyckliga dar!	Let's sing of the student's happy days!
Låtom oss bedja!	Let us pray!

2nd person plural: -en. Compare the examples below from the 1917 and 2000 Bible translations:

Bedjen och eder varda givet! [1917]	Ask and it shall be given unto you.
Be, så skall ni få. [2000]	

(b) Use: the imperative expresses a command, wish or piece of advice. It always represents the 2nd person present tense.

Koka upp såsen och låt den sjuda.
Bring the sauce to the boil and allow it to simmer.

Occasionally, in colloquial Swedish, a subject is inserted:

Kom hit du och titta på det här!
You come here and look at this!

This subject is strictly speaking redundant, but it is inserted on occasion either to underline a contrast or to give the command a friendly or encouraging tone:

Laga du maten, så ska jag städa!	You cook and I will tidy up.
Kom du, det är inte farligt!	Come on now, it's not dangerous.

The imperative may be made more palatable by the addition of a phrase meaning 'please':

Var snäll och ge mig ett äpple!/Ge mig ett äpple, är du snäll.
Please give me an apple!

Var god dröj!
Please hold the line. [said by telephonists]

Note: Swedish imperative sentences usually end with an exclamation mark, unless the actual imperative is very far from the end of the sentence (1305).

538   Conditional clauses

A further means of expressing mood is to use one of the following common kinds of conditional construction:

(a) Conditional clause (see also 1042(a)):

Om vi hade råd skulle vi köpa en ny bil.
If we could afford it we would buy a new car.

Om/Ifall du inte äter upp din smörgås, får du ingen efterrätt.
If you don't eat up your sandwich you won't get any dessert.

(b) Question clause:

Äter du inte upp din smörgas, får du ingen efterrätt.
If you don't eat up your sandwich you won't get any dessert.

The conditional is here expressed by question word order (see 1042(b)).

(c) Imperative clause (see 537, 10&-f.):

Ät upp din smörgås, så får du efterrätt.
Eat up your sandwich, then you'll get some dessert.

(d) A further means of expressing condition is the use of some adverbial expression:

Har du inte ätit upp din smörgås? I så fall får du ingen efterrätt.
Haven't you eaten up your sandwich? Then you'll get no dessert.

D   TRANSITIVE, INTRANSITIVE AND REFLEXIVE VERBS

539   Introduction

(a) Transitive verbs always have a direct object:

John köpte huset.   John bought the house.

(b) Intransitive verbs do not have a direct object:

Han sov.   He slept.

Note that the direct object of a transitive verb becomes the subject when the verb changes from active to passive: (see 547 below and 1032):

John	köpte	huset.	Huset	köptes	av John.
John	bought	the house.	The house	was bought	by John.
subject	*active verb*	*object*	*subject*	*passive verb*	*agent*

(c) Reflexive verbs (541) are formed using reflexive pronouns (301, 310ff.) and are intransitive.

(d) Certain verbs are ditransitive, i.e. they have two objects, a direct object and an indirect object:

Ingvar	gav	**Olle**	**boken.**
subject	*verb*	*IO*	*DO*
Ingvar	gave	Olle	the book.

There is a sizeable group of verbs which take two objects. This includes:

berätta tell; **(be)visa** show prove; **(er)bjuda** offer; **föreslå** recommend; **ge** give; **lova** promise; **lämna** leave; **låna** lend; **meddela** communicate; **misunna** envy; **räcka** hand; **skicka** send; **skänka** donate; **säga** tell; **sända** send; **undanhålla** withhold from; **unna** (not) begrudge; **vålla** cause.

The indirect object can also be expressed by means of a prepositional phrase (716(d), 727(q)):

Ingvar	gav	boken	till Olle.
subject	*verb*	*DO*	*IO*
Ingvar	gave	the book	to Olle.

In this last sentence it can be seen that **Olle** is linked only indirectly, via a preposition, to the verb.

540 Transitive and intransitive verbs

(a) Form: transitive and intransitive verbs often occur in pairs with very similar meanings and forms. In many cases the transitive verb is weak (Conj. I, II) while the intransitive is strong (Conj. IV):

Transitive	*Intransitive*
sätta IIa, place, set	**sitta** IV, sit
lägga IIa, lay, place	**ligga** IV, lie
bränna IIa, burn	**brinna** IV, burn
fälla IIa, fell	**falla** IV, fall
ställa IIa, stand, place upright	**stå** IV, stand
söva IIa, anaesthetise, put to sleep	**sova** IV, sleep (cf. **somna** I, fall asleep)
spräcka IIb, split, cleave	**spricka** IV, burst, split
sänka IIb, (cause to) sink	**sjunka** IV, sink

In some cases both equivalents are weak:

dränka IIb, drench, drown	**drunkna** I, drown
kyla IIa, chill, cool	**kallna** I, get cold, cool
släcka IIb, extinguish (flame)	**slockna** I, go out (flame)
väcka IIb, awaken, rouse	**vaka** I, stay awake
	vakna I, wake up

röka IIb, smoke   ryka IIb, give off smoke
trötta I, tire, make tired   tröttna I, tire, get tired

Some intransitive verbs may be made transitive by adding the prefix be-:

lysa   →   belysa
shine   illuminate

Others are: **bearbeta** treat; **bebo** inhabit; **begränsa** limit; **besegra** defeat; **besvara** answer; **bevaka** guard.

(b) A few Swedish verbs may be either transitive or intransitive: **sluta**, finish; **handla**, shop; **dricka**, drink.

Filmen slutade klockan 5.   The film *finished* at 5 o'clock. [intr.]
Jag slutade boken i går.   I *finished* the book yesterday. [tr.]

(c) Whereas Swedish often maintains quite firm distinctions between transitive and intransitive, employing two different (but occasionally related) verbs (cf. (a) above), many English verbs may be either. Compare:

The chimney s*moked*.   **Skorstenen rykte.** [intr.]
John *smoked* a cigar.   **John rökte en cigarr.** [tr.]

Other examples:

They *burned* the waste paper.   **bränna, -er, brände, bränt** [tr.]
The house *burned* to the ground.   **brinna, -er, brann, brunnit** [intr.]

Mary *left* this letter for you.   **lämna, -r, lämnade, lämnat** [tr.]
Mary *left* early.   **gå, -r, gick, gått** [intr.)

The Japanese *sank* the battleships.   **sänka, -er, sänkte, sänkt** [tr.]
The Vasa *sank* quickly.   **sjunka, -er, sjönk, sjunkit** [intr.]

He *drowned* the kittens.   **dränka, -er, dränkte, dränkt** [tr.]
He *drowned* in the lake.   **drunkna, -r, drunknade,
                                        drunknat** [intr.]

He *split* the log in two.   **spräcka, -er, spräckte, spräckt** [tr.]
His trousers *split*.   **spricka, -er, sprack, spruckit** [intr.]

Soldiers *blew* up the bridge.	**spränga, -er, sprängde, sprängt** [tr.]
The bomb *blew* up.	**explodera, -r, exploderade, exploderat** [intr.]

They *are growing* potatoes.	**odla, odlar, odlade, odlat** [tr.]
The potatoes *are growing*.	**växa, växer, växte, växt** [intr.]

The government has *frozen* wages.	**frysa, -er, fryste, fryst** [tr.]
The lake has *frozen* over.	**frysa, -er, frös, frusit** [intr.]

541 Reflexive verbs

(a) Form: for reflexive pronouns and other reflexive constructions see 301, 310ff. The reflexive verb construction is active but intransitive; the reflexive pronoun refers to the subject:

Transitive	*Reflexive*
Han lägger boken [object] **på bordet.**	**Han lägger sig** [reflexive object] **tidigt.**
He places the book on the table.	He goes to bed early.
Jag lär honom [object] **svenska.**	**Han lär sig** [reflexive object] **svenska.**
I teach him Swedish.	He learns Swedish.

(b) A number of verbs in Swedish may be used either transitively (with an object) or reflexively (with a reflexive object):

tvätta/ tvätta sig	wash
skära/ skära sig	cut (oneself)
gömma/ gömma sig	hide
böja/ böja sig	bend, submit
raka/ raka sig	shave
hejda/ hejda sig	stop (oneself)
känna/ känna sig	feel

e.g. *Transitive*	*Reflexive*
Sjuksköterskan tvättade patienten.	**Sjuksköterskan tvättade sig.**
The nurse washed the patient.	The nurse washed/had a wash.
Tjuven gömde stöldgodset.	**Tjuven gömde sig på vinden.**
The thief hid the stolen property.	The thief hid in the attic.

(c) Some verbs are only found in the reflexive form in Swedish:

gifta sig get married; **förkyla sig** catch a cold; **bege sig** go; **infinna sig** present oneself; **tilldra sig** occur; **förirra sig** get lost; **förivra sig** get carried away; **befatta sig** concern oneself (with).

Notice that many of these have a prefix in **för-**, **be-** or a verb particle.

(d) Many verbs which are reflexive in Swedish are not necessarily reflexive in English:

John reste sig.	John got up.
Han satte sig igen.	He sat (himself) down again.
Jag känner mig dålig.	I feel ill.
Hon klädde sig i svart.	She dressed in black.
Han borde uppföra sig bättre.	He should behave (himself) better.
De måste skynda sig.	They must hurry up.
Det kan jag inte erinra mig.	I can't remember that.

A number of these verbs indicate movement:

resa sig get up; **skynda sig** hurry up; **sätta sig** sit down; **närma sig** approach; **lägga sig** lie down; **röra sig** move [intr.]; **vända sig** turn [intr.].

Other verbs are reflexive when used intransitively in Swedish but are not reflexive in English:

avhålla sig abstain; **beklaga sig** complain; **bemöda sig** endeavour; **dra sig tillbaka** withdraw, retire; **föreställa sig** imagine; **förvåna sig** wonder; **förändra sig** alter, change; **glädja sig** rejoice; **visa sig** appear; **ångra sig** repent.

(e) In some cases an alternative to the reflexive form is an intransitive s-form of the verb (see 545 below).

Hans ögon tåras/tårar sig.	His eyes water.
De bara latas/latar sig.	They just laze about.
Folkmassan skingrades/skingrade sig.	The crowd dispersed.

Also: **harmas/harma sig** be indignant; **förargas/förarga sig** get annoyed; **glädjas/glädja sig** be happy.

E S-FORMS OF THE VERB AND THE PASSIVE

542 S-forms of the verb: form

	Infinitive	Present	Past	Supine	Meaning
Irregular forms are marked * in the table.					
I	baka/s	baka/s	baka/des	baka/ts	be baked
IIa	böj/as	böj/s	böjd/es	böj/ts	be bent
– stems in **-mj, -nj**:					
	vämj/as	vämj/es*	vämj/des	vämj/ts	be disgusted
II b	köp/as	köp/s	köp/tes	köp/ts	be bought
– stems in **-s**:					
	läs/as	läs/es*	läs/tes	läst/s	be read
III	sy/s	sy/s	sy/ddes	sy/tts	be sewn
IV	bjud/as	bjud/s	bjöd/s	bjud/its	be invited

(a) The present tense in **-s** is formed by adding **-s** directly to the stem (see (c) for exceptions). All other forms of the verb add **-s** directly to the active form. The only exceptions are IIb verbs with stems in **-s**, and I and IIa verbs with stems in **-mj, -nj**. These add **-es**:

> **Boken läses fortfarande.** The book is still read.

Others: **tämja** tame; **tänja** stretch; **skönja** perceive.

(b) In earlier Swedish the present s-passive of verbs of Conj. II and IV was formed by adding **-es** to the stem. This is still seen in formal Swedish, particularly on signs, but is rarely used in spoken or normal written Swedish:

> **Bär köpes här.** Berries bought here.
> **Båt uthyres.** Boat for hire.

(c) The participles (531f.) do not usually possess an **s**-form. There are some exceptions as regards the present participle, though these do not have a passive sense:

(i) Verbal use after the verbs **bli, ha, komma** in colloquial Swedish:

> **Han kom åkandes i sin bil.** He came driving in his car.

(ii) Adverbial use in some set phrases, both colloquial and archaic:

Vi fiskade både lovligt och olovandes.
We fished both legally and illegally.

Jag var, skam till sägandes, ganska lat.
I was, shame to say, rather lazy.

(d) The imperative (537) is unusual with s-verbs and never has a passive sense:

Djävlas inte med din lilla syster!
Don't annoy your little sister!

Skäms inte för det du gjort!
Don't be ashamed of what you've done!

543 S-forms of the verb: summary of use

S-forms of the verb have the following four distinct uses:

(a) The reciprocal: **De kysstes.** They kissed. See 544.

(b) The deponent: **Vi trivs här.** We like it here. See 545.

(c) Absolute use: **Nässlan bränns.** The nettle stings. See 546.

(d) The passive: **Huset målades.** The house was (being) painted. See 547f.

Note: There are two other distinct ways of forming the passive other than the s-form, namely with forms of **bli** + past participle (549) and with forms of **vara** + past participle (550). These are known as 'periphrastic forms'.

544 The reciprocal

The s-verb may indicate reciprocity, i.e. the subject both carries out an action and is the object of an action. The **-s** may be replaced by the pronoun **varandra** 'each other' (see 335). These verbs have, of necessity, a plural subject:

De träffas och talas vid. = De träffar varandra och talar med varandra.
They meet (each other) and talk (to each other).

Common reciprocal verbs are:

brottas I	wrestle	kyssas* IIb	kiss
enas I	unite	mötas* IIb	meet
förlikas I	be reconciled	pussas* I	kiss
försonas I	become reconciled	råkas I	meet
följas åt IIa	accompany (one another)	skiljas IIa	part
		retas* I	tease
hjälpas åt IIb	help (one another)	samlas* I	gather
kivas I	squabble	ses* V	meet
kramas* I	hug	slåss* IV	fight
tampas I	tussle		

Most of these verbs (*) also occur in an active form without -s. Cf.:

Han kramade henne.   He hugged her.
De kramades.   They hugged (each other).

545   The deponent

(a) Some s-verbs have an active meaning and are intransitive, i.e. they have passive form but active meaning.

Jag hoppas att de kommer.   I hope they come.
Det finns ingenting mer att säga.   There is nothing more to say.

Common deponent verbs are:

andas I breathe; **avundas** I envy; **blygas** IIa be ashamed; **brås (på)** III take after; **dagas** I dawn; **djävlas** I be nasty to; **envisas** I persist; **fattas** I be missing; **felas** I be missing; **finnas** IV be, exist; **färdas** I travel; **förolyckas** I lose one's life; **handskas** I treat; **hoppas** I hope; **kräkas** IIb vomit; **lyckas** I succeed; **låtsas** I pretend; **minnas** IIa remember, recall; **misslyckas** I fail; **nalkas** I approach; **randas** I dawn; **saknas** I be lacking; **skämmas** IIa be ashamed; **svettas** I sweat; **synas** IIb appear; **trivas** IIa be happy; **trängas** IIa jostle; **tyckas** IIb seem; **töras** IIa dare; **umgås** IV be in the company of; **vantrivas** IIa be unhappy; **väsnas** I be noisy; **åldras** I age.

Deponent verbs do not normally possess a form without **-s**. If such a form exists, then there is usually a marked difference in meaning between the verb with and the verb without **-s**. To all intents and purposes they are two distinct verbs. Cf.:

Hon tyckte att han var stilig.   She thought he was handsome.
Hon tycktes inte veta det.   She didn't seem to know that.

(b) Most deponent verbs are intransitive. Transitive deponents include:

andas in något breathe something in; **avundas någon/något** envy someone/something; **minnas någon/något** remember someone/something; **nalkas någon/något** approach someone/something.

(c) Deponents rarely form participles, but when they do, they first drop the -s:

åldras	→	**en åldrande kvinna** an ageing woman
lyckas	→	**ett lyckat försök** a successful attempt

546 Absolute use of the s-verb

A few s-verbs have an active meaning, like the reciprocal (544), but the action is unidirectional and the object understood. The meaning often incorporates the idea of habit or tendency. There are often forms without -s with similar meanings:

Deras hund bits	Their dog bites.
= Deras hund brukar bita mig.	Their dog usually bites me.
Nässlorna bränns.	Nettles sting.

Other s-verbs with absolute use are: **knuffas** jostle; **luras** deceive; **narras** fool; **nypas** pinch; **retas** tease; **rivas** scratch; **stickas** bite [of insects].

547 The passive: introduction

(a) Subject and agent

While active verbs often have a subject and an object, passive verbs may have a subject and an agent. In the transformation from active to passive the subject of the active construction becomes the agent of the passive construction, while the object of the active construction becomes the subject of the passive construction (see also 1002(d), 1032):

Active	**En kvinna**	**körde**	**bilen**
	subject		*object*
	A woman	drove	the car

Passive	**Bilen**	**kördes**	**av en kvinna**
	subject		*agent*
	The car	was driven	by a woman

Many passive constructions have no agent, however:

Bilen kördes försiktigt.	The car was driven carefully.

The reason for this is that in many cases the agent (or real subject) is unknown, unimportant or obvious from the context, and it is the action itself expressed by the verb or the object of the action (subject of the passive) that is the dominating idea:

Frukost serveras i skolorna kl. 11.	School lunch is served at 11.
Han dödades i en bilolycka.	He was killed in a car accident.
Mötet hölls i den stora salen.	The meeting was held in the big hall.

Some passive constructions, namely those in the impersonal passive, never have an agent. There is no direct English equivalent to these.

Nu ska det arbetas!	Now there will be some work done.
Här ska dansas, ser jag.	There's to be some dancing here, I see.

Some passive constructions employing an agent, whilst grammatically possible, are very unusual as an active construction reveals the grammatical relationship more clearly:

Bilen tvättades av honom.	→	**Han tvättade bilen.**
The car was washed by him.		He washed the car.

(b) There are three ways of expressing the passive (and one circumlocution):

(i) The s-passive (**-s** is added to the active form of the verb, see 542f.):

Äpplena skalas.	The apples are (being) peeled. [See 548.]

(ii) Forms of **bli** + past participle (i.e. periphrastic forms. For forms of the past participle, see 531):

Äpplena blir skalade. See 549.

(iii) Forms of **vara** + past participle (i.e. periphrastic forms. For forms of the past participle, see 531):

Äpplena är skalade. See 550.

(iv) **Man** etc. + active verb:

Man skalar äpplena. See 551.

548 The s-passive

In this, the most frequent type of passive construction, the s-form (542f.) stresses the action of the verb. Time is often unimportant in s-passive constructions, and the agent often unknown, immaterial or obvious from the context. This form is often found in the infinitive, and is very common in the past tense. S-passive constructions frequently indicate repetition, command or instruction. They are rather more common in written Swedish than in spoken, especially in newspaper style. In spoken Swedish, constructions with **bli** + past participle (549) or **man** + active verb (551) are often preferred.

Middag serveras klockan sju.
Dinner is served at seven.

Ordet söner uttalas med accent två.
The word 'söner' is pronounced with accent 2.

Felparkering straffas med böter.
Illegal parking is punishable by a fine.

Staden förstördes under kriget.
The town was destroyed during the war.

Boken måste läsas av alla studenter.
The book must be read by all students.

549 Forms of **bli** + past participle

The **bli**-passive usually expresses a definite isolated occurrence, often together with an adverbial expression of time or manner (607(a)(b)) and/or an agent. This form portrays an occurrence in which there is a transition from one state to another. In the present tense **blir** can indicate future (525(a)) and the **bli**-passive is thus more common in the past, perfect and pluperfect. It is common in the spoken language and in informal written Swedish.

Han blev påkörd av en bil igår och ena benet blev brutet.
He was hit by a car yesterday and one of his legs was broken.

Han har blivit vald till ordförande i klubben.
He has been elected chairman of the club.

England blev slaget 2-3 av Sverige i finalen.
England was beaten by Sweden 2-3 in the final.

Saken blir avgjord vid sammanträdet imorgon.
The matter will be decided at the meeting tomorrow.

Note: In colloquial Central Swedish **vart**, the past tense (and only extant) form of the verb **varda**, is sometimes heard in cases where one might expect **blev**:

Han vart påkörd av en bil igår.   He was hit by a car yesterday.

This form is not used in written Swedish.

550 Forms of **vara** + past participle

The **vara**-passive provides a picture of an object or state and stresses the result of an action or a completed transition. The past participle (531) possesses a strongly adjectival sense. This form is often found together with an agent and/or an adverbial expression of time or place (607(a)(b)).

Himlen är täckt av moln.	The sky is covered in cloud.
Hon är plågad av mygg.	She is tormented by mosquitoes.
Säden är förstörd av torkan.	The grain has been ruined by the drought.
Vi är bortbjudna i kväll.	We are invited out tonight.
Han har varit gift tidigare.	He has been married before.

551 Man etc. + active verb

See also 330. This construction is used as an alternative to the impersonal construction **det** + **s**-passive in which **det** is the formal as opposed to the real subject (see also 309(d), 1003):

Man skriver mycket i tidningarna om det.
A lot is written about it in the papers.
(= **Det skrivs mycket i tidningarna om det.**)

Man säger att det ska bli en ändring.
They say there'll be a change.
(= **Det sägs att det ska bli en ändring.**)

Man drack brännvin hela natten.
They were drinking brandy all night.
(= **Det dracks brännvin hela natten.**)
Brandy was being drunk all night.

Other impersonal active subjects frequently used are:

Någon:	**Någon sa det igår.**	Cf. passive:	**Det sades igår.**
Folk:	**Folk sa det igår.**		**Det sades igår.**
De:	**De sa det igår.**		**Det sades igår.**
Ingen:	**Ingen sa det igår.**		**Det blev inte sagt igår.**

552 Factors underlying the use of different passive forms

The reason why one particular form rather than another is used in a particular case is often difficult to discern. A number of different factors underlie the choice:

(a) The subject: there is a tendency to use **bli**-passives with personal subjects and s-passives with non-personal subjects.

Han blev påkörd av en lastbil förra veckan.
He was run over by a truck last week.

Det anses vara av sämre kvalitet.
It is considered to be of inferior quality.

This does not apply, however, to the perfect and pluperfect tenses:

Brita har utnämnts till ordförande.
Brita has been appointed chairperson.

(b) The agent: with a concrete agent, either **bli**-passives or s-passives are used, while with abstract agents s-passives are used. Compare:

Han överfölls/blev överfallen av rövare.
He was attacked by robbers.

Mördaren överfölls av ånger.
The murderer was overcome by remorse.

In cases where the **av** expression does not indicate the real agent of the activity but a means or cause (the diffuse passive), s-passives or **vara**-passives are used:

Läget präglas/är präglat av starka svängningar.
The situation is characterised by great fluctuations.

(c) Tense

(i) With the infinitive, and especially with modal auxiliaries (535), s-passives dominate:

Rummet ska städas innan pappa kommer hem.
The room must be tidied before Dad comes home.

Rapporten måste skrivas idag.
The report must be written today.

(ii) With the present tense s-passives are more common than periphrastic forms.

Bli + past participle often denotes future.
Vara + past participle has an adjectival sense.

S-passives denote a repeated action with terminative verbs, and a continuing action with durative verbs. Compare:

Dörrarna blir öppnade (om en timme).
The doors will be opened (in an hour).

Dörrarna är öppnade (nu).
The doors are opened (now).

Dörrarna öppnas (kl. 10).
The doors open (at 10 o'clock).

Diktatorn fruktas av alla.
The dictator is feared by everyone.

(iii) Past:

1   S-passives:

- can be used instead of **bli**-passives with terminative verbs:

Bilen stals/blev stulen.
The car was stolen.

Han utnämndes/blev utnämnd till professor.
He was appointed professor.

- are more common with terminative verbs when a repeated action is involved:

Rättsregler skapades ofta utifrån det konkreta fallet.
Laws were often created from the concrete case.

- are frequent with *durative verbs* or cases in which the action is stressed:

Borgar byggdes, nya städer grundades, källare grävdes.
Castles were built, new towns were founded, cellars were dug

När bröllopet firades, kom folk från hela bygden.
When the wedding was celebrated people came from the whole district.

- are also very common in cases of a single occurrence:

Ett rymningsförsök stoppades i sista stund.
An escape attempt was prevented at the last moment.

- are more common with modal auxiliary verbs:

Resultaten måste förbättras.
Profits must be improved.

2 **Bli**-passives:

- are more common when stressing the result of an action, especially when a qualifier is introduced:

Jag blev alltid vänligt emottagen.
I was always courteously received.

- are more common when stressing the result of an action, especially when there is a conditional:

Om man stal ett får blev man hängd.
If one stole a sheep one was hanged.

- are more common when stressing the result of an action, especially when an action was beginning:

Premiärministern blev (så småningom) älskad av folket.
The Prime Minister (eventually) came to be loved by the people.

3 **Vara**-passives tend to be adjectival:

Vikingarna var fruktade över hela Europa.
The Vikings were feared throughout Europe.

(iv) Perfect, pluperfect:

1 S-passives dominate even for single occurrences and completed actions:

Det sista glaset hade tömts för timmar sedan.
The last glass had been emptied hours before.

2 **Bli**-passives are used to stress a single completed event:

Han har som bekant blivit åtalad för rattonykterhet.
He has, as you know, been charged with drunken driving.

Bli-passives also draw attention to the subject:

> **Dessa skogar har blivit besparade tätbebyggelse (i motsats till andra skogar).**
> These forests have been spared urban development (as opposed to other forests).

Bli-passives are also used in the absolute passive construction (i.e. one lacking any adverbial of time or manner):

> **Det var ett under om en tavla blev såld.**
> It was a miracle if a picture was sold.

553   Differences in the use of the passive in English and Swedish

In many cases the use of the passive is much the same in the two languages. These notes concentrate on major differences.

(a) English passive = Swedish active:

(i) Swedish has **man** + active verb (551):

> It is more difficult than is generally supposed.
> **Det är svårare än man i allmänhet tror.**

(ii) 'There' + passive infinitive construction = Swedish active infinitive construction:

> There was nothing to be done.
> **Det fanns ingenting att göra.**

(iii) 'Be said to', 'be reputed to' = Swedish **lär, ska(ll)** (535):

> The food there is said to be good.
> **Maten där lär vara god.**

(b) Swedish passive = English active:

(i) **Det** + passive (impersonal passive) = 'there is/was' + noun (547(a)):

> **Det sjöngs och dansades hela natten.**
> There was singing and dancing all night.

Det talades om en ny giv.
There was talk of a new deal.

(ii) Some Swedish agentless **s**-passives = English intransitive verbs:

Dörren öppnades.
The door opened.

Hennes ögon fylldes med tårar.
Her eyes filled with tears.

Läget har förändrats/förvärrats/kan förbättras.
The situation has changed/deteriorated/may improve.

F COMPOUND VERBS

554 Introduction

A compound verb is one prefixed by a particle. In some compounds the particle forms an integral and inseparable part of the verb and remains attached to it in all circumstances. This kind of compound is known as *inseparable* (555). Such verbs inflect in the same way as in the uncompounded form. Compare:

stå – stod – stått stand   **bistå – bistod – bistått**
                                                                     support, assist

However, in other verbs the particle may become separated from the verb under some circumstances and in certain parts of the verb. Compare:

uppstiga, stiga upp rise, get up

This kind of compound is known as a *separable* compound (556).

555 Inseparable verbs

Inseparable compound verbs comprise:

(a) Most verbs compounded with nouns:

hungerstrejka (go on) hunger strike; **tjuvlyssna** eavesdrop; **rådfråga** consult.

Note 1: The common exception is **maskinskriva** 'to type':

Jag har suttit och skrivit maskin hela dagen.
I have been sitting typing all day.

Note 2: Some inseparable verbs are only used with a direct object:

Han bokförde dagens inkomster varje kväll.
He entered the day's takings in the book every evening.

In sentences with no direct object the separable form is used, the particle taking the place of the direct object:

Han har fört bok i 20 år.   He has kept the books for 20 years.

(b) Most verbs compounded with adjectives:

fullända complete; **storskratta** guffaw; **småle** smile; **godkänna** approve.

Note: Some adjective + verb compounds may be separated for stylistic reasons. In such instances the adjectival element reverts to its role as an adjective and agrees in number and gender with its predicate:

Rengör mina stövlar nu med en gång!   Clean my boots at once!
Gör mina stövlar rena nu med en gång!

(c) Most verbs compounded with other verbs:

brännmärka brand; **sprutmåla** spray paint.

(d) Verbs compounded with numerals and most verbs compounded with prepositions:

fyrdubbla quadruple; **undervärdera** underestimate; **överreagera** over-react.

(e) Verbs compounded with **själv-**:

självdö die naturally, die out; **självspricka** chap (skin).

(f) Verbs compounded with:

(i) Unstressed prefixes:

be-	**betala**	pay, pay for
för-	**förklara**	explain
ent-	**entlediga**	dismiss

(ii) Stressed prefixes:

an-	**anställa**	appoint
o-	**oroa**	worry
bi-	**bistå**	help, assist
sam-	**samtycka**	consent

er-	erhålla	receive
um-	umgås	associate with
före-	föredra	prefer
und-	undkomma	escape
här-	härstamma	originate
van-	vanhedra	disgrace
miss-	missunna	begrudge
väl-	välsigna	bless
när-	närvara	be present
å-	åskåda	watch

556 Separable verbs

These comprise two main groups, those that are usually separated into verb and particle (a) and those that are found in both separated or integral form (b):

(a) Certain Swedish verbs are always separated except in the participial forms, i.e. present and past participles. (See 531f.):According to modern usage this group comprises verbs whose particles are:

vilse	gå vilse	to get lost
	en vilsegången pojke	a lost boy
ihjäl	slå ihjäl	to kill
	Han blev ihjälslagen.	He was killed.
omkull	falla omkull	to fall over
	ett omkullfallet träd	a fallen tree
bort	resa bort	to go away
	Han är bortrest.	He has gone away.
igen	känna igen	to recognise
	ett igenkännande leende	a smile of recognition
om	köra om	overtake
	den omkörda lastbilen	the overtaken lorry

(b) Swedish verbs which may be either separated or integral indicate three general areas of meaning:

(i) Place:

upp	stiga upp	uppstiga	get up, rise
ned	stiga ned	nedstiga	go down, descend
in	räkna in	inräkna	include
till	strömma till	tillströmma	flock together
fast	frysa fast	fastfrysa	freeze fast
av	resa av	avresa	depart

från	ta ifrån	frånta	deprive
ut	låna ut	utlåna	lend out
(i)genom	gå genom	genomgå	go through
över	svämma över	översvämma	flood

(ii) Time:

för	förvarna	varna för	forewarn
före	föregå	gå före	precede

(iii) Action:

1 Beginning an action:

till	skruva till	tillskruva	screw tight
in	somna in	insomna	fall asleep
på	tända på	påtända	turn on, light

2 Ending an action (integral in past participle only):

av	stänga av	avstängd	shut off, switch off
upp	äta upp	uppäten	eat up
ur	dricka ur	urdrucken	drink up
ut	dö ut	utdöd	die out

557 Separable or inseparable forms – stylistic differences

In many cases in Swedish the separated and integral forms are identical in meaning. The separated forms are now used in the spoken language and in everyday written Swedish. The integral forms are reserved almost solely for official documents and more formal usage. Compare:

ta emot/emotta to receive
> **Vi tog emot våra priser.**
> We received our prizes.
> **Kungen emottogs av ambassadören.**
> The king was received by the ambassador.

härda ut/uthärda to endure
> **Jag härdar inte ut längre.**
> I can't stand it any longer.
> **Man kan knappast uthärda den tropiska hettan.**
> One can scarcely endure the tropical heat.

lägga ned/nedlägga to lay down
　　Hon lade ned böckerna på bordet.
　　She laid the books down on the table.
　　Kungen nedlade en krans på graven.
　　The king laid a wreath on the grave.

stiga ned/nedstiga descend
　　Vi steg ned i gruvan.
　　We went down into the mine.
　　Kristus hade nedstigit till dödsriket.
　　Christ had descended into the Kingdom of the Dead.

Others: **medtaga** bring along; **uppsöka** seek out; **tillsäga** inform; **sammanföra** bring together.

Notwithstanding these stylistic differences, the verbs are always compounded in their participial forms:

　　Fabriken är nedlagd.
　　The factory is closed down.　　　　[from **lägga ned**]

　　ett vänligt mottagande
　　a friendly reception　　　　　　　[from **ta emot**]

　　uppsökande journalistik
　　investigative journalism　　　　　[from **söka upp**]

558　Separable or inseparable forms – semantic differences

Certain Swedish verbs have separated and integral forms with different meanings (cf. English: 'take over' and 'overtake'). In Swedish the separated form usually has a literal meaning (physical or concrete), whereas the corresponding integral form has a figurative meaning:

Separated = Literal	*Integrated = Figurative*
Jag bryter av kvisten.	**Jag avbryter samtalet.**
I break off the branch.	I interrupt the conversation.
Han strök under ordet.	**Han underströk ordets betydelse.**
He underlined the word.	He emphasised the meaning of the word.
De steg över diket.	**Det överstiger mina krafter.**
They stepped over the ditch.	It exceeds my powers.

Sometimes the semantic difference is so great as to warrant regarding the two forms as two distinct verbs:

Bordsbenet gick av.	**Statsministern avgick.**
The table leg broke off.	The Prime Minister resigned.

Lampan lyser upp rummet.	**Vi upplyste honom om hans misstag.**
The lamp illuminates the room.	We enlightened him regarding his mistake.

Vi gick förbi hans hus.	**Vi förbigick honom vid prisutdelningen.**
We went past his house.	We passed over him in awarding the prizes.

Others: **ställa fram** put out/**framställa** present; **jaga in** drive in/**injaga** inspire; **komma ned** come down/**nedkomma** be delivered of; **bygga upp** build up/**uppbygga** edify.

Notwithstanding any semantic differences, the verbs are always compounded in their participial forms:

en avbruten kvist	a broken branch	**(bryta av)**
ett avbrutet samtal	an interrupted conversation	**(avbryta)**
en förbigående	a passer-by	**(gå förbi)**
Rummet var upplyst.	The room was lit.	**(lysa upp)**

559   Separable verbs – the position of the particle

See also 1021. The two parts of a separable verb, i.e. verb + particle, are always juxtaposed in a clause or sentence except:

(a) In a main clause with simple tense and a clausal adverbial (1007):

Jag tyckte aldrig om henne.	I never liked her.
Jag känner inte igen dig.	I don't recognise you.
Bordsben av stål går sällan av.	Steel table legs rarely break.

(b) When inversion in a main clause with simple tense means that the subject follows immediately after the verb:

Tycker du om henne?	Do you like her?
Kände ni igen honom?	Did you recognise him?
Det året skrevs pundet ner.	That year the pound was devalued.

(c) In an imperative constructed with a clausal adverbial:

Slå inte ihjäl honom!	Don't kill him!

Gå aldrig förbi hans hus!   Never walk past his house!

In all other cases verb and particle are juxtaposed. NB This is frequently at variance with English usage:

Många brev har kommit bort.	Many letters have gone astray.
Har du aldrig tyckt om henne?	Have you never liked her?
Stryk under ordet!	Underline the word!
Skriv upp det!	Write it down!
Jag ringer upp dem.	I will ring them up.
Låt mig stänga av den!	Let me switch it off.
Jag tar på mig mina finaste kläder.	I will put on my best clothes.

G SOME PROBLEM VERBS

In this section some problems of meaning are briefly outlined which are not dealt with in Modal verbs (535(b)), Transitive and intransitive verbs (540) or Reflexive verbs (541(d)). For problems of inflexion, double forms, etc. see 515f.

560   Translation into Swedish of some problem verbs

These notes isolate only very common problems. They are not dictionary definitions.

(a) Arrive/leave
1 arrive [of people] **anlända, komma**
The students arrive on Monday.
Studenterna kommer på måndag.

2 arrive [of trains, boats, planes, etc.] **ankomma**
The plane gets in at eight (o'clock).
Flygplanet ankommer klockan åtta.

1 leave [intransitive] **avgå, resa, åka, gå**
They left early.
De gick tidigt.

2 leave [transitive] **lämna**
They left their car in the car park.
De lämnade sin bil i parkeringsplatsen.

(b) Ask
1 enquire **fråga**
We asked him what he was called.
Vi frågade honom vad han hette.

2 ask [someone to do something] **be**
We asked him to come.
Vi bad honom komma.

3 ask [questions] **ställa**
The police asked us a lot of questions.
Polisen ställde en massa frågor.

(c) Change
1 alter **ändra, förändra**
The law has changed recently.
Lagen ändrades nyligen.

2 change one's mind **ändra sig**
He changed his mind several times.
Han ändrade sig flera gånger.

3 exchange [something for
something else: e.g. clothes] **byta**
He changed trains at Hallsberg.
Han bytte tåg i Hallsberg.

4 change gear, change money **växla**
The driver changed down.
Föraren växlade ner.

(d) Drive
1 drive a vehicle
[i.e. sit behind the wheel] **köra**
Olle drives a bus.
Olle kör buss.

2 travel [i.e. be driven] **åka**
We and the children drove to Norway this summer.
Vi och barnen åkte till Norge i sommar.

3 to provide the power
for something **driva**
What is it that drives him on?
Vad är det som driver honom?

(e) Feel
1 feel [transitive] **känna**
Suddenly he felt the pain.
Plötsligt kände han smärtan.

2 feel [intransitive] **känna sig**
He felt tired.
Han kände sig trött.

3. feel [deponent] **kännas**
It feels cold.
Det känns kallt.

(f) Go
1 go by vehicle **åka, resa, fara**
I am going to America.
Jag reser till Amerika.

2 go [generally; esp. walk, leave] **gå**
I really must go.
Jag måste verkligen gå.

(g) Grow
1 grow [intransitive] **växa**
Rice grows in China.
Ris växer i Kina.

2 grow [transitive] **odla**
People grow rice in China.
Folk odlar ris i Kina.

3 increase in size **öka**
The number of students is growing all the time.
Antalet studenter ökar ständigt.

(h) Know
1 know [facts] **veta**
Do you know what he is called?
Vet du vad han heter?

2 know [people] **känna**
Do you know him?
Känner du honom?

3 know [languages, specialisms] **kunna**
Do you know French?
Kan du franska?

(i) Live
1 dwell, reside **bo**
He lives in Stockholm.
Han bor i Stockholm.

2 be alive **leva**
Linné lived in the 18th century.
Linné levde på 1700-talet.

(j) Put
1 place horizontally **lägga**
Put the book on the table!
Lägg boken på bordet!

2 place upright **ställa**
Put the bottle on the table!
Ställ flaskan på bordet!

3 fix **sätta**
Put the curtains up!
Sätt upp gardinerna!

4 insert into **stoppa**
Don't put your hands in your pockets!
Stoppa inte händerna i fickorna!

(k) See
1 see **se**
Can you see the lighthouse from here?
Kan du se fyrtornet härifrån?

2 meet **träffa**
There's a Mr Smith to see you.
Det har kommit en herr Smith som vill träffa dig.

(l) Stop
1 movement **stanna**
She stopped the car.
Hon stannade bilen.

2 cease doing **sluta**
He stopped talking.
Han slutade tala.

(m) Think
1 hold an opinion **tycka**
I think it's a boring film.
Jag tycker att det är en tråkig film.

2 ponder **tänka**
She sat thinking about it.
Hon satt och tänkte på det.

3 intend **tänka**
He is thinking of buying a car.
Jag tänker köpa en bil.

4 believe **tro**
I think it might rain later.
Jag tror att det kommer att regna senare.

(n) Want
1 want [to do] **vilja**
I want to go home
Jag vill gå hem.

2 want [to have] **vilja ha**
I want a new car.
Jag vill ha en ny bil.

561   Translation into Swedish of the verb 'to be'

In addition to **vara**, five other Swedish verbs are regularly used to translate different senses of the English verb 'to be':

(a) ligga – used of towns, buildings, places and objects lying horizontally:

Sverige ligger i Skandinavien.	Sweden is in Scandinavia.
Kläderna låg utströdda över hela golvet.	The clothes were (lay) strewn across the floor.

(b) sitta – used of objects that are fixed in position:

Sitter nyckeln i låset?	Is the key in the lock?

Dina glasögon sitter på näsan.   Your glasses are on your nose.

(c) stå – used of objects that stand vertically, and when 'is' etc. indicates 'is written':

Bordet står i hörnet.	The table is (stands) in the corner.
Detta står på sidan tio i boken.	That is on page ten of this book.

(d) In order to indicate existence or transition (change of state) two verbs are used in preference to **vara**, namely **finnas** and **bli**:

Det finns många sjöar i Sverige.	There are a lot of lakes in Sweden.
Vad blev resultatet?	What was the result?

6 ADVERBS

A	FORM
601	Adverbs derived from adjectives
602	Other adverbs which are derivatives
603	Some simple adverbs which are not derivatives
604	Compound adverbs
605	Comparison of adverbs

B	FUNCTION
606	Introduction to adverb functions
607	Adverbs classified by meaning
608	Adverbs classified by function
609	Pronominal adverbs
610	Clausal adverbials
611	Adverbs qualifying the noun phrase
612	Adverbs qualifying the adjective/adverb phrase: amplifiers and diminishers

C	LOCATION AND MOVEMENT
613	Location and motion towards
614	Compounded forms indicating location/motion etc.

D	SOME DIFFICULT ADVERBS
615	Translation from Swedish
616	Translation into Swedish

A FORM

601 Adverbs derived from adjectives

(a) The majority of adverbs are formed from adjectives, and in principle adverbs may be formed from all adjectives (except the indeclinable adjectives (206) simply by adding the ending **-t** to the non-neuter singular form (202ff.):

snabb = quick [adjective]   **snabb***t* = quick*ly* [adverb]

The adverb and the neuter form of the adjective are often identical. It is, therefore, important, especially when translating into English, to distinguish between them. Compare:

Han var mycket vacker.	[Adjective, n.-n.]
He was very handsome.	

Huset var mycket vacker*t*.	[Adjective, n.]
The house was very beautiful.	

Han sjöng mycket vacker*t*.	[Adverb]
He sang very beautifully.	

Huset ligger mycket vacker*t*.	[Adverb]
The house is beautifully situated.	

Huset har en vacker*t* anlagd park. [Adverb]
The house has a beautifully laid out park.

(b) These adverbs in **-t** have two main functions in the sentence, as:

1   Adverbials of manner (see 1007(e), 1024):

Sov go*tt*!	Sleep well!
Du kom hem sen*t* i går kväll!	You came home late last night!

2   Amplifiers qualifying adjectives or adverbs (see 612(e)):

De var otrolig*t* vackra.	They were incredibly beautiful.
Han åkte hemsk*t* fort.	He drove awfully fast.

Notice the difference between:

Hon var en ovanlig*t* [adv.] vacker [adj.] flicka.
She was an unusually beautiful girl.

Hon var en ovanlig [adj.], vacker [adj.] flicka.
She was an unusual, beautiful girl.

Note: Sometimes, instead of an adverb of manner, Swedish prefers to use a predicative adjective. There is, as the English shows, a subtle difference in meaning:

Han gick bedrövat bort.   [Adverb]
He left dejectedly.

Han gick bedröva*d* bort.   [Predicative complement, 1006, 208(c)]
He left dejected.

(c) Adjectives ending in **-lig** form adverbs in three different ways:

(i) By adding **-en** (in some instances, marked *, this is the only option):

antagligen* presumably; **verkligen** actually; **tämligen*** fairly; **egentligen*** really; **tydligen** clearly; **möjligen** possibly; **onekligen** indubitably; **troligen** probably; **dagligen** daily; **bokstavligen** literally; **slutligen** finally; **nyligen***

recently; **ursprungligen** originally.

Note 1: There is no adjectival counterpart for a small number of adverbs in -**ligen**:

äntligen finally; **nämligen** actually.

Note 2: Some adjectives take the suffix -**ligen**: -**erligen**:

visserligen admittedly; **sannerligen** indeed; **synnerligen** exceedingly.

(ii) By adding -**vis** (= 'way', 'manner') to the neuter form of the adjective:

lyckligtvis happily; **naturligtvis** naturally; **rimligtvis** reasonably; **vanligtvis** usually; **möjligtvis** possibly; **nödvändigtvis** necessarily.

Note: -**vis** may also be added to some nouns to form adverbs:

bitvis here and there; **styckevis** piece by piece; **delvis** partly; **gradvis** gradually; **stegvis** step by step; **förhoppningsvis** hopefully; **inledningsvis** by way of introduction; **tidvis** at times; **jämförelsevis** comparatively; **förhållandevis** proportionately; **förslagsvis** tentatively; **undantagsvis** exceptionally; **händelsevis** by accident; **gruppvis** by groups; **klassvis** by classes.

(iii) By adding -**t** (see (a) above):

Notice, therefore, that the same adjectival stem may produce three different adverbs:

tydlig/	→	**tydlig/*t*** or **tydlig/*en***
obvious		obviously
naturlig/	→	**naturlig/*t*** or **naturlig/*en*** or **naturlig/*tvis***
natural		naturally

Those ending in -**ligt** are adverbs of manner (see 607(b), 1007(e), 1018f.).
Those ending in -**ligen** and -**ligtvis** are clausal adverbials (see 610, 1007, 1023).

Han är lyckligt gift.
He is happily married.

Han är lyckligtvis gift.
Happily [i.e. Fortunately] he is married.

Prinsen infann sig personligen. The prince attended in person.

(**d**) Present participles (532) may also be used as adverbs:

Hon har ett strålande vackert leende.
She has a radiantly beautiful smile.

Kristoffer är påfallande lat.
Kristoffer is remarkably lazy.

Han såg forskande på henne.
He regarded her quizzically.

Han svarade undvikande på frågan.
He answered the question evasively.

(e) Past participles in the neuter form (531) are also used as adverbs:

Hammarskiöld arbetade hängivet för fredens sak.
Hammarskiöld worked devotedly in the cause of peace.

Han dök upp helt oväntat.
He appeared unexpectedly.

602 Other adverbs which are derivatives

(a) Forms in -s, -es (old genitives):

alls at all; **annars** otherwise; **dags** time; **nyss** recently; **tvärs** straight; **dels ... dels ...** partly ... partly ... ; **någonstans** somewhere; **alldeles** completely; **särdeles** particularly; **avsides** secluded; **baklänges** backwards; **medsols, medurs** clockwise; **motsols** counter-clockwise; **förgäves** in vain.

(b) Forms in -a, -e:

lika in the same way; **ofta** often; **bara** only; **noga** carefully; **nära** close to; **stilla** calmly; **illa** badly; **hemma** at home; **sakta** slowly; **borta** away; **barfota** barefoot; **föga** little; **länge** for a long time; **framme** there (in front); **inne** in; **inte** not; **åtminstone** at least.

(c) Forms in -an, -en, -om (old datives):

ovan above; **undan** aside; **fjärran** distant; **samman** together; **redan** already; **sällan** rarely; **nästan** almost; **förresten** by the way; **bakom** behind; **fordom** in times past; **stundom** at times; **lagom** just right; **småningom** gradually; **enkom** solely.

(d) Forms in -städes, -stans (Expressing location (see 607(c)):

någonstans somewhere; **ingenstans** nowhere; **varstans** everywhere; **annanstans** elsewhere;

annorstädes elsewhere; **allestädes** everywhere; **ingenstädes** nowhere; **härstädes** here; **därstädes** there

Note: The suffixes -stans and -städes derive from stad in its original meaning of 'place' (cf. eldstad 'fireplace'; bostad 'abode', 'place of residence').

(e) Forms in **-ledes** (a productive suffix) and **-lunda** (expressing manner (see 607(b)):

> **således** accordingly; **likaledes** likewise; **brevledes** by letter; **annorledes** differently;
>
> **sålunda** thus; **någorlunda** fairly; **annorlunda** differently; **ingalunda** by no means.

(f) Forms in **-sin** (expressing time (607(a)):

> **någonsin, nånsin** ever

Note: **sin** was originally synonymous with **gång** 'time'.

(g) Forms in **-vart** (expressing direction):

någonvart somewhere; **ingenvart** nowhere

603 Some simple adverbs which are not derivatives

(a) Adverbs of time:

> **aldrig** never; **alltid** always; **då** then; **då och då** now and then; **förr** previously; **genast** immediately; **igen** again; **just** just; **nu** now; **strax** soon; **ännu** yet.

(b) Adverbs of place:

> **här, hit** here; **där, dit** there; **var, vart** where; **hem** home; **bort** away; **fram** forward; **in** in; **ner** down; **upp** up; **ut** out (see 613 for precise meanings).

(c) Adverbs of manner:

> **bra** well; **fort** quickly; **hur** how; **precis** precisely; **något** somewhat.

(d) Modal adverbs:

> **ju** 'you know'; **nog** 'probably'; **väl** 'I suppose' (see 615(f)); **ej, icke, inte** not.

(e) Conjunctional adverbs:

alltså therefore; **också** also; **så** so; **dock** however.

604　Compound adverbs

Compound adverbs are those formed from a simple adverb (see 603) plus a preposition or another adverb. The first element is nearly always an adverb. Of the following (a–h) and (q) are commonly found in Swedish:

(a) + ifrån:

härifrån [= 'från här'] from here; **därifrån** from there; **västerifrån** from the west; **bakifrån** from behind; **varifrån** [= 'ifrån var'] where . . . from; **inifrån** from inside; **bortifrån** from away; **hemifrån** from home.

(b) + åt:

häråt [= 'till/mot här'] this way; **hitåt** this way; **däråt** in that direction; **ditåt** in that direction; **bakåt** backwards; **framåt** forwards; **nedåt** downwards; **uppåt** upwards; **efteråt** afterwards.

(c) + ut:

norrut [= mot norr] northwards; **söderut** southwards; **österut** eastwards; **västerut** westwards; **förrut** before.

(d) + tills:

hittills [= till nu] hitherto; **dittills** [= till då] up to that point.

(e) + efter:

härefter [= från denna stund] after this; **därefter** after that; **hädanefter** henceforth; **varefter** [= efter vilket] after which.

(f) + på:

härpå [= på/efter detta] on/after that; **därpå** after that; **varpå** whereupon.

(g) + för:

därför therefore; **varför** why; **nedför** down; **uppför** up; **nedanför** below.

(h) + emot:

häremot [= emot detta] against this; **däremot** however; **varemot** against which.

The following (j)–(p) are less usual, and are found largely in bureaucratic or legal Swedish:

(j) + hän:

därhän [= till den punkten] to that; **dithän** to that; **varthän [= till vilken punkt]** where.

(k) + med:

härmed [= med detta] with that; **därmed [= med detta]** with that; **varmed [= med vilken]** with which.

(l) + om:

härom [= om detta] about this; **därom** about that; **varom** about which.

(m) + vid:

härvid [= ifråga om detta] in this connection; **därvid** with that; **varvid** at which.

(n) + till:

härtill [= till detta] to that; **därtill** to that; **vartill** to which; **nedtill** at the foot of; **upptill** at the top of; **intill** close to.

(o) + (ut)i:

häruti/häri [= i detta] in this (respect); **däruti/däri** in that; **varuti/vari** in which; **inuti/ini** inside; **borti** over there.

(p) + av:

härav [= av detta], **därav** of that; **varav** of which.

(q) Some other frequent compound adverbs are:

alltjämt still; **dessvärre** unfortunately; **därnäst** then; **jämväl** likewise;

kanske perhaps; **likväl** nevertheless; **ändock** still; **ännu** still; **ändå** yet; **ibland** sometimes; **numera** now; **omkring** around; **häromdagen** the other day; **nuförtiden** nowadays; **såhär** like this; **ånyo** anew.

There is a strong tendency nowadays to separate the preposition and adverb rather than use many of the less common compounds listed above.

Vad grälar ni om?	What are you quarrelling about?
(Varom grälar ni?)	

Kniven som jag skar mig med...	The knife that I cut myself on . . .
(Kniven varmed jag skar mig...)	

605 Comparison of adverbs

(a) Adverbs derived from adjectives possess the same comparative and superlative forms as the adjectives (cf. 233ff.), i.e. the **-t** of the adverb drops before the comparative or superlative ending is added:

Basic	*Comparative*	*Superlative*
tidigt early	**tidigare**	**tidigast**
sent late	**senare**	**senast**
högt highly	**högre**	**högst**

(b) **Väl, bra** compare as for the adjective **god**. **Illa** compares like **dålig**. **Mycket** compares like **mycken**. (See also 235.)

Basic	*Comparative*	*Superlative*
väl, bra well	**bättre**	**bäst**
illa badly	**sämre**	**sämst**
illa badly	**värre**	**värst**
mycket much	**mer(a)**	**mest(a)**

(c) Some other adverbs also compare by adding an ending **-are**:

Basic	Comparative	Superlative
fort quickly	**fortare**	**fortast**
länge for a long time	**längre**	**längst**
ofta often	**oftare**	**oftast**
nära close	**närmare**	**närmaste**
sakta slowly	**saktare**	**saktast**

Note also one adverb which changes its stem:

gärna willingly	**hellre**	**helst**

See also words ending in **-a** in 236(a)(iv).

(d) Adverbs ending in **-ligen, -tvis** do not usually compare.

(e) Adverbs formed from participles compare with **mer, mest** (cf. 236):

> **Jag har aldrig sett henne mer förtjusande vacker.**
> I have never seen her more charmingly pretty.

(f) For comparison of some adverbs of place see 237. The comparative and superlative forms are usually regarded as adjectives:

> **Hans namn stod främst på listan.**   His name was first on the list.

B FUNCTION

606 Introduction to adverb functions

Adverbs represent a particularly heterogeneous group as regards meaning and types of use. An adverb literally 'belongs to the verb', and it qualifies one of the following:

- the verb:
Hon sprang *fort.*   She ran quickly.

- an adjective:
Utsikten var *otroligt* **vacker.**   The view was unbelievably beautiful.

- an adverb:

Han sjöng *ovanligt* vackert.   He sang unusually beautifully.

- an entire clause:

Det blir *troligen* regn ikväll.   There will probably be rain tonight.
Vi har *inte* fått regn på en vecka.   We haven't had rain for a week.

607   Adverbs classified by meaning

(a) Time (answering the question: 'When?' **När?**):

> **aldrig** never; **alltid** always; **då** then; **då och då** now and then; **efter** after; **emellanåt** occasionally; **fortfarande** still; **förr** previously; **först** first; **förut** previously; **genast** immediately; **ibland** sometimes; **igen** again; **jämt** all the time; **länge** for a long time; **nu** now; **nyligen** recently; **någonsin** ever; **ofta** often; **redan** already; **sedan** then; **sist** finally; **snart** soon; **strax** soon; **sällan** seldom; **tidvis** from time to time; **ursprungligen** originally; **vanligen** usually; **ännu** still; **ånyo** anew.

This group may be further subdivided into:

(i) Point in time: **nu, då, förr, förrut**, etc.

(ii) Period of time: **länge, jämt**, etc.

(iii) Frequency: **aldrig, ofta, alltid, sällan, emellanåt**, etc.

(b) Manner (answering the question: 'How?' **Hur?**):

> **bra** well; **illa** badly; **väl** (see 615(f)); **noga** carefully; **fort** quickly; **ogärna** unwillingly; **sakta** slowly; **långsamt** slowly; **sålunda** thus (+ others in -lunda, -ledes: 602(e)).

(c) Place (answering the question: 'Where?'/'Where to?' **Var?/Vart?**) (see also 613):

> **här** here; **hit** here; **där** there; **dit** there; **hemma** at home; **hem** home; **borta** away; **bort** away; **inne** in; **in** in; **ute** out; **ut** out; **uppe** up; **upp** up; **nere** down; **ner** down; **framme** forward; **fram** forward; **hitåt** this way; **ditåt** that way (+ others in -åt: 604(b)); **varifrån** from where; **härifrån** from here (+ others in -ifrån: 604(a)), **annorstädes** elsewhere (+ others in -städes: 602(d)), **annanstans** elsewhere (+ others in -stans: 602(d)); **bakom** behind; **efter** after; **emellan** between; **emot** against; **förbi** past; **före** in front of; **igenom** through; **intill** close to; **inuti** inside; **jämsides** next to; **kvar** behind;

nedanför below; **nära** close to; **omkring** around; **ovan** above; **ovanpå** on top of; **ovanför** above; **samman** together; **fjärran** distant; **undan** away; **utanför** outside; **innanför** inside; **tillbaka** back; **ur** out; **överallt** everywhere; **utomlands** abroad; **utomhus** outdoors.

(d) Degree (answering the question: 'To what extent?' **Hur mycket?***)* (see also 612):

mycket a lot; **litet** (a) little; **föga** little; **ganska** rather; **lagom** just enough; **mest** mostly; **särskilt** particularly; **lika** as; **nästan** almost; **synnerligen** extremely; **utomordentligt** exceedingly; **ytterst** extremely; **tämligen** rather; **ungefär** approximately.

(e) Cause (answering the question: 'Why?' **Varför?**):

alltså therefore; **därför** which is why; **sålunda** thus; **nämligen** (see 615(f)); **följaktligen** consequently.

608   Adverbs classified by function

The heterogeneity of adverbs stands out most clearly with regard to their different functions. While some adverbs are semantically independent, for example the adverbs of manner in 607(b), in order to be able to establish the significance of many others one must look at the context. Compare:

Han försvann *plötsligt.*	He disappeared suddenly.
***Härmed* var samtalet slut.**	With this the conversation was ended.

Plötsligt modifies the action of the verb; it tells us how he disappeared. **Härmed** refers back to a previous statement which establishes the reason why the conversation ended. In 609–12 below the main types of adverbs classified by their function are set out.

609   Pronominal adverbs

As in the case of pronouns, the meaning of these adverbs is determined by their context. They may:

- point out:
Den där flickan är lång.
That girl is tall.

- refer back:

Vi kom dit. Sedan drack vi kaffe.
We arrived there. Then we drank coffee.

- refer forward:

Den flicka vi såg serverade oss.
That/The girl we saw served us.

See also 325ff., 329. Notice that whereas pronouns replace nouns, pronominal adverbs replace prepositional expressions of different kinds:

Bilen	**stannade**	**framför huset.**
Noun		*Prepositional expression*
The car	stopped	in front of the house.

Den	**stannade**	**där.**
Pronoun		*Pronominal adverb*
It	stopped	there.

The following are the main types of pronominal adverb:

(a) *Demonstrative:*

Först går vi *dit*, och sedan åker vi hem.
First we're going there, and then we'll go home.

***Hädanefter* måste du vara försiktig.**
Henceforth you will have to be careful.

Others: **här, hit, där, hädan, då,** compounds in **här-, hit-, där-, dit-** (see 604).

(b) *Relative:*

Den stad *där* jag är född heter Södertälje.
The town where I was born is called Södertälje.

Vi kom *dit* vi skulle.
We arrived at where we were going.

Den tid *då* jag arbetade där var mycket lycklig.
The time when I worked there was a very happy one.

Han ville veta *vad* det rörde sig om.
He wanted to know what it was about.

(For function as a subordinator, see 822.)

(c) *Interrogative:*

Notice that interrogative adverbs introduce both direct and indirect questions, i.e. both main and subordinate clauses, and that consequently the word order varies. See also 821, 1037, 1039(b).

Var **är ni någonstans?**	**Jag vet inte** *var* **vi är.**
Where are you?	I don't know where we are.
Vart **gick han?**	**Jag vet inte** *vart* **han gick.**
Where did he go?	I don't know where he went.
När **kommer du hem?**	**Jag vet inte** *när* **jag kommer hem..**
When are you coming home?	I don't know when I'm coming home.

(d) *Indefinite:*

Det måste finnas här *någonstans.*
It must be here somewhere.

Aldrig *någonsin* **har jag sett på maken.**
I have never ever seen the like.

Vi betalade ett *någorlunda* **skäligt pris.**
We paid a fairly reasonable price.

Hon sitter väl *någon annanstans.*
She must be sitting somewhere else.

610   Clausal adverbials

These adverbs qualify the clause as a whole rather than one particular word in the clause. For their function and position in the sentence see 1007, 1023, 1026f., 1031, 1043, 1045. Consider the adverb in the following sentences:

Det var en *verkligt* **svår uppgift.**
It was a really difficult task.

Verkligt qualifies the adjective **svår**.

Det var *verkligen* **trevligt att få träffa dig.**
It was really nice to see you.

Verkligen qualifies the clause **trevligt att få träffa dig**.

Clausal adverbials include:

1 Adverbs formed by adding -en, -tvis to adjectives ending in -lig (see 601(c)):

möljigen possibly; vanligen usually; naturligtvis naturally

Han kommer möjligen i morgon. (**= Det är möjligt att han kommer i morgon.**)	He is possibly coming tomorrow.
Naturligtvis dricker han öl. (**= Det är naturligt att han dricker öl.**)	Naturally he drinks beer.

2 Some other adverbs: **ju, nog, väl** (see 615(f)); **kanske** perhaps; **tyvärr** unfortunately; **gärna** willingly; **alltså** therefore; **kanhända**, perhaps; **ingalunda** by no means; **icke** not; **inte** not; **ej** not; **knappast** scarcely.

The main types of clausal adverbial are:

(**a**) Negations (and equivalents):

icke, inte, ej not; **ingalunda** by no means
knappt, knappast hardly; **omöjligen** not possibly

Det är knappt 15° i rummet.	It is scarcely 15° in the room.
Det är ingalunda fallet.	This is by no means the case.

Negations are sometimes regarded as a kind of modal adverb (see (b) below).

Note: **Ej** is usually only found in the written language: **ej genomfart** no thoroughfare.
Icke (not **inte**) is found in compounds, often calques: **en icke-rökare** a non-smoker; **icke-våld** non-violence; **icke-angreppspakt** non-aggression pact.

(**b**) Modal adverbs:

These show the speaker's attitude to the statement, his or her involvement or reservation, degree of certainty, etc. They include:

ju, nog, väl (see 615(f)); **sannolikt** likely; **minsann** indeed; **visserligen**, to be sure; **tyvärr, dessvärre** unfortunately; **lyckligtvis, dessbättre** fortunately.

Dessvärre har jag inte kunnat finna boken.
Unfortunately I have not been able to find the book.

Det är minsann inte så lätt.
It is indeed not so easy.

(c) Conjunctional adverbs:

These adverbs link clauses in a similar way to coordinating and subordinating conjunctions (see also 801ff.). However, a clause beginning with a conjunctional adverb has inverted word order (see also two-part constructions in (iv) below). Conjunctional adverbs can also be found within a clause:

Jan är student. Han reser *alltså* för halva priset.
Jan is a student. He travels therefore at half price.

Hon arbetar heltid i år. *Dessutom* sköter hon sitt hem.
She is working full-time this year. In addition she looks after her home.

The main relationships expressed in this way are the following:

(i) Opposition:

> **emellertid** however; **dock** moreover; **likväl** yet; **ändå** nevertheless; **ej heller** not . . . either

> **Det var besynnerligt. Emellertid var det sant.**
> It was strange. However, it was true.

> **Förslaget var lockande, men likväl oantagligt.**
> The proposal was attractive, but yet unacceptable.

(ii) Consequence or inference:

> **sålunda** thus; **således** consequently; **alltså** therefore; **därför** for that/this reason; **följaktligen** consequently; **fördenskull** for that reason.

> **Olle ligger sjuk för tillfället. Därför kan han inte komma.**
> Olle is ill at present. That is why he cannot come.

> **Det gäller sålunda att nå snabbast möjliga resultat.**
> It is therefore a question of achieving the fastest possible results.

(iii) Explanation or motivation:

> **ju, nämligen** (see 615(f))

Han vaknade först sent på dagen. Han hade nämligen glömt att dra upp väckarklockan.
He did not wake up until late in the day. He had forgotten to wind up his alarm clock, you see.

(iv) Sequel:

vidare furthermore; **slutligen** finally; **sammanfattningsvis** to sum up.

Han teg länge. Slutligen sa han nej.
He was silent for a long time. Finally he said no.

Notice that in two-part constructions of the type **både ... och** 'both ... and'; **såväl ... som** 'as well as ...'; **antingen ... eller** 'either ... or'; **varken ... eller** 'neither ... nor'; **vare sig ... eller** 'either ... or', the first element is a conjunctional adverb, while the second is a coordinating conjunction (see also 804).

In the constructions **dels ... dels** and **än ... än** both elements are conjunctional adverbs.

Han vill både ge ut sina pengar och spara dem.
He wants both to spend his money and to save it.

Det är inte praktiskt, för dels drar det för stora kostnader, dels kan det genomföras först om några år.
That's not practicable, partly because it incurs too high a cost, partly because it can only be implemented in some years' time.

611 Adverbs qualifying the noun phrase

These adverbs emphasise a particular noun phrase by making its significance in the statement more precise. They include:

bara only; **också** too; **inte ens** not even; **ännu** still; **redan** already; **just** just; **däremot** on the other hand; **endast** only; **särskilt** especially; **alldeles** completely; **åtminstone** at least; **inte helle** nor; **även** also, too, as well.

Redan nästa år tänker vi påbörja arbetet.
We are thinking of beginning work as early as next year.

Det är bara norrlänningarna som kan åka skidor i juni.
Only Norrlanders can ski in June.

612 Adverbs qualifying the adjective/adverb phrase: amplifiers and diminishers

(a) The adverb normally qualifies the verb in a clause or the entire clause. However, certain adverbs also qualify adjectives or other adverbs, especially those denoting degree or kind. Among these are the amplifiers and diminishers:

> **mycket** very, much; **särdeles** extremely; **synnerligen** exceedingly; **helt** completely; **alldeles** completely; **ganska** rather; **lagom** just right; **rätt** rather; **väldigt** very; **rysligt** awfully; **alltför** far too, much too; **för** too; **lite(t)** (a) little; **inte alls** not at all; **bra** well; **nog** sufficiently; **allt/alltmera** [before a comparative] ever, increasingly; **pass** [e.g. **hur pass? så pass**] much; **allra** . . . of all, very.

Det var en mycket intressant film.	It was a very interesting film.
Du skrev det mycket fort.	You wrote it very quickly.
Han är ganska ful.	He is rather ugly.
Vädret var lagom varmt.	The weather was pleasantly warm.
Det gick inte alls bra.	It did not go at all well.
Lagret var synnerligen välförsett.	The warehouse was especially well stocked.

(b) The amplifiers **allt**, **alltmer** and **allra** are used only with the comparative and superlative (see Chapter 2E):

Problemet blir allt större.	The problem is growing ever bigger.
Saken blir alltmera invecklad.	The affair is becoming increasingly complex.
Han brukar komma allra sist.	He usually comes last of all.
De allra flesta svenskar har teve.	The great majority of Swedes have TV.

Note: **Alltmer(a)**, not **allt**, is used before adjectives and adverbs which form their comparatives with **mer(a)**. See 236.

(c) When qualifying an adjective in the positive or an adverb, **mycket** = 'very' (for negative 'not very', see (f) below):

Han var mycket lång.	He was very tall.
De gick mycket fort.	They walked very fast.

(d) When qualifying an adjective in the comparative, or a verb, **mycket** = '(very) much, a lot':

Han var mycket längre än sin bror.	He was much taller than his brother.
Han sjöng mycket.	He sang a lot.

(e) In colloquial Swedish, adverbs formed from adjectives are often used as amplifiers. They provide a subjective tone and, as in English, soon pale in significance, losing their literal meaning:

Det blev förskräckligt varmt.	It became terribly hot.
Vi såg en fantastiskt bra match.	We saw a fantastically good match.
Jag har hemskt bråttom.	I am in an awful hurry.

(f) 'Not very' = **inte så väldigt, inte så hemskt**, etc.
When used with a negative, adverbs used in this way are preceded by the word **så**:

Hon är inte så väldigt ung.	She's not all that young.

C LOCATION AND MOVEMENT

613 Location and motion towards

(a) Among those adverbs denoting place (607(c)) are some which exist in two distinct but parallel forms. One form is used with verbs indicating location or rest at a place (**vara** be; **bo** live; **finnas** be; **sitta** sit; **stå** stand; **ligga** lie; **stanna** stop etc.). The other form is used with verbs indicating motion, either actual or imagined, towards a place (**åka** go; **fara** travel; **resa** travel; **gå** go/walk; **komma** come; **springa** run; **ringa** phone; **faxa** send a fax; **längta** long (for) etc.). The adverbs of this type are:

Location		Motion towards		See also:
var(?)	where (?)	**vart (?)**	where (to)	(b)(i), 616(d)
här	here	**hit**	(to) here	(b)(ii) below, 616(d)
där	there	**dit**	(to) there	(b)(ii) below, 616(d)
inne	in(side)	**in**	in(side)	(b)(iii) below
ute	out(side)	**ut**	out(side)	(b)(viii) below
uppe	up	**upp**	up	(b)(vii), (viii) below
nere	down	**ner**	down	(b)(iv) below
hemma	at home	**hem**	home	
borta	away	**bort**	away	(b)(v), (viii) below
framme	there, in front	**fram**	forward(s)	(b) below

Examples:

> **Han bor *här* hos oss. Han kommer *hit* imorgon.**
> He lives here with us. He is coming here tomorrow.

> **Barnen leker *ute* idag. De går *ut* tidigt på morgonen.**
> The children are playing outside today. They go out early in the morning.

> **Hans leker *nere* vid ån. Hans går *ner* till ån.**
> Hans is playing down by the river. Hans goes down to the river.

Notice that the motion involved need not always denote actual movement:

> **Jag ringde *dit* i morse.**   I rang there this morning.
> **Jag längtar *hem*.**   I am homesick.

Movement *within* a specific area is regarded as location, not as motion towards:

> **Jan springer *därborta* i parken.**   Jan is running about over there in the park.
> **Jan springer *bort* till parken.**   Jan is running off to the park.

(b) Notes on use:

(i) **Var, vart** are the only interrogatives of this type:

> ***Var* är Erik? *Vart* har han gått?**
> Where is Erik? Where has he gone?

> **Jag undrar, *var* han är. Jag undrar *vart* han har gått.**
> I wonder where he is. I wonder where he has gone.

These interrogatives should not be confused with **där, dit** as relative adverbs. Both translate English 'where'. See 616(d).

(ii) **Hit, dit** correspond to the (archaic) English 'hither', 'thither', but are common in all varieties of Swedish.

(iii) **Inne** also means 'in' in the sense of 'popular', 'trendy', 'in vogue':

> **Det är inne med manchesterbyxor i år.**
> Cords are in this year.

(iv) **Nere** can also mean 'depressed', 'in low spirits'.

(v) Compare:

Hon bor tre kilometer *bort.*
She lives 3 kilometres away.
[The idea is one of motion from the speaker towards home.]

När man är i Lund är Luleå långt *borta.*
When you're in Lund, Luleå is a long way off.

Borta can also mean 'absent-minded', 'not paying attention'.

(vi) **Framme** often means 'at one's destination':

När är vi *framme?*   cf. **När kommer vi *fram?***
When do we get there?

(vii) Compare:

De bor tre trappor *upp.*
They live on the third floor.
[The idea is one of ascending the stairs.]

Fåglarna bor *uppe* på taket.
The birds live up on the roof.

(viii) With the superlatives **högst** and **längst** colloquial Swedish often has **ut**, **upp**, **bort** instead of **ute**, **uppe**, **borta**:

Han bor *högst upp* i huset.   He lives right at the top of the house.
Det ligger *längst ut* vid havet.   It is right out by the sea.

Note 1: See 602(d)(g) for less common pairs of location – motion towards adverbs.

Note 2: See 604(b), 614(a) for adverbs compounded from an adverb + preposition to indicate motion towards.

614 Compounded forms indicating location/motion etc.

By means of compounding and the addition of derivational suffixes certain adverbs in 613 above can be given special locational, directional or temporal significance. (See also 604.)

(a) When the particle **-åt** is added to **hit, dit**, their directional significance is amplified:

> **hitåt** in this direction/over here [towards the speaker].
> **ditåt** in that direction/over there [away from the speaker].

(b) When the particle **-tills** is added to **hit, dit** they are given a time significance:

> **hittills** up to now, to date; **dittills** up to then.

(c) Note also:

(i) When **-städes** or **-stans** is added to forms of **någon, ingen, annan** a locational significance is implied:

> **någonstans** somewhere; **ingenstans** nowhere; **ingen annanstans** nowhere else; **någon annanstans** somewhere else; **annorstädes** somewhere else.

(ii) When **-sin** is added to **någon** a time significance is implied: **någonsin** ever.

D   SOME DIFFICULT ADVERBS

615   Translation from Swedish

(a) Därför, därför att:

därför, adverb = 'for this reason', 'consequently':

> **Det är varmt. Därför svettas jag.**   It is hot. That's why I'm sweating.
> **Det är alltså därför!**   So that is why!

därför att, conjunction = 'because', 'on account of', 'owing to'. It introduces a subordinate clause (see also 813):

> **Jag svettas, _därför att_ det är varmt.**
> I am sweating because it is hot.

> **Varför svettas du? _Därför/För att_ det är varmt.**
> Why are you sweating? Because it is hot.

(b) Eller hur? The equivalent of French _n'est-ce pas?_, German _nicht wahr?_, this phrase neatly concludes a question, removing the necessity found in English for repeating the verb and subject in a tag-question:

Du kommer hem till mig i kväll, eller hur?
You will be coming back to my place tonight, won't you?

Du har fått dina julklappar, eller hur?
You have received your Christmas presents, haven't you?

Colloquial Swedish often has **vad** (always pronounced /va/) for the same function:

Det stämmer väl inte, va?   That isn't right, is it?

(c) Först, redan:

(i) Först

1 first: **Jag kommer, men först ska jag byta om.**
             I'm coming, but first I have to change.

2 not until: **Det var först sedan hon kom hem (som) hon märkte det.**
             It was not until she got home that she noticed it.

3 only: **Först då sa han något.**
             Only then did he say anything.

             Jag kom hem först i morse.
             I only came home this morning.

(ii) Redan

1 already: **Ska du redan gå?**
             Are you going already?

2 even: **Redan en ytlig undersökning gav bevis.**
             Even a superficial investigation proved this.

3 as early as: **Redan på 1500-talet blev Sverige en nationalstat.**
             As early as the sixteenth century Sweden became a nation state.

(d) Förstås (pronounced /förståss/) derives from the **s**-passive form of the verb **förstå** (see 542). It is now used within a clause as a modal adverb:

Han tänker förstås inte göra det.
Of course/Naturally, he is not thinking of doing it.

Det förstås!
That's obvious!

(e) Gärna, hellre, helst, heller:

(i) Gärna

1 willingly, readily, by all means, with pleasure:

Följer du med? Ja, gärna!
Are you coming? Yes, by all means.

2 likes to: **Han tar sig gärna en öl.**
He likes to have a beer.

3 well: **Du kan lika gärna göra det.**
You might just as well do it.

4 certainly: **Han får gärna försöka.**
He can certainly try./He can try if he likes.

(ii) Hellre is the comparative form of **gärna** = 'rather', 'prefers to':

Han dricker hellre kaffe än te.   He prefers (drinking) coffee to tea.
Han skulle hellre dö än medge det.   He would rather die than admit it.

(iii) Heller was originally a variant form of **hellre**, but is now used only after a negative to convey 'neither', 'not either', etc.:

Jag hade inga pengar, och det hade han inte heller.
I had no money, and nor had he/he had none either.

Inte jag heller.   Nor/Neither do I.
Jag är väl inte döv, heller!   I'm not deaf, you know!

(iv) Helst is the superlative form of **gärna** = 'preferably', 'most of all':

När vill du åka? Helst idag.
When do you want to leave? Preferably today./Today, if possible.

Vill du att jag gör det? Helst inte.
Do you want me to do it? I'd rather not./Preferably not.

(f) Ju, nog, väl, nämligen, liksom: when unstressed these modal adverbs are employed subtly to change the sense of a statement or question by indicating the speaker's attitude to it. Notice that, when stressed, **nog** = 'enough', 'sufficient', **väl** = 'well'.

(i) **Ju** indicates that the speaker expects the listener to agree or to be familiar with what he is saying. **Ju** corresponds to English phrases such as 'you know/see', 'of course', etc.

Där kommer han ju!
There he comes now!

Det har jag ju aldrig sagt, eller hur?
I never said that, did I?

Du har ju varit i Stockholm tidigare?
You have been to Stockholm before, of course?

(ii) **Nog** often injects a note of doubt or uncertainty, in some cases conciliation. It corresponds to English phrases such as 'probably', 'I expect', 'I daresay', etc.

Han kommer nog i morgon.
He'll probably/presumably be here tomorrow.

Det är nog sant, men ...	That's probably true, but ...
Du har nog rätt.	I daresay you're right.
Det tror jag nog!	I should think so!

(iii) **Väl** generally expresses a hope, expectation or wish that the listener will agree, and as such corresponds to English 'surely', 'I suppose', 'I hope', 'I expect', etc. It may simply strengthen a statement (like **ju** (i) above) or express conciliation (like **nog** (ii) above).

Du kommer väl?	I hope you will come.
Du är väl inte sjuk?	You are not ill, are you?
Du har väl hört, att ...	You must have heard that ...
Det var väl det jag trodde.	That's just what I thought.

(iv) **Nämligen** provides new information, of which the listener is unaware. It corresponds to English phrases such as 'you understand', 'you see'. Cf. **ju** = 'as you already know', **nämligen** = 'as I am now telling you by way of explanation', 'you see'.

Du måste komma idag, i morgon är jag nämligen i Uppsala.
You will have to come today, tomorrow I am in Uppsala, you see.

Du måste komma idag, i morgon är jag ju i Uppsala.
You will have to come today, tomorrow I am in Uppsala as you know.

Nämligen can also mean 'namely':

Det fattas något här, nämligen en bra arbetsmiljö.
There is something missing here, namely a good working environment.

(v) **Liksom** = 'sort of', 'kind of'. This is often an empty filler found in colloquial Swedish.

Det där med miljön ligger liksom i tiden.
This environment business is kind of topical.

Jag sa liksom till honom ...
I sort of said to him ...

(g) Långt, länge:

långt = far (distance):
Hur långt är det till Göteborg?   How far is it to Gothenburg?

länge = long (time):
Hur länge bodde du i Sverige?   How long did you live in Sweden?

616 Translation into Swedish

This section outlines some common ways of rendering frequently encountered English adverbs in Swedish.

(a) 'So'

'So' may be an adverb or a conjunction.

(i) As an adverb:

1   In comparatives after a negative = **så** (see also 823(c)):

He is not so quick as he used to be.
Han är inte så snabb som han var tidigare.

2   Before result clauses = **så**:

I was so tired I went straight to sleep.
Jag var så trött att jag somnade omedelbart.

3   Pronominal adverb, referring back = **det** (see 309(f)):

| I think so. | **Det tror jag.** |
| I told you so. | **Jag sa väl det.** |

I had hoped he would win, and he did (so).
Jag hade hoppats han skulle vinna, och det gjorde han.

4   In exclamations = **så**:

So nice to see you again!   **Så trevligt att träffas igen!**

5   'So' = too = **det . . . också**, **med** (see 309(e) Note):

I'm hungry and so are you.   **Jag är hungrig och det är du med.**

(ii) As a conjunction: = **så, så (att)** (809, 817):

She asked me to go, so I went.   **Hon bad mig gå, så jag gick.**
Be careful so you don't catch cold.   **Se till så att du inte blir förkyld!**

(b) 'Then'

'Then' can be translated as **då**, **sedan** or **så**:

(i) **Då**   =

1   'at that time', 'at that moment', 'on that occasion':

You should have been with us then. **Du skulle ha varit med då.**
She was then fifty years old.   **Hon var femtio år gammal då.**

2   'in that case':

Are you awake? In that case/Then you had better get up at once.
Är du vaken? Då bör du stiga upp med detsamma.

Note: **Då** may also be:

1 a temporal conjunction (= **när**) (see 812(a), 823(l)):

Då vi kom hem, åt vi.　　　　　When we got home, we ate.

2 a causal conjunction (= **eftersom**) (see 813(b), 823(h)(ii)):

Då jag inte hade några pengar, kunde jag inte köpa dem.
As I didn't have any money, I could not buy them.

(ii) **Sedan** = 'after that', 'subsequently' (= **därefter, efteråt**)

First we cut the lawn. Then we did some weeding.
Vi klippte först gräsmattan. Sedan rensade vi ogräs.

Note: **Sedan** may also be:

1 a temporal conjunction (= 'after') (see 812(b)):

Sedan han hade gått, kritiserade alla honom.
After he had left, everyone criticised him.

2 a temporal conjunction (= 'since') (see 812(b)):

Sedan han for är hon inte sig lik.　　Since he left she has not been herself.

3 a preposition (= 'since', 'ago') (see 722(l)):

Jag har känt honom sedan kriget.　　I have known him since the war.

(iii) **Så** = 'after that', 'subsequently' (= **därefter, efteråt**)

Först kom Eva, så Gunilla.　　First came Eva, then Gunilla.

(c) 'Too'

(i) When it qualifies an adjective or adverb and expresses an excessive degree of something, 'too' = **för**:

Vägen är för lång att gå.　　The road is too far to walk.
Vi gick för fort sista biten.　　We walked too fast on the last bit.

(ii) When 'too' = 'also', 'as well' it is translated by **också** (written and spoken form), **även** (written and formal spoken form), **med** (spoken form only) (see (a)(i) 5 above):

Han fick en bok också.　　He received a book too.
Det tycker jag med.　　I think so too.

(d) 'Where': when translating 'where' one must ask two questions:

1　Is it an interrogative or a relative adverb?
2　Does it indicate location at a place or motion towards a place (see 613 above)?

The choice involved is expressed in this diagram:

WHERE

Interrogative:
1 location	**var (?)**	**Var är han? Jag undrar var han är.**
		Where is he? I wonder where he is.
2 motion	**vart (?)**	**Vart går han? Jag undrar vart han går.**
		Where's he going? I wonder where he's going.

Relative:
1 location	**där**	**Jag vet ett kafé där vi kan äta.**
		I know a café where we can eat.
2 motion	**dit**	**Jag vet ett kafé dit vi kan gå.**
		I know a café where we can go.

In colloquial Swedish **där**, **dit** are often replaced by **som** + preposition:

> **Jag vet ett ställe som vi kan äta lunch på.**
> I know a place that we can eat lunch at [cf: where we can eat lunch].

> **Jag vet ett ställe som vi kan gå till för att äta lunch.**
> I know a place that we can go to to eat lunch [cf: where we can go to eat lunch].

Notice that **där** can also be a demonstrative adverb = 'there'.

(e) 'Whenever', 'wherever'

English	*Remarks*	*Swedish*	*See examples*
'Whenever'	= 'at any time you like'	**när som helst**	2
'Whenever'	= 'no matter when' + clause = 'every time (that)' + clause	**varje gång**	4
'When ever?'	= 'When (on earth)?'	**när?**	
'Wherever'	= 'anywhere you like'	**var/vart som helst**	1
'Wherever'	= 'no matter where' + clause = 'everywhere (that)' + clause	**var/vart . . . än**	3
'Wherever?'	= 'Where (on earth)?'	**var/vart (i all sin dar)?**	

1 **Lägg det var som helst.**
Put it wherever you like.

2 **Du kan få komma när som helst.**
You can come whenever you like.

3 **Jag följer dig vart du än går.**
I'll follow you wherever you go.

4 **Varje gång jag ser honom tänker jag på dig.**
Whenever I see him I think of you.

Note: For rules governing the choice of **var/vart** see 613.

(f) 'However'

Although 'however' (= 'nevertheless') is rendered by Swedish **emellertid, dock,** Swedish has a number of other ways of rendering English idioms with 'however'.

English	Remarks	Swedish	See examples
'However'	used with adjective or adverb	**hur . . . än**	1, 2
'How ever?'	= 'How on earth . . . ?'	**hur (i all sin dar)?**	3
'However you wish'	= 'in whatever way you wish'	**hur som helst**	4
'However much/little'	= 'as much/little as'	**så mycket/lite(t) (som)**	5
'However much/little'	= 'no matter how much/little'	**hur mycket/lite(t) än**	6

1 **Jag kommer att köpa tavlan, hur dyr den än är.**
I'm going to buy the picture, however dear (it is).

2 **Hur tidigt jag än stiger upp, äter jag alltid frukost.**
However early I get up, I always have breakfast.

3 **Hur i all sin dar vet du det?**
How ever do you know that?

4 **Gör hur som helst!**
Do whatever you like!

5 **Man får så mycket man behöver.**
You get however much you need.

6   **Jag betalar inte räkningen, hur lite den än är på.**
     I'm not paying the bill, however little it is!

Note 1: 'However' used with 'much', 'little' is often omitted in English. This is not the case in Swedish.

    Much as I like him ...   **Hur mycket jag än tycker om honom ...**

Note 2: The finite verb is often omitted in English after 'however' + adjective or adverb. This is not so in Swedish.

    I'll pay the bill, however much (it is for).   **Jag betalar räkningen hur mycket den än är på.**

Note 3: **Hur som helst** renders English 'anyway', 'be that as it may' when followed by a clause.

    Hur som helst, så hoppas han ...   Anyway he hopes . . .

7 PREPOSITIONS

A   **INTRODUCTION**
701   Introduction to prepositions
702   Prepositional complements
703   Place of the preposition in Swedish
704   Prepositions and stress

B   **SIMPLE AND COMPOUND PREPOSITIONS:**
       The fifteen most common prepositions
705   **Av**
706   **Efter**
707   **Från**
708   **För**
709   **Genom (igenom)**
710   **I**
711   **Med**
712   **Mellan (emellan)**
713   **Mot**
714   **Om**
715   **På**
716   **Till**
717   **Under**
718   **Vid**
719   **Över**

C   **PREPOSITIONAL USE**
720   Some other prepositions of place
721   **På** or **i**? How to render English 'in', 'on', 'at', 'to' in Swedish
722   Some other prepositions of time and quantity
723   Prepositions and time
724   Time-when
725   Duration
726   Frequency
727   Some other prepositions of manner etc.
728   Some other parts of speech used as prepositions
729   English "of" and its equivalents in Swedish
730   Preposition in English – no preposition in Swedish
731   Preposition in Swedish – no preposition in English

A INTRODUCTION

701 Introduction to prepositions

Some seventy prepositions are among the 10,000 most common words in the Swedish language, and fifteen of them (see 705–719) belong to the most frequently used of all Swedish words. Prepositions are indeclinable words. They may be categorised in four different forms:

(a) Simple prepositions comprise a single morpheme: **av, i, på, om**.

(b) Compounded prepositions comprise:

(i) adverb + preposition compounds, where the adverb modifies the meaning of the simple preposition: **bakom, inunder, uppå**.

(ii) preposition + preposition, which usually offer merely a stylistic variation of a simple form: **utav, omkring.**

(c) Complex prepositions encapsulate the meaning of a phrase in two or more words: **för . . . sedan, på grund av, i och med, i fråga om**.

(d) Prepositions may also be formed from verbs, adjectives, nouns or other parts of speech (see 728): **angående, enligt, tack vare**.

The most easily identifiable kinds of prepositional relationship are those of time, place and manner.

702 Prepositional complements

In most instances Swedish prepositions precede the prepositional complement (the most common exceptions are noted under 703(b) and (c)). The prepositional complement is characteristically a noun, a pronoun in the object form or an infinitive form of the verb.

(a) Preposition + *noun phrase*

As in English the prepositional complement in Swedish is generally a noun or the object form of the pronoun:

> **i bilen** in the car; **med glädje** with pleasure; **utan honom** without him; **för ett år sedan** a year ago; **sedan min fars tid** since my father's time.

Notice, however, that the prepositions **utom** and **förutom** take the *subject* form of the pronoun, when the correlative itself is in the subject form (see also 727(g), (p)).

> **Alla utom jag hade något att äta.**   Everyone but me had something to eat.
> *but*
> **Jag träffade alla utom henne.**   I met everyone but her.

Note: In a few, well-defined instances, nouns forming prepositional complements retain old, inflected forms after the prepositions **till** (cf. 716(e)) and **i** (cf. 710(c)(vii)).

(b) Preposition + **att** + *infinitive phrase*

Swedish also has **att** + *infinitive phrase* as a prepositional complement, providing that the subject of the finite verb is the same as the hypothetical 'subject' of the infinitive. (English only rarely has the same facility, although the use of the preposition followed by the '-ing' form of the verb is an approximate equivalent.)

> **Det fanns inget att göra förutom att lyda.**
> There was nothing to do except (to) obey.

> **Han gick utan att säga någonting.**
> He left without saying anything.

> **Vi har aldrig haft några planer på att stanna här.**
> We have never had any intention of staying here.

Sometimes the use of a preposition before **att** + infinitive is optional, especially:

(i) after common verbs such as **be (om) att** 'request'/'ask to'; **hoppas (på) att**, 'hope to', etc.

(ii) after common adjectives such as **rädd (för) att** 'afraid to'; **beredd (på) att** 'prepared to', etc.

Note 1: By no means all Swedish prepositions may be combined with an infinitive in this way. Prepositions which exclusively indicate place, and the prepositions **före**, **innan** are not used with **att** + *infinitive phrase* as a prepositional complement.

> **Brukar du duscha innan du simmar?**   Do you have a shower before going for a swim?

Note 2: In formal usage **efter** (as a preposition of time) sometimes occurs with **att** + *perfect infinitive phrase* as a prepositional complement.

> **Efter att ha ätit, lade han sig.**   After eating, he went to bed.

Note 3: English expressions with 'by/in' + the '-ing' form of the verb are often rendered by **genom att** + *infinitive phrase* as a prepositional complement in Swedish.

Han undkom genom att spela död.
He escaped by pretending to be dead.

Han gjorde ett stort fel genom att låta dörren stå öppen.
He committed a grave mistake in leaving the door open.

(c) Preposition + *subordinate clause*

In Swedish a subordinate clause introduced by **att** or an interrogative word may be a prepositional complement. This is often the case with the prepositions **av, efter, för, genom, i, med, (e)mot, på, till, trots, utan, åt, över**. It is not possible always to use a preposition alone in this way in English, although, in many instances, an approximate English equivalent is the use of preposition + 'the fact that'.

Vi protesterar mot att vi inte har några jobb.
We are protesting about not having any jobs.

Är du säker på att han hotade dig?
Are you sure (of the fact) that he threatened you?

Jag tvivlar på om han vill hjälpa oss.
I doubt if he will want to help us.

Sometimes the use of a preposition before **att** + subordinate clause is optional, especially:

(i) after common verbs such as: **be (om) att** 'request'/'ask that'; **hoppas (på) att**, 'hope that'; **varna (för) att** 'warn that'; etc.

(ii) after common adjectives such as **rädd (för) att** 'afraid that'; **beredd (på) att** 'prepared to'; etc.

(iii) before indirect exclamations and commands:

Tack (för) att du är så snäll!
Thank you for being so kind.

Tänk (på) vilka faror du utsätter dig för!
Think what dangers you're exposing yourself to!

(d) Preposition + *prepositional phrase*

A preposition may have a prepositional phrase as a complement.

Vi har inte träffats sedan i våras.   We haven't met since last spring.

(e) Preposition + *adverbial phrase*

A preposition may have an adverbial phrase as a complement.

> **Det håller jag för helt osannolikt.**   I consider that to be highly unlikely.

Where the adverb is an adverb of place, it precedes the preposition in an adverb + preposition compound.

> **Varifrån kommer du?**   Where do you come from?
> **Han kröp inunder täcket.**   He crept under the cover.
> **Kom ut, därunderifrån!**   Come out from under there!

Note: Swedish uses special adverbial forms to render English preposition + adverbial phrases of place such as 'where . . . to' (**vart**), 'to there' (**dit**), etc. (613) and preposition + adverbial phrases of time such as 'until now' (**hittills**), 'not for long' (**inte länge**), etc.

(f) Preposition without complement

When used without a complement, prepositions often assume an adverbial role.

> **En smörgås med ägg på.**   A sandwich with egg on.
> **Bilen låg i diket och jag bredvid.**   The car lay in the ditch, with me
>   alongside.

703   Place of the preposition in Swedish

Swedish prepositions may be divided into three groups according to the position they assume with regard to the prepositional complement:

Pre-positioned prepositions precede the prepositional complement.

Parenthetical prepositions enclose the prepositional complement (typically a noun phrase, pronoun or adverb).

Postpositioned prepositions follow the prepositional complement.

(a) Pre-positioned prepositions

The majority of the 150 or so Swedish prepositions precede the prepositional complement, as most prepositions do in English:

> **bakom bilen** behind the car; **framför datorn** in front of the computer; **hos Olssons** at the Olssons'; **utan vatten** without water; **i augusti** in August;

trots hans hjälp despite his help

(b) Parenthetical prepositions

A small number of complex prepositions enclose the prepositional complement:

för . . . sedan	. . . ago
för . . . skull	for . . . sake
(p)å . . . vägnar	on behalf of . . .
sedan . . . tillbaka	for + expression of time
åt . . . till	towards, on the way to . . .
i . . . ställe	in place of, instead of . . .
på . . . när	to within . . .

Parenthetical prepositions invariably have a noun, adverb, noun phrase, pronoun or pronominal phrase as a prepositional complement (**för ett år sedan** 'a year ago'; **för min familjs skull** 'for my family's sake'; **i hans ställe** 'in his place').

(c) Postpositioned prepositions

(i) Postpositioned prepositions occur only in certain idiomatic expressions. Postpositioned forms are stressed in speech (as in English).

året om, året runt	all year round, through(out) the year
jorden runt, jorden över	the whole world over
hela natten igenom	all night long, all through the night
oss emellan	between you and me

(ii) When compounded with adverbs of place (613) prepositions appear as the final element of the compound. Most of these compounds are reserved for more formal written Swedish and are rarely enountered in the spoken language.

däribland among which; **därigenom** thereby; **däremot** on the other hand; **därutöver** in addition; **hemifrån** (away) from home.

Note also: **dessutom** in addition.

(iii) A form of postpositioning is also seen when the prepositional complement is emphasised by being moved into the initial (topic) position in the sentence or clause (see 1027). In such instances the postpositioned preposition appears as the last word in the sentence or clause, i.e. not immediately after the prepositional complement. Sometimes there is no prepositional complement at all.

Dig tycker jag om, men honom är jag rädd för.
You I like, but I'm scared of him.

Det borde du ha tänkt på.
That's something you should have thought of.

Säg ifrån om det gör ont!
Tell me if it hurts.

The same process is often seen in V-questions (1036(b)), exclamations, and infinitive and relative clauses. The prejudice against postpositioned prepositions in formal English is by no means as strong in Swedish:

Vad ska du laga det med?	What are you going to mend it with?
Vilket rörigt hus du bor i!	What a messy house you live in.
Båten vi reste med var röd.	The boat we travelled on was red.
en smörgås med kaviar på	a sandwich with caviar (on)

Note 1: A form of postpositioning is present in certain passive sentences (547ff.) although in this case the preposition usually follows the passive verb.

Han har inte hörts av sedan i somras.   He's not been heard of since last summer.

Note 2: Postpositioned **på** is used idiomatically (without English equivalent) in phrases with **ett sätt att** + infinitive.

ett sätt att bli rik på   a way of getting rich

704   Prepositions and stress

Prepositions are usually unstressed in Swedish unless postpositioned (see 703(c)(i)). Swedish prepositions are stressed, however, when used as particles in a verb phrase. *Verb + stressed particle* constitute a single unit of meaning (cf. 556ff.).

Compare:

'tycka om någonting	= have an opinion about something
preposition	
Vad 'tycker du om Sverige?	What do you think of Sweden?
tycka 'om någonting	= like something
particle	
Jag tycker mycket 'om Sverige.	I like Sweden a lot.

Particles comprise both stressed prepositions (**hälsa *på*** 'visit'; **hålla *med*** 'agree with'; **köra *om*** 'overtake'; **tycka *om*** 'like', etc.) and adverbs (**skriva *ner*** 'annotate'; **gå *bort*** 'die', etc.).

B   SIMPLE AND COMPOUND PREPOSITIONS: THE FIFTEEN MOST COMMON PREPOSITIONS

705   Av

Basically the preposition **av** suggests some kind of source or origin, a point of departure. However, **av** is not used to express relationships in space (i.e. actual location) and is rarely used with expressions of time (cf. **från** 707).

Av is used chiefly of materials which provide a starting point for a manufactured product or a creation in the widest sense, and also indicates the source (i.e. the cause) of a reaction.

Beyond this, **av** indicates the passive agent in Swedish (547ff.), and serves to indicate one type of quantity expression (the relationship of a part to the whole).

Sometimes **av** is replaced in colloquial Swedish by **utav**, especially in (b) and (c) (i) and (ii) below.

Agent	Origin material	Origin cause	Origin place	Measure	Possession
by	of/from	from/with by/for	off/from	of	of

(a) Agent: 'by'   **en tavla av Zorn**   a painting by Zorn
                        brev skrivna av ett barn   letters written by a child

Note: **Av** is also used as the agent in the following types of expression, which may be regarded as ellipted forms in which the verb (**gjort, sagt, tänkt**, etc.) is missing:

   Det var dumt/elakt/snällt av dig.   That's stupid/nasty/kind of you.

(b) Origin: material

(i) 'of'   **en ring av rent guld**   a ring of pure gold
                  en man av kött och blod   a man of flesh and blood

(ii) 'from'   **göra guld av järn**   to make gold from iron
(c) Origin: cause

(i) 'from'   **göra ngt av gammal vana**   to do sth from habit
                  Lär dig av erfarenhet!   Learn from experience!

(ii) 'with'   **gråta av glädje/av rädsla** to cry with joy/with fear

(iii) 'by'	**av misstag**	by mistake
	av en händelse	by chance
(iv) 'for'	**av brist på pengar**	for lack of money
	av vilken orsak	for what reason . . .?

(d) Origin: place

| 'off'/'from' | **Du kan köpa/låna/få det av honom.** |
| | You can buy/borrow/get it from him. |

(e) Measure: 'of'	**ingen/några/en del/hälften av . . .**
	none of/some of/part of/half of . . .
	i nio fall av tio	nine times out of ten

Note: In this sense **av** usually indicates only an incomplete portion of something. For that reason Swedish has **alla eleverna, hela klassen, båda eleverna** even where English would idiomatically have 'all of the pupils', 'all of/the whole of the class', 'both of the pupils' (339). Similarly, expressions of measure (**ett kilo potatis** 'half a kilo of potatoes'; **ett halvt glas mjölk** 'half a glass of milk'; etc.) do not require **av**. (See also 126f.).

(f) Possession: 'of'	**en art av hjortsläktet**	a species of the deer family
	i utkanten av staden	on the outskirts of town
	folk av samma ras/tro	people of the same race/faith
	en tavla av stort värde	a painting of great value

Note, however, that **av** may not always replace the possessive genitive (729).

(g) With nouns

Used after nouns **av** frequently indicates some kind of result or trace of a past action.

i egenskap av in the capacity of; **frukten av** the fruit(s) of; **förekomsten av** the occurrence of; **minnet av** the memory of; **resultatet/utfallet av** the result of.

(h) Unstressed **av** with verbs

bestå av consist of; **leva av** live off; **lida av** suffer from; **njuta av** enjoy

Note: See also (c)(i) and (ii) above.

(j) Stressed **av** with verbs

Stressed **av** often has a meaning which corresponds to English 'off':

> **betala av** pay off; **borsta av** brush off; **hålla av** be fond of; **klä av (sig)** undress (oneself), take (one's) clothes off; **runda av** round off; **stiga av (bussen, etc.)** get off (the bus, etc.); **skaka av** shake off.

706 Efter

Efter suggests 'following upon' and is frequently used in expressions of time ('after') and of place ('behind'), when some kind of sequence is intended (contrast **bakom** 720(c)).

Place	*Time when*	*Succession*	*Reference*	*Object of desire*
behind, after	after, since	after	(according) to; by	*verb/noun* + for

(a) Place

(i) 'behind'	**Han körde efter vår bil.**	He drove behind our car.
	Stäng dörren efter dig!	Shut the door behind you.
(ii) 'after'	**K kommer efter J i alfabetet.**	
	K comes after J in the alphabet.	
(iii) 'of'/'from'	**Märken/Spåren efter tio smutsiga små fingrar.**	
	The marks/traces of ten dirty little fingers.	

Note: In certain instances **efter** is synonymous with **utefter** (cf. 720(r)).

> **Han gick efter staketet tills han kom till en grind.**
> He walked along/followed the fence until he came to a gate.

(b) Time

(i) 'after'	**efter klockan tre**	after 3 (o'clock)
	efter jul	after Christmas
	Året 800 efter Kristus	(The year) 800 AD
(ii) 'since'	**Hon har varit sjuk efter olyckan.**	
	She's been ill since the accident.	

(c) Succession: 'after' **mil efter mil**   mile after mile

                                 den ena efter den andra   one after the other

(d) Reference

(i) '(according) to'   **Gå efter reglerna!**   Stick to the rules!

                                  efter bästa förmåga   to the best of one's ability

                                  ordna saker efter storlek   to sort things according to size

(ii) 'by'   **segla efter stjärnorna**   to sail by the stars

                                  spela efter gehör/noter   to play by ear/read music

(e) With nouns

Used with nouns **efter** often indicates a desire or search, etc. for something:

> **längtan efter** desire/longing for; **strävan efter** aspiration for; **sökandet efter** the search for.

(f) Unstressed **efter** with verbs

(i) indicates the object of a desire, search or similar purposeful action (often 'for' in English):

> **fråga efter** inquire about; **kippa efter andan** gasp for breath; **leta/söka efter** search for; **längta efter** long for; **ringa efter** phone for; **sträva efter** strive for; **törsta efter** thirst for.

(ii) has the meaning 'according to' (see (d) above): **rätta sig efter** 'adapt to'.

(g) Stressed **efter** with verbs

This often corresponds to stressed 'after' in English:

> **se efter** look after/take care of; **ta efter** take after/imitate; **Vad är du ute efter?** What are you after/What do you want?; **ge efter** give in.

707   Från

Från suggests origin, a point of departure or vantage, or marks the beginning of a period in time. **Ifrån** is preferred as the latter element in compound prepositional forms, as a stressed particle after verbs, and in heavily stressed positions.

Origin: time	Origin: place
(with effect) from	from

(a) Origin in time

(i) 'from' **en pjäs från 60-talet** a play from the (19)60s
minnen från barndomen childhood memories

(ii) 'with effect from' **från och med idag** from today

(b) Origin in place

'from' **ett brev från Amerika** a letter from America
Jag kommer från Sverige. I come from Sweden.

Försök att se det från hans synpunkt!
Try to see things from his point of view.

Note also: **undantaget från regeln** the exception to the rule.

(c) Unstressed **från** with verbs

avstå från abstain from; **bortse från** disregard (**bortsett från** = apart from); **skona någon från något** spare someone (from) something.

(d) Stressed **(i)från** with verbs

The form **ifrån** is preferred when used as a stressed particle with verbs, and usually expresses an idea similar to English 'away from'.

gå ifrån leave; **komma ifrån** get away from; **springa ifrån** run away (from); **säga ifrån** speak out.

708 För

För corresponds in usage to English 'for' in a wide range of senses, but special care is needed when rendering English 'for' + time expressions of duration in Swedish (725). Note that the construction **Vad . . . för?** (with postpositioned **för)** is commonly used in colloquial Swedish as an alternative to **varför?**

Vad gråter han för? Vad säger du det för?
What's he crying for? Why do you say that?

Time	Place	Manner	Intention, purpose	Indirect object	Genitive
for, at, 0	(in front) of	by, with	for	to, from	of

(a) Time

(i) 'for'	**en vän för livet**	a friend for life
	ett rum för natten	a room for the night
	Säg farväl för alltid!	Say goodbye for ever.
	för första gången	for the first time
	för evigt	for eternity
	vädret för 5 dygn framåt	the weather for the next five days
(ii) 'at'	**för ögonblicket**	at the moment
	för närvarande	at present
(iii) 0	**nuförtiden**	nowadays

Note : In many instances English 'for' + expression of time cannot be translated by Swedish **för**. Cf. 725.

(b) Place

(i) 'in front of'	**Håll handen för munnen när du gäspar!**
	Put your hand in front of your mouth when you yawn!
(ii) 'of'	**Stå inte i vägen för dem som jobbar!**
	Don't get in the way of those who're working!

(c) Manner

(i) 'by'	**Brukar du skriva du för hand?**
	Do you usually write by hand?
(ii) 'with'	**Köp det för egna pengar!**
	Buy it with your own money!

(d) Intention: 'for'	**en tidning för barn**	a newspaper for children
	pizza för avhämtning	pizza to go/takeaway pizza

ha ingen användning för något
to have no use for something

Note 1: The verb **använda**, however, is used with **till** (= 'for the purpose of') or with **som** (= 'in the capacity of'):

Vad använder du det till?	What do you use that for?
Han använder mig som slav.	He uses/treats me as his slave.

Note 2: **För** is often linked with **att** + *infinitive* to express purpose.

Han gick ut för att hjälpa henne.	He went out to help her.

(e) With indirect object (dative)

(i) 'to'
    beskriva/förklara/läsa något för någon
    to describe/explain/read something to someone

    Gå inte och prata för dig själv!
    Don't talk to yourself.

    presentera någon/något för någon
    to introduce someone/something to someone

    vara till hjälp/nytta/hinder för någon
    to be of help/of use/a hindrance to someone

    Det är nytt/främmande för mig.
    It's new/strange to me.

(ii) 'from'
    Göm det för honom!
    Hide it from him!

    Jag har inga hemligheter för dig.
    I've no secrets from you.

(iii) 0
    berätta något/tala om något för någon
    to tell someone something

Note: A similar usage is seen in expressions such as:

Blommorna dog för mig.	The flowers died on me.
Elden slocknade för mig.	The fire went out on me.
Någon har stulit plånboken för mig.	Someone has stolen my wallet.

(f) Genitive: 'of'
    chefen för företaget   the boss of the company
    tiden för avresan   the time of departure

(g) Replacive

(i) '(in exchange) for'
    kött för 45 kronor kilot
    meat for 45 crowns a kilo

Jag vill inte för mitt liv göra det igen.
I wouldn't do that again for the life of me.

(ii) 'for',	**Hon arbetar för två**	She works for two.
'on behalf of'	**Jag talar för alla.**	I speak for everyone.
	en gång för alla	once and for all

Note: **Betala** is followed by **för** when it means 'to pay in exchange for'.

Han betalade 50 kronor för kaffet.	He paid 50 crowns for the coffee.
Vad har du betalat för bilen?	What did you pay for the car?

However, when **betala** means 'to pay off' it is followed by the direct object without **för**.

Har du betalat bilen?	Have you paid for the car?

(h) Distributive

(i) 'by'	**dag för dag**	day by day
	steg för steg	step by step
(ii) 'for'	**ord för ord**	word for word

Note: A similar usage is seen in expressions such as: **var och en för sig (själv)** = 'separately'/'by ourselves (themselves)'.

(j) Enumeration: 0   **för det första, andra, etc.**   firstly, secondly, etc.

(k) Considering: 'for'	**Han är stor för sin ålder.**	He's big for his age.
	varmt för årstiden	warm for the time of year

(l) With nouns

föremål för an/the object of; **ett intresse för** an interest in.

(m) With adjectives

anklagad för accused of; **bra för** good for; **berömd för** famous for; **dålig för** bad for; **glad för** happy about; **känd för** renowned for; **orolig för** worried about; **rädd för** frightened of; **typisk för** typical of.

Note also: **ha lätt/svårt för något** 'to find something easy/difficult'.

(n) Unstressed **för** with verbs (see also (e) above)

akta sig för något watch out for something; **anklaga någon för något** accuse someone of something; **anse någon för något** consider/regard someone as something; **dö för** die for; **intressera sig för** be interested in; **misstänka någon för något** suspect someone of something; **skämmas för** be ashamed of; **straffa för** punish for; **tacka för** thank for; **varna för** warn about.

(o) Stressed **för** with verbs

dra för gardinerna draw the curtains; **se sig för** look out, take care; **ta för sig** help oneself.

709   Genom (igenom)

Genom and **igenom** correspond generally to English 'through' in all its prepositional meanings (place, time and manner). **Genom** is generally preferred when the meaning is clearly prepositional. **Igenom** is preferred as the latter element in a compound preposition, and also when the meaning is more or less adverbial, or when the preposition is stressed.

Place	*Time duration*	*Manner*
through	through(out)	through, by

(a) Place

(i) 'through'	**Katten kom in genom fönstret.** The cat came in through the window.
(ii) others	**en resa genom Asien** a journey across Asia
	Åk hem genom Danmark! Come home via Denmark.
	Röken går upp genom skorstenen. Smoke goes up the chimney.

Note: **Genom + hela** + *noun in definite form* often corresponds to English 'throughout':

Pesten spred sig genom hela landet.   The plague spread throughout the country.

(b) Time: 'through'   **konsten genom tiderna**   art through the ages

Note: US English 'through' meaning 'up to and including' is rendered by **till och med** (sometimes abbreviated **t.o.m.** or **tom**) in Swedish:

Öppet från mars till och med juni   Open March through June

(c) Manner

(i) 'through'	**genom hans hjälp**	through/thanks to his help

Jag får det genom en vän.   I'll get it through a friend.

(ii) 'by'   **fortplantning genom delning**   reproduction by fission

Note: **Genom att** + *clause* corresponds to English result clauses of the type:

    He saved her by running as fast as he could.
    Han räddade henne genom att springa så fort han orkade.

(iii) Mathematics: 'over'/'divided by'

    3/4 (tre genom fyra)   3 divided by 4

(e) Stressed **(i)genom** with verbs

    gå igenom en operation undergo an operation; **gå igenom någons ägodelar**
    go through someone's possessions.

710 I

The preposition **i** is the second most common word in the Swedish language (after **och** = 'and'). In addition to indicating certain locations in space and time (see also 721–726) it has a wide range of idiomatic usages.

Place	*Time when*	*Time duration*	*Frequency*	*Material*	*Condition*
in, at, on, etc.	in, to	for	0, per	in	in

(a) Location

(i) 'in'   **Jag bor i ett hus i staden.** I live in a house in town.
                         i New York, i Norge   in New York, in Norway
                         i östern   in the east
                         i en bok, i bilen   in a book, in the car
                         kaffe med grädde i   coffee with cream (in)

Note 1: In many instances English 'in' indicating a place relationship is rendered by **på** in Swedish (cf. 715, 721).

Note 2: The use of the preposition **i** in the following examples ('from' or no preposition in English) indicates clearly that not all of the Bible/newspaper is being read:

Han läser i Bibeln varje dag.	He reads (from) the Bible every day.
Jag satt och läste i tidningen.	I was reading the paper.

(ii) 'at'   **Båten lade till i Åhus.**   The boat docked at Åhus.

	Han är i skolan/i kyrkan.	He's at school/at church.
	Betala varorna i kassan!	Pay at the check-out.
(iii) 'on'	Han talar i telefonen.	He's on the phone.
	en rapport i radio/TV	a report on the radio/TV
	Han satte sig i gräset.	He sat down on the grass.
	Hon sitter i soffan.	She's sitting on the sofa.
(iv) 'of'	borgmästare i Wadköping	mayor of Wadköping
	mitt i staden	in the middle of (the) town
(v) 'from'	En lampa hängde i taket.	A lamp hung from the ceiling.
(vi) 'to'	gå i skolan/i kyrkan	to go to school/church

Note: The use of **i** suggests that one is a pupil at a school (**en elev i skolan**), a member of a church (**en medlem i kyrkan**), etc. But note **läsa på universitet(et)** 'to study at university'. If actual direction or mode of transport is of prime importance, it is possible to use **till skolan**, etc., especially with verbs other than **gå:**

Han cyklar till kyrkan varje vecka.	He cycles to church every week.

(vii) 'into'	Stoppa det i fickan!	Put it into your pocket.
	Kasta dem i fängelset!	Throw them into prison!

Note: 'Into' is, however, generally translated by **in i** in Swedish.

Vi gick in i huset.	We went into the house.
Jag körde rakt in i den andra bilen.	I drove straight into the other car.

However, Swedish is generally much more precise about expressing direction than English. Thus **upp i, ned i, ut i** are often used as more exact Swedish equivalents for English 'into':

Klättra ned i brunnen/upp i trädet!	Climb into the well/into the tree.
De gick ut i trädgården.	They went (out) into the garden.

'Into the kitchen' is idiomatically translated as **ut i köket**, unless the movement is clearly from outside the house into the kitchen, or unless the speaker himself is in the kitchen, i.e. the movement is towards the speaker. Thus:

Jag fick lämna gästerna i hallen och springa ut i köket.
I had to leave the guests in the hall and run out into the kitchen.
but:
Jag var ute i trädgården och fick springa in i köket när telefonen ringde.
I was out int he garden and had to run ito the kitchen when the telephone rang.

(b) Place (with parts of the body)

I is often used idiomatically with expressions with parts of the body (frequently without English equivalent). Such usage overlaps usage (a) above and (f) below. See also **om** (714) and **på** (715).

Han tvättade sig i ansiktet, slog sig i pannan och kliade sig i huvudet.
He washed his face, hit his forehead and scratched his head.

Jag skadade mig i tån, gjorde mig illa i foten och fick ont i magen.
I injured my toe, hurt my foot, and got stomach-ache.

Först tog de henne i handen, sedan drog de henne i håret.
First they took her by the hand, then they pulled her hair.

(c) Time

(i) 'in'	**i april, aldrig i livet**	in April, never in my life
(ii) 'for'	**Jag har bott här i 3 år.**	I've lived here for three years.
(iii) 'at'	**i början/slutet av året**	at the start/end of the year
(iv) 'of'	**den femtonde i månaden**	(on) the 15th of the month
(v) 'per'	**en gång i veckan**	once per week/a week
	90 km i timmen	90 km per hour (cf. 726)
(vi) 'to'	**fem minuter i tio**	five minutes to ten
(vii) 0	**i fredags, i våras**	last Friday/last spring
	i dag, i år	today, this year

(d) Material: 'in'

	en staty i brons	a statue in bronze
	måla i olja	to paint in oils
	arbeta i trä	to work in wood
	klädd i grönt/i ylle	dressed in green/in wool
	en skål i rödvin	a toast in red wine

(e) Condition, state

(i) 'in'	**i en förfärlig röra**	in a terrible mess
	i gott skick	in good condition
	Han är i trettioårsåldern.	He's in his thirties.
	Vi lever i fattigdom/lyx.	We live in poverty/luxury.
	dela något i tre delar	to divide something into three
(ii) 'at'	**vara i fred/i krig**	to be at peace/at war
(iii) 'on'	**vara i tjänst**	to be on duty

(f) Means or instrument

(i) 'in'	**uttrycka något i siffror**	to express something in figures

(ii) 'by'	**Han grep mig i kragen.**	He seized me by the collar.
	Jag tog henne i handen.	I took her by the hand.

(iii) 'at'	**i full fart**	at top speed

(g) 'in the form of': 0 **få någonting i present**   to receive something as a present

Hur mycket har du i lön/betalar du i skatt?
How much do you earn/How much tax do you pay?

Har du så mycket i kontanter/i småpengar?
Have you so much money in cash/small change?

(h) With nouns

en föreläsning/en lektion/läxor i a lecture/lesson/homework in; **kunskaper i** a knowledge of; **min like i** my equal in; **(en) lärare/professor i** a teacher/professor of.

(j) With adjectives

Used after adjectives **i** often denotes predominantly positive feelings towards people and things (compare **på** 715(j)):

förtjust/glad i fond of; **kär i** in love with; **tokig i** crazy about.

Also: **sjuk i** ill with.

(k) Unstressed **i** with verbs

dö i die of/from; **ta/få fatt i** get hold of; **ha ont i** have a pain in [+ part of the body]; **ha rätt i något** be right about something; **ta del i** participate in.

(l) Stressed **i** with verbs

hålla i något keep hold of something.

711 Med

The preposition **med** covers all straightforward meanings of English 'with'. In many instances, however, English usage renders **med** idiomatically.

Manner	*Possession*	*Measure*
with, by, in,	with	by

(a) Manner

(i) '(together) with'	**Åk med hela familjen!**	Travel with all the family.
	kaffe med grädde	coffee with cream
(ii) 'against'	**kriget med Norge**	the war against Norway
(iii) 'with'	**Ät med fingrarna!**	Eat with your fingers!
[i.e. 'using']	**se något med blotta ögat**	to see something with the naked eye
(iv) 'in' [i.e. 'using']	**prata med hög röst**	to speak in a loud voice
	med andra ord	in other words
	Skriv med bläck!	Please write in ink.
(v) 'by' [i.e.'using']	**Åk med buss/bil/tåg!**	Travel by bus/car/train!
	betala med check	to pay by cheque
	Skicka det med posten!	Send it by post.
(b) Possession: 'with'	**en man med sex fruar**	a man with six wives
	en smörgås med ägg (på)	a sandwich with egg (on)
(c) Measure: 'by'	**förlängt med 2 meter**	extended by two metres
	dela/multiplicera med 3	to divide/multiply by 3
	Priserna föll med 5%.	Prices fell by 5%.
	Räntan höjdes med 5%.	Interest was raised by 5%.
	seger med 5 mål mot 3	victory by 5 goals to 3
(d) Ellipsis: 'with'	**Upp med händerna!**	Up with your hands!
		Hands up!
	Ned med monarkin!	Down with the monarchy!
	Ut med er!	Out with you!/Get out!

(e) With nouns

> **förbindelse med** connection with; **fördel med** advantage with/of; **jämförelse med** comparison with; **likhet med** similarity to; **medlidande med** compassion for; **nackdel med** disadvantage of; **tålamod med** patience with.

(f) with adjectives and participles

(i) 'with'

> **bekant med** acquainted with; **belåten med** satisfied with; **enig med** in agreement with; **färdig med** finished with; **försiktig/noga/noggrann med** careful with; **förknippad med** connected/associated with; **(miss)nöjd med** (dis)satisfied with.

(ii) 'to'

förlovad med engaged to; **gift med** married to; **identisk med** identical to; **släkt med** related to; **jämfört med** compared to/with.

(iii) Others

full med full of; **jämnårig med** the same age as; **tillräckligt** (indecl.) **med** sufficient (+ noun); **ha dåligt med något** to have little of something.

Note1: **Med** is often used after an adjective, frequently without an English equivalent, when the speaker or writer is making a value judgement.

Det är svårt med svenska.	Swedish is difficult.
Det är modernt med gamla namn.	Old-fashioned names are modern.
Det var gott med lite mat.	It's nice to have a bite to eat.

Note 2: **Med** corresponds to English 'about' in adjectival phases such as:

Det bästa/roliga med dig är...	The best/funny thing about you is...
Det är något underligt/fint med det.	There's something strange/good about it.

(g) Unstressed **med** with verbs

(i) 'with'

börja/sluta med begin/end with; **gräla med** quarrel with; **(miss)lyckas med** (not) succeed with/in; **nöja sig med** be content with; **sätta igång med/ta itu med** get started with; **stå ut med** put up with; **vara tillfreds med** be satisfied with; **syssla med** busy oneself with.

(ii) 'to' (describing some kind of mutual activity)

förlova sig med get engaged to; **gifta sig med** get married to; **prata/tala med** talk to.

(iii) Others

räkna med count on; **ha råd med** afford; **slösa med** waste; **öka/minska med** increase/decrease by.

(h) Stressed **med** with verbs

Used with verbs stressed **med** usually indicates some kind of accompaniment or solidarity.

bli/följa/komma med accompany; **hålla med** agree with; **hänga med** accompany follow (a discussion line of reasoning, etc.); **vara med** attend, be present at.

Note the following phrases and idioms:

med en gång, med detsamma	at once/immediately
med stor sannolikhet	in all probability

gå med vinst/förlust	run at a profit/loss
Jag har (inte) tid med det just nu.	I have (no) time for that right now.
vara med barn	to be with child/pregnant
Det är inte mer med den saken.	There's no(thing) more to it.

712 Mellan (emellan)

Mellan (or its variant **emellan**, see Notes 1 and 2 below) corresponds to English 'between' as a preposition of place, time and manner.

(a) Place   **Jag bor/åker mellan Malmö och Lund.**
                   I live/travel between Malmö and Lund.

(b) Time   **Vi brukar träffas mellan 8 och 9.**
                   We usually meet between 8 and 9 o'clock.

(c) Manner   **Det löser vi mellan vänner.**
                   We'll solve that between friends.

(d) Quantity   **Mellan 200 och 250 människor väntas komma.**
                   Between 200 and 250 people are expected to come.

Note 1: **Emellan** is preferred as the latter element in compound prepositions: **mittemellan** = 'halfway/midway between'.

Note 2: **Emellan** is positioned immediately after the complement in certain instances:

oss vänner emellan	between (us) friends
sinsemellan	between themselves.

(e) With nouns

förhållandet mellan the relationship between; **skillnaden mellan** the difference between; **ett val mellan** a choice between.

(f) With verbs

skilja mellan distinguish between; **välja mellan** choose between/from.

713 Mot

Mot suggests movement in the direction of a point in space or time, but may also express contrast and comparison, and is used with a number of verbs, nouns and adjectives in more or less figurative senses.

Emot rather than **mot** is combined with adverbs to form compound prepositions (cf. (l) below) and is used as the stressed particle after certain verbs (cf. (k) below). Sometimes **emot** is also seen instead of **mot** when a preceding word ends in a consonant.

The form **gentemot** is sometimes used, especially in formal language, when the meaning is 'compared to' (see (e) below), or after certain nouns (see (g) below).

Motion	*Place*	*Time-when*	*Contrast*	*Comparison*
towards, to	against	towards	against	to

(a) Motion

(i) 'towards'	**Nu åker vi mot Stockholm.** We are now travelling towards Stockholm.
(ii) 'to', 'for'	**Tåget mot Malmö avgår från spår 7.** The train to/for Malmö is departing from platform 7.
(iii) 'against'	**Kör inte mot rött ljus!** Don't drive against red lights!

(b) Place

(i) 'against'	**Förbjudet att ställa cyklar mot fönstret.** Leaning cycles against the window is prohibited.
(ii) others	**ansikte mot ansikte** face to face **gränsen mot Norge** the border with Norway

(c) Time: 'towards' **mot slutet av augusti** towards the end of August

Det blir allt kallare fram mot jul.
It gets gradually colder towards Christmas.

Note: Two archaic verbs are used in set phrases with **mot** + *expression of time*:

Det lackar mot jul.	Christmas is a-coming.
Det lider mot kväll.	Night is drawing on.

(d) Contrast: 'against' **mot mina principer** against my principles
mot min önskan/vilja against my wishes/will
mot bättre vetande against my better judgement

(e) Comparison: **De kostar 50 kronor idag mot 40 igår.**
['compared to'] They cost 50 crowns today compared to 40 yesterday.

Det var ingenting mot vad jag har sett.
That's nothing compared to what I have seen.

(f) Replacive:	**mot kontant betalning**	for/against cash payment
['in exchange for']	**mot legitimation**	on proof of identity

(g) With nouns

Used with nouns, **mot** often denotes conduct, reaction or attitude towards something:

> **ett anfall/angrepp mot** an attack on/against; **en allergi mot** an allergy to; **ett brott mot** a crime against; **ett hot (gente)mot** a threat to/against; **invändningar (gente)mot** reservations about; **kampen mot** the fight against; **kritik mot** criticism of; **motvilja mot** disgust of; **ett medel mot** a remedy for; **medicin mot** medicine for; **motstånd (gente)mot** resistance against.

Note also: **i riktning mot** 'in the direction of'.

(h) With adjectives

Used with adjectives, **mot** usually denotes some form of conduct, reaction or attitude towards something:

> **allergisk mot** allergic to; **(o)artig mot** (im)polite to(wards); **elak mot** nasty to; **frikostig mot** generous towards; **grym mot** cruel to; **kritisk mot** critical of; **(o)rättvis mot** (un)fair to; **snäll mot** kind to; **sträng mot** strict with; **stygg mot** unkind to; **tacksam mot** grateful to; **(o)trogen mot** (un)faithful to; **skeptisk mot** sceptical about; **trevlig mot** nice towards; **uppriktig/ärlig mot** honest with; **vänlig mot** friendly with.

(j) Unstressed **mot** with verbs:

(i) denotes conduct, or a (usually negative) reaction towards something or someone:

> **demonstrera mot** demonstrate against; **bära sig illa åt mot någon** behave badly towards someone; **invända/protestera mot** protest against; **kämpa mot** fight against; **opponera sig mot** oppose; **ha någonting/ingenting mot** have something/nothing against; **le mot någon** smile at someone; **reagera mot** react against/towards; **försvara/skydda sig mot** defend/protect oneself against; **vaccinera sig mot** vaccinate oneself against.

(ii) Others:

> **byta något mot något** exchange something for something; **vetta mot** face, look onto; **gränsa mot** border.

(k) Stressed **(e)mot** with verbs

> **säga (e)mot** contradict; **ta emot** receive; **rusa (e)mot** come rushing towards.

(l) Some compound and complex prepositions formed with **emot**

Han kom framemot tiotiden.	It was getting on for ten when he came.
Vi bor mittemot skolan.	We live opposite the school.
Vi bor snett emot skolan.	We live almost opposite the school.
agera tvärtemot givna order	to act contrary to orders

> **Eurons värde gentemot dollarn har sjunkit de senaste månaderna.**
> Over recent months the euro has fallen in value compared to the dollar.

714   Om

The basic meaning of the preposition **om** suggests some kind of encompassment (see (a), (b), (c) below) but **om** also has a wide range of idiomatic usages.

Place	*Subject matter*	*Time*	*Frequency*
(a)round, *compass point* + of	about, on	in	per

(a) Location:

'(a)round'	**Han vek om hörnet.**	He went round the corner.
	en scarf om halsen	a scarf (a)round your neck

Note 1: **Om** is often used with parts of the body in phrases like the following (cf. also 721(d)(ii)):

Han är smutsig om händerna, kall om fötterna och våt om fingrarna.
His hands are dirty, his feet are cold and his fingers are wet.

Note 2: **Om** is used to express place with points of the compass: **norr om Stockholm** = 'north of Stockholm'.

(b) Subject matter:

'about', 'on'	**ett program om samer**	a programme about Sami
	en bok om Sverige	a book on Sweden
	Det är synd om henne.	It's a shame about her.

(c) Apportionment: **Vi var tre om belöningen.**
'sharing' There were three of us to share the reward.

De var många om de få platserna.
There were many people for the few seats.

(d) Time-when: 'in' **Kom om en vecka!** Come in a week.

Used with 'time-when' expressions **om** usually indicates a future occurrence. It is, however, rarely used with days of the week and never with dates or months. See also 724.

Note 1: Observe, however:

Ugglan jagar om natten och sover om dagen The owl hunts by night and sleeps by day.
långt om länge at long last

Note 2: **Om** is postpositioned in the phrase: **året om** (= **hela året**) 'all year round'.

(e) Frequency: 0 **Vi åker dit tre gånger om dagen (om året).**
(See 726.) We go there three times a day/a year.

Note: **Om** is postpositioned in the phrase: **många gånger om** = 'over and over'.

(f) With nouns

Used with nouns **om** usually denotes subject matter, 'on', 'with regard to', 'concerning', etc.

ansökan om a request for; **begäran om** a desire for; **ett beslut om** a decision on; **en bön om** a prayer for; **drömmen om** the dream of; **en fråga om** a question of; **historien om** the story of; **hoppet om** the hope of; **löftet om** the promise of; **en vision om** a vision of; **ett vad om** a bet/wager on.

(g) With adjectives

gott [indecl.] **om** plenty of; **ont** [indecl.] **om** little/a shortage of; **medveten om** aware/conscious of; **rädd om** [in phrases such as: **Var rädd om dig!** Take care of yourself]; **övertygad om** convinced of/about.

(h) Unstressed **om** with verbs

(i) subject matter: 'about', 'with regard to'

be om ask for request; **bråka/gräla om** quarrel about; **drömma om** dream about; **fråga om** ask about; **handla om** concern/be about; **komma överens**

om agree about; **prata/tala om** talk about; **tävla om** compete for; **övertyga om** convince about.

(ii) used after verbs expressing pervasive sensory qualities such as:

Det luktar om honom.	He smells.
Det skiner alltid om hans skor.	He always has a shine on his shoes.

(iii) Others

bry sig om care about; **ta hand om** take care of; **tycka synd om** feel sorry for; **vara synd om** be a shame/a pity about.

(j) Stressed **om** with verbs

hålla om någon embrace someone; **köra om** overtake; **tycka om** like.

In many instances stressed **om** signifies that something is done anew (often rendered by an expression with 're-' + *verb* in English):

Jag vill måla om hemma.	I want to (re-)paint the house.
Tänk om!	Think again!
Gör om det, om du törs!	Do that again if you dare!

715 På

På is a very common Swedish preposition that English renders in many ways. In recent years **på** has increased in popularity amongst Swedes, taking over some of the functions of other prepositions. (For example, **vid universitetet** 'at the university' now sounds old-fashioned or pedantic, and most Swedes prefer to say **på universitetet** (cf. **på skolan** 'at school'.) Phrases such as **i mitten av** 'in the middle of' are being replaced by **i mitten på**; and prepositional expressions like **namnet på någonting** 'the name of something' provide a paradigm for many analogous expressions (**en bild på** 'a picture of'; **titeln på** 'the title of', etc.).

Location	Motion	Time-when	Time-duration	Measure	Possession
on, in, at	to	on + day in + season at + festival	in (not) for	of, with	of

(a) Location

(i) 'on'	på bordet, på väggen	on the table, on the wall
	på en båt, på tåget	on a boat, on the train
	Vi bor på Storgatan.	We live on Storgatan.
	Vi kör på höger sida.	We drive on the right.
	Läs texten på sidan 35!	Read the text on page 35!
	Jag har inga pengar på mig.	I have no money on me.
(ii) 'in'	på landet, på gården	in the country, in the yard
	Vi ses på restaurangen.	See you in the restaurant.
	Jag jobbar på en bank.	I work in/at a bank.
	på ett hotellrum	in a hotel room
	inte ett moln på himlen	not a cloud in the sky
(iii) 'at'	på apoteket	at the chemist's
	på biblioteket	at the library
	på 6000 meters höjd	at a height of 6,000 metres

See 721 for an explanation of the difference in usage between **i** and **på** in expressions of location.

In a few instances, especially after verbs such as **låna**, **hämta**, etc., Swedish usage prefers a preposition of place where English has a preposition of direction.

Hämta paketet på posten!	Collect the parcel from the post office.
Jag lånade pengarna hos Olle.	I borrowed the money from Olle.
Jag tog en bok på hyllan.	I took a book from the shelf.

(b) Motion: 'to', 'on(to)'

Jag gick på bio/matchen.	I went to the cinema/game.
Han hoppade på bussen.	He jumped onto the bus.

See 721(b)(ii)) for an explanation of the difference in usage between **till** and **på** in expressions of motion.

(c) Time-when

(i) 'on' + day	på söndag/söndagarna	on Sunday/on Sundays
(ii) 'in' + season	på våren	in spring
+ part of day	på kvällen	in the evening
+ decade	på 90-talet	in the 90s
+ century	på 1100-talet	in the 1100s

(iii) 'at'	**på den tiden**	at that time
+ festivals	**på julen**	at Christmas
	på samma tid	at the same time

For a fuller explanation of **på** and other prepositions in time-when expressions, see 724.

(d) Duration

På renders 'in' in expressions which may be considered to answer the question 'How long does it take to . . . ?' and 'for' in a negative clause expressing a length of time during which a state, action or experience has not taken place. (See 725.)

> **Kan man köra härifrån till Lund på en timme?**
> Can you drive from here to Lund in an hour?

> **Han gör allt på väldigt kort tid.**
> He does everything in a very short time.

> **Jag har inte sett henne på länge/på flera år.**
> I haven't seen her for a long time/for several years/in several years.

(e) Measure

(i) 'of'	**en försening på 2 dygn**	a delay of two days
	ett fartyg på 3000 ton	a vessel of 3,000 tonnes
	ett barn på fyra år	a child of four (years)
	en rabatt på 25 procent	a reduction of 25 percent
	ett ord på sju bokstäver	a word of seven letters
(ii) 'with'	**en lägenhet på 3 rum och kök**	an apartment with three rooms and a kitchen

As will be seen from the above examples **på** is frequently used with expressions of measure containing some kind of numerical information.

(f) Genitive: 'of'	**färgen på huset**	the colour of the house
	namnet på gatan	the name of the street
	priset på bensin	the price of petrol
	den bästa tiden på året	the best time of the year
	början/slutet på boken	the beginning/end of the book
But compare:		
	i början/slutet *av*....	at the beginning/end of ...

På in this sense is used primarily with object to object relationships, rather than with people (although note: **namnet på mannen** = 'the name of the man'/'the man's name'). It is common after nouns expressing visible qualities and characteristics of objects (**färg, form, mått, bredd, höjd, djup, längd, storlek,** etc. and also **styrka, smak, kvalitet**).

Note: **På** may also express so-called objective genitive relationships (cf. 729(d)):

> **mordet på ärkebiskopen**   the murder of the archbishop

(g) Manner

The use of **på** as a preposition expressing relationships of manner is usually restricted to a few common phrases and idioms:

Vad heter det på svenska?	What's that in Swedish?
Det var bara på skämt.	It was only in jest/in fun.
på samma sätt, på detta sätt	in the same way/in this way
på måfå	at random
på nytt	anew, again
på förhand	in advance

Note also the idiomatic use of **på** in sentences such as:

Det var ett sätt att bli rik på.	That's one way of getting rich.
Det var mitt sätt att göra det på.	This was my way of doing it.

(h) With nouns (see also (f) above)

anfall/attack/angrepp på attack on/against; **bevis på** proof of; **brist på** lack of; **efterfrågan på** demand for; **exempel på** example of; **fortsättning på** continuation of; **förväntning på** expectation of; **jakt på** hunt/chase for; **lösning på** solution to; **prenumeration på** subscription to; **prov på** sample of; **svar på** answer to; **tanke på** thought of; **tillgång på** supply of; **överskott/överflod på** surplus of.

(j) With adjectives

Used after adjectives **på** often denotes predominantly negative feelings towards people or things (cf. **i** 710(j)). Note, however, that in such instances **på** is usually replaced by **över** when the prepositional complement is an **att** + *infinitive construction* or **att** + *subordinate clause.*

arg/sur på angry with; **avundsjuk på** envious of; **besviken på** disappointed in/with; **ledsen på** hurt/disappointed with; **svartsjuk på** jealous of; **trött på** tired of; **beredd på** ready for; **nyfiken på** curious about; **(o)säker på**

(un)sure about; **pigg på** keen on; **rik på** rich in; **bra på** good at; **dålig på** bad at.

(k) Unstressed **på** with verbs

(i) På is frequently encountered with verbs indicating one of the five senses when these are followed by a direct object, especially when the action involved is deliberate. Compare, for example:

> **Ser du månen? Ja, jag ser på den nu.**
> Can you see the moon? Yes I'm looking at it now.

höra/lyssna på listen to; **känna på** feel [i.e. sense of touch]; **lukta på** smell; **smaka på** taste; **ta på** touch; **titta/se på** look at.

(ii) På is often used after verbs indicating movements like shaking, raising, etc. with parts of the body:

> **Han höjde på ögonbrynen, ryckte på axlarna och skakade på huvudet.**
> He raised his eyebrows, shrugged his shoulders and shook his head.

(iii) På often denotes some kind of target or object for one's feelings:

> **bero på** depend upon; **hoppas på** hope for; **hälsa på** greet; **hämnas på** take revenge on; **irritera sig på** be irritated about; **kasta på** throw at; **klaga på** complain about/of; **koncentrera sig på** concentrate on; **lita på** rely on; **reagera på** react to; **ropa på någon** call (after) someone; **rösta på** vote for; **skjuta på** shoot at; **skylla på** blame; **skälla på** shout (in anger) at; **ta reda på** find out about; **tro på** believe in; **tröttna på** grow tired of; **tvivla på** doubt; **tänka på** think about; **vänta på** wait for.

(iv) Others:

> **brås på** take after; **bjuda på något** offer something; **klara sig på** manage on something; **livnära sig på** make a living out of.

(l) Stressed **på** with verbs

> **hitta på** think up; **hålla på att** + *verb*/**hålla på med** + *noun* be in the process of doing something; **hälsa på**, visit [a person]; **komma på** come across, encounter; **skjuta på** push; **skriva på** sign; **slå/sätta på** switch on; **ta på** put on.

716   Till

Principally the preposition **till** suggests movement or progression (up) to a destination or target. Often the idea of movement is figurative, and in this sense **till** may serve as part of a prepositional phrase expressing an indirect object relationship, especially with persons.

Till is also commonly used before time-when expressions, chiefly to express English 'until', but also in a number of other senses.

Till has retained remnants of old noun case-endings in a number of set phrases still commonly used in Swedish. Such forms after **till** often express manner (see **(e)** below).

Motion	*Time-when*	*Indirect object*	*Possession*
(up) to	until, for	to/for	of

(a) Motion

(i) 'to'	**Vi reste dit i fjol.**	We went there last year.
	tåget till Lund	the train to/for Lund
	Vi gick tidigt till sängs.	We went to bed early.
	Då kom han till makten.	Then he came to power.
(ii) 0	**Vi reser ofta till utlandet.**	We often travel abroad.

Note: **Till** may also express location in a few instances:

till höger/till vänster	on the right, on the left (*also*: to the right, left)
anlända till en plats	to arrive in/at a place

(b) Progression: 'to'   **(från) 15 till 20 personer**   (from) 15 to 20 people
öppet från mars till juli   open from March to July

(c) Time-when

(i) 'until'	**Stanna till i morgon!**	Stay until tomorrow!
	tills vidare	until further notice
	till dess	until then (by then)
Note also:		
	natten till tisdag	the night before Tuesday

till sist	at last

(ii) 'in time for' **Kom inte för sent till middagen!**
Don't be late for dinner!

Jag åker hem till jul/till våren.
I'm going home for Christmas/in the spring.

See also 724(l)(iv) for further details of **till** + expressions of time.

(d) Indirect object

(i) 'to', 0	**Skriv ett brev till mig!**	Write me a letter.
	Ring till dina föräldar!	Phone your parents.
	Vad sa du till henne?	What did you say to her?
(ii) for	**Ta med några till oss!**	Bring some for us!
	Köpte du en till mig?	Did you buy one for me?

Note: For more on the use of the indirect object, see 1022.

(e) Manner

Used in this way **till** usually forms part of set phrases. The nouns in these phrases sometimes retain the old case endings (129(h)).

Vi kom till fots.	We came on foot.
Hon fick det bara till låns.	She only got it on loan.
hus till salu	house for sale
vara till hjälp/nytta/hinder(s)	to be of help/use/a hindrance

(f) Till denotes 'by way of', 'for'

Hon är barnmorska till yrket.	She's a midwife by profession.
Han är blyg till naturen.	He's shy by nature
Vi känner honom till utseendet.	We know him by sight.
Vi känner henne till namnet.	We know her by name.
Vad får vi till middag?	What's for dinner?
till en början	for a start
till exempel	for example
till minne av	in memory of

(g) Genitive: 'of'

en förstad till Stockholm	a suburb of Stockholm

författaren till boken	the author of the book
nyckeln till huset	the key to/of the house
en vän/släkting till mig	a friend/relation of mine
en jätte till karl	a giant of a man

Note that, in this sense, **till** is often used to signify 'belonging to' where English has 'of' or 'for': **en ny skärm till datorn** 'a new screen for the computer'.

(h) Other usages

till min stora förvåning	to my great surprise
till följd av	as a result of
till ett pris av	at a price of
till varje pris	at any price

(j) With adjectives

användbar till usable as/for; **knuten/bunden till** attached to; **färdig till** ready to; **(o)skyldig till** (not) guilty of.

(k) With nouns:

(i) denotes conduct towards, attitude towards or relations with:

hat till hatred of; **kärlek till** love of; **hänsyn till** consideration (regard) for; **en anknytning till** a connection with.

(ii) denotes the cause or reason for something:

anledningen till the reason for; **bakgrunden till** the background to; **början till** the start of; **förklaringen till** the explanation for; **ett förslag till** a suggestion for; **idén till** the idea for; **initiativet till** the initiative for/behind; **en källa till** a source of; **motivet till** the motive for; **orsaken till** the reason for/cause of; **skälet till** the reason for.

(iii) denotes a comparison with or contrast to:

ett alternativ till an alternative to; **en motsats till** a contrast to; **en motsvarighet till** a counterpart to; **en synonym till** a synonym for.

(l) Unstressed **till** with verbs:

(i) denotes some kind of connection between things (figurative or physical), or a result or effect:

anknyta till connect with; **ansluta sig till** join; **användas till** be used for/as; **binda till** tie to; **duga till** be of use as; **hålla sig till** keep/restrict oneself to; **hänvisa till** refer to; **koppla till** connect to; **leda till** lead to; **tvinga någon till** force someone (in)to; **utveckla (sig) till** develop into.

(ii) denotes a change in status:

befordra till promote to; **förvandla till** change into; **upphöja till** raise to; **utse/utnämna till** appoint to; **välja någon till** elect someone as/to the position of; **översätta till** translate into.

(m) Stressed **till** with verbs

gå till (Hur gick det till?) come about (How did that happen?); **hjälpa till (Kan jag få hjälpa till med något?)** lend a hand (Can I help with anything?); **känna till** be familiar with; **lägga till** add; **se till** look after; **stå till** [in phrases such as **Hur står det till?** How do you do?]

717 Under

The preposition **under** has two chief functions; one is to express duration, one to express place (physical or figurative). Note that Swedish is often more precise than English when expressing prepositional relationships of place. **Under** is thus used to express location, or movement generally only if the movement is under something and then out again on the other side. Otherwise Swedish often prefaces **under** with an adverbial qualifier. Compare:

Hunden ligger under soffan.
The dog is lying under the sofa.

Hunden kröp in under soffan (och låg kvar där).
The dog crept under the sofa and stayed there.

Båten seglade under 15 broar.
The boat sailed under fifteen bridges.

Location	Time-duration	Measure	Manner
under, below, beneath under, by, in	during, for		under, below

(a) Place

(i) 'under'	**under mattan**	under the carpet
	Tyskland under Hitler	Germany under Hitler
(ii) 'below'	**lägenheten under vår**	the apartment below ours
	ett slag under bältet	a punch below the belt
(iii) 'beneath'	**under hans värdighet**	beneath his dignity

Note also: **under vägen** = 'en route', 'on the way'.

(b) Time

(i) 'during'	**under medeltiden**	during/in the Middle Ages
	under samtalet(s gång)	during the conversation
	någon gång under dagen	some time during the day
(ii) 'for'	**Det regnade oavbrutet under 40 dagar.**	
	It rained non-stop for 40 days.	

Note also: **under tiden** = 'in the meantime', 'meanwhile'.

(c) Measure

(i) 'under'	**barn under 15 år**	children under 15 years
	under 500 åskådare	fewer than 500 spectators
(ii) 'below'	**Temperaturen är under noll.**	
	The temperature is below zero.	

(d) Manner

Under is used in a number of instances to introduce the accompanying circumstances to an action or occurrence.

gå under fullständig tystnad	to walk in complete silence
under allmänt jubel	amid general merriment
under förutsättning att	on condition that
under dessa förhållanden	in/under these circumstances
resa under falskt namn	to travel under a false name
vara känd under namnet Jocke	to be known by the name Jocke

718   Vid

The preposition **vid** suggests adjacency or proximity (see also **bredvid** 720(g)), but is used in a number of figurative and idiomatic expressions in a freer sense.

Location	*Time-when*
by	around

(a) Location

(i) 'by'	**Han satt vid fönstret.**	He sat by the window.
	Värm dig vid brasan!	Warm yourself by the fire.
	en stad vid kusten	a town by/on the coast
	ett hus vid torget	a house by/on the square
(ii) 'at'	**sitta vid bordet**	to sit at the table
	studera vid universitetet	to study at university
(iii) Others	**slaget vid Waterloo**	the battle of Waterloo
	uppträda vid rätten	to appear in court

Note: **Invid**, usually used only of actual location, suggests closer proximity than **vid**, an idea generally strengthened by an adverb, **tätt invid, alldeles invid**:

> **en stuga alldeles invid vägen**   a cottage right by the side of/close to the road

(b) Time

(i) 'around'	**Vi ses vid tiotiden.**	I'll see you around ten-ish.
	vid 20 års ålder	around twenty years of age
	vid början av dagen	at the start of the day
	vid slutet av året	at the end of the year
(ii) Others	**vid ankomst/avgång**	on arrival/departure
	kärlek vid första ögonkastet	love at first sight
	vid den tiden/vid det laget	by that time

Note 1: **Vid** renders 'time-when' expressions corresponding to English 'in the event of' in instances such as:

> **Uppvisningen inställs vid regn.**   The show will be cancelled in the event of rain.
> **Kör försiktigt vid halka!**   Drive carefully in slippery conditions.
> **vid sjukdom/krig**   in the event of illness/war
> **vid detta tillfälle**   in this instance

Note 2: Possession: **Vid** suggests 'having' in certain set phrases, but this usage is no longer productive.

en man vid namn Jansson	a man by the name of Jansson
De är vid god hälsa.	They're in good health.
Han är vid gott lynne.	He's in good spirits.
hålla något vid liv, vara vid liv	to keep something alive, to be alive

(d) With adjectives

(o)van vid be (un)accustomed to, (un)used to.

(e) Unstressed **vid** with verbs

binda vid tie to; **fästa vid** fasten to/attach to; **hålla fast vid** hold onto, to insist; **stå fast vid** stand by (figurative); **vänja sig vid** accustom oneself to.

(f) Stressed **vid** with verbs

bränna(s) vid burn fast (i.e. stick to the pan).

719 Över

The preposition **över** suggests 'at a higher level than' and often renders English 'over' as a preposition of place and of measure.

Över is common after adjectives and verbs, where it is beginning to take over many of the usages of **av** and **för**.

Location	Motion	Time duration	Time-when	Measure
over, above	across, over	over	past	over

(a) Place

(i) 'over'	**lampan över bordet**	the lamp over the table
	Hoppa över staketet!	Jump over the fence.
(ii) 'across'	**Han simmade över ån.**	He swam across the river.
	bred över axlarna	broad across the shoulders
	Jag bor tvärs över gatan.	I live just across the street.
(iii) 'above'	**200 meter över havet**	200 metres above sea level

Hans röst hördes tydligt över bullret.
His voice could be heard clearly above the noise.

(iv) Others   **Ovädret var över oss på kort tid.**
The storm was upon us in a short time.

Tåget till Köpenhamn går över Malmö.
The train to Copenhagen goes via Malmö.

Note: **överallt** = 'everywhere':

   Han har varit överallt i Norden.   He's been everywhere in the Nordic countries.

(b) Time

(i) 'over'   **Vill du stanna över helgen?**
Do you want to stay over the weekend?

Jag arbetar över jul(en).
I'm working over Christmas.

Man kan spara mycket över en femårsperiod.
You can save a lot of money over a five-year period.

(ii) 'past'   **Klockan är fem över sex.**   It's five past six.
Klockan är över åtta.   It's past eight (o'clock).

(c) Measure

(i) 'over'   **Det kostar över 200 euro.**   It costs over 200 euros.
över 50 000 åskådare   over 50,000 spectators

(ii) 'beyond'   **Utsikten var vacker över all beskrivning.**
The view was beautiful beyond description.

Note: The compound form **utöver** is sometimes used to give emphasis in instances such as (c)(ii) above. **Utöver** may also be used to signify 'in addition to'. See 727(g).

(d) With nouns and adjectives

(i) **över** often suggests feelings towards:
   entusiasm över enthusiasm for; **glädje/lycka över** happiness over/at; **ilska över** anger over; **oro över** concern about/for; **sorg över** sadness at; **besviken över** disappointed over/with; **chockad över** shocked about/over; **förvånad över** surprised at; **generad över** embarrassed about/at; **glad över** happy

about; **häpen över** amazed at; **ledsen över** sorry about; **stolt över** proud of.

(ii) **över** also suggests superiority over:

makt över power over; **kontroll över** control of; **inflytande över** influence over (on).

(iii) Others

en karta över a map of; **en lista över** a list of; **ett minnesmärke över** a monument to.

(e) Unstressed **över** with verbs

(i) denotes superiority or control over:

bestämma över be master of/rule over; **disponera/förfoga/råda över** be in charge of; **vinna över** beat/win against.

(ii) Others:

förvånas över be surprised at; **grubbla över** to ponder; **klaga över** complain about; **skryta över** boast about; **skämmas över** be ashamed over (at); **undra över** wonder at.

(f) Stressed **över** with verbs

gå över exceed; **hoppa över** omit (**Vi hoppade över de där sidorna.** We skipped those pages); **se över** inspect check; **ta över** take over.

C PREPOSITIONAL USE

720 Some other prepositions of place

(a) Note that many of these prepositions also fulfil other functions (prepositions of time, manner, etc.).

(b) Prepositions of place:

	Main meaning	*Refer to*	*See also*
bakom	behind	c, below	
bland	among	d, below	
bortemot	in the direction of	e, below	722(d)
bortom	(on) the other side of	f, below	
bortåt	in the direction of	e, below	722(d)
bredvid	beside, next to, by	g, below	
framför	before, in front of	h, below	
förbi	past	j, below	
före	before, in front of	k, below	722(e)
hinsides	(on) the other side of	f Note, below	
hitom	(on) this side of	f, below	
hos	at (the home of)	l, below	
inför	before	m, below	
innanför	within, inside	n, below	
inom	within	o, below	722(g)
intill	close by	p, below	722(h)
inuti	inside	q, below	
jämte	beside	g Note, below	
kring	(a)round	s, below	722(j)
längs(med)	along	r, below	
nedanför	at the bottom/foot of	t, below	
nedför, nerför	down	v, below	
omkring	(a)round	s, below	722(j)
ovan	above	t, below	
ovanför	above	t, below	
ovanpå	on top of	t, below	
runt	(a)round	s, below	722(j)
undan	away from	u, below	
uppför	up	v, below	
ur	out of	w, below	
utanför	outside	n, below	
utanpå	on the outside of	x, below	
utefter	along	r, below	
utför	down	v, below	
utmed	along	r, below	
utom	beyond	y, below	727(p)
åt	to(wards)	z, below	727(q)
åt . . . till	towards	z Note 2, below	

(c) Bakom suggests 'behind' and is used both literally and figuratively. (See also **efter** 706.)

Hon stod bakom dig i kön.	She stood behind you in the queue.
Han är hjärnan bakom idén.	He is the brain behind the idea.

(d) Bland suggests 'among'.

Jag är bara en bland många.	I am just one among many.
bland annat, bland andra	among other things, among others

Note: If motion is implied, **bland** is often combined with an adverb, **in bland**, **ut bland**, etc.

Älgen försvann in bland träden.	The elk disappeared (in) among the trees.

(e) Bortemot and **bortåt** suggest movement towards or proximity to some kind of target, but are far less common than **till** (716) in expressions of motion, or than **omkring**, etc. (see (s) below) with expressions of place or quantity. **Inemot** is sometimes used in the same sense with time and numbers.

Han gick bortemot stationen.	He walked off towards the station.
Stället ligger bortåt Hindås till.	The place isn't far from Hindås.
Jag väntade bortemot en timme.	I waited for getting on for an hour.

(f) Bortom and **hitom** indicate location (or occasionally motion) 'beyond' or 'this side of' a given point respectively. They are, however, usually replaced in modern Swedish by **på andra sidan** + *noun with end article* and **på den här sidan** + *noun with end article* respectively.

Han bor bortom kyrkan.	He lives beyond the church.
Det finns två träd hitom ån.	There are two trees this side of the river.

Note: **Hinsides** ('on the other side of') is archaic and restricted in its use. It has a biblical ring, evoking the same flavour as 'the hereafter' in English.

Vem vet vad som väntar hinsides graven? Who knows what awaits us beyond the grave?

(g) Bredvid indicates 'beside' and is used both literally and figuratively.

Vill du sätta dig bredvid Olle?	Do you want to sit beside Olle?
Bredvid dig är hon rätt vacker.	In comparison to you she is quite lovely.

Note: **Jämte** is uncommon today, but may still be encountered in place of **bredvid**.

(h) Framför indicates 'in front of' and is used both literally and figuratively.

Bussen stannar framför affären.	The bus stops in front of the shop.
Plikten framför allt	Duty before all else
Jag föredrar kaffe framför te.	I prefer coffee to tea.

(j) Förbi indicates movement (or occasionally location) past a point in space (see 416 for 'past' in clock-time expressions).

Vi har väl inte åkt förbi huset?
Surely, we've not driven past the house?

Båten var redan förbi udden när den sjönk.
The boat was already past the headland when it sank.

(k) Före suggests 'before', usually in some kind of deliberate sequence.

Han stod före mig i kön.	He was before me in the queue.
Polisbilen körde före oss.	The police car drove in front of us.

(l) Hos suggests 'at the house of' (cf. French *chez*, German *bei*), but is also used figuratively to indicate 'in the works of', when referring to, for example, a writer, or 'in the soul of', when referring to a person's nature.

Jag var hos Olssons/hos doktorn igår.
I was at the Olssons'/at the doctor's yesterday.

Jag växte upp hos mina farföräldrar.
I grew up with my grandparents.

Det kan man läsa om hos Moberg.
You can read about that in Moberg('s works).

Det är något hos dig jag inte gillar.
There's something about you I don't like.

Hos is usually replaced by **till** (716) with verbs of motion, but notice:

Sätt dig hos mig i soffan!	Sit by me/next to me on the sofa.

(m) Inför suggests 'in the presence of' or 'at the prospect of/ahead of'.

Han står åtalad inför rätta.	He is appearing in court.
Vi ställs inför ett svårt problem.	We are faced with a grave problem.

förberedelser inför mötet   preparations for/ahead of the meeting

(n) Innanför, utanför suggest 'inside', 'outside' in the sense of restriction within or exclusion from an area (cf. below: **inom** (o), **inuti** (q), **utanpå** (x)). **Utanför** also suggests 'outside' in the sense of 'in front of' a place (cf. also **framför** (h), above).

innanför murarna	within the city walls
innanför Sveriges gränser	within the borders of Sweden
utanför storstadsområdena	outside the main cities
utanför västkusten	off the west coast

(o) Inom suggests 'within' in the sense of restriction to an area (often figurative). (Cf. also **innanför** (n), above, **inuti** (q), below).

inom synhåll/hörhåll/räckhåll	within sight/earshot/reach
ett stort namn inom branschen	a big name in the industry
Något inom mig säger …	Something inside me tells me …
inom ramen för vårt projekt	within the framework for our project

Note: **Inom** is compounded with certain nouns to form certain adverbial expressions:

Jag arbeta inomhus för det mesta	I work indoors most of the time.
Han har mycket inombords.	He has got a lot in him.
inomskärs	landward of the islands/skerries

(p) Intill (also **invid** (718(a) Note) suggests adjacency to a location.

ett hus intill kyrkan   a house by the church

(q) Inuti suggests 'inside' in the sense of restriction within a volume (cf. **innanför** (n), above). **Inom** (cf. (o) above) rather than **inuti** is preferred when expressing a corresponding idea in an abstract sense.

Titta inuti flaskan/paketet!   Look inside the bottle/packet.

Note: **Uti** ('in', 'inside') has a quaint, old-fashioned ring to it and is reserved mostly for poetry or deliberately affected language.

(r) Längs, utmed, utefter, längsmed all correspond to English 'along' in the sense of location or movement parallel with something. **Utmed, längsmed** and **utefter** often suggest a more pervasive presence or movement, cf. English 'all along'.

Det fanns inga hus längs vägen.   There were no houses along the road.

> **Vakterna gick utefter gränsen.**   The guards patrolled (along) the frontier.
> **Vi rodde utmed kusten.**   We rowed along/up/down the coast.

(s) Omkring, kring, runt suggest '(a)round' both in the sense of 'encircling' and in the sense of 'in the vicinity of'. **Omkring** perhaps gives a slightly less precise (i.e. less 'circular') impression than **kring** and **runt**.

> **Vi var tolv stycken runt bordet.**   There were twelve of us round the table.
> **Det var fuktigt omkring sjön.**   It was damp around the lake.
> **Temperaturen ligger runt noll.**   The temperature is around freezing.
> **Brukar ni dansa kring granen?**   Do you dance round the Christmas tree?

Note 1: **Runt** is postpositioned in a few set phrases such as:

> **Hon har rest jorden runt fem gånger.**   She has travelled round the world five times.
> **Han åkte land och rike runt.**   He drove the length and breadth of the country.

Note 2: **Kring** (and occasionally **omkring**) is used to indicate subject matter. In this sense it is less specific than **om** (714(b)).

> **Studier kring Strindbergs drama**   Studies in Strindberg's drama

(t) Ovan, ovanför, ovanpå all suggest 'above' with expressions of place, but they are not synonymous in Swedish. **Ovan** sounds poetic and affected in modern Swedish and may generally be replaced by **över** (719). **Ovanför** suggests 'at a higher level than'; it is more common than **ovan** but may also be replaced by **över** in most instances. **Ovanpå** suggests location 'on top of' something else.

> **Fåglarna svävade hogt ovan molnen.**
> The birds were hovering high above the clouds.

> **Benet gick av strax ovanför knäet.**
> His leg was broken just above the knee.

> **Ovanpå leran ligger ett tunt lager grus.**
> Above the clay is a thin layer of gravel.

Nedanför is *not* the opposite of **ovanför** (cf. **under** 717). **Nedanför** suggests a location corresponding to English 'at the foot of', 'at the bottom of', etc.

> **Han stod och väntade nedanför trappan.**
> He stood waiting at the bottom of the stairs.

Note: **Ovanför/nedanför** are used in informal Swedish to indicate 'north/south of':

> **Vi bor en bra bit ovanför Umeå.**   We live a good way north of Umeå.
> **Tåget spårade ur strax nedanför Gävle.**   The train was derailed just south of Gävle.

(u) Undan may render English 'away from' but its usage is restricted to a relatively small number of verbs. Stressed **undan** with a verb usually corresponds to English 'away'.

Han klarade sig undan polisen.	He got away from the police.
De flydde undan sina fiender.	They escaped from their enemies.
Lägg undan era böcker!	Put your books away!
sätta undan, ställa undan	to put away

(v) Uppför and **nedför/nerför** suggest movement 'up' and 'down' an incline. **Utför** suggests precipitous, often uncontrolled movement 'down' an incline or 'off from' a high point. All three words are also used adverbially.

Kör inte uppför/nerför backen!	Don't drive up/down the hill.
Vi gick uppför/nerför trappan.	We walked up/down the stairs.
Hon ramlade utför trappan.	She fell down the stairs.

Note: The English expressions 'uphill', 'downhill' are compounded in Swedish:

Vi cyklade nerförsbacke i 20 minuter.	We cycled uphill for 20 minutes.
Det var nerförsbacke hela vägen.	It was downhill all the way.
Firman är i utförsbacken.	The firm is going downhill.

(w) Ur suggests movement 'out of' (+ *volume*, see 721(a) Note 3). This idea is sometimes strengthened by an adverbial qualifier (**ut ur**, **fram ur**, etc.).

Hon drog kontakten ur väggen.	He pulled the plug out of the wall.
Kom ut ur rummet omedelbart!	Come out of the room at once!
Dricker du direkt ur burken?	Do you drink straight from the can?

Note: **Ur** also has a number of figurative uses.

Han målar ur minnet/ur egen fantasi.	He paints from memory/from his own imagination.
Jag var lite ur balans/ur form.	I was a little unbalanced/off form.
ur funktion/ur tjänst	out of order/off duty

(x) Utanpå suggests 'on the outside of' in the sense of being affixed to the outside of something, and is thus somewhat restricted in its usage. **Utanpå** is also used adverbially.

Etiketten satt (utan)på flaskan.
The label was on the outside of the bottle.

Han drog stövlarna utanpå byxorna.
He pulled his boots on over his trousers.

(y) **Utom** suggests 'beyond' with expressions of place, but it is only used in set phrases. When used to express place in a more figurative sense, it is rendered by a range of idioms in English.

Han är utom synhåll/utom hörhåll/utom räckhåll/utom fara.
He is out of sight/out of earshot/out of reach/out of danger.

Hennes föräldrar var utom sig av rädsla/sorg/glädje.
Her parents were beside themselves with fear/grief/joy.

Det är utom allt tvivel.	It is beyond all doubt.

(z) **Åt** usually suggests motion in the direction of a point in space, but in this sense its role has, in many instances, been taken over by **mot** (713) and **till** (716).

Åt vilket håll går vi nu?	Which direction are we going in now?
Det här går åt skogen/helvete.	This is going to pieces/hell!
Rummet vetter åt norr.	The room faces north.

Note 1: Expressions with **åt sidan** may often be rendered by 'away' or 'aside' in English. (cf. **undan**, (u) above.)

Han lade boken åt sidan och tittade upp.	He put the book aside and looked up.
Alla gick åt sidan när vi passerade.	Everyone stepped aside as we passed.

Note 2: Combined with **till** to form a parenthetical preposition, **åt . . . till** expresses motion in the direction of, or location.

De gick åt Uppsala till.	They walked towards Uppsala.
De bodde åt Uppsala till.	They lived on the way to Uppsala.

721 På or i? How to render English 'in', 'on', 'at', 'to' in Swedish

Care must be taken when rendering the English prepositions of place 'in', 'on', 'at', 'to' into Swedish. Dictionary definitions are insufficient to cover the wide range of idiomatic renderings, and it is difficult to formulate practical rules for the usage of **på** and **i** as prepositions of place. What follows is a list of hints rather than hard and fast rules, and some alternatives have been intentionally omitted. Only a keen observation of the idiomatic usages of **på** and **i** will lead to a thorough understanding of the way in which these two common prepositions are used.

(a) A rule of thumb (albeit one with many exceptions) is that Swedish usage requires:

(i) **På** + *a (two-dimensional) surface* (cf. English 'on' + *surface*)

(ii) **I** + *a (three-dimensional) volume* (cf. English 'in' + *volume/enclosed space*)

på = 'on' + *surface*	**i** = 'in' + *volume*
tavlan på väggen the picture on the wall	**möss i väggen** mice in the wall
duken på bordet the cloth on the table	**duken i lådan** the cloth in the drawer
antennen på taket the aerial on the roof	**hunden i huset** the dog in the house

Note 1: Some commonly used expressions require special care! Note the following:

på landet in the country(side)	**i landet** in the country (= state)
möta någon på gatan to meet someone in the street	**ett hål i gatan** a hole in the road
möta någon på gården to meet someone in the yard	**i trädgården** in the garden
inte ett moln på himlen not a cloud in the sky	**i himmelen** in heaven
båtarna på havet the boats on the sea	**fiskarna i havet** the fish in the sea
på vinden in the loft	**i öknen** in the desert
på hörnet on the corner	**i hörnet** in the corner
på åkrarna in the fields	**i skogen** in the forest
sitta på en stol to sit on a (dining) chair	**sitta i en fåtölj** to sit in an (easy) chair
Jag bor på Storgatan. I live in High Street.	**Hon bor i staden.** She lives in town/in the city.
på det här stället in this spot	**tala i telefon/radio/TV** to speak on the phone/radio/TV

Note 2: Geographical names are usually preceded by **i** (cf. English 'in', 'at') unless they refer to an island (**ö**) or a peninsula (**halvö**) when they are usually preceded by **på** (cf: English 'on'). (Note: 'to arrive in/at/on' = **anlända till**.)

    Jag bor på Gotland/på Färöarna.   I live on (the island of) Gotland/on the Faeroes.

Jag bor i Visby/i Thorshavn/i London.   I live in Visby/in Thorshavn/in London.

Notice also the use of **i** with larger islands which are also states (cf. English 'in'):

Han bor i Storbritannien/i Australien.   He lives in Great Britain/in Australia.

Island (Iceland) may be used with either **på** or **i**.

Note 3: Motion away from surfaces is often rendered by **från**: motion from out of volumes is often rendered by **ur**.

Han reste sig från pallen.	He got up from/off the stool.
Han reste sig ur fåtöljen.	He got up from/out of the armchair.

Some major exceptions to the rule of thumb in (a) above now follow.

(b) På + *public or commercial buildings* and *places of work, study or entertainment*

Except in one or two set phrases, Swedish idiom almost invariably uses **på** to signify location ('in', 'at', 'on') and sometimes also motion ('to', see (b)(ii) below) with nouns describing most kinds of public or commercial buildings and places of work, study or entertainment. As the examples indicate, these categories encompass a very wide range of nouns.

På + *public buildings*: **på flygplatsen** in/at the airport; **på hotellet** in/at the hotel; **på (järnvägs)stationen** in/at the railway station; **på rådhuset** in/at the town hall; **på sjukhuset** in/at the hospital; etc.

På + *places of work*: **på apoteket** in/at the chemist's; **på banken** in/at the bank; **på fabriken** in the factory; **på varuhuset** in/at the department store; etc.

På + *places of study*: **på daghemmet** in the kindergarten; **på gymnasiet** in the high school; **på universitetet** at the university; **på studieförbundet** at the evening class; **på kurs(en)** on the course. Note, however – **i skolan** at/in school. (But see Note 1 below.)

På + *places of entertainment*: **på bio(n)** at/in/on the cinema; **på bröllopet** at the wedding; **på dansen** at the dance; **på festen** at the party; **på hockeymatch(en)** at the (ice)hockey match; **på krog(en)** at/in the pub; **på museum/museet** at/in the museum; **på utställning(en)** at/the exhibition; etc.

(i) **På** = location

Except in one or two set phrases, Swedish idiom almost invariably uses **på** to signify location ('in', 'at', 'on') with nouns belonging to the categories above.

Vi var på ett kontor på banken.	We were in an office at the bank.
Han arbetar på IKEA.	He works at IKEA.
Hon är på ett möte på jobbet.	She's in a meeting at work.
Vi bodde på en liten lantgård.	We lived on a little farm.
Han är på sitt rum på hotellet.	He is in his room at the hotel.

Skola and **kyrka**, however, are two important exceptions to this general rule:

Vi träffades i skolan.	We met at/in school.
Han brukar städa i kyrkan.	He usually cleans up in the church.

Note 1: Observe the difference between the following:

Eleven är inte i skolan idag.	The pupil is not at school/in class today.
Läraren arbetar inte på skolan idag.	The teacher is not working at the school today.
eleverna på/vid Vasaskolan	the pupils at Vasa School

Note 2: Swedish also uses **på** with certain large private buildings and homes. (See also (e)(ii) below):

Kungaparet bor på slottet.	The king and queen live in/at the castle.

Note 3: Sometimes **vid** is used instead of **på** + place of work:

Han är student/lärare vid universitetet.	He's a teacher/student at the university.
Jag arbetar vid järnvägen	I work for the railway.

[**På järnvägen** may signify work on the actual tracks as a navvy.]

Jag arbetar vid gruvan.	I work at the mine.

[**På** is avoided here because of the overriding idea of a mine as an enclosed space (see (a) above). **I** would imply work as a miner in the actual mine shafts.]

Note 4: **På** is also used with many expressions indicating time off from work etc:

Han är (ute) på lunch/på kafferast.	He's at lunch/having a coffee break.
De är på semester/på utflykt.	They're on holiday/on an excursion.
Han är på permission.	He's on leave.

Note 5: **Hos** is invariably preferred to **på** when the prepositional complement is a noun or pronoun referring to a person. Compare:

Har du varit på bageriet/vårdcentralen?	Have you been to the bakery/health centre?
Har du varit hos bagaren/läkaren?	Have you been to the baker's/doctor's?

(ii) **På** = English 'to' indicating motion towards

Frequently English 'to' indicating motion towards a public or commercial building, a place of entertainment or enjoyment (but not a place of work or study: see **till**, 716) is rendered by Swedish **på**. Only if the idea of movement towards such a place is of prime importance is **till** used (cf. 716 and Notes 1 and 2 below). The clue here is the vague English 'to go to', which hardly indicates motion.

Vi gick på biblioteket/på museet/på IKEA.
We went to the library/to the museum/to IKEA.

Vi gick på (en) dans, på bio, på teater, på (en) nyårspremiär, på en utställning, på (ett) bröllop.
We went to a dance, to the cinema, to the theatre, to a new year première, to an exhibition, to a wedding.

Någon i köket kom upp på rummet med frukost varje morgon.
Someone from the kitchen came up to the room with breakfast each morning.

However, there are many exceptions to this basic rule:

Note 1: If the information conveyed seeks to emphasise the movement involved rather than the goal, English 'to' is best rendered by **till**. This makes clear that the movement is *to* a place rather than *at* a place.

    Ambulansen körde till sjukhuset.   The ambulance drove to the hospital.

Note 2: English 'to' signifying 'to' but not 'into', i.e. 'up to and no further', is rendered by **till** in Swedish. Compare:

    Jag gick på bio(n).   I went to the cinema [and saw a film there].
    Jag gick till bion och väntade.   I went to the cinema and waited [but did not go in].

Note 3: English 'to' + *articleless noun* is rendered in certain set phrases by *i* + *noun in definite form:*

    Alla barn måste gå i skolan/kyrkan.   All children must go to school/church.

or *till* + *noun in definite form*

    Jag brukar gå till stan en gång i veckan. I usually walk to town once a week.

Compare:

    Jag tycker om att gå på stan.   I like to go to town (i.e. to walk around the shops).

Note 4: Note also:

    Jag går på lunch nu!   I'm off to lunch now.
    När går du på semester/permission?   When do you go on holiday/leave?

(c) På + *mode of transport* = English 'on'

Det var nästan tomt på bussen, men det var många människor på tåget och ännu fler på tunnelbanan.
It was almost empty on the bus, but there were a lot of people on the train and even more on the underground.

Vi träffades på båten/på färjan/på spårvagnen/på flygplanet.
We met on the boat/on the ferry/on the tram/on the plane.

Note: English 'by' + *mode of transport* is generally rendered by Swedish **med**, or with a form of the verb **åka** + *0 preposition*.

    Jag reser helst med tåg.   I prefer to travel by train.
    Skicka brevet med flyg!   Send the letter by air/by plane.
    Vi åkte buss/bil/tåg/tunnelbana dit.   We went there by bus/car/train/underground.

(d) 'In', 'on' + parts of the body

(i) Again the basic rule of thumb is **på** + *surface*; **i** + *volume*

på + *surface*	i + *volume*
ett utslag på ryggen a rash on the back	**smuts i ögat** dirt in the eye
ett sår på läppen a sore on the lip	**löss i håret** lice in the hair

Note 1: Notice, however:

| **ett slag i ansiktet** | a blow in the face |
| **en bula i pannan** | a bump on the forehead |

Note 2: Notice the expressions **att ha ont i** ('to have a pain in', 'to have . . . ache') and **det gör ont i** ('my . . . . hurts' (cf. 142(b)).

| **Jag har ont i magen/armen.** | I have stomach-ache/My arm aches. |
| **Det gör ont i ryggen.** | My/Her (etc.) back hurts. |

Note 3: Note the use of **i** + parts of the body to render English 'by' in expressions such as:

| **hålla/ta/gripa någon i armen/i handen** | to hold/take/seize someone by the arm/hand |

Om (= 'round') is also used:

| **ett grepp om halsen/armen** | a grip around the throat/the arm |

(ii) **Om** (*not* **på**) is commonly used before parts of the body after certain adjectives and verbs where English has no preposition, employing a possessive instead.

Han är ren/smutsig/varm/kall/torr/våt/brun om fingrarna.
His fingers are clean/dirty/warm/cold/dry/wet/brown.

Jag fryser om tårna och svettas om händerna.
My toes are cold and my hands are sweaty.

Han torkade sig om fötterna och sedan tvättade sig om händerna.
He dried his feet and then washed his hands.

Note: However, in accordance with the basic rule:

| **Han är röd i ansiktet/våt i pannan** etc. | His face is red/His forehead is wet, etc. |

(e) Some further hints on how to translate English prepositions of place 'in', 'on', 'at', 'to' into Swedish.

(i) 'At' + *homes* **= hos**

English 'at' with the names or titles or professions of people, used to signify these persons' homes or place of work, is rendered by Swedish **hos** (cf. 720(l)).

Vi var hos Olssons igår.	We were at the Olssons' yesterday.
Han bor hos sin syster.	He lives at his sister's.
hos frisören/hos läkaren	at the hairdresser's/at the doctor's

Note: 'at home' is rendered by the adverb **hemma** (cf. 613).

(ii) 'at', 'in', 'on' + *address* **= på**

Han har en affär på Storgatan.	He has a shop on/in Storgatan.
De bor på nummer 12.	They live at number 12.
Jag bor på rum 220.	I'm staying in room 220.

(iii) 'At' + *places extending lengthways* **= vid**

Han stod vid disken/vid baren/vid gränsen/vid staketet.
He stood at the counter/at the bar/at the border/at the fence.

Karlstad ligger vid Klarälven.	Karlstad is on the River Klarälven.

Note:

vid sidan av	at/by the side of
på kanten av	at the edge of

(iv) 'To' indicating destination = till

Reste du ensam till Venedig?	Did you travel to Venice alone?
Kom till pappa!	Come to Daddy!
Adressera brevet till Ekgatan 5!	Address the letter to Ekgatan 5.

Note 1: If English 'to' denotes actual entry into a building or place, Swedish generally uses an *adverb* + i or på (cf. (a), (b) above).

Han gick in på banken, sedan upp på vinden och till slut ut i köket.
He went to the bank, then (up) to the loft and finally (in)to the kitchen.

Note 2: English 'to' is rendered by Swedish i or på in instances such as:

Detta är mitt första besök i staden/i Malmö/i Sverige/på ön.
This is my first visit to the city/to Malmö/to Sweden/to the island.

(v) 'To' + *verbs of fastening, tying*, etc. **= vid** (cf. 718(e))

Jag band hunden vid stolpen.	I tied the dog to the post.
Jag fäste repet vid masten.	I fastened the rope to the mast.

(f) Summary chart showing major usages of **i**, **på**, etc. corresponding to English 'in', 'on', 'at', 'to' with expressions of place:

Usage	In	On	At	To
volume (3D) (cf. (a))	i	–	–	**till**
surface (2D) (cf. (a))	–	**på**	–	**till**
places that extend lengthways (cf. (e)(iii)) –		**vid**	–	–
geographical names (cf. (a) note 2: (e)(iv)	i	**på**	i	**till**
addresses, streets (cf. (e)(ii),(iv))	**på**	**på**	**på**	**till**
public buildings (cf. (b))	**på**	–	**på**	**på (till)**
place of work, study (cf. (b))	**på**	**på**	**på**	**till (på)**
place of entertainment (cf. (b))	**på**	–	**på**	**på (till)**
transport (cf. (c))	–	**på**	–	–
names of people, titles, professions indicating place of home or work (cf. (e)(i))	–	–	**hos**	**till**

722 Some other prepositions of time and quantity

(a) Note that many of these prepositions also fulfil other functions as prepositions of place, manner, etc.

(b) Prepositions of time and quantity:

	Main meaning	Refer to	See also
à	at a price of	c below	
alltsedan	ever since	l Note 2 below	
bortemot	close to	d below	720(e)
bortåt	close to	d below	720(e)
cirka	approximately	j Note 2 below	
framemot	towards, close to	d below	
för . . . sedan	ago	f below	
före	before, by	e below	720(k)
inemot	close to	d below	
innan	before	e Note 2 below	812(d)
inom	within, in	g below	720(o)
intill	until	h below	720(p)

	Main meaning	*Refer to*	*See also*
kring	(a)round	j below	720(s)
omkring	(a)round	j below	720(s)
på . . . när	to within	k below	
runt	(a)round	j below	720(s)
sedan	since	l below	
sedan . . . tillbaka	since	m below	
ungefär	approximately	j Note 2 below	

(c) The preposition **à** suggests 'at a price of' or 'to a quantity no more than'. It is a loan word from French and may be replaced by **till** (716).

Vi har 15 à 20 biljetter kvar.	We have 15 to 20 tickets left.
biljetter à 500 kronor styck	tickets at 500 crowns each

(d) **Bortemot, bortåt, framemot** and **inemot** suggest proximity to some kind of target.

Jag väntade bortemot en timme.	I waited for about an hour.
Han var bortåt 80 år gammal.	He was about 80 years old.
Du kom framemot slutet av 1999.	You came towards the end of 1999.

(e) **Före** suggests 'before'.

Vi träffas igen före jul.	We'll meet again before Christmas.
År 55 f.Kr. (= före Kristus)	In the year 55 BC (before Christ)
Högmod går före fall.	Pride goes before a fall.

Note 1: **Före detta** (often abbreviated **f.d.**) is an indeclinable adverbial expression which renders English 'former', 'erstwhile', 'one-time', etc.

en före detta statsminister	a former Prime Minister

Note 2: **Innan**, more properly a conjunction (812(d)), is sometimes used as a preposition. See 728(b).

(f) **För...sedan** brackets the prepositional complement, and corresponds to English 'ago'.

Jag kom hit för 10 år sedan.	I came here ten years ago.

(g) **Inom** suggests 'within' referring to a future period of time.

Jag flyttar inom en vecka.	I am moving house within a week.
Vi ses igen inom inom kort.	We'll be seeing one another shortly.

(h) **Intill** suggests adjacency to a point in time or quantity:

Jag älskar dig intill döden.	I'll love you until I die.
Intill 20 barn befaras skadade.	Up to twenty children are feared injured.

(j) **Omkring, kring, runt** suggest '(a)round'. **Omkring** perhaps gives a slightly less precise impression than **kring** and **runt**.

Jag kommer kring den första.	I'll come around the first (of the month).
Vi brukar äta kring femtiden.	We usually eat at about five o'clock.
omkring 20 000 deltagare	around 20,000 participants

Note 1: **Runt** is postpositioned in some phrases:

Vi har öppet dygnet runt året runt.	We are open round the clock all year round.

Note 2: The adverbs **cirka** (often abbreviated **ca** when written) and **ungefär** (abbreviated **ung.**) are both commonly used before numbers in much the same way as the preposition **omkring.**

Han har bantat ungefär/cirka 25 kilo	He has lost/slimmed about 25 kilos.

(k) **På...när** (= '(to) within' + *expression of measure*) brackets the complement. It is only encountered in instances such as:

Du är inte på långt när så stark som du tror.
You're nowhere near as strong as you think.

Han gissade priset på 50 kronor när.
He guessed the price to within 50 crowns.

(l) **Sedan** marks the beginning of a period of past time and may usually be rendered by English 'since'. In spoken and sometimes also in informal written Swedish **sedan** is abbreviated to **sen** (short vowel). **Sedan** is also used adverbially ((607(a), 616(b)) and as a conjunction 812(b)).

Jag har inte sett dig sedan mars.	I haven't seen you since March.
De har varit borta sedan i julas.	They've been away since Christmas.

Note 1: **ända se(da)n** (less commonly **alltse(da)n**) renders English 'ever since' + *time-when expression.*

Han har varit så ända sedan barndomen.	He has been like that ever since his childhood.

Note 3: Notice the expressions:

se(da)n dess, alltsedan dess	since then
ända sedan dess	ever since then
för . . . sedan	ago (cf. 703(b))

(m) Sedan . . . tillbaka is a parenthetical prepositional expression which brackets the complement. It may render English 'for' + *expression of past time* in very special circumstances. (Usually 'for' indicating a period of time is rendered by **i** or no preposition in Swedish (cf. 725).) However, this construction does not always make clear whether or not the action or state still prevails. Used with a present tense verb **sedan...tillbaka** indicates that the action or state still prevails (cf. English 'has been . . . -ing').

Han bor/är bosatt i Lund sedan 30 år tillbaka.
He has been living in Lund for thirty years (and still is).

723 Prepositions and time

Relationships of time in Swedish are the object of much idiomatic variation, especially in the spoken language. Furthermore, Swedish differentiates quite clearly between a point in time (Time-when: 724) and a period of time (Duration: 725). For advice on how to render certain English prepositions into Swedish before time expressions, examine the tables summarising such usage:

'in', at, 'on' + definite time	724(a)(i)
'in', 'at', 'on' + indefinite and habitual time	724(a)(ii)
Swedish usage summarised	724(m)
'for' ('not . . . for') + duration	725(a)(b)
'during', 'over' + duration	725(c)
'in' + duration	725(e)
'in' + frequency	726(b)
clock time	416

724 Time-when

(a) Introduction

When considering which prepositions to use with expressions of 'time-when' in Swedish, it is often necessary to observe the difference between definite time and indefinite or habitual time.

(i) Definite time may refer to past, present or future, and specifies when a particular event has taken place, is taking place or will take place. In English this is usually achieved by specifying a date of some sort, or by giving the season, month, weekday or other unit of time by a word like 'this', 'last', or 'next'. The predominant preposition used with definite time-when expressions in Swedish is **i**, although no preposition is used with numbers in dates, etc. and **på** is sometimes used with the days of the week.

Definite time	See	Swedish prep.	English prep.
years	b below	0	in
dates	b below	0	on
clock time	b below	0	at
months	c below	**i**	in
seasons	d below	**i, på**	in
festivals	d below	**i, på**	at
parts of the day	d below	**i**	various
days of the week	e below	**i** + past **på** + future	on

(ii) Indefinite and habitual time may refer to past, present or future.

Indefinite time expressions may often be replaced by 'one' in English: 'I last saw him at night/on a Sunday/in (the) summer' = 'I last saw him one night/one Sunday/one summer'.

Habitual time expressions may often be replaced by 'every' in English: 'I see him on Thursday(s)/in (the) summer/at night' = 'I see him every Thursday/every summer/every night'. English prepositions used with indefinite and habitual time-when expressions are usually rendered by **på** in Swedish.

Indefinite and Habitual Time	See	Swedish prep.	English prep.
dates	b below	0	on
clock time	b below	0	at
months	c below	**i**	in
seasons	f below	**på**	in
festivals	f below	**på**	at
parts of the day	f below	**på**	in
days of the week	g below	**på**	on

(b) Time-when expressions with numbers (dates, years, clock-time).

No preposition in Swedish = 'in', 'on', 'at' in English (cf. 414ff.). Note, however, that written Swedish frequently prefaces year dates with **år** (= '(in the) year'), especially when such dates would otherwise begin a sentence.

> **Han föddes (år) 1917. År 1992 dog han.**
> He was born in 1917. In 1992 he died.

> **Han kom (söndagen) den femtonde juli.**
> He came on (Sunday) 15 of July.

> **Vi får lön den tjugofemte varje månad.**
> We get paid on the twenty-fifth of the month.

> **De ringer igen klockan tre.**
> They are going to phone back at 3 o'clock.

Note: Commercial Swedish has expressions like:

> **Fakturan betalades den tredje i femte.**   The invoice was paid on the third of the fifth.

(c) Time-when expressions and months. **I** in Swedish = 'in' in English.

> **Han kom i januari.**   He came in January [i.e. last January].
> **Han brukar komma i januari.**   He usually comes in January.
> **Han kommer i januari.**   He is coming in January [next January].

Note: The preposition **i** before the name of the month may be omitted if a year date follows (cf. (b) above):

> **Detta hände (i) juli 1956.**   This happened in July 1956.

(d) Definite time with seasons, festivals and parts of the day. **I** in Swedish = 'in', 'at' in English.

(i) Seasons and festivals

Note the suffixation of **-as** to the names of the seasons and the main Swedish festivals to signify recently past time.

> **Han föddes i våras/i somras/i höstas/i vintras.**
> He was born last spring/summer/autumn/winter.

> **Vi gifte oss i julas/i påskas/i midsomras.**
> We got married last Christmas/Easter/midsummer.

De gifter sig i vår.
They are getting married in spring (this spring, next spring).

However, **på** is often used with the names of the seasons (definite form) to signal past or future time. **På** is occasionally used with festivals (definite or indefinite form) to signal past time. **Till** is often used with festivals (definite or indefinite form) to signal future time. (See also (m) below.)

Vi kommer tillbaka på sommaren.
We'll be back in the summer [= this coming summer].

Han var sjuk på midsommar.
He was ill at midsummer [= last midsummer].

De tänker gifta sig till påsk.
They intend to get married at Easter.

Note: When a date is given the noun appears in the definite form with no preposition.

De tänkte gifta sig hösten 2002.	They planned on getting married in the autumn of 2002.

(ii) Parts of the day

Often English has an adverbial expression where Swedish has **i** + *noun*.

Past time	*Present time*	*Future time*
i förrgår the day before yesterday		**i övermorgon** the day after tomorrow
i går yesterday	**i dag** today	**i morgon** tomorrow
i morse/i förmiddags (earlier) this morning	**(i förmiddag)** (this morning)	**i morgon bitti** tomorrow morning
i eftermiddags (earlier) this afternoon	**i eftermiddag** this afternoon	**i eftermiddag** (later) this afternoon
i kväll (earlier) this evening	**i kväll** this evening	**i kväll** (later) this evening
i natt last night	**i natt** tonight	**i natt** (later) tonight
cf: also **i fjol** last year	**i år** this year	**i år** (later) this year

Note 1: Swedes are generally more precise when referring to parts of the day than English usage demands. Consequently, **i morse** is used only to refer retrospectively to the early morning period (i.e. **morgonen**, the time up until, say, 9 a.m. or 10 a.m. when one would normally greet people with **God morgon**). After that **i förmiddags** is used for the period up to noon, and **i eftermiddags** from noon until the end of the normal working day. (During the whole of this period the normal greeting is **God middag** or **God dag**.) **Kväll** is generally used of the period between the end of the working day and bedtime: **natt** of time later than bedtime. **Afton**, meaning 'evening', is generally encountered only in rather formal contexts and as a formal greeting: **God afton**.

Note 2: Note also: **i går eftermiddag, i går kväll, i går natt, i morgon eftermiddag, i morgon kväll**, etc. (Cf. (e) Note 1 below.)

Note 3: 'At midnight' is rendered **vid midnatt** (past, present and future). 'At midday' is difficult to render idiomatically in Swedish: **vid middag** may suggest 'during dinner'. Swedes tend therefore to say simply **klockan tolv**.

Note 4: Where English has 'in the morning' etc., Swedish usually has **på förmiddagen** etc. of past time and **under förmiddagen** of future time. In journalistic Swedish **på förmiddagen** etc. is usually also preferred to **i förmiddags** etc.

> **Presidenten anlände på eftermiddagen.**   The president arrived this afternoon.

(e) Definite time with weekdays. **I, på** in Swedish = 'on' in English.

English 'on' indicating definite time with a day of the week is rendered by **i** + *weekday* + **s** to refer to a day in the immediate past (i.e. 'last Sunday' etc.), and by **på** + *weekday* to refer to a day in the immediate future (i.e. 'next Sunday' etc.). The addition of **nu** before **på** corresponds closely to English 'this coming Monday' etc.

Definite time – past		*Definite time – future*	
Han kom	**i söndags** last Sunday	**Han kommer/ska komma**	**på söndag** next Sunday

Note 1: **i söndags morse, i söndags kväll**   on (last) Sunday morning/evening
         på söndag morgon, på söndag kväll   on (next) Sunday morning/evening

Note 2: No preposition is used if the weekday is followed by a date (cf. (b) above).

Note 3: Where English has 'on Sunday' etc. (= a particular but unspecified Sunday in the past) Swedish has **på söndagen**.

> **På söndagen sa en talesman ...**   A spokesman said on Sunday ...

(f) Indefinite and habitual time with seasons, festivals and parts of the day. **På** in Swedish = 'in', 'at' in English.

After **på** a season, festival or part of the day usually takes the definite form. However, in many instances the end article is optional after a festival.

Han kom på sommaren/julen/på kvällen.
He came in the summer/at Christmas/in the evening.

Påskliljorna slår ut på våren.
The daffodils bloom in (the) spring.

The definite plural form of the noun is often used (especially with seasons and parts of the day) to indicate a habitual occurrence.

Han brukar komma på kvällarna/på somrarna.
He usually comes in the evenings /in summer.

(g) Indefinite and habitual time with weekdays. **På** in Swedish = 'on' in English.

English 'on' indicating indefinite and habitual time with weekdays (i.e. 'on Sunday(s)', 'every Sunday' or 'one (unspecified) Sunday') is generally rendered by **på** in Swedish. The definite plural form of the weekday is often used to indicate a habitual occurrence. If the indefinite article is used before the weekday to indicate indefinite time, the preposition may be omitted, especially if a following phrase specifies the time ('many years ago', 'three years earlier', etc.).

Han kommer på fredagen/på fredagarna.
He comes on Friday/on Fridays (every Friday).

Han föddes på en söndag.
He was born on a Sunday (one Sunday).

Det hände (på) en måndag för länge sedan.
It happened one Monday a long time ago.

(h) 'This (next, last)' in definite 'time-when' expressions.

Swedish often expresses ideas such as 'last spring', 'this January', 'next Easter', etc. prepositionally (cf. (c), (d) and (e) above). However, these ideas may also be expressed adverbially in many instances.

See	Past time	Present time	Future time
	(förra + noun + end art.) 'last'	(denna, detta + noun) 'this'	(nästa + noun) 'next'
724(d)(ii)	förra året	–	nästa år
	förra månaden	denna månad	nästa månad
	förra veckan	denna vecka	nästa vecka
	förra helgen	denna helg	nästa helg
724(d)(i)	förra våren	–	nästa vår
724(d)(i)	förra julen	–	nästa jul
724(e)	förra söndagen	–	nästa söndag

Note 1: 'Last January', 'next April', etc. may be indicated by **i januari förra året, i april nästa år,** etc.

Note 2: **Sista veckan, sista söndagen,** etc. is only used to render 'last' when this means the last in a series ('final'). Thus:

Jag såg honom sista veckan i augusti.	I saw him (in) the last week in August.
Vi träffades förra veckan.	We met last week.

Compare:

idag för en vecka sedan	this day last week/a week ago today
idag om en vecka	this day next week/a week today [see (l)(ii).]

Note 3: Swedish has no preposition before ordinals + weekday or unit of time, or in expressions with **följande** and **förra** corresponding to 'the following' and 'the previous'.

De har öppet första söndagen i månaden.	They are open on the first Sunday in the month.
Han blev sjuk förra måndagen.	He was taken ill on the previous Monday.
Han dog följande fredag.	He died on the following Friday.

(j) 'Ago' = **för . . . sedan** (cf. 722(f))

Hon flyttade för sju år sedan.	She moved house seven years ago.

(k) Approximate time-when

Approximate 'time-when' is usually rendered by the prepositions **runt, omkring** (cf. 722(j)) or (with clock time and festivals especially) **vid** (cf. 718).

Han fyller år runt den tionde.	His birthday is around the tenth.
De brukar träffas vid jultiden.	They usually meet at Christmastime.
Vi äter vid ett-tiden.	We eat around one (o'clock).

Note: **På + -talet** is used to express time approximate to the nearest decade or century. (See 407(b).)

Han föddes på 1800-talet.	He was born in the 19th century.
Han skrev sin bästa böcker på 50-talet.	He wrote his best books in the fifties.

also:

Han levde på Napoleons tid.	He lived in the days of Napoleon.

(l) Other prepositional usage with time-when expressions

Paragraphs (a)–(k) above illustrate the major prepositional usages with a number of time-when expressions. Some less common usages follow below.

(i) **I** (cf. also 710) may be used before **förra, nästa, denna** expressions in (h) above to make clear that something has happened (is happening, will happen) 'in the course of . . . '. Such usage is most commonly found in journalese:

Regeringen förbereder sig på en ny lärarstrejk i nästa vecka.
The government is preparing for a new teachers' strike next week.

(ii) **Om** (cf. also 714) is used to render English 'in' before a future point in time.

När åker ni? Om en vecka.	When are you going? In a week.
Vi är nog alla borta om 100 år.	We'll probably all be gone in 100 years.
Om två år börjar han skolan.	In two years he'll be starting school.

Note: Note the use of **om** in:

Ugglan sover om dagen och jagar om natten.
The owl sleeps by day and hunts by night.

(iii) **På** (cf. also 715) is often used with the names of the seasons (definite form) to signify past or future time (cf. (d) above).

På + *noun* + *end article* is quite widely used in journalese where standard usage prefers **i** + *parts of the day* (cf. (d)(ii) above) or **i** + weekdays (cf. (e) above).

(iv) **Till** is sometimes used to indicate that an event is planned to take place in time for a festival or season.

Hon fyller 7 år till våren.	She will be seven in the spring.
Han börjar skolan till hösten.	He'll be starting school in the autumn.
Jag tror jag åker hem till julen.	I think I'll go home for Christmas.

(m) Table summarising prepositional usage with expressions of definite, indefinite and habitual time.

	Definite time-past	Definite time-present	Future		
centuries	på 1900-talet	på 2000-talet	på 2100 talet	(k)	Note
decades	på 90-talet	på 00-talet	på 10-talet	(k)	Note
years	(år) 1996		(år) 2025	(b)	
	i fjol	i år	–	(d)	
	förra året	–	nästa år	(h)	
seasons	i våras	i vår	i vår	(d)	
	förra våren		nästa vår	(h)	
	(på) våren 1955	nu på våren	(på) våren 2025	(l)	
months	i januari	i januari	i januari	(c)	
dates	den 15 juli	den 15 juli	den 15 juli	(b)	
weekdays	i söndags		på söndag	(e)	
	förra söndagen		nästa söndag	(h)	
weeks	förra veckan	denna vecka	nästa vecka	(h)	
part of week	förra helgen		nästa helg	(h)	
festivals	i julas	i jul	i jul	(d)	
	förra julen	–	nästa jul	(h)	
	på jul	–	till jul(en)	(l)	
day	igår	i dag	i morgon	(d)	
parts of day	i morse	i förmiddag	i morgon bitti	(d)	
	i eftermiddags	i eftermiddag	i eftermiddag	(d)	
clock time	klockan tio	klockan tio	klockan tio	(b)	
	vid tiotiden	vid tiotiden	vid tiotiden	(k)	
when?	för en vecka sedan	i detta ögonblick	om en vecka	(j), (l)	

	Indefinite time	Habitual time	See
years	–	varje år	
seasons	på våren	på våren/på vårarna	(f)
months	i januari	i januari	(c)
dates		den 15 (varje månad)	(b)
weekdays	på en söndag	på söndagen/	
		på söndagarna	(g)
weeks	–	varje vecka	
part of week	–	varje helg	
festivals	på jul(en)	på jul(en)/på jularna	(f)
day	på dagen	på dagen/dagarna	(f)
parts of day	på morgonen	på morgonen/morgnarna	(f)
	på eftermiddagen	på eftermiddagen/eftermiddagarna	
clock time	klockan tio	klockan tio	(b)
when?	någon gång	gång på gång	

725   Duration

(a) Introduction

With expressions involving a length or period of time in Swedish (duration), there are three major considerations, namely:

1   Does the expression of duration answer a (hypothetical) question **Hur länge?** (= '(For) How long?') with the English preposition 'for' (sometimes no preposition in English)?

2   Does the expression of duration answer a (hypothetical) question **När?** (= 'During what period?') with the English preposition 'during' (sometimes no preposition in English or 'over')?

3   Does the expression of duration answer a (hypothetical) question **Hur lång tid krävs?** (= 'How long – 'In what length of time'/'How much time is needed . . . ?') with the English preposition 'in'?

The table below gives a survey of the main prepositional usage in English and Swedish to express duration.

	See	English	Swedish
1	(b)(i)	for	**i** or 0
	(b)(ii)	not . . . for	**inte . . . på**
2	(c)(i)	during, for	**under** or 0
	(c)(ii)	over, for	**över**
	(c)(iii)	throughout	**hela** + noun + end article
3	(e)	in	**på**

(b) 'For' – **i**, no preposition, **(inte) . . . på**

(i) 'I have lived here for six years' – 'for' = **i** in Swedish

In many instances the preposition **i** may be omitted, especially before **nära, hela** (cf. omission of 'for' in English). **I** is usually retained, however, when the prepositional phrase introduces a sentence or clause.

Jag har bott här (i) 6 år.	I have lived here for six years.
Jag ska vara borta i tre månader.	I'm going to be away for three months.
Hon var döv (i) hela livet.	She was deaf all her life.
I många år försökte han rymma.	For (many) years he tried to escape.

In positive sentences with **länge** (= 'for a long time') the preposition **i** is always omitted (but cf. (ii) below):

Han har bott här länge.	He has lived here (for) a long time.

Note: Cf. also expressions with **sedan . . . tillbaka** (722(m)).

(ii) 'We've not met for many years' – 'not . . . for' = **inte . . . på** in Swedish

Vi har inte träffats på många år.	We've not met for many years.
Jag får inte resa på sex veckor.	I'm not allowed to travel for six weeks.
Jag har inte åkt skidor på länge.	I've not been ski-ing for a long time.

Note 1: 'For' + *future duration* is rendered by **för** in a small number of set phrases.

för alltid, för evigt, för gott	for always, for ever, for good
vädret för fem dygn framåt	the weather for the next five days

Note 2: Some other common expressions of duration with the preposition **i**:

i många dagar/veckor	for days/weeks (on end)
i många timmar/i timtal	for hours (on end)
i åratal, i evigheter	for years, for ages

Notice that **i** becomes **på** when these phrases occur in negative sentences (cf. (ii) above).

(c) 'During' – **under, över**

(i) 'We lived there during the war' – 'during' = **under** in Swedish

Vi bodde där under kriget.	We lived there during the war.
Vi var isolerade under stormen.	We were isolated during the storm.

Note: **under tiden 1–15 maj (under tiden första till femtonde maj)** = from 1 to 15 May/between 1 and 15 May.

(ii) 'We stayed there over the summer' – 'over' = **över**

Vi bodde där över sommaren.	We stayed there over/for the summer.
Stanna över helgen/julen!	Please stay over the weekend/Christmas.

(iii) 'Throughout' + *duration* = **under hela . . ./hela . . . (igenom)**

Note that **under** may be omitted before **hela** + *expression of time* (cf. English).

Vi letade hela natten (igenom).	We searched throughout the night.
Det regnade under hela matchen.	It rained throughout the entire match.

(d) 'From . . . to' = **från (och med) . . . till (och med)**

Vi reste från maj till juni.   We travelled from May to June.

Flyg för halva priset från och med 30 juni till och med 12 augusti!
Fly for half price from 30 June to 12 August (inclusive)!

(e) 'In' = 'In what length of time?' Duration indicating 'in a time of/in the space of' = **på** in Swedish.

Han målade huset på två dagar.   He painted the house in two days.

Note: Cf. also 726.

726 Frequency

Expressions of frequency answer the (hypothetical) question: 'How often?'

(a) Swedish generally uses **i** + *unit of time* in such instances:

en gång, två ganger	**i sekunden**	once, twice	a second
	i minuten		a minute
	i timmen/timman		an hour
	i veckan		a week/weekly

i månaden	once, twice a month
i seklet	a century
i livet, etc.	in a lifetime, etc.

But note three important exceptions:

en gång, två gånger	om dagen	once, twice a day/daily
	om året	a year/yearly
	om dygnet	a day (= 24 hrs)

(b) Idiomatically, however, frequency is also rendered by the preposition **på** most often when the sentence contains a superlative (cf. 233ff.) or an ordinal.

Det är andra gången på tio dagar som han är sjukskriven.
This is the second time in ten days that he's been off sick.

Det var det roligaste jag har hört på länge/på många år.
That's the funniest thing I've heard in a long time/for many years.

727 Some other prepositions of manner etc.

(a) Note that some of these prepositions also fulfil other functions (prepositions of time, place, etc.).

(b) Prepositions of manner etc.:

	Meaning	*Refer to*	*See also*
apropå	talking of . . .	c, below	
enligt	according to	d, below	
exklusive	excluding	e, below	
för . . . skull	for . . .'s sake	f, below	
förutan	without	o below	
förutom	in addition to	g, below	
inklusive	including	e, below	
i . . . ställe	in . . .'s place	h, below	
jämte	together with	j, below	720 (g) Note
plus	plus	e, below	805(d)
medels, medelst	by means of	k, below	
per	per	l, below	
på/å . . . vägnar	on . . .'s behalf	m, below	
trots	of	n, below	
utan	without	o, below	
utom	except for	p, below	720(y)
åt	for + *indirect object*	q, below	720(z)

(c) Apropå is from the French *à propos*, but with Swedified spelling. It is commonly used in Swedish.

Apropå dem, visste du att ...	Talking of them, did you know ...
Apropå ingenting (särskilt) ...	To change the subject ...

(d) Enligt is more common in written Swedish and corresponds to English 'according to/in accordance with'.

Enligt vad vi fick veta ...	According to what we have learnt . . .
lön enligt avtal	wages according to contract

(e) Exklusive, inklusive render 'excluding', 'including', but usage of these two words is more or less restricted to commercial Swedish, where, when written, they are usually abbreviated **exkl., inkl.** Another loanword, **plus**, is sometimes used instead of **exklusive**. Swedish alternatives for **exklusive, inklusive** are **utom** ((p) below) and **medräknat** (indeclinable) respectively.

Flygbiljetten kostar 750 euro exklusive/inklusive moms.
The plane ticket costs 750 euros excluding/including VAT.

(f) För . . . skull (= 'for X's sake') is a parenthetical prepositional expression, bracketing the prepositional complement, typically the s-genitive form of a noun or a possessive adjective in the non-neuter singular form.

Vi köpte det för barnens skull.	We bought it for the children's sake.
Vi älskar dig för din egen skull.	We love you for what you are.
Gör det för säkerhets skull!	Do it for safety's sake.
Du gör allt för pengars skull.	You'll do anything for money.

(g) Förutom suggests 'in addition to'. It is synonymous with **utöver** which suggests 'over and beyond'. The occasional use of **utom** (= 'with the exception of' (p), below) in Swedish in place of **förutom** can sometimes cause confusion. Note that **förutom** is followed by the subject form of the pronoun if the word to which the pronoun refers is itself a subject.

Jag ärvde aktierna förutom/utöver allt annat.
I inherited the shares in addition to everything else.

Det bor inga här förutom jag.
There's no one living here except for me.

(h) I . . . ställe (= 'in . . .'s place') is a parenthetical expression bracketing the prepositional complement, typically the s-genitive of a noun or a possessive adjective in the neuter singular form. In most instances **i . . . ställe** may be replaced by **i stället för** + *noun* or *possessive pronoun*. **I stället för** is usually preferred with nouns referring to inanimate objects.

Han kom i kungens ställe.	He came instead of the king.
Om jag vore i ditt ställe ...	If I were you/If I were in your shoes ...
Du kan åka i stället för mig.	You can go in my place.
Ta margarin i stället för smör!	Take margarine instead of butter.

(j) Jämte, meaning 'together with', is usually encountered only in formal language.

Presidenten jämte uppvaktning anländer till Stockholm idag.
The president and his entourage arrive in Stockholm today.

Note: **Jämte** is not a conjunction and cannot therefore coordinate elements in the clause. This is of importance when considering matters of congruence. (Note singular form of past participle below.)

Kungen jämte sin gemål var upptagen hela dagen.
The king and his consort were engaged all day.

(k) Medels or **medelst** suggesting 'by means of' is encountered only in formal language and officialese. It may usually be replaced by **genom** (709) or **med** (711).

Planerna innebär en förbättring av området medelst dikning.
The plans mean improving the area by means of ditching.

(l) Per renders the equally versatile English 'per' to express agent, frequency, distribution, time-when and other prepositional relationships. Originally commercial Swedish, **per** has now spread to general use.

Vi ordnar upp det per telefon.	We'll sort it out by phone.
20 kilo bagage per person	20 kilos of baggage per person

Note: When distribution and frequency occur together Swedish prefers **per ... och**:

Svenskarna dricker 140 liter kaffe per person och år.
Swedes drink 140 litres of coffee per person per year.

(m) På/å ... vägnar are formal expressions corresponding to English 'on behalf of'. The expression brackets the complement, typically the **s**-genitive of a noun or a possessive adjective in the plural form.

å styrelsens vägnar	on behalf of the board
Tacka dem på våra vägnar!	Thank them on our behalf/from us.

(n) Trots suggests some form of concession, like English 'in spite of', 'despite'. **Oaktat** is synonymous, but formal and archaic in tone, corresponding in style to

English 'notwithstanding'.

De kom tryggt fram trots ovädret.
They arrived safely despite the storm.

Note: The common expression **trots allt** may usually be rendered in English by 'after all'.

Han är bara barn, trots allt!   He's only a child after all/when all said and done.

(o) Utan (like the poetic archaism **förutan**) renders English 'without'. **Utan** is also used as a conjunction (cf. 823(f)(iii)).

Jag klarar mig bra utan dig.   I'm getting on well without you.

Note 1: Where there is no ambiguity, the article or possessive adjective is frequently omitted after **utan** in Swedish.

Gå inte ut utan hatt!   Don't go without your hat!

Note 2: Some idiomatic phrases:

att vara utan arbete	to be out of work
utan jämförelse	beyond comparison

(p) Utom renders English 'except (for)'. **Utom** rarely begins a sentence or clause, however, as Swedish prefers prepositional phrases such as **med undantag av** in initial positions. Note that **utom** is followed by the subject form of the pronoun if the word to which the pronoun refers is itself a subject.

Jag har träffat alla utom henne.   I have met everyone except her.
Alla utom jag har bil.   Everyone but me has a car.

(q) Åt often corresponds to English 'for' before an indirect object in Swedish (cf. **till** 716(d)(ii)).

Sätt fram lite mat åt honom!   Put out some food for him!
Jag köpte en skjorta åt pappa.   I bought a shirt for father.

Note: **Åt** is also used after a number of verbs: **anförtro sig åt** 'to confide in'; **glädja sig åt** 'to look forward to'; **le/skratta åt** 'to smile/laugh at'; **ägna sig åt** 'to devote oneself to'. Note also: **två åt gången** 'two at a time'.

728 Some other parts of speech used as prepositions

A number of other parts of speech, primarily participles, have taken on the role of prepositions.

(a) Angående, beträffande, rörande ('concerning') are usually confined to commercial and official language, although **angående** is not uncommon elsewhere.

Meningarna är delade angående denna sak.
Opinions are divided on this matter.

Beträffande Er order på trävaror
Re: your order for timber products

(b) Innan ('before') is actually a conjunction (cf. 812(d)), and **före** (720(k)) is to be preferred as a preposition. However, **innan** is often encountered in informal Swedish used as a preposition in expressions of time.

Vi ses väl innan jul.
We'll see one another before Christmas, won't we?

Note: **innan dess** = 'before then/beforehand'.

(c) Nära = 'near (to)' is primarily an adverb (see 607(c)), but it often serves as a preposition in place of the prepositional phrase **i närheten av**. **Nära** is often preferred when there is little emphasis on actual geographical proximity.

Vi bor nära flygplatsen.   We live near the airport.
Han var nära 90 år/döden.   He was close to 90/close to death.
Det var nära ögat!   That was a close shave!

(d) Näst = 'next to', usually in a figurative sense. For actual location **bredvid** is usually preferred (cf. 720(g)).

Han är bäst i klassen näst dig.
He's best in the class after you.

Göteborg är näst Stockholm Sveriges viktigaste handelsstad.
Next to Stockholm, Gothenburg is Sweden's most important trading centre.

(e) Oavsett and the less common **oansett, oberoende av** render 'regardless of'.

Alla är välkomna, oavsett ålder.   Everyone is welcome, regardless of age.

(f) Tack vare means 'thanks to'.

Tack vare din hjälp har jag   Thanks to your help I have

Note: **Till följd av** or **på grund av** should be used if the circumstances are unfavourable.

Hon dog till följd av fallet.   She died as a result of her fall.

(g) Visavi has, until recently, been used to render three distinct meanings in Swedish: 'opposite', 'towards' and 'concerning'. However, despite its versatility, **visavi** seems to be losing ground to the expressions **mittemot** ('opposite'), **(gente)mot** ('towards') and **angående** ('concerning') respectively.

Svenskarna har alltid varit frikostiga visavi Baltikum
The Swedes have always been generous towards the Baltic states.

Vad är din synpunkt visavi förslaget?
What's your point of view regarding the suggestion?

(h) Å, formerly synonymous with **på** ('on'), is now only encountered in a small number of set phrases.

å ena sidan . . . å andra sidan	on the one hand . . . on the other
å någons vägnar	on behalf of someone [cf. 727(m), 703(b)]

(j) Än (= 'than') usually assumes the status of a preposition when it precedes the subject of an elliptted clause. The 'subject' is thus made into an object, but always remains the subject when the verb is explicit:

snabbare än ljusets hastighet	faster than the speed of light
Han är äldre än mig.	He is older than me.

But:

Han är äldre än (vad) jag är.	He is older than I am.

729 English 'of' and its equivalents in Swedish

The English preposition 'of' is rendered in a great number of ways in Swedish. What follows is not complete but provides hints on how best to translate 'of' in many common instances.

(a) Summary table showing English 'of' and Swedish usage

'of'	Example	Swedish usage	Refer to
possessive genitive	the contents of the book	-s genitive	(b) below, 129
possessive genitive	the tops of the mountains	compound noun	(c) below
possessive genitive	–	på	(d) below, 715
		för	708
		till	716
		i	710
		vid	718
		över	719
		av	705
double genitive	a friend of yours	till	(e) below, 716
appositive genitive	the city of London	0	(f) below
partitive genitive	a cup of tea	0	(g) below
	half a pound of treacle	0	
	both of (all of, the whole of)	0, av	705
	some of, none of, many of, much of	0, av	705

'of'	Example	Swedish usage	Refer to
partitive genitive	half of, two of which of . . .?	**av**	705
material	a heart of stone	**av**	(h) below, 705
'comprising' + number	a flat of 6 rooms	**på**	(j) below, 715(e)
with dates	the first of May	0	(k) below
origin	the king of Sweden	**av, från**	(l) below
with compass points	East of Eden	**om**	(m) below,
	the north of England	0	714(a) Note
subject matter (= 'about')	I'm dreaming of a White Christmas	**om**	(n) below, 714(b)
following:			
demonstrative pronoun	that of/those of	0	(o) below
pejorative	that idiot of a policeman!	**till**	(p) below
verbs/adjectives + 'of'		various	(q) below

(b) English possessive genitive 'of' – Swedish s-genitive

English possessive genitive constructions with 'of' are perhaps most frequently and most easily rendered by Swedish s-genitive forms (cf. 129):

the meaning of life   **livets mening**
the contents of the book   **bokens innehåll**
the kingdom of the dead   **de dödas rike**

(c) English possessive genitive 'of' – Swedish compound noun

In some instances Swedish may make a compound noun (cf. 1111ff.), often with an s-link, where English has an 'of-genitive'.

the tops of the mountains   **fjälltopparna**
the leg of the table   **bordsbenet**

(d) English possessive genitive 'of' – Swedish preposition

English 'of' expressing a possessive/genitive relationship may also be rendered in Swedish by one of a number of prepositions. Such prepositional renderings may often be replaced by Swedish s-genitive constructions (cf. (b) above). Consider, however:

1   s-genitive constructions are usually more colloquial than all prepositional constructions other than those with **på**.

2 **s**-genitive constructions are rare (in English and Swedish) with so-called 'objective genitives'. In an objective genitive 'of' precedes a noun which fulfils the role of a weak object in the sentence or clause: 'The murder of Gustav III' indicates that someone murdered Gustav III and that Gustav III was only passively involved in (i.e. was the object of) the action. Examples of objective genitive constructions below are marked [obj. gen.].

(i) **På** is often used where English 'of' may be replaced by 'on'. Often **på** in such instances has a more colloquial ring than the **s**-genitive. (Cf. also 715.)

the roof of the school	**taket på skolan**
the captain of the ship	**kaptenen på skeppet**
the names of the children	**namnen på barnen**
the start/end of the day	**början/slutet på dagen**
the price of butter	**priset på smör**
the pursuit of happiness	**jakten på lyckan** [obj. gen.]
the murder of Gustav III	**mordet på Gustav III** [obj. gen.]

(ii) **För** is often used where English 'of' may be replaced by 'for' (708(f)):

a representative of the government	**en representant för regeringen**
the boss of the company	**chefen för firman**
milk instead of beer	**mjölk i stället för öl**

(iii) **Till** is often used in connections where a person is the owner or possessor 'of' something. **Till** is also used in a number of instances where English 'of' may be replaced by 'to' and after nouns indicating the cause of or a reaction to something. (Cf. also 716.)

the owner of the car	**ägaren till bilen**
the author of the book	**författaren till boken**
a father of twins	**en far till tvillingar**
the door of/to the house	**dörren till huset**
the cause of the fire	**orsaken till branden** [obj. gen.]

(iv) **I** renders English 'of' in instances where 'in' is also acceptable and in a number of idiomatic phrases (cf. also 710). **I** is almost invariably used if a prepositional genitive is required after a superlative in Swedish:

the world's richest man	**den rikaste mannen i världen**
the hero of the book	**hjälten i boken**
a professor of mathematics	**en professor i matematik**
your knowledge of Swedish	**dina kunskaper i svenska**

(v) **Vid** renders 'of' with individual battles + place names:

the battle of Lützen	**slaget vid Lützen**

Note: with the names of countries **för** is used:

the Battle of Britain	**slaget för Storbritannien**

(vi) **Över** may be used to render English 'of' after nouns suggesting something composed or drawn up to give a survey of (i.e. 'over') a particular subject (cf. also 719).

a bibliography of new books	**en bibliografi över nya böcker**
a survey of	**en översikt över**
a map of Lapland	**en karta över Lappland**
a view of the town	**en utsikt över stan**

(vii) **Av** is not commonly used to render English possessive genitive 'of'. Note, however:

the invasion of Norway	**invasionen av Norge** [obj. gen.]
a glimpse of the sun	**en skymt av solen** [obj. gen.]
a feeling of wellbeing	**en känsla av välbehag** [obj. gen.]

(e) 'A friend of yours'

Note the use of **till** + *personal pronoun/noun* in Swedish where English has a double genitive with 'of' + possessive adjective/**-s** genitive noun.

a friend of mine/yours/his	**en vän till mig/dig/honom**
a sister of Leif's/my uncle's	**en syster till Leif/till min farbror**

(f) 'The city of London' – appositive genitive

Swedish generally does not use a preposition corresponding to English 'of' in appositive genitive constructions.

the city of London	**staden London**
the month of May	**månaden maj/maj månad**
the Christmas/summer of '42	**julen/sommaren 42**

(g) English partitive expressions with 'of'

(i) 'A cup of tea' – no preposition in Swedish. Swedish generally has no preposition corresponding to English 'of' in partitive expressions.

a cup of tea	**en kopp te**
12 kilos of peas	**12 kilo ärter**

a pair of trousers   **ett par byxor**
a large number of Swedes   **ett stort antal svenskar**

Note also:

a sort of computer   **en sorts/ett slags dator**
a game of chess   **ett parti schack**

(ii) 'Both of', 'all of', 'the whole of', etc. are usually rendered in Swedish without a prepositional 'of'. (See 339, 347.)

He met all of the boys.   **Han träffade alla pojkarna.**
He met all of them.   **Han träffade (dem) alla.**
Both of the girls are married.   **Båda flickorna är gifta.**
Both of them are married.   **Båda två är gifta.**
He saw the whole of the country.   **Han såg hela landet.**

(iii) 'Some of', 'none of', 'much of', 'many of' are rendered in Swedish with **av** when followed by a pronoun. When followed by a noun, however, they may be rendered either by **av** + *noun in definite form*, or by 0 *preposition* + *noun in indefinite form.*

Some of them are eating lunch.   **Några av dem äter lunch.**
Many/None of the boys became ill.   **Många/Inga av pojkarna blev sjuka.**
      Många/Inga pojkar blev sjuka.

(iv) 'Half of', 'two of', 'Which of?' Swedish has **av** after words clearly indicating a part of the whole. (Cf. (ii) and (iii) above.)

Half of the workers have gone.   **Hälften av arbetarna har gått.**
Two of them were Swedes.   **Två av dem var svenskar.**
this part of the book   **den här delen av boken**
Which of the books do you want?   **Vilka av böckerna vill du läsa först?**

Note also:

The book is full of errors.   **Boken är full av fel.**

(v) 'The majority of' (see also 353(c)(d))

The majority of Danes voted no.   **Flertalet danskar röstade nej.**

But:

A majority of Danes voted no.   **De flesta danskar röstade nej.**

Note: **ett flertal danskar** = 'a number of Danes'

(h) 'A heart of stone' – 'of' + material = **av** in Swedish.

a statue of pure gold   **en staty av rent guld**
a chest of oak   **en kista av ek**
a heart of stone   **ett hjärta av sten**

(j) 'A boy of sixteen' – 'of' + numerical expression = **på** in Swedish. English 'of' signifying 'comprising' or 'amounting to' when followed by a number is often rendered by Swedish **på**.

a salary/a rent of 50,000 dollars	**en lön/en hyra på 50 000 dollar**
tax/interest of ten percent	**skatt/ränta på tio procent**
a boy of sixteen	**en pojke på sexton år**

(k) 'The first of May' – 'of' in dates = no preposition in Swedish. (See 724.)

the twenty-third of January	**den tjugotredje januari**

Note: Swedish has a commercial form for 'the fourth day in the fifth month', etc.

the fourth of the fifth	**(den) fjärde i femte**

(l) 'The king of Sweden' – 'of' indicates origin = **av, från** in Swedish. The sense of origin is stronger with **från** than with **av**. Compare the following:

the king of Sweden	**kungen av Sverige**
the Wizard of Oz	**trollkarlen från Oz**
of humble origin	**av ringa härkomst**
He comes from a good family.	**Han kommer från en god familj.**
Mr Ek of our Malmö office	**Herr Ek från vårt kontor i Malmö**
born of Swedish parents	**född av svenska föräldrar**

(m) 'East of Eden' – 'of' with points of the compass = **om**

'North of' = 'to the north of':

East of Eden	**öster om Eden**
a town to the south of Umeå	**en stad söder om Umeå**

But note: 'The north(ern part) of':

the north of England	**norra England**
the west of Sweden	**västra Sverige, Västsverige**

(n) 'I'm dreaming of a white Christmas' – 'of' expressing subject matter = **om** in Swedish. When English 'of' indicates 'about', 'on the subject of', it is often rendered by **om** in Swedish (cf. 714).

I dreamed of you last night.	**Jag drömde om dig i natt.**
I've never heard of that!	**Jag har aldrig hört talas om det!**

Note, however:

I think of you often.	**Jag tänker ofta på dig.**

(o) 'That of'. Note how Swedish renders the following type of expression:

The melting point of ice is lower than that of iron.
Isens smältpunkt är lägre än järnets.

British submarines are old. Those of the USA are considerably newer.
Brittiska u-båtar är gamla. Förenta staternas är betydligt nyare.

(p) 'That idiot of a policeman!' – 'of' in pejorative expressions. **Till** is sometimes used to render English 'of' in certain types of pejorative expressions and analogous expressions, although it is perhaps more common to use a suitable adjective + noun expression in Swedish.

That idiot of a policeman!	**Den idioten till polis!** [Note: no article]
	cf. **Den där dumma polisen!**
a giant of a man	**en jätte till karl**

(q) Verbs/Adjectives/ + 'of'. The use of Swedish prepositions corresponding to English 'of' after verbs and adjectives is idiomatic, as these examples illustrate:.

to boast of something **skryta över något**; to consist of/be composed of something **bestå av något**; to complain of something **klaga på något**; to cure someone of something **bota någon från något**; to remind someone of something **påminna någon om något**; to suspect someone of something **misstänka någon för något**; afraid of **rädd för**; conscious of **medveten om**; critical of **kritisk mot**; fond of **förtjust i**; full of **full med;** guilty/innocent of **skyldig/oskyldig till**; proud of **stolt över**; sure of **säker på**; tired of **trött på**.

Note that **av** is used in expressions such as:

That's good/kind/nice of you.   **Det var snällt av dig.**

730   Preposition in English – no preposition in Swedish

In a number of instances English has a preposition where Swedish has no preposition, chiefly:

(a) In many expressions of time (cf. 414ff., 724, 725(b))

She was born at six o'clock on the third of May in 1942.
Hon föddes klockan sex den tredje maj (år) 1942.

(b) In partitive genitives (729(g)):

a glass of/litre of milk   **ett glas mjölk/en liter mjölk**

(c) In appositive genitives (729(f)):

He visited the town of Lund in the spring of 1917.
Han besökte staden Lund (på) våren 1917.

(d) Swedish has no preposition corresponding to English 'by' after **åka** (go) + means of transportation used in a general sense:

to travel by bus/boat/train/car   **åka buss/båt/tåg/bil**

but note:

We went in our car.   **Vi åkte i vår bil.**

(e) Swedish has no preposition corresponding to English 'to' after certain common verbs:

to belong to **tillhöra**; to happen to someone **hända någon**; to reply to **besvara**; to teach something to someone **lära någon något**; to promise something to someone **lova någon något** etc.

731   Preposition in Swedish – no preposition in English

In a number of instances Swedish has a preposition where English has no preposition, chiefly:

(a) Before the complement of a verb (often **till** in Swedish, cf. 716).

Hon blev vald till president.	She was elected president.
Han döptes till Kurt.	He was christened Kurt.
Vi kallade honom för Kurre.	We called him Kurre.

(b) With many verbs where the Swedish preposition precedes a part of the body (cf. 721(d)(ii)).

Han tvättade sig om händerna.	He washed his hands.
De bara rycker på axlarna	They just shrug their shoulders.

(c) In verbal constructions where English transitive verbs with a direct object correspond to Swedish intransitive verbs with a prepositional object.

Hon har gift sig med en dansk.	She has married a Dane.
Tryck på knappen!	Press the button!
Det tvivlar jag på.	I doubt that.

Note also:

be om något request something; **bjuda på något** offer something; **dra i** pull;

gå in i enter; **imponera på** impress; **njuta av** enjoy; **svara på** answer; **öva sig i** practise; etc.

(d) In certain expressions of time with 'last' and 'this' (724(h)):

i fredags, i januari	last Friday, last January
i natt, i fjol	last night, last year
i kväll	this evening

(e) In expressions of frequency (726):

en gång i timmen/om året	once an hour/a year

(f) The preposition **med** is usually retained in absolute phrases of the following type in Swedish. 'With' is not always retained in English.

Han satt där med en hund vid sina fötter.
He was sitting there, (with) a dog at his feet.

(g) Prepositions of time and place are retained in Swedish after expressions such as 'as early/late as', 'as far as', etc.

De fick snö så sent som i maj.	They had snow as late as May.
Vi åkte så långt som till Kiruna.	We travelled as far as Kiruna.

8   CONJUNCTIONS

A   **COORDINATION AND SUBORDINATION**
801   Introduction
802   Position of conjunctions
803   Subordinators and indicators of subordination

B   **COORDINATING CONJUNCTIONS**
804   Introduction
805   Copulative conjunctions
806   Disjunctive conjunctions
807   Adversative conjunctions
808   Explanative conjunctions
809   Conclusive conjunctions

C   **SUBORDINATING CONJUNCTIONS**
810   Introduction
811   General subordinators
812   Temporal conjunctions
813   Causal conjunctions
814   Conditional conjunctions
815   Concessive conjunctions
816   Final conjunctions
817   Consecutive conjunctions
818   Comparative conjunctions
819   Descriptive conjunctions

D   **OTHER SUBORDINATORS**
820   Other subordinators, introduction
821   Interrogative pronouns and adverbs
822   Relative pronouns and adverbs

E   **SOME PROBLEM CONJUNCTIONS**
823   Translation into Swedish of some problem conjunctions

A   COORDINATION AND SUBORDINATION

801   Introduction

For main clause, subordinate clause, see 1009ff., 1020f., link position 1035, the form, function and position of subordinate clauses 1037–1043.

(a) *Coordination* involves the linking together of two clauses or elements of a similar kind. The link used is often a *coordinating conjunction* placed between the elements to be linked (see 803–809):

Hans och Greta lyssnar på jazz. Hans and Greta are listening to jazz.	[Subjects coordinated]
De sitter och lyssnar. They are sitting and listening.	[Verbs coordinated]
Jag tycker om Olle och Olle tycker om mig. I like Olle and he likes me.	[Main clauses coordinated]
Jag hoppas att han vinner och att han har rekordtid. I hope that he wins and that he gets a record time.	[Subordinate clauses coordinated]

(b) *Subordination* involves the incorporation of a subordinate clause (indicated by round brackets) into a main clause sentence (indicated by < >). The link word used is often a *subordinating conjunction* or other *subordinator* placed at the beginning of the subordinate clause (see 810–819).

<Jag tycker om Olle I like Olle *main clause* *independent*	**(därför att Olle tycker om mig)>.** because Olle likes me. *subordinate clause* *dependent*

In this example the subordinating conjunction is **därför att**. Notice how the subordinate clause here is subordinated to the main clause, i.e. dependent on it, and part of the larger main clause sentence (see 1041).

Compare coordination:

< Jag tycker om Olle > I like Olle *main clause* *independent*	**och** and	**< Olle tycker om mig>.** Olle likes me. *main clause* *independent*

There is often a hierarchy of clauses, one within another, by which clauses are subordinated:

> < **Jag tror** (att vi kan vinna /om vi anstränger oss/) >.
> I think that we can win if we exert ourselves.
> < A (B /C C/B)A >

In this example the subordinate clause marked C–C is subordinated to the subordinate clause B–B which in turn is subordinated to (actually the object of) the main clause sentence A–A (see 1041).

802 Position of conjunctions

(**a**) *Coordinating conjunctions* (801(a)) are found:

- Usually between the two sentence elements, phrases or clauses to be coordinated. See 801(a) above and 1035.

- At the beginning of the sentence:

  > *Och* **jag som litade på honom!**   And I trusted him!

Note: Certain conjunctions never appear at the beginning of the sentence; these include explanative, conclusive and comparative conjunctions (808f, 818).

The use of the conjunction does not usually affect the word order in the clause following. For double conjunctions, see 805(c).

(**b**) *Subordinating conjunctions* (801(b)) are found at the beginning of the subordinate clause:

Either between the main and subordinate clauses when the order is MC + SC

Or at the beginning of the sentence when the order is SC + MC.

> *Om* **vi hinner,** **tänker vi hälsa på Olssons.**
> If we have time, we are thinking of visiting the Olssons.
> *sub.* SC MC
> *conj.*

> **Vi** **tänker hälsa på Olssons,** *om* **vi hinner.**
> We are thinking of visiting the Olssons if we have time.
> MC *sub.*
> *conj.* SC

This applies to most adverbial clauses but not to attributive clauses, some consecutive clauses or indirect questions in which the subordinate clause cannot precede the main clause, and the conjunction or other subordinator (see 803) therefore cannot begin the sentence (see 1039).

Han frös	*så att* **han skakade.**	
He was so cold	that he was shaking.	
	sub. conj. – consecutive clause	

Vi frågade dem,	*om* **de ville följa med.**	
We asked them	whether they wanted to go along.	
	sub. conj. – indirect question	

Min lärare,	**som är svensk,**	**är mycket trevlig.**
My teacher,	who is Swedish,	is very nice.
	other subordinator –	
	attributive clause	

803 Subordinators and indicators of subordination

(a) Coordinating conjunctions normally consist of a single word, e.g. **och** 'and'; **men** 'but'; **eller** 'or', while subordinating conjunctions frequently consist of several words, often a combination of adverb or preposition + subordinating conjunction. Compare:

Vi kom till stationen	*efter* **tågets avgång.**
We got to the station	after the train had left.
	prep. + noun phrase

Vi kom till stationen	*efter det att* **tåget gått.**
	sub. conj. + subordinate clause

(b) Phrases may also be linked by a conjunctional adverb (610(c)) in a separate main clause. Compare:

Jag måste gå	*för* **det är sent.**	I must go because it's late.
	coord conj.	

Jag måste gå.	**Det är** *nämligen* **sent.**	I must go. It's late, you see.
	conjunctional adverb	

The function is the same in both cases, but the conjunctional adverb often comes first in the clause, causing inversion: finite verb – subject (FV–S) (cf. 1018), whereas subordinating conjunctions are found with subordinate clause (i.e. straight) word order: subject – finite verb (S–FV) (cf. 1018). Compare:

Olle klarade inte provet.	*Ändå* **fick han mycket hjälp.**
	conjuncional FV S
	adverb
Olle didn't pass the test.	Even so, he got a lot of help.

Olle klarade inte provet	***trots att* han fick mycket hjälp.**
	conj. S FV
Olle didn't pass the test,	even though he had a lot of help.

(c) Other subordinators include interrogative pronouns and interrogative adverbs and relative pronouns and relative adverbs. These differ from conjunctions in that they introduce a subordinate clause and constitute a sentence element in that clause at the same time:

Jag undrade *vem som* hade sagt det.	I wondered who had said that.
subord- FV	
inator	
+ subject	

Jag frågade *vad* han hade sagt.	I asked what he had said.
subordinator	
+ object	

Ön, *dit* han ska resa, heter Fårö.	The island he's going to is called
subordinator	Fårö.
+ adverbial	

(d) An *indicator of subordination* is not a word class or sentence element but a marker showing the clausal relationship. Such indicators are:

(i) An introductory word in the subordinate clause, e.g. subordinating conjunction, interrogative pronoun or adverb, relative pronoun or adverb. See 810, 820ff.

Han skrev *att* han tänkte emigrera.
He wrote that he was considering emigrating.

Vi frågade *varför* han tänkte göra det.
We asked why he was considering doing that.

Han visste inte *vart* han skulle åka.
He didn't know where he was going to go.

(ii) The position of the clausal adverbial immediately before the finite verb. See 1015(e).

Han sa (att) han *aldrig* skulle återvända.
He said he would never return.

(iii) The omission of **har** or **hade** where there is a supine. See 523(b).

Vi visste att han gått och tänkt på det i flera år.
We knew he had been thinking about it for several years.

(e) Not all subordinate clauses are introduced by a conjunction or other subordinator. Some have no introductory word because the words **att** or **som** have been omitted:

Jag tycker det är roligt. (cf. **Jag tycker att det är roligt.**)
I think it's fun.

Filmen vi såg var svensk. (cf. **Filmen som vi såg var svensk.**) [See 1040.]
The film we saw was Swedish.

B COORDINATING CONJUNCTIONS

804 Introduction

Section	Term	
805	Copulative	**och, samt** ('and'), **plus**
806	Disjunctive	**eller** ('or')
807	Adversative	**men** ('but'), **fast** ('though'), **(inte . . .) utan** ('not..'.) but
808	Explanative	**ty** ('for'), **för** ('for')
809	Conclusive	**så** ('so')

Conjunctional adverbs, see 805–809, 610(c).
Double conjunctions, see 805–809, 610(c)(iv)

There are very few coordinating conjunctions, but the conjunctional adverbs (802(b), 610(c)) fulfil almost the same function. Coordinating conjunctions are classified according to their function into: copulative, disjunctive, adversative, explanative and conclusive.

805 Copulative conjunctions

Copulative means 'connecting'.

(a) **Och** ('and') is the most frequent word in Swedish and is often pronounced /å/.

Och is used to link two main clauses:

Eva älskar Olle och Olle älskar henne.
Eva loves Olle and Olle loves her.

As in English, in lists **och** is often only inserted before the last item:

Han bar kavaj, byxor *och* **hatt.**
He was wearing a sports jacket, trousers and hat.

Note: **Och** is sometimes omitted as a stylistic device:

Han var stark, en väldig björn, byggd som en trädstam.
He was strong, a mighty bear, built like a tree trunk.

(b) Samt is usually found at the end of a list:

Det väntas hårt väder på Gotland, Öland samt längs Norrlandskusten.
Strong winds are expected for Gotland, Öland and along the coast of Norr-land.

Samt is usually restricted to formal style and cannot link clauses.

(c) Både . . . och 'both . . . and'. The coordination may be strengthened by the addition of the conjunctional adverb **både** to form **både . . . och**, which emphasises that both elements have equal weight:

Både **du** *och* **jag gillar sill.**
Both you and I like herring.

Vi borstar tänderna *både* **innan vi äter** *och* **innan vi lägger oss.**
We brush our teeth both before we eat and before we go to bed.

See 823(e).

Some other similar constructions are:

dels . . . dels partly . . . partly
såväl . . . som both . . . and [more formal than **både . . . och**]
inte bara . . . utan också not only . . . but also
ömsom . . . ömsom sometimes . . . sometimes . . .

(d) Plus is becoming common as a conjunction:

Stan har mycket att bjuda på: hotell, restauranger, barer *plus* **ett ovanligt fint museum.**
The town has much to offer: hotels, restaurants, bars plus an unusually fine museum.

For other conjunctional adverbs which have a copulative function see 610(c).

806 Disjunctive conjunctions

Disjunctive means 'alternative'.

(a) Eller

> **Pengar *eller* livet!**   Your money or your life!
> **Är det du *eller* jag som bestämmer?**   Is it you or me who decides?

(b) A number of 'double conjunctions' consist of a conjunctional adverb + **eller**. These strengthen the element of choice:

(i) Antingen ... eller:

> *Antingen* **är han verkligen sjuk *eller* (också/så) skolkar han idag.**
> Either he really is ill or else he is playing truant today.

Note: **antingen ... eller (också)** causes inversion in both clauses, but on occasions it is synonymous with **vare sig** (see (iii) below) meaning 'whether or not', and in this case it is followed by straight word order:

> **Du får äta upp din mat *antingen* du vill *eller* inte.**
> You must eat your food whether you want to or not.

(ii) Varken ... eller:

> **På min tid fanns v*arken* tv *eller* video.**
> In my day there was neither TV nor video.

(iii) Vare sig ... eller is usually only found in negative sentences:

> **Jag vill inte resa *vare sig* idag *eller* i morgon.**
> I wish to travel neither today nor tomorrow.

807 Adversative conjunctions

Adversative means 'opposite' and expresses a contrast, restriction or correction.

(a) Men ('but') links words, phrases or clauses:

> **Människan spår men Gud rår.**   Man proposes but God disposes.
> **Hon är intelligent men hemskt tråkig.**   She is intelligent but very boring.

Note 1: **Men** can be strengthened in different ways by the addition of the conjunctional adverbs **ändå** or **visserligen**:

> **Vädret var dåligt, *men ändå* hade vi det skönt.**
> The weather was bad, but nevertheless we had a good time.

> **Visserligen var du sjuk, *men* du kunde ha ringt.**
> You were admittedly ill, but you could have rung.

Note 2: **Men** is sometimes omitted for stylistic reasons:

> **Det regnade inte, bara droppade då och då från den grå himlen.**
> It didn't rain, just dripped now and then from a grey sky.

(b) Utan ('but') is similar to **men** but follows a negative (**inte, aldrig, sällan, knappt,** etc.) and introduces a second element contradicting the first (see 823(f)). Unlike **men, utan** implies the same subject in both clauses:

> **Hon var inte full *utan* bara trött.**
> She wasn't drunk but just tired.

> **Han ägde aldrig lägenheten *utan* hyrde den.**
> He didn't ever own the flat but rented it.

(c) Fast ('but') is often similar in use to **men,** but is colloquial and restrictive:

> **Vi har fått en lägenhet, *fast* den är bara liten.**
> We have got a flat but it is only small.

Note: **Fast(än)** ('although') is a subordinating conjunction (cf. 815(a)):

> **Vi bor i en lägenhet *fast(än)* den inte är vår.**   We live in a flat although it's not ours.

Compare the word order used with **fast** as a coordinating conjunction:

> **Vi bor i en lägenhet *fast* den är inte vår.**   We live in a flat but it's not ours.

Opposition can also be expressed by the conjunctional adverbs **dock** 'yet'; **likväl** 'yet'; **emellertid** 'however', 'nevertheless'; **ändå** 'yet'.

808 Explanative conjunctions

Explanative means 'explaining'.

För, ty ('for', 'as') always link complete clauses:

> **Han kommer inte *för* han är sjuk.**
> He isn't coming as he is ill.

Note 1: **Ty** is now rarely seen:

> **Vägen var våt, *ty* det hade nyligen regnat.**
> The road was wet as it had recently been raining.

Note 2: The conjunctional adverbs **ju, nämligen** also express explanation (see 615(f)):

> **Han kommer inte. Han är *nämligen* sjuk.**   He isn't coming. He's ill, you see.
> **Han kommer inte. Han är *ju* sjuk.**   He isn't coming. He's ill, of course.

809 Conclusive conjunctions

Conclusive means 'in conclusion', 'as a result'.

Så ('so') links only clauses and expresses a conclusion or result:

Det är sent, *så* vi går väl inte ut nu.
It's late so I suppose we won't be going out now.

Bilen är sönder, *så* jag måste ta bussen idag.
The car has broken down so I have to take the bus today.

Note: Conclusion may also be expressed by means of the following conjunctional adverbs:

alltså 'therefore'; **därför** 'consequently'; **följaktligen** 'consequently'.

Bilen är sönder. Därför måste jag ta bussen idag.
The car has broken down. That is why I have to take the bus today.

C SUBORDINATING CONJUNCTIONS

810 Introduction

See also 1037ff.

---

811 I *General subordinators*

Explicative
* indirect speech **att** that
* indirect question   **om** whether
See also **som** (822).

II *Semantically differentiated subordinators*

812	Temporal	**då** when; **när** when; **tills** until; **inte . . . förrän** not ...until; **innan** before; **medan** while; **sedan** after, since; **alltsedan** ever since; **efter det att** after; **under det att** while; **i och med att** as soon as; **så snart som** as soon as; **så ofta (som)** as often as.
813	Causal	**för att** because; **eftersom** as, because; **därför att** because; **då** as; **emedan** because; **genom att** in that; **på grund av att** because; **som** as.
814	Conditional	**om** if; **ifall** if; **såvitt** in so far as; **såvida** provided that; **på villkor att** on the condition that; **förutsatt att** provided that; **bara i den mån som** only in so far as.

815	Concessive	**fastän** although; **fast** although, **trots att** though; **även om** even though; **om . . . så** even if; **samtidigt som** at the same time as.
816	Final	**för att** in order that; **på det att** that.
817	Consecutive	**så att** so that; **så att** so that.
818	Comparative	**lika . . . som** as . . . as; **såsom** as; **liksom** as; **än** than; **ju . . . desto** the . . . the; **som om** as if.
819	Descriptive	**genom att** by the fact that; **i det att** in view of the fact that; **utan att** not that.

Subordinating conjunctions are more complex than coordinating conjunctions as they often comprise a compound or word group, in many cases a combination of an adverb or preposition + **att** or **som**. In this way they are able to express many subtle semantic distinctions.

Simple subordinating conjunctions are: **att, om, då, när, tills, innan, medan, sedan, som, fast**.

Compound subordinating conjunctions are: **huruvida, alltsedan, eftersom, emedan, såvida, däremot, liksom,** fastän.

Word groups as subordinating conjunctions are: **därför att, för att, genom att, på det att, i det att, utan att, så att, även om**.

811 General subordinators

The general subordinators are **att** 'that' **om** 'whether'. These merely indicate that the clause they introduce is a subordinate clause. They impart no other meaning.

(a) Att ('that') is as important among subordinating conjunctions as **och** is among coordinating conjunctions. It is always pronounced /att/ unlike the infinitive marker (518), which is often pronounced /å/. The conjunction **att** may often be omitted (1040) as in English. **Att** is used most often to introduce a statement in indirect speech, and follows a verb of saying or reporting:

Han sa *att* han arbetade hårt.
(Cf. direct speech: **Han sa: Jag arbetar hårt.**)
He said that he was working hard.

See also 1041 for main clause order after **att**.

(b) **Om** corresponds to **att** but is used to introduce indirect questions formed from yes/no questions (1036). Unlike **att, om** may not be omitted:

Vi undrade om han arbetade hårt.
(cf. direct question: **Vi undrade: Arbetar du hårt?**)
We wondered whether he was working hard.

Om is also used as a conditional or a concessive conjunction (814, 815).

(c) General subordinators may introduce subject and object clauses and clauses constituting the predicative complement, attribute or adverbial in the sentence, while the semantically differentiated subordinators (812–819) may only introduce adverbial clauses, see 1038(a)(b).

812   Temporal conjunctions

Temporal means 'time-based'.

(a) **När, då** 'when'. As a temporal conjunction **när** is more common in spoken Swedish and **då** in written Swedish:

När/Då **han hade parkerat bilen, gick han in.**
When he had parked the car he went in.

Nu när 'now that':

Nu när **vintern är här, ser allting trist ut.**
Now that winter has arrived everything looks very sad.

Note 1: **När** is also an interrogative adverb, see 609(c), 821:

När **tänker du åka?**   When are you thinking of leaving?

Note 2: **Då** is also a causal conjunction ('as') in both written and spoken Swedish, see 813, and an adverb ('then'), see 616(b):

Då **måste vi hjälpa dig.**   Then we have to help you.

(b) **Sedan** as a temporal conjunction has two meanings:

(i) *Sedan* **han hade parkerat bilen, gick han in.**
After he had parked the car he went in.

(ii) *Sedan* **han försvann har hon varit ledsen.**
Since he disappeared she has been very depressed.

Note 1: **Sedan** is also an adverb (see 616(b)):

Sedan **gick vi hem.**   Then we went home.

Note 2: **Sedan** is also a preposition (see 722(l)):

> **Sedan jul har det varit dåligt väder.**   Since Christmas there has been bad weather.

(c) Medan ('while'):

> **Medan gräset gror, dör kon.**
> While the grass is growing the cow dies. [Swedish proverb]

Other expressions indicating roughly the same idea are: **under det att**; **under tiden att**; **så länge som**; **just som**.

(d) Innan, (inte) förrän ('before'):

> **Innan vi gick hem tackade vi värdinnan.**
> Before we went home we thanked the hostess.

Förrän is used when there is a negative in the main clause, or after **knappt**:

> **Du kan *inte* springa *förrän* du har lärt dig att gå.**
> You can't run before you've learnt to walk.

Note 1: **Inte förrän** can also mean 'not until':

> **Vi kommer *inte förrän* vi har lagat bilen.**
> We won't be there until we've mended the car.

Note 2: **Innan** may also be a preposition used colloquially (728(b)):

> **Innan jul måste vi träffas.**   Before Christmas we must meet.

See also (e) below and 823(d).

(e) Tills ('until') is a contraction of the prepositional phrase **till dess att**:

> **Vänta *tills* vi kommer!**   Wait until/till we get there! [See 823(k).]

Notice: 'not until' **inte förrän**.

(f) Efter det att ('after'):

> **Efter det att vi kom iland, åt vi lunch.**
> After we went ashore we ate lunch.

Occasionally the preposition **efter (706)** is incorrectly used as a conjunction.

(g) Notice also: **så länge som** 'as long as'; **så snart som** 'as soon as'; **så ofta som** 'as often as'.

813   Causal conjunctions

Causal means 'reason', 'cause'.

(a) För att, därför att, emedan ('because', 'as', 'since') usually begin a subordinate clause following a main clause, whereas **eftersom** clauses may either precede or follow the main clause. **Därför att** and **eftersom** tend to be encountered more frequently in written Swedish.

> **Det här ska du få,** *för att* **du har varit så snäll.**
> You shall have this as you have been so kind.

> **Vi åkte till Sverige** *därför att* **vi ville plocka svamp.**
> We went to Sweden because we wanted to pick mushrooms.

> *Eftersom* **han inte kommer måste vi börja utan honom.**
> As he isn't coming we will have to begin without him.

> **Vi måste börja utan honom** *eftersom* **han inte kommer.**
> We will have to begin without him as he isn't coming.

Note 1: **Emedan** is more formal and now rarely encountered:

> **Försöket misslyckades** *emedan* **det var illa förberett.**
> The attempt failed as it was badly prepared.

Note 2: **Därför att** should not be confused with the conjunctional adverb **därför** (= 'which is why', 'for that reason'). Compare:

> **Vi ville plocka svamp.** *Därför* **åkte vi till Sverige.**
> We wanted to pick mushrooms. That's why we went to Sweden.   (See also 610(c)).

(b) Då ('as')

> *Då* **han inte svarade på mitt brev, ringde jag honom.**
> As he didn't answer my letter I rang him.

Då is also a temporal conjunction (= 'when'), 812(a), and an adverb, 616(b), 823(b).

814   Conditional conjunctions

Conditional means 'expressing a condition'. See 1042 for different kinds of conditional clause.

(a) Om, ifall ('if', 'whether'), **såvida, såvitt** ('as long as').

The most common coordinating conjunction is **om**:

> *Om* **du är snäll, ska du få godis.**
> If you are good you can have some sweets.

In spoken and informal written Swedish **ifall** is common:

De undrade ifall vi ville följa med.
They wondered whether we wanted to go along.

Jag följer med *såvida* ni inte har någonting emot det.
I'll come too if you haven't any objections.

Det går bra *såvitt* inga problem uppstår.
It'll be fine as long as no problems arise.

Note 1: **Såvitt** can also be an adverb:

Såvitt jag förstår problemet, är det så här.
As far as I understand the problem, it is like this.

Note 2: **Huruvida** is sometimes used to avoid duplication of **om**:

Det är fråga om *huruvida* han kommer att lyckas.
It is a question of whether he will succeed.

(b) Förutsatt att ('provided that'):

Förutsatt *att* detta är riktigt, kan vi slå till.
Provided that/Assuming this is correct, we can act.

(c) Om . . . inte ('unless'):

Om du *inte* ger dig med detsamma, så skjuter vi.
Unless you/If you don't surrender at once we'll shoot.

815 Concessive conjunctions

Concessive means 'expressing a concession'.

(a) Fast, fastän, trots att ('although'):

Han är på gott humör *fast* han är sjuk.
He's in good spirits although he's ill.

Fastän is usually only found in written Swedish.

Note: **Trots att** should not be confused with the preposition **trots** ('despite', 'in spite of'), see 727(n).

(b) Note also concessive expressions such as the following, expressing 'however' (Cf. also 616(e)(f).):

Det var ett rum, *om än* aldrig så litet.
It was a room, however little.

Hur . . . än:

> **Han blir aldrig arg, *hur* mycket man *än* irriterar honom.**
> He never gets angry, however much one annoys him.

816 Final conjunctions

Final in this sense expresses an intention. **För att** ('in order to'):

> **Vi måste avskeda personal *för att* vi ska rädda företaget.**
> We have to sack staff in order to save the company.

817 Consecutive conjunctions

Consecutive means 'as a result', 'in consequence'.

(a) Så att, så . . . att ('so that', 'so . . . that'):

> **Han drack så att han blev sjuk.**
> He drank so that he became ill.

> **Han sprang så fort att han blev alldeles röd i ansiktet.**
> He ran so fast that he got quite red in the face.

(b) Så: 'In order that' (**så . . . inte** 'lest'/'in order that . . . not')

> **Ta mormor i armen så (att) hon inte snavar i trappan.**
> Take grandma's arm so (that) she doesn't trip on the stairs.

Note 1: **Så:** '(and) as a result' is also used as a coordinating conjunction (cf. 809). Main clause statement order (subject–finite verb) (NB position of adverb **inte**).

> **Jag var alldeles tillplattad, så jag visste inte vad jag skulle säga.**
> I was completely bowled over, so I didn't know what to say.

Note 2: **Att** is often omitted in these **så att** constructions in spoken Swedish.

818 Comparative conjunctions

Comparative means 'expressing a comparison' (See also 242).

(a) (Lika) som ('as . . . as') (see 823(c)):

> **Jag är lika stor som min bror.**   I'm as big as my brother.

(b) (Så)som ('as' = 'in the way that'):

De gjorde (så)som de hade blivit befallda.
They did as they had been told.

Note: **Såsom** frequently becomes abbreviated to **som** in these constructions in spoken Swedish.

(c) (Lik)som ('as' = 'in the same way that)':

Han vann nu liksom han hade gjort så många gånger förr.
He won now as he had done so many times before.

Note: **Liksom** frequently becomes abbreviated to **som** in these constructions in spoken Swedish.

(d) Än ('than'):

Programmet var tråkigare än jag hade väntat mig.
The programme was more boring than I had expected.

(e) Ju . . . desto; ju . . . ju ('the' + comparative . . . 'the' . . . + comparative):

Ju mer jag lär känna honom, desto bättre tycker jag om honom.
The more I get to know him the better I like him.

Notice the fixed order of clauses; the subordinate clause introduced by **ju** must come first. The main clause with **ju . . . desto . . .** has inversion.

Ju högre löner vi har, ju högre standard får vi.
The higher our salary, the higher will be our standard of living.

819 Descriptive conjunctions

Descriptive in this sense means 'commenting'.

(a) Genom att ('in that', 'by the fact that'):

Han räddades genom att kamraterna ingrep.
He was saved in that his friends intervened.

(b) I det att ('in so far as', 'in view of the fact that'):

Den svenska ekonomin har en stor svaghet i det att makten är koncentrerad till ett fåtal stora företag.
The Swedish economy has a major weakness in that the power is concentrated in a few large companies.

(c) Utan att ('without'):

Det gäller att utöka vårt inflytande i området utan att någon oroas av utvecklingen.
It is a matter of increasing our influence in the area without anyone becoming uneasy about developments.

Note: **Inte utan att** ('not that' + negative): this rather convoluted form is still quite common in Swedish. Notice that Swedish does not require a negative with the finite verb following **inte utan att**:

Det är inte utan att jag tycker att det ar lite kallt här.
It's not that I don't think it's a bit cold in here.

D   OTHER SUBORDINATORS

820   Other subordinators, introduction

821	Interrogative pronouns	**vem** who; **vad** what; **vilken** which; **vilket** which; **vilka** which; who.
821	Interrogative adverbs	**när** when; **var** where; **vart** where . . . to; **hur** how; **varför** why; **varifrån** where . . . from.
822	Relative pronouns	**som** who; which; **vars** whose; **vilken** which; **vilket** which; **vilka** which, who.
822	Relative adverbs	**där** where; **dit** where . . . to; **då** then.

Pronouns and adverbs used to introduce a subordinate clause are also subordinators.

821   Interrogative pronouns and adverbs

These include the pronouns: **vem, vad, vilken, vilket, vilka,** and the adverbs: **när, var, vart, hur, varför, varifrån.** See 361ff., 609(c).

These words introduce v-questions (see questions 1036), and when they are used to form subordinate clauses, i.e. indirect questions, no other conjunction is required before them:

Jag undrade, *vart* han hade tagit vägen.
I wondered where he had got to.
(Cf. direct question: **Jag undrade: *Vart* har han tagit vägen?**)

When an interrogative pronoun is the subject of a subordinate clause, however, the word **som** is introduced as a subject marker (see 367):

Jag undrar *vem* som kysser henne nu.
I wonder who is kissing her now.

822 Relative pronouns and adverbs

These include the pronouns: **som, vars, vilken, vilket, vilka, vad,** and the adverbs: **där, dit.** See also 369ff, 609.

(a) Som is the most frequent of all subordinators, and forms relative clauses.

Brevet (*som*) jag skickade till honom var maskinskrivet.
The letter that/which I sent him was typewritten.

Flickan *som* vann priset heter Eva.
The girl who won the prize was called Eva.

See also: 370(c), 823(j).

(b) Vilken:

Jag vet inte *vilken* du menar.
I don't know who/which you mean.

(c) Vars supplies a genitive form for **som**, only when referring to a singular noun or pronoun. It is usually only found in written Swedish. In spoken Swedish the construction **som** + preposition is preferred (see 372(d)). Compare:

En man *vars* namn jag inte känner, kom fram till mig.
A man whose name I don't know came up to me.

En man *som* jag inte vet namnet *på*, kom fram till mig.
A man whose name I don't know came up to me.

(d) Där, dit:

Han hittade en skog *där* det fanns massor av svamp.
He found a forest where there were lots of mushrooms.

Han har hittat en skog *dit* vi kan gå för att plocka svamp.
He has found a forest where we can go to pick mushrooms.

See also 616(d) 'where'.

E   SOME PROBLEM CONJUNCTIONS

823   Translation into Swedish of some problem conjunctions

Many English conjunctions have direct equivalents in Swedish, e.g. 'that' = **att**, 'if' = **om**, etc. However, the same word in English is often a conjunction, preposition and adverb and each part of speech may possess at least one equivalent in Swedish. The conjunction form is one that introduces a clause with a finite verb. While many Swedish prepositions may govern an infinitive, they can only do so if there is no change of subject:

> **För att få veta det måste han fråga mig.**
> In order to find out he has to ask me.

> **Han svarade utan att se på mig.**
> He replied without looking at me.

If there is a change of subject, the sense can only be conveyed by means of a conjunction and following clause.

(a) 'After':

(i) As a conjunction before a full clause (i.e. one with a finite verb), use **efter det att**. Either **det** or **att** can be omitted.

> We travelled to Ipswich after we had made our decision.
> **Vi åkte till Ipswich *efter det att* vi hade beslutat oss.**
> **Vi åkte till Ipswich *efter att* vi hade beslutat oss.**
> **Vi åkte till Ipswich *efter det* vi hade beslutat oss.**

(ii) As a conjunction before a non-finite clause (1050), use **efter att**:

> We travelled to Ipswich after we had made our decision.
> **Vi åkte till Ipswich *efter att* ha beslutat oss.**

(iii) As a preposition, use **efter** (see 706):

> After Christmas   **Efter jul**

(b) 'As':

(i) When 'as' = 'for', use **för (ty)** (See 808):

> He disappeared as he was afraid.
> **Han försvann *för (ty)* han var rädd.**

(ii) When 'as' = 'while', use **medan** (see 812(c)):

As he was speaking he went red.
Medan **han talade rodnade han.**

(iii) When 'as' = 'because', use **eftersom/då** (see 813(a), 616(b) Note):

As he will not be coming we will begin.
Eftersom (Då) **han inte kommer börjar vi.**

(iv) When 'as' = 'like', use **(lik)som** (see 818):

Now as before it is difficult.
Nu *(lik)som* **förr är det svårt.**

Notice also:

Blind as he was, he could find his way home.
Fastän **han var blind, kunde han hitta hem./**
Blind som han var, kunde han hitta hem.

(c) 'As . . . as . . .' :

(i) When a comparison is made in a positive clause, use **lika . . . som**:

You are as gifted as your sister.　　**Du är** *lika* **begåvad** *som* **din syster.**

(ii) Otherwise use **så . . . som**:

I'm not as gifted as my sister.　　**Jag är inte** *så* **begåvad** *som* **min syster.**

(d) 'Before':

(i) As a conjunction after a positive main clause, use **innan**:

We called in to see him before we came here.
Vi hälsade på honom *innan* **vi kom hit.**

(ii) As a conjunction after a negative main clause, use **förrän** (See 812(d)):

It was not long before he arrived.　　**Det dröjde** *inte* **länge** *förrän* **han kom.**

Note 1: As an adverb = 'earlier', 'previously', use **förr, förut, tidigare**:

I have never been in Sweden before.　　**Jag har aldrig varit i Sverige** *förr/förut/tidigare.*

Note 2: As a preposition of time, use **före, innan** (see 722f):

We met Jan just before Christmas.　　**Vi träffade Jan strax** *före/innan* **jul.**

Note 3: As a preposition of place = 'in front of', use **före, framför, inför** (see 720(k),(h),(m) respectively as each has its own area of use):

The boy stood before his father.　　**Pojken stod** *framför* **sin far.**

(e) 'Both':

(i) As a conjunction use **både . . . och**:

Both Erik and Eva were language students.
Både Erik *och* Eva var språkstuderande.

Note: As an indefinite pronoun, where 'both' can be replaced by 'the two', use **båda** (see 805(c), 347):

Both students were intelligent.   **Båda studenterna var intelligenta.**

(f) 'But':

(i) As a conjunction after a positive main clause, use **men**:

The essay is long but does not say much.
Uppsatsen är lång *men* säger inte så mycket.

(ii) As a conjunction after a negative main clause when the second clause does not directly contradict the first, use **men**:

The essay is not long but it is very boring.
Uppsatsen är inte lång *men* den är mycket tråkig.

(iii) As a conjunction after a negative main clause when the second clause directly contradicts the first, use **utan**:

The essay is not long but actually quite short.
Uppsatsen är inte lång *utan* egentligen ganska kort.

Note: When 'but' is a preposition, and can be replaced by 'except', use **utom**:

All the students but one are gifted.
Alla studenterna *utom* en är begåvade.

(g) 'Either':

(i) As a conjunction, 'either . . . or' (meaning 'one of A or B') after a positive, use **antingen . . . eller**:

He must be either fifty or fifty-one years old.
Han måste vara *antingen* femtio *eller* femtioett år gammal.

(ii) As a conjunction 'either . . . or' (meaning 'both A and B') after a comparative, use **både . . . och**:

He is older than either you or me.   **Han är äldre än *både* dig *och* mig.**

(iii) As a conjunction, 'either . . . or' (meaning 'both A and B') after a negative, use **varken . . . eller**:

He did not come either yesterday or today.
Han kom *varken* igår *eller* idag.

Note 1: As an adverb, use **heller** (615(e)):

He cannot come either.   **Han kan inte komma *heller*.**

Note 2 : As an indefinite pronoun ('one of A or B'), use **vilken som helst** (358):

Take either of them.   **Ta *vilken som helst* av dem.**

Note 3: As an indefinite pronoun ('both A and B'), use **båda** (347):

People stood on either side of the road.   **Folk stod på *båda* sidor om vägen.**

(h) 'Since':

(i) As a conjunction, when 'since' = 'after', use **sedan**:

How long is it since you saw your father?
Hur länge är det *sedan* du såg din pappa?

(ii) As a conjunction, when 'since' = 'because', 'as', use **eftersom, då, emedan**:

Since you are here anyway, you could help wash up.
***Då* du ändå är här, kan du hjälpa till och diska.**

Note 1: As a preposition, when 'since' = 'after', use **sedan** (cf. 722(l)):

It has been very warm since Easter.
Det har varit mycket varmt *sedan* påsk.

Note 2: As an adverb, when 'since' = 'since that time', use **sedan dess** (see also 812(b)):

I have not been there since.   **Jag har inte varit där *sedan dess*.**

(j) 'That':

(i) As a conjunction, use **att**:

They said (that) they were pleased. **De sa *att* de var glada.**

Note 1: As a relative pronoun, when 'that' = 'which', 'who(m)', use **som** (370):
He bought the house (that) we liked so much.
Han köpte huset (*som*) vi tyckte så mycket om.

Note 2: 'That' can also be a demonstrative pronoun in Swedish: **denna, den där**, etc. (325f.)

Note 3: In cleft sentences (see 1048) in Swedish the relative pronoun **som** is used for 'that':

It was my idea that won the prize.   **Det var min idé *som* vann priset.**
     i.e. **det är/var X som . . .**

Compare the use of the conjunction **att** in existential sentences (see 1033):

It was my idea that he should come.   **Det var min idé *att* han skulle komma.**
     Det is formal subject, **att han skulle komma** is real subject.

(k) 'Till', 'until': **tills** or **förrän**?

(i) As a conjunction, when 'till' occurs in a positive clause, use **tills**:

We will wait till the rain stops.   **Vi väntar *tills* det slutar regnar.**

(ii) As a conjunction, after a negative, use **inte . . . förrän**:

We cannot begin until he arrives.   **Vi kan inte börja förrän han kommer.**

Note 1: Sometimes, for stylistic reasons **först när** is preferred to **inte . . . förrän**:

Not until we were ready did I begin.   ***Först när* vi var färdiga började jag.**

Note 2: As a preposition, use **till**:

from morning to night   **från morgon till kväll**

(l) 'When' (See 821):

(i) As a temporal conjunction, use **när, då**:

I want to speak to him when he gets here.
Jag vill prata med honom *när* han kommer.

Twenty years ago, when I still believed in Socialism . . .
För 20 år sedan, *då* jag ännu trodde på socialismen . . .

Note: As an interrogative adverb, use **när?**:

When are you leaving?   ***När* åker du?**

(ii) 'Since when?' = **Sedan när, Hur länge?**

Since when have you been smoking cigars?
***Sedan när/Hur länge* har du rökt cigarrer?**

(iii) 'Hardly . . . when' = 'no sooner than' = **knappt . . . förrän**:

I had hardly sat down when the telephone rang.
Jag hade *knappt* satt mig *förrän* det ringde i telefonen.

Note the translation of 'when' in certain phrases: 'when young' **i min ungdom**; 'when passing' **i förbigående**; 'when bathing' **under/vid badning**.

(iv) As a concessive conjunction, use **fastän**.

How could you do it, when you knew it was wrong?
Hur kunde du göra det, *fastän* du visste att det var fel?

(v) As a relative pronoun, use **som** (see 370):

I will never forget the day (when) I won the Vasa Race.
Jag glömmer aldrig den dagen (*som*) jag vann Vasaloppet.

9 INTERJECTIONS

901   Introduction
902   **Ja, nej, jo**, etc.
903   Reactions in conversation
904   Expressions of feeling, exclamations
905   Commands
906   Imitations
907   Polite expressions
908   Expletives

901 Introduction

(a) Interjections belong primarily in the spontaneity of the spoken language where the tone given them is important. They are in many cases some of the oldest words in the language and some of the most primitive. They are found primarily in spoken language and rarely in written. Interjections are uninflectable but may vary in form. They often possess a simple phonological structure of either vowel + consonant (**oj!**) or consonant + vowel (**fy!**). They constitute a clause on their own, often coming first in the sentence. They are, therefore, often marked off from other information by a comma:

> **Aj, det gör ont!**   Ow, that hurts!

(b) Interjections represent a very economical use of language. Compare:

> **Aj!**   *with*   **Jag slog mig på tummen med hammaren!**
> Ow!   *with*   I hit my thumb with the hammer!

(c) The distinction is sometimes made between primary and secondary interjections, the latter being words from other parts of speech now employed as interjections: **hjälp!** 'help'; **snälla** 'dear'; **välkommen** 'welcome'. These are often expletives: **Gode Gud!** 'Good God!' or imperatives: **Grattis/Gratulerar!**, 'Congratulations!'

902 Ja, nej, jo, etc.

(a) Uses of **ja/nej**. The Swedish equivalents to 'yes', 'no' represent a reaction to a yes/no question (1036). In each case their correlate is the question.

Ska vi gå på bio ikväll? – Ja (, det ska vi/vi ska gå på bio ikväll).
Shall we go to the cinema tonight? – Yes (, we shall/we'll go to the cinema tonight).

Nej (, det ska vi inte/vi ska inte gå på bio ikväll).
No (, we won't/we won't go to the cinema tonight).

(b) Use of **jo**. If the question is a negative one and the reaction stresses a positive response, **jo** is used:

Tänker du *inte* gå på bio? Jo (, det gör jag faktiskt).
Aren't you thinking of going to the cinema tonight? Yes (, I am actually).

Jo also contradicts a negative statement:

Det kommer *inte* att regna idag. Jo, det tror jag visst det!
It won't rain today. Yes, of course it will!

Note: In Northern Sweden and in Finland-Swedish dialect jo is used generally for ja.

(c) Use of **javisst, jaha, jaså**. A stronger form of agreement with the question is indicated by **javisst** or **jovisst** (see (b) above) (= 'yes', 'certainly'). Agreement with a statement containing new information is often indicated by **jaha** in colloquial Swedish. Surprise at a statement is sometimes indicated by **jaså**, but this can have several shades of meaning depending upon intonation, such as, for example, indifference.

(d) Ja, jo is used in colloquial Swedish to introduce a positive statement or question:

Ja/Jo, det kan vara sant förstås.   Well, that may be true of course.
Ja/Jo, vad ska vi göra nu?   Well, what shall we do now?

In introducing a warning or correction **nåja** is used:

Nåja, nu kan det vara nog pojkar!   Now that's enough boys!

Note: All kinds of other spoken variants with differences of intonation are found, e.g. **jaa, jaja, jajamän(san), joo, jojo, nää, nähä, tja** (= 'well'), **nja** (a hybrid form expressing grudging agreement cf. **nej** + **ja**), **okej**.

903 Reactions in conversation

(a) Some interjections express the reaction of one partner in a conversation to what is said by the other, or are used to attract attention or ask for repetition.

Hörni, små barn! Det är dags att ni går och lägger er.
Now then, kids. It's time for you to go to bed.

Hallå däruppe! Vad fasan gör du?
Hey, you up there! What in heaven's name are you doing?

– Jag talade ju om existentialismen. – *Hursa!*
'I was speaking about Existentialism.' 'What!'

(b) The interjection **va** now has several uses:

(i) The listener asks the speaker to repeat:

– Se upp för helvete, Stefan! – Va?'   'Look out, damn it, Stefan!' 'What?'

(ii) Unstressed **va** at the end of an utterance requests confirmation:

Vi går neråt stan, va?   What do you say to going to town?

Va is fast replacing **eller hur**, but is generally regarded as less cultivated.

(iii) Unstressed **va** at the end of an utterance may denote a command:

Sakta i backarna, va!   Slow down, won't you!

(iv) **Va** is used to mark the introduction of a new topic:

Min gamle lärare, va, han var ju otroligt korkad.
My old teacher, you know, he was unbelievably dense.

904 Expressions of feeling, exclamations

Interjections often represent a spontaneous reaction to a situation, such as:

Pain, discomfort: **aj, o, å**

Aj, vad det gör ont!   Ow, that hurts!

Surprise, delight: **åh, oj, ojoj, ojdå, hoppsan, nämen, va**

Oj, vad vackert!   Oh, how beautiful!
Hoppsan! Eva har fallit i bassängen. Whoops! Eva has fallen in the pool.

Relief: **gudskelov**

Han klarade sig oskadd, gudskelov!   He escaped unhurt, thank goodness.

Disgust or disapproval: **usch, fy**

> **Usch, vad hemskt!**   Ugh, how horrible!
> **Fy dej!**   Shame on you!
> (NB Object form of pronoun)

Annoyance or discomfort: **ack, puh**

> **Puh, vad det var varmt idag!**   Phew, it's hot today!

Disparagement: **asch, äsch, bah**

Disagreement: **pytt(san)**

Joy: **hurra, bravo**

Doubt: **hm, äh**

Religious feeling: **halleluja, amen**

905 Commands

These often merge with imperatives (see 537), and may be classified according to the person(s) to whom they are directed:

- To animals: **kusch, hut** [to dogs] (lie) down!; **fot** [to dogs] heel!; **ptro** [to horses] whoah!
- To children: **sch** shh!; **hyssj** hush.
- To soldiers: **halt** Halt; **giv akt** Attention!; **lediga** (stand) at ease; **marsch** march!

Notice also: **pst!** as in English.

Many of these derive from other word classes: **varsågod, hjälp, förlåt.**

906 Imitations

These interjections are onomatopoetic, i.e. they imitate sounds of different kinds:

(a) Sounds made by animals and humans:

vov(vov)	(dog)	**gnägg**	(horse)
miau	(cat)	**kuckeliku**	(cockerel)
muu	(cow)	**krax**	(crow)

bää	(sheep)	**kvitt**	(bird)
nöff	(pig)	**pip**	(bird)
surr	(bee)		
tralala	(singer)		

(b) Sounds made by man-made objects: **pang** bang; **tick-tack** tick tock; **bing-bång** ding-dong; **klang** boing; **krasch** crash; **dunk** thud.

(c) Other sounds: **plask** splash; **pladask** flop.

(d) Verbs are often formed from interjections of this type:

> **prassla** rustle; **spraka** crackle; **knarra** creak; **knaka** creak; **susa** sigh; **vina** whine; **klucka** gurgle; **skvalpa** splash, slop; **jama** miaouw, mew; **gnägga** whinny; **bräka** bleat; **gala** crow [of rooster etc.]; **kvittra** chirp, twitter; **pipa** cheep, squeak, whistle.

(e) Nouns may often be formed from interjections of this type:

> **ett plask** a splash; **en krasch** a crash.

907 Polite expressions

(a) On meeting and parting:

> **hej** hello; **hejsan** hi there; **goddag** good morning, how do you do?; **tjänare**, hi; **välkommen** (pl. **välkomna**) welcome; **adjö** goodbye; **farväl** farewell; **hej då** 'bye; **hej, hej** (in response to **hej då**).

(b) At mealtimes:

> **skål** cheers; **smaklig måltid** bon appétit, enjoy your meal.

(c) Seasonal greetings:

> **Gott Nytt År** Happy New Year; **Glad Påsk** Happy Easter.

(d) Thanks and apologies:

> **förlåt** sorry; **ursäkta** pardon me; **för all del** don't mention it; **tack** thank you; **tack för maten** thank you for the meal; **tack för sist** thank you for the last time [a polite Swedish phrase used when meeting someone again after having previously been entertained by them].

(e) Others:

grattis (gratulerar) congratulations; **grattis på födelsedagen** Happy Birthday!; **prosit** bless you!; **varsågod** here you are; **hursa?** what did you say?; **hallå** hey there! (see also 903).

(f) Please:

Swedish has no word corresponding exactly to English 'please'. A number of constructions apply in different circumstances:

Varsågod ta plats!	Please take a seat.	[Formal]
Vänligen rök inte!	Please do not smoke.	[Formal]
Var snäll/god och hjälp mig!	Please give me a hand.	[Informal]
Snälla, stäng av teven!	Please turn off the TV.	[Informal]

908 Expletives

(a) Most swearwords and many coarse exclamations are interjections. The following list is not exhaustive:

förbannat; fy katten; Gode Gud; (dra åt) helvete; kors; fan; fasen; himmel; jävlar; jävlaranamma; skit; satan.

(b) In order not to offend innocent ears Swedes employ a variety of milder euphemisms, some based on the above expletives:

förbaskat; fy farao; jesses; helsicke; dra åt Hälsingland; sjutton; jäklar; jääärnspikar; fasingen; fasicken; fanders.

10 SENTENCE STRUCTURE AND WORD ORDER

A   **SENTENCE ELEMENTS**
1001   Word classes and sentence elements
1002   Subject
1003   **Det** as impersonal and formal (place-holder) subject
1004   Finite and non-finite verb
1005   Direct and indirect object
1006   Complement
1007   Adverbial
1008   The order of sentence elements

B   **PHRASES**
1009   Introduction
1010   The noun phrase
1011   The verb phrase
1012   The adjective phrase
1013   The adverb phrase
1014   The prepositional phrase

C   **MAIN CLAUSE WORD ORDER – BASIC POSITIONS**
1015   Main clause and subordinate clause
1016   FV1, FV2 and the position of the subject
1017   Sentence types
1018   Main clause positions

D   **SUBORDINATE CLAUSE WORD ORDER – BASIC POSITIONS**
1019   Subordinate clause positions
1020   Differences between main clause and subordinate clause positions

E   **ORDER WITHIN POSITIONS**
1021   Order of non-finite verbs and verb particles
1022   Order of objects and complements
1023   Order of clausal adverbials
1024   Order of other adverbials and the passive agent
1025   Order within positions – summary

F   **MAIN CLAUSE TRANSFORMATIONS**
1026   The base clause
1027   Topicalisation
1028   The weight principle

1029   Adverbial shift
1030   'Light' elements
1031   Negation
1032   Passive transformation
1033   Existential sentences and the place-holder
1034   Extra positions
1035   Link position
1036   Questions

G   SUBORDINATE CLAUSES
1037   Form of the subordinate clause
1038   Function of the subordinate clause
1039   Position of the subordinate clause in the sentence
1040   Clauses with no indicator of subordination
1041   Main clause word order in **att**-clauses
1042   Conditional clauses
1043   Independent clauses

H   EMPHASIS
1044   Emphasis and positions
1045   Fronting
1046   Raising
1047   Duplication
1048   Cleft sentence

J   ELLIPSIS
1049   Introduction
1050   Non-finite clauses
1051   Verb omission and subject omission
1052   Apposition and the predicative attribute
1053   Main and subordinate clause word order, the extended scheme: summary

A   SENTENCE ELEMENTS

1001   Word classes and sentence elements

Previous chapters of this book have been concerned with word classes, that is with classification according to the form or meaning of words. In this chapter the functions of words and word groups in the sentence, i.e. sentence elements, are examined. A comparison of the two viewpoints can be made from the following analysis:

Du	har	inte	tvättat	bilen	idag.	
You	have	not	washed	the car	today.	
pronoun	*verb*	*adverb*	*verb*	*noun*	*adverb*	*Word class*
subject	*verb*	*adverbial*	*verb*	*object*	*adverbial*	*Sentence element*

In section A the different sentence elements or building blocks are each examined in some detail, whilst in 1008 these are located in a scheme showing their relative order in the sentence. Section B examines phrases built around each of a number of word classes, and shows how these phrases form sentence elements. The sentence scheme, with its seven positions, is explained for the main clause in section C, for the subordinate clause in section D. The seven positions are analysed in greater depth in section E, whilst possible movement of elements within positions (transformations) and possible additional positions are dealt with in section F.

1002   Subject

(a) In a Swedish clause, as in English, the subject is usually explicit. The form of the subject varies considerably. It may be:

A noun phrase:

> **Regnet föll i timmar.**   The rain fell for hours.
> **Sven åkte skidor.**   Sven went ski-ing.
>
> **Den lilla flickan med rött hår sjöng.**   The little girl with red hair sang.

A pronoun:

> **De sjöng Luciasången.**   They sang the Lucia song.

An adjective:

> **Blått är vackert.**   Blue is beautiful.

An infinitive phrase:

> **Att ljuga är ju fult.**   It is bad to lie.

A subordinate clause:

Att så många går arbetslösa är en stor skandal.
That so many people are out of work is a great scandal.

(b) The subject (S) is usually placed next to the finite verb (FV), and its position relative to the verb often helps to indicate sentence type:

Åke vann.
S – FV = Statement   Åke won.

Vann Åke?
FV – S = Question   Did Åke win?

But notice also that Swedish has inverted statements:

I fjol vann Åke två gånger.   Last year Åke won twice.
FV – S = Statement

Imperative clauses often have no subject:

Gå härifrån!   Get out of here!
Var försiktig!   Be careful!

1003   Det as impersonal and formal (place-holder) subject

(a) As a subject in many descriptions of weather and some other constructions, **det** ('it') lacks any real meaning. Its function is by means of its position to indicate sentence type, i.e. statement:

Det regnar/snöar/haglar.   It's raining/snowing/hailing.
Det blir mörkt snart.   It will be dark soon.
Det är kallt härinne.   It's cold in here.
Det är bullersamt.   It's noisy.

Det used in this way is also known as the *impersonal subject*.

(b) When the subject of a sentence is postponed, i.e. moved to the right in the sentence, an anticipatory **det** ('there', 'it') must be inserted. This additional subject is known as the *formal subject* (FS) or place-holder subject, and the postponed subject is known as the *real subject* (RS):

Det sitter två patienter i väntrummet.
FS   RS
There are two patients sitting in the waiting room.

Compare:

> *Två patienter* sitter i väntrummet.
> S

This kind of construction is known in English as an *existential sentence* (see 1033) as it is found with the verb 'to be', thus expressing existence. Its use in Swedish is less restricted in that many different intransitive verbs are used. The real subject may be of two kinds:

Type 1
Real subject = Indefinite noun phrase   Formal subject = 'there'
> *Det* ligger *inga brev* på ditt bord.
> FS   RS
> There are no letters on your desk.

Type 2
Real subject = Infinitive phrase   Formal subject = 'it'

> *Det* är intressant *att resa utomlands.*
> FS   RS
> It's interesting to travel abroad.

Type 1 is used to avoid beginning a sentence with an indefinite noun phrase, i.e. a new idea. In Type 2 **det** is used to replace a postponed 'heavy' (i.e. long or stressed) subject (see 1033). Compare: *Att resa utomlands* är **intressant.**

1004 Finite and non-finite verb

(a) A Swedish clause usually contains a finite verb, i.e. a verb showing tense, mood or voice. Finite forms include:

Present tense: **Han *kör* långsamt.**
                          He drives slowly.

Past tense: **Han *körde* långsamt.**
                          He drove slowly.

Imperative: ***Kör* långsamt!**
                          Drive slowly!

Present and past passive: **Bilen *körs/kördes* långsamt.**
                          The car is/was driven slowly.

Subjunctive: **Det *vore* kul att kunna köra.**
                      It would be fun to be able to drive.

(b) There may be more than one finite verb in the sentence:

Barnen ligger och sover.	The children are (lying) asleep.
Pappa sitter och läser.	Dad is (sitting) reading.
Gå ut och tvätta bilen!	Go out and wash the car.

With more than one finite verb the subject is placed either immediately *before* or immediately *after* the first verb:

Barnen ligger och sover.	The children are asleep.
Ligger barnen och sover?	Are the children asleep?

(c) If there are both finite and non-finite verbs in the clause, the finite verb is often an auxiliary verb and comes first in the chain. The finite verb may be a temporal auxiliary, indicating tense:

De *har/hade* rest.	They have/had left.
Han *blev* inkallad.	He was called up.

The finite verb may be a modal auxiliary:

De *skulle* resa.	They were going to leave.
Han *lär* kunna förstå tio språk.	He is said to understand ten languages.

(d) Non-finite verbs forms usually occur together with a finite verb. (For one exception, the omission of **har/hade** in the subordinate clause, see 1051, 523(b).)

Non-finite forms include:

Infinitive:	**Jag måste *springa*.**	I have to run.
	Jag tycker om *att sjunga*.	I like singing.
Supine:	**De har *sprungit* bort.**	They've run away.
Present participle:	**De kom *springande*.**	They came running.
Past participle:	**Barnen är *bortsprungna*.**	The children have run off.

(e) Several infinitives may occur together:

Han säger sig inte *kunna börja skriva* på uppsatsen ännu.
He says that he is not able to begin writing the essay yet.

(f) In some cases after a modal auxiliary both an infinitive and a supine may be found:

Han borde *ha tänkt* på det.   He should have thought of that.
Han borde *kunnat tänka* på det.   He should have been able to think of that.

Note: The presence of two supines is, however, a colloquialism:

*Han hade kunnat gjort det.   He would have been able to do it.

In written Swedish this is: **Han hade *kunnat göra* det.**

1005   Direct and indirect object

(a) Direct objects are found with transitive verbs (see 540):

Farfar byggde *stugan* själv.   Grandpa built the cottage himself.
Någon har stulit *hans cykel*.   Someone has stolen his bike.

(b) Both direct and indirect objects are found with ditransitive verbs (see 540). The *direct object* (DO) is usually an inanimate object affected by the action of the verb, while the *indirect object* (IO) is an animate being that is the recipient of the action:

De skickade *mormor en vacker julklapp*.
         IO   DO
They sent grandma a beautiful Christmas present.

As in English, the Swedish indirect object precedes the direct object unless the indirect object has a preposition. Compare:

Jag lånade *studenten min bok*.   I lent the student my book.
        IO   DO

Jag lånade *min bok till studenten*.
        DO   IO

(c) The prepositional object consists of a preposition + noun phrase:

Jag bjöd honom *på en kopp te*.   I invited him to a cup of tea.
           Prep. Obj.

(d) The object usually comes directly after the non-finite verb:

Jag har läst *boken*.   I have read the book.

It may, however, begin the sentence:

> ***Den boken** har jag inte läst.*   I haven't read that book.

Object clauses (see 1039(a)) generally come at the end of the sentence:

> **Han har inte frågat idag *om vi vill komma.***
> He hasn't asked today whether we want to come.

For the position of unstressed object pronouns and the reflexive object pronoun see 1030.

(e) The form of the object varies. It may be:

A noun phrase:
> **De köpte *det gamla huset.***
> They bought the old house.

> **Olle träffade *flickan* igår.**
> Olle met the girl yesterday.

A pronoun:
> **Olle träffade *henne* då.**
> Olle met her then.

An infinitive phrase:
> **De fortsatte *att skriva.***
> They continued writing.

> **Hon började *sjunga.***
> She began singing.

A phrase in direct speech:
> **Han sa: *'Eva är sjuk'.***
> He said, 'Eva is sick.'

A subordinate clause:
> **Hon frågade *om vi ville komma.***
> She asked whether we wanted to come.

> **Jag vet *att han är dum.***
> I know he is stupid.

1006 Complement

(a) The predicative complement is usually found in the same position as the object. It is found with a copular verb. Copular verbs fulfil two main functions:

1   They describe a state: **vara** be; **heta** be called; **verka** seem; **tyckas** seem; **se . . . ut** look (like).

Det är *vår*. Han är *gammal*.   It is spring. He is old.

2   They result in a change: **bli** be; become; **utse . . . till** appoint to ; **göra . . . till** make into.

Det blir *vår*. Han blir *gammal*.   It will be spring. He is growing old.

Other intransitive verbs may also be used as copular verbs, e.g. **gå, stå, sitta, ligga**:

De gick sorgsna bort.   They went away despondent.
Skogen stod grön.   The forest stood green.
Snön låg djup.   The snow lay deep.
Vi satt tysta.   We sat in silence.

Passives are also used as copular verbs:

Hjalmar kallades Frida av sina skolkamrater.
Hjalmar was called Frida by his fellow pupils.

(b) Complements are of three kinds and agree in gender and number with either subject or object:

Subject complement:
   Flickan är *ung*.   The girl is young.
   Huset är *gammalt*.   The house is old.
   Väggarna är *vita*.   The walls are white.
   Hon är *professor*.   She is a professor.
   De är *sjuksköterskor*.   They are nurses.

Object complement:
   De utsåg Carlsson till *ordförande*.   They elected Carlsson as chairman.
   Det gjorde dem *ledsna*.   It made them sad.
   De har målat huset *rött*.   They have painted the house red.

Free complement:
   ***Trött och nervös* gick hon på semester.**
   Tired and nervous she went on holiday.

   Hon gick *trött och nervös* på semester.

(c) Complements may be:

A noun phrase:
   Bilen var en *skrothög*.   The car was a heap.
   Vem är *det*? Det är *han*.   Who is it? It's him.

An adjective phrase:
    Bilen var *splitterny*.   The car was brand new.

A subordinate clause:
    Det är *vad jag sa*.   That's what I said.
    Ett resultat blir *att priserna stiger*.   One result is that prices will rise.

1007   Adverbial

(a) Adverbials are of two kinds: *clausal adverbials* (sometimes called 'sentence adverbials') and *other adverbials* (sometimes called 'content adverbials').

Clausal adverbials usually modify the sense of the clause as a whole:

    Vi brukar *inte* åka båt till Sverige på sommaren.
    We don't usually go by boat to Sweden in the summer.

Other adverbials generally answer the questions: how? where? when? why?:

Vi brukar inte åka båt	*till Sverige*	*på sommaren.*
	[where?]	[when?]

(b) Clausal adverbials are usually adverbs:

    Är han *egentligen* så intelligent som han tror?
    Is he really as intelligent as he believes?

    Följer hon *kanske* med på bio ikväll?
    Is she maybe coming to the cinema tonight?

(c) Other adverbials are of the following kinds:

Adverb phrase:	**Han arbetar *fort*.** He works quickly.
Prepositional phrase:	**Han arbetar *i verkstan*.** He works in the workshop.
Noun phrase:	**Han arbetar *hela kvällen*.** He works all evening.
Subordinate clause:	**Han arbetar *när han kan*.** He works when he can.

> **Han arbetar *om han får betalt.***
> He works if he gets paid.

Adjective phrase: **Rädd och hungrig bröt han sig in i stugan.**
Afraid and hungry he broke into the cottage.

(d) Clausal adverbials are usually classified into the following types:

Modal adverbs: **Han är *tyvärr* dum.**
He is, alas, stupid.

Pronominal adverbs: **Nu går vi *dit.***
Now we're going there.

Conjunctional adverbs: **Jan är student. Han reser *alltså* billigt.**
Jan is a student. That's why he travels cheaply.

Prepositional phrases: **Han är *trots allt* bäst.**
He is nevertheless best.

Negations: **De är *inte* här.**
They are not here.

(e) Other adverbials are often classified as:

Manner adverbial: **Han arbetar *långsamt.***
He works slowly.

Place adverbial: **Han arbetar *hemma.***
He works at home.

Time adverbial: **Han arbetar *nästa vecka.***
He works next week.

Condition adverbial: **Han arbetar *om han får tid.***
He works if he has time.

Cause adverbial: **Han arbetar *därför att han måste.***
He works because he must.

Instrument: **Han tvättade bilen *med en svamp.***
He washed the car with a sponge.

Comparison: **Han är pigg *som en mört.***
He is as fit as a fiddle [*lit.* as a roach].

(f) Clausal adverbials come *after* the finite verb (or after the subject in inverted word order) in the main clause, and *before* the finite verb in the subordinate clause:

> **Vi hade *inte* parkerat olagligt.**
> We had not parked illegally.

> **Vi förklarade, att vi *inte* hade parkerat olagligt.**
> We explained that we had not parked illegally.

(g) Other adverbials come either at the end of the sentence or at the beginning of the sentence:

> **Vi hade parkerat *där hela dagen.***   We had parked there all day.
> ***Där* hade vi parkerat *hela dagen.***
> ***Hela dagen* hade vi parkerat *där.***

Note: Occasionally, in more formal Swedish, the other adverbial is moved to the position usually occupied by the clausal adverbial (see 1029):

> **Vi hade *hela dagen* låtit bilen stå där.**   We had allowed the car to stand there all day.

1008 The order of sentence elements

The account of Swedish word order presented here is based largely on an original positional scheme developed by Paul Diderichsen for Danish, a syntactically very similar language. Whilst most systems for learning word order are based on rules indicating the relative location of only two elements, Diderichsen's sentence scheme has the great advantage of being a topographical scheme which maps the clause, indicating the relative positions of all the elements in the clause simultaneously. The names of the positions have been changed in the account that follows in order to adapt more closely to traditional grammatical terminology:

Main clause (MC):

Topic	Finite verb	(Subject)	Clausal adverbial	Non-finite verb	Object/ Complement/ Real subject	Other adverbial
T	FV	S	CA	NFV	O/C	OA
I morse	**hade**	**hon**	**ännu inte**	**packat**	**väskan**	**när vi kom.**

This morning she still hadn't packed her case when we arrived.

Subordinate clause (SC):

Conjunction	Subject	Clausal adverbial	Finite verb	Non-finite verb	Object/ Complement	Other adverbial
conj.	S	CA	FV	NFV	O/C	OA

eftersom	jag	inte	hade	sett	det nya barnet	tidigare.

as I hadn't seen the new baby before

For Topic see 1027. For definitions of clause see 1017 below. This scheme and its significance for word order and sentence construction are examined in detail in the sections that follow.

B PHRASES

1009 Introduction

(a) Phrases consist of a head word (H) alone or have a head word with optional determiners coming before or after the head (prepositioned or postpositioned). There are specific rules for the five different kinds of phrase (see 1010ff.):

två *lärare* från Hull
H (Noun phrase)
two teachers from Hull

ganska *nöjd* med resultatet
H (Adjective phrase)
fairly pleased with the work

nästan *skrika* åt honom
H (Verb phrase)
almost shout at him

mycket *fort*
H (Adverb phrase)
very quickly

ett stycke *innanför staketet*
H (Prepositional phrase)
a little way inside the fence

(b) Determiners may be:

- Functional, i.e. express quality or degree: *några* flickor 'some girls'. These usually come before the head.

- Descriptive, i.e. modify the headword: **flickorna** *från Finland* 'the girls from Finland'; **slutet** *på boken* 'the end of the book'. These mostly come after the head, but occasionally come before the head: *milt* grön 'pale green'; *hånfullt* leende 'smiling mockingly'.

(c) Phrases are of two kinds:

- *Endocentric* phrases have a head word plus possible determiners and can have the same function as the head alone. These include the noun phrase (with a noun or pronoun as head), adjective phrase (with an adjective or participle as head) and adverb phrase (with adverb as head). (The head word is in italics.)

Den lilla *flickan* är söt.	The little girl is pretty.
***Hon* är intelligent också.**	She is also intelligent.
ganska *dåligt*	fairly bad
just *nu*	just now

- *Exocentric* phrases have a combination of words that cannot be dissolved without the syntactic function being altered. These include the prepositional phrase (with preposition + noun phrase as head) and the verb phrase (with the verb as head). (The head word is in italics.)

pojken *med den vita mössan*	the boy with the white cap
Han lär kunna *spela* fiol.	She is said to be able to play the violin.

(d) Characteristic of the clause (1021ff.) is a combination of phrases, with the verb phrase and noun phrase forming a *nexus* (the relationship of subject + finite verb). The only exception is the command using the imperative where there is no explicit subject: **Kom! Sluta! Sjung ut!** The order of elements in the nexus is important in determining which type of clause we are dealing with (cf. **Det regnar** 'It's raining', with **Regnar det?** 'Is it raining?'). The nexus is the core of the clause.

All of the five types of phrase dealt with below can, as we shall see later, form an element in the clause.

1010   The noun phrase

(a) A noun phrase (NP) comprises a noun or pronoun as head word with possible determiners. The determiners may be prepositioned or postpositioned. If the noun phrase is a pronoun the determiners can only be postpositioned. (The head word is in italics.)

nyfikna *barn*	inquisitive children
***folk* som pratar för mycket**	people who talk too much
alla *människor*	all people
***individer* från medelklassen**	individuals from the middle classes
min *cykel*	my cycle
***perioden* innan sekelskiftet**	the period before the turn of the century

i Kalles *plånbok*	in Kalle's wallet
förslaget att ge upp	the proposal to give up
första *dagen*	the first day
en lika dum *fråga* som den han ställde	a question as silly as the one he asked
denna *fråga*	this question
hon som skrattade	she who laughed

(b) The noun phrase is the building block used in many different constructions. The syntactical functions of the noun phrase are as:

- Subject (see 1002)
  Den nya bilen har luftkonditionering.
  The new car has air conditioning

- Direct (accusative) object (see 1005)
  Ylva köpte *Svenska Akademiens grammatik* åt Phil.
  Ylva bought the Swedish Academy grammar for Phil.

- Indirect (dative) object (see 1005)
  Han gav *sin fru* pärlor på bröllopsdagen.
  He gave his wife pearls for their anniversary.

- Subject complement (see 1006)
  Hon är *den bästa lärare jag har haft*.
  She is the best teacher I have had.

- Object complement (see 1006)
  Alla kallar henne *Charlie*.
  Everyone calls her Charlie.

- Adverbial (see 1007)
  Han pluggade *hela natten*.
  He was studying all night.

- Determiner
  Den där cykeln skulle jag vilja ha.
  I would like that bicycle.

- Quality attribute
  Vi köpte *ett kilo* kaffe.
  We bought a kilo of coffee.

- Epithet
Danskarna gillar *drottning* **Margrethe.**
Danes like Queen Margrethe.

- apposition
Charlie, *den nya institutionschefen,* **är enormt flitig.**
Charlie, the new head of department, is very hard working.

- governed by a preposition
Uppsatsen ligger *i det bruna kuvertet.*
The essay is in the brown envelope.

(c) Prepositioned determiners and attributes

Determiners						*Adjective*	*Head*
Totality	Demon-strative	Possession	Quantity	Selection	Comparison	*attribute*	*word*
			en				släkting
			två			unga	syskon
		Olles	många			konstiga	släktingar
alla	dessa	mina				vackra	saker
	denna			sista			dag
inga					sådana	tråkiga	filmer

Translations: a relative; two young siblings; Olle's many strange relatives; all these, my beautiful things; this last day; no such boring films

Adjective attributes (see 208):

> **en glad man** a happy man; **ett stormande hav** a stormy sea; **en avbruten gren** a broken branch; **en röd liten stuga** a little red cottage; **vackra svenska flickor** beautiful Swedish girls.

> **den från daghemmet bortsprungne pojken**
> the boy who had run away from the day centre

These come before the head.

Instead of the adjective attribute we may find:

Genitive attribute: *Eriks* **bil** Erik's car; *gårdens* **ägare** the owner of the farm.

Measurement attribute: *ett kilo* **mjöl** a kilo of flour; *en hel meter* **tyg** a whole metre of cloth.

Epithet: *farbror* **Olof** Uncle Olof; *diktaren* **Shakespeare** the writer Shakespeare.

(d) Postpositioned attributes

(i) General postpositioned attributes

• Adverb	**resan** *hem* the journey home
• Prepositional phrase	**mannen** *från Mallorca* the man from Majorca
• Pronoun	**rånaren** *själv* the robber himself
• Relative clause	**flickan** *som jag känner* the girl that I know
• Att-clause	**den tanken** *att man skulle dö* the idea that one would die
• Indirect question clause	**frågan** *hur det skulle gå* the question of how it would go
• Comparative clause	**en sådan fin bil** *som du har* a fine car like you have
• Conjunctional sub clause	**tiden** *innan du kom* the time before you arrived
• Infinitive phrase	**löftet** *att återvända* the promise to return
• comparative phrase	**en lika stor lön** *som din* a salary as big as yours

(ii) Appositions

These are reduced clauses where the head of the apposition acts as a complement.

Olle /som var/, min skolkamrat under många år
Olle /who was/ my school friend for many years

Anna /som är/, vår lärare, har blivit sjuk.
Anna /who is/ our teacher, has fallen ill.

Satsdelarna, t.ex. subjekt och objekt, är problematiska.
The sentence elements, e.g. subject and object, are problematical.

(iii) Predicative attribute

en krigsman /, som var/ rustad till tänderna
a warrior, /who was/ armed to the teeth

(iv) **Med**-phrase attribute

pojken med händerna i fickorna (= pojken som har...)
the boy with his hands in his pockets (= the boy who has...)

(e) Definite and indefinite noun phrases (see 208, 221)

Definite noun phrases refer back to a familiar (given) idea. Indefinite noun phrases introduce a new idea.

> **Jag träffade *en ljus och en mörk flicka. Den ljusa flickan* var sötast.**
>   *indefinite NP*   ← *definite NP*
> I met a fair and a dark girl.   The fair girl was prettiest.

> **Nu ska jag visa dig *en trevlig sak.***
>   *indefinite NP*
> Now I will show you something nice.

Only indefinite noun phrases may form the real subject (i.e. when the subject is postponed, see 1003):

> **Det inträffade en olycka på motorvägen.**
> An accident happened on the motorway.

Definite noun phrases allow a complement that agrees (see 208):

> **Äpplena är goda.**   The apples are good.

Only definite noun phrases may be duplicated (see 1047):

> **Cykeln, den har blivit stulen.**   The cycle, it has been stolen.

(i) Indefinite noun phrase (see 208):

> **Köpte du smör?**   Did you buy butter?
> **Hästar är trevliga djur.**   Horses are lovely animals.

The indefinite noun phrase consists of a naked noun, or one preceded by:

- an indefinite article   *en* **bil** a car
- adjective attribute(s)   *billigt danskt* **smör** cheap Danish butter
- a measurement attribute   *en liter* **vin** a litre of wine
- a combination of these   *många vackra* **damer** many beautiful ladies

(ii) Definite noun phrase

The definite NP consists of a proper noun (name) or a noun with end article.

> ***Nilsson* har blivit sjuk.**   Nilsson has fallen ill.

Hittade du *smöret?*	Did you find the butter?

The noun in the definite noun phrase may be in the naked form, or be preceded by a definite attribute expressing totality, possession, selection, or by a demonstrative:

alla **människor** all people; *min* **cykel** my bicycle; **i** *Kalles* **plånbok** in Kalle's wallet; *första* **dagen** the first day; *denna* **fråga** this question.

1011 The verb phrase

(a) The verb phrase may contain just one finite verb or a combination of several verbs (see 501). As we are aware from word order rules, the verb phrase can therefore be discontinuous, that is it may bracket other words (**I förrgår** *blev* **han** *utsparkad* 'Yesterday he was thrown out')

(b) A narrow view of the verb phrase would show the following structures:

- finite verb (FV) (see 1004)

  Han skriver brev.
  He is writing letters.

- FV + one or more non-finite verbs (NFV) (see 523ff., 532)

  Han har skrivit flera brev
  He has written several letters.

  Han måste kunna skriva ett brev till sin mor.
  He must be able to write a letter to his mother.

- FV (+ NFV) + verb particle – particle verbs (see 559)

  Han har skrivit ut alla detaljerna för hand.
  He has written out all the details by hand.

- FV (+ NFV) + preposition – prepositional verbs

  Han hade letat efter boken.
  He had looked for the book.

- FV (+ NFV) + reflexive pronoun (see 541)

  Han har inte rakat sig på flera dagar.
  He hasn't shaved for several days.

(c) Verb phrases consisting of a finite (+ non-finite) verb plus preposition are of two kinds:

1   Those with an unstressed preposition, prepositional verbs:

        Vad 'tycker du om Sverige?   What do you think of Sweden?

2   Those with a stressed preposition (or adverb), particle verbs:

        Tycker du verkligen 'om Sverige?   Do you really like Sweden?

Some further examples:

Unstressed preposition		*Stressed preposition*
av	**njuta av** enjoy	**hålla av** be fond of
efter	**fråga efter** enquire about	**se efter** look after
(i)från	**avstå ifrån** abstain from	**såga ifrån** speak out
för	**intressera sig för** be interested in	**ta för sig** help oneself
i	**dö i** die from	**hålla i något** keep hold of something
med	**syssla med** busy oneself with	**hålla med** agree with
(e)mot	**reagera mot** react to	**ta emot** receive
om	**tycka synd om** feel sorry for	**måla om** repaint
på	**hälsa på** greet	**hälsa på** visit
till	**duga till** be of use	**hjälpa till** lend a hand
under	**lägga något under** put something underneath	**stryka under** underline
över	**klaga över** complain about	**se över** inspect

(d) A few verbs take both a reflexive pronoun and particle:

        Vi bryr oss inte om det.   We don't bother about it.

(e) Copular verbs (e.g. **vara**, **bli**) (see 1006(a)) are devoid of real meaning and take an obligatory subject complement:

        De är sjuka.   They are ill.
        Vi är studenter.   We are students.
        Han blev president.   He became President.

(f) Transitive verbs have a direct object, intransitive verbs have no object and ditransitive verbs have both an indirect and direct object (see 539).

Jag slog honom.	I hit him.
Vi sov i tio timmar.	We slept for ten hours.
Han gav henne ett halsband.	He gave her a necklace.

(g) We also use the terms *main verb* (i.e. head in the verb phrase) and *auxiliary verbs*, which are themselves of two kinds:

- Temporal auxiliary **(vara, ha,** see 523ff):
  Han har redan gått.   He has already left.

- Modal auxiliary **(ska, vill, måste, bör,** etc., see 535):
  Vi måste tyvärr gå nu.   We have to leave now, unfortunately.

(h) Verbs have tense, aspect, mood and voice:

(i) Tenses include infinitive, present, past, perfect, pluperfect and future (see Chapter 5B).

(ii) Aspect expresses the viewpoint from which the user views the action of the verb and is of three kinds:

- *Perfective* indicates that the action is completed:
  Plötsligt började det regna.   Suddenly it began to rain.

Notice that the adverbial of time often indicates completion:
  Lars köpte en ny bil igår.   Lars bought a new car yesterday.

- *Imperfective* indicates that the action is not yet completed:
  Jan har varit borta i tre veckor (och är fortfarande borta).
  Jan has been away for three weeks (and is still away).

- *Progressive* indicates an action that is continuing:
  Han håller på att laga bilen.   He is mending the car.

This can also be shown by 'pseudo-coordination' with **och**:

  Studenterna stod och väntade.   The students stood waiting.

(iii) Mood is the relationship between the speaker and listener (see 534–538), i.e. how the speaker wishes his utterance to be regarded. This can be expressed in many ways, e.g. word order, clause structure, use of adverbials, use of modal verbs or use of inflexion.

Statements and questions often use a simple verb (or modal auxiliary plus main verb):

Staden har 250 000 invånare.   The town has 250,000 inhabitants.
Har alla studenterna kommit?   Have all the students come?

Commands often use an imperative:

Sitt ner!   Sit down!
Håll tyst!   Keep quiet!

Hypothetical cases may use a simple verb in the past subjunctive:

Om jag vore miljonär skulle jag köpa ett franskt vinslott.
If I were a millionaire I would buy a wine chateau in France.

Wishes can be expressed by a simple verb in the present subjunctive or the verb **må** (535(b)(vii)):

Gud bevare oss!   God protect us!
Må det gå dig väl!   May you fare well!

Uncertainty as to the reliability of a statement is expressed using **lär** (535(b)(x)):

Han lär inte klara sin examen.   They say he won't get his degree.

Possibility or ability is expressed using **kunna** plus infinitive (535(b)(ii)):

Han kan springa fort.   He can run fast.
Det kan bli sol imorgon.   It can be sunny tomorrow.

(iv) Voice is the distinction between active and passive (see 547ff.). In the active voice the grammatical subject and the agent (person or thing causing the action) are the same (notice the direction of the action shown by the arrows):

En gammal man körde taxin.   An old man was driving the taxi.
     →

In the passive voice the subject is the patient (person or thing acted upon by the verb) and there may be an agent preceded by **av**:

Taxin kördes av en gammal man.   The taxi was being driven by an old
     ←   man.

Agentless passives are frequent:

Taxin kördes fort.   The taxi was being driven fast.
     ←

(j) But we should perhaps also include objects and complements in the verb phrase, which then looks like this:

Head /Verb	Particle	Indirect object Bound SC Real subject	Direct object Bound OC Nexus infinitive	Bound adverbial	Free adverbial
sätta	upp		en tavla	i hallen	i kväll
beröva		barnen	deras hopp		
bli			trött		
göra		honom	glad		
höra		flickorna	komma		
rakade			sig		

Translations: hang up a picture in the hall tonight; deprive the children of their hope; get tired; make him happy; hear the girls arrive; shaved (himself)

1012 The adjective phrase

(a) The adjective phrase consists of an adjective or participle alone as head or with possible adverbial determiners (see 612). These determiners are primarily adverbs.

> **ganska lång** rather long; **två meter lång** two metres long; **komiskt högtidlig** comically formal; **tidvis mycket effektiv** occasionally very efficient

In a few cases adjectives have postpositioned determiners: **gott nog** 'good enough'

(b) Adjective phrases function as:

- Predicative complement (i.e. subject or object complement) (see 308):
  De är väldigt lyckliga. They are extremely happy.
  Han gör henne mycket lycklig. He makes her very happy.

- Prepositioned adjective attribute to the head in a noun phrase (see 308):
  en inte särskilt rolig middag a not very interesting dinner
  ett alltför långsamt tempo too slow a tempo
  en för rockkonserter olämplig lokal an unsuitable venue for a rock concert

1013 The adverb phrase

(a) The adverb phrase often consists of an adverb alone, though it may have adverbial determiners. Only adverb determiners may be prepositioned (see 612):

mycket långsamt	very slowly
helt tillfälligt	completely by chance

Prepositional phrases used adverbially may be postpositioned:

ute på landet	out in the country
ut genom fönstret	out through the window

(b) The adverb phrase functions primarily:

- As clausal adverbial (see 1007):
  Han betalar aldrig. — He never pays.
  De tycker egentligen inte om det. — They don't really like it.

- As determiner to a nominal:
  Inte bara vi kommer att drabbas. — Not only we will be affected.

- As sentence adverbial (see 1007):
  Där bor Roger. — That's where Roger lives.
  Lene sprang snabbt. — Lene ran fast.

- As determiner to an adjective or adverb (see 612):
  Han blev väldigt glad. — He was very happy.
  De skriver kolossalt snabbt. — They write extremely quickly.

- To introduce a subordinate clause
  Vi vaknade när solen kom upp. — We woke when the sun rose.

1014 The prepositional phrase

(a) The prepositional phrase consists of a preposition plus a prepositional complement (see 702). This complement is governed by the preposition and can consist of a noun phrase, an infinitive phrase or a subordinate clause:

Studenten med den vita mössan är min bror.
The student with the white cap is my brother.

Han funderade på att skrika efter hjälp.
He thought of shouting for help.

Han grubblade på hur det skulle vara att bli miljonär.
He thought of what it would be like to become a millionaire.

In some prepositional phrases we can see signs of old case endings: **till sängs** 'to bed'; **till salu** 'for sale'.

(b) The prepositional phrase can function as:

- Postpositioned attribute to a noun phrase (NB The noun phrase is a prepositional complement to a new prepositional phrase):

  bussen från stationen   the bus from the station

- Sentence adverbial (see 1007):
  Vi gick längs ån.   We walked along the river.

- Clausal adverbial (see 1007):
  Utan tvekan är det beklagligt.   It is, without doubt, regrettable.

- Prepositional object (see 1005(b)):
  Han väntade tåligt på sin tur.   He waited for his turn.

- Complement (see 1006):
  Han är på dåligt humör.   He is in a bad mood.

C MAIN CLAUSE WORD ORDER – BASIC POSITIONS

1015   Main clause and subordinate clause

(a) A clause is a sentence or part of a sentence usually including a subject and a finite verb. While a main clause (MC) can occur on its own, a subordinate clause (SC) usually occurs together with a main clause and may be regarded as forming part of that clause. Compare:

Hon får godkänt i sin examen. Det gläder oss.
MC   MC
She will pass her exam. This pleases us.

Att hon får godkänt i sin examen gläder oss.
SC = subject   FV   O
That she will pass her exam pleases us.

Jag vet ännu inte *om jag kan göra det.*
                  SC = object
I don't know yet whether I can do it.

Jag betalar dig *när vi träffas.*
               SC = OA-time
I'll pay you when we meet.

Some subordinate clauses do occur as sentences without a main clause, however (see 1043):

Om jag bara kunde göra det!   If only I could do it!

(b) Many (but not all) subordinate clauses begin with a subordinating conjunction (see 810ff., 1037, 1040):

Jag vet inte *om* han kommer idag.
I don't know whether he's coming today.

Jag tror (*att*) han kommer idag.
I think (that) he's coming today.

Vi tyckte (*att*) det var en vacker sång.
We thought (that) it was a beautiful song.

(c) The main clause may in principle begin with any sentence element (see 1018, 1027) while the subordinate clause usually begins with the subordinating conjunction (if present), followed by the subject (cf. (b)). Notice that inverted word order (verb – subject) is much more common in Swedish than in English:

Main clause

Topic	FV	S	CA	NFV
Imorgon	**måste**	**jag**	–	**arbeta**
Tomorrow I have to work.				

Subordinate clause

Matrix	Conj.	S	CA	FV	NFV	O/C	OA
(Han sa)	**att**	**han**	–	**måste**	**arbeta**	–	**imorgon**
He said that he had to work tomorrow.							

Note: Many Swedish grammars use Diderichsen's original terminology for the positions in the clause, namely **F v n a V N A** for main clause and **k n a v V N A** for subordinate clause where F = Fundament, v, V = verbal, n, N = nominal, and a, A = adverbial, k = conjunction (see 1008).

(d) In subordinate clauses the temporal auxiliary **har/hade** may be omitted in formal written Swedish:

Vi tackar för det varuprov (som) du (har) skickat.
We thank you for the sample of merchandise (that) you have sent.

(e) In main clauses the clausal adverbial is usually placed after the finite verb, whereas in subordinate clauses it comes before the finite verb:

MC: **Han   kan *inte*   dansa.**
       FV   CA
He can't dance.

SC: **Han sa, att han** *inte* **kunde dansa.**
　　　　　　　　CA　　FV
　　He said that he couldn't dance.

For the structure of clauses, see 1018ff.

1016 FV1, FV2 and the position of the subject

Swedish main clauses can be divided into two main types according to the position of the finite verb (FV) in the clause (see 1004): in FV1 clauses the finite verb comes first in the clause, and in FV2 clauses it comes second. Notice, however, that in our word order scheme the finite verb always occupies position 2 in FV1 clauses, and the initial position (Topic, see 1027, 1055) remains unfilled. Put another way, in FV1 clauses the topic = 0 (zero), which is in itself a kind of marker for particular types of clause.

Type	1 Topic	2 FV	3 Subject	4 Clausal adverbial	5 Non-finite verb	6 Object
FV1						
1	–	**Läser**	**du**	–	–	**svenska?**
Can you read Swedish?						
2	–	**Läs**	–	–	–	**dina läxor!**
Do your homework!						
3	–	**Måtte**	**du**	**aldrig**	**ångra**	**ditt beslut!**
May you never regret your decision!						
FV2						
4	**Han**	**läser**	–	–	–	**svenska.**
He reads Swedish.						
5	**Idag**	**läser**	**han**	–	–	**svenska.**
Today he's reading Swedish.						
6	**Varför**	**läser**	**han**	–	–	**svenska?**
Why does he read Swedish?						

From these examples it is clear that FV1/FV2 distinguishes certain sentence types (see 1017): FV1 clauses (T=0) are either yes/no questions (1), commands (2) or optative clauses using **må/måtte** or the subjunctive (3). FV2 clauses are either statements (4, 5) or v-questions ((6), cf. 1036(b)).

It is also clear that, while FV1 clauses often have inverted word order (FV – S), FV2 clauses may have either straight (S – FV) or inverted (FV – S) order. In subordinate clauses (see 1019f.) straight word order (S – FV) is usual.

1017   Sentence types

See 1016 above for a definition of FV1/FV2. The main sentence types in Swedish are as follows:

(a) Statement	FV2 straight:	**Han kommer hem imorgon.** He's coming home tomorrow.
	FV2 inverted:	**Imorgon kommer han hem.** Tomorrow he's coming home.
(b) Question (see 1036)		
(i) Yes/no question	FV1 inverted:	**Kommer han hem imorgon?** Is he coming home tomorrow?
(ii) V-question	FV2 inverted:	**När kommer han hem?** When is he coming home?
(c) Command	FV1 usually no subject (inverted)	**Kom (du) hem nu!** (You) Come home now!
(d) Optative	Usually FV1 inverted	
(i) **Må, måtte:**		**Måtte det gå dig väl!** May everything go well for you!
(ii) Subjunctive:		**Vore jag bara ung igen!** Were I but young again!

1018   Main clause positions

The following table shows different kinds of main clause word order according to the basic scheme.

Topic	Finite verb	(Subject)	Clausal adverbial	Non-finite verb	Object/Complement	Other adverbial
Statement						
1 Han	packar	–	–	–	väskorna.	
2 Han	hade	–	ännu inte	packat	väskorna	imorse.
3 Imorse	hade	han	ännu inte	packat	väskorna.	
4 Väskorna	hade	–	ännu inte	packats	–	imorse.
5 Vi	ger	–	–	–	Olle boken	ikväll.
6 Sedan	blev	de	tyvärr	–	arga.	
7 Det	sitter	–	redan	–	en polis	i vardags-rummet.
8 Det	har	–	redan	kommit	tre poliser.	
9 Det	regnade	–	–	–	–	ständigt i tre dagar.
10 (När vi kom,)	hade	mor	redan	hunnit laga	middag.	
Question						
11 När	brukar	de	–	komma	–	till staden?
12 –	Brukar	de	aldrig	komma	–	till staden?
Command						
13 –	Ring	–	inte	upp	dem	nu!
Optative						
14 –	Måtte	du	aldrig	få ångra	dig!	
15 –	Vore	jag	bara		ung	igen!
Conditional clause with question word order						
16 –	Kommer	du	inte	–	–	imorgon, (så blir jag arg.)

Translations: 1 He is packing the cases. 2 He still hadn't packed the cases this morning. 3 This morning he still hadn't packed the cases. 4 The cases still hadn't been packed this morning. 5 We will give Olle the book this evening. 6 Then alas they got angry. 7 There is already a policeman sitting in the living room. 8 Three policemen have already arrived. 9 It rained constantly for three days. 10 (When we arrived) mother had already had time to make dinner. 11.When do they usually come to town? 12 Don't they usually ever come to town? 13 Don't ring them up now! 14 May you never regret it! 15 If only I were young again! 16 If you don't come tomorrow (I will be angry).

Notes on main clause positions:

(a) Main clause statements and questions always have a finite verb and usually a subject. All other positions may be left vacant. The subject may occupy the topic position (1, 2, 4, 5). The subject may alternatively occupy the position immediately following the finite verb (3, 6, 10–12,14–16). Even with impersonal verbs a subject must be inserted (9). When there is both a formal subject and a real subject the latter is postponed to the object position (7, 8).

(b) The initial (topic) position is always occupied in statements and v-questions (1–11), but is vacant in yes/no questions (12), commands (13) and optatives (14, 15), i.e. in FV1 clauses. Only one sentence element may occupy the topic position at any one time (1–11).

(c) There may be more than one non-finite verb (10, 14, for verb particles see 1021).

(d) There may be more than one clausal adverbial (2, 3, 4).

(e) There may be more than one other adverbial (9).

(f) There may be more than one object or complement (5).

(g) There may be a link position preceding the topic and occupied by a coordinating conjunction (see 1035).

(h) There may be an extra position inserted before the topic position but after any link, or after the other adverbial position or both (see 1034).

D   SUBORDINATE CLAUSE WORD ORDER – BASIC POSITIONS

1019   Subordinate clause positions

The following table shows examples of different kinds of subordinate clause word order.

Matrix	conj.	Subject	Clausal adverbial	Finite verb	Non-finite	O/C	Other adverbial
1 Vi frågade	om	han	ännu inte	(hade)	packat	väskorna.	
2	Eftersom	de	inte	(hade)	sagt visste vi	ett ord,	
							inget.
3 Vi tyckte	(att)	det	inte	var	–	så roligt	längre.
4 Om vi är tysta, och	om	vi	inte	busar,	–	–	får vi se på TV.
5 Hon undrade om		det	inte	fanns	–	mer mat	hemma.
Independent clause 6	Om	du	bara	visste	–	allt!	
7	Att	ni	aldrig	blir	–	trötta!	
8 Kanske	–	chefen	inte	sitter	kvar	–	så länge.

Translations: 1 We asked whether he still hadn't packed the cases. 2 As they hadn't said a word, we didn't know anything. 3 We thought (that) it wasn't fun any longer. 4 If we are quiet and if we do not misbehave we may watch TV. 5 She wondered whether there wasn't more food in the house. 6 If you only knew everything! 7 How come you never get tired! 8 Perhaps the boss will not stay so long.

Notes on subordinate clause positions:

(a) The subject position is always occupied. If there are both a formal and a real subject the latter is postponed to the object position (5).

(b) The finite verb **har, hade** may be omitted when acting as a temporal auxiliary, i.e. when there is a supine (1, 2).

(c) The subordinating conjunction **att** may sometimes be omitted (3) (see 1040).

(d) There is a link position preceding the conjunction, sometimes occupied by a coordinating conjunction (see 1034). (See example 4 above.)

(e) For independent clauses (with subordinate clause word order) see 1043.

(f) There is an extra position inserted after the other adverbial position (see 1034).

1020   Differences between main clause and subordinate clause positions

See also 1015. What follows is a summary of the major differences:

(a) While the main clause begins with any sentence element (the topic), the subordinate clause almost invariably begins with the conjunction and subject (and needs no topic). Occasionally, however (see 1019 example 3 and 1040), the conjunction **att** may be omitted in the subordinate clause. Thus, while main clause word order may either be subject–verb (straight) or verb–subject (inverted), subordinate clause order is usually subject–verb (straight).

(b) In the main clause the clausal adverbial comes immediately after the finite verb. In the subordinate clause the clausal adverbial comes immediately before the finite verb.

(c) The main clause must always have a finite verb, but in the subordinate clause the finite verb **har/hade** may be omitted when there is a supine.

E   ORDER WITHIN POSITIONS

In many sentences there is more than one element in the CA, NFV, O/C and OA positions. In this section the relative order of these elements within positions is examined.

1021 Order of non-finite verbs and verb particles

See also 1004.

(a) In the case of separable compound verbs (555ff.) the separable particle occupies the non-finite verb position. When the separable verb is in the non-finite form both verb and particle occupy this position:

T	FV	S	CA	NFV	O/C	OA
Vi	*ringde*	–	inte	*upp*	honom	**igår.**
We didn't ring him up yesterday.						
Vi	**brukar**	–	inte	*ringa upp*	honom	**på kvällen.**
We don't usually ring him up in the evening.						
Han	**blir**	–	inte	*uppringd*	–	**på kvällen.**
He doesn't get rung up in the evening.						

(b) When there is a different non-finite verb, the particle immediately precedes it:

T	FV	S	CA	NFV	O/C	OA
Han	**ser**	–	inte	*ut att vara*	**en brottsling.**	
He doesn't look like a criminal.						

(See 1053.)

1022   Order of objects and complements

See also 1005f. This paragraph also deals with the position of real subjects (see 1003).

(a) The order of objects is usually as in English, i.e. a prepositionless object precedes an object with a preposition:

Han lånade   *boken*   *till Nils.*
            –prep.   +prep.
He lent the book to Nils.

Vi bad	*honom* IO	*(att) skynda sig.* DO = Infinitive phrase	We asked him to hurry up.

If neither object is preceded by a preposition, then the indirect object precedes the direct object:

Han lånade	*Nils* IO	*boken.* DO	He lent Nils the book.

This is also the case for pronominal objects:

Han lånade	*honom* IO	*den.* DO	He lent him it.

Note: When the object is a subordinate clause, the prepositional object may precede the preposition-less object:

Han sa	*till alla* IO	*att Eva var sjuk.* DO = SC	He told everyone that Eva was ill.

(b) The direct object precedes the object complement:

Partiet omvalde idag	*Olof Olsson till* DO	*partiets ordförande* OC

The Party today re-elected Olof Olsson as party chairman.

(c) The subject complement usually precedes all objects:

Han är värd	*en belöning.*	He is worthy of a reward.
SC	DO	

Note: There are some exceptions in set phrases:

Det är mödan värt.	It is worth the effort.
Han var alltid situationen vuxen.	He was always equal to the occasion.

(d) The real subject in existential sentences precedes the subject complement:

Men det finns	*inte många lägenheter* RS	*outhyrda* i Stockholm. SC

But there aren't many flats unoccupied in Stockholm.

(e) To summarise the relative order of elements within the object/complement position:

Real subject – Subject complement – Indirect object – Direct object – Object complement

---

(f) Reflexive pronouns and unstressed object pronouns are placed in the subject position immediately after the finite verb:

T	FV	S	CA	NFV	O/C	OA

Då   **lärde**   **han** *sig*   **aldrig**   –   **språket.**
Then he never learned the language.

Jag   **gav**   *honom den*   **inte.**
I didn't give him it.

Note: An exception to this is a clause with a complex verb (see 1030).

1023   Order of clausal adverbials

See also 610, 1007.

The order is usually:

1   Short modal adverbs (610(b)): **ju, nog, väl, då**.

2   Short pronominal adverbs (609) or conjunctional adverbs (610(c)): **alltså, därför, ändå, dock**.

3   Longer modal adverbs (610(b)) or prepositional phrases: **antagligen, visserligen, verkligen, egentligen, faktiskt**.

4   Negations: **inte, aldrig**.

The relative order when all of these are present in the sentence is shown by these examples:

	1	2	3	4	
De har	*ju*	*därför*	*faktiskt*	*aldrig*	**rest utomlands.**

They have therefore actually never travelled abroad.

Vi får   *väl*   *ändå*   *trots allt*   *inte*   **ge upp.**
We must nevertheless despite everything not give up.

1024 Order of other adverbials and the passive agent

See also 1007.

(a) The order of other adverbials is rather flexible. Two rules of thumb seem to apply:

Adverbials of manner usually precede those of place and time (manner–place–time = MPT):
Long adverbials usually follow the MPT group.

The order is, therefore, usually:

1   Adverbial expressions of *manner* (607(b)) or *degree*:

 noga carefully; **försiktigt** carefully; **långsamt** slowly; **ordentligt** properly; **i hög grad** to a high degree; **i ringa omfattning** to a very limited extent; etc.

2   Adverbial expressions of *place* (607(c)):

 här here; **där** there; **hemma** at home; **på Öland** on Öland; **i staden** in town; etc.

3   Adverbial expressions of *time* (607(a)):

 igår yesterday; **på förmiddagen** in the morning; **nästa vecka** next week; **år 2010** in 2010; **dagen därpå** on the following day; etc.

4   Long adverbial expressions, such as *cause, condition*, etc.:

 av ett eller annat skäl for one reason or another; **på goda grunder** for good reasons; **om du håller med** if you agree; etc.

Notice the alternatives in the table below (and see 1029):

1 Manner	2 Place	3 Time	4 Other long adverbials
Han reste plötsligt	bort	igår	av någon anledning.

He suddenly left yesterday for some reason.
(Cf. Han reste av någon anledning plötsligt bort igår.)

| Vi träffades av en händelse | i London | förra året. | |

We met by chance in London last year.
(Cf. Vi träffades av en händelse förra året i London.)

| Han kom – | hem till mig | flera gånger | för att han var ensam. |

He came back to my place several times because he was lonely.

| Han är född – | i Birmingham | år 1944 | under en tysk bombräd. |

He was born in Birmingham in 1944 during a German bombing raid.
(Cf. Han är född under en tysk bombräd år 1944 i Birmingham.)

The alternative order here is the result of a desire to emphasise the final element in the sentence.

(b) Notice that the passive agent (see 547) usually comes immediately before the other adverbial expressions:

Vi blev   uppringda   *av Svenssons* på hotellet   häromkvällen.
                          agent   OA-place   OA-time
We were rung up by the Svenssons at the hotel the other day.

The agent comes immediately after the object:

Han beviljades avsked   *av styrelsen*   igår.
            O   agent   OA-time
His notice was accepted by the board yesterday.

1025   Order within positions – summary

1	Topic	any element from 2–7 below
2	Finite verb	present or past or imperative or subjunctive
3	(Subject)	reflexive pronoun – subject – unstressed object
4	Clausal adverbial	short modal adverb – short pronominal adverb – longer modal adverb – negation
5	Non-finite verb	infinitive(s) or supine(s) or participle (infinitive or supine +) verb particle
6	Object/Complement	reflexive pronoun – real subject – subject complement – indirect object – direct object – object complement
7	Other adverbial	passive agent – manner adverbial – place adverbial – time adverbial – long adverbials

F MAIN CLAUSE TRANSFORMATIONS

This section deals in detail with movements within the (very flexible) Swedish main clause. These transformations are often made for different stylistic reasons.

1026   The base clause

For the purposes of applying transformation rules a basic main clause structure for Swedish is assumed, as follows:

1	2	3	4	5	6	7
Topic	Finite verb	Subject	Clausal adverbial	Non-finite verb	Object/ Complement	Other adverbials
Han	tänker	–	inte	sälja	bilen	i vår.

He's not thinking of selling the car this spring.

This base clause begins with the subject, i.e. has straight word order, and has all other positions filled (except the subject). In the paragraphs below possible variations of this order are examined. In paragraphs 1027–1031 these variations largely involve changes for stylistic effect, whereas in paragraphs 1032–1034 the changes involve a more radical re-disposition of elements.

1027 Topicalisation

See also 1015f., 1045. For the base clause, see 1026 above.

(a) Topicalisation involves placing one of the sentence elements from positions 2 to 7 in the base clause in the topic position, thus displacing the subject to position 3. The most frequent topicalisation is of adverbial expressions indicating when or where the action of the clause is taking place.

1	2	3	4	5	6	7
T	FV	S	CA	NFV	O/C	OA

Base sentence:

Han	tänker	–	inte	sälja	bilen	i vår.

He's not thinking of selling the car this spring.

1 OA to Topic:

I vår	tänker	han	inte	sälja	bilen.	

2 Object to Topic:

Bilen	tänker	han	inte	sälja	–	i vår.

He's not thinking of selling the car this spring.

3 CA to Topic:

Inte	tänker	han	–	sälja	bilen	i vår.

He's not thinking of selling the car this spring.

4 NFV + Object to Topic:

Sälja bilen	tänker	han	inte	göra	–	i vår.

5 It is also possible to topicalise direct speech (object):

'Tusan!'	utropade	han.

'Blast!',he exclaimed.

1	2	3	4	5	6	7
T	*FV*	*S*	*CA*	*NFV*	*O/C*	*OA*

6 The complement may also be topicalised, though this may tend to sound affected:

Hemskt **var** **det.**
Horrible it was.

7 In spoken Swedish the finite verb may be topicalised (cf. also 4 above):

Skriver **gör** **han** **sällan.**
(= **Han skriver sällan.**)
He seldom writes.

Notice that in examples 4 and 7 when the finite verb is topicalised an additional finite verb **gör/gjorde** must replace it as the 'place-holder'. The function of the place-holder is to indicate sentence type. Compare:

Skriver han inte?	= yes/no question	Doesn't he write?
Skriver gör han inte.	= statement	(*lit.*) Write he does not.

This also applies to the place-holder **det** as formal subject, see 1033.

(b) It is common to find as topic a subordinate clause which is an Other adverbial:

1	2	3	4	5	6	7
T	*FV*	*S*	*CA* ·	*NFV*	*O/C*	*OA*

När vi kom hem	drack	vi	alltid	–	kaffe.	

When we got home we always drank coffee.

(Cf. Vi	drack	–		alltid	–	kaffe	när vi kom hem.)

Om Olle är snäll	får	han	–		–	en glasspinne.	

If Olle is good he can have an ice–cream.

(Cf. Olle	får	–	–		–	en glasspinne om han
är						snäll.)

(c) Notice that (with the exception of ((a)4) above) only one sentence element usually occupies the topic position at any one time. This means, for example, that only one adverbial may be topicalised:

Vi åkte	till Stockholm	i våras	→	I våras	åkte vi	till Stockholm
	OA-place	OA-time		OA-time		OA-place

We went to Stockholm last spring.

→	Till Stockholm	åkte vi i våras.
	OA-place	OA-time

1028 The weight principle

(a) The weight principle can be formulated as follows: unstressed familiar information (a short element) tends to be placed to the left in the sentence, while heavy new information (a long element) tends to be placed to the right in the sentence. Thus the natural balance in most sentences accords with 'end weight'. This applies to spoken and most informal written Swedish.

> **Han blev redaktör för tidningen år 1945 när han var bara 21 år.**
> T   FV   C   OA   OA
> He became editor of the paper in 1945 when he was just 21 years of age.

(b) The implications of this are summarised here and explained in greater detail in the paragraphs that follow and in 1044ff.:

(i) Elements losing their stress may move leftwards.

(ii) Occasionally, as in the case of **inte**, this leftward movement is not accommodated within the positional scheme; see 1031.

(iii) Some subjects introducing new information, and therefore stressed, are postponed (moved rightwards), in the case of infinitive phrases and subordinate clauses to the extra position; see 1033ff.

(iv) In passive transformation both leftward and rightward movement of sentence elements occurs simultaneously; see 1032.

(v) Clauses that are not formed in accordance with the weight principle are found in formal written Swedish. They often involve leftward movement of very heavy phrases and thus have 'left weight' (cf. 1029).

1029 Adverbial shift

(a) A common feature particularly in written Swedish is the leftward shift of an adverbial expression (OA) to the clausal adverbial (CA) position (see also 1007, 1028), a transformation known as 'adverbial shift':

1   **Han blev   institutionschef   i fjol.**
              subject complement   OA
     He became head of department last year.

1a **Han blev   i fjol   institutionschef.**
      OA   subject complement
   Last year he became head of department.

In (1) above the informational value of the written sentence is ambiguous: neither element after the verb receives particular emphasis. In the spoken sentence it would be possible to use voice stress:

Han blev institutionschef i 'fjol.

When, as in (1a), the OA is moved leftwards the element **institutionschef** is consequently moved rightwards and becomes stressed. It is now an element 'heavy' in information. The reason for the shift is, then, often to leave another element in the final stressed position.

Further examples of this kind of adverbial shift are:

2 **Han har stannat   hemma   under de senaste dagarna.**
                 OA-place   OA-time
   He has stayed at home the last few days.

2a **Han har   under de senaste dagarna   stannat   hemma.**
            OA-time   OA-place
   The last few days he has stayed at home.

3 **Han ska ta kontakt med firman   när tiden är mogen.**
                                    OA = SC
   He will get in touch with the firm when the time is ripe.

3a **Han ska   när tiden är mogen   ta kontakt med firman.**
           OA = SC
   When the time is ripe he will get in touch with the firm.

4 **Vi väntar   med att ge honom nyheten   tills imorgon.**
             DO   OA-time
   We will delay giving him the news until tomorrow.

4a **Vi väntar   tills imorgon   med att ge honom nyheten.**
             OA-time   DO
   We will delay until tomorrow giving him the news.

(b) Other adverbials which are relatively 'light' can be placed in the CA position without disturbing the balance:

Han ska *imorgon* åka till Stockholm.
He's going to Stockholm tomorrow.

Vi ska *så småningom* bygga en sommarstuga.
We will eventually build a summer cottage.

Är vi *då* mogna för beslut?
Are we then ready to take a decision?

Han började *snabbt* gå förbi busskön.
He began quickly to pass the bus queue.

(c) Adverbials of place are rarely moved left, whilst adverbials of time are often moved. Compare:

5 **Han har bott i norra England *i tio år*.**
He has lived in the North of England for ten years.

5a **Han har *i tio* år bott i norra England.**
He has lived for ten years in the North of England.

But:

5b ***Han har *i norra England* bott i tio år.**
(This sentence is impossible in Swedish.)

(d) A movement in the opposite direction, i.e. movement of the clausal adverbial to the other adverbial position, is largely restricted to the spoken language, and is undertaken in order to provide the otherwise unstressed clausal adverbial with a measure of stress:

6 **Han har *faktiskt* studerat svenska i tre år.**
    CA
He has actually studied Swedish for three years.

6a **Han har studerat svenska i tre år *faktiskt*.**
            CA
He has studied Swedish for three years, actually.

7 **Det finns ju *också* rätt många iranier.**
There are of course quite a lot of Iranians too.

7a **Det finns ju rätt många iranier *också*.**
There are also, of course, quite a lot of Iranians.

8 **Du är *alltså* inte klok!**
You must be mad!

8a **Du är inte klok *alltså*!**
You are mad, you know!

1030 'Light' elements

Light elements are short unstressed sentence elements, usually object or reflexive pronouns. In constructions without a non-finite verb these tend to move leftwards to occupy the 'subject' position, thus preceding the clausal adverbial.

T	FV	S	CA	NFV	O/C	OA
1 **Jag**	**känner**	–	inte	–	ˡ honom.	
I don't know him.						
2 **Jag**	**känner**	honom (light DO)	inte.			
I don't know him.						
3 **Jag**	**gav**	honom (light IO)	inte	–	ˡ boken. (DO)	
I didn't give him the book.						
4 **Jag**	**gav**	honom (light IO)	inte	–	ˡ den. (DO)	
I didn't give him it.						
5 **Jag**	**har**	inte	gett	–	honom den. (IO – DO)	
I haven't given him it.						
6 **Jag**	**gav**	honom den (light IO-light DO)	inte.			
7 **Då**	**har**	han	inte	lärt	sig svenska.	
Then he hasn't learned Swedish.						
8 **Då**	**lärde**	han sig (light IO)	inte	–	svenska. (DO)	
Then he didn't learn Swedish.						

In a sentence with a complex verb or two objects (5, 7) in which the DO is unstressed, it occupies only the O/C position. This word order is thus obligatory in such cases. In a sentence with a finite verb alone, the DO occupies the object position only when it is relatively stressed (see also 1, 4 above). This is often the case when expressing a contrast:

Jag känner inte ˡ **honom, men jag känner** ˡ **henne.**

Compare this case with the emphatic (i.e. heavily stressed) topic (see 1045(b)):

|Honom känner jag inte, men |henne känner jag.

1031   Negation

(a) The main forms of negation in Swedish are the clausal adverbs **icke, inte, ej, aldrig, ingalunda, knappt, knappast** (see also 641(a)). When these negate the entire clause they occupy the clausal adverbial (CA) position. Consider the following examples of negative sentences with different forms of the verb:

Present tense:
Jag äter inte ost.
I don't eat cheese.

Past tense:
De sa aldrig något.
They never said anything.

Future:
Jag ska inte göra det.
I won't do that.

Det kommer aldrig att hända.
That will never happen.

Perfect, pluperfect:
Jag har/hade aldrig sett honom!
I have/had never seen him.

Imperative:
Gör aldrig det!
Never do that!

Infinitive:
Vi uppmanade dem att aldrig göra om det.
We urged them never to do that again.

Notice in this last example that in Swedish the negative 'splits' the infinitive, i.e. comes between the infinitive marker **att** and the infinitive itself.

(b) The negative occupies different positions relative to the finite verb in main and subordinate clauses.

Main clause:

T	FV	S	CA	NFV	O/C	OA
Ikväll	*tänker*	**Per**	*inte*	**laga**	**mat.**	
Per	*tänker*	–	*inte*	**laga**	**mat**	**ikväll.**

Per is not thinking of making dinner tonight.

Subordinate clause:

Matrix	Conj.	S	CA	FV	NFV	O/C	OA
Per sa	**att**	**han**	*inte*	*tänkte*	**laga**	**mat**	**ikväll.**

Per said that he was not thinking of making dinner tonight.

(c) Only light elements (see 1030) and the subject in inverted clauses may intrude between the negative and the finite verb:

T	FV	S	CA	NFV	OC	OA
Han	**tvättade**	**sig** (light IO)	**inte**	–	–	**igår kväll.**

He didn't wash yesterday evening.

| **Han** | **fick** | **den** (light DO) | **inte** | – | – | **förrän i fredags.** |

He didn't receive it until last Friday.

| **I går** | **fick** | **han den** (S, light DO) | **inte.** | | | |

Yesterday he didn't get it.

(d) On occasion in inverted statements the negative may come between the finite verb and the subject:

> **Idag kommer Peter *inte*.**   Peter is *not* coming today.
> **Idag kommer *inte* Peter.**   *Peter* isn't coming today.

This accords with the weight principle (see 1028) in so far as the word that receives particular emphasis comes last.

(e) Negating pronouns and the negated object.

For **ingen** etc. and **inte någon** etc. see 343ff. Notice, also, however, that **inte någon** etc. rather than **ingen** etc. must be used:

1   When there is both a FV and NFV in the clause.

2   When the negated pronoun is the object/complement of a subordinate clause.

Main clause:

T	FV	S	CA	NFV	O/C	OA
Jag	**hade**	–	**inte**	**gjort**	**någonting.**	

I hadn't done anything.

Subordinate clause:

Matrix	Conj.	S	CA	FV	NFV	O/C	OA
Jag sade,	**att**	**jag**	**inte**	**hade**	**gjort**	**någonting.**	

I stated that I hadn't said anything.

Note: When qualifying objects or real subjects, **ingen** etc. + the noun it qualifies are occasionally found in the clausal adverbial position; the negative sense seems to attract them to this position. This may, however, often be regarded nowadays as a rather affected form.

Main clause:

T	FV	S	CA	NFV	O/C	OA
Jag	**hade**	–	**inte**	**fått**	**några pengar**	**den veckan.**

I hadn't received any money that week.

Jag	**hade**	–	**inga pengar**	**fått**	–	**den veckan.**

Jag	**har**	–	**inte**	**hört**	**någonting**	**om detta.**

I haven't heard anything about that.

Jag	**har**	–	**ingenting**	**hört**	–	**om detta.**

Subordinate clause:

Matrix	Conj.	S	CA	FV	NFV	O/C	OA
Han påstår	**att**	**det**	**inte**	**finns**	–	**någon Gud.**	

He maintains that there is no God.

Matrix	Conj.	S	CA	FV	NFV	O/C	OA

| Han påstår att | det | ingen Gud | finns. | | | |

Han sa att han inte hade – några pengar.
He said that he hadn't had any money.

Han sa att han inga pengar hade.

1032 Passive transformation

For passive forms and usage, see 547ff. The transformation from active to passive is a method of moving 'light' information leftwards and 'heavy' information rightwards in the sentence. There are two main reasons for passive transformation:

Reason 1. The object in the base (active) sentence is unstressed and some other element needs to be emphasised.

Reason 2. The subject in the base sentence is unknown or unimportant ('agentless passive').

Examples of passive transformations (italics indicates stress):

	Active		*Passive*
1	**Man stal *bilen*.**	→	**Bilen *stals*.**
	Someone stole the car.		The car was stolen.
2	**Man omvalde *honom*.**	→	**Han *omvaldes*.**
	They re-elected him.		He was re-elected.
3	**Man har bjudit *oss*.**	→	**Vi har blivit *bjudna*.**
	They have invited us.		We have been invited.
4	***Olof Lundén* intervjuade honom.**	→	**Han intervjuades *av Olof Lundén*.**
	Olof Lundén interviewed him.		He was interviewed by Olof Lundén.

In examples 1–3 an expression containing an unimportant subject becomes an agentless passive expression with emphasis on the verb. In example 4 the subject in the base sentence is important, and in order to emphasise it, it is moved rightwards according to the weight principle (1028).

Further examples:

5 **Eleverna (S) tyckte mycket** *om* **henne.**   → 5(a) **Hon (S) var mycket** *omtyckt.*
The pupils liked her a lot.   → 5(b) **Hon (S) var mycket omtyckt**
                                                       av eleverna (agent).

If the object of the base sentence (**henne**) is not to receive emphasis, but this is rather to be placed on some other element, then passive transformation moves this object leftwards to become a natural (unstressed) topic. Now the verb (**omtyckt**) is emphasised, or alternatively the agent (**av eleverna**) if it is present.

Notice that, of the two methods possible for radically altering emphasis in the sentence, topicalisation (see 1027, 1045) is only possible for the main clause, while passive transformation is possible for both main and subordinate clause:

6 **Eleverna tyckte mycket om henne.**

Henne tyckte eleverna mycket om.   [Active MC]
Hon var mycket omtyckt *av eleverna.*   [Passive MC]
Jag har hört, att hon var mycket omtyckt *av eleverna.*   [Passive SC]

1033   Existential sentences and the place holder

See also 1003.

(a) When the subject consists of new, heavy information which we do not wish to introduce immediately at the beginning of the sentence, it is possible to postpone it, i.e. to move the subject rightwards. The postponed subject is then referred to as the real subject (RS). An extra subject known as the formal subject (FS) or place-holder subject, usually **det**, is in this case inserted in the vacant Topic or Subject position:

1a   *En polis* **sitter i köket.**   A policeman is sitting in the kitchen.
     S

1b   *Det* **sitter** *en polis* **i köket.**   There's a policeman is sitting in the
     FS   RS   kitchen.

2a   *Att sluta röka* **är svårt.**   Stopping smoking is difficult.
     S

2b   *Det* **är svårt** *att sluta röka.*   It's difficult to stop smoking.
     FS   RS

3a *Vad du säger* **spelar ingen roll.**   What you say doesn't matter.
   S

3b *Det* **spelar ingen roll** *vad du säger.*   It doesn't matter what you say.
   FS   RS

It is clear from these examples that there are two main types of existential sentence:

Type 1 has a real subject that is an indefinite noun phrase (1b).

Type 2 has a real subject that is either an infinitive phrase (2b) or an indirect question (3b).

(b) The order in the existential sentence is as follows:

T	FV	S	CA	NFV	O/C	OA	X_2 (see 1034)
Type 1:							
1 **Det**	**sitter**	–	**inte ofta**	–	**en polis**	**i köket.**	
There isn't often a policeman sitting in the kitchen.							
2 **I köket**	**sitter**	**(det)**	**inte ofta**	–	**en polis.**		
There isn't often a policeman sitting in the kitchen.							
3 **I morgon**	**kommer**	**(det)**	**kanske**	–	**en hel skolklass.**		
Tomorrow perhaps a whole school class will come.							
4	**Sitter**	**(det)**	–	–	**en polis**	**i köket?**	
Is there a policeman sitting in the kitchen?							
5 **Det**	**har**	–	–	**skrivits**	**mycket strunt**	**i tidningen på sistone.**	
There's been a lot of rubbish written in the paper lately.							
Type 2							
6 **Det**	**är**	–	–	–	**svårt**	–	**att sluta röka.**
It's difficult to stop smoking.							
7 **Det**	**gör**	–	–	–	**ingenting**	–	**vad du säger.**
It doesn't matter what you say.							
8 **Det**	**förvånade**	–	–	–	**mig**	–	**att du vann.**
It surprised me that you won.							

When an adverbial expression is topicalised, **det** is sometimes omitted (2, 3). **Det** and the verb may be inverted in yes/no questions (4), and **det** is found in passive constructions (5). In these examples **det** is devoid of real meaning. It functions as a place-holder subject, occupying the vital subject position and thereby indicating sentence type. Compare:

> **Sitter (det) en polis i köket?** = Yes/no question (verb – subject order)
> **Det sitter en polis i köket.**   = Statement (subject – verb order)

Note: In South and West Swedish dialects **där**, **här** often replace **det** as place-holder:

Där finns inga ägg i kylskåpet.   There are no eggs in the fridge.

1034   Extra positions

Extra positions are necessary in the word order scheme on occasion in order to accommodate either free elements outside the clause, clauses as real subject, or object clauses. They are located as follows (X):

X_1	T	FV	S	CA	NFV	O/C	OA	X_2
1 **Olof,**	**han**	**är**	–	–	–	**sjuk.**		
2 **I Lissabon,**	**där**	**dansar**	**de.**					
3	**När han kom,**	**brukade**	**han**	–	**kyssa**	**oss,**	–	**Maja och mig.**
4	**Det**	**har**	–	**alltid**	**förvånat**	**mig**	–	**att han kunde vara så fräck.**
5	**Det**	**är**	–	**inte**	–	**sant**	–	**att tiden läker alla sår.**
6	**Det**	**är**	–	–	–	**roligt**	–	**att spela tennis.**
7	**De**	**frågade**	–	–		**honom**	**igår**	**om Lasse var hemma.**
8	**Jag**	**överlåter**	**det**	**nu**	–	**till dig**	–	**att köpa brödet.**

1 Olof, he is ill.
2 In Lisbon, there they dance.
3 When he arrived he used to kiss us, Maja and me.
4 It has always surprised me that he could be so cheeky.
5 It's not true that time heals all wounds.
6 It's fun playing tennis.
7 They asked him yesterday whether Lasse was at home.
8 I leave it to you to buy the bread.

The extra position(s) may be added to the scheme in order to accommodate duplicates (see 1047). This is the case in examples 1, 2, 3 above. Also found in the extra position are heavy elements such as subordinate clauses and infinitive phrases, usually represented in the main clause by a formal subject **det** (see 1003, 1033) as in examples 4, 5, 6, 7 above. The different elements occupying the extra positions in these examples are as follows:

1 Correlative to topicalised subject.
2 Correlative to topicalised OA-place.
3 Correlative to object.
4 Real subject, subordinate clause.

5   Real subject, subordinate clause.
6   Real subject, infinitive phrase.
7   Object clause.
8   Object clause represented by **det**, formal object in main clause.

1035   Link position

A link position (L) is added before all other positions in cases of coordination of main or subordinate clauses (see 801). The link position itself is, however, not regarded as part of the clause but as a unit between clauses.

Main clause:

L	X_1	T	FV	S	CA	NFV	O/C	OA	X_2
...och	–	vi	brukade	–	alltid	leka	–	därborta i trädgården.	

... and we always used to play over there in the garden.

L	X_1	T	FV	S	CA	NFV	O/C	OA	X_2
...men	Olle,	han	är	–	–	–	dum, –		han.

... but Olle, he's stupid, he is.

L	X_1	T	FV	S	CA	NFV	O/C	OA	X_2
...så	–	därför	lekte	vi	aldrig	–	med honom.		

... that's why we never played with him.

Subordinate clause:

	L	Conj.	S	CA	FV	NFV	O/C
(Jag hoppas att han vinner)	och	att	han	–	har	–	rekordtid.

(I hope that he wins) and that he gets a record time.

The link position may be occupied by a coordinating conjunction (804ff.). For extra positions see 1034. For conjunction position in the subordinate clause see 1019.

1036   Questions

See also 1016f. This section deals with direct questions. For indirect questions, see 820f., 1037(b), 1038(a). For answers to positive and negative questions, see 902.

There are four different constructions:

(a) Yes/no question

This is so called because of the expected answer – **ja/nej** or **jo, kanske, tyvärr,** etc. Such questions contain a suggestion and anticipate affirmation or denial. They have inversion of finite verb and subject.

X (cf. 1034)	T	FV	S	CA	NFV	O/C	OA
–	–	**Åker**	**du**	–	–	–	**bort imorgon?**
Are you leaving tomorrow?							
		Sålde	**du**	**inte**	–	**huset?**	
Didn't you sell the house?							
–	–	**Har**	**ni**	**aldrig**	**läst**	**bibeln?**	
Have you never read the Bible?							
–	–	**Kan**	**jag**	–	**få se**	**hennes brev?**	
Can I see her letter?							
–	**I morgon,**	**åker**	**du**	–	–	**bort då?**	
So tomorrow, you'll be leaving then?							
Huset,	**(då)**	**sålde**	**du**	**inte**	–	**det?**	
The house, didn't you sell it?							

Alternative questions are sometimes regarded as a separate type, but usually represent a duplication of the yes/no question:

X (cf. 1034)	T	FV	S	CA	NFV	O/C	OA
–	–	**Ska**	**vi**	–	**ta**	–	**till vänster eller till höger här?**
Should we turn right or left here?							

(b) V–question

This is so called because of its form. The topic is an interrogative adverb or pronoun, most but not all of which begin with v-: **vad, vem, vilken, var**, etc. plus **hur, när**. V–questions usually have inversion of the finite verb and subject, but see examples 6–8 below where the v–word is subject.

X (cf. 1034) T		FV	S	CA	NFV	O/C	OA
1 –	**Vad**	**såg**	**han**	–	–	–	**därborta?**
What did he see over there?							
2 –	**Vem**	**är**	**den här Olsson?**				
Who is this Olsson?							
3 –	**Vart**	**åker**	**vi**	–	–	–	**på sommaren?**
Where are we going in the summer?							
4 –	**När**	**kommer**	**vi**	–	–	–	**hem ikväll?**
When will we get home tonight?							
5 –	**Hur**	**vågade**	**de**	–	**säga**	**det?**	
How dared they say that?							

Notice that the v-question requests information about a specific sentence element, e.g. in (1) object, (2) predicative complement, (3) OA-place, (4) OA-time, (5) OA-condition.

X (cf. 1034) T		FV	S	CA	NFV	O/C	OA
6 –	**Vem**	**gick**	–	–	–	–	**ut just nu?**
Who went out just now?							
7 –	**Vad**	**händer**	–	–	–	–	**på kontoret?**
What happens at the office?							
8 –	**Vilka barn**	**kommer**	–	**inte**	–	–	**i morgon?**
Which children are not coming tomorrow?							
9 –	**Hurdant väder**	**hade**	**ni**	–	–	–	**i Grekland?**
What kind of weather did you have in Greece?							

Note: In some complex questions there is a combination of yes/no question and indirect question:

Q: **Vet du, när han kommer?**	Do you know when he's coming?
(cf. Vet du det? När kommer han?)	Do you know? When is he coming?
A: **Ja, det vet jag.**	Yes, I know.
or:	
Ja, han kommer i morgon.	Yes, he's coming tomorrow.

(c) Questions in statement form

Sometimes question intonation plus the possible addition of an adverbial particle (**ju, väl,** etc.) or tag (**inte sant, eller hur, va,** etc.) is sufficient to indicate a question:

T	FV	S	CA	NFV	O/C	OA	X_2
Du	**är**	–	**väl**	–	**trött**	**nu?**	
You must be tired now?							
Du	**reser**	–	**alltså**	–	–	**i morgon?**	
You're leaving tomorrow, then?							
Han	**röker**	–	**inte**	–	–	–	**va?**
He doesn't smoke, does he?							
Leif Eriksson	**upptäckte**	–	–	–	**Amerika,**	–	**inte sant?**
Leif Eriksson discovered America, didn't he?							

(d) Other types of question

Some exclamations are in question form with inversion (FV – S):

Ska jag ha tagit mutor?   Am I supposed to have taken bribes?
Hur vackert är det inte här!   How beautiful it is here! (*lit.* 'is it
                                     not?')

Note: Most exclamations have straight word order (S – FV). Cf.:

Vilken båt han har!   What a boat he has!
Vilken båt har han?   What boat does he have?

Some commands are in question form:

Olle, vill du komma genast!   Olle, will you come right away!
Kan du vara snäll och stänga fönstret!   Can you please close the window!

G   SUBORDINATE CLAUSES

See also 801ff. (coordination and subordination) and 1019f. This section
comprises a brief introduction to the form and function of subordinate clauses
(1037f.), their position in the sentence (1039), and an account of some problem
areas as regards the word order and structure of subordinate clauses (1040–1043).

1037   Form of the subordinate clause

Some characteristics of subordinate clauses and basic positions within the
subordinate clause are given in 1019f. above. As can be seen from that initial
account, most subordinate clauses have an introductory word termed
(*subordinating*) *conjunction*. A common classification of subordinate clauses is
by the nature of this introductory word. The main types are then:

(a) *Relative clauses* introduced by a relative pronoun or relative adverb:

Flickan *som jag träffade igår* var mycket vacker.
The girl that I met yesterday was very beautiful.

Ön *dit han åkte i fjol* ligger i skärgården.
The island he went to last year is in the archipelago.

(b) *Indirect questions* introduced by an interrogative pronoun, interrogative adverb or interrogative conjunction:

Jag vill veta, *vad han gör.*
I want to know what he's doing.

De frågade, *varför vi inte kom till festen.*
They asked why we didn't come to the party.

Vi undrar, *om det är möjligt.*
We wonder whether it's possible.

(c) *Conjunctional clauses* introduced by a subordinating conjunction:

Anna sa *att hon inte ville dansa.*
Anna said that she didn't want to dance.

***När vi kommer dit*, äter vi middag.**
When we get there we'll have dinner.

***Om vädret är fint* tänker vi åka till stugan.**
If the weather is fine we're going to go to the cottage.

1038 Function of the subordinate clause

Subordinate clauses can be classified according to their function in relation to the sentence, i.e. according to the sentence element which they represent in the larger main clause sentence:

(a) Subject and object clauses (see also 1002, 1005) include:

(i) Most **att**-clauses:

***Att du är frisk* gläder mig.** [subject]
I am pleased that you are better.

Jag tycker inte om *att du ljuger.* [object]
I don't like your lying.

Att-clauses as object used often to be preceded by an adjective phrase (adjective + preposition) (see 518(b)(iii)). In many cases the preposition may now be omitted:

Jag är säker (på) att du kommer att vinna.
I'm certain you'll win.

Vi är oroliga (för) att hon misslyckas.
We are worried that she will fail.

Note: This construction is also possible with other subordinators:

Jag är osäker (på) hur vi klarar det.   I'm unsure how we will manage it.

(ii) Indirect question clauses:

Det är okänt, *vem som kommer.* [real subject]
It is not known who is coming.
(Cf. V-question: **Vem kommer?**)

Jag frågade henne, *vad jag skulle göra.* [object]
I asked her what I should do.
(Cf. V-question: **Vad ska jag göra?**)

Han frågade, *om jag ville följa med.* [object]
He asked whether I wanted to go along.
(Cf. Yes/no question: **Vill du följa med?**)

Subject clauses are often the real subject in an existential sentence, see 1033.

(b) Adverbial clauses (see also 1007) are conjunctional clauses and include:

(i) Temporal clauses (indicating time):

Vi åker *när Olle kommer.*
We will leave when Olle arrives.

Då han sa detta blev jag arg.
When he said that I got angry.

Medan vi satt och åt, pratade hon hela tiden.
While we were sitting eating she talked the whole time.

(ii) Conditional clauses (indicating condition):

Om du är snäll, **ska du få en kaka.**
If you are good you can have a cake.

Ifall du kan göra det, **är det bra.**
If you can do that, that's fine.

(iii) Comparative clauses (indicating comparison):

Han är inte så stark *som han borde vara.*
He is not as strong as he should be.

Han är starkare *än han var förr.*
He is stronger than he was.

(iv) Consecutive clauses (indicating consequence):

Jag var så arg *att jag genast gick därifrån.*
I was so angry that I left immediately.

Han låste skåpet så *(att) det inte gick att öppna igen.*
He locked the cupboard so it could not be opened again.

(v) Causal clauses (indicating cause):

Han fick en kaka *därför att han var snäll.*
He got a cake because he was good.

Eftersom han var snäll **fick han en kaka.**
As he was good he got a cake.

(vi) Final clauses (indicating intention):

Man måste stödja honom *för att han inte ska snubbla.*
We have to support him so that he doesn't fall over.

Jag stängde fönstret *så att det inte skulle dra på honom.*
I closed the window so that he wouldn't be in a draught.

(vii) Concessive clauses (indicating concession):

Fastän han inte var snäll, **fick han ändå en kaka.**
Although he wasn't good he still got a cake.

Trots att det regnade, **åkte vi till stugan.**
Despite the fact that it was raining, we went to the cottage.

Även om jag hade råd, **skulle jag inte köpa bil.**
Even if I could afford it I wouldn't buy a car.

(c) Attributive clauses:

(i) Relative clauses with **som**:

Jag vill köpa en sådan bil, *som Olssons har.*
I want to buy a car like the Olssons'.

A useful distinction is made between **som**-clauses which form a unit of meaning together with the noun phrase to which they refer, i.e. restrictive relative clauses, which restrict the meaning of the noun phrase, and those which are merely an afterthought or parenthesis, i.e. non-restrictive. Restrictive relative clauses use a determinative pronoun (without end article on the noun; see 329) while non-restrictive clauses use a demonstrative pronoun or end article:

Restrictive:
/De elever som ska följa med på bussen/ bör samlas här klockan tio.
/Those pupils coming on the bus/ should gather here at ten o'clock.

Non-restrictive:
De eleverna/, som ju också är mycket unga förresten,/ är mycket otrevliga.
Those pupils/, who are very young by the way,/ are very unpleasant.

To test, ask the question: **Vilka bör samlas här kl. 10?** Answer: **De elever som ska följa med på bussen.**

But the answer to the question: **Vilka är mycket otrevliga?** is: **De** or **Eleverna.**

Restrictive relative clauses are sometimes called necessary relative clauses. Non-restrictive relative clauses are sometimes called unnecessary relative clauses. Non-restrictive relative clauses are usually enclosed within commas (see 1302(b)). See also determinative pronouns (329).

(ii) Relative clauses without **som**:

Hon är den vackraste flickan *jag någonsin har sett.*
She is the most beautiful girl I have ever seen.

(iii) Some **att**-clauses:

Risken att vi skulle förlora matchen **var mycket liten.**
The risk that we might lose the match was very small.

(iv) Some indirect question clauses:

Frågan *om vi borde gå med i facket* **har diskuterats mycket.**
The question whether we should join the union has been discussed a lot.

1039 Position of the subordinate clause in the sentence

See also 1018f. for main and subordinate clause positions, and 1038 for functions of subordinate clauses. Subordinate clauses in most cases comprise sentence elements in larger main clause sentences (see also 801(b)) as follows:

(a) Subject and object clauses occupy the T or X_2 position

T	FV	S	CA	NFV	O/C	OA	X_2
For translations see 1038(a)							
Att du är frisk (S)	gläder	–	–	–	mig.		
Det (FS)	gläder	–	–	–	mig	–	att du är frisk. (RS)
Att du ljuger (O)	tycker	jag	inte	om.			
Jag	tycker	–	inte	om	–	–	att du ljuger. (O)

(b) Most adverbial clauses (temporal, conditional, causal, comparative, concessive) occupy the T, CA or OA positions:

T	FV	S	CA	NFV	O/C	OA
När Olle kommer	åker	vi	–	–	–	ut till stugan.
When Olle arrives we will go out to the cottage.						
Vi	åker	–	–	–	–	ut till stugan när Olle kommer.
Vi	åker	–	, när Olle kommer,	–	–	ut till stugan.
Om du är snäll	ska	du	–	få	godis.	
If you are good you shall have some sweets.						
Du	ska	–	–	få	godis	om du är snäll.
Du	ska	–	, om du är snäll,	få	godis.	

Notice that subordinate clauses occupying the CA position are stressed and are only found in written Swedish.

(c) Some adverbial clauses (final, consecutive) usually occupy the OA position:

T	FV	S	CA	NFV	O/C	OA
For translations see 1038(b)						
Man	**måste**	–	–	**stödja**	**honom**	**för att han inte ska snubbla.**
Jag	**blev**	–	–	–	**så arg**	**att jag genast gick därifrån.**

(d) Attributive clauses which are associated with subject, object or complement occupy the same position as these, i.e. T, S or O positions:

T	FV	S	CA	NFV	O/C
Min bror, som är läkare, S	**tjänar**	–	–	–	**mycket pengar.**
My brother, who is a doctor, earns a lot of money.					
Igår	**kom**	**min bror, som är läkare.** S			
Yesterday my brother, who is a doctor, arrived.					
En sån bil, som Olssons har, O	**tänker**	**vi**	–	**köpa.**	
Vi	**tänker**	–	–	**köpa**	**en sån bil som Olssons har.**
Hon	**är**	–	–	–	**den vackraste flicka jag har sett.** C

1040 Clauses with no indicator of subordination

See 803(d) for indicators of subordination. Some subordinate clauses do not begin with an introductory word which marks them as subordinate, nor do they have clausal adverbials whose position would indicate them as subordinate. These clauses are of two main types:

(a) Clauses corresponding to **att**-clauses

These often contain verbs of saying, thinking and perceiving e.g. **säga** 'say'; **tro**, **tycka** 'think'; **se** 'see'.

MC base:

Jag tror det alltid blir tråkigt.
I think it'll always be boring.

Det blir alltid tråkigt.
It'll always be boring.

Vi tycker det ofta är ytterst obehagligt.
We think it's often very unpleasant.

Det är ofta ytterst obehagligt.
It's often very unpleasant.

Hon sa hon hade läst brevet.
She said she had read the letter.

Hon hade läst brevet.
She had read the letter.

The subordinate clause in each case here has the same main clause structure as the base.

Note: **Att** is usually retained after forms of **veta**:

Vet du att han är sjuk?   Do you know he's ill?

(b) Clauses corresponding to **som**-clauses

In some relative clauses it is possible to omit **som** if the **som**-clause is a restrictive relative clause (see 1038(c)(i)), and if it has its own subject, i.e. when **som** is object or prepositional object:

Boken (som) du lånade mig var mycket spännande.
The book you lent me was very exciting.

Här är en rolig historia (som) ni säkert kommer att skratta åt.
Here's a joke you're bound to laugh at.

1041 Main clause word order in **att**-clauses

For main and subordinate clause order see 1015, for main clause order 1018, for subordinate clause order 1019, for major differences 1020.

(a) The following statements hold good for most subordinate clauses in written Swedish:

(i) There is no topic, unlike the main clause, and the order is usually both straight and fixed: conjunction – subject – finite verb (but cf. (b)(i) below).

(ii) The clausal adverbial precedes the finite verb.

(iii) An adverbial subordinate clause may itself form the topic of a main clause sentence (1039(b)):

Eftersom de inte kom,	**gick**	**han.**
T	FV	S

As they didn't come he left.

(b) In spoken Swedish (occasionally in written Swedish), and especially in clauses introduced by **att, därför att, för att, så att** (sometimes **eftersom, fastän**) there is frequently found:

(i) A non-subject following the conjunction as a kind of 'topic' in the **att**-clause, and inverted (FV – S) word order:

Nils sa,	**att**	**idag**	**kommer**	**han**	**hit.**
	Conj.	'Topic'	FV	S	
Nils said	that	today	he's coming		here.

(ii) The clausal adverbial following the finite verb in the **att**-clause:

Nils sa,	**att**	**han**	**kommer**	**inte**	**imorgon.**
	Conj.	S	FV	CA	
Nils said	that	he	isn't coming		tomorrow.

In these cases the conjunction **att** functions almost as a colon, and the second clause is regarded as a main clause, i.e. a statement in direct speech. The reported speech retains the MC word order of the original. Cf.:

Nils sa: 'Idag kommer jag dit.'
Nils sa: 'Jag kommer inte imorgon.'

Note: This main clause word order only appears in the att-clause when the sentence (e.g. **Nils sa**) is a positive statement (see also 1041(a)). Should the sentence be a negative statement then the usual order in the subordinate clause obtains:

Han sa aldrig, att vi alltid måste vara uppmärksamma.
He never said that we always had to be attentive.

(c) When an adverbial (temporal, conditional) clause is moved to the front of an **att**-clause two structures are possible as alternatives to the base sentence:

Base sentence:

Jag tror att jag ska köpa en båt om jag vinner på tipset.
I think I'll buy a boat if I win the pools.

1 Jag tror att, om jag vinner på tipset, så ska jag köpa en båt.
                                          FV S

For the use of **så** in such cases see 1047(c).

2 Jag tror att jag, om jag vinner på tipset, ska köpa en båt.
                  S   FV

Type (1) is common in spoken Swedish (cf. (b)(i) above), while type (2), which retains subordinate clause order, emphasises the subject (**jag**) of the **att**-clause.

1042 Conditional clauses

See also 538. There are three main types of conditional clause:

(a) Clause introduced by **om/ifall**

> **Om du skriver till honom (så) får du veta vad som har hänt.**
> If you write to him you'll find out what has happened.
> (Cf. **Du får veta vad som har hänt om du skriver till honom.**)

These clauses usually occupy the T or OA position, see 1039(b). If the **om**-clause comes first in the sentence it is often duplicated by the word **så** (cf. 1047).

(b) Clause with question word order

Some conditional clauses omit **om** and express the condition solely by means of inversion. These are FV1 clauses.

> **Kommer du imorgon, kan du träffa henne.**
> If you come tomorrow, you can meet her.
> (Cf. **Om du kommer imorgon, kan du träffa henne.**)

> **Vore jag rik, kunde jag köpa villan.**
> If I were rich I could buy the house.
> (Cf. **Om jag vore rik, kunde jag köpa villan.**) [See 536(c).]

Such clauses with question word order are very common. They always come first in the sentence and represent an intermediate form between main and subordinate clause structure. They possess inverted word order (FV – S). An inserted clausal adverbial will follow the finite verb, unlike the case with most subordinate clauses:

> **Kommer du inte imorgon, så blir jag arg.**
> FV   CA
> If you don't come tomorrow I will be angry.

Compare:

Om du inte kommer imorgon, så blir jag arg.

This kind of inversion to indicate condition also occurs in written English, where conditionals formed with the subjunctive sometimes have inverted word order:

Had we but world enough, and time . . .
Were you to agree to this, it would be disastrous.

(c) Imperative clause

Some conditional clauses express the condition by means of an imperative. They are, therefore, FV1 clauses with main clause word order as in (b). Note that in such clauses the **så** that duplicates the imperative/condition in the following clause is compulsory (cf. 1047(c)).

Skriv till honom, så får du veta vad som har hänt.
Write to him, then you'll find out what has happened.

Kom hit Olle, så får du godis.
Come here, Olle, and you can have some sweets.

Note: A similar function may often be expressed by a statement:

Vi tittar i tidningen, så får vi se, vad vi har att välja på.
We'll look in the paper, then we'll know what we can choose from.

1043 Independent clauses

There are five main types of sentence in which the order is that of the subordinate clause, but in which there is no accompanying main clause. These may be called 'independent clauses'.

(a) Answers to questions using **(där)för att:**

(Varför åker ni inte bort i år?) För att/Därför att vi inte har råd.
(Why aren't you going away this year?) Because we can't afford it.

(b) Clauses introduced by **kanske, kanhända** and the less frequent **månne, månntro:**

Kanske/Kanhända han redan har gjort det.
Perhaps he has already done it.

This represents a contraction of an earlier main clause sentence:

Det kan ske/hända (att) han redan har gjort det.
MC   SC

Note: **Kanske** may also introduce a main clause, causing inversion:

Kanske har han redan gjort det.
T   FV S

(c) Clauses expressing an exclamation. A main clause verb may on occasion be understood in these constructions:

(Tänk) Att det alltid ska bli så här!
(Fancy) that it always has to be like this!

(Det förvånar mig) Att du inte skäms!
(I'm surprised) that you're not ashamed of yourself!

Så dum jag ändå var!
How stupid I was nevertheless!

Som han pratade hela kvällen!
How he talked all evening!

Tycker du om jordgubbar? Om (jag gör)!
Do you like strawberries? You bet (I do)!

(d) Clauses expressing a wish. These are introduced by **om**:

Om jag ändå hade talat om det för honom!
If only I had told him!

Om is usually accompanied by **ändå** or **bara**. The wishes expressed in such clauses are often unreal and the verb is also found in the past or subjunctive without any introductory word:

Vore det ändå så lätt!   If it were only so easy!

Note: Occasionally such exclamations are introduced by **den som**:

Den som ändå kunde spela piano!   If I could only play the piano!

H EMPHASIS

1044 Emphasis and positions

(a) A governing principle in the utterance is that information supplied by a real or implied context ('familiar' information) is placed before new information (see also 1028f.):

Implied context: **Vad gjorde Ulla?**

Ulla	**köpte blommor igår.**
Ulla	bought flowers yesterday.
Familiar	*New*

Implied context: **Ulla köpte blommorna igår.**

De var	**hemskt vackra.**
They	were awfully pretty.
Familiar	*New*

The familiar information, often the jumping off point for the sentence, is called the *theme* and the new information imparted, the point or message, is called the *focus*.

Ulla	**köpte**	**blommor igår.**
Theme	*Focus*	

Igår	**köpte**	**Ulla blommor.**
Theme	*Focus*	

As the new information often tends to be longer or 'heavier' than the familiar information, the focus tends to follow the weight principle of *end-weight* (see 1028):

Ulla	**köpte blommorna på blomsterhandeln mitt emot stationen.**
Theme	*Focus*

Ulla bought flowers at the florists opposite the station.

So it is normal for emphasis to be placed on words at the end of the sentence. The end of the sentence is a natural stress position and we talk of *end-focus*:

Han körde *bil i torsdags*.   He drove last Thursday.

Han körde *i torsdags en gammal Chevrolet i blått och rött med rostiga dörrar*.
Last Thursday he drove an old blue and red Chevrolet with rusty doors.

Notice that in this last example the principles of end-weight and end-focus override the normal word order, as the (very long) object is preceded by an adverbial expression of time in Swedish.

(b) In spoken Swedish it is possible to use intonation to place emphasis on any element in the sentence without altering the word order:

Ulla köpte blommor i går.	i.e. not Eva
Ulla *köpte* blommor i går.	i.e. they were not free
Ulla köpte *blommor* i går.	i.e. not fruit
Ulla köpte blommor *i går*.	i.e. not today

This is not, of course, possible in written Swedish and therefore various different strategies must be adopted to provide an unequivocal marking of elements, e.g.:

Fronting: **Igår köpte Ulla blommor.**
(See 1045 below.)

Raising: **Den filmen tycker jag inte var så spännande.**
(See 1046 below.)
In my opinion that film wasn't very exciting.

Duplication: **Ulla, hon köpte blommor i går.**
Hon köpte blommor i går, Ulla.
(See 1047 below.)

Cleft sentence: **Det var Ulla som köpte blommor i går.**
Det var i går som Ulla köpte blommor.
Det var blommor som Ulla köpte i går.
(See 1048 below.)

(c) The end of the sentence is not the only stress position in Swedish. The initial position can accommodate a stressed element:

Mig lurar ni inte så lätt!	Me you can't fool so easily!
I Stockholm trivdes jag inte.	In Stockholm I didn't really feel at home.
Inte gör vi det idag!	We're not doing that today!

See also 1045(b).

1045 Fronting

(a) Natural topics

The topic or fronted element most frequently represents given information which the reader/listener is already familiar with, i.e. an element which is 'light' in information, often the theme (see 1044).

The topic may comprise familiar personal and demonstrative pronouns, pronominal adverbs, nouns in the definite and adverbial expressions of time. These frequently serve to link sentences together. Of these the adverbial expressions, whilst not strictly speaking comprising familiar information, do present background information of less significance than what follows.

Examples of natural topics:

> *Vi* hade länge behövt en semester, så *i våras* åkte vi till Stockholm. *Där* träffade vi våra goda vänner Olssons och *vi* trivdes väldigt bra. *De* har en stor villa på Lidingö. *Villan* har femton rum och egen swimmingpool. *I en hel vecka* låg vi bredvid poolen. *Det* var härligt må du tro! *Sedan* måste vi tyvärr åka hem.
>
> We had needed a holiday for a long time, so last spring we went to Stockholm. There we met our good friends the Olssons and had a great time. They have a big house on Lidingö. The house has fifteen rooms and its own swimming pool. For a whole week we lay beside the pool. It was lovely, you know! Then, sadly, we had to come home.

(b) Emphatic topics

A different kind of topic is one representing new information, i.e. an element 'heavy' in information, the focus. Such emphatic topics often include the object, verb phrases, infinitive phrases and negations, most of which already have emphasis, but gain extra emphasis in this way:

> *Öl* gillar han inte, men *vin* älskar han.
> Beer he does not like, but he does like wine.

> Han brukar skriva felfritt, men *ett fel* gjorde han.
> He usually writes faultlessly, but one mistake he did make.

> *Aldrig* ses vi mer i detta liv.
> Never again will we meet in this life.

> *Pengar* hade han inga.
> He didn't have any money.
> *Skicka bort pojken till internatskola* ville de inte.
> They didn't want to send the boy away to boarding school.

> *Springa efter flickor* kan han, och *supa* kan han, men *arbeta* vill han inte.
> He can chase after girls, and drink, but he won't work.

> *Att skriva en så förskräckligt ogrammatisk svenska* borde vara straffbart.
> Writing such awfully ungrammatical Swedish should be a punishable offence.

1046   Raising

(a) Raising is a kind of fronting (1045) for emphasis. As seen above, fronting in the main clause involves moving a sentence element from its usual position in the base clause to the initial position within the same clause. Raising, however, takes an element from a subordinate clause and makes it the topic in the sentence (matrix), thereby 'raising' it from its original clause:

Jag tror inte   (att) *det programmet* **var så lyckat.**
Matrix   *Subordinate clause*

Det programmet   **tror jag inte var så lyckat.**
That programme I don't think was so successful.

In this case the subject of the subordinate clause, **det programmet**, has become the topic in the sentence and is emphasised. The effect is to split subject and predicate in the original subordinate clause and to conflate this with the main clause (cf. cleft sentence 1048). The word order is also changed from straight to inverted. Notice that **att** is deleted in the new clause. The construction is common, especially in spoken Swedish. Raising frequently occurs in **att**-clauses and infinitive phrases that are complements to the verbs **säga** 'say'; **tänka** 'think'; **tro** 'think'; **veta** 'know'; **anse** 'consider', etc.:

Honom **vet jag att du inte kan stå ut med.**
(← **Jag vet att du inte kan stå ut med** *honom.*)
Him I know you can't stand.

Nästa vecka **tror jag att jag åker på semester.**
(← **Jag tror att jag åker på semester** *nästa vecka.*)
Next week I think I'll go on holiday.

(b) A certain kind of raising may also occur in cleft sentences (cf. 1048). In this instance the object may be raised to become the complement in the cleft sentence:

Base sentence: main clause:
Han har lånat hennes bil.
He has borrowed her car.
Cleft sentence (cf. 1048):
Det är hennes bil han har lånat.
It's her car he has borrowed.

Subordinate clause:
Jag tror det är hennes bil han har lånat.
I think it's her car he borrowed.

Raising:
Det är hennes bil som jag tror han har lånat.
It's her car I think he has borrowed.

1047 Duplication

(a) The duplication of a sentence element by means of a pronominal word is common in spoken Swedish. Most frequently duplicated in this way are indefinite or article-less forms. The effect of duplication is to emphasise the free element placed in the extra position outside the clause (see 1034).

(b) Most elements can be duplicated at the front of the sentence, rather fewer at the end of the sentence:

Subject:

Olof, han är sjuk.
Olof, he's ill.

Han är sjuk, *Olof.*
He's ill, Olof.

–

Jag kan inte göra det, *jag heller.*
I can't do it either.

Object:

Eva, henne tycker jag inte om.
Eva, her I don't like.

Jag tycker inte om henne, *Eva.*
I don't like her, Eva.

Complement:

En rik man, det har han alltid varit. –
A rich man he has always been.

Clausal adverbial:

–

Det är inte till salu nu, *inte.*
It's not for sale now.

Note: A similar construction, **Inte är det till salu nu, inte**, involves fronting with resultant inversion as well as end duplication. Duplication of **inte** is common in spoken Swedish:

Kan du hjälpa mig? Inte idag, inte!	Can you help me? Not today I can't.
Du får inte lov att göra det, inte.	You won't be allowed to do it.

Other adverbial:

Förr, så spelade jag mycket golf. –
Previously I used to play a lot of golf.

I Uppsala, där trivdes jag under min studietid. –
In Uppsala I enjoyed my student days.

–	**Då gör vi det, *då*.** Then we'll do that, then.
–	**Du sjunger så vackert, *så*.** You sing so beautifully.

Verb:

***Sjunga*, det kan jag minsann inte.** I definitely can't sing.	–
***Ljuger*, det gör hon hela tiden.** Lie, she does it all the time.	–

When a finite verb is duplicated, the construction **det + gör (gjorde)** usually represents it:

***Fiskar*, det gör hon ju gärna.** [See 1034, 1027(a).]
She likes to fish.

The non-finite verb, more seldom duplicated, is represented in the main clause by **det + är/var**:

***Att tala ryska*, det är ju inte lätt, det inte!**
Speaking Russian, that isn't easy that!

This last example shows several duplications.

(c) Pro-forms:

When a subordinate clause precedes a main clause, the subordinate clause may be duplicated in the main clause by a so-called 'pro-form' (here an adverb, e.g. **så**, **där**). This may be due to the desire to avoid confusion with a question:

***När vi kom fram*, så kokade vi kaffe.**
SC = OA-time
When we got there we made coffee.

***Därute i skogen vid sjön*, där vill jag bo.**
SC = OA-place
Out in the forest by the lake, that's where I want to live.

1048 Cleft sentence

(a) It is possible to focus on a particular element by using the construction **Det är/var X som...** 'It is/was X who/which/that...'

***Han* skickade mig två exemplar av boken förra veckan.**
Det var *han* som skickade mig två exemplar av boken förra veckan.
(It was) he (who) sent me two copies of the book last week.

The subject in the base sentence has become the predicative complement in a new main clause and is emphasised, while the remainder of the base sentence is appended in the form of a relative clause. The original sentence is thus cleft in two, the transformation involving both a kind of topicalisation and an addition to the base sentence. Elements of the base sentence other than the subject may also be emphasised in this way:

> **Det var *två exemplar av boken* (som) han skickade mig förra veckan.**
> [direct object in base]
> **Det var *till mig* (som) han skickade två exemplar av boken förra veckan.**
> [indirect object in base]
> **Det var *förra veckan* (som) han skickade mig två exemplar av boken.**
> [Other adverbial in base]

(b) When a sentence element is extracted it retains its original form. Thus:

> **Hon skrattade.**   → **Det var hon som skrattade.**
> She laughed.   It was she who laughed.

But:

> **Du ska vända dig till henne.** → **Det är henne du ska vända dig till.**
> You should approach her.   It is her you should approach.

(c) When a prepositional phrase is involved, the whole phrase is usually moved:

> **Det var i Värmland som jag träffade honom.**
> ← **Jag träffade honom i Värmland.**
> It was in Värmland that I met him.

With separable compound verbs and prepositional verbs the preposition remains with the verb, and does not move with the following noun phrase:

> **Det var en gammal Opel som vi körde om.**
> ← **Vi körde om en gammal Opel.**
> It was an old Opel we overtook.

(d) The cleft sentence is very common in questions:

> **Var det han som kritiserade regeringen?**
> Was it he who criticised the government?

> **Är det jag som måste bestämma?**
> Is it I who should decide?

> **Är det först på söndag som hon kommer?**

Is it not until Sunday that he's coming?

Är det öl han dricker?
Is it beer he's drinking?

Är det i staden vi ska träffa dem?
Is it in town that we're going to meet them?

J   ELLIPSIS

1049   Introduction

A clause normally contains a subject and finite verb. There are, however, exceptions to this pattern:

(a) Commands may often lack a subject:

   Rök inte härinne!   Don't smoke in here!

(b) In some subordinate clauses **har/hade** is omitted before the supine (cf. 523(b)):

   De sa, att de åkt till Sverige i fjol.
   They said they had gone to Sweden last year.

(c) There are a number of frequent cases in which the clause contains an object or other adverbial but has no finite verb and most often no subject (see 518(b), 1050(b)). These are cases of ellipsis or abbreviation of an original subordinate clause, and represent a striving for economy of expression:

   Vi bad dem om att vi skulle få följa med.
   We asked them whether we would be allowed to go along.

   Vi bad dem om att få följa med.
   We asked them to be allowed to go along.
In the paragraphs below only a selection of common constructions of this type is given. Many are infinitive phrases, and the internal order in such phrases and their position in the sentence are shown in 1050(d).

1050   Non-finite clauses

Non-finite clauses are those lacking a finite verb. They are of various kinds:

(a) Ellipted adverbial clauses

In order for this ellipsis to be possible the subject must be the same in both the sentence and the subordinate clause. These clauses include:

(i) Temporal clauses:

> **Efter det att vi gått på teatern, åt vi middag.**
> After we went to the theatre, we ate dinner.

> **Efter att ha gått på teatern, åt vi middag.**
> After having gone to the theatre, we ate dinner.

(ii) Final clauses:

> **Han reste sig för att han skulle kunna se bättre.**
> He stood up so that he could see better.

> **Han reste sig för att kunna se bättre.**
> He stood up so as to be able to see better.

(iii) Most comparative clauses:

> **Det är bättre att han dör än att han ger oss.**
> It's better that he dies than that he surrenders.

> **Det är bättre att dö än att ge sig.**
> It's better to die than surrender.

(iv) Clauses after certain prepositions:

> **Han klarade provet genom att han pluggade varje kväll.**
> He got through the test in that he studied every night.

> **Han klarade provet genom att plugga varje kväll.**
> He got through the test by studying every night.

> **Han gick utan att han sa adjö.**   →   **Han gick utan att säga adjö.**
> He left without saying goodbye.

(b) Object and infinitive constructions (see also 518(a)(iii))

With some verbs of perception, saying and thinking (**höra** 'hear'; **se** 'see'; **känna** 'feel'; **säga** 'say'; **påstå** 'claim'; **anse** 'consider'; **tro** 'think'; **tycka** 'think'; etc.) the object phrase may take the form of an object + infinitive:

> **Vi såg att han åkte bort.** → **Vi såg honom åka bort.**
> We saw that he left.   We saw him leave.

In this example **honom** is both the object of **såg** and the implied subject of **åka bort**.

> **Jag hörde att hon spelade gitarr.** → **Jag hörde henne spela gitarr.**
> I heard that she was playing the guitar.   I heard her play the guitar.

Some verbs have a reflexive pronoun as object:

> **De sa att de var trötta.** → **De sa sig vara trötta.**
> They said that they were tired.

(c) Subject and infinitive constructions. These may be seen as a development of the object + infinitive construction seen in (b) above. The object of the object + infinitive construction is topicalised, becoming the subject of a passive:

> **Man påstår att han är intelligent.**
> People say that he is intelligent.

> **Man påstår honom vara intelligent.**   Object + infinitive
> **Han påstås vara intelligent.**   Subject + infinitive

Here the subject of the sentence and the non-finite clause is the same. With the verbs **tyckas** (seem); **anse** (consider); **förefalla** (seem); **verka** (seem) the infinitive **vara** may be omitted:

> **Han verkar (vara) intelligent.**   He seems (to be) intelligent.

(d) Word order in non-finite clauses

(i) Positions within subordinate clauses and elliptical constructions:

Matrix	Conj.	S	CA	FV	NFV	O/C	OA	
	Efter det att	vi	–	–	gått	–	på teater	(åt vi middag.)
	Efter	–	–	–	att ha gått	–	på teater	(åt vi middag.)
Vi såg	att	han	–	åkte	–	–	bort.	
Vi såg	–	–	–	–	–	honom åka bort.		
Han verkar	–	–	–	–	(vara)	intelligent.		

(For translations see (a)–(c) above.)

Notice that the adverbial may split the infinitive in Swedish:

> **Jag hoppas att jag snart får träffa dig igen.** →
> **Jag hoppas att *snart* få träffa dig igen.**
> I hope to meet you again soon.

Even heavy OAs may do this:

> **Jag hoppas *att* i min nuvarande ställning *kunna* fortsätta att tjäna mitt land.**
> I hope in my present position to be able to continue to serve my country.

(ii) Position of non-finite clauses in the sentence: cf. 1039.

T	FV	S	CA	NFV	O/C	OA	X₂
Efter att ha gått på teater	åt	vi	–	–	middag.		
Han	steg	–	–	upp	–	–	för att kunna se bättre.
Han	verkar	–	–	(vara)	intelligent.		
Vi	såg	–	–	–	honom åka bort.		

1051 Verb omission and subject omission

(a) Some verbs expressing general movement (e.g. **gå**, **åka**, **springa**, **resa**, etc.) may be omitted between certain auxiliaries, e.g. **vill**, **ska**, **måste** and adverbs of motion (613):

Han vill åka hem. → Han vill hem.	He wants to go home.
Han ska bort.	He is going away.
Han måste ut.	He has to get out.
Måste vi till staden?	Do we have to go to town?
Han måste på teatern.	He has to go to the theatre.
Du måste ifrån Stockholm.	You have to get out of Stockholm.
De måste ut ur det här fängelset.	They have to get out of this prison.

(b) The finite verb is usually omitted in comparative clauses:

Hon sjunger som en fågel (sjunger).	She sings like a bird (sings).
Hon är äldre än jag (är).	She is older than I (am).

Note: In the ellipted clause the pronoun must have the same form it would have in the complete clause. Compare, for example:

Mari älskar orientering mer än mig. (= mer än hon älskar mig) [Object form]
Mari loves orienteering more than me. (= more than she loves me)

Mari älskar orientering mer än jag. (= mer än jag gör) [Subject form]
Mari loves orienteering more than I. (= more than I do)

(c) The verbs **har/hade** may be omitted in formal written Swedish (cf. 523(b)) before a supine in the subordinate clause.

(d) Omission of the second of two identical subjects is possible only when both of the following conditions are fulfilled:

1 The subject precedes the verb.
2 The clauses concerned are main clauses coordinated with the conjunctions **och** 'and'; **men** 'but'; **eller** 'or'; **utan** 'but'.

Examples:

Mari bor i Umeå och (hon) trivs jättebra där.
Mari lives in Umeå and (she) loves it there.

Compare:

Mari bor i Umeå och där trivs hon jättebra.

Gustav Adolf dog egentligen inte vid Lützen utan (han) dödades vid Breitenfeld ett år tidigare (enligt Jersild).
King Gustav Adolf did not actually die at Lützen but (he) was killed at Breitenfeld a year earlier (according to Jersild).

The conjunction **att** may be deleted together with the subject:

Jag vet att hon bor i Umeå och (att hon) studerar vid universitetet.
I know that she lives in Umeå and (that she) studies at the university.

1052   Apposition and the predicative attribute

Postpositioned qualifiers often represent deletion of some kind:

(a) Apposition (usually a deleted relative clause):

Åkes bil, (som är) en Volvo, har gått 1000 mil.
Åke's car, (which is) a Volvo, has done 6,000 miles.

Institutionens nuvarande chef, (som heter) Åke Svensson . . .
The present head of the department, (who is) Åke Svensson . . .

(b) Predicative attribute:

Hon gick genom skogen (och var) klädd i jacka och stövlar.
She was walking through the forest (and was) dressed in a jacket and boots.

en buss, (som är) full med passagerare
a bus, (which is) full of passengers

1053 Main and subordinate clause word order, the extended scheme: summary chart

Sentences below exemplify rules for positions discussed above.

		X_1	L	T	FV	S	CA	NFV	O/C	OA	X_2
MAIN CLAUSE – STATEMENTS											
1026	1			Han	har	–	inte	tvättat	bilen	idag.	
1027	2			Idag	har	han	inte	tvättat	bilen.		
1027	3			Till Lund	reste	vi	–	–	–	i våras.	
1027	4			Bilen	har	han	inte	tvättat.			
1027	5			Sedan	blev	hon	tyvärr	–	mycket arg.		
1027	6			Vacker	var	hon	inte.				
1027	7			Sälja bilen	tänker	han	inte	(göra).			
1027	8			Inte	tänker	han	–	sälja	bilen	än.	
1027	9			'Tusan!'	sa	han.					
1021	10			Vi	tycker	–	inte	om	honom.		
1021	11			Han	ser	–	inte	ut att vara	en brottsling.		
1022	12			Jag	har	–	–	lånat	Nils boken.		
1021	13			Cyklisten	blev	–	inte	omkörd	–	av bilen.	
1023	14			De	har	–	ju faktiskt	rest	–	utomlands.	
1024	15			Chefen	beviljades	–	–	–	–	avsked	av styrelsen i går.
1024	16			Vi	kom	–	–	–	–	med tåg till stan i går.	
1033	17			Det	sitter	–	nämligen	–	en polis	i köket.	

		X_1	L	T	FV	S	CA	NFV	O/C	OA	X_2
1033	18		–	Det	är-	–	–	troligt	–	–	att han vinner.
1033	19			Det	har	–	alltid	varit	en gåta	–	varför han dog.
1034	20			Han	sa	–	inte	–	–	–	att han skulle bort.
1034, 1047	21	Lars,	–	han	är	–	–	–	sjuk,	–	han.
1034, 1047	22	Inte	–	–	gör	vi		det,		inte.	
1035	23		(Han kommer)	men han	tänker		inte	stanna		länge.	

QUESTIONS

		X_1	L	T	FV	S	CA	NFV	O/C	OA	X_2
1036	24				Sålde	du	inte	–	huset?		
1036	25				Har	du	aldrig	läst	boken?		
1036	26				Kan	jag	–	få se	hennes brev?		
1047	27	Huset,		–	sålde	du	inte	–	det?		
1036	28			Vad	är	–	–	–	–	på kontoret?	
1036	29			Du	är	–	väl-	–	trött	nu?	
1036	30			Han	röker	–	inte,	–	–	–	eller hur?

	X_1	L	T	FV	S	CA	NFV	O/C	OA	X_2
COMMANDS AND OPTATIVES										
1016f., 31				**Ring**	–	inte	upp	dem	nu!	
1016f. 32				**Skriv**	(du)	–	–	–	till honom!	
1016f 33				**Måtte**	det	–	gå	dig	väl!	
1016f 34				**Vore**	jag	bara	–	ung	igen!	
CONDITIONAL CLAUSES WITH QUESTION WORD ORDER										
1042 35				**Går**	du	inte genast,	–	–	–	ringer jag till polisen.
ATT-CLAUSES WITH MAIN CLAUSE WORD ORDER										
1041 36	Nils sa att		idag	kommer	han.					
1041 37	Nils sa att		han	kommer	–	inte	–	–	imorgon.	

Matrix	Conj.	S	CA	FV	NFV	O/C	OA	X₂
SUBORDINATE CLAUSES								
1037 38 Vi frågade	om	de	ännu inte	(hade)	packat	väskan	ordentligt.	
1037 39	Eftersom	de	ännu inte	(hade)	sagt	ett ord		(förstod vi inte.)
1040 40 Vi tyckte	(att)	det	inte	var	–	roligt	längre.	
1035 41 Om vi är tysta, och	om	vi	inte	busar,	–	–	–	får vi se på TV.
INDEPENDENT CLAUSES								
1043 42	Därför att	vi	inte	har	–	råd.		
1043 43	Om	du	bara	visste	–	allt!		
1043 44	Kanske	han	redan	har	gjort	det.		
NON-FINITE CLAUSES								
1050 45	Efter	–	–	–	att ha gått	–	på teatern, åt vi middag.	
1050 46 Vi såg		honom	–	–	åka	–	bort.	
1050 47 Jag	–	–	–	hörde	henne spela	gitarr.		
1050 48 Han påstås	–	–	–	vara	dum.			

Translation of examples: 1 He hasn't washed the car today. 2 Today he hasn't washed the car. 3 We travelled to Lund last spring. 4 He hasn't washed the car. 5 Then alas she got very angry. 6 Beautiful she was not. 7 He's not thinking of selling the car. 8 He's not thinking of selling the car yet. 9 'Blast!' he said. 10 We don't like him. 11 He doesn't look like a criminal. 12 I have lent Nils the book. 13 The cyclist was not overtaken by the car. 14 They have actually travelled abroad. 15 The boss's notice was accepted by the board yesterday. 16 We came to town by train yesterday. 17 There's a policeman sitting in the kitchen, you see. 18 It is probable that he will win. 19 It has always been a mystery why he died. 20 He didn't say that he was going away. 21 Lars, he's ill, he is. 22 We're not doing that, we're not. 23 (He's coming) but he's not thinking of staying for long. 24 Didn't you sell the house? 25 Have you never read the book? 26 Can I see her letter? 27 The house, didn't you sell it? 28 What happened at the office? 29 You're tired, aren't you? 30 He doesn't smoke, does he? 31 Don't ring them up now! 32 (You) Write to him! 33 May things go well for you! 34 If I were only young again! 35 If you don't leave immediately I shall call the police. 36 Nils said that he was coming today. 37 Nils said that he's not coming tomorrow. 38 We asked whether they still hadn't packed the case properly. 39 As they still hadn't said a word, we didn't think it was funny any longer. 41 If we are quiet and we don't misbehave, we can watch TV. 42 Because we can't afford it. 43 If you only knew everything! 44 Perhaps he has already done it. 45 After having gone to the theatre we ate dinner. 46 We saw him go away. 47 I heard her playing the guitar. 48 He is considered to be stupid.

11 WORD FORMATION

1101   Introduction

A   AFFIXATION
1102   Swedish and foreign affixes
1103   Productivity
1104   Prefixes
1105   Table of prefixes
1106   Suffixes
1107   Table of suffixes
1108   Retrogradation
1109   Zero suffix

B   COMPOUNDING
1110   Introduction
1111   Compound nouns – forms by word class
1112   Compound nouns – form of links
1113   Guide to noun links
1114   Compound nouns – meaning
1115   Compound adjectives and numerals – forms by word class
1116   Compound adjectives – meaning
1117   Compound verbs – forms by word class and the particle verb
1118   Compound adverbs, conjunctions and prepositions
1119   Derivational compounding

C   EXPRESSIVE FORMATION
1120   Hypocorism
1121   Onamatopoetic formation
1122   Contamination, euphemism, folk etymology

D   ABBREVIATION
1123   Clippings and blends
1124   Acronyms

E   FOREIGN INFLUENCES ON SWEDISH
1125   Types of foreign influence
1126   Latin and Greek
1127   German
1128   The Nordic languages and Finnish
1129   French
1130   English
1131   Other languages

F	**CONVERSION**
1132	Adjective to noun
1133	Noun to adjective
1134	Adverb to adjective
1135	Verb to noun

1101 Introduction

(a) Many words in Swedish are directly descended from Proto-Indoeuropean, Common Germanic or Common Norse, i.e. the languages from which Swedish itself has developed. Examples of such indigenous words are:

> **man, kvinna, far, mor, bror, syster, and, fisk, get, gås, hund, ko, älg, al, ask, bok, hassel, lind, rönn, berg, dal, en, två, tre – tio, jag, mig, du, dig, vad, arm, fot, kind, knä**

New words in Swedish have arisen by a number of different processes:

1	Affixation	– adding a prefix/suffix to an existing root
2	Compounding	– adding a root to a root
3	Abbreviation	– shortening words, sometimes to their initial letters
4	Borrowing	– importing words from other languages
5	Expressive formation	– e.g. forming a pet name or imitating a sound
6	Conversion	– i.e. using a word from one word class as if it belonged to a different class.

(b) These processes may be illustrated by the following examples, many based on the root **vän** 'friend':

1 AFFIXATION

Prefix		*Root*		
o	+	**vän**	→	**ovän**
un	+	friend	→	enemy

Root		*Suffix*		
vän	+	***lig***	→	**vänlig**
friend	+	ly	→	friendly

Root		*Suffix*		
vän	+	***skap***	→	**vänskap**
friend	+	ship	→	friendship

2 COMPOUNDING

djur	+	**vän**	→	**djurvän**
animal	+	friend	→	animal lover

användare	+	**vänlig**	→	**användarvänlig**
user	+	friendly	→	user friendly

vän	+	**ort**	→	**vänort**
friend		town	→	twin town

3 ABBREVIATION

fotografi	→	**foto**
photograph	→	photo

4 BORROWING

from German	**bundsförvant** = ally, friend
from French	**kompanjon** = (business) companion, friend
from English	**partner** = (business) partner, friend
from other languages	**kollega** = colleague, friend [from Latin]

5 EXPRESSIVE FORMATION

kompanjon	→	**komp**	+	*is*	→	**kompis**
partner						chum

		bäst	+	*is*	→	**bästis**
		best				best friend

6 CONVERSION

Adjective	→	*Noun*
djup	→	**djup -et**
deep	→	(the) deep

(c) Modification

Notice that the first element (FE) in a compound typically modifies the second or subsequent element (SE): **hustak, biltak, skiffertak** are all kinds of **tak** ('roof'). In both derivatives and compounds it is the final element to which any inflexional ending is attached, and consequently this element which determines the word class:

fri	+	**tid**	→	**fritid**	cf. **fritiden**	(noun)
free		time	→	spare time		

o	+	**van**	→	**ovan**	cf. **ovana**	(adjective)
un	+	accustomed	→	unaccustomed		

rost	+	**fri**	→	**rostfri**	cf. **rostfritt**	(adjective)
rust	+	free	→	stainless		

god	+	**het**	→	**godhet**	cf. **godheten**	(noun)
good	+	ness	→	goodness		

This means that, while prefixes never alter the word class (e.g. in **van** → **ovan** both are adjectives), suffixes are frequently used for this very purpose (e.g. in **god** → **godhet** adjective changes to noun).

A AFFIXATION

1102   Swedish and foreign affixes

(a) Chronology:

Early Swedish had different means of forming words from those used nowadays. Many of these word formation elements disappeared during major linguistic developments as early as the Viking Age. Only a few of them have remained productive over the centuries, e.g.: **-ing/-ning** in early Swedish **viking, drottning, penning, skilling** also in more recent formations **gamling, raring, snygging, hårding, mobbning, tackling**.

The number of affixes was later severely reduced and many of them became non-productive. In medieval Swedish new affixes developed to take their place, which were of two main kinds:

(i) Indigenous final elements in compounds became *productive* affixes (see 1103):

e.g. Old Swedish

likr	= 'body', 'figure', 'appearance'	→ **-lig** in: **dödlig, gudlig, nylig, daglig**
samber	= 'same'	→ **-sam** in: **fridsam, mödosam**
domber	= (meaning varies, abstract)	→ **-dom** in: **mandom, sjukdom, guddom, kristendom**
skaper	= (form, type)	→ **-skap** in: **vänskap, fiendskap, herrskap, boskap**
leker	= (meaning varies, abstract) →	**-lek** in: **kärlek, storlek, väderlek**

(ii) A great number of words, especially abstract terms, were borrowed from Low German in the Middle Ages. Many of these provided affixes that became productive with Swedish stems at that and later periods:

be-, bi-	betala, bilägga	**-bar**	uppenbar
för-	förlåta, fördärva	**-het**	kyskhet
sam-	samband, samåkning	**-inna**	furstinna
-ande	meddelande, ordförande	**-ska**	synderska

(iii) In more recent times Swedish has received a fresh wave of productive affixes via loanwords of Romance origin:

> rea*list*, prole*tär*, regiss*ör*, servi*tris*, restaur*ant*, akt*iv*, kultur*ell*, centr*al*, intellig*ent*, ajourn*era*

(b) The introduction into the language of foreign affixes often results in two word formation elements with the same meaning existing side by side in the lexicon. A major distinction can be made here between Germanic affixes (i.e. indigenous words + German loans) and Romance affixes (mostly Latin and French loans, some having been borrowed via English):

e.g. PREFIXES

Germanic			*Romance*		
o-	olaglig	=	in- (ir-, im-, il-)	illegal	(unlawful)
sam-	samarbete	=	ko-	kooperation	(cooperation)
själv-	självlärd	=	auto-	autodidakt	(self-taught)
åter-	återuppbygga	=	re-	rekonstruera	(reconstruct)

Note: **Själv-** and **åter-** are not strictly speaking prefixes, see 1103(c).

e.g. SUFFIXES

Verb	*Noun (Person)*	*Noun (Activity)*	
Germanic			
granska	**granskare**	**granskning**	
inspect	inspector	inspection	
Romance			
inspektera	**inspektör**	**inspektion**	
inspect	inspector	inspection	

Verb	*Noun (Person)*	*Adjective*	*Noun (Abstract)*
Swedish			
tillverka	**tillverkare**	—	**tillverkning,** **tillverkande**
produce	producer		production
Romance			
producera	**producent**	**produktiv**	**produktivitet**
produce	producer	productive	productivity

1103 Productivity

(a) A productive affix or word element has two features:

1. It is possible to describe grammatically and/or semantically the elements which can be included.

2. It produces a derivative whose meaning is easily predicted from the meaning of the basic word.

For example, **-bar** is an adjective suffix meaning '**möjlig att X**' where X is a verb. So we can form:

användbar usable	= **möjlig att använda** possible to use
tänkbar conceivable	= **möjlig att tänka** possible to think
förnyelsebar renewable	= **möjlig att förnya** possible to renew, etc.

Potentially it should be possible to add a productive affix to any word of a particular grammatical or semantic type. Thus **-bar** is an adjective suffix which potentially can be added to all transitive verb stems. (It is an adjective suffix but is also deverbal, see 1106). This must be contrasted with very frequent but non-productive affixes which are lexical forms, i.e. they are only found with the loanwords they accompany and do not give rise to any new formations in Swedish. These are all borrowed from other West European languages, e.g.:

kon- (←Latin con-): **konflikt, konsonant, konservativ**

kon- is not used to form new Swedish words.

(b) The meaning of a new formation may be more or less transparent. For example, **en fiskburgare** and **en ostburgare** are fairly obviously kinds of **hamburgare** ('hamburger') but made with fish or cheese. **En bankomat** is discernible as deriving from **bank** + **automat** ('dispenser') i.e. a cash dispenser. However, whilst the word **mjuk** ('soft)' in **mjukglass** ('soft ice') is understandable, it is not immediately obvious in **mjukvara** ('software') or in **mjukporr** ('soft porn'). The last two words are examples of a new formation or loan that is lexicalised and where one or more of the individual elements have lost or adapted their original meaning.

(c) Some roots frequently found in compounds may come to be regarded as productive affixes. This happened frequently in Old Swedish (see 1102(a)(i) above) and is still occurring. The meaning of the root usually becomes vaguer and more generalised when it is used as an affix, e.g.:

-vänlig: originally an independent root – an adjective – meaning 'friendly', used first in e.g. **barnvänlig** = '**vänlig mot barn**'.

Nowadays it is found in the less easily predictable:

användarvänlig, fotvänlig, hudvänlig, figurvänlig, lekvänlig, miljövänlig, sittvänlig.

This process can be seen in words with the following affixes:

(i) Prefixes	**själv-**	**självdö, självfinansiera, självdeklaration**
	åter-	**återförena, återanvända, återbäring, återbruk**
(ii) Suffixes	**-artad**	**vulkanartad, lavinartad**
	-fattig	**solfattig, kalorifattig**
	-fri	**alkoholfri, trafikfri, vapenfri**

-full	praktfull, värdefull
-lös	livlös, föräldralös, uddlös, tandlös, mållös
-nära	hudnära, figurnära, kustnära
-riktig	sittriktig, moderiktig, funktionsriktig

Root-forming prefixes are marked in the table in 1105 thus /efter/ **efterskrift**.

(d) Some vogue affixes and word elements of recent years from the cultural and political debate are listed below.

anti- (← Latin) originally in: **antites, antipati, antibiotikum, antiklimax**. Recently in words denoting persons: **antikommunist, antiimperialist**; most recently in vogue words: **antirasist, antivåld, antihjälte, antikropp, antirökkampanj, antiauktoritär**.

köns- as in: **könsroll, könsfördomar, könsdiskriminering, könskvotering**.

miljö- as in: **miljöförstöring, miljöfråga, miljövård, miljöfarlig, miljöskydd**.

pseudo- (← Greek) originally in: **pseudonym**; recently in: **pseudohändelse, pseudoproblem, pseudovetenskaplig**.

-cid (← Latin) originally in: **herbicid, pesticid**; new formations are: **biocid, ekocid, genocid**.

-krati (← Greek) originally in: **demokrati, aristokrati, plutokrati**; new formations are: **meritokrati, teknokrati, byråkrati**.

-mat (← Greek) originally in: **automat**; new formations are: **tankomat, bankomat, tvättomat**.

See also the lists of productive affixes in 1104, 1106, 1107.

1104   Prefixes

(a) A prefix is a morpheme which introduces a word, coming before the root, but which itself cannot form a root, e.g.:

o	+	ro	→	oro	(cf. English un + rest→
prefix		*root*			unrest)

(b) Several different prefixes may express the same basic meaning: For example negation (see also 1105) can be expressed by:

o-	olycklig	il-	illegal
dis-	disharmoni	in-	intolerant
icke-	ickevåldspolitik	non-	nonaggression

(c) The same prefix may also occur in derivatives of a number of different word classes. Unlike suffixes (see 1106), prefixes do not alter the word class, e.g.:

o +	**djur**	→	**odjur**	o +	**lycklig**	→	**olycklig**
neg.	*noun*		*noun*	*neg.*	*adjective*		*adjective*

o +	**gilla**	→	**ogilla**	o +	**gärna**	→	**ogärna**
neg.	*verb*		*verb*	*neg.*	*adverb*		*adverb*

(d) Prefixes are either stressed or unstressed.

Stressed prefixes comprise a large group forming nouns, adjectives and verbs:

- stressed indigenous prefixes: **ansvar, otrevlig, misstolka, samarbete**
- stressed loan prefixes: **antikommunist, illegal, prorektor**

This distinction is often a grey area, however, as most productive affixes have at one time been borrowed, including for example the prefixes **an-** and **miss-** from medieval Low German.

Unstressed prefixes are few and are used primarily to form verbs, for example **be-** and **för-**, both originally from Low German loans: **besvara, förvara**.

In the table in 1105 prefixes are classified according to the way in which they modify the meaning of the stem to which they are added.

1105   Table of prefixes

This is not an exhaustive list. The symbol /   / = root forming compound – see 1103(c)(ii) for explanation.

Prefix	Sense	Examples	Translation

1 NEGATIVE and PEJORATIVE

o-	not	olycklig	not happy = unhappy
	not	ovän	not friend = enemy
	not	ogilla	not like = disapprove of
	bad	ovana	bad habit

Note 1: Used especially with adjectives ending in **-bar, -lig, -ig, -isk, -sam** and with some nouns.
Note 2: Nouns may either be negative, **olycka** ('accident') or pejorative, **ogräs** ('weed)'.

in-	not	**intolerant**	not tolerant = intolerant
il-	not	**illegal**	not legal = illegal
im-	not	**impopulär**	not popular = unpopular
ir-	not	**irreparabel**	not repairable = irreparable
non-	not	**nonaggression**	non-aggression
a-	not	**asymmetrisk**	not symmetrical = asymmetrical
/icke-/	not	**icke-europeisk**	non-european

Note: **icke-** is often used for English loan translations, **icke-rökare** 'non-smoker'.

Prefix	Sense	Examples	Translation
miss-	not	misslyckad	not succeeded = failed
	bad	missljud	bad sound = discord
van-	badly	vantrivas	get on badly
	badly	vansköta	look after badly
des-	wrongly	desillusionerad	with wrong illusion = disillusioned
dis-	wrongly	disharmonisk	with wrong harmony = disharmonious

2 PEJORATIVE

kvasi-	falsely	kvasivetenskaplig	falsely scientific = quasi-scientific
pseudo-	falsely	pseudoklassisk	falsely classical = pseudo-classical
krypto-	secretly	kryptofascist	secretly fascist = crypto-fascist

3 REVERSATIVE or PRIVATIVE

de-	reverse action	denationalisera	reverse nationalise = privatise
des-	deprive of	desarmera	deprive of armament = disarm
/av-/	deprive of	avfolka	deprive of population = depopulate

4 ATTITUDE

kon-	together with	konkurrera	run together = compete
		kontext	with the text = context
kor-	together with	korrelat	relate with = correlative
kom-	together with	kompensation	pay for = compensation
kol-	together with	kollaborera	work with = collaborate
ko-	together with	koordinera	work with = coordinate
sam-	together with	samarbeta	work together with
/med-/	together with	medresenär	[accompanying traveller] = fellow passenger
sär-	separate from	särbeskattning = separate taxation	tax separately from
pro-	in favour of	prokommunist = pro-Communist	in favour of Communism
anti-	against	antikommunist = anti-Communist	against Communism
gen-	against	genstridig	fighting against = rebellious
/mot-/	resistance to	motståndare = opponent	person standing against something
kontra-	corresponds to	kontrapunkt	counterpoint
	against	kontrarevolution	counter-revolution

5 SIZE or DEGREE

för-	extremely	försupen extremely drunken =	alcoholised
hyper-	beyond	hypermodern	beyond modern = hypermodern
super-	beyond	supermakt	beyond a power = superpower
ultra-	beyond	ultramodern	beyond modern = ultramodern
ärke-	beyond	ärkefiende	beyond enemy = arch-enemy
mini-	little	minisemester	little holiday = mini-break
maxi-	big	maxipack	large pack

Note: These loan prefixes are productive.

under-	too little	undernärd	too little nourished = undernourished
över-	too much	överansträngd	too much strained = overwrought

Prefix	Sense	Examples	Translation

6 LOCATION (time or place)

Prefix	Sense	Examples	Translation
/för(e)-/	before	företrädare	going before = predecessor
post-	after	postskriptum	after the text = postscript
/efter-/	after	efterskrift	after the text = postscript, epilogue
sub-	under, below	subtropisk	below the tropics = tropical
/under-/	under, below	underjordisk	under the ground = subterranean
bi-	beside	biprodukt	additional product = by-product
ur-	original	urskog	original forest = virgin forest
/medel-/	between	medelvärde	in-between value = average/median value
neo-	new	neoklassicism	new classicism = neoclassicism
/ny-/	new	nyår	New Year
		nyanställa	recruit (verb)
ex-	former	exkung	ex-king

7 LOCATION or DIRECTION

Prefix	Sense	Examples	Translation
trans-	across	transportera	carry across = transport
/över-/	across	överföra	send across = transmit
ex-	from	export	(goods) carried out from = export
/ut-/	from	utförsel	sending out from = export

8 DIRECTION (time or place)

Prefix	Sense	Examples	Translation
an-	to, towards	ankomma	come towards = arrive
/till-/	to, towards	tillsända	send to = remit
för-	away from	fördriva	drive away
/bort-/	away from	bortgång	going away = death
/borta-/	away	bortamatch	away match
/undan-/	away from	undanta	take away = exclude
und-	away from	undgå	go away = escape
re-	back, again	regruppera	group together again = regroup
gen-	back, again	gengångare	person who comes back = ghost
/åter-/	back, again	återse	see again
fort-	again	fortplanta	plant again = reproduce
/vidare-/	further	vidareutbildning	further education
/slut-/	end	slutskede	end stage
pre-	before	preludium	playing before = prelude
post-	after	postmodernism	after modernism = post-modernism

9 NUMBER

Prefix	Sense	Examples	Translation
/halv-/	half	halvcirkel	semicircle
mono-	one	monoteism	one god = monotheism
/en-/	one	ensidig	one sided = biased
bi-	two	bilateral	two sided = bilateral
di-	two	dikotomi	two classes = dichotomy
tve-	two	tvetydig	two meanings = ambiguous
/två-/	two	tvåspråkig	two languages = bilingual
/dubbel/	two	dubbelbeskattning	double taxation
poly-	many	polygami	many wives = polygamy
/fler-/	many	flerfärgad	multicoloured
/mång-/	many	mångmiljonär	multimillionaire

multi-	many	multifärgad	multicoloured

Prefix	Sense	Examples	Translation
pan-	all	panamerikansk	pan-American
/all-/	all	allsidig	all sides = comprehensive

10 OTHERS

auto-	self	autodidakt	self-taught = autodidact
/själv-/	self	självlärd	self-taught
vice-	deputy	vicepresident	vice-president
pro-	instead of	prorektor	pro-rector

11 TRANSITIVISATION

be-	bo	live	→	bebo	inhabit
be-	segra	win	→	besegra	defeat
be-	svara	reply	→	besvara	respond to
för-	neka	refuse	→	förneka	deny
för-	tiga	be silent	→	förtiga	keep secret

Note: There are three different kinds of combinations in the above list:

1 Foreign prefix + foreign root: **kor-relat**
2 Indigenous prefix + indigenous root   **ny-år, tve-tydig**
3 Combination of foreign and indigenous elements **mång-miljonär, hyper-dålig, vice-ordförande**

1106   Suffixes

(a) A suffix is a morpheme which ends a word. It comes after the root, but cannot itself form a root, e.g.:

vetenskap	+	lig	=	→	vetenskaplig
(science		-ly			scientific)
root		suffix			

Unlike prefixes, suffixes are frequently used in order to alter the word class, e.g.:

ludd	+	ig		→	luddig
(fluff		-y			fluffy, vague)
noun		adj. suffix			adjective

färg	+	a		→	färga
(colour					colour)
noun		verb suffix			verb

klar	+	het		→	klarhet
(clear					clarity)
adjective		noun suffix			noun

It is sometimes useful to be able to denote not only the nature of the converting suffix – noun suffixes form nouns – but also the word class of the original word. Thus *denominal* words are formed from nouns, *deverbal* words from verbs and *deadjectival* words from adjectives.

Productive deadjectival noun suffixes include **-het, -ism, -itet**:

> **svag** weak – **svaghet** weakness; **huligan** hooligan – **huliganism** hooliganism; **populär** popular – **popularitet** popularity

Productive deverbal adjective suffixes include **-bar, -ig, -sam**:

> **stapl[a]** stack – **stapelbar** stackable; **tål[a]** tolerate – **tålig** (patient); **prat[a]** talk – **pratsam** talkative

Productive deverbal suffixes include: **-ande, -are: rengör[a]** – **självrengörande** self-cleaning; **jogg[a]** – **joggare** jogger

A large group of deverbal nouns have the suffix **-ing/-ning**:

> **mobb[a]** bully– **mobbning** bullying; **tyngdlyft[a]** lift weights – **tyngdlyftning** weight-lifting; etc.

Productive deadjectival verb suffixes include **-na**:

> **sval** cool – **svalna** cool down; **blek** pale – **blekna** grow pale

The same suffix may in combination with different stems result in different meanings: **arbet*are*** 'worker', is a person who works, **mät*are*** 'meter', is an object which measures. The converse is also true; several suffixes may express the same basic meaning, e.g. **utvandr*are*, emig*rant*, res*ande*, inspekt*or*, kondukt*ör*** are all people carrying out some activity, e.g. **utvandra, emigrera, resa**, etc. (See also 1107.1.)

The same suffix may also occur in derivatives of several different word classes, e.g.: **-ing** may be added to:

- proper nouns: **Småland** → **smålänning**
- adjectives: **sjuk** → **sjukling**
- verbs: **uppkomm[a]** → **uppkomling**

In the table in 1107 suffixes are classified according to the word class of the resultant derivative and further sub-classified according to *either* the way they modify the meaning of the stem to which they are added *or* the word class of the stem.

(b) In some cases the derivative may also have a different stem vowel from its base word:

(i) NOUN	→ NOUN	**Värmland**	**värmlänning**
(ii) ADJECTIVE	→ NOUN	**lång**	**längd**
		tung	**tyngd**
		glad	**glädje**
(iii) ADJECTIVE	→ VERB	**tam**	**tämja**
		tom	**tömma**
		full	**fylla**

(c) In some cases we can talk of a zero-suffix (0-suffix, see 1109). Here the base is a verb and the derivative its stem, which may often form an abstract noun:

lyft[a] → lyft   e.g. **lönelyft** (salary) raise

1107   Table of suffixes

This is not an exhaustive list. V = verb, N = noun, A = adjective, e.g. V- = Verb ending in ... , N- = noun ending in ... , L = Latin derivation, F = French derivation

Group/Suffix	Added to stem	Sense	Examples	Notes
1 NOUN-FORMING				
PEOPLE				
Masculine and Feminine				
-are	V-a	person	**läsare**	
		agent of action	**mätare**	
-ande	V-a	agent	**studerande**	
-ende	V-vowel	agent	**gående**	
-ant/-ent	V-era	agent	**emigrant**	
		agent	**konsument**	
-(a)tor	V-era	agent	**diktator**	
-graf		agent	**fotograf**	
-is		agent	**kompis**	hypocorisms, see 1120
-ist	V-a, N	occupation	**cyklist**	
		philosophy	**Marxist**	
-iker	N-ik	occupation	**kritiker**	
-log		occupation	**sociolog**	
-an		nationality	**amerikan**	
-es		nationality	**kines**	
-(i)er		nationality	**belgier**	
-it		nationality	**muskovit**	
-at		person	**demokrat**	
-är/	N-tion	occupation	**funktionär**	see also 2 below

Group/Suffix	Added to stem	Sense	Examples	Notes
-är/-jär		occupation	finansiär, pionjär	
Masculine				
-are		occupation	lärare	
-ör	V-era	occupation	regissör	
-ing/-ling	V, N, A	origin	krympling, värmlänning, sjukling	
Feminine				
-(ar)inna	V-a, N	occupation	värdinna	
-(er)ska	V-a, N-are	occupation	sjuksköterska	
-(ö)rska		occupation	frisörska, kassörska	
-essa/-issa	N	occupation	prinsessa	
	N	occupation	abbedissa, profetissa	
-ös	N-ör	occupation	dansös	
-ris	N-ör	occupation	servitris	
ACTIVITY				
-(n)ing	V-a	activity,	skrivning	
-ande	V-a	result of activity	skrivande	
-ende	V-vowel	result of activity	leende	
-an	V-a	abstract	början	
-else	V	abstract	jämförelse	
-(a)tion, -sion, -ition	V-era	abstract	funktion	
			inform/era	→ information
			fung/era	→ funktion
			explod/era	→ explosion
			kompon/era	→ komposition
-grafi, -ologi		abstract	fotografi, sociologi	
Zero suffix	V-a		glid, lyft	see 1109
STATUS				
-het	A	status	brottslighet, svaghet	
-lek	A	dimension quality	storlek kärlek	
-dom	N, A	status condition	ålderdom sjukdom	
-skap	N	condition	vänskap	
-ska	A	abstract	ondska	
-an	see Activity	feelings	önskan	
-else		feelings	frestelse	
-sel		feelings	blygsel	
-ande		feelings	medlidande	
-nad			tystnad	
-(n)ing			förvåning	
-itet	A	status	neutralitet	
-ism		views	socialism	

Group/Suffix	Added to stem	Sense	Examples	Notes

2 ADJECTIVE-FORMING

FROM VERBS

-bar	V-a	possible	hörbar	
-lig	V-a, V-vowel		rörlig, trolig	
-abel	V-era	possible	diskutabel	
-aktig	V	tendency	varaktig	
-ig	V	inclination	slarvig	
-sam	V	inclination	arbetsam	
-sk	V	inclination	glömsk	
-en	V	inclination	närgången	
-sen	V	inclination	överlägsen	
-(a)tiv	V-era	inclination	kontemplativ	

FROM NOUNS

-(a)d/t	N	which have X	enarmad	
-(is)erad	N	which have X	transistoriserad	
-ig	N	which have X	tvåstavig	
-enlig	N	according to	lagenlig	
-mässig	N	corresponding to	planmässig	
-aktig	N	characteristic of	dåraktig	
-artad	N	of	granitartad	
-(i)sk	N	belonging to	brittisk	
-lig	N	belonging to	mänsklig, vänlig	
-al	N-um	belonging to	central	
-ell	N	belonging to	kulturell	
-ant	N-ans/-ens	L, F	elegant	
-ent	N	L, F	intelligent	
-iv	N-ion/-sion	F	aktiv	
-är	N	F	reaktionär	
-ös	N	F	nervös	

FROM ADJECTIVES

-lig/-lik	A	tendency to	sjuklig, jämlik	
-aktig	A	close to	gulaktig	often colours
-artad	A	having the property of	storartad	

3 VERB-FORMING

FROM NOUNS

-a/-era	N	treat, provide with	adressera färga	
	N	remove	damma avfrosta	(addition of prefix)
-a/-era	N	place in	decentralisera burka paketera	

Group/Suffix	Added to stem	Sense	Examples	Notes
-a/-era	N	do, produce,	tvätta, fynda, golfa	
		make the object of	kritisera	
	N	use	cykla	
		be, act as	basa	
			vikariera	
			förklara	(addition of prefix)
	N	make into	amerikanisera, bolagisera	

FROM ADJECTIVES

-a	A	make, change into	lugna	
-na	A	become X	svartna, mörkna, gulna, blekna	
-a (+ mutation)	A	make X	värma	
-ja (+ mutation)	A	make X	glädja	

OTHERS

Pronoun	address as	dua	
Interjection	say	heja	

1108   Retrogradation

The most usual method of word formation is for nouns to be formed from verbs:

Verb		Noun		Noun
skriva	→	skrivning	→	skrivande

But sometimes the process is reversed and (compound) verbs are formed from (compound) nouns:

Verb		Noun		Compound Noun		Compound Verb
(försäkra	→	försäkring	→)	brandförsäkring	→	brandförsäkra
(röka	→	rökare	→)	kedjerökare	→	kedjeröka
(rädda	→	räddning	→)	livräddning	→	livrädda

This process is known as retrogradation or 'back-formation' and is very common in newspaper style. It often produces ephemeral formations:

folkparksturnera, storupprusta, enhetstala, buktala, djupfrysa, marknadsföra, momsbelägga, ugnsteka, korrekturläsa, hjärntvätta, iscensätta, planlägga, dammsuga, svartlista.

1109 Zero suffix

Nouns are occasionally formed directly from the stem of verbs after deletion of the infinitive **-a** ending:

Noun	*Verb*		*Noun*	*Verb*	
dropp	←	**dropp[a]**	**flyt**	←	**flyt[a]**
drip		drip	fluency		flow

Others include: **fusk, glid, riv, smäll, spill, stöt, svinn, åk.**

Many new formations of this kind are compounds: **avhopp, utsläpp, uttag, lönelyft, påhitt.**

B COMPOUNDING

1110 Introduction

(a) Whereas in English compounds are either written as one or two words or sometimes hyphenated, Swedish usually writes them as one word:

local train	**lokal|tåg**
bed|room	**sov|rum**
flower pot/flower-pot/flower|pot	**blom|kruka**

Note: There is an increasing tendency (strongly resisted by linguists) to separate compounds in some varieties of Swedish in the English manner (see also 1130):

> *****personal matsal** [normally **personalmatsal**] staff cafeteria

This may result in some strange (and comic) phrases: ***rök fritt (rökfritt), *en lång hårig flicka (en långhårig flicka),* en sjuk gymnast (en sjukgymnast), *kyckling lever (kycklinglever)**.

Compounds may be formed from all word classes. In nearly every instance the second or subsequent element (SE) determines the word class, as it this element that usually takes inflexional endings.

Compound nouns are most frequent, and within this group nouns are the most frequent type of first element (FE): **sol|sken.**

Nouns also form the most common FE in compound adjectives: **kvälls|öppen.**

On occasion a phrase may form the FE in a compound: **tvåvåning|s|hus, hundraår|s|minne.**

An unusual group of noun compounds consists entirely of an imperative phrase:

ett far|väl, ett kryp|in, ett håll|igång, ett stå|hej, en förgät|mig|ej, ett kom|ihåg

Combinations of word class are found in 1111, 1115, 1117f., etc.

(b) Compounds consist of two (or more) elements which may occur as independent words, but the relationship between the elements does not often represent equal weight. In most compounds there is a head word, usually the SE, which indicates the basic meaning, accompanied by a descriptive element, the FE:

hus|tak

Other possible types of **tak** are: **bil|tak, sol|tak, vagn|tak, halm|tak, skiffer|tak,** and in a figurative sense **löne|tak, utlåning|s|tak,** etc.

The main types of syntactic relationship between the elements are:

(i) *Determinative*, i.e. where one element determines or describes the type of head word, as in **hus|tak** above. Here the compound may be replaced by the SE + a prepositional expression or a genitive:

hus|tak	= **taket på huset, husets tak**
blå|svart	= **en blå nyans av en svart färg**
idrott|s|klubb	= **klubb för idrott**
svensk|amerikan	= **svensk som utvandrat till Amerika**

Determinative compounding is most frequent among compound nouns and adjectives. Many compound verbs are not compounds proper but are formed by retrogradation (see 1108). Many compound verbs are separable compounds comprising a stressed particle + verb (see 1117). For compound adjectives see also 1115f., and for compound adverbs see 1118.

(ii) *Copulative*, i.e. where the two elements are of equal status, e.g. **blå|gul, byx|kjol**. Here the compound can be substituted by 'FE *and* SE' or 'FE = SE':

blå|gul	= **blå + gul**
byx|kjol	= **byxor + kjol**
ett Sverige-Norge samarbete	= **ett samarbete mellan Sverige och Norge**
en pojk|vän	= **en pojke + en vän**

(iii) *Possessive compound.* This type expresses some characteristic feature of a person or animal, providing a metonymic image (i.e. the part stands for the whole):

vilje|stark	= som har stark vilja
röd|skinn	= (person) som har rött skinn [i.e. a native American]
grå|ben	= (djur) som har grå ben [i.e. wolf]
tjock|skalle	= (person) som har tjock skalle [i.e. numskull]

(c) Some recent very productive first and final elements that work in much the same way as prefixes and suffixes are:

First element:

engångs	engångs|bestick, engångs|flaska
fick	fick|förpackning, fick|räknare
mjuk	mjuk|start, mjuk|valuta
noll	noll|bemanning, noll|tillväxt
när	när|demokrati, när|radio
snabb	snabb|kaffe, snabb|mat
trivsel	trivsel|skapande, trivsel|vikt

Second or subsequent element:

aktion	flykting|aktion, fred|s|aktion
bank	blod|bank, lägenhet|s|bank
burgare	ost|burgare, fisk|burgare
getto	betong|getto, student|getto, stor|stad|s|getto
knutte	data|knutte, kultur|knutte, charm|knutte, muskel|knutte
landskap	kontor|s|landskap, skol|landskap
medveten	miljö|medveten, mode|medveten, kvalitet|s|medveten
riktig	fot|riktig, sitt|riktig
roll	kvinno|roll, kön|s|roll
åldern	atom|åldern, rymd|åldern, data|åldern, guld|åldern

1111 Compound nouns – forms by word class

(a) Compound nouns may have as their FE a number of different word classes:

FE	Example
NOUN	hus|tak, parkering|s|mätare, gatu|belysning
PROPER NOUN	Ericsson|direktör, Strindberg|s|pjäs
NOUN PHRASE	sexrum|s|lägenhet, alleman|s|rätt, engång|s|förpackning
ADJECTIVE	fri|tid, hög|hus, lokal|tåg, sjuk|kassa
VERB	tvätt|medel, sov|rum, gå|gata, ha|begär, strö|jobb

VERB PHRASE	gör-det-själv-|möbler, slit-och-släng-|samhället
PREPOSITION	över|klass, mellan|vägg
PREPOSITIONAL PHRASE	undervatten|s|kamera,
	mellankrig|s|åren,
	dygnetrunt|service
NUMERAL	åtti|talet, fyr|takt, fem|kamp
ADVERB	väl|stånd, nu|tiden, ute|liggare,
	hemma|marknad
PRONOUN	jag|roman, all|rum, hon|kön
INTERJECTION	ja|sägare, nej|kampanj

(b) Some general guidelines apply to the form of the FE:

(i) Nouns are usually found in their basic form, without inflexional endings:

finans|politik	←	finanser	+	politik
atlant|flyg	←	Atlanten	+	flyg

Exceptions: A small number of loanwords whose plural ends in –a, and most FEs using **öga, öra**:

**fakta\|blad, data\|operatör, narkotika\|smugglare
ögon\|bryn, öron\|inflammation, örn\|gott**

(But see also 1112 for vowel reductions and links:)

(ii) Adjectives are usually found in their basic form, without inflexional endings:

snabb|val	cf.	ett snabb*t* val
blå|märke	cf.	ett blå*tt* märke
grov|arbete	cf.	ett grov*t* arbete
fin|byxor	cf.	fin*a* byxor

Exceptions: **andre\|styrman** (ordinal numbers), **lille\|bror, stora\|syster** (definite), **små\|företagare** (plural), **fler\|pack, äldre\|omsorg** (comparative).

(iii) Verbs are found as their stem:

älsk|värd	←	älska + värd
rid|häst	←	rida + häst
gå|gata	←	gå + gata

Exceptions: To facilitate pronunciation some verb stems add **-e** or more rarely **-s** or when used as FE:

läse|sal	←	läs[a] + sal
drick|s|pengar	←	drick[a] + pengar

(iv) When the FE in a compound adjective is an adverb formed from an adjective this FE is found in the adjectival form, i.e. without **-t**:

trög|flytande	←	trögt + flytande

hög|utbildad   ←   högt + utbildad

Exception: högt|uppsatt.

1112   Compound nouns – form of links

In this paragraph and 1113 only compound nouns are discussed. See 1111(b) for other methods of linking. The linking of compound nouns is complex and no hard and fast rules exist; all that can be given are some guidelines.

(a) Two element compounds: NOUN (with or without modification) + NOUN

Five main methods are employed:

1 NOUN + NOUN

ett bil|däck	← en bil	+	ett däck
en blixt|inspektion	← en blixt	+	en inspektion
en telefon|sluss	← en telefon	+	en sluss
en turist|byrå	← en turist	+	en byrå
ett trä|hus	← (ett) trä	+	ett hus

2 (NOUN minus final -a/-e) + NOUN (but cf. 5 below)

en flick|skola	← en flicka	+	en skola
(en) käll|sortering	← en källa	+	en sortering
ett pojk|namn	← en pojke	+	ett namn
en lärar|lön	← en lärare	+	en lön

Note: FEs ending in -mme also drop one m:

en tum|sugare	← en tumme	+	en sugare
en tim|arbetare	← en timme	+	en arbetare

BUT: **en kaffe|kopp, vete|mjöl, ett firma|namn, en pizza|deg, ett villa|område**

3 NOUN + s + NOUN

ett parkering|s|hus	← en parkering	+	ett hus	
en byte|s|balans	← ett byte	+	en balans	
en skriv|bord|s|lampa	← ett skriv|bord	+	en lampa	(see (b) below)
ett röd|vin|s|glas	← ett röd|vin	+	ett glas	(see (b) below)

4 NOUN in -ja → -je + NOUN

ett kedje|byte	← en kedja	+	ett byte
en vilje|styrka	← en vilja	+	en styrka

Note also: **ett familj|e|hem, ett familj|e|bidrag** but **ett kampanj|bidrag**.

5 (NOUN + case ending in **-u,-o,-e,-a**) + NOUN

ett vecko|slut	← **en vecka**	+	**ett slut**
ett varu|hus	← **en vara**	+	**ett hus**

Of these, type 5 is largely non-productive, comprising lexicalised relic roots (but notice some new formations: **ett lyckopiller, ett kvinnoparti, en skilsmässoför-handling**).

Minor methods include:

6 NOUN in consonant + **-la** (→ consonant + **-el**) + NOUN

en tavel|krok	← **en tavla**	+	**en krok**
ett våffel|järn	← **en våffla**	+	**ett järn**

Exceptions are words in **-lla** and a few others:

ett hyll|plan	← **en hylla**	+	**ett plan**
en käll|förteckning	← **en källa**	+	**en förteckning**
(en) pärle|mor	← **en pärla**	+	**en mor**
ett pärl|fiske	← **en pärla**	+	**ett fiske**

7 POLYSYLLABIC NOUN in **-te** → **-ts** + NOUN

en arbet|s|narkoman	← **ett arbete** + **en narkoman**
en ansikt|s|lyftning	← **ett ansikte** + **en lyftning**

Cf. bisyllabic nouns retain the **-e**: **lyte – lyte|s|komik, bete – bete|s|mark**.

The way in which the ending is decisive to the form of the link is shown in much greater detail in the guide to noun links in 1113.

(b) Three element compounds

Notice that compound nouns whose FEs themselves are compounds tend to differ from those which have a simple FE in that a majority of them employ the link **-s** after the second element:

en fot + en boll	→	**en fot|boll**	NOUN + NOUN
en boll + en plan	→	**en boll|plan**	NOUN + NOUN
en fotboll + en plan	→	**en fot|boll|s|plan**	NOUN + s + NOUN

Note 1:The use of **-s** is limited by the nature of the final syllable of the FE, cf. 1113: **motor|trafik|led**.

Note 2: When the final element in a compound FE naturally drops a final -a this is sometimes replaced by an -e before subsequent elements are added:

en skola + en inspektör → en skol|inspektör → en grund|skol|e|inspektör

The major dilemma is, however, that posed by the s-link (see 1113).

1113 Guide to noun links

Initial element	Examples
(a) NOUN + NOUN	
FE in stressed vowel	armé|kår, bi|kupa, bro|öppning, bastu|bad, by|fåne, sjö|gräs
FE in -s	ras|diskriminering
FE in -'sje' sound	bransch|organisation, marsch|fart, lunch|korg, kurs|ändring, bagage|hylla, garage|port
FE in -s + consonant	plast|kort, fisk|ben, disk|bänk
FE in unstressed -el, -en, -er, -ar, -on	segel|båt but: handel|s|balans vatten|glas but: tentamen|s|prov finger|avtryck but: fader|s|gestalt sommar|lov, hallon|buske
FE in participial -ande, -ende	yttrande|frihet, boende|kostnad
FE in -else	rörelse|mönster, fängelse|straff
FE in stressed -eri, -i	bryggeri|chef, geologi|elev, filosofi|lärare, konditori|kund
FE in stressed -ist	turist|byrå, nudist|läger
FE in stressed -ad, -all, -an, -at, -ell, -em, -et, -ett, -ik, -iv, -log, -om, -on, -ur, -yr	promenad|skor, kravall|polis, vulkan|utbrott, internat|skola, kapell|mästare, problem|barn, tapet|våd, biljett|lucka, fysik|bok, arkiv|bild, katalog|pris, ekonom|utbildning, person|bevis, kultur|krock, martyr|död
(b) NOUN in unstressed -e/-a (loses -e/-a) + NOUN	
FE is bisyllabic non-neuter in -a/-e	flick|skola, ång|panna, pojk|streck
FE ends in -are	lärar|lön, arbetar|kvarter

But: mästare + kock →   mäster|kock

mästare + kupp →   mäster|kupp

(c) NOUN in **-ja** (changes to **-je**) + NOUN

olje|plattform, kedje|reaktion

(d) NOUN in **-erska, -inna** (changes to **-erske, -inne**) + NOUN

sköterske|elev, grevinne|titel

(e) NOUN + **s** + NOUN

FE is a compound   **barn|bidrag|s|fråga, motor|båt|s|färd, last|bil|s|förare**

Note: This does not apply to elements ending in **-are** in three (plus) element compounds:

yrkeslärar|utbildning, världsmästar|tävling|s|vinnare

FE ends in **-(n)ing, -ling**	**parkering|s|plats, tidning|s|bud, älskling|s|färg**
FE ends in stressed **-itet**	**nationalitet|s|beteckning, universitet|s|rektor**
FE ends in **-(t)ion**	**motion|s|cykel, religion|s|kunskap**
FE ends in stressed **-är**	**pensionär|s|träff, karaktär|s|drag**
FE ends in **-dom, -het, -lek, -skap**	**visdom|s|ord, snabbhet|s|premie, kärlek|s|bevis, sällskap|s|resa**
FE ends in **-nad**	**byggnad|s|firma, marknad|s|föring, överlevnad|s|instinkt**
FE ends in **-ator, -tor** (referring to people)	**diktator|s|fasoner, kontor|s|personal**

(f) NOUN + NOUN or NOUN + **s** + NOUN

Monosyllabic FE
ends in consonant

tall|barr, hund|koppel, tåg|resenär, eld|själ
BUT: **stad|s|mur, strid|s|vagn, hav|s|utsikt, krig|s|byte, kök|s|golv, stat|s|kassa** (all with shortened vowel in FE); **fred|s|plan, svar|s|talong, gård|s|plan, värld|s|omsegling, kropp|s|byggnad, kväll|s|promenad, rum|s|upplevelse, själ|s|frände, skydd|s|nät, tvång|s|tröja**

Note: Some monosyllabic nouns may link either with **-s-** or without:

bord|s|dryck	but: **bord|lampa**
död|s|annons (shortened vowel in FE)	but: **död|grävare**
skog|s|industri	but: **skog|fattigdom**

1114   Compound nouns – meaning

In this section all kinds of FEs are dealt with, unlike 1111f. The syntactical and semantic relationship between the FE and SE in a compound can be clarified by expanding the compound into a phrase (see also 1110), e.g.:

halm|tak   = **tak av halm**
(FE denotes material, content)

arbet|s|rum   = **rum där man arbetar**
(SE = adverbial of place)

barn|skrik   = **barns skrik**
(FE is subject of activity in SE)

Various classifications can be made on this basis:

(a) Verbal activity in SE:

FE is subject:	**hund|skall**	=	**hundens skall, att hund skäller**
FE is object :	**sjuk|vård**	=	**vård av sjuka, att man vårdar sjuka**
FE is adverbial:	**tåg|resa**	=	**resa med tåg, att man reser med tåg**

(b) Verbal activity in FE:

SE is subject:	**rull||trappa**	=	**trappa som rullar**
SE is object:	**rid|häst**	=	**häst som man rider**
SE is adverbial:	**skriv|maskin**	=	**maskin som man skriver med**

(c) No verbal activity in either FE or SE:

Adverbial relationship

- place	**äng|s|blommor**	=	**blommor på ängen**
- time	**semester|vecka**	=	**vecka under semestern**
- means	**ång|lok**	=	**lok som drivs med ånga**
Material or content	**byx|tyg**	=	**tyg som man syr byxor av**
Possessive relationship	**arbetar|hustru**	=	**hustru till en arbetare**

(d) FE is an adjective:

FE is complement:	**små|barn**	=	**barn som är små**

(e) Possessive compounds: See 1110 (b) 3.

1115   Compound adjectives and numerals – forms by word class

(a) The same types of links used to form compound nouns (see 1112) also apply in the formation of compound adjectives. The FE is here often a noun:

1	FE + adjective	**blixt|snabb**
2	FE -a/-e + adjective	**pojk|aktig**
3	FE + s + adjective	**näring|s|riktig**
4	FE + link in -e/-a + adjective	**olje|skadad**
5	FE + case ending + adjective	**vecko|lång**
6	FE in -la (→ -el-) + adjective	**mussel|formig**
7	FE in -te (→ -ts-) + adjective	**arbet|s|skygg**

(b) Compound adjectives may have as their FE a number of different word classes:

FE	Example
NOUN	**rost|fri, miljö|vänlig, is|kall, flam|säker**
NOUN PHRASE	**iögonen|fallande**
ADJECTIVE	**mörk|grön, ny|rik, snar|lik**
VERB	**älsk|värd, kör|klar, skriv|kunnig**
PRONOUN	**själv|säker, hel|svensk**
ADVERB	**väl|behövlig, ut|fattig**
PREPOSITION	**under|jordisk, över|full**
PREPOSITIONAL PHRASE	**pånytt|född**
NUMERAL	**fyr|stämmig, fem|faldig**

(c) For general rules applying to the form of the FE, see 1111(b), 1112f.

(d) Compound numerals (units of measurement are found in the singular)

två\|hundra\|trettio\|sju, halv\|annan, etc.

1116   Compound adjectives – meaning

(a) FE is a noun:

(i) FE is the agent (SE is a participle):   **fukt\|skadad = skadad av fukt**

(ii) FE is the object (SE is a participle):   **förtroende\|ingivande = som inger förtroende**

(iii) FE is an adverbial:
- time: **natt\|öppet**   **= öppet på natten**
- place: **värld\|s\|erfaren**   **= erfaren om världen**

- manner: maskin|skriven   = skriven på maskin
- degree, type: brand|gul   = gul som brand
- defining SE: sitt|riktig   = riktig att sitta i

(b) FE is an adjective (SE is a participle):

lätt|lagad   = lätt att laga
snabb|gående   = som går snabbt

(c) FE is an adjective (with or without hyphen)

blå|gul   = blå och gul
svensk-amerikansk   = svensk och amerikansk

Note: **svenskt-engelskt samarbete** (= **svenskt och engelskt samarbete**) but: **svensk-engelskt lexikon** (**svenska till engelska**).

(d) FE is a verb (SE is an adjective defining FE):

kör|säker   = säker att köra

1117 Compound verbs – forms by word class and the particle verbs

For general rules applying to the form of the FE see 1111(b). For verbs formed by retrogradation see 1108.

(a) The types of links used to form compound nouns (see 1111) also apply in the formation of compound verbs.

(b) Compound verbs may have as their FE a number of different word classes:

FE	Example
NOUN	**namn|ge, övning|s|köra, kedje|röka, arbet|s|vägra, syssel|sätta**
ADJECTIVE	**svart|måla, lam|slå, små|le, god|känna (BUT gott|göra), ren|göra**
NUMERAL	**fyr|dubbla**
PRONOUN	**själv|dö**
ADVERB	**ut|se, väl|signa**
VERB	**sprut|måla, frys|torka, ös|regna**
PREPOSITION	**genom|skåda, över|glänsa**
PREPOSITIONAL PHRASE	**omhänder|ta, ifråga|sätta, tillintet|göra**
ADVERBIAL PHRASE	**smyg|röka**

(c) Most compound verbs are, however, of two main types:

(i) Verbs whose FE is a noun or adjective:

> **del|ta, sol|torka, bok|föra, sjö|sätta, råd|fråga, damm|suga, klar|göra, vit|måla, kal|hugga**

(ii) Verbs whose FE is a particle (*particle verbs*)

A verb particle is a preposition or adverb which is stressed and used together with a verb, the two elements together comprising one unit of meaning.

> **Han** *skrev* ‿*under* **avtalet.**   He *signed* the agreement.

In the participial forms (present and past participle) the verb particle forms a prefix to the verb:

> **Bilen som** *körde om* **oss krockade med en buss.**
> The car that overtook us crashed into a bus.

> **Den** *omkörande* **bilen krockade med en buss.**
> The car overtaking us crashed into a bus.

> **Vi** *tycker om* **vår chef.**
> We like our boss.

> **Vår chef är mycket** *omtyckt.*
> Our boss is very popular. (*lit.* 'liked')

Some compound verbs are always one word, i.e. the prefix is inseparable:

> **om|ge, til|låta, ut|bilda**

Some compound verbs are always two words (except in the participial forms); the prefix is separable:

> **koka över, hålla med, slå ihjäl (cf. ihjälslagen)**

Sometimes the integral and separated forms of compound verbs exist side by side. In such instances they form three distinct types:

- the one-word and two-word forms indicate a stylistic distinction:

Formal	*Informal*
igen|känna	**känna igen**
recognise	

- the one-word and two-word forms indicate a semantic and stylistic distinction:

	Figurative	*Literal*
	av|bryta	**bryta av**
	interrupt	break off

- sometimes the semantic distinction is so great that the two forms can be regarded as two completely distinct verbs:

	av|gå	**gå av**
	resign	break in two

1118 Compound adverbs, conjunctions and prepositions

(a) They are of three main kinds of compound adverbs:

1 ADVERB + ADVERB

Most indicate location or motion towards a place:

här\|uppe, där\|nere, hit\|upp, dit\|in, här\|hemma

2 ADVERB + PREPOSITION

The usual prepositions forming the SE are: **-ifrån, -åt, -efter, -på, -för, -emot**:

här\|ifrån, ned\|åt, var\|efter, här\|på, upp\|för, där\|emot

In formal written Swedish there are many compounds in **där-** (= **detta**). These are rarely found in spoken Swedish :

där\|av, där\|efter, där\|med, där\|på, där\|till, där\|vid

3 PREPOSITIONAL PHRASE (i.e. preposition + noun/adjective)

i\|stället, till\|freds, till\|väga

(b) Compound conjunctions (in which only the FE is a conjunction) include:

där\|för, i\|fall, så\|vitt, så\|vida

(c) Compound prepositions include: **fram\|emot, allt\|sedan**

1119   Derivational compounding

A compound element may itself be a derivative of another word:

olycksdag   ← olycka   + dag
               derivative

tryckfrihet   ← tryck   + frihet
                              derivative

Some words are reminiscent of this type but differ in that their derived SE does not exist as an independent word:

   ordförande, nybörjare, dörrknackare, väskryckare, pristagare, femåring

There is no word ***förande, *börjare, *knackare, *ryckare, *tagare** or ***åring**. These words are based on phrases: **knacka på dörren, rycka en väska, ta priset, (som är) fem år.**

They have been formed by a composite process of compounding and affixation.

This also applies to adjectives: **blåögd, tremotorig, ordhållig, rödnäst, gudfruktig.**

C EXPRESSIVE FORMATION

1120   Hypocorism

Hypocorisms are familiar or 'pet' forms. They derive in three different ways:

(a) Addition of suffix **-is**, often to abbreviations:

godsaker	+ **-is**	→ **godis**	goodies
daghem	+ **-is**	→ **dagis**	creche
gratulerar	+ **-is**	→ **grattis**	congrats
tjock	+ **-is**	→ **tjockis**	fatty [noun]

Note also: the loan words **fringis**, 'fringe benefits'; and **poppis** (indeclinable adjective), 'popular'.

(b) Nicknames:

   Bosse → Bo, Karl → Kalle, Jan → Janne, Nils → Nisse, Ulf → Uffe, Lars → Lasse, Margareta → Maggan, Sigurd → Sigge, Susanne → Sussi

Note: In Old Swedish many personal names were similarly abbreviated. The resultant forms are often used as given names in modern Swedish:

Johannes → Johan, Jan, Hans; Margareta → Greta; Nikolaus→ Nils; Laurentius → Lars.

(c) Addition of -(s)a/-e to an abbreviated form:

sosse(← socialist), **brorsa** (← bror), **syrra** (←syster), **matte** (← matematik), **moppe** (←moped).

1121 Onomatopoetic formation

(a) These include words that are imitations of various sounds (see also 905):

(i) Childish imitations: **vovvov, miau, bää, nöff.**

(ii) Others: **bing-bång, plask.**

(b) In some cases verbs may be formed from such sounds:

knarra, bräka, pipa, prassla.

1122 Contamination, euphemism, folk etymology

(a) Contamination involves conflating two words of similar meaning to form a new word, and it can thus be creative:

undersam (← **underlig** + **sällsam**)

(b) Euphemism involves the replacement of a word (often an interjection) which may cause offence by one less likely to do so (cf. English 'By God!' → 'By Golly!'):

fy fasingen (← **fy fan!**); **jäklar** (← **djävlar**)

(c) Folk etymology involves a misinterpretation of the original meaning often of a loan from a foreign language:

följetong from French *feuilleton*
ungkarl from German *Junker*
pumps from English 'pumps' = ladies shoe without a heel
ostburgare, 'cheeseburger', from **hamburgare** (← Hamburg!)

D   ABBREVIATION

1123   Clippings and blends

Clipping involves the reduction of a morpheme or part of a morpheme, e.g. **bio** ←
biograf.

(a) Initial reduction (the beginning of a word disappears):

Reduction of a whole morpheme	*Reduction of part of a morpheme*
(bi)cykel	**(automo)bil**
	(omni)buss
	(violon)cello

(b) Final reduction (the end of a word disappears):

Reduction of a whole morpheme	*Reduction of part of a morpheme*
livs(medelsaffär)	**bio(graf), snus(tobak)**
	lok(omotiv), doa(kör)
	kolla(tionera), foto(grafi)
	chark(uteri), läsk(edryck)
	rea(lisation), kval(ificer)a

(c) When the middle of a word disappears this is known as a *blend* ('telescope' or
'medial' reduction):

Reduction of a whole morpheme	*Reduction of part of a morpheme*
te(kopps)fat	**mo(torho)tell**
brand(kårs)chef	**mo(torveloci)ped**
öppet(hållande)tider	**m(er)oms(ättningsskatt)**
	alko(hol)testa
	flex(ibel arbets)tid

1124   Acronyms

When the process of reduction leaves only an initial letter or letters in a word, the
result is known as an acronym.

(a) Alphabetisms:

These are words formed from initials and pronounced as letters of the alphabet:

> **bh (bysthållare), TV (television), LO (Land|s|organisation), UD (Utrike|s|-**
> **departementet), VM (Värld|s|mästarskap), OS (Olympiska spelen)**; **ett**
> **SMS** text message.

(b) Respelling of alphabetisms:

These are words formed from initials but written (and sometimes inflected) as words in their own right: **be|hå, teve** (see also above).

(c) Acronyms pronounced as words:

These are words formed from initials but pronounced as words in their own right: **SACO** /sɑːkω/, **SAS** /sas/, **SAAB** /sɑːb/, **AMS** /ams/, **SAF** /saf/; **hiv(-smittad)** /hiːv/, **AIDS(-sjuka)** /ɛiːds/.

(d) Hybrid forms (alphabetism + noun etc.):

> **P-plats (parkeringsplats), T-bana (tunnelbana), u-land (utvecklingsland), u-båt (undervattensbåt), k-pist (kulsprutepistol), CD-skiva, prao-elev (praktisk arbetslivssorienteringselev), EU-domstolen (Europeiska Unionens domstol), kabel-TV (kabeltelevision)**

Note: A small number of abbreviations which are contractions (i.e. they comprise the first and last letters of the full form) are traditionally seen with a colon. See 1304(c).

E   FOREIGN INFLUENCES ON SWEDISH

1125   Types of foreign influence

(a) A distinction is often made in Swedish between *foreign* words and *loan* words. Foreign words retain some feature of spelling, pronunciation or inflexion which are obviously alien to Swedish.

Foreign spelling and/or pronunciation:

> **juice, boulevard, game, copyright, cocktail, layout, show, cowboy, bookmaker, manager, müsli, heat, service, outstanding, playa, fightas**

Foreign inflexion (but see also 118):

jeans, cornflakes, boots	s-plural
designer	s-plural (or **designer**)
centrum	def. **centrumet**, pl. **centrum/centra**

In the case of word groups from foreign sources we can talk of *loan phrases* or *quotations*:

> **sales promotion, selfmade man, up to date, all right, fighting spirit, comme il faut, anno dazumal**

(b) Loanwords are those assimilated into Swedish patterns of spelling, pronunciation or inflexion (e.g. the adaptation of French loans to Swedish spelling so as to retain approximately the same sound). They are therefore often, within a short time, regarded as Swedish:

> corps → **kår**, balcon → **balkong**, pièce → **pjäs**, lieutenant → **löjtnant**, régisseur → **regissör**, actrice → **aktris**, parapluie → **paraply**, famille → **familj**, fabrique → **fabrik**, mannequin → **mannekäng**, juste → **schysst**, tape → **tejp**, pizza → **pizza, pizzor** (pl.), fight → **fajt(as)**

(c) Sometimes the wrong form of a word is borrowed, e.g. the so-called *keps words* from English where an English plural form was used as a Swedish singular:

caps (pl.)	→ **en keps**	potatoes (pl.)	→ **en potatis**
babies (pl.)	→ **en bebis**	jumpers (pl.)	→ **en jumpers**

A *keps* word is often provided with a Swedish plural form: **kepsar, potatisar, bebisar, jumpersar.**

(d) *Calques* (loan translations) represent a borrowing of the underlying idea(s) in a word, usually a compound or derivative, and the translation of these ideas into the target language. Calques are relatively rare in Swedish. Some examples are:

Latin	con-scientia	→	Sw **samvete**
English	iron curtain	→	Sw **järnridån**
English	maiden speech	→	Sw **jungfrutal**
English	nuclear family	→	Sw **kärnfamilj**
English	chain smoke	→	Sw **kedjeröka**
German	Schadenfreude	→	Sw **skadeglädje**
German	Haßliebe	→	Sw **hat-kärlek**
German	Gastarbeiter	→	Sw **gästarbetare**
French	dernier cri	→	Sw **sista skriket**
French	le tiers monde	→	Sw **tredje världen**
French	humour noir	→	Sw **svart humor**

(e) *Semantic extension* is the borrowing of a meaning from a foreign language and its addition to the meaning of an existing indigenous word. For example, **en duva** and **en hök** in Swedish meant 'a dove' and 'a hawk', two types of bird, but have gained the meanings 'peace lover' and 'warmonger' from American English in the 1960s. The expression **få kalla fötter** now means 'to have doubts about doing something'. Note also: **Det är upp till dig** 'It's up to you', and **ett album**, which used to be 'a book for collecting photos or stamps', and is now also 'a collection of musical pieces on a record, tape or CD/DVD'.

(f) For neologisms that do not exist in the supposed donor language, e.g. **Han är fit for fight**, see 1130(b) new English formations.

1126   Latin and Greek

(a) Very early loans into the Germanic languages include **kärra** (L *carrus*), **marknad** (L *mercatus*), **köpa** (L *caupo*). Christian missionaries speaking Anglo-Saxon, Friesian and Saxon introduced many Latin and Greek words into Swedish in the Viking Age. Many Greek words were transmitted via Latin:

> **altare** (L *altare*), **biskop** (G *episkopos*), **brev** (L *breve scriptum*), **kyrka** (G *kyriakon*), **kloster** (L *claustrum*), **kristen** (L *christianus*), **påsk** (medieval Latin *pascha*), **påve** (L *papa*), **präst** (L *presbyter*), **ängel** (G *angelos*), **djävul** (L *diabolus*, G *diabolos*)

Others include: **vin, mynt, koppar, öre, kittel, fikon, frukt, peppar, senap, lejon, persika, ros, källare, kök, mur, planta.**

(b) Loans since the Reformation tend to be via High German, French and English and are of high frequency in the arts and sciences:

Architecture:	**sockel** (L), **plint** (G), **villa** (L), **kamin** (L)
Printing:	**manus** (L), **ark** (L), **kursiv** (L), **fraktur** (L), **antikva** (L), **korrektur** (L)
Philosophy:	**ateism** (G), **humanism** (L), **metafysyik** (G), **hypotes** (G)
Chemistry:	**kemi** (G), **klor** (G), **fosfor** (G), **aluminium** (L), **radium** (L)
Medicine:	**anatomi** (G), **bacill** (L), **nerv** (L), **astma** (G), **operation** (L)
Linguistics:	**fonetik** (G), **dialekt** (G), **etymologi** (G), **fonem** (G), **finit** (L), **inversion** (L), **singular** (L)

Neologisms using Latin and Greek stems include: **akupunktur, astronaut, agronom, biograf, elektricitet, megafon, olympiad, pornografi, prefabricera, prenumerera, radio, telefon, television, socionom.** Words in -tek: **bibliotek, diskotek, mediotek (mediatek)**. Words in -mat: **automat, bankomat, datamat, tvättomat.**

(c) Many and Greek affixes have proved productive in Swedish:

Latin: **ab-, ad-, anti-, bi-, de-, dis-, ex-, il-, im-, in-, inter-, ir-, ko-, kon-, kontra-, kor-, kvasi-, non-, pre-, post-, pro-, re-, sub-, trans-, ultra-, vice-.**

Greek: **-al, -an, -ans, -ant, -arium-, -ator, -ens, -ent, -ik, -ism, -itet, -iv, -on, -or, -tion, -(i)um, -us**, adjectives in **-al, -at**, verbs in **–era.**

1127   German

(a) The total number of Low German (i.e. North German) words of all kinds borrowed into Swedish, mostly in the 14th century, is very high, but tends to be concentrated in the following fields:

Trade:	betala, frakt, ränta
Urban life:	rådhus, stad, borgmästare
Crafts, guilds:	gesäll, bagare, verkstad
Foodstuffs:	skinka, medvurst, socker, sirap
Tools, goods:	läder, hyvel, verktyg
Titles:	herre, fru, fröken

(b) The influence led to both replacement of Old Swedish words and an extension of the vocabulary, e.g. vardha was replaced by bli(va); skön, ansikte and språk were added to the existing fager, anlete, mål.

(c) As significant as lexical borrowing is the introduction via many loanwords of frequent loan affixes which were later used to form new derivatives: *an*komst, *be*tala, *bi*stå, *för*stå, *und*komma, god*het*, lärar*inna*, fäng*else*, ro*lig*, läs*bar*, pojk*aktig*.

See 1102ff.

(d) Since the 16th century most loans from German have been from High German, and have included many originally French words. High German loans tend to concentrate in the following fields among others:

Military:	fänrik, furir, fäste, stab
Mining:	blyerts, granit, schakt, skiffer, skikt
Banking:	bank, kassa, rabatt

German loans from later periods include:

16th century:	artig, blank, citron, dunkel, främling, förnäm, kastanj, ordentlig, väsentlig; (verbs) ankomma, besiktiga, erinra, förolämpa, omkomma, ordna, passera, skaffa, trotsa
17th century:	fantastisk, forell, hurtig, inbilla, offentlig, porslin, putsa, riktig, träffa, ungefär, ur, överraska
18th century:	avträde, drivhus, forska, katrinplommon, mejsel, mutter, skärp, snaps, stadshus, synpunkt, upplysning, vals
19th century:	stormakt, ståndpunkt, utlandet, bestick, förvånansvärd, pilsner, referat, snälltåg, tax, tomat, vemod, årtionde
20th century:	(calques) gästarbetare, hatkärlek, kedejhus, kombivagn, mindervärdighetskänsla, självhäftande, triviallitteratur, upparbeta, utvecklingsland, hudnära (and others in -nära), miljövänlig (and others in -vänlig), kropssriktig (and others in -riktig)

(e) Despite several subsequent attempts to 'purify' the language of the many German loans, most recently in the late 19th century, most such loans are now well assimilated into the Swedish system of pronunciation, orthography and inflexion and no longer seem alien.

1128 The Nordic languages and Finnish

(a) Danish

(i) Loans from Low German in the late Middle Ages were often transmitted to Swedish via Danish:

koger, bägare, drabba, beveka, förlora, belåten, förmögen, svag

(ii) Danish loans into Swedish from later periods include:

17th century:	**klöver, ruter** (in a pack of cards)
18th century:	**dana, undvara, eftermäle**
19th century:	**betingelse, slank, genombrott, hänsyn, gräll, framhäva, säregen, försändelse, levebröd, obönhörlig, tillnärmelsevis, förståelse, spydig, lyhörd, upplevelse**
20th century:	**bil, besvikelse, häleri, begivenhet, upphovsrätt, samfärdsel**

(b) Norwegian

Written Norwegian was until the last hundred years difficult to distinguish from written Danish, and only a few loans are easily attributable: **rabalder, samröre, huldra, slalom, luftled.**

An early loan is **lämmel**; a recent loan phrase is **Ha det!**, Be seeing you!

(c) Finnish

From the Middle Ages:	**pojke**
More recent loans:	**pjäxa, sisu, känga, rappakalja, jenka**

1129 French

(a) French loans entered Swedish particularly in the 17th and 18th centuries, and tend to concentrate in the following fields:

Diplomacy:	**allians, ambassadör**
Literature and theatre:	**poesi, balett, ridå**
Food:	**dessert, choklad, glass**

Furniture:	**möbel, fåtölj, byrå, persienn**
Fashion:	**blus, parfym, frisyr, negligé**
Family:	**kusin, familj, mamma, tant**

(b) Many French loans still have end stress: **barrikad, brutal, medalj, intressant, idé, hotell, engagemang, ingenjör, petitess.**

(c) Assimilation of pronunciation and spelling of French loans were greatly facilitated by Carl Gustaf Leopold's *Afhandling om svenska stafsättet*, 1801, which made many astute recommendations for re-spelling, subsequently adopted by dictionary writers:

hard c	>	k	**kaffe, kredit, klass**
silent -e	>	zero	**princip, not**
-que	>	-k	**fabrik, bank, risk**
-ce	>	-s	**balans, existens, polis**
-ll	>	-lj	**biljett, briljant, familj, fåtölj**
-ch	>	-sch	**affisch, mustasch, broschyr**
ai	>	ä	**affär, porträtt, suverän**
eu	>	ö	**adjö, möbel**
ou	>	u	**kusin, kuvert**
u	>	y	**byrå, staty** (later also: **kostym, volym, tortyr, frisyr**)

1130 English

(a) English loans into Swedish date back to the 17th century. They are found mainly in the following fields:

Communications:	**lok, sliper, bicykel**
Cloth, clothing:	**pläd, ulster**
Food, drink:	**paj, biff, whisky**
Games, sport:	**bridge, krocket, sport, träna**
Business:	**check, jobb(a), strejk, bojkott**
Press, politics:	**intervju, reporter, konservativ**
Others:	**manager, slum, turist**

20th century:

Transport and communications:	**radio, container, motell, transistor, e-mailadress, frukost-TV, datavirus**
Clothes:	**blazer, bikini, jeans, jumper, overall, shorts**
Foods:	**chips, cola, juice, ketchup**
Others:	**designer, fans, hobby, kalla kriget, korsord, outsider, party, service, spray(a)**

(b) Types of modern English loans in Swedish:

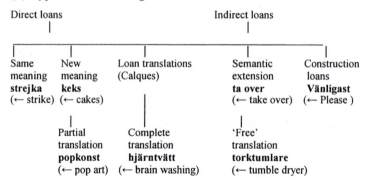

Direct loans   Indirect loans

Same meaning	New meaning	Loan translations (Calques)	Semantic extension	Construction loans
strejka (← strike)	**keks** (← cakes)		**ta over** (← take over)	**Vänligast** (← Please)

| | Partial translation **popkonst** (← pop art) | Complete translation **hjärntvätt** (← brain washing) | 'Free' translation **torktumlare** (← tumble dryer) | |

(i) *Direct loans* may be divided into:

- those that have the same meaning as the original (**team, image**)

- those in which some semantic change has taken place (**city** in Swedish refers only to the town centre, **kex** are not cakes but biscuits, **soul** is only a kind of music)

- loan phrases (**practical joke**)

(ii) *New English formations* are those where a new formation in Swedish is based on English patterns but does not originate from an English-speaking country: **en freestyle** is in Swedish not only a kind of swimming but also a personal stereo or walkman; **en babysitter** is not someone who looks after a baby but a kind of baby chair. Swedes use **after ski** where the English use 'après ski'.

(iii) *Indirect loans* may be divided into loan translations, which may in their turn be a partial translation (**grapefrukt, hårdrock, stretchbyxor**) or a complete translation which is literal (**befolkningsexplosion** 'population explosion'; **kedjerökare** 'chain smoker'; **mjukvara** 'software'; **kedjereaktion** 'chain reaction'; **utvärdera** 'evaluate'; **soffpotatis** 'couch potato'; **gyllene fallskärm** 'golden parachute'; **släppa katten ur säcken** 'let the cat out of the bag') or a 'free' translation (**bandspelare** 'tape recorder'; **brädsegling** 'sail boarding'; **allsång** 'community singing'; **krockkudde** 'air bag').

(iv) *Semantic extension* involves imparting a new meaning to an existing Swedish word:

Det är inte min huvudvärk om du inte köper mitt argument.
It's not my headache if you don't buy my argument.

Det är upp till dig!   It's up to you!

(v) *Construction loans* involve borrowing a structure type rather than a word or phrase. There are several major new developments of this type:

1 The introduction of the English apostrophe (Swedish usually has no apostrophe before the genitive -s):

   *Köp maten hos Kalle's!   Buy your food at Kalle's!

2 Writing compounds as two separate words (Swedish properly has them as one word):

   *Sko mässa Shoe Fair; ***hemma video** home video; ***kontroller kabel** controller cable

3 Another practice of this type is to impart a new and generalised use to the pronoun **du**, which is increasingly used to replace **man**:

   *Om du äter mycket engelsk mat blir du fet.
   If you eat a lot of English food you get fat.

4 The use of **mer, mest** with adjectives where an inflexional comparison might have been expected:

   Svärföräldrarna visade sig vara mer formella än vi hade väntat oss.
   The in-laws proved to be more formal than we had expected.

5 Verbs with the redundant particle **upp, ner**:

   Han startar upp ett nytt företag. He is starting up a new company.
   Vi måste kolla upp statistiken. We will have to check up the statistics.
   De har stängt ner fabriken. They have closed down the factory.

(c) Adaptation of English loans:

(i) Pronunciation and spelling:

- vowels (diphthongs) unchanged: **milkshake, sound, mountainbike, make up**

- adaptation to Swedish pronunciation:

Pronunciation	Spelling	
ä	a	**blazer**
	ai	**raid**
	ay	**spraya**
	ej	**fejka, tejp, strejka, mejla**
aj	aj	**tajt, paj**

Note also retained spellings: **design, drive, guide, sightseeing**

Sw. u	u	**lunch, muffin, punk**
Sw. y	y	**city, jury, rally**
sh	ch	**charter, chips, choke**
y	j	**jet, juice, gin, jogga**
v	·w	**wire (also vajer), swing, show**
w	w	**walkie talkie, weekend**
t	th	**thriller, thinner**

(ii) Form

Plural forms of nouns may be retained (s-plurals) or adapt to Swedish inflexion:

sweatshirts, revolvrar, guider, jobb (but see also 'keps words', 1125(c).)

Adjectives are in many cases easy to adapt to Swedish patterns:

-al → -ell:	**formell, audiovisuell**
-y → -ig:	**snobbig, trendig**

Verbs are also very easy to adapt to Swedish patterns: **coacha, fightas**

-ate → -era:	**indikera, laminera, sofistikerad**
-ize → -isera:	**standardisera, organisera, miniatyrisera**

1131 Other languages

(a) Italian

Food:	**cappucino, lasagne, pasta, zucchini, spaghetti**
Music:	**adagio, piano, intermezzo, violin, diva**
Banking:	**konto, diskonto, ditto, saldo, giro**
Others:	**libero, fiasko, fascist, vendetta, marina**

(b) Spanish:	**paella, siesta, albino, kokos, guerilla, silo**

(c) Russian:	**gulag, kosmonaut, töväder, pogrom, bolsjevik, vodka**

(d) Others:

Arabic:	**alkohol, siffra**
Greenlandic:	**anorak, kajak, iglo(o)**
Japanese:	**karate, judo, origami, kimono**
Turkish:	**kebab**

F CONVERSION

For conversion from one word class to another by means of affixation see 1106f.

1132   Adjective to noun

(a) Complete nominalisation (see 230) occurs when the adjective takes end article or plural endings: **en unge – ungen – ungar – ungarna**. Often, however, only some of these endings are used: **en liten, de små, lillen/lillan, gulan, vitan, höger-n, vänster-n, fett-et, vilt-et, djup-et, grund-et, brant-en, hög-en, lugn-et**.

(b) Certain nationality words (see 229) and other words describing persons are derived from adjectives: **en svensk -en, -ar, -na; en tysk –en, -ar, -na; en dansk -en, -ar, -na; en liberal; en konservativ; en militär**.

(c) In many cases of the 'adjectival noun' (see 227ff.) the noun is understood but not usually supplied. Swedish differs from English in that the adjectival noun is also found in the singular: **en döv** ('a deaf person') – **den döve** (masc.)('the deaf man') – **den döva** (fem.)('the deaf woman') – **de döva** ('the deaf').

Many adjectives are used in this way, especially in the plural, including:

> **de sjuka** the sick; **de gamla** the old; **de fattiga** the poor

Notice especially singular adjectival nouns of the following kinds:

> **det enda** the only thing; **det sista** the last thing; **det bästa** the best thing; **det goda** the good thing

(d) In some cases the adjective is used nominally where the noun could easily be supplied:

> **Alla de gamla / människorna / var trötta efter den långa promenaden.**

1133   Noun to adjective

Some colour words and others have converted from nominal to adjectival use. They are usually indeclinable: **rosa** 'pink'(from Latin *rosa*) **beige** (from Italian *bambagia* ('cotton') via French).

Others include: **slut, släkt, pyton, toppen** (only used predicatively).

Some nouns have had an intermediate stage as an adverb: **fel**, **lagom** (originally dative plural of the noun **lag**).

1134 Adverb to adjective

This small group includes adverbs in **-vis**: **delvis, portionsvis, gradvis**.

Others include: **bra, annorlunda, ringa, nog, avsides, utsocknes, fjärran**, all indeclinable adjectives.

1135 Verb to noun

(a) The noun denotes the action of the original verb (usually neuter): **flyt-et, glid-et, lyft-et, åk-et**.

(b) The noun denotes a tool with which the action is carried out (usually non-neuter): **fläkt-en, lyft-en, tork-en**.

(c) A number of nouns have been formed from an imperative verb phrase: **krypin, farväl** (also interjection), **givakt** (also interjection), **förgätmigej, hålligång, komihåg**.

12 ORTHOGRAPHY

A   SYMBOLS AND SOUNDS
1201   Letters of the alphabet, pronunciation
1202   Clarification of letters and the alphabet and numerals
1203   Diacritics

B   SPELLING
1204   Miscellaneous spelling rules
1205   M and N spelling rules

C   SMALL AND CAPITAL LETTERS
1206   Small or capital letters?
1207   The use of capital letters in simple proper nouns: **Är Sven svensk?**
1208   The use of capital letters in proper nouns comprising two or or more
        words: **Förenta staterna**
1209   The use of capital letters in compound proper nouns: **Sydamerika**
1210   The use of capital letters in abbreviations

D   MISCELLANEOUS
1211   Hyphenation
1212   Figures or words?
1213   One word or two?

A   SYMBOLS AND SOUNDS

1201   Letters of the alphabet, pronunciation

There are twenty-nine letters in the Swedish alphabet:

A B C D E F G H I J K L M N O P Q R S T U V W X Y Z Å Ä Ö

In modern Swedish **Q** and **W** are only encountered in proper names (**Ewa Granquist, Qatar, Wales**) and a few loanwords (**quisling, know-how**).

The letter **W** (**dubbelt v**) is regarded as a variant of the letter **V** (or **enkelt v**). The word **wc**, for instance, is pronounced as if written **vc** and web addresses (**www**) are pronounced as if spelt **v – v – v**. The letter **W** is frequently omitted when listing the letters of the alphabet, and is usually integrated with **V** in entries in dictionaries, phone books, encyclopaedias, etc.

In phone books and many other listings of names the surname **Carlsson** (and variants) is integrated with entries for **Karlsson**.

1202 Clarification of letters of the alphabet and numerals

When it is necessary to clarify spelling, over a poor telephone line for example, the following names are used within Sweden for the letters and numerals:

A	**Adam**	**U**	**Urban**
B	**Bertil**	**V**	**Viktor**
C	**Cesar**	**W**	**Wilhelm**
D	**David**	**X**	**Xerxes**
E	**Erik**	**Y**	**Yngve**
F	**Filip**	**Z**	**Zäta**
G	**Gustav**	**Å**	**Åke**
H	**Helge**	**ä**	**ärlig**
I	**Ivar**	**ö**	**Östen**
J	**Johan**		
K	**Kalle**	**0**	**nolla**
L	**Ludvig**	**1**	**etta**
M	**Martin**	**2**	**tvåa**
N	**Niklas**	**3**	**trea**
O	**Olof**	**4**	**fyra**
P	**Petter**	**5**	**femma**
Q	**Quintus**	**6**	**sexa**
R	**Rudolf**	**7**	**sjua**
S	**Sigurd**	**8**	**åtta**
T	**Tore**	**9**	**nia**

1203 Diacritics

Note that the Swedish letters **Å, å, Ä, ä, Ö, ö** are separate letters, not accents or diacritics on **A, O**.

The following diacritics are, however, found in Swedish:

(a) Acute accent: this is found in around one hundred loans from French: **idé** 'idea'; **kafé** 'café'; **armé** 'army'; **entré** 'entrance'; **succé** 'success' (notwithstanding the French spelling *succès*). It is also found in some Swedish names: **Linné, Wessén, Tegnér**. It is also used with capitals: **LINNÉ**.

(b) Grave accent

This is rare, apart from the preposition à (a loan from French, see 722(c)), pronounced as short **a**:

    tre biljetter à 50 kronor   three tickets at 50 kronor

In loans that have become familiar in Swedish it is often omitted: **ampere, kortege**.

(c) Circumflex is rare nowadays: **crême fraiche** (**ê** is pronounced as long **e** or long **ä**), but it is often omitted: **entrecote** rather than **entrecôte, hotell** 'hotel' rather than **hôtel** (**ô** is pronounced as long **å**).

(d) In some loanwords, especially names and titles from European languages the indigenous accents are sometimes retained:

    São Paulo, señor, müsli, Škoda

(f) In internet and e-mail addresses the Swedish letters **å, ö, ä** become **a, o, a**. **Södertälje** becomes **Sodertalje**, **Växjö** becomes **Vaxjo**, **Skånska** becomes **Skanska**, etc. Sometimes the old telegraphese **aa, oe, ae** are used instead.

B SPELLING

1204   Miscellaneous spelling rules

(a) lätt + tuggad = lättuggad easy to chew

One of a potential sequence of three identical letters is dropped in compound and inflected forms:

    till + låta = tillåta allow

(b) -ck and **-kk**

The combination **-kk-** occurs very rarely in a single phoneme in Swedish and only in loanwords (e.g. **akkja** 'sledge' [from Sami]; names **Jokkmokk, Pekka**). Instead **-ck** is used to indicate a preceding short vowel:

koka cook (verb)	*but* **kock** chef
tak roof	*but* **täcka** to cover
lok locomotive	*but* **lock** lid

Note 1: However, the combination **-kk-** may occur in compound words, as the final letter of one word and the initial letter of another:

> **tackkort** thank you card; **kokkonst** art of cooking; etc.

Note 2: Note the spelling **och** (pronounced /ock/ or /å/).

(c) -c and **-k**: except when used in the combination **-ck** the letter **c** is encountered relatively infrequently in Swedish (but note the common proper names, **Carl, Carlsson,** etc.). **C** is usually pronounced hard in Swedish (as in English 'helicopter'), but there are exceptions. Hard **c** in loanwords is often changed to **k** in spelling over a period of time:

> **karusell** ('roundabout'), **kompakt, helikopter, diktator, skoter**
> *but*: **clown, cowboy, container, controller, carport, cardigan.**

Sometimes Swedish usage is unsure: **akryl/acryl, disko/disco.**

(d) Before the spelling reform of 1906 the **v** sound was represented by **hv-** at the beginning of some words, **-fv-** medially and **-f** finally. One may still encounter forms like **hvad (vad), hvem (vem), gräfva (gräva), bref (brev)** in older texts.

(e) The initial combination **ps-** is pronounced /s/ in the words **psalm** and **psaltare** and derivatives. In all other cases **ps-** is pronounced as written.

(f) z and **zz**: the letters **z** (pronounced /s/) and **zz** (pronounced /ts/) are generally seen only in loanwords and proper nouns:

> **azalea, pizza, razzia** ('raid'), **zulu, zink, zigenare** ('gypsy'), **zodiak, Mai Zetterling, Anders Zorn, Zambia, Nya Zeeland.**

Where English has **z** many corresponding words in Swedish have **s**:

> **sebra, Sion, gasell, Brasilien, hasselnöt** ('hazel nut').

(g) Some orthographical points mentioned elsewhere in this book:

(i) **industrien** or **industrin**?	cf. 133(e)
(ii) **knäet** or **knät**?	cf. 133(e)
(iii) **salen** or **saln**?	cf. 133(d)(ii)
(iv) **staden** or **stan**?	cf. 133(d)(iii)
(v) **dagen** or **dan**?	cf. 133(d)(iii)
(vi) inflection of adjectives in **-id**	cf. 203(f) Note
(vii) inflection of adjectives ending in a vowel	cf. 203(a)
(viii) personal pronoun forms	cf. 301
(ix) **någon, sådan,** etc.	cf. 341, 328
(x) verbs with long and short forms	cf. 515

1205   M and N spelling rules

(a) A final **m** is not doubled in the spelling of Swedish words even after a short vowel:

   dum, hem, rum, program.

(There are three exceptions: **damm** 'dust'; **lamm** 'lamb'; **ramm**, 'battering ram'.)

(b) A final **n** is not doubled in the spelling of many common Swedish words, even after a short vowel:

allmän	**han**	**kan**	**män**
an	**hon**	**man**	**sen** (from **sedan**)
den	**innan**	**min**	**sin**
din	**in**	**mun**	**vän**
en	**igen**	**men**	**än**

But note also the following:

   grann, sann, tunn, fann (from **finna**), **hann** (from **hinna**), **känn** (from **känna**).

(c) Between vowels **m** and **n** are doubled after a short vowel:

   dumma, hemmet, rummet, programmen, mannen, kunna, denna, inne.

Note: The only exception is **pilgrim** – **pilgrimen** – **pilgrimer**.

(d) In most cases (exceptions are found in (e),(f),(g) below) a word containing a double **m** or double **n** drops one **m** or **n** if a consonant is added immediately afterwards in the inflected form of the word:

ett nummer	**numret**
en sommar	**somrar**
gammal	**gamla**
glömma	**glömde**
hammare	**hamra**
känna	**kände**
tunn	**tunt**
sann	**sant**

Note: This does not apply in cases where an -s is added:

(i) to a noun to form a genitive expression: **ett lamms bräkande.**
(ii) directly to a verb to give the s-form of the verb: **jag minns inte; det känns varmt; det finns inte.**

(e) When the stem of a word ends in **-nn**, this is retained before the endings **-bar**, **-het** and **-sam**, and before other endings beginning with **-l** or **-r**:

kännbar, tunnhet, gynnsam, kvinnlig, sinnrik.

Before other endings a single **-n** is used:

känslig, bränsle.

(f) In stems in **-mm** the double **m** is usually replaced by single **-m** before all suffixed endings:

förnimbar (← förnimma), glömsk, tömning, skamlös, grymhet.

(g) In compound words **-mm** and **-nn** are retained (unless the rule in 1204(a) applies: cf. **damm + moln = dammoln**):

tunnbröd, brunnsvatten, lammkött, dammkorn.

B SMALL AND CAPITAL LETTERS

1206   Small or capital letters?

Swedish usage is at variance with English usage in the matter of small and initial capital letters. There is a trend in present-day Swedish towards using small letters in all but the most clear-cut examples according to the guidelines below. An initial capital letter is used:

(a) To start a sentence, as in English. Note, however, that names like **von Linné**, **af Geijerstam**, etc. and dates and numbers are best avoided at the beginning of a sentence.

(b) After a colon introducing direct speech (cf. 1304), or similar:

Jan frågade: Vad gör du?   Jan asked: 'What are you doing?'

Note, however, that the colon is followed by a small letter if it does not introduce direct speech, but merely a list.

Olssons säljer olika osorters frukt: apelsiner, äpplen, persikor, osv.
Olssons sell different kinds of fruit: oranges, apples, peaches, etc.

(c) To show respect. An initial capital letter may be used to show respect in the following instances:

(i) When referring to the Godhead:

Gud, Jesus Kristus, Fadern, Herren, Skaparen, Frälsaren, etc.

Note: In recent Swedish Bible translations pronouns referring to the Godhead have not been given capital letters.

(ii) In more formal letters. In formal or business correspondence the second person pronouns (**Ni, Er, Du, Din**, etc.) are sometimes written with an initial capital letter. Nowadays these 2nd person pronouns usually have small letters in personal correspondence.

(iii) In royal titles:

Leve Hans Majestät Konungen!   Long live His Majesty the King!

Normally other titles and epithets are rendered with small letters (cf. 1207(e)(i)), but there are exceptions, especially when the title has almost the status of a name:

År 800 kröntes Karl den Store till kejsare.
In 800 Charlemagne was crowned Emperor.

Stockholm grundlades av Birger Jarl.
Stockholm was founded by Birger Jarl (Earl Birger).

År 1349 flyttade Sankta Birgitta till Rom.
In 1349 Saint Bridget moved to Rome.

(**d**) To write the word **I** 'ye'. The (now archaic) Swedish 2nd person plural pronoun **I** (cf. 301(e) Note 3) is always seen written with a capital letter.

Note: English 'I' (1st person singular pronoun) is rendered by Swedish **jag**, not spelt with a capital letter unless it begins a sentence or follows a colon introducing direct speech.

1207 The use of capital letters in simple proper nouns: **Är Sven svensk?**

A simple proper noun in Swedish is a name and begins with a capital letter. Such names may be grouped into four categories:

(**a**) Names given to people, animals, boats, cars, houses, etc.:

Elsa, Tommy, Karo, Sessan, Golf, Tallbacken, etc.

(**b**) Place names:

Sverige, Stockholm, Vänern, Indalsälven, Värmland, Kebnekaise, etc.

Note: Street names written as one word always have an initial capital letter:
Kungsgatan, Avenyn, Järnvägstorget.

(**c**) Names of firms, institutions, organisations, etc.:

Volvo, Landsorganisationen, Socialstyrelsen, Operan.

Note 1: Capital letters are also used in the following and similar instances:

Jag har köpt en ny Ford.	I have bought a new Ford.
Det var första gången jag flög i en Boeing.	It was the first time I flew in a Boeing.
Köp en bra tv! Köp en Hitachi!	Buy a good TV! Buy a Hitachi!

Note 2: Small letters are used for the following:

riksdagen (the Swedish) parliament; **armén** the Army; **flottan** the Navy; **flyget** the Air Force.

(d) Titles of books, plays, films, etc.:

Nässlorna blomma, Fadren, Smultronstället, Ödessymfonien, etc.

(e) Note, however, the following cases, which have small initial letter in Swedish:

(i) Titles given to people:

herr Alm, fru Ek, fröken Asp, professor Hellström, kung Carl Gustaf, president Kennedy.

There are occasions on which titles are written with an initial capital letter. Cf. 1206(c) above.

(ii) Nouns derived from names:

Charles Darwin but **en darwinist** (also: **darwinistisk**); **Vidkun Quisling** but **en quisling**; **Judas Iskariot** but **en judas.**

Nouns originally derived from names after long use may lose the sense of being a name (cf. (c) Note 1 above) and therefore have lower case:

en chippendalemöbel a piece of Chippendale furniture; **dieselmotor** diesel engine; **falukorv** Falun sausage; **mausergevär** Mauser rifle **swedenborgianismen**; **parmesanost** Parmesan cheese; **röntgen** X-ray; **vichyvatten** soda-water.

This is the case even when the compound is truncated, leaving only the proper noun phrase:

en flaska beaujolais(vin)	a bottle of Beaujolais (wine)
en stor karljohan(svamp)	a big Penny Bun (mushroom)
en ung sanktbernhard(hund)	a young St Bernard (dog)

(iii) Nouns and adjectives derived from place-names:

en stockholmare a Stockholmer; **en svensk** a Swede; **en engelsman** an Englishman; **atlantisk** Atlantic; **europeisk** European.

(iv) Nouns and adjectives signifying religious or political persuasion:

en kristen a Christian; **en jude** a Jew; **en socialist** a Socialist; **katolsk** Catholic; **kommunistisk** Communist.

Note: The names of Sweden's political parties and organised churches are frequently written with small letters though usage does vary here:

centerpartiet/Centerpartiet; metodistsamfundet/Metodistsamfundet.

(v) Names of weekdays, months, seasons and festivals in the calendar:

söndag, måndag, mars, april, höst, vinter, jul, påsk, midsommar.

(vi) Units of measurement formed from personal names: **watt, ampere**, but **Fahrenheit, Celsius.**

1208 The use of capital letters in proper nouns comprising two or more words: **Förenta staterna**

(a) The general rule in Swedish is that only the first word of a proper noun expression of two or more words takes an initial capital letter:

Förenta staterna the United States; **Drömmar om rosor och eld** *Dreams of Roses and Fire* [book title]; **Röda havet** the Red Sea; **Klippiga bergen** the Rocky Mountains; **Göta kanal** the Göta Canal; **Lule älv** the River Lule älv.

This means that it is often the article which, as the first word in the expression, takes the initial capital letter.

Den flygande holländaren the Flying Dutchman; **Det sjunde inseglet** *The Seventh Seal* [film title]; **Ett drömspel** *A Dreamplay* [drama title].

But historical events and periods generally have small letters:

första världskriget the First World War; **slaget vid Hastings** the Battle of Hastings; **franska revolutionen** the French Revolutionen.

(b) However, any of the words in a proper noun expression may themselves be proper nouns (cf. 1207(a)–(c)), in which case they too are capitalised.

Republiken Sydafrika the Republic of South Africa; **August Strindberg**; **Ford Mondeo**; **Gösta Berlings saga** *The Tale of Gösta Berling* [book title].

Note 1: Street names comprising two or more words usually begin each element with a capital letter:

Södra Vägen, Östra Hamngatan, etc.

An exception is made when a name in the s-genitive form precedes a word like **gata, torg,** etc.:

Gustaf Adolfs torg.   Cf. also 137(f).

Note 2: Points of the compass used adjectivally have a small letter: **norra England** 'Northern England'; **västra Sverige** 'Western Sweden'. But note, as a prefix: **Nordengland, Västsverige.** (Cf. 1209(b)).

Note 3: Names based on compass points have capitals when referring to clearly delineated areas: **Norden** (NB capital letter) 'Scandinavia'; **norden** 'the north'; **den amerikanska Södern** 'the American South'.

Note 4: **Ön Man** the Isle of Man; **Ön Wight** the Isle of Wight.

Note 5: Well-known place names for which there is no Swedish equivalent usually have capital letters commencing each element:

Mount Everest, Mont Blanc, El Salvador.

(c) Names of firms, institutions, organisations, etc.

There are no hard and fast rules for how to capitalise the names of firms, etc. when these comprise more than one word. It is left up to the individual firms to decide the normal spelling for their particular name. Some common examples are:

Röda korset, Folkets hus, Förenta nationerna, Europeiska unionen, IFK Göteborg, Dagens Nyheter, Ord och Bild.

Note: Names of institutions etc. preceded by **Kungliga** (= '(The) Royal') [often abbreviated **Kungl.** in the written language], **Föreningen, Sällskapet** (= 'Society'), **Sveriges, Stockholms,** etc. are written with a capital letter on the second word:

Kungliga Operan The Royal Opera; **Föreningen Rädda barnen; Sällskapet Naturens vänner; Sveriges Radio; Göteborgs Symfoniorkester.**

(d) Fixed epithets without the definite article often have a capital letter:

Röde Orm; Musse Pigge Mickey Mouse; **Johannes Döparen** John the Baptist.

1209   The use of capital letters in compound proper nouns: **Sydamerika**

A proper noun may be incorporated into a compound noun (see 1111) in two different ways. In both instances the compound itself usually begins with a capital letter.

(a) As the first element of the compound:

en Stockholmstidning a Stockholm newspaper; **Volvoledningen** the management of Volvo; **en Mozart-opera** a Mozart opera; **en Zorntavla** a Zorn painting; **en Bellmansvisa** a Bellman song.

Note that exceptions include names for species of animals, plants, etc. which have a proper noun as their first element are usually spelt with a small initial letter:

> **gotlandsruss** Gotland pony; **ölandstok** potentilla; **kinakål** Chinese leaves.

(b) As an element within the compound:

> **Sydamerika** South America; **Mellansverige** Central Sweden; **Storstockholm** Greater Stockholm

Note that the proper noun element loses its initial capital letter here. Except in well-known geographical concepts, some variation does occur in forms such as **Sommarsverige/sommarsverige** 'Summer Sweden', etc.

1210 The use of capital letters in abbreviations

Capital letters are used in abbreviations if the abbreviated word does, itself, begin with a capital letter.

KB	=	**Kungliga Biblioteket**	the Royal Library
Sthlm	=	**Stockholm**	

However, there are many more occasions when capital letters are used in abbreviations even though they would not normally be used if the word were written out in full.

VD	=	**verkställande direktör**	Managing Director
AB	=	**aktiebolag**	limited company

There are no rules for such practice; only familiarity with the language and a good list of abbreviations will make clear the correct forms.

Note 1: Roman numerals used to signify the succession of kings, popes, etc. are always capitalised:

> **Carl XVI Gustaf**

Note 2: Chemical symbols (**Ka, H20, Fe**, etc.) conform to an international standard, and are thus identical in English and Swedish.

D MISCELLANEOUS

1211 Hyphenation

The following basic rules for word division may prove helpful on occasions when dividing a word is unavoidable.

(a) Compound words

Compound words may be divided into their separate elements:

träd-gård   **Stock-holm**
sam-arbets-vilja   **för-kär-lek**

Prefixes and suffixes may be treated in the same way:

an-befall-a   **juster-bar**

Note: The link **-s** tends to go with the first element: **livs-medels-butik**.

(b) Hyphenation of simple words

Two equally valid principles are employed for word division:

1 The morpheme principle divides words according to their morphemes:

mur-ar   **tras-ig**

All kinds of endings can be hyphenated according to this principle:

parker-ing   **hertig-inna**   **spion-era**
bil-en   **mörk-are**

2 The single consonant principle implies adding one consonant to the second syllable:

mu-rar   **tra-sig**

When no morpheme boundary exists this principle must be applied:

lyd-de   **dum-mare**   **åt-tio**

Two vowels can also be hyphenated: **akvari-um**, **idé-erna**.

Exceptions:

(i) Consonant clusters **ng**, **gn** should accompany the syllable preceding the division: **eng-elsk**, **vagn-arna**.

(ii) Consonant groups denoting **sj**-sounds are usually not hyphenated: **ma-skin**, **sta-tion**.

(iii) The letter **x** is always kept with the first syllable: **väx-ande**.

1212 Figures or words?

In written Swedish cardinal numbers are given either as figures or as words. If numerals are not too long they are given as words in running text.

(a) Words are, therefore, generally used in expressions for 1–19 and for round numbers from 20 to 90.

(b) Figures are used:

(i) For large numbers: **251 000 invånare**.

(ii) With units of measurement given as abbreviations: **50 kg, 500 m**^{2}.

(iii) In dates and times: **1918, 15.15** (see 414ff.).

Larger numbers are written as groups of three counted from the end:

    1 250 000 (en miljon tvåhundrafemtio tusen)

(iv) Prices: **Biljetten kostar 50 pund**.   The ticket costs £50.

See also 401.

1213   One word or two?

Compounds are always written as one word. They are distinguished by their single word accent: cf. **'femton** 'fifteen' **'fem 'ton** 'five tonnes'.

However, not all expressions involving two or more words may be written as compound forms.

(a) Semantic differences

Occasionally there may be a difference in meaning between two or more words written separately and compounded:

    Han var herre över allt i denna by.
    He was lord over everything in this village.

    Han var känd överallt i byn.
    He was known everywhere in the village.

Cf. also **grön sak** 'green thing'; **grönsak** 'vegetable'; **kanhända** 'maybe'; **kan hända** 'can happen'; etc.

(b) Stylistic differences

In many instances the difference between two or more words written separately and compounded is merely a matter of style and practice. One finds, for example:

i övrigt	but	**ihåg, ihjäl, ihop, ifall**
för övrigt	but	**förutom**
till sist, till synes	but	**tillbaka**

For separable and inseparable verbs, see 554ff.

(c) The following should be written as two (or more) words:

> **före detta, framför allt, i dag, i kväll, till godo, över huvud taget.**

(d) Alternatives are sometimes found in genitive expressions:

en tremeters plank	or	**en tremetersplank**
ett 50-minuters program	or	**ett 50-minutersprogram**

(e) The following are written as one word:

> **ibland, tillsammans, isär, tillbaka, återigen.**

13 PUNCTUATION

1301	Punctuation marks
1302	The comma
1303	The full stop
1304	The colon
1305	The exclamation mark
1306	Direct speech
1307	Quotations
1308	The apostrophe
1309	The hyphen
1310	The dash
1311	Addresses
1312	Dates

1301   Punctuation marks

In many cases English and Swedish practice is the same as regards punctuation. This section is a résumé of the most important points of use, and also includes some of the main differences between English and Swedish use.

The names of the principal punctuation marks (**skiljetecken**) in Swedish are:

.	**punkt**
,	**komma**
:	**kolon**
-	**bindestreck**
—	**tankstreck, pratminus, talstreck**
( )	**bågparenteser**
{ }	**klammerparenteser**
[ ]	**hakparenteser**
< >	**vinkelparenteser**
;	**semikolon**
'...' ''...'' »...»	**anföringstecken, citationstecken**
?	**frågetecken**
'	**apostrof**
!	**utropstecken**
@	**snabel-a** (only in e-mail addresses)

1302   The comma

The comma is used between groups of words that are relatively independent of each other. In certain cases the length of a sentence requires a comma to make it more readable. Therefore, completely hard and fast rules are not possible. The comma is used chiefly:

(a) Between main clauses in the same sentence linked with a conjunction (but see (d) below):

> **Landslaget vann matchen, och alla gick hem glada.**
> The national team won the match, and everyone went home happy.

> **Han försökte komma in, men dörren var låst.**
> He tried to get in, but the door was locked.

A comma is not required, however, when the subject is the same in both clauses and is omitted in the second clause:

> **Landslaget vann matchen och åkte hem.**
> The national team won the match and went home.

(See also (d) below.)

(b) Around a subordinate clause which is not strictly necessary in the sentence (non-restrictive clause (see 1038(c)(i)):

> **Hans första stora framgång, att han redan vid 14 års ålder vann 100 meter-löpet, blev avgörande för hans utveckling.**
> His first great achievement, that at the age of 14 he won the 100 metres, was decisive for his development.

The comma is, however, not used to indicate necessary (restrictive) clauses (see 1038(c)(i)):

> **Det är klart att vi ska bjuda honom.**   It's obvious we should invite him.
> **den sortens bil som inte rostar**   the kind of car that doesn't rust

(c) Around (lengthy) subordinate clauses to mark a pause when the passage is read. This is particularly common when the subordinate clause begins the sentence:

> **Staden såg obebodd ut, eftersom ingen rök steg upp ur skorstenarna.**
> The town looked deserted, as no smoke rose from the chimneys.

Om man ser närmare på resultatet, förstår man varför vetenskapsmännen blev så chockerade.
If one looks more closely at the result, one can understand why the scientists were so shocked.

(d) When one of the coordinating conjunctions (cf. 802(a), 804ff.) is omitted:

Han var kraftigt byggd, nästan lite för tjock, snarare under än över medellängd.
He was powerfully built, almost a little too fat, under rather than over average height.

In this sense the comma is used in lists:

Vi ska köpa ris, kött, sallad och ärter.
We are going to buy rice, meat, lettuce and peas.

Han kom, han såg, han segrade.
He came, he saw, he conquered.

Note: The addition of the comma with **dels . . . , dels; än . . . , än; ju . . . desto . . .**:

Än var de glada, än djupt bekymrade.   One moment they were happy, the next worried.

(e) Around words which are in apposition, or words which are a parenthetical addition to the sentence such as tags:

Max von Sydow, den berömde svenske skådespelaren, uppträder i många hollywoodfilmer.
Max von Sydow, the famous Swedish actor, appears in many Hollywood films.

Du vill väl vara med, eller hur?   You do want to come, don't you?

(f) Before **men**, **utan** when a contrast is emphasised and when **men** or **utan** is followed by more than just one or two words (cf. 807):

Han har inte mycket pengar, men troligen mer än tillräckligt.
He doesn't have much money, but presumably more than sufficient.

Compare:

Han är rik men snål.   He is rich but mean.

(g) In order to separate interjections (cf. 901f.), forms of address, etc. from the main body of the sentence (cf. also 1034):

Ja, det vill jag gärna göra!   Yes, I'll do that by all means!
Hej, hur står det till?   Hi, how are things?

Mina damer och herrar, nu börjar vi.
Ladies and gentlemen, now we shall begin

(h) Note the following occasions when the use of the comma in English is *not* reflected in Swedish.

(i) Around adverbs like 'however', 'too', 'though':

This, however, is uncertain.   **Detta är emellertid osäkert.**

(ii) After introductory and closing phrases in letters:

Dear Mr Smith,   **Bäste herr Smith!**
Yours sincerely,   **Med vänlig hälsning**

(iii) A colon is sometimes preferred when introducing direct speech in Swedish (cf. 1304).

(j) Note the difference in usage of the comma in certain numerical/mathematical expressions in English and Swedish:

(i) Comma in Swedish, decimal point in English:

5,62   5.62

(ii) Comma in English, space (or sometimes a full stop) in Swedish

3,000   **3 000**
4,567,890   **4 567 890**

1303   The full stop

The full stop is used chiefly:

(a) At the end of a sentence.

(b) In many abbreviations: **bl.a. (bland annat); e.Kr. (efter Kristus);** etc.

Note: Exceptions include internationally accepted abbreviations for measurements (**cm, km**) and abbreviations comprising the initial capital letters of two or more words (**EU, HKH**).

(c) In certain numerical/mathematical expressions (cf. 410, 414, 416):

kl. 13.25 (pronounced **klockan tretton och tjugofem**); **Stockholm 21.4 1992**

Note: The English decimal point is represented by a decimal comma in Swedish (cf. 1302(j)).

1304   The colon

The colon is used in the following ways:

(a) Before quotations, dialogue in a play or thoughts in direct speech coming after a lead verb. In this case the word after the colon has an initial capital letter:

Han frågade: – Vad gör du här?   He asked: 'What're you doing here?'

Jean: I kväll är fröken Julie galen igen; komplett galen!
Jean: Tonight Miss Julie is crazy again, quite crazy!

(b) Before lists, examples, explanations and summaries:

Du ska ta med tre blanketter: en vit, en röd och en blå.
You must bring three forms: one white, one red and one blue.

(c) In some numerical expressions and a few abbreviations:

250:95	**250 kronor (och) 95 öre**
1:a	**första**
S:t	**sankt**
n:r	**nummer** [see 1125]

(d) Before all kinds of endings added to a figure, a letter, an acronym, etc.:

3:e gången	the third time
25:an	the number 25 (bus, tram, etc.)
LO:s regler	the rules of LO [see 129(d) Note 2]
Gustaf III:s död	the death of Gustaf III

Note: This means that genitive s-endings on an abbreviation are preceded by a colon in Swedish:

avd:s personal   the dept's staff

1305 The exclamation mark

The exclamation mark is used after exclamations, greetings, commands (imperative verb forms (537)) and introductions to letters:

Vad vackert det var!	How beautiful it is!
Skynda dig!	Hurry up!
Lycka till!	Good luck!
Hej, Bosse!	Hi, Bosse.
Bäste Magnus!	Dear Magnus,
Kära Eva!	Dear Eva,

Note: If the exclamation, greeting, command, etc. is followed by a clause, the exclamation mark is usually best omitted:

Skynda dig, annars hinner vi inte med bussen. Hurry up, otherwise we'll miss the bus.

But NB: direct speech:

Skynda dig! skrek hon.	'Hurry up!' she shouted.

1306 Direct speech

(a) The most common Swedish convention for indicating direct speech is the use of the dash (**pratminus**) before each speaker's comments. A new line is started each time there is a change of speaker.

− Vad heter du? frågade polisen.
'What's your name?' asked the policeman.

− Martin, kom svaret.
'Martin,' came the reply.

(b) If the words indicating direct speech precede the direct speech itself, a colon is used in Swedish where English has a comma:

Geir säger: − Minns du den här yxan, Ravnkel?
Geir says: 'Do you remember this axe, Ravnkel?'

− Ja, svarar Ravnkel. Det är en bra yxa.
'Yes,' replies Ravnkel. 'It's a good axe.'

(c) Swedish may also use inverted commas round direct speech, instead of introducing it with a dash. Note that the form of the inverted commas ("...") differs from that in English ("...").

(d) Swedish may also use guillemets ›...›› round direct speech. In printed Swedish these marks always point to the right.

1307 Quotations

Inverted commas, single ('...') or double ("...") are usually used around direct quotations:

> **Strindberg kallade jorden för en 'jämmerdal'.**
> Strindberg called the world a 'vale of tears'.

However, when the quotation is not taken directly from speech or a written work, but is, for example, merely the name of a book, film, play, etc., Swedish rarely uses inverted commas:

> **Har du läst Nessers Återkomsten?**
> Have you read Nesser's *The Return?*

> **Jag tycker att Tystnaden är Bergmans bästa film.**
> I think that *The Silence* is Bergman's best film.

(See: Use of capital letters 1207(d).)

Note: A judicious use of inverted commas may sometimes help avoid an ambiguity when using quotations:

> **'Messias' kommer till Stockholm till jul.** (i.e. the oratorio, not the man)

1308 The apostrophe

(a) The apostrophe is used (sparingly!) to show that certain letters have been omitted in less common elisions.

> **'Dag ropa' han.** = **God dag ropade han.** 'G'day,' he shouted.
> **Jag såg 'na.** = **Jag såg henne.** I saw 'er.

Note: No apostrophe is used in the following: **dan (dagen); stan (staden); sa (sade); ha (hava)**.

(b) Unlike English, Swedish does not normally use an apostrophe to indicate a possessor (i.e. genitive) (see 129):

> **hundens ägare** the dog's owner
> **Evas mamma** Eva's mother

1309 The hyphen

The hyphen is used:

(a) In some compound names:

> **Karl-Erik, Peterson-Berger, Uppsala-Ekeby AB**

(b) In many compounds with **icke**:

> **icke-rökare** non-smoker
> **icke-socialistisk** non-Socialist

(c) To replace **och** in compounds like:

> **Sverige-Norgeavtal** Sweden-Norway agreement
> **nord-sydlinje** north-south line

(d) To avoid repetition of the second element of a compound in expressions such as:

> **sön- och helgdagar = söndagar och helgdagar**
> Sundays and holidays
>
> **färg- och parfymhandel = färghandel och parfymhandel**
> paint and perfume shop

Note: When the first element of the compound is the repeated element it is not replaced by the hyphen:

> car prices and repairs = **bilpriser och bilreparationer** (not *bilpriser och -reparationer)

(e) In compounds and before suffixes where the first element is an acronym:

> **LO-kongressen** the Swedish trades Union Confederation Congress; **en IOGT-are** an IOGT member.

(f) In compounds where the first element is a number:

> **2000-talet** 21st century; **50-öring** 50-öre piece; **75-årsdag** 75th birthday; **1952-orna** the class of 1952.

But there is no hyphen if the number is written out:

> **förstamajtalare** May Day speaker; **tvåvåningshus** two-storey house.

1310   The dash

The dash (double the length of the hyphen) is used:

(a) To indicate a pause before an unexpected conclusion to a statement:

> **Han ville ha en Jaguar, men fick – en Lada.**
> He wanted a Jaguar but got – a Lada.

(b) As brackets around a parenthetical phrase, before an exclamation, etc.:

> **Jag fick inte – i varje fall inte då — be om ursäkt.**
> I was not able – at least not then – to apologise.

(c) Between figures and names of places to indicate period, extent, distance, etc.:

> **Sträckan Malmö–Lund måste vara 15–20 kilometer.**
> The stretch between Malmö and Lund must be about 15–20 kilometres.

> **Stängt 12–14.**
> Closed 12 to 2.

1311   Addresses

Here follow some examples of letters, addressed according to the advice of the Swedish post office. Note especially the straight, left-hand margin (in both typed and hand-written addresses) and the absence of punctuation.

(a) Address within Sweden:

> **Åke Åkerström**
> **Kungsgatan 24**
> **824 93 HUDIKSVALL**

The title (if there is one) is written out in full (**Herr**, **Fru**, etc.) unless very long, or a Latin abbreviation (**Fil mag** etc.). Titles are often dropped nowadays in favour of first name and surname alone. The street number always follows the street name. The street name is best written out in full.

(b) Addressee living in a block of flats:

> **Robert Olsson**
> **Storkgatan 5, 2 tr**
> **403 10 GÖTEBORG**

(c) E-mail addresses follow the international pattern:

carl.nilsson@translexab.se

but notice that Swedish å, ä, ö are not used, see 1203(f).

Note 1: If writing from abroad to any address in Sweden the nationality marker **SE** should be placed before the post code, and separated from it with a dash: **SE–104 19 Stockholm**.

Note 2: The sender usually writes his own address preceded by **Avs:** or **Avsändare** at the top on the back of the envelope, to ensure that the letter can be returned unopened in the event of non-delivery.

Note 3: When sending private correspondence Swedes usually write as a letterhead only the name of their post town and the date where English convention requires the full address: **Göteborg, 2003-05-14**.

1312   Dates

(a) In running text the convention is **den** + date in figures (sometimes written out in full) + month written out + year in figures, thus:

Vi träffades den 14 [pronounced as an ordinal number **fjortonde**] **maj 2003.** We met on the 14th of May 2003.

(b) On letterheads the convention is year (in full or just the last two digits), month (always given in two digits, i.e. 01 for January, 06 for June) and date (always given in two digits), thus:

2003 - 05 - 14 or **2003-05-14** or **2003/05/14**
2003.05.14
2003 05 14 or
030514

LINGUISTIC TERMS

This list comprises only those terms that may not be familiar to a student of language or those that are not already explained in the text. In some cases these are not directly transferable to English grammar.

ABSTRACT NOUNS refer to unobservable notions, e.g., **svårighet** difficulty; **musik** music; **påstående** assertion.

ADJECTIVE PHRASE consists of an adjective or a participle with optional words which modify or limit its meaning, e.g. **Han är *(ganska) dum*** He is rather silly.

ADVERB PHRASE consists of an adverb with optional words which modify or limit its meaning, e.g. **Han körde *(ganska) fort*** He drove (quite) fast.

ADVERBIAL (see CLAUSAL ADVERBIAL, OTHER ADVERBIALS)

AFFIX is a prefix added to the beginning or a suffix added to the end of a word, e.g. *o*lycklig unhappy; god*het* goodness.

AGENT is the person or thing carrying out the action in a passive construction, e.g. **Bilen kördes *av inspektören*** The car was driven by the inspector.

AGREEMENT is a way of showing that two grammatical units have a certain feature in common, e.g. plural **min*a* hund*ar*** my dogs; neuter **slott*et* är stor*t*** the castle is big.

ANAPHORIC reference means that a word refers back to a previous word or words, e.g. **Olle är sjuk. *Han* har druckit för mycket** Olle is ill. He (i.e. Olle) has drunk too much.

APPOSITION is where two noun phrases describe the same phenomenon, e.g. ***Olle, min bror*, är sjuk** Olle, my brother, is ill.

ASSIMILATION is the process whereby a sound changes to become more like or even identical with another sound, e.g. pronunciation of **min bror** as /mimbror/. The two sounds may merge completely, as in the case of **-d** in the past tense of the verb **använda + -e → använde**.

ATTRACTION is a grammatical error often caused by the speaker's losing sight of the true agreement and becoming distracted by another word, e.g. ***Typiskt* för detta barn är en viss blyghet** ('A certain shyness is typical of this child') should read **Typisk** to agree with **(en) blyghet**.

ATTRIBUTIVE is used to describe adjectives that precede the noun and modify it, e.g. **ett** *stort* **hus** a big house.

CLAUSAL ADVERBIAL denotes an adverb modifying the sense of the clause as a whole, e.g. **Han är** *inte* **dum** He's not stupid; **De är** *aldrig* **lata** They are never lazy.

CLAUSE usually comprises a NOUN PHRASE and a VERB PHRASE (SUBJECT and PREDICATE): **Han läste denna bok** He read this book.

COLLECTIVE NOUNS are nouns denoting a group, e.g. **familj** family; **boskap** cattle; **ärter** peas.

COMMON NOUNS are all nouns that are not PROPER NOUNS e.g. **en hund** a dog, **två dramer** two dramas; **svagheter** weaknesses.

COMPLEMENTS express a meaning that adds to (or complements) that of the subject or object. They can be either an ADJECTIVE PHRASE or a NOUN PHRASE, e.g. **Olle och Sven är** *intelligenta.* **De är** *studenter.* Olle and Sven are intelligent. They are students.

COMPLEX VERB is one that has two or more parts: **Jag** *har ätit sniglar* I have eaten snails.

COMPOUND VERB is a verb consisting of a STEM and a prefixed PARTICLE, which may be inseparable or separable from the stem, e.g. *betala* pay, but **köra** *om/om*köra overtake.

CONGRUENCE (= AGREEMENT)

CONJUGATION denotes the way a verb is inflected, its pattern of endings, and also a group of verbs with the same endings, e.g. past tenses in: Conj. I **kalla-de**; Conj. IIb **köp-te**; Conj. III **bo-dde**.

COPULAR verbs (or copulas) link the noun or adjective COMPLEMENT to the subject, e.g. **Eva blev läkare** Eva became a doctor; **Sven** *blev* **besviken** Sven was disappointed.

COPULATIVE means 'linking', (see COPULAR).

CORRELATIVE is the word or phrase that a pronoun replaces or refers to. For example, the correlative **Filmen** is replaced by the pronoun **som** in **Filmen som vi såg var urfånig** The film we saw was really silly.

COUNT NOUN is a noun that describes an individual countable entity and therefore usually possesses a plural form, e.g. **bok, böcker**, book, books; **ägg, ägg** egg, eggs; **pojke, pojkar** boy, boys.

DECLENSION denotes the different ways of INFLECTING the noun in the plural, e.g. **flick*or*** girls; **pojk*ar*** boys; **park*er*** parks; **äppl*en*** apples; **m*ä*n** men. It is also used to describe adjective + noun constructions such as the indefinite declension of the adjective, e.g. **en sådan liten bil** a little car like that, or the definite declension of the adjective, e.g. **den lilla bilen** the little car.

DEFINITE refers to a previously mentioned entity, cf. ***Tjuven* har stulit klockan** The thief has stolen the clock. The indefinite refers to a new entity, e.g. ***En tjuv har stulit klockan*** A thief has stolen the clock.

DERIVATIVE refers to a word derived from a STEM, usually by the addition of an AFFIX, e.g. ***angå*** concern, ***begå*** commit, ***föregå*** precede and **en gå*ende*** a pedestrian are all derivatives of the verb **gå** go.

DIRECT OBJECT refers to a person or thing directly affected by the action of a (transitive) verb, e.g. **Pojken slog *bollen/sin syster*** The boy hit the ball/his sister.

DUPLICATION involves the repetition of a subject, object or adverbial, usually in a pronoun or adverb form, e.g. ***Olle,* han är inte dum, *han*** Olle, he isn't stupid, he isn't.

DURATIVE VERB (or verb of duration) denotes a continued action (e.g. **sova** sleep), a constant change (e.g. **växa** grow) or an intermittent action (e.g. **droppa** drip).

ELLIPSIS involves the omission of a word or word group in the sentence, e.g. **Jag ville röka men jag fick inte (*röka*)** I wanted to smoke but I was not allowed to (smoke).

END FOCUS is the principle that new, unfamiliar information comes at the end of the sentence, e.g. **Han åkte sedan *till Venedig*** Then he went to Venice.

END WEIGHT is the principle that long, heavy expressions come at the end of the sentence, e.g. **Han åkte sedan *med en gammal lastbil utan strålkastare*** He then travelled in an old truck without lights.

FIGURATIVE SENSE is a sense other than the literal, e.g. **Det kostar skjortan!** It costs an arm and a leg [*lit.* 'the shirt'].

FINITE VERB is a verb whose form shows tense, mood or voice (active/passive) (cf. NON-FINITE VERB).

FOCUS is new information imparted in an utterance (i.e. its message), e.g. **Eva *åker till Tunisien imorgon*** Eva is going to Tunisia tomorrow.

FORMAL SUBJECT is **det** in cases when the REAL SUBJECT is postponed, e.g. ***Det* (FS) sitter en gubbe (RS) därborta** There's an old man sitting over there.

FRONTING is moving an element to the beginning of the sentence. Compare **Vi älskar rödvin** We love red wine and **Rödvin älskar vi** Red wine we love.

GENDER can be by sex (**karlen – han** the chap – he; **tjejen – hon** the lass – she) or grammatical gender (**ett hus** a house; **ett barn** a child; **en matta** a carpet).

GRAMMATICAL SUBJECT (= FORMAL SUBJECT)

HOMONYM is a word that is identical in spelling to another word, e.g. **komma** = either 'to come' or 'comma'.

IDIOM(ATIC) indicates a usage that is not readily explicable from grammar.

IMPERATIVE is the mood of the verb expressing command or warning or direction, e.g. **Kom!** Come on!; **Rör om!** Stir!

IMPERSONAL constructions do not involve a person but usually the impersonal pronoun **det**, e.g. **Det snöar** It's snowing.

IMPLIED SUBJECT is actually an object which functions as subject in a non-finite clause, e.g. **Vi bad *honom* skriva en rad** We asked him to drop us a line.

INDECLINABLE describes a word that does not inflect, e.g. the adjectives **bra** good; **utrikes** foreign; **öde** deserted. These take no endings for gender or plural.

INDEFINITE (cf. DEFINITE)

INDIRECT OBJECT is usually a person or animal benefiting from an action: e.g. **Vi gav *honom* pengarna** We gave him the money.

INFINITIVE PHRASE is a phrase consisting of an infinitive accompanied by optional words which modify it, e.g. **att skriva brev** to write a letter.

INFLECT means to change form by modifying an ending, e.g. the verb **skriva** write, inflects **skriv, skriva, skriver, skrev, skrivit, skriven**, etc.

INFLEXIBLE (= INDECLINABLE)

INFLEXION (see INFLECT)

INTERROGATIVE means question, e.g. an interrogative pronoun asks a question: ***Vem* var det?** Who was that?; ***Varför* kom du hit?** Why did you come here?

INVERTED word order denotes verb – subject order, e.g. **Idag åker vi** Today we leave.

MATRIX is that part of a main clause sentence remaining when the subordinate clause is removed, e.g. ***Eva lovade* att hon skulle skriva till oss** Eva promised that she would write to us.

MORPHEME is the smallest part of a word expressing some meaning: in the word **bilarna** 'the cars' there are three morphemes: **bil** 'car' **ar** (plural morpheme) **na** (definite morpheme).

MUTATED VOWEL is one that changes in different forms of the word, e.g. **o** → **ö** in **son – söner** (son – sons); **stor – större** (big – bigger).

NOMINAL means noun or acting as a noun, e.g. ***Simning* är roligt** Swimming is fun; ***Att simma* är roligt** To swim is fun.

NON-COUNT NOUN is a noun, often denoting an abstract or substance, that does not usually take a plural, e.g. **mjöl** flour; **bensin** petrol; **luft** air; **vatten** water; **glädje** joy.

NON-FINITE VERB forms are those forms not showing tense or mood, namely infinitive, supine and participles.

NOUN PHRASE is a noun often accompanied by one or more words before or after the noun which modify it, e.g. **en vacker dikt som jag lärde mig** a beautiful poem that I learned.

NUMBER is a collective term for singular and plural usually marked by an ending, e.g. **två pennor** two pens.

OBJECT (see DIRECT OBJECT, INDIRECT OBJECT)

OTHER ADVERBIALS (or content adverbials or sentence adverbials) are usually an adverb, noun phrase or subordinate clause denoting manner, place, time or condition, e.g. **Han åker** *med tåg* (Manner) *till Stockholm* (Place) *i morgon* (Time) *om han har tid* (Condition) He will travel by train to Stockholm tomorrow if he has time.

PARENTHETICAL means bracketing, e.g. the prepositional expression *för* **10 dagar** *sedan* ten days ago.

PART OF SPEECH means word class, e.g. noun, adjective, verb, conjunction, etc.

PARTICLE is a stressed adverb or preposition appearing together with a verb to form a single unit of meaning, a particle verb, e.g. *om* in **köra om** 'overtake'; *ned* in **skriva ned** 'write down'.

PARTITIVE indicates that a part is implied, e.g. *en del av* **pengarna**, some of the money; *en flaska* **vin** a bottle of wine; *ett kilo* **potatis** a kilo of potatoes.

PEJORATIVE means deprecating as in e.g. **din dumma åsna** you stupid ass.

PERIPHRASTIC means paraphrasing.

POSTPOSITIONED means coming after something.

PREDICATE forms the only compulsory part of the clause other than the SUBJECT. The predicate is the verb plus any object, complement or adverbial: **Han** *spelar (piano dagligen)* He plays (the piano every day).

PREDICATIVE(LY) indicates that an element is found after the verb.

PREDICATIVE COMPLEMENT is a word or word group (often a NOUN PHRASE or ADJECTIVE PHRASE) which complements, i.e. fills out, the subject, e.g. **Hon är** *hans lärare* **och hon säger att han är** *lat* She is his teacher and she says that he is lazy.

PREPOSITIONAL PHRASE consists of a preposition plus a prepositional complement (usually a NOUN PHRASE or INFINITIVE PHRASE), e.g. **flickan** *med det långa håret* the girl with the long hair; **flickan gick** *utan att säga adjö* the girl left without saying goodbye.

PRE-POSITIONED means coming in front of something.

PRODUCTIVE implies that a word class or method of word formation is still being used to produce new words, e.g. the suffix **-vänlig** in **sittvänlig** comfortable to sit in.

PROPER NOUNS are names of specific people, places, occasions or events, books, etc. e.g. **Olle; Stockholm; Krig och fred.**

RAISING is the practice of moving an element from a subordinate clause to the front of the main clause (see FRONTING), e.g. *Det* **sa Pelle att vi inte skulle göra** Pelle said that we should not do that (← **Pelle sa att vi inte skulle göra** *det*.)

REAL SUBJECT is the postponed subject, e.g. **Det är roligt** *att dricka vin* It's nice to drink wine (see FORMAL SUBJECT).

RECIPROCAL or RECIPROCATING indicates a mutual activity in either the pronoun, (**De älskar varandra** They love one another) or in the verb (**De kysstes länge** They kissed for a long time).

REFLEXIVE applies to both pronouns and verbs. Reflexive pronouns refer to the subject in the same clause. They have a special form in the 3rd person, e.g. **Han har rakat** *sig* He has shaved (himself). Reflexive verbs incorporate such a pronoun: **De har** *lärt sig* **svenska** They have learned Swedish.

SEMANTIC denotes the meaning of words.

SIMPLE VERB is one that only consists of one word, e.g. *hjälp!* help!; (**han**) *sover* (he) sleeps; (**han**) *gick* (he) went.

STATEMENT is a declarative sentence or clause ending with a full stop.

STEM is the part of the verb common to all of its forms and onto which the inflexional endings are added, e.g. *dansa/*, *dansa/r*, *dansa/*de, *dansa/*t.

SUBJECT is a NOMINAL sentence element which together with the PREDICATE forms a clause.

SYLLABLE consists of a vowel plus one or more consonants, e.g. **ö, dö, rör, röst, in-du-stri-ar-be-ta-re.**

TAG QUESTION in English consists of verb + subject (+ negative) at the end of a statement to invite a response from the listener: He likes salmon, doesn't he? In Swedish **va?** or **eller hur?** usually suffice: **Han gillar lax,** *eller hur?* He likes salmon, doesn't he?

TERMINATIVE VERBS denote an action or process implying a state of change or leading to a change or cessation, e.g. **somna** fall asleep; **låsa** lock.

TOPIC is the position at the beginning of all main clause STATEMENTS and V-QUESTIONS. It is usually occupied by the subject, e.g. *Vi/Studenterna* **tycker om öl** We/The students like beer. But in Swedish, non-subjects, especially ADVERBIAL expressions of time or place, often occupy the topic position, e.g. *I morgon* **spelar jag fotboll** Tomorrow I'm playing football.

V-QUESTION is a question introduced by an INTERROGATIVE pronoun or adverb (many of which begin with the letter **v** in Swedish), e.g. **vad, vem, varför, när, hur**, etc.

VERB PHRASE consists of a FINITE VERB alone or several finite and non-finite verbs in a chain, e.g., **Han** *reser* He is travelling; **Han** *måste kunna springa* He must be able to run.

VOICED indicates a consonant produced with vibration of the larynx, e.g. **b, d, g, v, m, n, r, l**.

VOICELESS indicates a consonant produced without vibrating the larynx, e.g. **p, t, k, f, s, z**.

SHORT BIBLIOGRAPHY

GENERAL ON SWEDISH

Språkvård
Nysvenska studier
Arkiv för Nordisk Filologi
Svenskans beskrivning (Förhandlingar vid sammankomst för att dryfta frågor rörande svenskans beskrivning) 1–, 1964–
Lars-Gunnar Andersson, *Vi säger så*, Stockholm, 2000
Björn Collinder, *Svenska. Vårt språks byggnad*, Stockholm, 1971
Catharina Grünbaum, *Strövtåg i språket*, Stockholm, 1996
Ulf Teleman, *Manual för grammatisk analys av talad och skriven svenska*, Lund, 1974
Erik Wellander, *Riktig svenska. En handledning i svenska språkets vård*. 4th edn, Stockholm, 1973
Åke Åkermalm, *Modern svenska, Språk- och stilfrågor*, 2nd edn., Stockholm, 1972

SWEDISH DICTIONARIES

Ulla-Britt Kotsinas, *Norstedts svenska slangordbok*, Stockholm, 1998
Ture Johannisson and K.G. Ljunggren (eds), *Svensk handordbok. Konstruktioner och fraseologi*, Stockholm, undated
Nationalencyklopediens ordbok, 3 vols, Höganäs, 1995
Ralf Svenblad, *Norstedts förkortningsordbok*, Stockholm, 1998
Svensk ordbok, Stockholm, 1986
Svenska akademiens ordlista över svenska språket, 12th edn, Stockholm,
Olof Östergren *et al.*, *Nusvensk ordbok*, Stockholm, 1919–1972

SWEDISH GRAMMAR

Erik Andersson, *Grammatik från grunden*, Uppsala, 1993
Natanael Beckman, *Svensk språklära för den högre elementärundervisningen*, 9th edn, Stockholm, 1964
Harold Borland, *Swedish for Students*, London, 1970
Björn Collinder, *Svensk språklära*, Lund, 1974
Britta Holm and Elizabeth Nylund Lindgren (eds), *Deskriptiv svensk grammatik*, Stockholm, 1977

Philip Holmes and Ian Hinchliffe, *Swedish. An Essential Grammar*, London, 1997
Nils Jörgensen and Jan Svensson, *Nusvensk grammatik*, Stockholm, 1986
Ebba Lindberg, *Beskrivande svensk grammatik*, 2nd edn, Stockholm, 1980
Hans Lindholm, *Svensk grammatik. Lärobok i svenska som främmande språk*, Lund, 1986
Ulf Teleman, Staffan Hellberg and Erik Andersson, *Svenska Akademiens grammatik*, 4 vols, Stockholm, 1999
Olof Thorell, *Svensk grammatik*, 2nd edn, Stockholm,1977
Elias Wessén, *Vårt svenska språk*, Stockholm, 1968
Elsie Wijk Andersson, *Ny Grammatik, Det svenska språkets struktur*, Uppsala, 1981

MORPHOLOGY

Sture Allén, *Tiotusen i topp: Ordfrekvenser i tidningstext*, Stockholm, 1972
Sture, Allén, Mats Eeg-Olofsson, Rolf Gavare and Christian Sjögreen, *Svensk baklängesordbok*, Stockholm, 1981
Anders Bodegård, *Tänk efter*, Stockholm, 1985
Staffan Hellberg, *The Morphology of Present-Day Swedish*, Stockholm, 1978
Staffan Hellberg, *Sanningen om svenskan*, Gothenburg, 1984
Ferenc Kiefer, *Swedish Morphology*, Stockholm, 1970
Arto Kirri, *Studier över passivkonstruktioner i nysvenskt skriftspråk*, Åbo, 1975
Per Montan and Håkan Rosenqvist, *Prepositionsboken*, Stockholm, 1982
Bengt Nordberg, *Det mångskiftande språket*, Malmö, 1985

SYNTAX

Lars-Gunnar Andersson, *Form and function of subordinate clauses*, Gothenburg, 1975
Paul Diderichsen, *Elementær dansk grammatik*, 3rd edn, Copenhagen, 1962
Lars-Johan Ekerot, "Syntax och informationsstruktur", in *Svenska i invandrarperspektiv*, ed. Kenneth Hyltenstam, Lund, 1979, pp. 79–108
Lars Holm and Kent Larsson, *Svenska meningar*, 2nd edn, Lund, 1980
Nils Jörgensen, *Meningsbyggnaden i talad svenska*, Lundastudier i nordisk språkvetenskap Serie C nr 7, Lund, 1976
Ulf Teleman, "Bisatser i talad svenska", in *Svenskt talspråk*, ed. Gösta Holm, Stockholm, 1967

WORD FORMATION

Lars-Erik Edlund and Birgitta Hene, *Lånord i svenskan*, Stockholm, 1996
Philip Holmes and Ian Hinchliffe, *Swedish Word Formation*, Hull, 1996

Bo Seltén, *Ny svengelsk ordbok*, Lund, 1993
Ragnhild Söderberg, *Svensk ordbildning*, Stockholm, 1971
Olof Thorell, *Svensk ordbildningslära*, Stockholm, 1981
Olof Thorell, *Att bilda ord*, Stockholm, 1984

ORTHOGRAPHY AND PUNCTUATION

Svenska skrivregler, Svensk språknämnden, 2nd edn, Stockholm, 2001
Skrivregler för svenska och engelska från TNC, Stockholm, 2001
TT-språket, 5th edn, Stockholm, 1983
Gunilla Widengren, Tom Carlsson and Christer Hellmark (eds), *Manus. Handbok för redaktörer*, Stockholm, 1989

ENGLISH GRAMMAR

Alvar Ellegård, Åke Englund and Östen Rudal, *Engelsk grammatik*, Stockholm, 1978
Arvid Gabrielson and Daniel Elfstrand, *Engelsk grammatik för universitet och högskolor*, 4th edn, Stockholm, 1960
Randolph Quirk, Sidney Greenbaum, Geoffrey Leech and Jan Svartvik, *A Comprehensive Grammar of the English Language*, London, 1985
Jan Svartvik and Olof Sager, *Modern engelsk grammatik*, Stockholm, 1971
Jan Svartvik and Olof Sager, *Engelsk universitetsgrammatik*, Stockholm, 1977

INDEX

English words are in *italics*, Swedish words are in **bold**. Words are listed in Swedish alphabetical order, namely **a . . . z, å, ä, ö**. Reference is to paragraph, not page;
n indicates Note.

a 131, 136, 138, 140, 143, *see also* Indefinite
  article
à 722(c), 1203(b)
Abbreviation 1101, 1123–24
Abbreviations 416(a)*n*, 1210, 1303(b)
  gender 110(a)
  of ordinal numbers 411(h)
about 714, 729(n)
above 719, 720(t)
according to 706(d), 727(d)
Acronym 1124
across 719(a)
Acute accent 1203(a)
Adaptation of foreign loans 1125(a)
addition: in addition to 727(g)
Addresses 721(e), 1311
Adjectival forms 201–220
  according to meaning 209(b), 211–213
  after genitive 223(a)
  after personal pronoun 223(f)
  after possessive pronoun 317(c)
  basic (non-neuter, positive) 202, 232
  comparative *see* Comparative of
    adjectives'
  declensions *see* Definite declension of
    adjectives; Indefinite declension of
    adjectives
  definite *see* Definite declension of
    adjectives
  ending in: **-a** 201, 202, 217, 218, 220,
    241(d); **-e** 201, 204(a), 217, 219, 220,
    227(b), 240(c)(d); **-t** 201, 202
  indefinite *see* Indefinite declension of
    adjectives
  neuter 202f.: adjectives lacking 203(l);
  plural 202, 203(k), 204, 218(a): masculine
    220(b); with double subject 209; with
    singular subject 210(a)
  positive 232: adjectives without 238
  superlative *see* Superlative

  with **sorts** and **slags** 130(d), 223(a)
Adjective phrase 1012
Adjectives 201–245
  agreement 201, 208f.: lack of 210–214
  as nouns (nominalised) 215, 227–231:
    female 218(c); genitive 227(c); male
    227(b); people 228
  attributive use 201, 203(l), 206(e), 207,
    208, 211(d)
  beginning with **o-** 236(a)
  comparison of *see* Comparative of
    adjectives
  derived from: adverbs 206(d), 238(a);
    nouns 206(d); prepositions 238(a)
  endings *see* Adjectives ending in
  forms *see* Adjectival forms
  indeclinable 206, 218(b), 219(c), 220(b),
    236(a), 239
  independent 215, 227
  of location 224(b), 238(a), 241(g)
  order in attributive use 207
  participial 206(a), *see also* Past
    participle, Present participle
  possessive *see* Pronouns, possessive
  predicative use 201, 203(l), 206(e), 208,
    211(d)
  qualifying human beings 203(l)
  which are also adverbs 206(b)
Adjectives ending in:
  consonant 201(b)
  vowel 203(a)
  -a 206(b), 236(a): **-tida** 206(b)
  -d 203(f)(h), 236(a)*n*: **-ad** 204(a), 236(a);
    -id 203(f)
  -e 206(a), 236(a): **-nde** 219(b), 236(a)
  -g: **-ig** 202(b), 236(a), 601(c), **-lig** 601(c),
    1102(a)
  -k: **-esk** 202(b), 236(a)*n*; **-isk** 202(b),
    236(a); 233(b)
  -ell 202(b)

-m 203(k), 233(b);
-sam 203(k), 1102(a)
-n: -en 204(c), 233(b), 236(a)*n*; -nn 203(j)
-r: -bar 202(b), -er 204(b), 233(b);
-är 202(b)
-s 206(c), 236(a): -es 206(c);
-is 206(c)*n*; -os 206(c)*n*;
-us 206(c)*n*; -ös 202(b), 206(c)*n*
-t 203(b)(e), 236(a)*n*
-v: -iv 202(b)
Adverbial 1007
as topic 1027
cause 1007(e), 1024(a)
clausal (sentence) 601(c), 610, 1007,
1016(d): order 1023, 1026; position
803(d), 1007(f), 1008, 1015(e),
1020(b), 1029; splitting infinitive
1031(a), 1050(d)
condition 1007(e), 1024(a)
content *see* other
degree 1024(a)
det referring to 309(e)
duplication of 1047(b)
other (content) 1007, 1018(e), 1025: order
1024; positions 1007(g), 1008, 1029
place 1007(e), 1024(a), 1029(c)
predicative 811(c)
sentence 1007(a)
time 1007(e), 1024(a), 1029(c)
Adverbial shift 1007(g)*n*, 1029
Adverb phrase 1007(c), 1013
Adverbs 601–616
comparison 238(a), 346(p), 605
compound 604, 614
conjunctional 603(e), 610(c), 803(b),
804–809, 1007(d), 1023; causing
inversion 803(b)
demonstrative 609(a)
derived from: adjectives 601, 605; nouns
601(c)*n*; participles 601(d)(e), 605(e);
others 602
function of 606, 608
interrogative 609(c), 803(c)(d), 821,
1037(b)
meaning of 607
modal 603(d), 610(b), 1007(d), 1023
of cause 607(e)
of degree 607(d)
of manner 601(b)(c), 602(e), 607(b)
of motion (direction) 602(g), 603(b),
607(c), 613, 614, 1051(a)
of place (location) 238, 602(d), 603(b),
605(f), 607(c), 613, 614
of time 602(f), 603(a), 607(a), 614
pronominal 609, 1007(d), 1023:
indefinite 609(d)

qualifying the adjective/adverb phrase
601(b), 612
qualifying the noun phrase 611
relative 609(b), 803(c), 822, 1037(a)
simple, not derivatives 603
see also Adverbial
Adverbs ending in:
-a 602(b); -lunda 602(e), 607(b)
-e 602(b)
-m: -om 602(c), 604(l)
-n: -an 602(c); -en 601(c), 602(c), 605(d),
610; -ifrån 604(a), 607(c); -sin 602(f),
614(c)
-s 602(a); -ledes 602(e), 607(b); -vis 601(c),
605(d), 610; -städes 602(d), 607(c),
614(c); -stans 602(d), 607(c), 614(c);
-tills 604(d), 614(b)
-t 601; -ligt 601(c); ut 604(c); -vart 602(g);
-åt 604(b), 607(c), 614(a)
af Leopold, Carl Gustaf 1129(c)
Affixation 1101, 1102–1109
Affixes
productivity 1103
after 706, 812(b)(f), 823(a)
against 711(a), 713
Age 408
Agent (passive) 547–550, 552(b), 1024(b),
1032
ago 722(f), 724(j)
Agreement
of adjectives *see* Adjectives
of pronouns 305–307
aldrig 603(a), 1023, 1031(a)
all (of) 339, 729(g)
at all 358
all etc. 339, 346(n), 729(g)
with adjective 208(b)
with possessive pronoun 320(l)
allesamman 339(g)
allihop etc. 339(g)
allra 242(f), 612(a)(b)
alls 343*n*, 345*n*
allt (adv) 242(e), 612(a)(b)
allt vad 373(b)
allting 339(d)
alltsamman 339(g)
alltsedan 722(l)*n*
alltså 603(e), 809*n*
along 706(a)*n*, 720(r)
Alphabet *see* Letters (of the alphabet)
Alphabetism 1124(a)
although 807(c)*n*, 815(a)
among 720(d)
Amplifiers 612
an 131, 136, 138, 140, 143, *see also* Indefinite
article

Anaphoric substitution 360
and 803(a), 805, 1051(d)
andra 320(l), 340, 346(g), 411
den andra etc. 340
angående 728(a)
anhörig 231
Animals 102(a)(b), 106(a)
　addressing 303
　names given to 1207(a)
　pronouns for 305, 307
　sounds made by 906
ankomma, anlända 560(a)
annan etc. 208(b), 340
annanstans 340(b)*n*, 609(d)
annars 340(b)*n*
another 340(d)
Answers, short 309(f)
antingen . . . **eller** 209(b), 806(b), 823(g)
använda . . . **till/som** 708(d)*n*
any 336, 341, 346, 358
anybody, anyone 341, 358
Apostrophe 1308
　in genitive 129(b), 1308(b)
　to show omission of letters 1308(a)
Apposition 1052(a), 1302(e)
　with genitive 130(d)
　with **sin** 320(h)
approximately 141, 346(d), 407(a), 722(j)*n*,
　724(k)
apropå 727(c)
around 714, 718(b), 720(s), 722(j)
arrive 560(a)
Articles 131—143
form: definite 132—135, 222
　indefinite 131
　omitted in Swedish 139f.
　position 143
　usage 136—142, 221—226, *see also* Definite
　　article, Indefinite article
as 808, 813, 818(b)(c), 823(b)
as . . . *as* 818(a), 823(c)
ask 560(b)
at
　place 710(a), 715(a), 718(a), 720(l), 721
　time 708(a), 710(c), 724
　others 710(e)(f), 716(h)
att:
　conjunction 811(a), 823(j): omitted
　　803(d)*n*, 1051(d)
　infinitive marker 518
Attraction
　in adjective agreement 214
　with **sin** 320(d)
　with **slags** 130(d)
Auxiliaries *see* Verbs, auxiliary
av 705, 729

　with passive agent 547ff., 552(b)
avgå 560(a)
away 613
away from 720(u)
Back formation 1108
bad 235
bakom 720(c)
barn 211(c)
be 506, 515(a), 560(b)
be 561
because 813(a)
before 720(h)(k)(m), 722(e), 728(b), 812(d),
　823(d)
behalf: on behalf of 708(g), 727(m)
behind 706(a), 720(c)
below 717
beneath 717(a)
berries 104(b), 117(a)
beside 706(a)*n*, 720(g)
besluta 516(g)
betala 516(b)
betala för 708(g)*n*
beträffande 728(a)
better 235(a)(b)
between 712
beyond 719(c)(f), 720(y)
biljon (billion) 404(b)
bland 720(d)
Blend 1123(c)
bli 508, 515(a), 561
　passive with 547(b), 549, 552
　with **det** 309(b)(d)(f)(g)
　with future sense 525(a)
blitt 515(a)*n*
blotta 224(a)
blå 203(a), 217*n*
bo 505, 560(i)
boats 305(a)
Body, parts of 142(a), 323, 721(d), 731(b)
Book titles 1207(d), 1208, 1307
Borrowing
　from English 1130;
　from Finnish 1128;
　from French 1129;
　from German 1127;
　from Greek 1126;
　from Latin 1126
bort(a) 603(b), 613
bortemot 720(e), 722(d)
bortom 720(f)
bortåt 720(e), 722(d)
both (of) 137(k), 336, 347, 729(g), 805(c),
　823(e)
bra 203(a)*n*, 603(c), 605(b), 612(a)
　comparison 235(a)
bre(da) 506, 515(b)

bredvid 720(g), 728(d)
bringa 506, 516(b)
brinna 540(a)
bräda 121
bränna 540(a)
Buildings 721(b)
but 803(a), 807, 823(f), 1051(d)
by 705(a)(c), 706(d), 708(c)(h), 709(c), 710(f),
    711(a)(c), 718(a), 720(g), 721(c)*n*(d)*n*,
    722(e)
byta 560(c)
båda 137(k), 447, 729(g), 823(e)(g)
    with possessive pronoun 320(l)
bådadera 336
både (. . . och) 209(b), 805(c), 823(e)(g)
bägge 347
bäst 235(a)(b), 605(b)
bättre 235(a)(b), 605(b)
böra 535
början 120(f)

Calque 1125(d)
Capital/small letters
    abbreviations 1210
    days, months, etc. 415(a), 1207(e)
    Godhead 1206(c)
    names: people 1207(a), 1208(a)*n*; places
        1207(b), 1208, 1209(b)
    pronouns 1206(c),
    religious and political persuasion 1207(e)
    spelling with 1206–1210
    titles: books etc. 1207(d), 1208; people
        1206(c), 1207(e)
Centuries 407(b), 411(a), 724(k)*n*
change 560(c)
Chemical symbols 1210*n*
Circumflex 1203(c)
cirka 722(j)*n*
Clauses
    adverbial 802(b), 811(c), 1038(b), 1039(b),
        1038(b)(c); ellipted 1050(a); position
        1041(c)
    att 1038; **att** omitted 803(d), 1019(c),
        1020(a), 1040(a), with main clause
        order 1041, order, summary 1053
    attributive 802(b), 1038(c), 1039(d)
    base 1026
    causal 1038(b), 1039(b)
    comparative 1038(b), 1039(b), 1050(a),
        1051(b)
    concessive 359, 1038(b), 1039(b)
    conditional 1038(b), 1039(b), 1041(c),
        1042: with question order 1018,
        1042(b); order, summary 1053
    conjunctional 1037(c), 1038(b)
    consecutive 802(b), 1038(b), 1039(c)

    definition of 1015(a), 1050(a)
    det refers to 309(e)
    FV1 1016
    FV2 1016
    imperative 1002(b), 1042(c)
    independent 1015(a), 1018, 1043: order,
        summary 1053
    indirect question 366f., 802(b), 1038
    main *see* Main clause
    non-finite 1050
    object 811(c), 1034, 1038(a), 1039(a);
        position 1005(d)
    optative 1016ff.
    order, summary 1053
    relative *see* Relative clause
    som 1038(c), 1039(d); **som** omitted
        803(e)*n*, 1040(b)
    subject 811(c), 1038(a), 1039(a),
        1040(b)
    subordinate *see* Subordinate clause
    temporal 1038(b), 1039(b), 1041(c)
        1050(a)
Cleft sentence 823(j)*n*, 1046(b), 1048
    and **sin** etc. 320(f)
Clipping 1112, 1123(a)(b)
Clock time 402(b), 416, 724(b)
close by 720(p)
close to 722(d), 728(c)
Clothing 142(a), 323
Colon 1304, 1306(b)
Comma 401*n*, 1301, 1302
Commands 905, 1016(c)
    see also Imperative

Comparative of adjectives 232–245
    absolute 235(e)*n*, 243
    adjectives missing some forms 238f.
    in -**are** 206(a), 219(c), 232, 233, 237(a)
    in -**re** with a change of stem 206(a), 219(c),
        232, 234, 237(a), 238(a)
    irregular 232, 235
    summary 245
    with **mer** 232, 236, 237(b)
Comparative of adverbs 238(a), 346(p), 605
compared to 713(e)
Comparison 1007(e)
    of adjectives *see* Comparative of adjectives;
        Superlative
    and **sin** etc. 320(e)
    of adverbs *see* Comparative of adverbs
    with **än, som** and pronouns 324
Compass points 224(b), 1208(b)*n*
    with **om** 714(a)*n*, 729(m)
Complement 1006, 1018(f)
    det as 309
    duplication 1047(b)
    form of 1006(c)

free 1006(b)
object 201, 208(c), 210, 1022(b)(e)
order of 1022, 1025
position 210, 1008, 1027
predicative 201, 811(c), 1006(a)
prepositional 702, 703(b)
subject 201, 208(c), 210, 1006(b),
    1022(c)(d)(e)
verb, with preposition in Swedish 731(a)
Compounding 1101, 1110−1119
Compounds:
    adjectives;1115; meaning 1116
    adverbs 604, 614, 1118(a)
    conjunctions 1118(b)
    dividing 1211(a)
    English 1110(a)
    first element 1110(a)
    forms by word class 1111
    form of links 1112f.
    including en-/ett- 402n
    links 1113
        meaning 1114
    names with hyphen 1309
    nouns 1111−1114
    or separate words 1213
    numerals 1115
    prepositions 1118(c)
    second element 1110(a)
    verbs 1117
    see also Verbs, compound
concerning 728(a)
condition: on condition that 814(a)
Conditional 534f.
    to indicate mood 535, 538
    with någon 346(k)
    see also Clauses, conditional;
        Conjunctions, conditional
Conjugations of verbs 501(b)
    first (I) 502
    second (II) 503f.; IIa 503(a); IIb 503(b),
        504
    third (III) 505, 506
    fourth (IV) 506n, 507−514: minor
        gradation series 513; a-o-a-a 511;
        i-a-u-u 510; i-e-i-i 508; y/(j)u-ö-u-u
        509; ä-a-u-u 512
    see also Verbs, forms
Conjunctions
    adversative 807
    causal 813
    comparative 802(a)n, 818
    concessive 815
    conclusive 802(a)n, 809
    conditional 814
    consecutive 817

coordinating 801(a), 802(a), 803(a),
    804−809, 1051(d): omitted 1302(d);
    position 1018(g), 1019(d), 1035
copulative 805
descriptive 819
disjunctive 806
double 610(c), 805(b), 806(b)
explanative 802(a)n, 808
final 816
interrogative 1037(b); position of 802,
    1008, 1035
problem, translation into Swedish 823
subordinating 801(b), 802(b), 803(a)(d),
    810−819, 1015(b), 1037; compound
    810; simple 810; word order 802(b),
    1015(c); word group 810
temporal 812
consequently 809n
Consonant doubling 113(g), 114(g)(j), 133(k),
    233(c), 503(a), 1205(c)
Contamination 1122(a)
Contractions 133(d)
Conversion 1101, 1132−35
Coordination 801(a), 1035
Copulative compounding 1110(b)
Correlative 1034
Correspondence 301(e)n, 303(a)n, 326(c)n,
    1206(c), 1302(h), 1305
    Yours faithfully/sincerely 317(d)n
    see also Addresses
Counting 402(b)
Countries 104(a), 137(g), 229
Currency 406(a)

Danish loans 1128(b)
Dash 1301, 1304(a), 1310
Dates 414f., 724(b)(d)n(e)n, 729(k), 730(a),
    1212(b)
    full stop in 1303(c)
    in letters 1312
Dative, ethical 312
Days 415
    gender 102(c); parts of 724(d)(f); with
        article 137(e); with preposition
        724(d)(e)(f)(g)(h)
de:
    article 201(a), 222(a), 301(d), see also
        Definite article, front
    demonstrative 137(k), 222(a)n, 325f.
    determinative 329
    pronoun 301(d), 305(c), 307, 325f, 329:
        impersonal use 551
de som/dem som 329(b)n
Decades 407(b), 411(a), 724(k)n
Decimal comma/point 410(b)n, 1302(k)

Declension of adjectives *see* Definite
    declension of adjectives; Indefinite
    declension of adjectives
Declensions of nouns 101(d), 111
    first 112
    second 113
    third 114
    fourth 115
    fifth 116
    sixth 117
    seventh 118
    see also Plural of nouns
Definite article
    end 132–135, 137ff., 222, 224, 304(a)*n*,
      333: indicating possession 142, 323;
      omitted 130(b), 140f, 223, 225, 241(g),
      329(a), 333; with demonstrative
      326(b); with nominalised adjective
      215(c)
    front (adjectival) 201(a), 221–226, 301(d):
      with ordinal numbers 411(b); omitted
      224, 225, 240(g)(h)
Definite declension of adjectives 201, 202,
    204, 217–226
    as adjectival noun 228(b)
    of superlative 241
    summary of use 226
see also Adjectival forms
Degree 212
dej 301(b)
del:
    -del 412(a)
    en del av 346(c)
dels . . . , dels 1302(d)*n*
dem 301(d), 305(c), 326(c), 329(b)
Demonstrative 222(a)*n*(b), 223(c), 325–328
den
    article 201(a), 222(a), *see also* Definite
      article, front
    demonstrative 137(k), 222(a)*n*, 325f.
    determinative 329
    pronoun 305(b), 306, 325, 329
den där etc. 325f.
den här etc. 137(k), 222(b), 325f.
denna etc. 223(c), 325f., 724(h)
denne 325
dens 329(b)
densamma etc. 327
Deponent *see* s-verbs
deras 316ff.
Derivational compounding 1119
despite 727(n), 815(a)*n*
dess 316ff.
det:
    article 201(a), 222(a), *see also* Definite
      article, front

demonstrative 137(k), 222(a)*n*, 305(b), 309,
    325f., 329; as place-holder 1003, 1033;
    uses 308f., 551, 616(a)
    determinative 329
    pronoun 301, 305(b), 307
Determinative compounding 1110(a)
Diacritics 1203
Diaeresis 1203(e)
Diderichsen's positional scheme 1008, 1026
dig 301(b), 303(a), 310ff.
Diminishers 612
din, ditt, dina 315ff.
Direct speech 1302(h), 1305, 1306
    as topic 1027
direction: in the direction of 720(e)
Dissimilarity 242
Distribution 338
dit 603(b), 609(b), 613, 616(d), 820, 822
divided by 410
dock 807(c)
dom 301(d)
double 406(d)
Double definition 221f
down 613, 720(v)
downhill 720(v)*n*
dozen 405(a)
dra(ga) 511, 515(a)
dratt 515(a)*n*
driva 560(d)
drive 560(d)
du 303(a)
-**dubbelt** 406(d)
duplicate 406(d)
Duplication 1034, 1047
during 717(b), 725(c)
dussin 405
dylik etc. 328
då:
    adverb 603(a), 609(b), 616(b), 1023
    conjunction 812(a), 813(b), 820,
      823(b)(h)(l)
dålig 235, 605(b)
där 603(b), 609(b), 613, 616(d), 820, 822
    as formal subject 1033(b)*n*
därför 615(a), 809*n*, 813(a)*n*
därför att 615(a), 813(a), 1041(b), 1043(a)
dö 506
död 230(b)

each 331f., 336f.
each one 333
each other 313, 335
Eder, Edert, Edra 301(e)*n*, 316(b)
efter 706, 812(f)
    with infinitive phrase 702(b)*n*, 823(a)
efter (det) att 812(f), 823(a)

eftersom 813(a), 823(b)(h), 1041(b)
egen 223(a)
either 336, 823(g)
either . . . or 806(b)
ej 603(d), 610(a), 1031(a)
eller 803(a), 806(a), 1051(d)
eller hur? 363*n*, 615(b)
Ellipsis 210, 213, 320(a), 711(b)(d), 728(j),
    1049–1053
else 340(b)*n*
em (= eftermiddag) 416(a)*n*
emedan 813(a), 823(h)
emellan 703(c), 712
emellertid 807(c)
emot 713, 728(g)
Emphasis *see* Stress
'en 301(e)*n*
en:
    article 131, 141, *see also* Indefinite article
    numeral 402: **en till** 340(d)
    pronoun 330
ena 220(a), 402
    den ena . . . den andra 340(c)
End article *see* Definite article, end
End focus 1044(a)
enda 220(a), 406(d)*n*
endera 336
Endocentric phrases 1009(c)
English, The 229
English loans
    apostrophe 1130(b)
    construction loans 1130(b)
    indirect loans 1130(b)
    table of loan types 1130(b)
enkel 406(d)*n*
enligt 727(d)
ens (pronoun) 330
er, ert, era personal pronoun 303(b)(c),
    reflexive pronoun 310ff., possessive
    pronoun 316ff.
eran 301(c)
'et 301(e)*n*
ett:
    article 131, *see also* Indefinite article
    numeral 402
etta 406(a)
Euphemism 1122(b)
eventuell etc. 346(q)
ever 602(f), 614(c)
-ever 358f.
ever since 722(l)*n*
every 331–333
every other 334
every (single) one 333
everyone 339(e)
everything 339(d)

except for 727(p)
Exclamation 368, 522(e), 904, 1043(c), 1305
    in question form 1036(d)
Exclamation mark 1301, 1305
excluding 727(e)
Exhortations 905, 907
Existential sentence 309(d), 1003(b),1023(d)
    word order 1033
exklusive 727(e)
Exocentric phrases 1009(c)
Expletives 901, 908
Expressive formation, 1101, 1120–1122
Expressions of feeling 904
Extra positions 1018(h), 1028(b), 1019(f),
    1034, 1047(a)

-faldigt 406(d)
Familiar information 1038, 1044(a)
far, in so far as 819(b)
fast 807(c), 815(a)
fastän 807(c)*n*, 815(a), 823(b)(l), 1041(b)
fattas 309(d)
feel 560(c)
fel 139(e)
Feminine *see* Adjectives, as nouns; Nouns,
    feminine
Festivals 102(c), 137(e), 724(d)(f)(h)(l),
    907(c)
few 354*n*, 355
a few 341(a)*n*, 355(b)
fewest 356
Figures or words 1212
Finland-Swedish 902
finna 510
finnas 309(d), 510
Finnish loans 1128(c)
first 411
First element 1101
firstly 411(e)
fjärdedel 413(e)
fler(a) 208(b), 235(e)*n*, 351
flertal 729(g)
flest(a) 235(e)*n*, 352f.
fm (= förmiddag) 416(a)*n*
Focus 1044(a), 1048(a)
-fold 406(d)
folk 211(b), 330(d)*n*, 551
Folk etymology 1122(c)
foot: at the foot of 720(t)
for:
    conjunction 808
    preposition: indirect object 716(d), 727(q);
    reason, cause 705(c), 708; time
    expressions 708, 710(c), 717(b), 725;
    others 713(a), 716(e)(f)
Foreign influence

types of 1125
Foreign words and loan words 1125(a)
    assimilation 1125–32
former 326(c)*n*
Forms of address 224(b), 225(a), 302(b)*n*,
    303(b), 304, 1302(g)
fort 603(c), 605(c)
Fractions 102(f), 124*n*, 412f.
fram 603(b), 613
framemot 722(d)
framför 720(h), 823(d)
framme 613
French loans 1129
Frequency 138(b), 406(c), 411(g), 714(e), *see
    also* Prepositions, of time
from 705(b)(c)(d), 706(a), 707, 708(e), 710(a),
    725(d)
front: in front of 708(b), 720(h)(k)(n)
Fronting 1045, 1046(a)
Fruits 117(a)
frysa 516(g)
fråga 560(b)
från 707, 729(l)
från (och med) 725(d)
Full stop 1301, 1303
fullmäktig 231
Future of the past 527
Future perfect tense 526
Future perfect of the past 528
Future tense 525ff.
    using perfect 523(e)
    using present 520(d)
fyrti(o) 401*n*
få:
    pronoun, adjective 208(b), 238(c), 355
    verb 506, 535
fåtal 355(b)*n*
färre 356
föda(s) 521(a)*n*
föga 354*n*
följaktligen 809*n*
följande 139(e), 223(e), 724(h)*n*
för:
    adverb 612(a), 616(c)
    conjunction 808, 823(b)
    preposition 708, 729(d)
för att 708(d)*n*, 813(a), 816, 1041(b), 1043(a)
för . . . sedan 703(b), 722(f), 724(j)
för . . . skull 703(b), 727(f)
förbi 720(j)
före 702(b)*n*, 720(k), 722(e), 728(b), 823(d)
före detta 722(e)*n*
föregående 139(e), 223(e)
förlåt 363*n*, 906(d)
förr 603(a)
förra 137(k), 724(h)

förrän 812(d), 823(d)(k)
först 615(c)
först när 823(k)*n*
första 411
förstås 615(d)
förut 823(d)
förutan 727(o)*n*
förutom 702(a), 727(g)
förutsatt att 814(b)
förändra 560(c)

gammal 205(b), 207(a), 235(a)
ganska 612(a)
ge 506, 515(a)
Gender
    abbreviations 110
    and adjectives 201ff.
    and articles 132ff.
    common see Non-neuter nouns
    double 109
    natural 211 see also Nouns, masculine;
        Nouns, feminine
    nouns 101(c)
    rules for determining 102–110: by form
        103, 105, 107;
        by meaning 102, 104
    see also Neuter nouns; Non-neuter nouns
Genitive
    appositive 729(f), 730(c)
    double (*a . . . of* + possessive pronoun)
        317(d)*n*, 322, 729(e)
    explicative 130(e)
    form 129: with -a, -o or -u 129(f); with
        apostrophe 129(b); with -s 129, 227(c),
        729(b)(d); without -s 129(c)
    group 130(c)
    Latin 129(e)
    names 129(b)(c), 130(c)(d)
    nouns ending in -s 130(e)
    of measurement 130(e), 223(a)
    Old Swedish 129(f)
    partitive 729(g), 730(b)
    prepositional 130(e)
    relative pronouns 372
    use 130
    without article 130(b), 223(a)
genom 709
genom att 702(b)*n*, 709(c)*n*, 819(a)
gentemot 713, 728(g)
Gerund in English 519(c)
go 560(f)
god 235(a)(b)
goddag 907(a)
good 235(a)(b)
Grammatical terms without article 139(b)
gratis 206(c)

grattis 907(c)
Grave accent 1203(b)
Greetings 1006, 1305
gross 405
grow 560(g)
grå 203(a), 217*n*
Guillemet 1301, 1306(d)
gå 506, 560(a)(f)
gång 406(c), 616(e)
gärna 605(c), 615(e)
göra 504, with det 309(f), *see also*
    Place-holder

ha 504, 515(a)
    as auxiliary 501, 523f, 531(c); omitted in
        subordinate clauses 523(b), 524(e),
        531(c), 803(d), 1004(d), 1015(d),
        1018(b), 1014(c), 1049(b), 1051(c)
half (of) 413, 729(g)
half past 416(a)
hallå 907(e)
halv 413(a), 416
halva 137(k), 224(a), 413(c)
halvannan 413(c)*n*
halvt 411(d)
han 304(c), 305f.
hans 316f., 319f
hardly 823(l)
hardly any 346(h)*n*
hej 907(a)
hela 137(k), 224(a), 339(c), 724(c), 729(g)
heller 615(e), 823(g)
hellre 605(c), 615(e)
helst 605(c), 615(e), *see also . . .* som helst
hem 603(b), 613
hemma 613
henne 305(a)
hennes 316ff.
her/hers 316, 319ff.
here 613
heta 309(g), 504
High German loans 1127(d)
himmel 133(b)*n*
his 316, 319ff.
historia 133(j)
hit 603(b), 613
hitom 720(f)
home 613
Homonyms 128
hon 304(c), 305f.
honom 305(a)
hos 720(l), 721(b)*n*, (e)
how 820f.
however 616(f), 807(c), 815(b)
Human beings 102(b), 106(a), 116(d)*n*,
    117(a)

addressing 303
adjectives qualifying 203(l), 211(d)
    female 218; male 219(e)(f), 220, 411(c)
    pronouns 305(a)(b), 306, 307, 325*n*
    sounds made by 906(a)
hundra(de) 401(n), 404(a), 414(a)
hundred(s) 401*n*, 404
hur 603(c), 616(f), 820f.
hur . . . än 140(e), 616(f), 815(b)
hurdags 416(b)
hurdan etc. 361, 364(c)*n*
hursa 363*n*
huvud 115(d)
Hyphen 1211, 1301, 1309
Hypocorism 1120
hålla på att 521(b), 522(f)
hälft 413(b)
här 603(b), 613
    as formal subject 1033(b)*n*
härom- 340(d)*n*

i 710, 721, 729(d)
    genitive, dative 702(a)*n*
    parts of body 710(b)
    time expressions 416, 710(c), 724, 725(b),
        726(a)
I (pronoun) 301(e)*n*, 1206(d)
i det att 819(b)
i och med 710(l)
icke 610(a), 1031(a), 1309(b)
if 814(a)
if only 814(b)
ifall 814(a), 1042
igenom 703(c), 709
illa 605(b)
Imitations 906
Imperative 501(a), 534, 537, 905, 1016ff.,
    1049(a), 1305
    form 537(a): plural 517, 537(a)*n*
    order 1016ff.: summary 1053
    -s verbs 541(d)
    with subject 538(b), 1056
Impersonal constructions 304(b), 309(d)(h),
    551
in 603(b), 613
in
    place 710(a)
    time 710(c), 714(d), 715(a)(c), 721, 724,
        725(e), 726(a)
in(side) 613
in bland 720(d)*n*
in i 710(a)*n*
in that 819(a)
including 727(e)
Indefinite article 131, 136–143
    with indefinite adjective 208(b)

with **sådan** 328
Indefinite declension of adjectives 201–216
  as adjectival noun 228(b)
  for possessive pronouns 317(d)
  neuter singular 202, 203, 209(b), 210, 213,
    215: adjectives lacking 203(l)
  non-neuter singular 202, 209(b); for people
    227(b); for published titles 211(e);
    with neuter nouns 222(d)
  singular for groups 212
  use 208, 216, 223(a)
  see also Adjectival forms
Indeterminate object 309(j)
Indicative mood 534
Indigenous words 1101
Infinitive 501–515, 518f., 1004(e)
  form 501–515, 542
  perfect 501(a)
  present 518
  split 1031(a), 1050(d)
  use 518f.; as noun 104(d)*n*, 518(b); as verb
    518(a); for English gerund 519; in
    English and Swedish 519
  see also Object and infinitive construction;
    Subject and infinitive construction
inför 720(m), 823(d)
-ing forms 519(c), 521(b), 533
ingalunda 1031(a)
ingen etc. 343ff., 729(g)
impersonal use 551; with adjective 208(b);
  with noun 1031(e); with possessive
  pronoun 320(l)
ingendera etc. 336
inklusive 727(e)
innan:
  conjunction 812(d), 823(d)
  preposition 702(b)*n*, 722(e)*n*, 728(b)
innan dess 318(b)
innanför 720(n)
inne 613
inom 720(o), 722(g)
inside 720(n)(q)
inst. 326(c)*n*
Institutions 137(d), 721(b), 1207f.
Instrument (adverbial) 1007(e)
inte 610(a), 1023, 1028(b), 1031(a)
  duplication 1047(b)*n*
inte alls 343*n*, 345*n*, 612(a)
inte bara . . . utan också 805(b)
inte förrän 812(d)
inte någon etc. 344f., 1031(f)
inte . . . på 725(b)
inte utan att 819(c)*n*
Interjections 901ff., 1302(g)
intet 343
intill 720(p), 722(h)

into 710(a)
Intonation 1044(b)
inuti 720(q)
Inverted commas 1306(c), 1307
Inverted word order *see* Word order
it 305, 309
Italian loans 1131(a)
its 318 ff.

ja 902
jag 301(a), 302(a)
  substituted by **man** 330(c)
jaha 902(c)
jaså 902(c)
javisst 902(c)
jo 902(b)(d)
ju 603(d), 610(b)(c), 615(f), 808*n*, 1023
ju . . . desto 242(g), 351(d), 818(e)
ju . . . ju 242(g), 351(d), 818(e)
just 357, 603(a), 611
just som 812(c)
jämte 720(g)*n*, 727(j)

kallas 309(g)
kanhända 1043(b)
kanske 1043(b)
keps words 118(c)*n*, 1125(c)
kind:
  a kind of 328
  kinds of 130(d)
  what kind of . . . ? 361, 364
Kings 411(f), 1206(c)
klocka 106(f), 305(a), 416
klä(da) 506, 515(b)
knappast 1031(a)
knappt 823(l), 1031(a)
know 560(h)
koka 516(b)
komma (vb) 513, 560(a)
kommer att 525(b)
kring 720(s), 722(j)
kunna 504, 535, 560(h)
kvart 413(e), 416
  en kvarts 413(e)
kyrka: i kyrkan 710(a)*n*, 721(b)
känna 560(e)(h)
känna sig 560(e)
kännas 560(e)
käraste/käresta 231*n*
köra 560(d)

la 515(c)
lagom 357
Lakes 102(e), 137(f)
Languages 229(a)
last 238(b), 724(h), 731(d)

lat 203(l)
latest 238(b)
latter 326(c)*n*
le 506
least 356
leave 560(a)
Left weight 1038(b)
less 356
Letters (of the alphabet)
   capital/small *see* Capital/small letters
   gender 104(c)
   listed 1201f.
   plural 116(e)
   z 1204(f)
   å 1203
   ä 1203
   ö 1203
Letters *see* Correspondence
leva 560(i)
ligga 540(a), 561
Light element 1030, 1031(c)
lik 242(b)
lika ... som 242(a), 818(a), 823(c)
likadan ... som 242(a)
like this 328
likna 242(b)
liksom 615(f), 818(c), 823(b)
likväl 807(c)
lilla 205(a)
lillan 205(a)*n*, 230(a)
lillen 205(a)*n*, 330(a)
Link position 1018(g), 1019(d), 1035
lite(t) 140(f), 346(b), 354, 355(a)*n*, 612(a)
liten 205(a)n, 207(a), 230(a), 235(a)
little 354
   a little 346(b), 354
live 560(i)
Loan phrases 1125(a)
Loan translation 1125(d)
Loanwords
   adjectives 203(c)(e)
   nouns *see* Nouns, foreign origin
   spelling 1204
   with accents 1203
Locations 137(d), 224(b)
   geographical 104(a), 224(b), 721(a)*n*
   possessive pronoun 318(a), *see also*
      Placenames
long: as long as 814(a)
lot: (a) lot(s) (of) 348ff.
Low German loans 1127(a)
långt 605(a), 615(g)
låta 535
lägga 504, 515(c), 540(a), 560(j)
lämna 560(a)
länge 605(a), 615(g)

så länge som 812(c)(g)
längs(med) 720(r)
lär 535, 553(a)

Main clause 1015
   and commas 1302
   order of sentence elements 1008,
      1015–1023, 1026ff, 1036
   summary 1053
   types 1016f.
   see also Clauses
majority 729(g)
man
   noun 117(f), 121
   pronoun 211(a), 303(a), 304(c), 330
      English influence 1130(b)
      and possessive pronoun 320(l); with
      active verb as alternative to s-passive
      547(b), 551, 553
many 349, 729(g)
Materials 120(c), 137(g), 729(h)
Mathematical expressions 402(b), 410, 709(d)
Mealtimes 137(e)
means: by means of 727(k)
Measure 127, 212, 410(b)*n*, 705(e), 711(c),
   715(e), 717(c), 1212(b)
med 616(a)(c), 711, 721(c)*n*
medan 812(c), 823(b)
medels(t) 727(k)
mej 301(b)
mellan 712
men 803(a), 807(a), 823(f), 1051(d), 1302(f)
mer 235(e), 236f, 351, 605(b)(e)
   with **vad, vem** 340(b)*n*
mest(a) 235(e), 236f, 241(e)(f), 352f.,
   605(b)(e)
   den/det mesta etc. 352f.
mig 301(b), 302(a), 310ff.
miljard (milliard) 404
miljon (million) 404, 1302(j)
millennium 411(a)
min, mitt, mina 316ff.
mindre 356
minst 356
minuter 416(a)
mista 516(c)
mittemot 728(g)
Modal auxiliaries *see* Verbs, modal auxiliary
Months 102(c), 415, 724(c)
more 235(e), 236f, 351
most 235(e), 236f, 352f.
mot 713, 728(g)
motsvarande 139(e)
much 348, 729(g)
Musical instruments 139(a)

my/mine 316, 322
mycket 140(f), 235(a), 242(e), 348, 350,
    605(b), 612
mygga 121
må(nde) 535, 1016f.
många 208(b), 235(a), 320(l), 349, 729(g)
mången 140(e), 349*n*
månne 1043(b)
månntro 1043(b)
måste 535
måtte 535, 1016f.
människa 106(e), 305(a)

'n 301(e)*n*
'na 301(e)*n*
Names 304, 1201, 1207
    compound 1309(a)
    in -**a**, -**e** 106(b)
    see also Nouns, proper; Placenames; Street
        names
Nationality 140(a), 207(a), 224(b), 229
nedanför 720(t)
nedför 720(v)
Negated object 1031(f)
Negation 610(a), 1013(d), 1023, 1031
Negative statements 341, 343ff., 346(h)(l),
    812(d), 1031
neither 336
neither . . . nor 806(b)
nej 902(a)
ner 603(b), 613
nere 613
nerför 720(v)
Neuter nouns:
    by form 105
    by meaning 104
    definite forms 132ff.: with adjective 221ff.;
        see also Definite article
    for animals 102(b)*n*
    for human beings 102(a)*n*, 105(a)
    plural forms 113–119
nevertheless 807(c)
New English formations 1130(b)
New information 1028, 1044(a)
Newspaper titles 211(e)
next with time expressions 724(h)
next to 720(g), 728(d)
Nexus 1009(d)
ni 303(b)(c)
Nicknames 1120(b)
nio 401*n*
no (interjection) 902
no (pronoun) 343ff.
no matter who/what 359
no-one 343ff.
nobody 343ff.

nog 603(d), 610(b), 612(a), 615(f), 1023
noll 401*n*
nolla 406(a)
Nominalisation of the adjective 227–230
    see also Adjectives as nouns
Non-neuter nouns
    by form 103, 107, 112ff., 118
    by meaning 102
    definite forms 132ff.: with adjective 221ff.;
        see also Definite article
    indicating person but not gender 306
    plural 112–119
none (of) 336, 343ff., 729(g)
Norden 1208(b)*n*
north of 729(m)
Norwegian loans 1128(b)
not a 343ff.
not any 343ff.
not for 725(b)
not one 343(b)*n*
not only . . . but also 805(b)
not that with negative 819(c)*n*
not until 812(d)*n*(e)
nothing 343ff.
notwithstanding 728(e)
Noun phrase 1007(c), 1010
Nouns
    abstract 101, 105(a), 107(b)(c),120(b),
        133(c), 137(a), 213
    adjectival 129(f), 215(b)(c), 227ff.: female
        218(c); male 219(e)(f); nationality
        229f.; past participle 531(c)
    collective 120(d), 122(f): pronoun
        referring to 307; with adjective 211,
        212, 213; with *many* 350
    common 101(a)
    compound 1110–1114, 1119, 729(c): form
        of link 1112; gender 109(c); spelling
        1204, 1205(g), 1209; *see also*
        Compounds
    concrete 101(a)
    count 101(b)
    declensions 111ff.; *see* Declensions of
        nouns
    definite forms: alternative 134(d)*n*; instead
        of possessive 318(b); *see also* Definite
        article
    derived from names 1207(e)
    endings: *see* Nouns ending in
    feminine 106, 219
    formed from other parts of speech 104(d)
    gender: *see* Gender
    homonyms 128
    indefinite forms: *see* Plural of nouns,
        Singular of nouns
    irregular forms: *see* Plural of nouns

masculine 106(a)(e), 217, 220
non-count 101(b), 208(a)
plural forms: *see* Plural of nouns
proper 101(a), 129(c–e), 139(c), 219(f); for
    places 104(a) *see* Place names; spelt
    with small or capital letters 1207ff.;
    with adjective 219(f), 225(a)
singular forms: *see* Singular of nouns
verbal 120(a)
Nouns ending in:
consonant 112(a)(d), 113(a)(g), 117(a),
    133(a)
vowel 113(a), 114(g)(j), 115(a), 116(a)
  -a 103, 106(b), 112(a)(b), 114(f), 116(b),
    119(b); -inna 106(c); -ska 106(c)
  -d: -nad 103, 114(a)
  -e 106(b), 113(a)(c):-ande 105(a), 116(d);
    -are 103, 117(a)(d)(e)*n*, 119(b), 133(d),
    134(g); -else 103, 115(b); -ende 105(a),
    117(a), 120(a)*n*; -ie 115(c); -je 115(c)
  -é 133(f)
  -g -(n)ing 103, 113(a), 119(b), 1102(a)
  -i 133(e); -eri 105(a)
  -k -tek 105(b); -lek 113(a), 1102(a); -ik
    103
  -l 133(d); -al 107(d), 114(k); -el 112 (c),
    113(a)(d), 114(e), 117(e)*n*, 133(b),
    134(e)
  -m 113(g), 133(k); -dom 103, 113(a),
    1102(a); -em 105(b); -ism 103; -um
    105(a), 114(f), 117(c), 133(f)(g)
  -n 113(d)(g), 133(b)(k); -an 120(f), 133(c);
    -en 113(a)(d), 114(e), 116(e)*n*, 133(b),
    134(e); -ion 103; -on 117(a); -tion 103,
    119(b)
  -o 115(c): -bo 115(c)
  -p -skap 107(a), 1102(a)
  -r 113(d), 133(d); -er 112(c), 113(a)(d)(e),
    114(e), 117(a)(e)(f), 119(b), 133(b),
    134(e)-(g); -or 114(d), 133(b)
  -s 134(j); -ans 103; -ens 103;
    -is 113(a)
  -t -ant 103; -at 107(c); -ent 107(b); -het
    103, 119(c)
  -u 115(c)
  -v -iv 105(b)
  -y 114(c)
  -å 115(c)
  -ä 133(e), 114(c)
  -ö 115(c), 133(e)
Now planes (verb tense) 529f.
nu när 812(a)
Number
  and adjectives 201ff.
  differences between English and Swedish
    124f.

Numbers
  cardinal 401–410: form 401; gender 102(f);
    use 406–410; with adjective 208(b)
  clarification 406(a), 1202
  figures/letters 1212
  indefinite 407(a)
  long 1212(b)
  no article 140(f)
  nouns 406
  of with 729(j)
  ordinal 401, 411–413; definite 220(a),
    224(b), 225(b); form 401, 1212(b);
    time 726(b); use 411–413; with var
    332(a)
någon etc. 208(b), 320(l), 341, 344–346, 551,
    729(g)
någondera etc. 336
någonsin 609(d)
någonstans 609(d)
någorlunda 609(d)
något till 346(f)
nåja 902(d)
nämligen 610(c), 615(f), 808*n*
när 609(c), 616(e), 812(a), 820f., 823(l)
nära 605(c), 728(c)
närmaste 231
näst 728(d)
nästa 139(e), 223(e), 231, 724(h)

oansett 728(e)
oavsett 728(e)
oberoende av 728(e)
Object 539ff., 1018(f)
  direct 1005, 1016: position 1030
  duplication 1047(b)
  form 1005(e)
  indirect 1005(b), 1024
  order 1005(b), 1020, 1025
  position 1005(d), 1008, 1027, 1030
  possessive pronoun referring to 319
  prepositional 702, 1005(c)
  reflexive pronoun referring to 310f.
Object and infinitive construction 311(a),
    320(c), 518f., 533, 1050(b)
Object complement *see* Complement, object
och 802(a), 805(a), 1051(d)
också 603(e), 611, 616(a)(c)
odla 560(g)
of 126, 130(a)(f), 705(b)(e)(f), 706(a),
    708(b)(f), 710(a)(c), 715(e)(f), 716(g),
    729
off 705(d)
officer 117(d)
ofta 605(c); så ofta som 812(g)
olik 242(d)
om

conjunction 811(b), 814(a), 1037(b), 1042,
    1043(d): with subjunctive 536(c)
preposition 703(c), 714, 729(m)(n): with
    parts of body 714(a)*n*, 721(d); with
    time 724(l), 726(a)
om . . . bara 814(b)
om . . . inte 814(c)
om än 815(b)
omkring 720(s), 722(j), 724(k)
on 710(a)(e), 714(b), 715, 721
    with time 724
ond comparison 235(a)
one
    numeral 402, 406(a)
    pronoun 228(d), 326(c), 330(a), 340(d)*n*,
        360
(the) one 402(c); *the one . . . the other* 340(c)
one another 313, 335
one of these 336
Onomatopoetic words 906, 1121
ont 142(b), 721(d)*n*
opposite 728(g)
or 803(a), 806(a), 1051(d)
order: in order to 816
oss 302(b), 310ff.
our/ours 316
out of 720(w)
out(side) 613, 720(n)(x)
ovan 720(t)
ovanför 720(t)
ovanpå 720(t)
over 709(d), 719, 725(c)

pair 125(a)
par 211(c), 307, 403*n*
Participles *see* Past participle, Present
    participle
Particle verbs 1117(c)
Passive 542f
    diffuse 552(b)
    forms: choosing 552; in **-es**
        542(a)(b); in **-s** 541, 547f., 552; with
        bli 547(b), 549, 552; with **vara** 547(b),
        550, 552
    impersonal 309(d), 547(a), 551, 553(b)
    use 543, 547ff.: as copular 1006(a); in
        English and Swedish 553; in forms of
        address 304(b);
    with **sin** etc. 320(g)
    word order 1033
Passive agent *see* Agent
Passive transformation 1032(b), 1034
past 416, 719(b), 720(j)
Past participle 501ff., 531
    as adjectival noun 228(b), 531(c)

as adjective 203(e)(g)(h), 204(a)(c), 207(a),
    219(a), 220(a), 228(b), 236(a), 531(c)
as adverb 601(e)
form 501–516, 545(c)
in **-ad** 219(a), 236(a), 531
in **-d** 236(a)*n*, 502, 503(a), 531
in **-en** 236(a)*n*, 531
in **-t** 236(a)*n*, 503(b), 531
in passive 531(c), 547(b), 549f.
Past tense 501(a)
    form 501–516
    summary 501
    use 522, 526f.
pastimes 139(a)
Pejorative expressions 303(a)*n*, 321, 729(p)
people 330(d)*n*
per 710(c), 727(l)
per 332(b), 727(l)
Perfect tense 501(a), 523
    form 501–516: summary 501, 514
    use 523, 529f.
Phrases 1009–1014
    adjective 1012
    adverb 1013
    noun 1010
    prepositional 1014
    verb 1011
piece: a piece of 140(g)
place: in . . . 's place 727(h)
Place-holder:
    subject (**det**) 309(d), 1003, 1027, 1033
    verb (**göra**) 1027, 1047(b)
Place names 102(e), 104(a), 129(c)(e), 137(f),
    721(a)*n*
    with capital letter 1207f.
    with possessive pronoun 318(a)
please 537(b), 907(f)
Pluperfect tense 501(a)
    form 501–516: summary 501, 514
    use 524, 529f.
Plural forms of adjectives *see* Adjectival
    forms
Plural of nouns 101(d), 111–119
    alternative: definite 134(d); indefinite
        112(d)*n*, 116(d)*n*, 117(e)*n*, 119(a)
    'borrowed' forms 120(f)
    collective forms 121
    definite 132, 134: **-a** 134(d)*n*; **-en** 117(e)(f),
        118(c), 134(d)(e)(g);**-na** 112(f), 113(h),
        114(m), 134(a)(b)(f)(g); **-ne** 134(a)*n*;
        summary 135; with adjectives 221ff.
    different, with different meanings 128
    indefinite 111–123, 136: **-a** 117(c), 134(k);
        -ar 113, 119, 120(a); **-er** 114; **-i** 134(k);
        -n 116; **-or** 112; **-r** 115; **-s** 118; zero
        116(e)*n*, 117;

with vowel change 114(a)(j)(k), 117(f)
irregular 116(c)
nouns lacking 120, 134(j)
predictability of 119
summary 123
usage: differences between English and
    Swedish 123f.; for measures of
    quantity 127
with stress shift 114(d)
plus 727(e)
plus 727(e)
polis 121
Political belief 140(a), 1207(e)
Popes 411(f)
Possessive *see* Genitive
Possessive compound 1110(a)
Pratminus 1301, 1306(a)
Predicative attribute 208(c), 811(c), 1010(d),
    1052(b)
Prefixes 1104
  anti- 1103(d)
  be- 1102(a)
  bi- 1102(a)
  dis- 1104(b)
  för- 1102(a)
  icke- 1104(b)
  kon- 1103(a)
  köns- 1103(d)
  miljö- 1103(d)
  o- 1102(b), 1104(b)
  pseudo- 1103(d)
  sam- 1102(a)(b)
  själv- 1102(b), 1103(c)
  åter- 1102(b), 1103(c)
  attitude 1105
  degree 1105
  direction 1105
  German 1102(a)
  location 1105
  negative 1105
  number 1105
  pejorative 1105
  privative 1105
  reversative 1105
  Romance 1102(a)
  stressed 1104(d)
  table of 1105
  transitivising 1105
  unstressed 1104(d)
Prepositional phrase 1007(c)(d), 1014, 1023
Prepositions
  and stress 703(c), 704–711, 713–716, 718f.
  complex 701, 703(b)
  compound 701, 703(c), 712*n,* 713(l)
  of manner 701, 708–717 *passim,* 727,
  of measure 711–719 *passim,* 722

of place 701, 705–719 *passim,* 720f.
of time 701, 705–719 *passim,* 722, 723ff.
parenthetical 703(b), 727(f)(h)(m)
position 703: postpositioned 703(c), 712*n,*
    720(s)*n,* 722(j)*n;* pre-positioned
    703(a); in relative clauses *see*
    Pronouns, relative
presence or absence in English and
    Swedish 730f.
showing possession 318(b)
simple 701, 705–719
with pronoun 314
Present infinitive 518
Present participle 501ff., 532
  as adjectival noun 105(a), 116(d), 228(b),
    532(b)
  as adjective 206(a), 219(b), 228(b), 236(a),
    532(b)
  as adverb 532(b), 601(d)
  as verb 532(b)
  form 501–516, 545(b)
  in English 533
  s-form 542(c)
Present tense 501(a), 520f.
  form 501–516: summary 501, 514
  use 520f., 529f.
Price 138(a), 337, 1212(b), 1304(c)
  at a price of 722(c)
Pro-forms 1047(c)
Productive affixes 1102(a), 1103(a)
  -mat 1103(d)
  -nära 1103(c)
  -ning 1102(b)
  -riktig 1103(c)
  -ris 1102(a)
  -vänlig 1103(c)
  -är 1102(a)
  -ör 1102(a), b)
Productive first element/second element
    1110(a)
Productivity 1103
Professions 106(d), 116(d)*n,* 117(a), 140(a)
Pronouns
  adjectival 220(a), 340(c)
  demonstrative 309(c), 325–328, 339(b)
  determinative 329
  emphatic 314f.
  indefinite 330–360
  interrogative 358, 361–368, 803(c)(d),
    821, 1037(b)
  negating 1031(e), *see also* **ingen, inte**
    någon, intet
  object 301–309, 310, 1030: emphatic use
    314(b); unstressed 1020(f), 1030
  personal 301–309

possessive 223(b), 301, 303(a)*n*, 316–324,
330; *a friend of mine* etc. in English
317(d)*n*, 322, 729(e); as form of
address 303(a); in English, end article
in Swedish 323; inversion 207(b)*n*;
reflexive 319f.; *see also* Genitive
reciprocal 313
reflexive 301, 310ff., 315(b), 541: position
1020(f), 1030
relative 223(d), 369–373, 803(c), 822,
1037(a)
subject 301–309: emphatic use 314(a)
Proverbs 137(b)
provided that 814(b)
Punctuation marks 1301ff.
put 560(j)
på 715, 721, 727(m), 729(d)(j)
with time 724, 725(b)(e), 726(b)
på ... när 703(b), 722(k)
på ... sidan 720(f)
(p)å ... vägnar 703(b), 727(m)

Quality 130(e), 207(a)
Quantity 126f., 207(a)
quarter 413(e)
Question 1016ff., 1036
alternative 1036(a)
complex 1036(b)*n*
direct 367
in cleft sentence 1048(d)
in statement form 1036(c)
indirect 366f., 811, 821, 1037(b)
order, summary 1053
tag 615(b), 1036(c)
V-question 1016ff., 1036(b)
with **någon** 341, 346(j)(l)
yes/no 902(a), 1016ff., 1036(a)
see also Adverbs, interrogative; Pronouns,
interrogative
quite 346(f)
Quotations 1307
Raising 1046
ream 405(d)
redan 615(c)
regardless of 728(e)
Reinforcement 242
Relationships 225(a)
Relative clause 1037(a), 1038(c)
necessary/restrictive 140(a)*n*, 1038(c)
unnecessary/non-restrictive 1038(c),
1302(b)
see also Adverbs, relative; Pronouns,
relative
Religion 140(a), 1207(e)
Retrogradation 1108
rena 224(a)

resa (vb) 560(a)(f)
ris 405(d)
Rivers 102(e)
Root 1101, 1104, 1106
round 714, 720(s), 722(j)
runt 703(c), 720(s), 722(j), 724(k)
Russian loans 1131(a)
rå(da) 506, 515(b)
rädd 203(g)*n*
rätt 139(e), 612
rörande 728(a)

s-genitive 129f., 729(b)
double 130(e)
s-verbs 313*n*, 542–548
absolute use 546
deponent 545
passive *see* Passive, forms in -s
reciprocal 544
sa (sade) 515(c)
sake: for ... 's sake 727(f)
saknas 309(d)
salig 223(a)
same 327
samma 139(e), 223(e), 327
samma ... som 242(a)
samt 805(b)
School subjects 213
score 405(b)
se 506, 560(k)
Seasons 102(c), 137(e), 724(d)(f)(h)(l)
Second element 1101
second 411(d)
sedan 616(b), 722(l), 812(b), 823(h)
sedan dess 318(c), 722(l)*n*, 823(h)
sedan ... tillbaka 703(b), 722(m)
see 560(k)
sej 301(b)
sekel 407(b)
-self 310f., 315
Semantic extension 1125(e)
semi- 413(a)*n*
senast 238(b)
Sentence elements 1001–1008
Sentence types 1011
several 351(c)
sida: åt sidan 720(z)*n*
side: (on) this/the other side of 720(f)
sig 301(b), 310ff., 330
Similarity 242
simma 516(f)
sin, sitt, sina 316, 318(b), 319f, 330
since 706(b), 722(l)(m), 812(b), 813(a),
823(h)
single 406(d)
Singular of nouns:

definite forms 132f.: alternative short and
    long 133(d)(e)(f); summary 135; *see
    also* Definite article
differences between English and Swedish
    usage 137–141
for the quantity expressed 126
nouns lacking 114(l)*n*, 122
nouns with two forms 112(d)*n*, 121
sist 238(b), 724(h)*n*
sitta 540(a), 561
Size 207(a)
själv etc. 224(a), 310, 315, 555(e)
skola (skulle) 504, 535, 553(a)
    future 525(c)(d), 529f.
skola: i skolan 710(a)*n*, 721(b)*n*
skriva 508
skulle *see* **skola**
skål 907(b)
slags 130(e), 223(a), 364(d)
slik etc. 328
sluta 516(g), 560(l)
Small letters *see* Capital/small letters
små 205(a), 217*n*, 230(a), 238(c)
smått 205(a)*n*
snart: så snart som 812(g)
so 309(e), 616(a), 809
so that 817
som:
    conjunction 140(b), 242(a), 818: with
        pronoun 324; with superlative 241(h)*n*
    relative pronoun 329, 369f., 373, 820, 822,
        823(j)(l): omitted 370(c), 803(d)*n*,
        1040(b)
    subject marker in relative clauses 366, 821
    . . . som helst 346(m), 358f, 616(e)(f)
some 336, 341f., 346
some of 729(g)
some . . . , others 346(g)
somebody 341
somehow 341(a)*n*
someone 341
something 341
sometimes 805(c)
somewhat 341(b)*n*
somlig 342, 346(g)
sorts 130(d), 223(a), 364(d)
Sounds, imitated 906
Spanish loans 1131(a)
Spelling
    -m, -n 1205
    personal pronouns 301(b)(d)
    sådan 328(a)
    sedan 722(l)
    small or capital letters *see* Capital/small
        letters
    various 1204f.

spite: in spite of 727(n), 815(a)
spä(da) 506, 515(b)
Squares, names of 137(f)
stackars with pronoun 314(b)
stanna 560(l)
Statement 1016ff.
    word order, summary 1053
stop 560(l)
stoppa 560(j)
Straight word order *see* Word order
Street names 137(f), 1207(b)*n*, 1208(b)*n*,
    1311(b)
Stress:
    adjectival phrases 224
    compound verbs 555(f)
    determinative 329
    front article and demonstrative 222(a)*n*
    plural nouns 114(a)(c)(d)
    själv 315(a)
    word order 1028–1031, 1039(b),
        1044–1048
Stress positions 1044
styck 337
stycken 406(b)
ställa 540(a), 560(b)(j)
ställe: i . . . ställe 703(b), 727(h)
största delen 352f.
stå 506, 540(a)
Subject 1002, 1018(a)
    double 209
    duplication 1047(b)
    form 1002(a)
    formal 309(d), 1003(b), 1018(a), 1019(a),
        1033f.
    impersonal 551, 1003(a)
    implied 311(b), 320(c)
    position 1102(b), 1004(b), 1008, 1025;
        postponed 1003(b)
    omission 1051(d)
    possessive pronoun referring to 319
    real 1003(b), 1018(a), 1019(a), 1024(d)(e),
        1033f.
    reflexive pronoun referring to 310
Subject and infinitive construction 1050(c)
Subject marker 366f, 821
Subjunctive 534, 537, 1016ff.
Subordinate clause 801(b), 1015, 1016ff.,
    1302
    and raising 1046
    as object 1022(a)*n*
    expressing similarity 242(a)*n*
    form 1037
    function 1038
    interrogative 366f.
    negated 1031(f)

order of sentence elements 1008, 1019f.:
  summary 1053;
main clause order 1041, 1042(b)(c)
position 1027(b), 1039: as topic 1027(b)
position of conjunction 802(b)
punctuation 1302
and conjunction 803(d)
with no indicator of subordination 1040
see also Clauses
Subordination 801(b)
  indicators of 803(d)
Subordinators 801(b), 803(c)
  general 811
Substances 120(c), 137(h)
such 328
Suffix:
  -a 1102(b)
  -al 1102(a)
  -ande 1102(a)
  -ant 1102(a)
  -are 1102(b)
  -artad 1103(c)
  -as 724(d)
  -bar 1102(a)
  -ell 1102(a)
  -ent 1102(a)(b)
  -era 1102(b)
  -fattig 1103(c)
  -fri 1103(c)
  -ful 1103(c)
  -ion 1102(b)
  -is 1120(a)
  -ist 1102(a)
  -itet 1102(b)
  -iv 1102(a)(b)
  -krati 1103(d)
  -lös 1103(c)
Suffixes 107, 119, 1106 ; *see also* Nouns
  ending in
  adjective-forming 1107
  deadjectival 1106(a)
  denominal 1106(a)
  deverbal 1106(a)
  expressing: people 1107, activity 1107,
    status 1107
  noun-forming 1107
  table of 1107
  verb-forming 1107
Superlative:
  of adjectives 139(f), 232–245
  of adverbs 605
  absolute 235(e)*n*, 244
  adjectives lacking, or lacking positive 238
  as adjectival noun 228(b)
  compound adjectives 237
  inflexion 241

forms: -ast 219(d), 232, 233, 237(a),
  238(a), 241(c); -st 220(a), 232, 234,
  237(a), 238(a), 241(d)
  with mest 232, 236, 237(b)
  irregular 235, 241(d)
  with time 726(b)
  without article 224(b), 225(c), 241(g)(h)
Supine 501ff., 531, 1004(f)
  double 1004(f)*n*
  form 501–516
  summary 501, 514
Swearwords 908
Swedish and foreign affixes 1102
så 603(e), 616(a)(b), 809
så (att) 616(a), 817, 1041(b)
så . . . som 823(c)
(så)som 818(b)
sådan etc. 208(b), 328
såvida/såvitt 814(a)
säga 504, 515(c)
sälja 504
sämre 235(a)(c)(d), 605(b)
sämst 235(a)(c)(d), 605(b)
sätta 504, 540(a), 560(j)

't 301(e)*n*
ta 511, 515(a)
tack 907
tack vare 728(f)
tala 516(b)
talking of 727(c)
-tal(s) 407
tatt 515(a)*n*
Temperature 409
Tenses of verbs
  compatibility 529
  complex 501(a)
  continuous, in English 521
  forms 502–517: summary 501, 514
  progressive, in English 521(b)
  simple 501(a)
than 728(j), 818(d)
thanks to 728(f)
that
  conjunction 811(a), 823(j)
  demonstrative pronoun 325f.
  relative pronoun 370, 729(o)(p), 822 (a)
the 132ff., 136, *see also* Definite article
the English 229
the . . . the (with comparative) 242(g), 351(d),
  818(e)
their/theirs 316, 319f.
Theme 1044(a)
then 616(b), 812(a)*n*(b)*n*, 820
Then planes (verb tense) 529f.

there 613
therefore 809*n*
there is/are 309(d)
these 325f.
think 560(m)
this
    pronoun 325f.
    with time expressions 724(h), 731(d)
those 325f
thousand(s) 401*n*, 404
    punctuation 410*n*, 1302(j)
through 709
throughout 709(a)*n*, 725(c)
tid: under tiden att 812(c)
tidigare 823(d)
Tilde 1203(d)
till 716(c), 812(e), 823(k)
till 716, 720(l)(z)*n*, 721(b)*n*(e), 724(l),
    729(d)(e)(p), 823(k)
    where no preposition in English 731(a)
    with dative 702(a)*n*
    with **dess** 318(c)
    with **en/ett** 340(d)
    with genitive 129(f), 702(a)*n*
    with personal pronoun 322
till (och med) 725(d)
tills 812(e), 823(k)
tillsammans med 711(a)*n*
time: what time? 416(b)
Time
    clock 416, 724(b)(k), 1212(b), 1303(c)
    prepositions 723–726, 730(a)(d), *see also*
        Prepositions, of time
Time marker 522(a), 525(a)
Time planes 529
tio 401*n*
Titles (for people) 137(j), 304(a), 1206(c),
    1307 *see also* Book titles; Newspaper titles;
    Kings; Popes
tjog 405(b)
tjugo 401n
tjugonde 401*n*
to 708(e), 710(a), 711(f), 710(c), 713, 715(b),
    716, 720(z), 721
together with 711(a), 727(j)
too 616(c)
    too many 348*n*, 350
Tools 102(g)
top: on top of 720(t)
Topic (position) 1008, 1016, 1018(a), 1020(a),
    1025, 1027, 1041(b), 1045f.
    emphatic 1045(b)
    in subordinate clause 1041(c)
    natural 1045(a)
Topicalisation 1027, 1048(a)
towards 713, 720(z), 722(d), 728(g)

Towns 318(a)
Trade 140(a)
Transport 721(c), 730(d)
treble 406(d)
Trees 102(d), 104(b)
trenne 403(b)
tretti(o) 401*n*
trettionde 401*n*
triplicate 406(d)
tro 505, 560(m)
trots 727(n), 815(a)*n*
trots att 815(a)*n*
trä(da) 506, 515(b)
träffa 560(k)
tu 403(a)
tusen 404(a), 414(a)
tusende 404(a)
tvenne 403(b)
tve- 403(c)
tvinga 516(f)(g)
två 347(b)*n*, 403
two 403
the(se) two 347(a)
Two-verb constructions 518f.
ty 808, 823(b)
tycka 560(m)
tänka 525(a)*n*, 560(m)
tör (torde) 535

undan 720(u)
under 717
under 717, 725(c)
under det att 812(c)
ungefär 722(j)*n*
unless 814(c)
until 716(c), 722(h), 812(d)(e), 823(k)
up 613, 720(v)
uphill 720(v)*n*
upp(e) 603(b), 613
uppför 720(v)
ur 720(w)
ursäkta 363*n*
ut 603(b), 613
ut ur 720(w)
utan
    conjunction 807(b), 823(f), 1051(d),
        1021(f)
    preposition 727(o)
utan att 819(c)
utanför 720(n)
utanpå 720(x)
ute 613
utefter 720(r)
utför 720(v)
uti 720(q)*n*
utmed 720(r)

utom 702(a), 720(y), 727(p), 823(f)

va as tag 903(b)
vad 373, 820ff.
vad? 361, 363, 615(b)
vad för? 361, 364
vad som 366f., 373
var indefinite pronoun 208(b), 331f., 411(g);
    interrogative pronoun 361f, 603(b),
    609(c), 613, 616(d)(e), 820f.
var för sig 332(b)*n*
var och en etc. 320(l), 333
var sin etc. 223(b)*n*, 320(j)
vara 513
    in passive 531(c), 547(b)
    with **det** 309(b)(d)(f)(g)
varandra (varann) 313, 331, 335, 547
varannan etc. 208(b), 331, 332(a), 334,
    411(g)
vardera etc. 137(k), 336
vare sig . . . eller 806(b)
varenda etc. 208(b), 331, 333
varför 820f.
varifrån 820f.
varje 208(b), 331f., 346(n)
varken . . . eller 209(b), 806(b), 823(g)
vars 223(d), 372, 820, 822(c)
vart(?) 603(b), 609(c), 613, 616(d)(e), 820f.
vart (from **varda**) 549*n*
vederbörande 139(e), 223(e)
vem 320(l), 820f.
vem? 361f.
vems? 362
Verb endings:
    summary chart 514
    see also Verbs
Verb particle 541(c), 704, 713
    order 1021, 1051(c)
    position 559
    prefix 555(f)
Verb prefixes
    be- 541(c)
    för- 541(c)
    inseparable 555(f)
    separable (particles) 556ff.
Verb stem 501
    in consonants 501(a), 507
    in vowel 501(a), 505
    in **-a** 502
    in **-d** 503(a)
    in **-e** 505
    in **-g** 503(a)
    in **-j** 503(a), 541(a)
    in **-k** 503(b)
    in **-l** 503(a)
    in **-m** 503(a)

    in **-n** 503
    in **-o** 505
    in **-p** 503(b)
    in **-r** 503(a)
    in **-s** 503(b), 542(a)
    in **-t** 503(b)
    in **-v** 503(a)
    in **-x** 503(b)
    in **-y** 505
    in **-å** 505
    in **-ö** 505
Verbs:
    auxiliary 309(f), 501, 1004(c), *see also*
        modal auxiliary *below*
    complex 1030
    compound 554ff, 1117, form 555f.;
        inseparable 555, 557f.; meaning
        556(b), 558; separable 558ff., 1021(a);
        style 557
    constructions with two 521(b)
    copula(r) 201, 1006(a)
    deletion 1051
    deponent 543, 545
    ditransitive 539(d), 1005(b)
    duplication of 1047(b)
    durative 552(c)
    ending in **-era** 502
    ending in **-s** *see* s-verbs
    finite 1002(b), 1004, 1008, 1016, 1018(a),
        1020(c): order 1025; as topic 1027
    forms 501–517; alternative 516; long and
        short 515; modal auxiliary 535; plural
        517; summary 501, 514; *see also*
        Conjugations of verbs; Imperative;
        Past participle; Present participle;
        Supine; Tenses of verbs
    impersonal 1018(a)
    intransitive 539f., 1006(a); in English,
        passive in Swedish 553(b)
    irregular: second conjugation 504; third
        conjugation 506
    modal auxiliary 501(a), 504, 534f.,
        1004(c)(f): forms 535
    mood 534–538
    non-finite 1004, 1008, 1018(c): as topic
        1027; order 1021, 1025
    of motion omitted 1051(a)
    principal parts 501
    problem, translation into Swedish 560
    reciprocal 313*n*, 543f.
    reflexive 310f., 539, 541
    indicating movement 541(d),
    alternating with s-form 541(e)
    strong 501(b), 507–514, *see also* 504*n*
    terminative 552(c)
    transitive 539f., 1005(a)

weak 501(b), 502–506
  summary 514
  with vowel gradation, *see* Conjugations of
    verbs, fourth
very 348*n*
veta 504, 560(h)
  with **det** 309(f)
vi 302(b), 304(c)
vid 718, 721(b)*n*(e), 724(k), 729(d)
vilja 504, 525(c)*n*, 535, 560(n)
vilka? 320(l), 361ff.
vilkas(?) 362, 372(c)
vilken! etc. 140(e), 208(b), 368
vilken(?) etc. 361, 363, 365
vilken (relative) 369, 371, 820f., 822
vilken etc. **som** 366f.
vilken som helst 358, 823(g)
vilkendera? etc. 361, 365*n*
vilkens etc. 372(b)(c)
vilket 371(b)
visavi 728(g)
visserligen 807(a)*n*
Vogue affix 1103(d)
vår, vårt, våra 316ff.
våran 301(c)
väl 603(d), 605(b), 610(b),6715(f), 1023
värre 235(a)(d), 605(b)
värst 235(a)(d), 605(b)
växa 504, 516(e), 560(g)
växla 560(c)
V-question 1016ff., 1036(b)

Wages 138(b)
want 560(n)
way:
  a way of + *-ing* 703(c)*n*
    by way of 716(f),
    in the (same) way 818(b)(c)
Weather 309(h)
Weeks 415(d), 724(h)(m)
Weight principle 1028, 1044(a), 1045(b)
Weights and measures 120(e)
what 373, 820f.
what (a) . . . *!* 140(e), 368
what? 361, 363, 367
whatever 358f.
when 812(a), 820f., 823
whenever 616(e)
where 613, 616(d), 820ff.
wherever 616(e)
whether 811(b)
which (relative) 370f., 820ff.
which? 361, 365, 820
whichever 359(d)
while 812(c)
who(m)? 361f, 367, 820f.

who(m) (relative) 369, 370, 820, 822
whoever 358f.
whole 224(a), 339(c), 729(g)
whose 820, 822
whose? 361f.
Wish 1043(d)
with 705(c), 708(c), 711, 715(e)
within 720(n)(o), 722(g)
  to within 722(k)
without 727(o), 819(c)
Word class 1001
Word division 1211
Word groups as subordinating conjunctions
  810
Word order 1008–1053
  adjectives 207
  causal clauses 813(a)
  conjunctions 802
  differences between English and Swedish
    207(b)
  for emphasis 210, 214, 1044–1048
  inverted 1002(b), 1015(c), 1016, 1020(a)
    adjectives 207(b)*n*
    after conjunctional adverb 803(b)
    in conditional statements 1044
    in negative statements 1031(c)(d)
    in questions 1036(b)
    in subordinate clauses 1041(b)
    with **antingen** 806(b)
  ju . . . desto 818(e)
  separable verbs 559
  short answers 309(f)
  själv 315(a)
  straight 1016, 1020(a), 1026
  så 817(b)
  within positions 1025
worse 235(a)(c)(d)
worst 235(d)

Year 414, 724(b)(d)(h)(m)
yes (interjection) 902
Yes/no question 902(a), 1016ff., 1036(a)
yet 807(c)
you 303f, 304(c), 330
your/yours 316
ytterligare 340(d)*n*

Zero suffix 1109

å 728(h)
åka 560(a)(d)(f), 721(c)*n*, 730(d)
år 414(b)
århundrade 407(b)
åt 720(z), 727(q)
åt . . . till 703(b), 720(z)*n*
åtskilliga 351(c)*n*

äkta 220(b)
än 242(c), 728(j), 818(d)
   with pronoun 324
än ... , än 1302(d)*n*
ända sedan 722(l)*n*
ändå 242(e), 807(a)*n*(c)
ännu 242(e), 603(a), 611
ärta 121

öga 116(d)(g)*n*
öka 560(g)
ömsom ... ömsom 805(c)
öra 116(d)(g)*n*
över 703(c), 719, 725(c), 729(d)
överallt 719(a)*n*